RITCHIE OLD TESTAMENT COMMENTARIES

What the Bible teaches

PSALMS

J.M. Flanigan

GENERAL EDITOR **W.S. STEVELY**

ISBN 1 904064 02 7

WHAT THE BIBLE TEACHES

40 Beansburn, Kilmarnock, Scotland

Typeset by John Ritchie Ltd.
Printed by The Bath Press, Avon, England.

CONTENTS

CONTRIBUTOR

J.M.FLANIGAN

Jim Flanigan had the great privilege of being raised in a christian home in Northern Ireland. He was saved as a young man and received into the Parkgate Assembly, Belfast in 1946. In 1972 he resigned from full-time employment in response to the call of God to give more of his time to the work of the Lord. Most of this has been in ministering the Word of God, bringing before the Lord's people the unique glories of the Person of Christ. This ministry has resulted in him travelling widely in the British Isles, the USA, Canada, Australia and Israel, in the last of which he maintains a special interest. Jim has brought to his growing written ministry his own delightful style which is orderly, accurate, and Christ-centred. This latest work continues to express these features.

ABBREVIATIONS

ASV	American Standard Version (the American variant of the RV)
AV	Authorised Version (known in the USA as the King James Version)
JFB	Jamieson, Faussett and Brown Commentary
JND	New Translation by J.N. Darby
JPS	Jewish Publication Society Old Testament
LXX	Septuagint (ancient translation of the Old Testament into Greek, often quoted in the New Testament)
NASV	New American Standard Version
Newberry	The AV as edited by Thomas Newberry; also known as "The Englishman's Bible"
NIV	New International Version
NKJV	New King James Version
NT	New Testament
OT	Old Testament
Rotheram	Rotherham's Emphasised Bible
RSV	Revised Standard Version (revision of the American Standard Version)
RV	Revised Version (published in England; revision of the AV)
TWOT	Theological Word Book of the Old Testament, edited by Harris, Archer and Waltke
YLT	Young's Literal Translation

PREFACE

The publishers have commissioned this Old Testament series of commentaries to complement the completed set of New Testament commentaries issued under the general title "What the Bible Teaches". Together they seek to provide an accessible and useful tool for the study of, and meditation on, Scripture.

While there is no shortage of commentaries currently available on the various books of the Old Testament it was felt that there was no complete series which sought simply to apply the message of Genesis through to Malachi to the concerns of believers today.

The authors of these volumes are not scholars of the original languages and rely on others for guidance on the best modern views of word meanings and similar matters. However all the authors share the conviction that the Bible in its entirety is the Word of God. They believe it to be reliable, accurate and intended "for our learning" (Rom 15.4). This view has been explained further by the Editor in a short series of articles that appeared in "The Believers Magazine", also published by John Ritchie Ltd., in 1999.

The two Testaments fit together so that principles and illustrations from the Old are brought to bear on issues that arise on nearly every page of the New. Knowledge of the Old is therefore an indispensable aid to the proper understanding of the New. In particular the Lord Jesus can be seen in prophecy and picture again and again. He, Himself, as described in the Gospels, is an exemplar of this approach to the Old Testament through His constant reference to people and incidents whose histories are recorded for us and to those prophetic statements that applied to Him.

Given this understanding of the nature and purpose of the Scriptures the main lessons of the books are considered and applied to our circumstances today by authors experienced in preaching and teaching the Word of God.

Since no attempt is being made to produce an academic series the technical apparatus has been kept to a minimum. Where authors have judged it of value attention is drawn to linguistic and other issues, and, where appropriate, reference is made to the numerical system devised by Strong to allow the reader without knowledge of the original languages to gain access to the various lexical aids which have adopted this system. For clarity, numerical references to NT words only are given in italics, following the practice used in Strong's Concordance.

The system of transliteration generally used is that adopted by the *Theological Wordbook of the Old Testament* (TWOT), edited by Harris, Archer and Waltke and published by Moody Press, Chicago 1980. However, there are occasions when account has been taken of the commonly recognised English spelling of some Hebrew words.

References to Scripture without attribution are taken from the Authorised (King James) Version. Where other translations are quoted the source is given. Measurements given in the Authorised Version have been translated, where appropriate, into their metric equivalents.

Since the commentaries do not necessarily follow a verse-by-verse approach, and to save space and cost, the text of Scripture is not included. It is assumed that all readers have available a copy of the Bible.

The complete Old Testament is expected to be covered in around fifteen to eighteen volumes. These will not appear in the order in which they are found in the Scriptures but simply in order of completion by the authors commissioned for the series.

W.S. STEVELY

BIBLIOGRAPHY

Armfield, H.T. *The Gradual Psalms*. London: J.T.Hayes, 1874.
The author calls his commentary, "A Treatise on the Fifteen Songs of Degrees...based on Ancient Hebrew, Chaldee, and Christian Authorities". Helpful, but sometimes heavy.

Barnes, Albert. *Notes on the Book of Psalms*. London: George Routledge & Sons.
Critical, explanatory, and practical. A most useful commentary.

Bellett, J.G. *Short Meditations on the Psalms.* London: A.S. Rouse, 1892.
The title aptly describes this small, sweet volume.

Boice, James Montgomery. *Psalms.* Grand Rapids, Michigan: Baker Books, 1996.
An expositional commentary. Soundly fundamental, but based on the NIV Text which will not appeal to some readers.

Brenton, Sir Lancelot C.L. *The Septuagint with Apocrypha*. USA: Hendrickson, 1986.
A most helpful edition of the Septuagint, giving the complete Greek text with a parallel English translation.

Clarke, Arthur G. *Analytical Studies in the Psalms*. Kilmarnock: John Ritchie, 1979.
W.E. Vine commends this work as a "comprehensive and useful volume". The writer himself says that the studies are intended to be merely suggestive. There is much alliteration.

Cohen, Dr A. *The Psalms.* London: The Soncino Press, 1945.
A most interesting and useful commentary written especially with Jewish readers in mind. It gives the Hebrew text along with the English translation of the Jewish Publication Society. A brief introduction to each Psalm supplies any known background information.

Cox, Samuel. *The Pilgrim Psalms.* Minneapolis, USA: Klock & Klock, Reprint, 1983.
A very helpful work on the "Songs of Degrees" - Psalms 120-134.

Darby, J.N. *Practical Reflections on the Psalms*. (Collected Writings, Vol. 17). London: Stow Hill, 1965.

Darby, J.N. *Psalms*. (Collected Writings, Vol. 13, pp. 241-352). London: Stow Hill, 1965.

Darby, J.N. *Psalms*. (Synopsis of the Books of the Bible, Vol. 2). London: Stow Hill, 1965.
Mr Darby has not written extensively on the Psalms, but whatever he has written will be appreciated by the thoughtful reader.

Davidson, James. *Proper Psalms on Certain Days*. London: John Heywood, 1879.
A small commentary compiled to associate certain Psalms with selected days in the christian Calendar. Some useful information.

Davies, T. Witton. *The Psalms (LXXIII-CL).* Edinburgh: The Century Bible, T.C. & E.C. Jack.

A companion to the volume by Davison (below) but tending to be hypercritical at times.

Davison, W.T. *The Psalms (I-LXXII).* Edinburgh: The Century Bible, T.C. & E.C. Jack

A concise, compact commentary on Psalms 1-72. Based on the RV.

De Burgh, William. *The Book of Psalms.* Dublin: Hodges, Smith & Co., 1860.

An excellent commentary, well described as being "critical, devotional, and prophetical".

Delitzsch, F. *Psalms*. (Keil & Delitzsch Commentary, Vol. 5). Grand Rapids, Michigan: Eerdman's, 1975.

Scholarly and conservative, with much quotation in Hebrew. Not easy to read.

Dennett, Edward. *Pilgrim Songs.* London: A.S. Rouse, 1897.

A small, but delightful, treatise on the "Songs of Degrees" - Psalms 120-134.

Gaebelein, Arno C. *Psalms.* (The Annotated Bible). New Jersey: Loizeaux Brothers, 1979.

Brief and concise, being only a part of the whole "Annotated Bible", but soundly reliable.

Grant, F.W. *The Psalms*. (The Numerical Bible). New Jersey: Loizeaux Brothers, 1897.

Not all readers will either follow or appreciate Grant's numerical structure in his work, but the commentary will, nevertheless, repay careful study.

Horne, George. *The Book of Psalms*. London: Ward, Locke & Co.

Quite a large volume on the Psalms, giving, as the writer says, "...their application to Messiah, to the Church, and to individuals".

Keller, Phillip. *A Shepherd looks at Psalm 23*. Grand Rapids, Michigan; Zondervan, 1970.

A devotional commentary on one of the best-loved Psalms, written by a shepherd.

Kidner, Derek. *Psalms 1-72.* (Tyndale Commentaries). Leicester: Inter-Varsity Press, 1973.

Kidner, Derek. *Psalms 73-150.* (Tyndale Commentaries). Leicester: Inter-Varsity Press, 1975.

Two excellent commentaries, compact yet comprehensive.

Kinney, LeBaron W. *Acres of Rubies.* New Jersey: Loizeaux Brothers, 1946.

A book of Hebrew word studies for the English reader, much of it relevant to the Psalms.

Kirkpatrick, A.F. *The Book of Psalms*. Cambridge University Press, 1939.

A most excellent commentary, often quoted and referred to by many other expositors. Has a lengthy introduction to the whole Psalter and an introduction to each individual Psalm.

MacBeath, John. *Psalms of the Heart*. Belfast: Ambassador Productions Ltd.

The writer himself says that, "The present book is simply an attempt to

put in brief and direct form some significant and useful lessons plucked out of the heart of each Psalm".

Maclaren, Alexander. *The Life of David.* London: Hodder & Stoughton, 1888.
This intriguing little book traces the life and character of David throughout his Psalms, dealing with his early days, his exile, his kingship, and his tears. A precious volume.

Maclaren, Alexander. *The Psalms.* Minneapolis: Klock & Klock, Reprint, 1981.
Maclaren's writings are choice. These three volumes, with his own translation, must rank very highly among all commentaries on the Psalms.

Meyer, F.B. *David, Shepherd Psalmist King.* Marshall, Morgan & Scott.
A devotional study, in the style which is characteristic of F.B. Meyer, tracing the varied periods and experiences in the life of the shepherd boy who became king.

Montgomerie, John. *The Alphabet of God.* Inverness: R. Jeans, 1940.
An interesting study of the twenty-two stanzas of Psalm 119, with comments on the particular Hebrew letter with which each line of each stanza commences.

Morgan, G. Campbell. *Notes on the Psalms.* Grand Rapids, Michigan: F.H. Revell, 1947.
Very brief, but helpful nonetheless, using the text of the ASV.

Murphy, James G. *Psalms.* Minneapolis: James Family Publishing, 1876.
A clear, concise, easily read commentary.

Oesterley, W.O.E. *The Psalms.* London: S.P.C.K., 1939.
Containing some useful information but not the most helpful of commentaries. Much textual criticism and not much of Messiah. Would need to be read with discrimination.

Perowne, J.J. Stewart. *The Book of Psalms.* (One-volume edition). Grand Rapids, Michigan: Zondervan, 1976.
Spurgeon called this commentary, "A masterpiece of extraordinary learning and critical skill". It is an invaluable aid in any study of the Psalms.

Phillips, John. *Exploring the Psalms.* New Jersey: Loizeaux Brothers, 1988.
Very readable, very sound, but very anecdotal.

Plumer, W.S. *The Book of Psalms.* Edinburgh: Banner of Truth, Reprint, 1975, 1978, 1990.
The most excellent and comprehensive of all the commentaries listed here. Both doctrinal and devotional, appealing to the mind and to the heart. A "must" for every student of the Psalms.

Pridham, Arthur. *Notes and Reflections on the Psalms.* London: James Nisbet & Co., 1869.
A helpful commentary, essentially practical, yet recognising a prophetic intention in each Psalm. True to the Person of Christ as Messiah.

Reynolds, Edward. *An Explication of Psalm 110.* Pittsburgh: Soli Deo Gloria, Reprint, 1993.
Perhaps the most comprehensive commentary on Psalm 110, rich

with thoughts of Christ. A 17th Century work, for many years out of print, but now available as Volume 2 of "The Works of Edward Reynolds".

Rotherham, Joseph Bryant. *Studies in the Psalms.* London: H.R. Allenson Ltd., 1911.
A scholarly treatise by the translator of "The Emphasised Bible".

Samuel, E. Bendor. *The Prophetic Character of the Psalms.* London: Pickering & Inglis.
The writer, with his Jewish background, has given us what the foreword calls, "Another literary treasure...a guide into sweet and untrodden paths of spiritual instruction".

Smith, George Adam. *Four Psalms.* London: Hodder & Stoughton.
A helpful and interesting little meditation on Psalms 23, 36, 52 and 121.

Spurgeon, C.H. *The Treasury of David.* USA: Hendricksen Publishers.
This massive work is invaluable, not only for Spurgeon's own commentary on each Psalm, but also for the explanatory notes and quotes drawn from an endless variety of other expositors. It is a rich storehouse which is the product of more than twenty years labour in which every single verse of the Psalter is commented upon so suitably. Every believer should read "The Treasury of David".

Spurrell, Helen. *A Translation of the Old Testament Scriptures.* London: James Nisbet, 1985.
An interesting, if not indispensible, translation of the Old Testament.

St. John, Harold. *Psalms.* (The Collected Writings). Glasgow: Gospel Tract Publications, 1989.
The usual helpful, pithy style of Harold St. John. Commentary on Psalms 1-88 and on the Songs of Degrees, with two addresses on Psalms 107 and 119.

Stuart, C.E. *The Book of Praises.* (Assembly Writers Library, Vol. 5). Glasgow: Gospel Tract Publications, 1981.
A brief but most useful treatise on the Psalms.

Weiss, Benjamin. *The Book of Psalms.* London: Wm. Oliphant & Sons, 1852.
A very old commentary; not easy to read but the student will find it helpful.

Wigram, G.V. *A Study of the Psalms.* Oak Park, Illinois: Bible Truth Publishers.
Notes, rather than commentary, but much helpful information in the Introductory Remarks.

Wilson, T.E. *The Messianic Psalms.* New Jersey: Loizeaux Brothers, 1978.
Regarded by many as the finest commentary on the Messianic Psalms. A delightful study, beautifully written, and easily read. Full of devotion to Christ.

THE BOOK OF PSALMS

INTRODUCTION

1. Introductory Remarks

The Psalms are the very heart of Holy Scripture. The Book of Psalms has been called "The Prayer and Praise Book of Israel", but, of course, the Psalms are not the exclusive property of that favoured nation. Believers of all ages have sung them and have revelled in the sweetness of these inspired songs. It seems as though every human emotion and every spiritual ambition finds expression in the poetry of the Psalms. There is praise and prophecy; there is duty and devotion; there is grief and gladness; there is joy and sorrow, tragedy and triumph, tears and laughter, trial and trust. There is language here, somewhere, to express the thoughts and feelings and desires of every child of God. There are dispensational Psalms, devotional Psalms, doctrinal Psalms, penitential Psalms, prophetical Psalms, practical Psalms, and imprecatory Psalms, with comfort and correction, instruction and direction, encouragement and reproof.

The Saviour Himself, however, has provided the key to the most profitable of all meditations, that is to find Christ in the Psalms. Here we may find His sufferings and His glory, His feelings and His tender inner experiences. On that memorable first day of the week on the way to Emmaus, and later in Jerusalem in the midst of His disciples, He showed those early believers that He was in all the Scriptures, and He made special reference to the Psalms (Lk 24.27, 44). Indeed certain Psalms are called "Messianic" because, apart from Himself, the Messiah, there can be no ultimate understanding or fulfilment of those particular Psalms.

2. Title

The Book of Psalms is called by the Jews, in Hebrew, T^{e}HILLIM (8416), which means "praises". The word has a root in Hebrew which means "to make a jubilant sound". The English "Psalms" is a transliteration of the Title in the Greek Septuagint, "Psalmoi", which means "Songs". The word "Psalter" is from the Greek "Psalterion", denoting a harp or other stringed instrument. Note that the Book of Psalms begins with "Blessed" and ends with "Hallelujah". Praises indeed!

3. Authors

Although often referred to as "The Psalms of David", actually a little less than half of the one hundred and fifty Psalms are specifically assigned to David in the titles, though Psalms 2 and 95 are attributed to David in the New Testament (Acts 4.25; Heb 4.7). There are several other named authors, so that the Psalms are, by their titles, distributed as follows.

1. Seventy-three Psalms are attributed to David.
2. Twelve Psalms are by Asaph.
3. Eleven are by the sons of Korah
4. Two Psalms bear the name of Solomon (72 and 127)
5. One Psalm is by Heman the Ezrahite (88)
6. One Psalm is by Ethan the Ezrahite (89)
7. One Psalm is by Moses the man of God (90)

The authorship of many Psalms is unknown. These are sometimes referred to as "the orphan Psalms". It should be noted, too, that at times the prepositions in the titles cannot be determined with certainty. Is it "By...", or "For...", or "To..."? This, in some cases, makes it difficult to identify the author positively.

The Psalms therefore cover a period of Hebrew history of at least twelve hundred years from Moses to the Maccabees, the earliest Psalm being that of Moses.

4. Survey and Summary

The most ancient manuscripts, and Jewish tradition, have divided the Psalms into five books. Both F. Delitzsch and A.C. Gaebelein quote from the Midrash, a Hebrew Commentary on the Old Testament. The comment on Psalm 1.1 is, "Moses gave to the Israelites the five books of the Law and corresponding with these David gave them the five books of the Psalms". It is not certain who collected and collated the Psalms, though some have mentioned Ezra the priest and scribe as being the inspired librarian. There being five books, this is therefore a Pentateuch, and Jews have referred to them as "The Pentateuch of David". Many expositors have remarked on the correspondence between the five books of Psalms and the five books of Moses, so that it is thought that the first book of Psalms corresponds to the book of Genesis, the second to the book of Exodus, the third to Leviticus, the fourth to Numbers, and the fifth to Deuteronomy. The five books of the Psalter are not equal in size, but are as follows, each book concluding with a doxology.

BOOK 1	Psalms 1-41	Ends with a benediction and a double "Amen, and Amen"
BOOK 2	Psalms 42-72	Ends with a benediction and a double "Amen, and Amen"
BOOK 3	Psalms 73-89	Ends with a benediction and a double "Amen, and Amen"
BOOK 4	Psalms 90-106	Ends with a benediction, an "Amen" and a "Hallelujah"
BOOK 5	Psalms 107-150	Ends with a call to praise and a "Hallelujah"

1. The Genesis Book. The Psalms of the first book seem to have the character of the book of Genesis in that they deal much with man. Here is man as God intended him to be and man as he actually is. Here is the godly man and the ungodly man. In Psalm 8 we have the first man, and, with other Psalms, an anticipation of the second Man, the Son of Man. It is thought that in Psalms 9 and 10 we have a prediction of the coming man of sin, the wicked one. The perfect Man is in Psalm 40.

2. The Exodus Book. Here are the counsels of God concerning Israel. It has been said that this is the story of Israel's ruin and redemption. It is a story of a remnant nation crying for deliverance and finding salvation in the coming King, their Redeemer. The section concludes with a Kingdom Psalm where the glory of Israel's Messiah fills the whole earth, reminiscent of the ending of the book of Exodus where the glory of the Lord filled the tabernacle.

3. The Leviticus Book. This section, somewhat shorter than the previous two sections, is likened to the book of Leviticus because of its obvious concern with the Sanctuary. There are frequent references to holiness, to the congregation, and to Zion. Eleven of the twelve Psalms bearing the name of Asaph appear in this book. Asaph was a Levite and a leading singer when the Ark was brought from its long exile to Jerusalem (1 Chr 15.17, 19). King David made him leader of the choral worship (1 Chr 16.4, 5). The inclusion of the Psalms of Asaph in this section is in accord with its Levitical character.

4. The Numbers Book. This is a wilderness section. It commences in Psalm 90 with the prayer of Moses, the man of the wilderness, and it ends in Psalm 106 with a rehearsal of the failures and rebellions of the nation in the wilderness. Throughout the section there are specific references to the wilderness (for example Ps 95.8), and there are aspirations after the promised land of Canaan (Ps 105.8-11). It is truly the book of Numbers in character.

5. The Deuteronomy Book. In the heart of this closing book of Psalms is that great Psalm 119 where in almost every verse there is reference to the Word of God. It is of note that in His wilderness experience our Lord Jesus quoted exclusively from the book of Deuteronomy. That book is one of retrospect, where forty years of wilderness journeyings are recounted. But there is also a restating of the counsels of God and the claims of the Law, together with an anticipation of blessing and prosperity in the Promised Land. All of these great considerations are to be found in the fifth book of the Psalms. The concluding five Psalms of this section all begin and end with a resounding "Hallelujah".

Is this then a divine arrangement? C.E. Stuart speaks for many when he writes, "Enough for us to know, and own, that the different authors wrote in words taught of the Spirit... And we may add our belief, that the arrangement of the different Psalms in the order in which they have come down to us is not of human origin, but is the carrying out of a Divine purpose. Hence there is a moral order in the arrangement of this book, as there is in other books of the inspired volume". And again he writes, "As we have said, there must be a moral order, for manifestly they are not arranged chronologically. This is patent since Psalm 137, written after the Babylonish captivity commenced, directly precedes a whole series (138-145), from the pen of the sweet Psalmist of Israel (2 Sam 23.1)".

5. The Messianic Psalms

There are some sixteen Psalms which are referred to as being "Messianic". This is, of course, an adjective formed from the title "Messiah". Now, while it is true that the Lord Jesus may be seen in many Psalms as the ultimate Blessed Man, there are certain Psalms which in a special and particular way speak of the Messiah. It has been thought by some that to be truly Messianic a Psalm must be quoted in the NT with reference to the Messiah. This may be generally true but there are three exceptions. Psalms 24, 72 and 89, are undoubtedly Messianic but are never quoted in the NT with reference to Christ.

Each of the Messianic Psalms, with the exception of Psalm 110, has a primary association, an original and initial reason for its being written. It may describe the experience of the Psalmist at that time, or be associated with some great event or circumstance, but when it is read and studied it becomes obvious that the contents go beyond the writer and his experiences, and that it is necessary to see the Messiah in the Psalm for its true fulfilment. The Messianic Psalms are Psalms 2, 8, 16, 22, 24, 40, 41, 45, 68, 69, 72, 89, 91,102, 110 and 118.

These lovely Psalms range from eternity to eternity. They expound the personal, moral, mediatorial, and official glories of the Messiah. They present His Godhead glory, His incarnation, His sinless life, His rejection, His sufferings, His death, His resurrection and ascension, His present priestly ministry, His millennial reign and future glory.

The Messianic Psalms deserve sincere and serious study. They will richly repay and reward time spent in meditation upon them, for a study of these Psalms is nothing less than a study of Christ Himself.

6. The Alphabetical Psalms

There are several Psalms which, in the Hebrew, have an alphabetical arrangement wherein certain verses or lines of the Psalm all commence with the same letter of the Hebrew alphabet. These are sometimes called the "Acrostic Psalms". Of course, in the translating of the Hebrew this alphabetical arrangement is unavoidably lost. The best known of the alphabetical Psalms is Psalm 119, where the arrangement is complete with twenty-two groups of verses with eight verses in each group and the eight verses of each group all beginning with the same particular letter of the Hebrew alphabet. This letter is indicated at the head of each section in most editions of our Bible. In Psalms 9, 10, 25 and 34, there is an irregular arrangement. Psalm 37 is another perfect example and other alphabetical Psalms are Psalms 111, 112 and 145.

7. Glossary

In the titles and in the text of the Psalms certain Hebrew words appear, not translated into English but transliterated, that is to say that the Hebrew characters have been replaced with Roman equivalents so that the words have been Anglicised for us. In most cases the meaning of these words is adequately clear, but at times there is still doubt as to the intended relevance of the word in the message of the particular Psalm.

Some of these words are familiar enough but they are all appended here for readers who may be interested in those which are not so well known.

(i) In the Text.

Two of these words appear in the body of the text of the Psalms.

(a) HIGGAION (1902). This word is found transliterated in Psalm 9.16. It is also found in Psalms 19.14 and 92.3, but in these instances it has been translated. It has the thought of a meditation or soliloquy. It is translated "meditation" in Psalm 19.14, and "solemn sound" in Psalm 92.3.

(b) SELAH (5542). This lovely word occurs seventy-one times in the Psalms. Elsewhere it is found only in the book of Habakkuk, in ch. 3.3, 9, 13. The word may come from one of two roots:- SALAH meaning, "to pause", or SALAL meaning, "to lift up". Many think that a "Selah" is a direction to both musicians and singers to lift up music, hearts and voices in a solemn meditation and adoration. Alexander Maclaren, however, speaks for others when he writes, "The Selah is probably a direction for an instrumental interlude while the singer pauses".

(ii) In the Titles.

Numerous Hebrew words appear in the titles of a number of Psalms. The following is a list of these, in alphabetical order, and as used in the AV, indicating their meanings and the Psalms in which they occur. It will, of course, be profitable, perhaps necessary, to comment more fully upon these meanings in the exposition, and to consider their relevance to their particular Psalms.

AIJELETH SHAHAR (365, 7837). "The Hind of the Morning". Psalm 22.

ALAMOTH (5961). From ALMA, "a virgin, a maiden". Psalm 46.

ALTASCHITH (516). "Destroy not". Psalms 57, 58, 59, 75.

GITTITH (1665). "Winepress". Possibly a musical instrument from Gath. Psalms 8, 81, 84.

JEDUTHUN (3038). A Levite, leader of the praises, a chief singer. Psalms 39, 62, 77.

MAHALATH (4257). "Sickness, sadness". Psalm 53.

MAHALATH LEANNOTH (4257, 6031). "Sickness; humiliation". Psalm 88.

MASCHIL (4905). "Instruction". Psalms 32, 42, 44, 45, 52, 53, 54, 55, 74, 78, 88, 89, 142.

MICHTAM (4387). "An engraving, a poem, or meditation". Psalms 16, 56, 57, 58, 59, 60.

MUTHLABBEN (4192). "Death of the Son". Psalm 9.

NEGINOTH (5058). "Stringed instruments". Psalms 4, 6, 54, 55, 61 (as NEGINAH), 67, 76.

NEHILOTH (5155). "A Flute" (Strong), but some say "Possessions". Psalm 5.

SHEMINITH (8067). "Upon the Octave" or "The Eighth". Psalms 6, 12.

SHIGGAION (7692). "Praise". Psalm 7.

SHOSHANNIM (7799). "Lilies". Psalms 45, 69.

SHUSHAN-EDUTH (7802). "Liliy of Testimony". Psalm 60 and Psalm 80 (plural).

BOOK 1

PSALM 1

Introduction

In the early days of Israel's entry into the land of Canaan, Joshua remembered the word of the Lord which had come to them through Moses. In accordance with the decree, he gathered the people at the two mounts, Gerizim and Ebal, in the vale of Shechem, and he divided their tribes, six on one mount and six on the other. "These shall stand upon mount Gerizim to bless...And these shall stand upon mount Ebal to curse". So the Lord had commanded, and at the two mounts they had read the whole law. It was a story of blessing and cursing, for obedience and disobedience to the law (Deut 11.29; 27.12-13; Josh 8.33-35).

In this first Psalm it is as if one is standing on those two mounts. The Psalm is so obviously divided into two parts. Verses 1-3 are, as it were, on Mount Gerizim, describing the blessedness of the obedient man. Verses 4-6 are on Mount Ebal, proclaiming the judgment of the disobedient.

The Psalm begins with "Blessed". It is a plural word, and an exclamation, "O the blessednesses ...". The ministry of the Saviour also commenced thus on another mount, with a pronouncement of blessing (Mt 5.1-3). And as in this opening Psalm there are two men, two ways, two destinies, and fruit and chaff, so it is in that opening ministry of the Lord Jesus in what is called the "Sermon on the Mount".

Ancient Jewish tradition believed that at one time the first two Psalms were one. The repetition of several words would make this possible, but the difference in tone and content makes it improbable. However, these two Psalms may be viewed as the vestibule, the antechamber, to the whole Psalter, as if the rest of the Psalms are but an exposition of the contents of these two.

Verses 1-3: The Righteous Man

The blessed man is described both negatively and positively. He is a man separated from the world around him. The men of the world are described as ungodly, as sinners, and scornful. That man is blessed who will not walk with them, nor stand with them, nor sit with them. He will have nothing of their counsel, their way of life, nor their settled interests. Notice the three-fold gradation of the character, the pursuits, and ambitions of the men of the world. It is a downgrade of evil. The righteous man must not heed their counsel or walk by it, for it is the way of sinners and it leads to the seat of the scoffer. Morally he must not walk, or stand, or sit, with them. The man who pursues the blessedness of the godly will refuse any such link with the ungodly, whatever be the phase of that ungodliness. He will stand his ground against the world. As another has said, "I cannot walk with those who dishonour Him, and honour Him in my walk" (J.N. Darby).

However, there is a positive side. The Psalmist not only tells what the blessed man will not do, but tells also what he actually will do. He will delight in the law of the Lord. Since "LORD" is printed here in the AV in capitals, as again in the closing verse of the Psalm, this indicates that it is the great name "Jehovah", and true blessedness is to be found in a constant meditation in His Word. This is the only divine title employed in this Psalm. Whether in the daylight of prosperity and joy, or in the night seasons of affliction and sorrow, the believer's resort should ever be to His Word. It ought to be remembered too, that, in the days of many of the Psalmists, their Bible was very small. Perhaps indeed, in David's time, they had not more than the five books of Moses. How privileged are those who today have a full and complete volume of inspiration. How these should delight to be constantly in that Word in meditation.

The blessed man who so continually meditates will be like a firmly planted tree; not a wild tree, but cultivated, flourishing by the refreshing rivers of communion with God. He is the subject of divine care and he bears fruit seasonably. There is nothing premature or untimely. All is morally suitable to the occasion and all is for the pleasure of God. The leaves are evergreen. The acts and deeds and words of this blessed man will abide and prosper. Of course, the ultimate and truly "Blessed Man" is none other than our Lord Jesus Himself.

Verses 4-6: The Ungodly Man

The second part of the Psalm deals with the character and the perdition of the ungodly, in contrast with the blessing of the godly. This section begins more forcibly than the AV would suggest. It is, "Not so the ungodly - not so" (LXX). The ungodly are like chaff. The wind will scatter them. They are light and lifeless. They are rootless, fruitless, and valueless. It is all reminiscent of the ministry of John Baptist who warned of the purging of the threshing floor. The true wheat was safe. It would abide, and that was assured, but the worthless chaff would be scattered by the wind and burned.

So the doom of the ungodly is sealed. They will forever disappear. They will not stand in the judgment and they have no place among the righteous. The way of the righteous is being constantly observed by the Lord - "He knoweth the way that I take" (Job 23.10). "He may try me", Job concedes, but the end will be as refined gold, precious and abiding. The way of the ungodly will perish. When the righteous inherit the kingdom and enter into the joy of their Lord the ungodly will go into everlasting punishment (Mt 25.34, 46). What a fearful end, to be lost for ever.

Notes

The names and titles of God are many and varied, each conveying some particular glory of Divine Persons. The different titles are equally beautiful but they need to be distinguished.

There are two Hebrew words translated "Lord" - "Jehovah" and "Adonai", but when the title "LORD" is printed in capital letters in the AV this always indicates that it is the great name "Jehovah". Since this will occur so very many times in the Psalms, it is appropriate to quote the following explanation as given in the introduction to the "Newberry" Bible. "The signification is, - He that always was, that always is, and that ever is to come. We have it thus translated and interpreted in Rev 1.4...It is a combination in marvellous perfection of the three periods of existence in one word, the future, the present, and the past".

PSALM 2

Introduction

This is the first of those Psalms which are called "Messianic". C.H. Spurgeon entitles it, "The Psalm of Messiah the Prince". Its Messianic and prophetic character is confirmed for us in that it is quoted seven times in the NT, always with reference to the Lord Jesus, the Messiah. It is quoted twice in the Acts of the Apostles (4.24-28; 13.33), twice in the Epistle to the Hebrews (1.5; 5.5), and three times in the Revelation (2.27; 12.5; 19.15). Notice, with reference to the quotation in Acts 4.25, that, while the human author of this Psalm is not identified in the Psalter, nevertheless the apostles attributed the Psalm to David. In its original and primary association the Psalm may have reference to the establishment of David upon his throne. In spite of the opposition of enemies, and David had many, he was Jehovah's anointed, and as such his coronation and enthronement is a foreshadowing of his greater Son, the Messiah. The Psalm is truly prophetic.

The twelve verses of Psalm 2 are divided obviously and poetically into four stanzas with three verses in each. It is likewise obvious that there are four speakers, four voices to be heard, one in each of the sections.

1. In the first section, verses 1-3, it is the voice of man in rebellion against Jehovah.
2. In the second section, verses 4-6, Jehovah, in wrath, speaks in reply.
3. In the third section, verses 7-9, Messiah speaks, declaring the divine decree concerning Him.
4. In the fourth section, verses 10-12, the Spirit speaks, calling upon men to be reconciled.

Verses 1-3: The Voice of Man

The Psalm begins with an ironic "Why?". "To what purpose?". "For what reason?". O the futility of revolt against Jehovah! The nations are raging. The people are vainly meditating malice against Jehovah. The kings of the earth array themselves in opposition to God. They will have no "King of kings" to rule over them. The rulers sit in evil counsel, devising their rebel plans. There is an unholy confederacy between Jew and Gentile to oppose the Lord and His Anointed. The apostles saw a fulfilment of it in Herod and Pontius Pilate with the Gentiles and the people of Israel, puny men allied in rebellion against the Prince of Peace (Acts 4.25-27). It is a wicked coalition which persists in our own day. "The mystery of iniquity doth already work" (2 Thess 2.7). Men will have nothing of divine restraint. The bands and cords of morality and spirituality they will break asunder and cast away. In every sphere of society a lawless spirit rages. What will it be when all restraint has been removed and men are left to vent their passions and wills as they desire?

Verses 4-6: The Voice of Jehovah

In the second solemn stanza heaven replies. How terrible when Jehovah laughs! The Almighty sits above them, enthroned in glory, unmoved by their futile, arrogant opposition to Him. He laughs at their foolish and puny defiance of Deity. But now He will speak. In His anger, in His wrath, Jehovah will confound them. In His sore displeasure He will vex them. There is doubtless an anticipation here of the future days of vengeance of which our Lord spoke in Luke 21.22. There will be a series of judgments during the great tribulation (Mt 24.21) which will make the plagues of Egypt seem as nothing. When the Saviour read the opening verses of Isaiah 61 in the Nazareth synagogue (Lk 4.16-20), He ceased His reading abruptly in the heart of a sentence. He had not come then to inaugurate the day of vengeance but patience is at an end in these verses, and heaven moves in judgment. Let men know that, in spite of their opposition and their arrogance and defiance, Jehovah has established His King upon the hill of His holiness. It is as if the purpose of God is already fulfilled and the true King reigns.

Verses 7-9: The Voice of the Messiah

The third section introduces the voice of that King, the Lord's Anointed. "I will declare the decree", He says. He will allow men to hear the holy converse between Jehovah and Messiah, between Father and Son. "Thou art My Son", is the confirmation of an eternal relationship. There is no beginning to this unique Sonship. The expression is quoted three times in the NT (Heb 1.5; 5.5; Acts 13.33), and it has been suggested that there is a golden thread running from Psalm 2 through all these citations. That golden thread is the humanity of Christ. The anointed King of Psalm 2 must be a Man. The Messiah of Hebrews 1 is also Man. So is the Priest of Hebrews 5 and the Saviour of Acts 13. He who is the Son eternally has been begotten into manhood to be recognised in humanity for what He has ever been in deity, the Son of God (Lk 1.35). In Acts 13.33 Paul states that Jesus was raised up among them. This is a reference to His manhood. So heaven's King and Kingdom are assured. As for the Son, the throne is His. The nations are His inheritance. Not only Israel and Canaan, but the nations and the uttermost parts of the earth are His by divine decree. The hand that held the mocking reed and then was pierced by men at Calvary will hold the sceptre, a rod of iron to break the oppressors, and rule the Kingdom for God with equity. This is the divine decree, now made known by the Son.

Verses 10-12: The Voice of the Spirit

The Psalm closes with a fourth stanza. It is an appeal for wisdom and reconciliation. It is an appeal to kings and to judges and to men of the earth everywhere to render due homage to Jehovah and to His Anointed with fear and trembling. "Kiss the Son". Notice that the word "Son" in v.12 is different from that in v.7. In v.7 it is the Hebrew BEN (1121), as in *Ben*-jamin, but in v.12 it is the Aramaic BAR (1248), as in *Bar*-abbas. Does not this emphasise the universal claims of the Messiah and the universality of the Spirit's appeal to both Jew and Gentile alike? Together, in the early part of the Psalm, these had been allied against Christ, but now the gracious appeal goes out to all. There is urgency too, for in a little while His anger will kindle. Happy is that man who finds refuge in Him. As the first Psalm begins, so the second Psalm ends - "Blessed". Blessed are all they who take refuge in Him.

Notes

In Acts 13.33, where the AV reads, "God hath fulfilled the same unto us...in that he hath raised up Jesus again", note that the RV and JND, with others, omit the word "again". This is not the raising up of Jesus again from the dead, in resurrection, as in vv. 30 and 34. It is His being raised up amongst them as a man, as was David in v.22, "He raised up unto them David". This is obviously not resurrection. So, "Of this man's seed hath God...raised unto Israel a Saviour, Jesus (v.23). In connection with this true manhood, the apostle quotes the second Psalm in v.33. A Man had been raised up among them who was God's Son.

PSALM 3

Introduction

The two Psalms, 3 and 4, are companion Psalms. They form a pair, being a morning and an evening hymn. As indicated in the title of Psalm 3, the sad background is that of 2 Samuel 15. David is in exile, a fugitive from the rebellion of Absalom and the treachery of Ahithophel. With those who still followed him faithfully he had crossed the Brook Kedron to the relative safety of Olivet and the mountainous desert beyond. He had left Jerusalem in sorrow. With head covered, and barefoot, they had gone over to the Mount of Olives, weeping as they went up the western slope of the mount. There were many sad days and nights to follow and these two Psalms were born during those days of the king's exile. Does not the Lord allow it so that the sorrows of His people often give birth to the sweetest songs and meditations?

Psalm 3 is in four stanzas of equal size, with two verses in each. There are three "Selahs", occurring after the first, second, and fourth stanzas. They are concerned firstly with David's lament, but then with his revived confidence, his peace in his circumstances, and his renewed trust in Jehovah.

Verses 1-2: The Lament of the Exile

He begins with a heart cry to Jehovah, "Lord how are they increased that trouble me! many are they that rise up against me". It is almost an echo of 2 Samuel 15.12, "The conspiracy was strong; for the people increased continually with Absalom". This was sorrow indeed, that his own beloved Absalom, his trusted counsellors, and so many of his people, had forsaken him, but there was a deeper hurt yet, and a more severe wound. Many there were who said, "There is no help for him in God". Could it be true? Had God, too, forsaken him? And was there some ground for believing that it could be so? Poor David! Is his conscience stinging? Is he remembering the shame of his so recent sin with Bathsheba (2 Sam 11.2-5)? Shimei curses him along the hillside, throwing stones and casting dust at him and his followers. David accepts it resignedly, saying that perhaps the Lord had bidden it. This is a sad lament indeed, concluding with the first of the "Selahs". Let the singer and the reader pause. Let them be silent, lifting up their hearts in solemn meditation, musing with sadness upon the trials of a man deserted and despised by his own son and by his own people.

Verses 3-4: Confidence in Jehovah

Again David uses the great name Jehovah. He will breathe the holy name six times in the Psalm. "But thou, O Lord, art a shield for me", he exclaims. It is not the ordinary word for a conventional shield which he uses. Jehovah is a buckler, wrapping him around, surrounding him on every side from the enemies that abound. In confidence now he feels himself completely protected by the presence of Jehovah, and, with the same assurance, he now looks forward. "My glory!", he cries, "and the lifter up of mine head". What is this, that this exile in the desert, this fugitive in the wilderness, can so anticipate better days? He who had left Jerusalem with bowed and covered head, in the shame of rejection, will yet return to his palace, and to glory, with his head lifted high. David had looked across the valley to the holy hill. He had earlier brought the Ark of the Covenant to the tabernacle on Mount Zion (2 Sam 6.12-17), and he now lifts his eyes towards that holy mount. "I cried unto the Lord with my voice", he says. Why does he say, "with my voice"? Because this is not just a silent prayer from the heart. The voices of his enemies were lifted up against him and he will lift up his voice too. He will call to Jehovah, and from the holy hill Jehovah will hear and answer. Again, "Selah". It is time once more to pause and reflect with the Psalmist.

Verses 5-6: Peace in the Storm

The third stanza provides the grounds upon which the Psalm is called,

"A Morning Hymn". Another night has passed. The rejected king has lain down and slept and has now awaked. In the midst of trouble he has had restful sleep. He has known peace in the storm and, as a new day dawns, he can face it with a calm confidence, for Jehovah has sustained him. The same Jehovah who, incarnate in a later day, will say to the storm on the Galilean Lake, "Peace, be still", has even now calmed the troubled sea of life for his tried saint. So, awakened after sleep and rest, David can say, "I will not be afraid". Though they may number tens of thousands who are against him on every hand, he cannot trust and be afraid at the same time. If his enemies are "round about" him, well, so is Jehovah, and, that being so, he cannot fear.

Verses 7-8: Trust in the Trial

There is no "Selah" after the third stanza. Why? Is there a holy impatience to come to the triumphant call of the fourth? "Arise, O Lord; save me, O my God". Does David now speak in such a confident anticipation that he can exult as if his prayer is already answered? "Thou hast smitten all mine enemies upon the cheek bone; thou hast broken the teeth of the ungodly". Another has written, "The language seems to be taken from a comparison of his enemies with wild beasts. The cheek bone denotes the bone in which the teeth are placed, and to break that is to disarm the animal" (Albert Barnes). Jehovah has rendered the enemies of the king toothless and harmless. He has fractured their jaws and broken their teeth and they are helpless. Salvation is the Lord's! Jehovah delights to bless his people. Shimei may curse; Jehovah will bless. It is a beautiful conclusion to the Psalm. Enemies may abound; evil may appear to triumph; trials may come like the billows of a troubled sea; but God will bless His people in it all. Now David may cry, "Selah". Pause and think. Meditate on these great things. Lift up the heart in gratitude to God who protects and preserves and ever provides for His needy saints.

Notes

For comments on the meaning and significance of "Jehovah", occurring six times in this Psalm, see the footnote at Psalm 1.

PSALM 4

Introduction

This is the first Psalm with a superscript. There are some expositors and commentators, as Thirtle, Scofield, the Companion Bible, and a later writer, A.G. Clarke, who believe that the superscript of a Psalm may in fact be a subscript of the preceding Psalm. Most commentators do not agree with this proposition, preferring to follow the Hebrew Bible and the Septuagint, understanding the superscriptions to be indeed titles, as indicated in the AV, JND, RV, RSV, and Spurrell, with others.

As Psalm 3 was a morning hymn, so this Psalm 4 is an evening hymn. The two Psalms are companions. They are the twin meditations of a troubled soul, and therefore of great blessing to saints in distress. C.H. Spurgeon says, "The Psalm…is another choice flower from the garden of affliction. Happy it is for us that David was tried, or probably we should never have heard these sweet sonnets of faith".

Fifty-five Psalms are committed to the care of the Chief Musician. This is the first of them. It was David himself who introduced music and song into the national worship, and the Chief Musician appears to have been the Director of Music with a special collection of Psalms in his care (1 Chr 6.31, 32; 15.16-22; 25.1, 7). "Neginoth" indicates stringed instruments, rather than wind instruments, and was probably a direction as to the preferred accompaniment of the Psalms so entitled.

The structure of this Psalm is very similar to that of Psalm 3. Again there are four stanzas of two verses each, with the "Selah" at the end of the first and second stanza. It is thought that the "Selah" at the end of Psalm 3 may be a connecting link between the morning and the evening hymns.

Verses 1-2: A Plea to God, and to Men

Psalm 4 perpetuates the cry of the preceding Psalm. "Hear me when I call", David pleads. There follows a title of God which is to be found only here in the Bible, "O God of my righteousness". Believers of every age and dispensation may intelligently employ this lovely form of address to God. By nature and by practice all have been but poor sinners, but in Christ, by grace, the believer has been given a righteous standing before God and the desire and power to live righteously before men. It is all of grace and of God. He is the author, the giver, the sustainer, and the rewarder of all and any righteousness His people have. He is the God of our righteousness.

Notice how David pleads for help now, perhaps on the basis that God has helped him in the past. Notice, however, that the words "when I was" are italicised. Omitting these may indicate a present tense, suggesting that even then, in his trouble, David was conscious of the divine presence, saying, "Thou hast enlarged me in distress". Jehovah will always come to the aid of His people in their sorrows and may safely be trusted to hear their prayers at all times. J.N. Darby's rendering of the second clause in the Psalm is very beautiful; "In pressure thou has enlarged me". It is an anomaly. Pressure tends to constrict and constrain, but in the pressure of affliction Jehovah enriches and enlarges His saints. Out of circumstances of sorrow and pain He brings forth sweetness and joy.

Having spoken to the Lord, David now speaks to men. It is well to commune with God first. Conflict with the enemy will be easier when there is prior communion with God. The Hebrew suggests that David actually uses a title of dignity in addressing those who oppose him. "Sons of men", he calls them. But in spite of their natural greatness they are vain. "Leasing" in v.2 is an old word for lying. For how long do they vainly imagine they can continue to turn the king's glory into shame? It was a fearful and dangerous path they were pursuing, despising the Lord's anointed. It is a time to pause, to reflect, to meditate upon the foolishness of it all. "Selah".

Verses 3-4: The Elect and the Enemy

In their folly David would have them know this, that Jehovah had set apart a people for Himself. Whatever men may say or do against His elect, they are the Lord's, set apart for Him. They are His peculiar possession and treasure. The remembrance of this should have a two-fold effect. For the elect it brings comfort and courage. He keeps them for Himself and his ear is open to their every cry. For the enemies it sounds a warning, "Who shall lay anything to the charge of God's elect?" (Rom 8.33). They are the apple of His eye and it is a serious thing to hurt them. Jehovah will hear when they call. It therefore behoves the enemies of God and His people to stand in awe, to tremble, to search their hearts, to take advantage of the quiet of the night, to be still and to muse upon their ways. Away from the clamour of the crowd a man should use the quietness to assess what is right and to see the folly of opposing God. Again, "Selah".

Verses 5-6: Sacrifice and Solace

The Psalmist renews his appeal to them. "Offer the sacrifices of righteousness, and put your trust in the Lord". There was a way back to God. It was a righteous way, by sacrifice. This had been His way since the first sin in Eden. Having offered the required offering, then it was simple trust. To every repentant sinner, so coming, He would be, as He was to the Psalmist, "God of my righteousness".

Having addressed both God and men, David resorts to sweet meditation and personal communion with the Lord. Men may question, "Who will show us any good?", but David knew from experience that Jehovah was the author of all that was good. He reminisces. He remembers the High Priestly blessing of Numbers 6.24-26, and he makes it his prayer, both for himself and for his followers: "LORD, lift thou up the light of thy countenance upon us". If the face of God would shine upon them it would lighten the path of affliction. How it would relieve the dark night of exile if Jehovah would but shine upon them.

Verses 7-8: Peace and Joy at Evening

The time of harvest was always a season of rejoicing in Israel. When the corn and wine, the harvest and the vintage, were increased and plentiful and safely gathered in, then there was a special joy. But it is possible, even in affliction, to have a gladness in the heart greater than the joy of a plenteous harvest. The Psalmist knew this, and he closes his evening hymn with expressions of calm repose in his God. He would sleep in peace. Let his enemies pursue him and plot his destruction. Let them plan his hurt and seek his life. Jehovah would keep him and he would rest in safety. Is it not probable that he slept more soundly than Absalom and more tranquilly than Ahithophel? Note this cluster of lovely words. There is light, gladness, peace, and safety. And all this is theirs, of every age, who rest in the Lord.

PSALM 5

Introduction

In many of the Psalms the titles contain Hebrew words, the meanings of which have sometimes gone into obscurity. We cannot, therefore, be dogmatic about their interpretation.

"Nehiloth" in our present Psalm is believed by many to be a wind instrument, such as the flute (Strong, 5155). Others say it is not a musical instrument at all but that the word means "inheritance" or "possession". If the former meaning is accepted then the flute is the preferred musical accompaniment to the singing of the Psalm. If the latter is the meaning then the Psalm is seen to be much occupied with the blessings, the possessions, the rich inheritance of those who trust in Jehovah.

Verses 1-3: A Morning Meditation

David now continues, as in preceding Psalms, to cry to Jehovah. This Psalm may belong to the same period of David's exile during Absalom's rebellion. Note how he pleads; "my words...my meditation...my cry...my voice...my prayer". There are petitions both audible and inaudible. "Give ear", he asks, "consider...hearken...O Jehovah...my King, and my God". It is a cry from the heart, sincere and thoughtful. It is touching to hear David exclaim, "My King". It is a recognition of the delegated character of his own monarchy. There was a greater sovereignty than his. This is intelligent address to God. There is reverence but urgency. Another day is dawning and in the morning hour David will begin that day with God. Observe how he "directs" his prayer. It is the word for arranging, ordering, marshalling. The Psalmist arranges his prayer in an orderly fashion. As the priest might have laid the sacrifice in order upon the altar so he lays his petitions and his worship before God in his morning devotions.

Verses 4-6: The Folly of the Wicked

David communes with a God who has no pleasure in wickedness or evil, nor in the foolishness of the workers of iniquity. God and evil cannot dwell together. What serious words are gathered together here to describe the sinfulness of the sinner. Wickedness; evil; iniquity; lying; deceit. David's

God abhors violence and deceit and these very things will characterise the usurper of a future day (2 Thess 2.9). But we are reminded of that Blessed One of whom, in a later day than David's, the prophet writes, "He hath done no violence, neither was any deceit in His mouth" (Is 53.9). In Him Jehovah found pleasure, and said so, "My beloved Son, in whom I am well pleased" (Mt 3.17; 17.5).

Verses 7-8: Worship and Witness

As for David personally, he will look towards the house of the Lord and worship. As Daniel opened his windows towards Jerusalem and kneeled to pray, so David looks toward the holy temple. Of course the temple, "exceeding magnifical" (1 Chr 22.5), was not yet built, but there was nevertheless a tabernacle on Mount Zion. The holy Ark of the Covenant dwelt there, as the symbol presence of Jehovah. The word "temple" is applied to the house of God in Shiloh in Samuel's day (1 Sam 1.9; 3.3). To this place David would look and pray early in the day, in the fear of the Lord, and he prays, as he does in Psalm 23, for Jehovah's leading in paths of righteousness. He pleads for clear guidance, that he might walk a righteous path, a path that would be both a testimony and a rebuke to his enemies.

Verses 9-12: Justice and Joy

The enemies of God and His people both think and speak wickedness. Paul will later quote David's description of them when writing to the saints at Rome: "Their throat is an open sepulchre; with their tongues they have used deceit" (Rom 3.13). "Very wickedness", says the Psalmist, unfaithful and flattering in their evil speech. They conceive this wickedness in the degradation of their inner beings. Their throats are corrupt as sepulchres, and their speech is correspondingly vile. God will destroy them, he had avowed in v.6. So be it. "Destroy thou them, O God", he now cries in v.10. Like the rebels of the second Psalm, their counsels are evil and their transgressions are many. They have merited the destruction for which David prays.

But those who trust will rejoice. Those who love Jehovah's name can shout for joy. The Lord is their defender. As with an encompassing shield they are wholly protected with His favour. Jehovah is round about His people. He blesses the righteous and they are joyful in Him. "Let them rejoice", says the Psalmist. "Let them ever shout for joy". "Let them…be joyful". The joy of the Lord is the strength of His people (Neh 8.10). Remembering all that Jehovah is to them and all that He has done for them, they have a right to rejoice.

Notes

It will be observed that there is language in some Psalms which is not now fitting for the New Testament believer. Certain Psalms, such as 58, 69, 83 and 137, are known as

"Imprecatory Psalms". It will be noted in the commentary on these Psalms that these maledictions do not reflect the spirit of this age of grace but belong essentially to an old dispensation. The believer today still recognises the wickedness of men and abhors it, and knows that men will of necessity be judged for it, but he cannot rightly pray for their destruction, nor does he cry for vengeance as Old Testament saints often did. In this new dispensation the preachers of the gospel of the grace of God plead with men to be reconciled to God, and they faithfully warn the unrepentant. They offer salvation and pardon in that message, but, alas, many will not respond and will perish accordingly.

PSALM 6

Introduction

A certain number of Psalms have been called "The Penitential Psalms". Perhaps the greatest example of these is the touching Psalm 51. Others are Psalms 32, 38, 102, 130 and 143. They are Psalms of mourning and penitence, a grieving over sin and a pleading for mercy. Psalm 6 is the first of these "Penitential Psalms". There may be no specific confession of sin here, but the anguish and the language is truly that of a real penitent who feels the weight of the wrong which he has done.

It is a Psalm of David, who commits it, as he does with fifty-four other Psalms, to the care of the Chief Musician, to be preserved in his collection. "Neginoth" means "stringed instruments", and apparently indicates that such should be employed in preference to wind instruments. "Sheminith" means "the eighth" or "an octave". F.W. Grant's comment is very beautiful, "The flutes are silent, and the music of the stringed instruments, better fitted to express the deeper emotions of the heart, follows them: and, indeed, in the bass notes, upon the octave". These musical directions would be well understood by the Chief Musician and the singers of that day, but today the full meaning of some of these words is not clear even to the best scholars of the Hebrew language. However, this is, as Spurgeon remarks, "a proof of the high antiquity of these Psalms...proofs of their being what they profess to be, the ancient writings of King David of olden times". We cannot be certain, but it is probable that this Psalm belongs to the period between David's sin with Bathsheba and Absalom's rebellion.

Verses 1-3: A Plea for Pity

The penitent Psalmist is obviously expecting and deserving chastisement and rebuke. In a spirit of true repentance he neither denies nor refuses this. He must submit to it, but asks that the rebuke come not to him in Jehovah's anger. "Whom the Lord loveth he chasteneth", and, "no chastening for the present seemeth to be joyous, but grievous" (Heb 12.6, 11), but David grieves mostly that he should be the subject of Jehovah's displeasure. He cannot ask for justice so he prays for pity and pleads his frailty. "I am weak", he cries, "have mercy". In body and in soul he feels the weight of his wrong. The sense of sin is a heavy burden. Listen to the groanings of this sorrowful man in the oft repeated, "O Lord; O Lord; O Lord; O Lord; O Lord". Five times in four verses does he so plead, crying, "How long?". It is the cry of an anguished soul. He longs that the chastisement should be over and done. He is suffering physically, mentally, and spiritually. Body and soul are alike weary with it all. He dreads both the severity and the extent of Jehovah's displeasure with him for his sin. How long before the clouds will lift and the sun break through? How long before the night passes and a new day dawns? O Lord, how long?

Verses 4-7: Travail and Tears

It is a consistent and understandable fact, that by sinning the enjoyment of the presence of God is lost. It was so even with our first parents in Eden. One cannot have both sin and the consciousness of the divine presence. David grieves the absence of the Lord and pleads, "Return, O Lord". That saint is miserable who, having known the presence of the Lord, has now lost it because of sin. David has an earnest three-fold prayer, "Return...deliver...save". In sincere and simple language he cries for salvation. It has already been remarked that he cannot plead justice, for justice would condemn him for what he has done. He pleads for mercy, therefore, and he pleads it in the plural - "Save me for thy mercies' sake". Whether a plurality of mercies is intended here, in the way that a plural would normally be understood, meaning many, or whether it is the Hebraistic way of expressing greatness, vastness, magnanimity, it does not matter. God's mercy is great. "Abundant mercy", writes an apostle of a later day (1 Pet 1.3). The Psalmist knows this and pleads accordingly.

He dreads death. He reasons that in the grave there is no remembrance of former things, and therefore no penitence, or praise. To those under law, with their partial revelation of conditions after death, and in the depressed state of soul in which the Psalmist was at that time, death was indeed the valley of the shadow and there was a certain mystery of stillness and silence. But why does David here, at this point in the Psalm, think of death? Does he fear that death might overtake him before his reconciliation with Jehovah? Does that kindred Psalm 32, particularly vv. 3 and 4, indicate that David was so affected physically by his remorse and regret that he actually lived in fear of death? It is no light matter to realise that one has sinned against the Lord. Day and night, sleeplessly, he wept and groaned and prayed, until, physically, he was drained of strength and energy. In utter weariness he groaned. His tears watered his bed by night and bedewed his couch by day and there was no rest. His grief is reflected in his sunken eyes. He has aged prematurely and, sadly, his enemies know it.

Verses 8-10: Answered Prayer

But suddenly he bids his enemies depart. They are workers of iniquity and he wants neither their company nor their criticism. Jehovah has heard him to the shame and confusion of his persecutors. Three times again in swift succession David uses the great name, Jehovah. Jehovah has heard his weeping and his supplication and has received his prayer. David's weeping had a voice - "the voice of my weeping". His tears were sincere, more eloquent than words, and the Lord heard. His supplications and his prayers were wet with his tears and Jehovah has heard. Now, as he is restored, it is the penitent's added plea that his enemies should be as he had once been, sore vexed and ashamed.

Notes

In v. 5 the word translated "grave" is SH^{e}OL (7585), which is the Hebrew equivalent of the Greek "Hades". The word occurs sixty-five times in the Hebrew of the OT, sixteen of these being in the Psalms. Its first occurrence is in Genesis 37.35 where it is translated, as it often is, "the grave", as here in this Psalm. It may be misleading that it is equally often translated "hell", as, for instance, in Psalm 16.10, for it is to be distinguished from "Gehenna" (1067) which is the place of torment, called "hell fire" (Mt 5.22). SH^{e}OL has been called the abode of the dead, the unseen world, the place of departed spirits, where the dead have ceased from the activities of this life. It is not, of course, the literal earthy burying place. William Hoste has called it "the grave-land". It is the abode of the spirits of the dead to which the grave admits.

PSALM 7

Introduction

This Psalm has been called "The Song of the Slandered Saint". It is a delightful paradox that saints can sing in circumstances such as those envisaged in Psalm 7. It is a "Shiggaion" (7692*)* of David. The word means "praise", but it is apparently not praise in the usual sense of that word. It has been interpreted as a "wandering ode". There is a certain variable, almost erratic, movement in the poetry, alternating between comfort and joy, between sorrow and solace, between trial and trust, as changing as are the life experiences of the saints themselves. "Shiggaion" occurs elsewhere only in Habakkuk 3.1, spelled "Shigionoth".

David has been slandered by one "Cush", a Benjamite. We have no historical record of anyone by that name and, therefore, we cannot identify him accurately. At least three suggestions have been made. First, he was a fellow tribesman of Saul, and may have been a courtier of the king, previously unmentioned in Scripture. Or, the word may be a pseudonym for Saul himself. Again, though unlikely, it may be a veiled reference to Shimei who later cursed David. The word means "black" or "sun-burnt", and in Jeremiah 13.3 and Amos 9.7 it is translated

"Ethiopian". Whoever he was, this Cush was a black-hearted man who was slandering David to King Saul. But in spite of the slander David will praise.

Verses 1-5: Refuge from the Oppressor

The Psalm begins and ends with those great titles, "Jehovah Elohim" (430) and "Jehovah Elyon" (5945). "Jehovah", says David, "is my God, and He is the Most High". This latter was the title used by Melchizedek in Genesis 14.19-20 when blessing Abram. It is good, in our trials, to recognise the majesty of God. In such an One David will "trust" (2620), and the thought is that of taking refuge from his pursuers. He is as one being hunted and he will, as it were, shelter himself as in a rock, safe in that refuge while the enemy crouches outside like a lion lying in wait to devour him. His only help and hope is in his God. There is none else able to deliver him. Jehovah alone can protect him from his oppressors. David may well be thinking of those defenceless lambs which he had shepherded in the fields of Bethlehem. Had he not, for them, slain a lion, and a bear (1 Sam 17.34-36)? Will Jehovah his God now deliver him from the lion that waits to rend him? Note the blending of fear and faith, of trust and triumph, in keeping with that meaning of "Shiggaion" that we have seen in the title.

The slandered David pleads and protests his innocence. Had he requited evil to him who was at peace with him? He appeals to the One who knew the truth of it all, and again he uses the language of the opening verse of the Psalm, "O Lord my God". Such is his confidence in his innocence that he can, with impunity, ask Jehovah to judge his case. If he is found guilty of the accusations being levelled against him he is prepared to have both his honour and his glory brought to the dust. Indeed, not only his honour, but his very life would be forfeit. If there is iniquity in his hands he will accept the consequences. But, he maintains, so far from that, he had in the past actually delivered the man who was his enemy without cause. Not once, but twice, had he spared the life of the sleeping Saul. How remarkably does this language agree with David's words to Saul in 1 Samuel 24.11-12: "Know thou and see that there is neither evil nor transgression in mine hand, and I have not sinned against thee; yet thou huntest my soul to take it. The Lord judge between me and thee". In that hill country of En-gedi David had entered the cave where the king slept, and had cut off a piece of the king's garment but spared his life. Again, in the wilderness of Ziph, David had, for the second time, an opportunity to slay Saul, but had again spared him who was seeking his life. Listen to his touching address to Saul then: "Wherefore doth my lord thus pursue after his servant? for what have I done? or what evil is in mine hand?" (1 Sam 26.18). "Yea", he says now, as he remembers, "I have delivered him that without cause is mine enemy". The first section of the Psalm ends with the "Selah". It is time for a pause, for reflection, and for praise too.

Verses 6-10: Judgment and Justice

David now asks for the setting up of a great tribunal, "Arise, O Lord". It is an ardent cry, a passionate plea, that Jehovah should sit in divine arbitration and judge the nations. Has heaven been silent while David's enemies raged? Has the Lord removed Himself from the scene and from the plight of His servant? "Arise", David pleads, "Awake!...Return!" Before the assembled peoples who would encompass the throne in such a tribunal David is willing that his case should be heard and judged by the Lord. He knows his innocence and He knows that Jehovah will judge righteously. He knows that such righteous judgment will vindicate him and establish his integrity before his oppressors. Prophetically, this looks on to that judgment of the nations of which the Lord Jesus spoke in Matthew 25. It will be a vast assembling of the nations when the Lord will acknowledge the righteousness of the righteous and bring to an end the wickedness of the wicked. David is now looking beyond the thought of his own personal vindication and anticipating the day when all evil will be judged and righteousness will be established on the earth. The Psalmist is mingling desires for his own personal judgment with thoughts of the judgment of nations. "The Lord shall judge the people", he says, "judge me, O Lord". God alone can try the hearts and reins, the motives and inward hidden thoughts of men. With divine omniscience He will assess, and judge accordingly. In such a tribunal David's defence is of God. Literally, this is, "My shield is with God", or, "upon God", or, "borne by God" (J.N. Darby; F.W. Grant; F. Delitzsch). The thought is that of the warrior's shield being borne by the armour bearer, ready at hand for the defence of the warrior. David's shield was with God. His defence was near at hand when Jehovah was there. Like the Son of David of a later day, he is happy to commit himself to Him that judges righteously (1 Pet 2.23). God will always be the Saviour of the upright in heart.

Verses 11-17: Retribution or Vindication?

Although there will be a future day of judgment, in fact there is an on-going divine reckoning now, and the Lord is angry with the wicked every day. If he, the wicked, turns not in repentance, then Jehovah sharpens His sword and bends His bow in readiness to judge the evil. If there is no repentance then there must be retribution. The instruments of death and judgment are already prepared. Righteous judgment is even now determined. In holy indignation God will move against the evil-doers.

"Behold!" The Psalmist summons us to look with him to the wicked and his end. It is a fearful sight. The sinner travails with iniquity. He conceives mischief and brings forth falsehood. It is akin to the truth of James 1.15, "Sin, when it is finished, bringeth forth death", for judgment must surely come. The wicked man digs a pit and himself falls into it. The background would be a familiar one to men of the desert and the wilderness. The hunter has dug a hole to entrap his prey, but he stumbles into the trap he has made for others. So would it be with David's slanderers. What they had imagined for David would come back upon their own heads in God's righteous judgment. They would fall into their own snare.

As for David, he praises Jehovah in it all. The Psalm concludes with a note of assurance and a song of praise. How often in the Psalm does he speak of righteousness, and, in accord with that righteousness, the Psalmist sings praise to the name of Him whom he calls "Jehovah Elyon", the Lord Most High. As Daniel told Nebuchadnezzar the King of Babylon, "The most High ruleth in the kingdom of men" (Dan 4.25). With such an One, who, in His sovereignty, is in perfect control of all things and all men, David could safely leave his judgment and his vindication. So should each saint learn from the good example of David to leave his case with God. He is righteous and may be confidently trusted to do what is right.

Seek not to vindicate thyself, nor plead
In thine own cause, for thou wilt surely err.
Best leave it to thy God, He faileth not;
Let Deity, my soul, thy suit prepare.

PSALM 8

Introduction

Psalm 8 is a truly Messianic Psalm, being quoted four times in the NT with reference to the Lord Jesus. He Himself quotes it once, in Matthew 21.16, Paul quotes it twice (1 Cor 15.27 and Eph 1.20-22), and the writer of the Epistle to the Hebrews quotes it once, in ch. 2.6-9. These NT citations will be noticed in more detail in the exposition.

The title indicates that this is another of those Psalms which are committed to the care of the Chief Musician, to form part of that special collection of Psalms. Also in the title is the word "Gittith" (1665), for which several meanings have been suggested. F.W. Grant cites an anonymous writer who sums these up very beautifully. He quotes, "Some Hebrew scholars would regard it as the name of a musical instrument peculiar to Gath, where David once sought shelter from the unrelenting persecution of Saul. Just as there was among the Greeks a Dorian Lyre, which had a wide celebrity on account of its excellent sweetness, so, it is suggested, for this Psaltery, "Gittith", was borrowed by David from the citizens of Gath, and thence introduced by him on account of the superior sweetness of its tone and beauty". He continues, "But a more likely derivation may be found for this title "Gittith", in a Hebrew root, signifying "wine-press". And now it is an autumnal song chanted by the vine-dressers at the joyful vintage-season". Of course, as Grant himself suggests, both of these interpretations may have significance in the Psalm. W.S. Plumer cites the Chaldee version which has the title, "A Psalm of David to be sung upon the harp that came from Gath". But again he quotes one Scott, who says, "'Gittith' is perhaps the name of some tune, which David had learned when in Gath, or from the Gittites". But Hengstenberg has an important comment when he says, "It is worthy of remark that all the three Psalms distinguished by this name are of a joyful, thanksgiving character" (See Psalms 81 and 84)

The date of this Psalm is not known for certain though some have fixed it, as with other Psalms of David, at around 1050 BC. It does not appear to be either celebrating, or associated with, any particular circumstance in the Psalmist's life or experience. However, there are touches in the Psalm which are reminiscent of David's shepherd life. How often, during the night watches, the shepherd boy of Bethlehem must have contemplated the glory of the heavens. As Plumer writes, "One thing seems clear, that even if the Psalm was not written during David's shepherd life, it must at least have been written while the memory of that time was fresh in his heart, and before the bitter experience of his later years had bowed and saddened his spirit". The scope of the Psalm is very wide, looking back to Eden and forward to the glorious reign of the Messiah, from the first Adam to the last Adam.

Verses 1-2: Wonder and Worship

It will be readily noticed that the Psalm begins and ends with the same lovely words, the same ascriptions of praise and the same expressions of wonder at the greatness and glory of God. It is like a jewel enclosed by, and encased in, two golden clasps. The Psalm concludes in the same spirit of worship with which it began. It is good when in meditation and study the reader is not diverted from a worshipping spirit. Rather should all contemplation of divine things increase our appreciation of God and help towards an intelligent and devoted address to divine Persons.

Jehovah's name is exalted. There is a greatness which can neither be expressed nor expounded, and the Psalmist can only exclaim, "How excellent!" (117). This word has been variously translated "great, illustrious, glorious, wonderful, magnificent, renowned". The name of the Lord is that by which He has made Himself known, but there is a limitation to human language and understanding, and so there are times when the worshipper can only but bow in wonder and cry as the Psalmist, "How excellent is thy name". The devout man will adore even when he can no longer apprehend or even enquire.

There is much coming and going between heaven and earth in this Psalm. There is an ascending and descending which begins in the opening verse. Jehovah's name is excellent in the earth and His glory is set above the heavens. "O LORD our Lord" is "O Jehovah our Adonai", "Jehovah our sovereign Lord". Jehovah is the Proprietor, Ruler, Possessor and Governor of everything. He is acknowledged on earth and His glory is established above the heavens. The Jews spoke of three heavens, as indeed Paul did (2 Cor 12.2). There was the aerial heaven of the atmosphere and the birds, then the stellar heaven or the heaven of the stars, and the third heaven was that dwelling place of God which in the Epistle to the Hebrews is called "heaven itself" (Heb 9.24). But above the heavens, supreme in His divine majesty, Jehovah sits in excellency. His name is known on earth and His glory is above the heavens.

It is in the wonder of the ways of God that such inscrutable and indescribable glory should be acknowledged by babes and sucklings, who give testimony to Him to the silencing of His enemies. It is not necessary to spiritualise this and to interpret these infants as being babes in faith, new-born souls. Our Lord Jesus Himself applied the words to children of His day. When such little ones acclaimed Him in the temple court, crying "Hosanna to the Son of David", and the priests and scribes complained in their displeasure, He said to them, "Yea; have ye never read, Out of the mouth of babes and sucklings thou hast perfected praise?"(Mt 21.15, 16). And again, in Matthew 11.25, at the end of a sad chapter, the Saviour said in His prayer of thanksgiving, "I thank thee, O Father, Lord of heaven and earth, because thou hast hid these things from the wise and prudent, and hast revealed them unto babes". Some expositors, however, as Gaebelein and Grant, do interpret these babes and sucklings as newly converted souls, believers who are young in the faith. If some object to the thought of "sucklings" engaging in the praise of Jehovah, it may be remarked here that Hebrew mothers nursed their children much longer than is the custom in Western culture. It will be remembered that Hannah did not wean the young Samuel until he was old enough to be left in the temple with Eli and to worship the Lord there (1 Sam 1.22-28).

But who is the enemy, and the avenger. These may be collective nouns, describing in a general way those who are at enmity with God and His people. It is more likely, however, that they indicate a person, who may be none other than the arch-enemy himself, Satan. The word "avenger" is a strong word. Perowne says, "It denotes one who thirsts for or breathes revenge". This, of course, is characteristic of the Devil whose judgment is already determined, and it must be particularly bitter for him to know that Jehovah can use the lispings of babes to silence him. Things that little children have said have often been used to the confounding of the adversaries.

Verses 3-4: The Creator and the Creature

How often the shepherd boy of Bethlehem must have lain in the fields among the flock, contemplating the skies. Sometimes by day, as in Psalm 19, sometimes by night, as here in Psalm 8, David must often have considered the infinite vastness and splendour of the heavens, the immeasurable distances of space, the glory of the sun and the brilliance of the moon, and the innumerable stars all keeping their appointed place in the firmament. It was all the work of Jehovah's fingers. He had embroidered the skies with a heavenly beauty and had ordained and established the vast solar system for His own glory. T.E. Wilson, quoting Carlyle, calls it "The silent palace of the Eternal".

Such contemplation is humbling to man. "What is man", the Psalmist asks, "and the Son of man?". Considering the greatness of the creator and the littleness of the creature, why should Jehovah be mindful of man at all or deign to visit him? Our English word "man", occurring twice here in v.4, is, in fact, the translation of two different Hebrew words. The first is ENOSH (582), meaning man in his frailty. The second is ADAM (120) which, although linking man with the clay and the ground, is, nevertheless, man in his dignity as God's vicegerent in the creation. But what is man in any case? Whether in his frailty or in his dignity, how insignificant is the creature, that Jehovah should condescend to visit him, as indeed He did in Eden so long ago (Gen 3.8). And what of that subsequent visitation of grace, when a divine Person, the Son of God Himself, tabernacled among men for thirty-three wondrous years, visiting David's Bethlehem, living in the despised Nazareth, and sojourning in Judea, Samaria, and Galilee. What is man, that the Creator should so think of him?

Verses 5-9: Glory and Honour

Now although man may indeed be insignificant and frail, yet Jehovah has given him a certain greatness in the creation. Two words in v.5 need comment - "little" and "angels". This word "little" may mean little in degree, a coming short just a little, or, it may have to do with time, indicating "for a little while". Since excellent expositors disagree, and since there is a sense in which both things are true, it must be left to the reader to decide which is contextual.

The word translated here as "angels" is ELOHIM (430). This is that title of God which is found as early as Genesis 1.1, "In the beginning ELOHIM created the heaven and the earth". Man was created in the image and likeness of the Creator and, in his innocence, was given a sovereignty and dominion in the creation a little lower than the Creator Himself. This is the only place in the OT where ELOHIM is translated "angels" but in Hebrews 2.7, where this verse is quoted, the word "angels" was preferred by those who translated the Hebrew Scriptures into Greek, in what is known as the Septuagint version.

The man was crowned with glory and honour. He had, as it were, a crown, a throne and a sceptre. The dominion was at his feet, subject to him. The creatures obeyed him, and in his authority he gave them names (Gen 2.19). The dominion was threefold. The man could look around, or look up, or look down. The beasts of the field, the birds of the air, and the fish of the sea, were all in his domain.

This lovely picture is, of course, initially true of the first Adam, the man in Eden. But the Psalm is undoubtedly prophetic, as Hebrews 2 proves, and it therefore points forward to the second Man, the last Adam, the Lord from heaven, even our Lord Jesus (1 Cor 15.45, 47). The former loveliness of Eden has been forfeited by man because of sin, but Jehovah never departs from an original purpose, and His purpose is that man should yet have dominion as it was at the first. The beauty of it all may be seen fulfilled during the life and ministry of Jesus, when wild beasts, winds and waves, disease and demons, and death itself were all subject to Him. But the ultimate fulfilment will come to pass when, in millennial splendour, He will have dominion from sea to sea, and will rule from the river to the ends of the earth (Ps 72.8). In that day the whole earth will be filled with His glory and the prayers of David the son of Jesse will be ended (Ps 72.20). When Messiah sits in glory and reigns over the earth, David has nothing more to pray for.

Remembering this, the reader will return to that spirit of worship of the opening verse of the Psalm. How excellent is Jehovah's name in all the earth!

PSALM 9

Introduction

As with the titles of many other Psalms, the title of this Psalm incorporates a strange and unusual word; in this case the word is "Muthlabben" (4192). This is often taken to mean "The death of the Son", but Spurgeon and others prefer "The death of the Champion" and quote the Chaldee which has, "The death of the Champion who went out between the camps". If this is accepted, there is an obvious reference to David's victory over Goliath of Gath, and the sentiments of the Psalm would certainly accord with this. It is a Psalm of triumph celebrating victory over the enemies of Jehovah and His people, and it is one of those fifty-five Psalms which are committed to the care of the Chief Musician. Because of the constantly changing strain in the Psalm it is difficult to give a methodical outline or division of the verses. As Alexander Maclaren so beautifully writes of it, "The diamond is turned a little in the hand, and a differently tinted beam flashes from its facets".

It should be noticed that there is a certain affinity with Psalm 10. They are linked by an acrostic arrangement which, although irregular, is nevertheless interesting and instructive. To quote F.W. Grant, "Two Psalms, which in the Septuagint and Vulgate are united together, as in a real way they are by an alphabetic arrangement which, though irregular and even defective, can be distinctly traced, and which runs through them both".

He continues, "May not the irregularity itself be designed?". Viewed prophetically, the two Psalms have to do with Israel's deliverance from enemies within and without, and from a wicked or lawless person, until the Most High reigns. The verses in which the acrostic arrangement is missing are those verses which deal with that lawless one and his evil rule (Ps 10.2-11), so that, as Grant observes, "We see then that the Psalm is as it should be, and that its irregularity as well as its regularity are alike of God". He feels that a little enthusiasm over this inspired pattern should be pardoned!

Verses 1-6: Praise to the Most High

The Psalmist praises with the assurance of a four-fold "I will". This is in response to a four-fold "Thou hast" on the part of Jehovah. Of Jehovah he says,

"Thou hast maintained my right"
"Thou hast rebuked the heathen"
"Thou hast destroyed the wicked"
"Thou hast put out their name for ever and ever".

This remembrance of Jehovah's power calls for a holy celebration and there is an outburst of praise to the Most High. So does the Psalmist sing his fourfold acknowledgement:

"I will praise thee, O LORD"
"I will shew forth all thy marvellous works"
"I will be glad and rejoice in thee"
"I will sing praise to thy name".

His praise is firstly to Jehovah. He then uses that millennial name of God with which the seventh Psalm concludes, "The Most High". This great name is to be found first in Genesis 14 where it occurs four times in vv. 18-22. Jehovah is El Elyon (5945), Possessor of heaven and earth, Proprietor, the mighty Creator, Upholder, and Owner of all things. By this name will Jehovah be known in that day when He reigns unchallenged and supreme in kingdom splendour. But David recognises this supremacy already and ascribes praise accordingly.

It is fitting yet that Jehovah should be praised and that His people should sing with joy as they recount His mercies and contemplate His greatness. He still maintains the cause of His people. He still judges righteously and one day will finally rebuke the nations and blot out the name of the wicked forever. All memorials of His enemies shall one day perish with them, and for ever. Well does the Psalmist sing of gladness and joy and praise with his whole heart.

Verses 7-12: A Refuge in Trouble

This next section of the Psalm begins with a "But", to emphasise the contrast between Jehovah and His enemies. Those enemies shall perish; they shall go into oblivion, with every memory of them, but Jehovah shall endure for ever. The thought seems to be echoed in Psalm 102.26-27 as cited in Hebrews 1.11-12 – "They shall perish, but thou remainest". Jehovah is, after all, "the Same". It is a divine title. He is the "I AM", the unchanging, ever-abiding, immutable One who will sit eternally upon His throne when those who have challenged Him have perished in His righteous judgment.

Note the repeated mention of this righteous character of God's judgment. Men can be partial in their judgments. Jehovah is impartial. Men may be respecters of persons and can be open to bribery and corruption to pervert the course of justice. Jehovah is no respecter of persons, but judges righteously, as Peter reminded the household of Cornelius in Acts 10.34, and as Paul reminded the men of Athens at Mars' Hill in Acts 17.31. Indeed it is as if Paul is actually quoting Psalm 9.8 on that occasion: "He shall judge the world in righteousness".

Now, the remembrance of this righteousness of God, if it be a terror to God's enemies, is a comfort to those who love Him. He will be a refuge for His people in times of trouble. He will be a resort for them in their times of distress and oppression. "Refuge" (4869) is a particularly precious word. Strictly, and literally, it is "A high tower; a high fortress". When His people are assailed they may run to this refuge, safe above the threatenings of the enemy below. Those who know Him, trust Him. None can trust Him who do not know Him. Trust is an intelligent leaning upon Jehovah by those who know Him. His name is His character, and, knowing His character, the saints can trust Him. "I know whom I have believed, and am persuaded that he is able to keep…" (2 Tim 1.12). Jehovah has never forsaken those who seek Him. So, for generations, His people have sung;

> O hope of every contrite heart,
> O joy of all the meek,
> To those who fall, how kind Thou art;
> How good to those who seek!

The exhortation to sing is almost to be expected. Jehovah dwells in Zion but the Gentile peoples around must hear of His doings. "People" of v.11 is a plural word, "peoples" (5971). It signifies the Gentiles. His people sing and the peoples hear. Zion resounds with Psalms and the surrounding nations hear the declarations of His mighty works.

When Jehovah makes inquisition, when He holds an inquest concerning the blood of His oppressed and martyred saints, He will remember and avenge. "How long?", those martyrs of a later day will cry. "How long, O Lord, holy and true, dost thou not judge and avenge our blood" (Rev 6.10). Justice may seem to linger and delay, but vindication is sure. The cry of the afflicted will not be forgotten.

Verses 13-14: A Personal Petition

From remarks which are general and national and all-embracing David now pleads very personally and individually. "Have mercy upon me, O Lord". "Be gracious unto me, O Jehovah" (JND). Poor David had many enemies. There were many who hated him and would have destroyed him. Many of them were his enemies wrongfully. They hated him without a cause (Ps 69.4). A thousand years later the same would be true of the Son of David, the Messiah (Jn 15.25), but it was true also of David himself.

But what a joyful transition is this, between vv. 13 and 14. From the gates of death Jehovah lifts him to the gates of Zion. It has been said that the Psalmist divided his time between praising and praying. From his prayer at the gates of death he is lifted to praise at the gates of Zion. How often does Jehovah allow His people to be brought low so that He may uplift them to the very gates of heaven in praise for deliverance? From the dark valley of the shadow of death He lifts them to the light and glory of heaven itself. His everlasting arms are ever underneath them, causing them to rejoice in His salvation.

Verses 15-18: The Doom of the Wicked

It is a principle, an unchanging principle, that men reap what they sow. In the very heart of this section the Psalmist calls for a solemn meditation upon what he has to say. With a "Higgaion" (1902) and a "Selah" (5542), he calls, in a doubly emphatic way, for a pause to consider, ponder, think, meditate on what he has said. The enemies of God and His people have fallen into the pit of their own digging. They are ensnared in the snare of their own making. They have become entrapped in the trap which they had set for the godly. It is like the wicked Haman hanged on the gallows that he had prepared for the good Mordecai (Est 7.10). Jehovah, who judges the wicked, is revealed, by His very judgments, to be what He is, a righteous God. He is known by the judgment which He executes. So must He eventually banish the wicked, with nations of men who forget God. How simple a thing does forgetfulness appear to be, but to forget God is unpardonable. So did the rich fool of the Saviour's parable forget the God who had given the increase in his harvest (Lk 12.16-21). The man had planned and plotted and schemed but had left God out of all his plans and thoughts. "Thou fool!"

But the poor and needy ought not to fear. Dependence upon God shall never be forgotten by Him. Men in their independence may forget Him, but He will never forget those who, in their need, are cast upon Him in expectation of His help. The hope and trust of the meek will be rewarded.

Verses 19-20: The Frailty of Man

The Psalm concludes with a powerful plea from the Psalmist that Jehovah should arise and that the nations should be judged in His sight. "Put them in fear", he cries. He has a two-fold end in view. "Let not man prevail". "Let them know that they are but men". Twice he uses the word "man". It is the Hebrew word ENOSH (582). It is mortal man in his frailty; man in his human weakness. With all his learning, his acquired knowledge, his supposed wisdom, his genius, his conquests and his wealth, he is, in the end, just "enosh", a frail creature. God has richly blessed him and endowed him, and yet he forgets God. But Jehovah will judge him.

With another "Selah", the song of victory concludes. The reader must meditate upon the ultimate triumph of a righteous God

PSALM 10

Introduction

Psalms 9 and 10 are so intimately connected that some ancient versions, such as the Septuagint and the Vulgate, have regarded them as one Psalm. Those who accept this unity of the two Psalms point to the fact that Psalm 10 has no title and that this implies a continuity with the preceding Psalm. There is, however, a completeness in each of the Psalms which seems to suggest two separate compositions, albeit by the same Psalmist. We have already noticed that there are other instances of Psalms which form a pair, but which are, nevertheless, complete in themselves - Psalms 1 and 2, and Psalms 3 and 4. So it is with Psalms 9 and 10.

As has been remarked on Psalm 9, the two Psalms are, in their original Hebrew, closely linked by an irregular acrostic arrangement. Had this acrostic form continued uninterrupted and undisturbed it might have signified order throughout. But the break implies the reverse. Here is envisaged a disorder occasioned by enemies within and outside the nation. The longest break in the acrostic arrangement, which commences with the opening verse of Psalm 9, occurs in those verses which particularly describe the lawless one, vv. 3-11 of Psalm 10. When this description of the wicked one is complete, then the acrostic form will resume. Alexander Maclaren speaks of "the calm flow of devotion and persistency of prayer", but then adds, "The description of the wicked is as a black rock damning the river, but it flows on beneath and emerges beyond".

The prophetic import of these Psalms must not be overlooked. They anticipate those days which are called by the prophet, "the time of Jacob's trouble" (Jer 30.7), and this adds interest to that other expression which is to be found in both Psalms 9 and 10, but nowhere else - "times of trouble" (Ps 9.9; 10.1). In these troubled times of the great tribulation the lawless one will persecute the nation until his eventual destruction at the coming of the Messiah who will then restore order and reign unchallenged in millennial glory.

Verses 1-11: The Cry and the Cause

"Why?" How many of His saints in every age have so called to Jehovah out of sorrow and pain? How often have His people called out from their perplexity and bewilderment and He does not seem to hear? Why, at times, when they want Him near, does He seem so far away? "Why standest thou afar off, O Lord?". To the Psalmist, Jehovah appears to be watching from a distance. Why does He hide Himself in these times of trouble? Would the burden be easier to bear if He were near? Did not Mary and Martha feel exactly the same when they exclaimed through their tears, "Lord, if thou hadst been here" (Jn 11.21, 32)? And did not even those who loved Him once ask, "Master, carest thou not" (Mk 4.38)? Maybe it is the hiding of His face, even more than the trouble, which perplexes His saints, and perhaps, as with the sisters of Bethany, His delay is to encourage trust and to teach that He has greater things in mind for His saints than what they ask. Well it is for the believer who can sing sincerely,

When darkness seems to veil His face,
I rest on His unchanging grace;
In every high and stormy gale
My anchor holds within the veil.

The sufferer must ever remember too, that if Jehovah seems at times to be distant, it is not really so. He is always a very present help in trouble for His saints and His hiding of Himself temporarily is but part of His plan and purpose for their ultimate good. As Spurgeon says, "The refiner is never very far from the mouth of the furnace when his gold is in the fire".

The problem here is an old problem. There is a contrast between the wicked and the poor, and the wicked, in his arrogance and pride, seems to prosper. Why does Jehovah apparently stand aloof from this? How, or why, can the wicked man continue, with impunity, in his wickedness? There follows, through until v.11, a long list of indictments against the lawless one. It is all so similar to Paul's description of fallen humanity in general in Romans 3.10-18, but here the indictments are particularly applicable, prophetically, to that man of sin, the arch-persecutor of God's saints in a day to come (2 Thess 2.3-4).

In his haughtiness the wicked persecutes the poor. This may indeed mean those who are materially poor, whom he despises because of their poverty. It may, however, mean the humble poor, those who are poor in spirit, whom our Lord commended in Matthew 5.3. Others, including JND, prefer to translate "afflicted", but perhaps the several ideas are closely connected. Those who are poor, whether poor in spirit or poor in this world's goods, are liable to be the afflicted objects of the contempt of the wicked, despised because of their poverty. The latter part of v.2, "let them be taken in the devices that they have imagined", may be a petition reminiscent of vv. 15-16 of the preceding Psalm, praying that the persecutor may fall into the pit which he has made for others or be entrapped in his own snare. Others think that this is not a petition but that "let them be" should be rendered "they are", or, "they shall be", meaning that, as the persecutor has planned, so it is; they shall be caught in the wicked devices which they have invented. But again, even if the AV translation is preferred, the thought may still be that the judgment of the wicked is already assured. There is really no need to petition; they shall yet reap what they have sown.

The wicked boasts of his desires, glorying in the depraved imaginations of his heart, and in his perversity he actually commends that covetousness which Jehovah abhors. In his pride he is not at all concerned with the thoughts of God. He thinks and plans materialistically only. If by covetousness a man can enrich himself and escape poverty, that, to the wicked, is to be commended. In his pride and self-sufficiency he has no desires after God, and, indeed, the solemn thought in v.4 may be that in his thinking there is no God.

The ways of the wicked seem always to succeed, to the grief of others. As for God's purposes, the wicked man does not, cannot, see them; they are far removed from his vision. And, as for his enemies, he treats them with the utmost contempt, blowing at them in derision. He fears no adversity or adversaries. In his arrogance he boasts that there is no adversary that can move him.

The evil character of this wicked one is appalling. There is cursing, deceit, fraud, mischief, vanity. What a catalogue of vices! There may be an allusion to a poisonous serpent. The venom is in his mouth and under his tongue. It is the character of one who, himself, is called "that old serpent" (Rev 12.9; 20.2). But notice, too, the cowardice and craft which are linked here with his cruelty. He lurks in secret places waiting for the innocent. He hides himself, like a lion in a covert, watching with cunning until he can spring upon his prey. He is a callous and cruel murderer of the poor, ensnaring men as in a net or a web. In his guile he may crouch and feign humility. The deception will catch some unawares, and, while he appears humble and harmless, the unsuspecting will be brought down by those strong men who help him. And now what folly is this? Is it ignorance or arrogance to think that God will not see or remember his evil ways and doings? Does he not know, has he not heard, of omniscience? Even the poor handmaid Hagar could say, "Thou God seest me" (Gen 16.13).

The solemn indictments are concluded. It is as if the witnesses have testified against the wicked man one after another and the case against him is heard. It is time to petition Jehovah to act in judgment.

Verses 12-18: The Lord is King

"Arise, O Jehovah!" So did David cry in Psalm 7.6. There is a double reason for this call to Jehovah. There is the desire for divine judgment and righteous retribution against the oppressor; the request that at last Jehovah should lift up His hand to protect the afflicted and to punish the wicked. But there is this consideration also, that it cannot be for ever tolerated that puny man should despise the Almighty. The wicked man has boasted in his presumption that Jehovah will not require an account of what he has done. He has oppressed the poor and has treated the God of the poor with contempt. It will not, must not, be overlooked. The warning of Jehovah in another Psalm is most applicable, "These things hast thou done, and I kept silence; thou thoughtest that I was altogether such an one as thyself: but I will reprove thee, and set them in order before thine eyes" (Ps 50.21). Though He may appear to have forgotten, it is not so. "God requireth that which is past" (Eccl 3.15). Jehovah sees, and knows, and remembers, and will eventually requite. When, at the last assize, the books are opened, there will be a divinely accurate account of all that has been done and He will judge accordingly. But that righteous judgment, which should be a terror to the wicked, is a comfort to the afflicted. The humble poor trust in Him. As a righteous Judge He is the Helper of the fatherless. "In thee the fatherless find mercy", said the prophet (Hos 14.3). As Spurgeon says, in his quaint way, "God is the parent of all orphans".

The Psalmist continues in his prayer for justice and judgment. He pleads that the arm of the wicked should be broken. The arm is a symbol of strength and power. He cries that this might be shattered and that Jehovah should search out every trace of evil in the tyrant and judge it, until nothing remains. Jehovah is King, and that eternally, for ever and ever, and there is no room in His realm for rebellious nations. In that day of Messiah's glory His angels will gather out of His kingdom "all things that offend and them which do iniquity" (Mt 13.41).

The Psalm ends on a note of thanksgiving. Jehovah, in the greatness of His everlasting Kingship, has heard the prayer of the meek. He touches their hearts. He graciously bends to hear their cry. From the majesty of His throne He stoops to listen to the voice of the humble. The time will come when the man of the earth will oppress His people no longer. God will vindicate His people and do justice to the fatherless. Let His saints rest in this, that the ultimate triumph of the Lord is assured and one day the oppressor will be no more.

PSALM 11

Introduction

The Davidic authorship of this Psalm is not questioned, but the exact date of its composition and the circumstances in which it was written are uncertain. Some think that the Psalm belongs to those days when David was in Saul's palace, loved by many but feared by the jealous king whose intent was to slay him. In a variety of ways Saul had plotted against David's life, and the advice of some timid friends apparently was that he should flee. Others feel that the Psalm refers to the days just prior to Absalom's rebellion, when the conspiracy against David was growing stronger and it seemed wise to escape. The situation described in the Psalm would correspond to both of these circumstances but there is no title to the Psalm which would confirm either.

David has known perhaps every experience of life. He seems to have trodden all those paths which are the common lot of saints, and so many of his Psalms have been born in the midst of trials. Often in these experiences David had friends and advisors who, like Job's friends, were "miserable comforters" (Job 16.2). At times he has to rebuff these well-meaning advisors and encourage himself in the Lord, and this is just what he does in this short Psalm.

Verses 1-3: Faith or Flight?

It may be indeed, as many think, that this Psalm belongs to that period in David's life when he was under persecution from Saul. David was yet in the palace and true to the king, but was the victim of the jealousy and envy of an insecure Saul who, more than once, had tried to kill him. Those friends would have meant well who said, "Flee as a bird to your mountain". They feared for David's life at the hand of Saul. But David had slain lions and bears and giants and was in no mind to flee from Saul. Besides, he was now the king's son-in-law, with responsibilities in the court. He was loved, too, by Jonathan, and by Saul's servants and household, and by all Israel and Judah (1 Sam 18.1, 5, 16). He could well have said, as Nehemiah did, "Should such a man as I flee?" (Neh 6.11).

Of course, the time would come when David must flee. It would eventually be the prudent thing to do. But he seems to imply here that there is some timidity and fear with his advisors which is not compatible with trust in Jehovah. Unless there is some indication to the contrary, why should he flee whose repose is in his God? Should he, at the first sign of danger, escape like some feeble fluttering bird to the hills of Judea? How can they suggest such a thing to a man like David? For a man whose refuge was in Jehovah, a flight to some hiding place in the Judean mountains was not a first consideration. David recoils from such a suggestion, avowing his trust in Jehovah.

But the advisors continue to press their argument. Conditions were waxing worse. It was as if the enemy had already bent his bow and made ready the arrow upon the string. The wicked were poised to shoot. They would do it privily (652), that is to say, unsuspectingly, suddenly, under cover, perhaps in darkness. David may be upright in heart but his enemies were not. They would not regard his uprightness, but would assail him mercilessly.

David's counsellors now reinforce their counsel with this; "If the foundations be destroyed, what can the righteous do?". If the foundations and pillars of society and morality be pulled down, this is anarchy. What then can the righteous achieve in such circumstances? Would it not be better to flee?

Verses 4-7: Righteousness and Retribution

David's faith, and the reasons for it, are in sharp contrast to the fear and timidity of his well-meaning counsellors. Jehovah was in His holy temple (1964). There was, of course, at that time, no "temple magnifical" (1 Chr 22.5). That had yet to be built by Solomon in a later day. Although the tabernacle was called "temple" when it was pitched at Shiloh in the days of Eli and the young Samuel (1 Sam 1.9), nevertheless it seems the more probable that David is thinking here of that heavenly palace of Jehovah. His throne was there, in the heavens, and this was David's refuge. Jehovah was sovereign. Nothing could happen without the knowledge and consent of the throne. God was in control and David could rest in that. The throne of the Almighty was immutable and it was safe to trust.

Jehovah was omniscient. The eyes of Jehovah never close. He is ever, always, watchful. "He that keepeth Israel shall neither slumber nor sleep" (Ps 121.4). And not only do His eyes behold, but His eyelids try the children of men. The comment of Spurgeon is interesting. He says, "As men, when intently and narrowly inspecting some minute object, almost close their eyelids to exclude every other object, so will the Lord look all men through and through. God sees each man as much and as perfectly as if there were no other creature in the universe". He goes on to quote one Stephen Charnock who writes, "...a metaphor taken from men, that contract the eyelids when they would wistly and accurately behold a thing". Jehovah does not only see but He knows intimately all our circumstances, and in this confidence David could rest in the midst of danger.

It is a principle in every age and with all His saints that Jehovah tries (974) the righteous. It is not at all inconsistent with His love for His people that He should so try them. "Whom the Lord loveth he chasteneth" (Heb 12.6). Such chastening is not pleasant, but it is not to be despised. It is like the refining of gold, so that any dross may be removed and the precious thing rendered the more precious by the refining. Job knew this, who said, "When he hath tried me, I shall come forth as gold" (Job 23.10).

With the wicked it is so different. The evil and the violent man is the object of righteous anger and there is an awful progression of judgment. Upon the wicked He shall rain snares, fire and brimstone, and a horrible tempest. The heavens will be opened for a fearful pouring down of judgments upon the impenitent. Delitzsch thinks that these snares (6341) are "a whole discharge of lassoes which may be compared to a noose thrown down from above". The wicked are entrapped. The judgment is inescapable and inevitable. There is fire and brimstone. The lost soul cries, "I am tormented in this flame" (Lk 16.24). The cup of wrath is full. The wicked will drink the very dregs of it with not a drop of water to cool the tongue. The horrible tempest is a burning wind, from which, likewise, there is no escape. This is their portion who persist, unrepentant, in their wickedness. "How shall we escape, if we neglect so great salvation?" (Heb 2.3).

Because He is righteous in Himself, Jehovah loves righteousness. He looks for it in His people, and His countenance smiles upon His saints who live righteously. He expects them to be as He is. "Be ye holy; for I am holy" (1 Pet 1.15-16). They are the great contrast in the world to the ungodly. Jehovah beholds them, observes them, and delights in their uprightness.

Notes

It will be noticed that in the superscription of this Psalm, and of several other Psalms, the words "A Psalm" are italicised (as in the AV) or bracketed (as in JND). This indicates that these words have been supplied by the translators and are not in the original Hebrew text, which simply reads "Of David". This has led some to query, or even deny, the Davidic authorship of these Psalms, and to suggest a Davidic collection rather than a Davidic composition. To quote Plumer, however, "The words *A Psalm* are not found in the Hebrew, but are properly supplied in the Septuagint, and other versions ancient and modern, including the English. There is no good reason for doubting that David was the author".

PSALM 12

Introduction

For notes on the "Chief Musician" see the introduction to Psalm 4, and for an explanation of "Sheminith" (8067) see the introduction to Psalm 6.

That this Psalm is a Psalm of David is not questioned, but the time and occasion of its composition cannot be determined with certainty. David had several difficult periods in his life to which the sentiments of the Psalm would have been applicable. Some think that it may describe his circumstances when, as a youth, he was domiciled in the court of the jealous King Saul whose constant intent was to kill him. Some think that it may have been composed during that time when David had to flee from Saul, a fugitive in the caves and woods of desert and wilderness. Others think that it belongs to those sad days when Absalom had usurped the crown and David was exiled from his throne and his kingdom. In any of these times there were those who were treacherous, chief of whom, of course, were his own son Absalom, and his former friend and counsellor Ahithophel.

Prophetically it is not difficult to see a foreshadowing of the reign of that arch-deceiver, the lawless one, the man of sin. The deceptions and the strong delusion of the days predicted in 2 Thessalonians 2.3-12 can be clearly envisaged in these verses. When the godly of this age have gone from the earth, iniquity will abound and the faithful of that day may so suitably employ the language of this Psalm. The Psalm is in two equal parts. The first describes the flattery and deceit of the words of wicked men, and their arrogance. The second describes the purity of the words of the Lord and His care for His own.

Verses 1-4: The Words of the Wicked

"Help, LORD!" (3467) (3068). It is a cry from the heart of a man in some distress, and, as Plumer remarks, "The word *help* does not call merely for some aid, but for full and effectual deliverance". He says again, "By far the most common rendering of the first verb in this verse is *save;* after that *deliver, preserve, avenge, rescue, help*". The Psalmist is under great pressure. He is burdened with the decline of godly and faithful men. "The godly man ceaseth...the faithful fail". This has been the lament of saints in many an age. Did not Paul write in his day, "This thou knowest, that all they which are in Asia be turned away from me" (2 Tim 1.15). Elijah felt it keenly too, and cried, though mistakenly, "I, even I only, am left" (1 Kings 19.14). There can never be, in any age, a complete and utter failure of testimony, for God never leaves Himself without a witness. Nevertheless, there are times when that witness is at a low ebb and the complaint of the Psalmist is understandable, with those of the prophet and the apostle.

The insincerity with which the ungodly converse with each other is now noted. It is universal, this hypocrisy, every one with his neighbour saying one thing and thinking another. They flatter with their lips but speak with a double heart. Literally this is "a heart and a heart". With one heart they faun and flatter, saying things which might please. With another heart they harbour mischievous thoughts and intents. It is duplicity and it is vanity. They have two hearts, one to speak smooth words and the other to imagine mischief.

Jehovah must, and will, deal with such. He ever desires sincerity and truth. Every Levitical offering was required to be without blemish and without spot. There was no blemish externally, and when the inner parts were exposed there was no spot there. This was how it was in perfection with God's beloved Son, but men in general were different. Of Jesus it was said, "He hath done no violence, neither was any deceit in his mouth" (Is 53.9). This was how Jehovah desired it. Flattering lips speaking hypocrisies, and tongues speaking proud things, are an offence to Him and He will cut them off.

Men boast that the tongue is their strength. "With our tongue will we prevail", they say. Plumer writes, "Hundreds may say it, yet millions think it. The forms of speech, on which wicked men rely, are slander, flattery, boasting, scorning, lying, misrepresentation". The same men say, in their arrogance and presumed independence, "Our lips are our own". They will refuse to be subject to divine restraint or moral law. They will do and say as they like. They will not be accountable. "Who is lord over us?", they say. "We may speak as we please. We have power and liberty to do so and will not be bound or recognise any lordship over us". Such is the attitude of depraved men, but it will not go unjudged.

Verses 5-8: The Words of the Lord

Jehovah speaks. He hears the groaning of the needy and He knows the oppression of the afflicted. God has always, in every age, heard the cries of His people. How early was it written, "They cried...And God heard their groaning...And the Lord said, I have surely seen the affliction of my people...I know their sorrows" (Ex 2.23-24; 3.7). The sighs of the saints rise to Him. He hears, and He sees, and says, "Now will I arise". At times He may seem to delay, but He will eventually, in His own time, respond to the call of the humble and needy who wait for Him. Men may oppress, and "puff" (6315) at the saints. It is as if to say that with the breath of their lips they could blow them away. It is the thought of scorning; making light of them; treating them with contempt. But Jehovah will preserve His saints and set them in safety.

When Jehovah makes a promise His people may safely rely on that promise. How do the words of the Lord contrast with the words of the wicked? His words are pure words, and precious. They are not yea and nay, but yea and amen (2 Cor 1.18-20). There is no ambiguity or double meaning, as there is with the words of men. The word "pure" is often linked with gold; here it is with refined silver. There is no alloy. The number seven, in the Jewish mind, was indicative of perfection. Silver purified seven times in the furnace was silver perfectly pure. Only the precious metal remained. So is His Word who has promised. Spurgeon comments, "The Bible has passed through the furnace of persecution, literary criticism, philosophic doubt, and scientific discovery, and has lost nothing but those human interpretations which clung to it as alloy to precious ore. The experience of saints has tried it in every conceivable manner, but not a single doctrine or promise has been consumed in the most excessive heat".

Upon this Word then, the saints can safely rely, and, looking forward, the Psalmist speaks with assurance. Notice the repeated, "Thou shalt...thou shalt". Jehovah will keep and preserve His people. And it is the same in every generation of saints, and forever. "Kept by the power of God", writes Peter in a day much later than the Psalmist's (1 Pet 1.5).

The wicked may walk round about. They may outnumber the godly minority and encompass the saints on every side, but the promise of the preservation of the godly remains. In those godless conditions where base and vile men are esteemed and exalted; when wickedness not only prevails but is admired and desired, the believer can cry, "Help, Lord", and wait on Him, trusting His faithful Word for protection and deliverance.

PSALM 13

Introduction

See the introduction to Psalm 4 for notes on the Chief Musician.

It is generally accepted that Psalm 13 is a Psalm of David, but, as with many of David's other Psalms, it is not possible to establish with any certainty the period of David's life to which it belongs. It is, of course, and so obviously, the cry of a soul in some distress. Luther says, "This is a prayer full of the sighings and groanings of an afflicted heart in the hour of darkness, and almost overwhelmed, under that darkness, with the extreme of grief and sorrow, and driven to the greatest strait of mind". The Psalm may have been born, as others of David's Psalms, in the days of his persecution by King Saul, but, again, may reflect the sad days of his exile from his rebellious son Absalom.

Perhaps the very uncertainty of its original association helps to make it the Psalm of all those saints who, in every age, have been brought to the limits of despair and plunged in sorrow. Its sentiments are those of every godly soul at some time or other, and especially of those who suffer persecution for God and Christ. As Spurgeon remarks, "If the reader has never yet found occasion to use the language of this brief ode, he will do so ere long, if he be a man after the Lord's own heart".

There are three sections in this short Psalm. Its six verses may be divided equally into three parts with two verses in each part. The first section is all mourning. The second has to do with praying. The third concludes the Psalm with singing. Murphy writes, "In the three couplets of this Psalm we have an expostulation, a petition, and a confession of faith. It reminds us of the time when David said in his heart, I shall now perish one day by the hand of Saul (1 Sam 27.1)", but, he continues, "His cry rises from sadness into hope".

Verses 1-3: Mourning

How long? How long? Four times David cries out his lament. It is a fourfold call of distress, of despondency almost bordering on despair. How long will the Lord forget him? Forget him? Forsake him? Leave him exposed to the power of his enemy? This is a sad indictment of Jehovah, to think that He had forgotten His child. Yet, in anguish of heart it has been the thought of many a believer, weary with constant sorrow, that God has forgotten. Engulfed in unremitting sadness so many saints in all ages have wrongly imagined that they have been forgotten. How long? For ever? How similar was the lament of the nation several centuries later; "Zion said, The Lord hath forsaken me, and my Lord hath forgotten me". Jehovah's answer came so tenderly; "Can a woman forget her sucking child, that she should not have compassion on the son of her womb? yea, they may forget, yet will I not forget thee" (Is 49.14-15). As for the second part of the question, "For ever?", much rather can the child of God reply with confidence, "Never!". There cannot be even a momentary forgetfulness on God's part. He can never forget His child. He has said, "I will never leave thee, nor forsake thee" (Heb 13.5).

"How long", the plaintiff continues, "How long wilt thou hide thy face from me?". Indeed Jehovah may at times hide His face. But He can never forget. He may hide His countenance in displeasure but not in indifference. He may hide Himself so as to encourage His saints to trust Him and to be more dependent upon Him. How the two sisters of Bethany missed the presence of the Lord in their sorrow. "Lord, if thou hadst been here!" (Jn 11.21, 32). They had sorrow upon sorrow before the Master came to them. Their brother Lazarus was sick. They sent messengers to the Lord to Bethabara. He did not come. Lazarus died. Still the Saviour had not come. The grief! The disappointment! The burial! Four days of mourning! At last He came. Why did He delay? The answer is plain, if at first strange. "Now Jesus loved Martha, and her sister, and Lazarus...therefore...he abode two days still in the same place where he was". (Jn 11.5-6). He delayed because He loved them and His love had greater things in store for them than what they desired. They would see His glory. Had He hidden His face from them for four days? Yet He had not forgotten those whom He loved. Even that soul overwhelmed with the deepest sorrow and crushed by suffering, may still trust in Him, saying with poor Job, "Though he slay me, yet will I trust in him" (Job 13.15), and singing with others -

> Simply trusting every day,
> Trusting through a stormy way;
> Even when my faith is small,
> Trusting Jesus, that is all.

"How long?"; still, in the agitation of his heart the Psalmist appeals. How long must he continue with daily sorrow in his heart? Day after day his grief had persisted while he examined his thoughts and took counsel in his soul. One thing after another suggests itself to his restless heart. Thoughts arise, are considered and then abandoned. He is bewildered. Was there some reason? Was there any reason? Was there no reason? Perowne quotes Luther, who says, "His heart is like a raging sea, in which all sorts of counsels move up and down; he tries on all hands to find a hole through which he can make his escape; he thinks on various plans, and still is utterly at a loss what to advise". Yet, as Alexander Maclaren remarks, "Hope itself despairs, and despair yet hopes".

David will soon sing again in confidence and in assurance, but the cry is repeated once more, "How long?" "How long shall mine enemy be exalted over me?" If, at first, David was concerned with his sorrow as it affected himself, now he is concerned about the reaction of his enemies. They would rejoice over his calamities. They would mock him. They would exult at his grief. And David's enemies were God's enemies! How then would all this affect the testimony for God? His enemies must not prevail. God's honour is at stake. He turns from his mourning to true praying.

Verses 3-4: Praying

David's appeal is to Jehovah, whom he calls, "My God". The Psalmist knows Jehovah in a most personal way. "Consider" (5027), he entreats. "Look upon me". "Hear me", he pleads. He is asking that Jehovah would see and hear and enlighten his eyes. He would not wish to sleep the sleep of death in this sad condition. That would be to die in the dark and in despair. If only the Lord would answer his cries and bring light into his darkness, then perhaps he could say with another, "Lord now lettest thou thy servant depart in peace" (Lk 2.29). "Their eyes were holden", it is said of those two who walked to Emmaus with sad hearts. But then it is said, "Their eyes were opened" (Lk 24.16, 31).

Once again David is concerned about the enemy he had mentioned in v. 2. The child of God has adversaries who would rejoice over his troubles. In a joyful triumphalism the enemies of God and His people would exult over the discomforts and failures of the saints. Those who troubled the Psalmist would rejoice when he was moved. The word "moved" (4131) is a sad and solemn word. It implies a wavering and a fall, being removed off course. How sad indeed when a believer so falls. How good when, like the apostle at the end of life, the saint can say, "I have finished my course" (2 Tim 4.7). David longs for restoration of communion so that the enemy may have no cause to exult.

Verses 5-6: Singing

"I have trusted…I will sing", says David, in the concluding words of this little Psalm, and he gives his reasons. David trusted (982). How often in his Psalms he speaks of his trust in Jehovah. In all his sorrow and trouble the Psalmist had a trust in God which was a confidence that really should have banished care. It is akin to that which the apostle exhorts in Philippians 4.6, "Be careful for nothing". If the heart of the believer confides in the Lord with prayer and thanksgiving, then, says the apostle, the peace of God will prevail in that trusting heart. David, confiding in the mercy, the loving-kindness, the goodness, of God, can rejoice, and in his joy he avows, "I will sing".

The Psalmist could look forward with confidence to brighter days because he could look back and remember Jehovah's gracious dealings with him in the past. The Lord had dealt bountifully with him in former days and his heart could now rejoice in anticipation of salvation from out of his sorrow. Memories of the past gave birth to confidence for the future. How like Paul again, who wrote, "Who delivered us…and doth deliver: in whom we trust that he will yet deliver us" (2 Cor 1.10).

So the short Psalm ends on a note of triumph, and how different is the end from the beginning. As Maclaren so fittingly comments, "The sad minor key of 'How long?' if coming from faithful lips, passes into a jubilant key, which heralds the full gladness of the yet future songs of deliverance". From mourning the Psalmist has gone on to singing, and the turning point is praying. What an encouraging lesson for saints of all ages.

PSALM 14

Introduction

Here is yet another Psalm committed to the care of the Chief Musician, the Director of Music. For comments on the title see the introduction to Psalm 4.

The historical reason or occasion for the writing of this Psalm is not clear. Some feel that it belongs to that period in David's life between his taking of the stronghold of Jebus in 1 Chronicles 11 and the return of the Ark from its captivity in 1 Chronicles 15-16. This may be the captivity referred to in v.7 of the Psalm. Whatever the primary association, the general sentiments expressed in the Psalm are common to the godly in every age.

Many will have noticed the resemblance between Psalms 14 and 53. The Psalmist, by the Holy Spirit, has given us an inspired repetition of truth most distasteful and unpalatable to the carnal mind. It may be that Psalm 14 is the earlier and original form of the Psalm, and that the "Maschil" Psalm 53 is a revision with a slight modification made to adapt the Psalm to the public service of the time. It should be noted that while in Psalm 14 the title "Jehovah" (3068) is predominant, in Psalm 53 it is the title "Elohim" (430) which occurs frequently, and "Jehovah" does not appear there at all.

This Psalm has seven verses. As with many other series of "sevens" in Scripture, these are divided into four and three. For example, the seven Feasts of Jehovah in Leviticus 23, the seven Parables of the Kingdom in Matthew 13, the seven Letters to the Churches in Revelation 2-3, and the seven Seals of the Scroll in Revelation 5 are all so divided. The first four verses of the Psalm are plainly concerned with the depravity of man. The last three verses are the manifestation of Jehovah as the refuge of His people.

Verses 1-4: The Depravity of Man

"The fool!" What an indictment. The Hebrew word NABAL (5036) is derived from a verb (5034) which denotes to fade and wither. As the autumnal leaves wither, and fall into decay and worthlessness, so is man morally without God. The fool! Plumer, quoting Morison, writes, "It is worthy of note that the corresponding word in Arabic signifies an atheist, an unbeliever". Spurgeon suggests that Trapp hits the mark when he calls him, "that sapless fellow, that carcase of a man, that walking sepulchre...withered and wasted, dried up and decayed".

Two questions arise, closely related. First, is the atheism of this fool a theoretical atheism or a practical atheism? Second, what is intended by the expression "in his heart"? Some will point out that the words "There is" are in italics in the AV and have therefore been supplied by the translators. Literally, what the fool says is, "No God!". What does he mean? Is this a philosophic, formulated denial of the existence of Deity? Then he truly is a fool. He flies in the face of that evidence of eternal power and Godhead, clearly seen in the creation around us (Rom 1.20). Note, however, that he does not say, "No Jehovah", but, "No Elohim" (430). It may well be that this fool is not denying that there is indeed an eternally existent Jehovah, but is saying rather that he will not recognise the right of the mighty and powerful Elohim to possess and rule over him. This is a practical atheism, which is atheism nonetheless, denying the sovereign rights of the great Proprietor of all things. There may be a God, this fool admits, but there is no God for me. How like another of whom the Lord Jesus spoke, who left God out of all his reckoning and was also called a fool (Lk 12.16-20).

Now this man speaks "in his heart", when he says, "No God". Is this the personal, unspoken reasoning of the fool? Is he an atheist secretly? Or is he an atheist in desire? Matthew Henry says, in his quaint way, "(The fool) cannot satisfy himself that there is none [i.e. no God], but he wishes there were none, and pleases himself with the fancy that it is possible there may be none. He cannot be *sure* there is one, and therefore he is willing to *think* there is none". Fool indeed, living as if there were no God, "even as they did not like to retain God in their knowledge" (Rom 1.28).

Jehovah looked down (8259) from heaven. The thought is that of looking intently as from a watchtower. From heaven to earth the divine intelligence looks upon men to see if there are any that understand and seek God. This is God seeking any who might be seeking Him. Was there any understanding at all among the children of men? No! There were no enquirers after divine things, and, in both a positive and a negative way, the Psalmist indicts the whole human race. He says "They are all gone aside...there is none that doeth good". Then, in an emphatic repetition of this latter indictment, he says, "No, not one". Paul quotes this in Romans 3.11-12. In the divine court mankind has been arraigned, Jew and Gentile alike. The fullest and most diligent enquiry has been made. The verdict has been given. "There is no difference". "They are all together become filthy" (444). It is moral corruption. With all this Isaiah 53 concurs; "All we like sheep have gone astray; we have turned every one to his own way". Both universally, collectively, and individually, men have gone after sin.

"Have they no knowledge", the Psalmist laments, "these workers of iniquity?". They are not only forgetful of God but they are devourers of His people, eating them up as a man eats bread, with enjoyment, and in their depravity they have no inclination whatsoever to call upon the Lord.

This is the solemn conclusion concerning mankind naturally and in general. If there should be any who are different, or any exceptions, it is not by nature but by the grace of God. By nature and by practice all men are sinners, all men and every man coming under the solemn indictment.

Verses 5-7: The Manifestation of Jehovah

"There were they in great (6343) fear (6342)". Literally, "They feared a great fear". It will be noticed that the two words "great" and "fear" are closely related. It is an emphasis of the fear, which is a great dread, awesome and terrible, causing the coward to tremble. What is this? Are those who devour the saints cowards at heart? As Spurgeon remarks, "As cowards are cruel, so all cruel men are at heart cowards". What produces this fear that makes the coward tremble? It is the realisation that God Himself, whom they have despised, is in the generation of the righteous. Balaam learned it, and said as he looked at the camp of Israel, "The Lord his God is with him, and the shout of a king is among them" (Num 23.21).

These depraved men, not content with their own corruption, having despised the Lord, they despise also those who trust in Him. The "poor" of the verse are the afflicted and humble, the poor in spirit whom the Lord Jesus Himself commends in Matthew 5.3. They make Jehovah their refuge (4268). He is their shelter, their hiding place, and they are accordingly despised by the self-sufficient men of the world. The carnal mind is enmity against God and scorns those who trust in Him, and yet, in reality, is in fear.

God is manifested therefore, as the refuge of His people. He is in the generation of the righteous and they know Him. Prophetically the Psalm looks forward to that day when Israel of the "diaspora", the dispersion, will be re-gathered in Eretz Israel, their own Promised Land. The Psalmist longs for that ultimate manifestation of God, when His redeemed people will rejoice with Him and Zion will be the centre and source of blessing for a millennial earth. "Jacob" was the name of the old supplanter and beguiler. "Israel" is the name of the renewed Jacob, the man whom God touched in grace, who became a prince with God. In that coming day of glory all will rejoice and be glad. The grace of God will preside supreme over the failings of Jacob and the glory of Israel alike, and Jehovah shall send the rod of His strength out of Zion (Ps 110.2). For that day David longs. It is the aspiration and the anticipation of all those who love His appearing.

PSALM 15

Introduction

Those who are acquainted with the Psalms will at once notice a striking similarity between Psalm 15 and Psalm 24. This short Psalm is composed of a question and an answer, and the sentiments expressed bear a close resemblance to the questions and answers of Psalm 24. References to the holy hill and to the house are to be found in each Psalm, and the descriptions of the moral fitness of Jehovah's guests in His house are also very much alike.

Observe though, that there is also a sharp contrast here with the preceding Psalm 14. There it was the character of the atheistic fool. There it was moral corruption and a carnal opposition to God and to His saints. Here it is the character of the upright man, the man of God.

This Psalm is David's. There is no dedicatory title apart from this, and there is no indication of the primary reason for it or the circumstances in which it was composed. However, the similarity with Psalm 24 may suggest that it was written about the time of the bringing back of the Ark of the Covenant to its dwelling place behind curtains on the Mount Zion (2 Sam 6.12-17).

The five short verses are divided unequally into two sections. The first verse is the first section; it asks the question. The remainder of the Psalm is the second section and gives the answer to the question.

Verse 1: The Question

The question is addressed to Jehovah. This is important. The enquiry is made to the divine Proprietor of the house and the hill. When once a man understands something of the greatness and the holiness of God and the eternal self-sufficiency of Jehovah, then he must ask the question, "Lord, who shall abide in thy tabernacle? who shall dwell in thy holy hill?". The tabernacle on the hill was the dwelling place of God among His people. Who could abide where He was? Who could dwell where He dwelt? Isaiah, who had seen the glory of God in ch. 6 of his prophecy, had similar questions, and indeed found similar answers (Is 33.14-15). The two words, "abide" (1481) and "dwell" (7931) are different. The first suggests a sojourning, a lodging. There is a temporary aspect to it, corresponding with the temporary nature of the tabernacle or tent itself. The second word has the thought of dwelling more permanently, residing, settling down, remaining. This is in keeping with the permanence of the holy hill, Mount Zion. But whether sojourning or abiding, the divine requirements are just the same for those who would come to the Holy Presence. Here, where Jehovah dwells, even the holy seraphim veil their faces. It is a solemn thing to enter the place where they cry, "Holy, holy, holy"(Is 6.2-3). Who indeed can abide there? Who can dwell there?

Verses 2-5: The Answer

The divine answer to the question describes the character of the man who will be accepted by Jehovah. Of course, in its perfection this description will suit only the blessed Lord Jesus, as does the similar description in Psalm 24. A man's ways and works and words, and even the thoughts of his heart, must be examined.

The acceptable man will walk uprightly (8549). This word is variously translated in the AV as "without blemish; without spot; sincere; complete; perfect". Such was the requirement in Israel's offerings to Jehovah and such must be the walk of the man who is fit to be received in the dwelling place of God.

This walk will be accompanied by righteous works. In contrast to the workers of iniquity in the world, the deeds of the upright man will be marked by that which is just and right. He will constantly work righteousness. Righteousness will be the habit of his life.

The words of this man agree with his walk and with his works. He speaks truth, and he speaks it with his heart. This is not lip service, thinking one thing and saying another. It is truth in the inward parts. The words, therefore, are sincere. There is no deceit or flattery or lying speech. "Blessed are the pure in heart", the Saviour taught (Mt 5.8), and from a pure heart this man of God will speak what is true.

He will not be guilty of backbiting with his tongue. The word "backbiting" (7270) has the thought of "playing the spy" with the intention of slandering and tale bearing. The morally upright man will not go about slyly exploring the lives of others with a malicious intent. Not only so, but neither will he take up or entertain slander which is told him about his neighbour. He will neither give nor take stories about others which would do harm or cause pain to a neighbour. He will not readily believe ill reports, nor trade in them. There is a wicked mischievousness which the saint must shun. It has been the cause of much hurt among neighbours and has spoiled many a previously happy relationship.

The righteous man, with a holy discernment, will know when to despise and when to honour. There are those who, being despicable in themselves, must be contemned (959), treated with the contempt which they deserve, and rejected as unsuitable companions for the godly man. There are others who must be esteemed and honoured for their fear of the Lord. There should be too, an admirable unselfishness about the saint. He will always be a man of his word. Should he make an arrangement or enter into a commitment which might turn out to be unprofitable to him, or to his loss, he will, nevertheless, be bound by his word. Even though his prior promise should be to his hurt, his word is his bond. This is honourable.

Nor will he, in a covetous spirit, take advantage of his less privileged brother, lending his silver and exacting usury. There may be, of course, an acceptable commercial practice, entered into to the mutual advantage of lender and borrower alike, but the callous and cruel grinding of the poor is to be detested (Deut 23.19-20). Extortion is a hateful thing, born out of covetousness. It is not the character of the man who would abide in the house of God. Allied to this covetous spirit is the practice of taking bribes to pervert the course of justice.

The man of God will eschew this also, and he who accepts the bribe is alike guilty with him who offers it.

Those who cultivate the desirable moral character so described in this short Psalm will never be moved. Such a man is well founded and safely anchored. He is like Mount Zion itself which cannot be removed but abideth for ever (Ps 125.1).

PSALM 16

Introduction

Psalm 16 is entitled "Michtam of David", but the meaning of "Michtam" (4387), is not fully known. Six Psalms bear this title. After Psalm 16, Psalms 56-60 are all "Michtam" Psalms and they are all Psalms of David. The word comes from a root which signifies "to cover" or "to hide", but another view understands the word to mean "engraven", perhaps in gold, as letters engraved on a monument, so that these six Psalms have become known as "David's Golden Psalms". Luther translates the word "a golden jewel". Some have combined the suggested meanings and have found in these Psalms precious truths, hidden, as it were, like the mysteries, or sacred secrets, of the NT, but brought out for us by the Holy Spirit as precious as the most fine gold, truths worthy to be engraved in our hearts. In Psalm 16 there are primary references to David and prophetic references to Christ. It is the third of the Messianic Psalms and is quoted by both Peter and Paul and perhaps also by the writer of the Epistle to the Hebrews (Acts 2.25-31; 13.35-37; Heb 2.13).

The Psalm is so unified and so compacted together that divisions and sub-divisions of its eleven verses are difficult. Verses 1-7, however, have to do with the prayer and preservation of the faithful, and verses 8-11 predict the prospect and pleasure of the Messiah.

Verses 1-7: The Prayer and Preservation of the Faithful

In the world of the ungodly, every believer may well pray with David, "Preserve me, O God". The word "preserve" (8104) is most often translated "keep". Along with its noun form, "keeper", it may be found so translated more than three hundred times in the AV. The thought is of a shepherd keeping his flock, of a garrison of soldiers keeping a city, or of a bodyguard guarding the monarch. Another Psalm gives abundant assurance to the saint that such a prayer for preservation will certainly be heard and answered. "Behold, he that keepeth Israel shall neither slumber nor sleep. The Lord is thy keeper...The Lord shall preserve thee...he shall preserve thy soul. The Lord shall preserve thy going out and thy coming in" (Ps

121.4, 5, 7-8). It was, too, the prayer of the Lord Jesus for His own on that last evening in the Upper Room. While He had been with them He had kept them as His little flock, but now He was leaving them in an adverse world. "Holy Father", He prays, "keep...those whom thou hast given me". "Keep them from the evil" (Jn 17.11,15).

David has a reason, an argument, why his prayer for preservation should be heard. He has put his trust in God. He has made God his refuge. The name of God which David uses here is that of El (410). It is the singular name of the Almighty, the Omnipotent. It is often connected with divine attributes, as "A jealous God" (Ex 20.5); "A merciful God" (Deut 4.31); "The faithful God" (Deut 7.9); "The mighty God" (Is 9.6). It is compounded to make that beautiful title, El Shaddai, God All-Sufficient, first occurring in Genesis 17.1. To such a One David makes his plea, "Preserve me, O God".

Notice that, in two verses, David employs three divine titles. Having first addressed his prayer to El, he now speaks, in v. 2, of Jehovah (3068), and then of Adonai (136). This variety of titles is both interesting and important. They present God in three aspects. He is God, the Almighty and Omnipotent One. He is the eternal, ever-existent, self-sufficient Jehovah. He is Lord and Master, Proprietor and Owner of the saints who acknowledge His sovereign rights. David says, with Elisabeth in Luke 1.43, with Mary in John 20.13, and with Thomas in John 20.28, "My Lord".

There is some difficulty with the last clause of v. 2, which is variously translated and interpreted. Many prefer the rendering of those versions which follow the thought of the RV and RSV, "I have no good beyond thee", in which case the Psalmist is disclaiming any merit of his own and simply stating that all, and everything, of good that he possesses has come from God, and that he has nothing apart from Jehovah. This is very true of course, but other expositors, however, in the context, prefer to stay with versions such as the AV and JND, and understand David to say that he has nothing of goodness that he can offer or extend to Jehovah the All-sufficient One. Indeed the LXX renders it, "Thou hast no need of my goodness", and Helen Spurrell's rendering is, "My charitable gifts are nought to Thee".

The opening words of v. 3 would seem to reinforce this latter view. David has nothing really with which he can enrich his God, but he can enrich the saints of God who are the excellent (117) of the earth, in whom Jehovah delights. The saints (6918), the holy ones, are the nobles of earth. They are the elite, the true aristocracy, and Jehovah finds His pleasure in them. If the Psalmist, then, cannot add anything to Him who in His greatness needs nothing, he will extend his goodness to God's people.

Jehovah is the one true God and has ever been a jealous God (Ex 20.5). He abhors idolatry. Those who hasten after another God have a sad and sorrowful prospect. Spurgeon quotes the quaint saying of Matthew Henry who says, "They that multiply gods multiply griefs to themselves; for whosoever thinks one god too little, will find two too many, and yet hundreds not enough". David will have nothing to do with such. The nation had worshipped a golden calf in the wilderness, so soon after their redemption from Egypt. The days of the judges were idolatrous times, and Israel was again to be plagued with idolatry in the reign of certain kings who were to follow David. David would have no part in idolatry. He would not join with them in their libations of blood. Gentiles were known to drink the blood of their sacrifices, sometimes indeed the blood of human sacrifices, as in the worship of Molech and Chemosh. It was a horrible practice associated with the idolatrous worship of their gods. Israel was, from time to time, infected with much of paganism, but the Psalmist's portion was in the one true Jehovah, and he would in no way have fellowship with such worshippers or their gods. He will not even mention the names of the gods of the heathen, and in this he was in accord with God's word through Moses, "And make no mention of the name of other gods, neither let it be heard out of thy mouth" (Ex 23.13). David repudiates these foul and vile practices and abhors utterly the idolatry with which they were associated.

He now speaks of his inheritance in Jehovah, his portion and his cup. It was what he had chosen and it was secure. Jehovah maintained it. It was in His hand. All that David had and all that he desired was in his God. Perowne quotes one Savonarola who remarks so beautifully, "What must he not possess who possesses the Possessor of all?". David's cup, his sustenance, his daily food and his refreshment were in the Lord. Dumb idols could never offer what the Psalmist had in Jehovah. The lines had fallen unto him in pleasant places. There is an allusion here to the ancient custom of marking out allotments with measuring lines. Some, on occasions, might complain about the portion allotted to them. But David is not speaking of an earthly inheritance. Spiritually and morally, his portion in the Lord was a good and pleasant heritage. He was satisfied with his lot and he must bless Jehovah who had guided him into this choice of divine things. In the night seasons, so conducive to quiet thought and meditation, David would commune with his own heart and rejoice in the Lord. "Reins" (3629) expresses the innermost being of a man, his emotions and his feelings, his affections and deepest thoughts.

Verses 8-11: The Prospect and Pleasure of the Messiah

It must be remembered that this is a Messianic Psalm, and is quoted by both Peter and Paul with reference to Christ (See note in the Introduction above). Much of the Psalm, of course, is true of David who wrote it, but with v.8 the reader now enters the truly Messianic portion. How perfectly were these the words of the Lord Jesus, "I have set the Lord always before me". The word "always" (8548) is translated "continually" fifty-three times in the AV. The thought is of continuity and constancy. The Lord Jesus was the perfect Servant of Jehovah. He could say, "He wakeneth morning by morning, he wakeneth mine ear to hear as the learned" (Is 50.4). The ear of the Saviour was always open to know the will of His Father and His meat was to do the will of Him who had sent Him (Jn 4.34). Later in the Psalm Messiah will anticipate His place at the right hand of Jehovah, but now, in devoted and dedicated service, He can say, "He is at my right hand, I shall not be moved". He walked resolutely and steadfastly in the path of God's pleasing and would not be deterred or deflected. In the doing of the will of God the Saviour rejoiced. He had come to do that will and He did it. He did it perfectly and delighted to do it. With the gladness and joy of doing the will of God there came rest, both of mind and body. The Lord Jesus, physically wearied at Sychar, could yet, in the energy of communion with the Father, minister to a needy Samaritan woman (Jn 4.6,31-34). His human weariness found refreshment in the will of God and He could rest in safety and assurance.

The connecting participle, "For", indicates the grounds for David's personal assurance. He could safely rest, for there was a future of glory. "Hell" is SH[e]OL, the "Hades" of the NT (see the footnote to Psalm 6). It was not the end. Jehovah would not abandon His servant David forever in that grave-land of the departed. He could rest in this assurance, that there would be a resurrection of the body and that one day there would be pleasure at God's right hand. It is interesting to note that only David and Job use the expression "My Redeemer". Their sentiments are the same. There may be sorrows and difficulties now, but the future is bright for those who can say, "My Lord", and, "My Redeemer". (See Ps 19.14 and Job 19.24-27)

Now, if all this was true of David, how particularly true it was of Him who is called the "Holy One", the Beloved. In his great Pentecostal message to the nation Peter calls upon this Psalm to show that the resurrection of Christ was a subject of prophecy. David, being a prophet, was speaking in Psalm 16 of that resurrection (Acts 2.24-31).

Verse 10 of the Psalm has been the subject of much controversy, especially those words, "Thou wilt not leave my soul in hell". Many expositors understand this to mean that the Lord Jesus did, in the language of the Creed, descend into hell, into SH[e]OL, to where OT believers were until the payment of their ransom price in the death of the Redeemer. It is taught that He then led captivity captive and took those saints with Him into glory. Whether this is true or not must be decided by other Scriptures. It would be reading too much into Psalm 16 to say that this is what David is here teaching about the Messiah. The Lord Jesus died. His body was buried by two friends. On the third day He rose again and is now at God's right hand in the heavens. It was not possible that death or the grave could hold Him, or that His holy body could see corruption. This is what Psalm 16 is predicting. The Saviour was incomparable, impeccable, and incorruptible. F.W. Grant's comment is beautiful, "It was a pathway of life, therefore, even though it led through death; in which His flesh dwelt in confident hope, that He would not abandon His soul to Hades, nor suffer piety such as His to see corruption"

The Man of sorrows is now the Man in the glory. The pathway of His lovely life has led Him to the right hand of God in the heights. The sepulchre was not the end. The word "presence" (6440) is, in the AV, rendered "face" almost four hundred times. The perfect Servant now rests in the light of the countenance of God. Fulness of joy! Pleasures for evermore! "Delights for ever", says the LXX. "An eternity of enjoyments", says Spurrell. To finite minds the joys of eternity are past comprehending, but this is certain, that where the Saviour is, His saints shall be also. His presence there in glory is the pledge that one day His people shall be with Him to enjoy the pleasures of that lovely place.

So does the prayer for preservation end with this note of assurance. Is this what Peter means when he says of the inheritance which is "reserved in heaven for you, Who are kept by the power of God" (1 Pet 1.4-5)? The inheritance is being kept for the saints and the saints are being kept for the inheritance. All is well.

PSALM 17

Introduction

The title of this Psalm is "A Prayer of David", and four other Psalms have the word "prayer" in their titles. Psalms 86 and 142 are, similarly, prayers of David. Psalm 90 is entitled "A Prayer of Moses the man of God", and Psalm 102 is "A Prayer of the afflicted, when he is overwhelmed, and poureth out his complaint before the Lord". The afflicted one of Psalm 102 may, of course, have been David himself, writing anonymously and dedicating the Psalm to all those who at any time suffer for their faithfulness to God.

There is nothing in this Psalm by which we can determine the occasion of its writing. It is a petition which may have been David's at many times and in many circumstances during his troubled life, especially under Saul's persecution of him. The sentiments expressed have been those of the afflicted people of God in every age. As Maclaren says, "The background is the familiar one of causeless foes round an innocent sufferer, who flings himself into God's arms for safety, and in prayer enters into peace and hope".

The fifteen verses are difficult to divide and sub-divide. The whole Psalm is a complete petition and any lines of demarcation of thought are not very clear. However, three parts may be observed. In verses 1-5 the Psalmist pleads his integrity. In verses 6-12 he prays for protection from his enemies. In verses 13-15 he anticipates his eventual glorification. These three movements in the Psalm are marked by a repetition of a divine name or title. "O Jehovah", the Psalmist says in v.1. "O God", he says at the beginning of the second section in v.6. This is the title El (410), on which see the note to Psalm 16.1. The third section commences at v.13, where again it is "O Jehovah".

Verses 1-5: A Prayer for Vindication

David's prayer is addressed to Jehovah, who has already tried him. "Hear the right, O Lord". He pleads that his cause is just and righteous. It seems right therefore that he should be heard and he is appealing for justice. His prayer is a cry (7440), and the word so rendered here has not been used before in the Psalms. It indicates a shout or a loud ringing cry such as was common in Eastern custom and culture, whether expressing joy or grief. As Spurgeon so aptly remarks, "If our prayer should like the infant's cry be more natural than intelligent, and more earnest than elegant, it will be nonetheless eloquent with God. There is a mighty power in a child's cry to prevail with a parent's heart". The Psalmist's cry is sincere. There is nothing feigned (4820). There is no hypocrisy or pretence. There is no subtlety or deceit. There is no craft or guile. It is with a clear conscience that David can appeal to Jehovah.

David is anxious for a divine judgment of his case and his cause. Men may accuse and abuse and misrepresent and slander. They have done this with the prophets and with the apostles and with the Saviour Himself. The Psalmist knows that the decision which will come from the presence of God will be a righteous decision. He can safely leave that sentence with the Lord. Although this Psalm is not reckoned among those which are called "Messianic", yet how beautifully do these words apply to the Lord Jesus, of whom it is written that "when he was reviled, reviled not again...but committed himself to him that judgeth righteously" (1 Pet 2.23). The eyes of the Lord will behold with equity, discerning what is right and issuing judgment accordingly.

Jehovah had already proved (974) and tried (6884) His servant David. Both these words, but especially the latter, have to do with the testing of metals. In its noun form this word is actually translated "goldsmith" in Isaiah 40.19; 41.7; 46.6, and also in Nehemiah 3.8, 31, 32. It is also rendered "refiner" in Malachi 32-3. As gold is smelted in the fire to be purged of dross, if such be there, so had Jehovah tried the Psalmist and found nothing. This does not mean of course, that David was sinless, but rather that there was none of that deceit or hypocrisy of which he had spoken. Not only so, but the Lord had visited him in the night. In those dark and quiet hours, when, in the silence, freed from the distractions of the world, a man may have private and personal thoughts, Jehovah had searched him and found nothing. David had purposed, too, that as his thoughts were so would his speech be. His words were true and sincere, corresponding with the inner thoughts of his heart. He had determined that no wrong word would escape his lips.

Not only in thought and in speech, but in deed also, the Psalmist had walked right paths. As far as men around him were concerned, he would not live as they lived or behave as they behaved. His heart, his tongue, and his actions were in agreement. Lip and life were in accord, and he had been kept so by the Word of God. Its cleansing power had preserved him. As another Psalm puts it, "Wherewithal shall a young man cleanse his way? by taking heed thereto according to thy word" (119.9). For His disciples the Saviour prayed, "Sanctify them through thy truth: thy word is truth" (Jn 17.17). There was, and there is, a destroyer intent on the ruin of lives and testimonies, and it was an older and sadder David who, having succumbed, cried, "Behold, thou desirest truth in the inward parts: and in the hidden part thou shalt make me to know wisdom. Purge me with hyssop, and I shall be clean" (Ps 51.6-7). Was David always conscious of his weakness? Is this why he asks, "Hold up my goings in thy paths, that my footsteps slip not"? Or, as some think, should this be more correctly rendered, "When thou holdest my goings in thy paths, my footsteps slip not" (JND)? Either way, the principle is the same. In his own strength the believer will fail. David knew this. He needed a Shepherd of whom he could sing, "He leadeth me in the paths of righteousness for his name's sake" (Ps 23.3).

Verses 6-12: A Prayer for Preservation

David's appeal is to the marvellous lovingkindness, or mercy, of God. "Marvellous" is an interesting word. It signifies "set apart; different; distinguished" (6395). Such is the nature of God's mercy towards His people in their weakness, and the Psalmist knows this. He can safely cast himself upon such goodness. There is a mighty right hand and a loving heart ever willing to defend and preserve those who trust Him.

Perhaps no part of the human body is more precious, more tender, than the eye, and the pupil, here called the apple, is the very centre of that tenderness. How carefully do men guard it and protect it from hurt. "Keep me", David prays, "keep me as the apple of thine eye". He is asking for an intimate shielding from harm and danger. "Hide me", he continues, and then uses an equally tender analogy. He pictures the parent bird, sheltering her brood in the covert of her wings with a mother's love and care. It was a familiar imagery and the Lord Jesus Himself used it in His lament over Jerusalem in Luke 13.34. David longs that Jehovah would similarly protect him and he cries, "Keep me; hide me".

The cry becomes urgent. His enemies are deadly and would encircle him with their malice as they themselves are encircled with the selfishness of their luxurious living. David likens them to hunting hounds dogging his steps, or to a lion seeking his prey. In ravenous wickedness they would pull him to the ground and devour him. They are cruel oppressors of the godly and only the might and the mercy of Jehovah can provide the necessary protection.

Verses 13-15: A Prayer for Glorification

David now anticipates deliverance from his enemies, and future glory, but his cry continues with urgency, "Arise, O Jehovah". He calls upon the Lord to confront the enemy. This is the force of the word "disappoint" (6923), as in the AV. He desires that Jehovah should intervene, that He should forestall the enemy in his wicked designs, and cast him down. Does he here call the enemy Jehovah's sword, when he says, "The wicked, which is thy sword"? Some revisers prefer, "deliver my soul from the wicked by thy sword". F.W. Grant, however, insists that there is no such preposition in the Hebrew text, and he retains the common version as being more in accord with the original. The italicised words of v.13 may then be omitted so as to read, "deliver my soul from the wicked, thy sword". "This", says Grant, "gives the fuller thought. If the lawless persecutor be, after all, God's sword, then how simple for Him to turn it aside!".

Does this same textual problem arise in the next verse? "From men which are thy hand, O Lord"? Again Grant says that there is no preposition, so as to make the reading "deliver...from men by thy hand". The italicised words of the AV, "which is" (v.13) and "which are" (v.14), seem, however, to give the sense, so that men of the world become, unwittingly, the sword and the hand of Jehovah in the working out of His purpose, and He can remove them as easily as a man moves his hand. So has He used Emperors and Caesars, Kings and Pharaohs, to accomplish His plans. It is an evidence of His sovereignty. "The most High ruleth in the kingdom of men" (Dan 4.17).

These men of the world are earth-dwellers. They have their portion here and now. All that they have is for a little season. It is transient, fleeting, passing away. Though they do not recognise it, all that they have has come from God. He is no respecter of persons, and He has in His goodness provided for them. He has filled their coffers and their barns in spite of their ingratitude. But all is transitory. They will leave it to their children, and for them eternity will be empty. They have lived for time and have not laid up treasure in heaven. As Spurgeon so aptly and eloquently remarks, "How fine a description have we here of many a successful merchant or popular statesman; and it is, at first sight, very showy and tempting, but in contrast with the glories of the world to come, what are these paltry molehill joys. Self, self, self, all these joys begin and end in basest selfishness; but oh, our God, how rich are those who begin and end in thee!".

"As for me", says David. He is not envious of these brief pleasures of the worldling, for there is, for the saint, an abiding glory and a joy that will never end. He anticipates that glad day when, with fellow-saints, he will behold the face of his God. It will be in a righteous state and standing that believers will dwell in the divine presence. "They shall see his face", writes John of a later day (Rev 22.4). If though now we see Him not, yet, believing, we rejoice with joy unspeakable and full of glory (1 Pet 1.8), what will it be to be in His presence where there is fullness of joy and pleasures for evermore (Ps 16.11)?

"I shall be satisfied, when I awake, with thy likeness", says the Psalmist. He may indeed die. His body may sleep for a little while in the grave. But to awake in the likeness of God will be satisfaction. At his original creation man was made in the image and glory of God (Gen 1.26-27; 1 Cor 11.7). This image has been sadly obscured by the fall and by subsequent centuries of sinning, but one day, in resurrection beauty, the believer will awake in His likeness. While Christ is the perfect expression of this, nevertheless every saint will, in that day, be fashioned like unto His body of glory. Such anticipations prevent the believer from being envious of the men of the world, and on this high note this Psalm which is a prayer reaches its noble conclusion.

PSALM 18

Introduction

This Psalm has been called "The Song of a Grateful Heart", and this indeed describes the sentiments expressed therein. With variations, alterations, and omissions, the Psalm is to be found again in 2 Samuel 22.1-51. Spurgeon quotes from Kitto's "Pictorial Bible" which comments, "The Rabbins reckon up seventy-four differences between the two copies, most of them very minute. They probably arose from the fact that the poem was, as they conjecture, composed by David in his youth, and revised in his later days, when he sent it to the chief musician". Much of the revision certainly belongs to a period towards the close of David's life since it is the composition of one who is both a warrior and a king (see vv. 34 and 43). Its being delivered to the Chief Musician indicates that it was to be used in the public worship of the temple.

On the "Chief Musician" see the introduction to Psalm 4.

David, though King, is happy to be called "The servant of the Lord", as of course were Abraham, Moses, Joshua and Job, and the apostles of the Lord Jesus. He expresses his gratitude for deliverance from his enemies, and particularly from Saul. There is both retrospection and anticipation for he rightly concludes that the God who has delivered him in the past will help him in the future.

The Psalm, though not usually counted among those that are termed Messianic, has, nevertheless, many references which are very applicable to the Messiah, and part of v.2 with v.49 may be seen quoted in Hebrews 2.13 and Romans 15.9. As F.W. Grant remarks, "a greater than David shines through continually".

The following suggested divisions may be helpful for an orderly meditation. Verses 1-3 are a prologue, a brief preface to the whole, in which the Psalmist avows his love and his intentions. Verses 4-19 recall, with poetic eloquence, his deliverance by Jehovah. In verses 20-29 he maintains that God has been righteous in thus delivering him. Verses 30-45 again recount the victories of the past, and anticipate similar victories in the future. Verses 46-50 are a joyful epilogue envisaging the ultimate triumph of David's greater Son.

Verses 1-3: The Prologue

David confesses a deep love, a tender affection, for Jehovah, whom he knows in such a personal way that he uses the pronoun "my" nine times in two verses. "My strength; my rock; my fortress; my deliverer; my God; my strength; my buckler; my salvation; my high tower". The imagery is mostly of a military character, reminiscent of the days of David's continual struggles with his enemies, when the rocks and crags of the wilderness were his defence and his fortresses. But the mighty God is his true rock and fortress, his defence, and the strength and power of his deliverance. In his God David has found refuge, a high tower to which to retreat, and a shield from every foe. It seems but natural that he should exclaim, "I will love (7355) thee, O Lord". The word is intense. It is a fervent love, an affection of the deepest kind, and it gives rise to an equally fervent desire to praise the Lord. He who has delivered his servant is praiseworthy and a continuing joy in praising him will assure salvation from the enemy for "The joy of the Lord is your strength" (Neh 8.10).

Verses 4-19: Distress and Deliverance

It is a strange but beautiful paradox that the sorrows of the saints can be set to music and described in the most sublime poetry. So have hymn writers of all ages sung of the distresses of the godly. David here remembers how the sorrows of death and hell had encompassed him. Two different words, in vv. 4 and 5, are here translated "compassed" in the AV, they are different but they are cognate (661; 5437). David was encircled by the sorrows of impending, threatening death. He felt hemmed in by the sorrows of the grave (SH[e]OL - 7585). They were as cords which wrapped themselves around him. They were like floods which enveloped him and snares which lay before him and made him afraid. Death and the grave and the prevailing ungodliness frightened him. He was straightened in his distress, frightened by the affliction, the cruel oppression of his adversaries. As Spurgeon comments, "He was like a mariner broken by the storm and driven upon the rocks by dreadful breakers, white as the teeth of death. Sad plight for the man after God's own heart".

In his distress he called out, crying aloud to Jehovah his God. That cry of distress reached into the sanctuary and Jehovah heard the call of His afflicted servant. "Temple" (1964) is not, of course, Solomon's temple of a later day. Nor does it here appear to mean that tent on Mount Zion where the Ark rested. It was the sanctuary in the heavens, the dwelling place, the palace of Jehovah, as in Psalm 11.4. David's cry on earth was heard in the sanctuary in heaven. It has been pointed out that the imperfect tenses of the verbs of v.6 indicate that this was David's habit in those difficult days, so that the verse might be rendered: "In my distress I would call upon Jehovah, and unto my God would I cry: He would hear my voice out of His temple, and my cry before Him would come unto His ears". This was David's habitual experience and his wont, to call upon his God and be granted divine deliverance.

Jehovah's prompt and powerful response to the cry of His servant reminds David of Sinai. How majestically Jehovah had revealed Himself then, and how similarly had He appeared for the deliverance of many of His saints since Sinai. To Moses, to Joshua, to judges and to prophets, He had shown Himself mighty to save. He was the God of the impossible. He could move mountains in His anger, shaking the very pillars of the creation. In language akin to that of Job (ch. 26) David sings of the power which made the hills tremble, and this was the power which had accomplished his deliverance from his enemies. This too, was the power which, in a later day would shake Philippi with an earthquake and open prison doors for the apostles.

The Sinai comparison continues with references to smoke and fire. These are symbols of the anger and wrath of God against sin and against His enemies. Jehovah will be angry with those who oppress His people. "Our God is a consuming fire" (Heb 12.29). It is a fearful thing to oppose Him or His people. As another Psalm has it, "The fire shall devour them" (21.9), and in another place, "The anger of the Lord…shall smoke against that man" (Deut 29.20). These Oriental symbols would be well understood by the early readers of David's Psalms. There is an intensity and energy here as Jehovah moves to deliver His child. The earth is shaken, there is flaming fire to consume and an issuing smoke to confuse. It is divine power manifested against the enemies of God and good.

Jehovah moves heaven and earth to defend and deliver His people. He bowed the heavens and came down. David employs the same symbolic language in Psalm 144.5. As in a storm the dark clouds seem to lower and almost touch the earth, so had God stooped in His wrath to deal with His enemies. Darkness was no impediment to Him. He put it under His feet and made it His secret place as He rode upon the cherubim in the midst of the storm. The dark waters and thick clouds around Him were His pavilion (5521), His tabernacle, His dwelling place. The angels are His chariots, like the wings of the wind. The cherubim are the grand symbolic representations of majesty, intelligence, power, and energy of movement (see Ezekiel 1 and 10). How puny are the human enemies of One who in omnipotence rides upon the cherub in the midst of the storm, and how safe are those whom He defends and delivers.

The brightness of His glory pierces the dark clouds. There are lightnings and thunderings and voices and fire just as observed by John in a much later century (Rev 4.5). Notice the awesome extremes of glory as Jehovah moves to scatter His enemies; there is hail and fire. Observe again that John of the Revelation saw exactly the same mingling of hail and fire when God acted in judgment (Rev 8.7). It seems as though the very foundations of the world are shaken when Jehovah rises in His anger. There is a cosmic upheaval. Ocean beds and deep ravines are both discovered and uncovered. He will shake heaven and earth to deliver His suffering servant. David acknowledges divine intervention. His salvation has come from above and he has been lifted out of the waters of affliction. He is like another, Moses, who was "drawn out of the water" and accordingly called MOSHEH (Ex 2.10). It was a deliverance from a cruel Pharaoh, the avowed enemy of God's people. David, as Moses, is drawn (MASHA - 4871) out of the waters from the wrath of the enemy. The enemy was strong, too strong for David himself, and an enemy who hated him. They had prevented him (6923), he says. "Prevent" is an old English translation of the word which has already occurred in v.5. It means to "confront" or "forestall". The cunning foe had barred his way and blocked his path in the day of his distress, but Jehovah was his support and stay. The Lord, who takes pleasure in His people, had not only delivered him, but had brought him out of his straightened circumstances into a large place. Like Joseph, brought from the prison to the palace, David is brought from the cave Adullam to the throne, from the desert to the court.

Verses 20-29: Righteousness and Recompense

The Psalmist now avows that Jehovah has been righteous in delivering him. He had, after all, walked in the ways of the Lord, he had kept his hands clean and there had been no wilful departure from his God. In spite of his failings David can assert his integrity in that the statutes of the Lord were ever before him and he had not, with wicked intent, put them from him. He had lived upright before Him whom he repeatedly calls, "My God", and he had kept (8104) himself, guarded himself, from iniquity. He was indeed a man after God's own heart. So, according to his righteousness, Jehovah had recompensed him, and this maintained Jehovah's righteousness also. It was but right that God should deliver His upright servant from wicked men. Clean hands and a pure heart, as in Psalm 24, called for acceptance with Jehovah, who rewarded the merciful with mercy, and the pure with purity. But note that the two words translated "froward" in v.26 are different words. "With the froward (6141) thou wilt shew thyself froward (6617). Froward men are crooked men, perverse, twisted. Jehovah, in response, will resist such men. He will oppose them and wrestle with them and show His displeasure. Such is the difference in these two words. It is an important distinction to be observed.

It is the way of Jehovah to help the humble and bring down the proud. The afflicted people of whom the Psalmist speaks, are the poor and needy. The high looks of which he speaks, belong to the haughty spirit. This is the principle of which Mary sings, "He hath put down the mighty...and exalted them of low degree" (Lk 1.52). The same thought is in the ministry of John Baptist too; "Every valley shall be exalted, and every mountain and hill shall be made low" (Is 40.4; Lk 3.5). It is Peter's word also; "God resisteth the proud, and giveth grace to the humble" (1 Pet 5.5). Indeed it is the opening ministry of the Saviour Himself, who taught, "Blessed are the poor in spirit: for theirs is the kingdom of heaven" (Mt 5.3).

So would David abide in the comfort of the light. Again he calls Jehovah "My God", and the God whom he knows so personally will light his lamp for him, and enlighten his darkness. In the corresponding 2 Samuel 22.29, David says, "Thou art my lamp, O Lord". It is said that the prevailing custom in Arabia and Egypt, and in neighbouring countries, was to light the lamps at sunset and keep them burning throughout the night hours. The poorest of the people would, if necessary, forego food rather than be without oil for the lamp. The child of God is ever averse to darkness. Does not David say in another place, "The Lord is my light and my salvation; whom shall I fear" (Ps 27.1)? Darkness has always been the emblem of distress and fear. Light is the emblem of comfort and of knowledge. In the holy city, the new Jerusalem, there is unfading light, "for the glory of God did lighten it, and the Lamb is the light thereof" (Rev 21.23).

Fearlessly then, David the warrior can run through a troop (1416). In the strength of the Lord he can engage any band or company of marauding enemies. Once again he says, "My God". By his God he can with confidence assail the fortresses of his enemies. In God he need fear no foe, whether in attack or defence. Note the same spirit in the apostle of another generation, who writes, "I can do all things through Christ which strengtheneth me" (Phil 4.13).

Verses 30-45: Victories - Past, Present, and Future

The Psalmist delights to recount, again and again, what God has wrought. He now recalls what God has done for him and through him, and, taking comfort from past experiences he can face the future with confidence. For, as for God, His way is perfect. There is no limit to this perfection. As Plumer so beautifully expresses it, "God's way is perfectly just, perfectly wise, perfectly holy, perfectly good, perfectly sure to prevail, perfectly honourable to Himself, perfectly safe to His people". Not only is His way perfect, but His Word is equally so. It has been tried by His saints of every age and is as pure gold, refined and free from dross.

David boldly challenges men with the question, "Who is God (433) save the Lord?". Plumer again comments so interestingly, "Here first in the Psalms occurs the name ELOAH, rendered 'God'. It occurs more than fifty times in the Scriptures, but only four times in the Psalms. It is the singular of ELOHIM. Many have supposed that this name specially refers to God as an object of religious worship. That idea may well be prominent in this place". Who, indeed is God, save Jehovah? Is He not Creator, Upholder, Sustainer, of the vast universe? Do the lifeless gods of the heathen have the attributes which He has? Do they have the sovereignty and glory and power of Eloah? The questions are rhetorical. They do not really require an answer. Jehovah alone is worthy of adoration and worship. Who therefore is a rock save our God? David has already spoken of Jehovah as his rock in v.2 of this Psalm. It is a fitting symbol of strength, stability and salvation. It is Jehovah, unchangeable, immovable, and immutable. What other supposed deity is a rock save our God?

David the warrior-king now ascribes all the glory of his victories to God. He will speak of his girdle, his feet, his hands, his bow, and his shield. Has he triumphed in battle? Then it was God who girded him with strength. God, whose way is perfect in v.30, makes His servant's way perfect also. It is the same word. God had given him the surefootedness of the hind, swift to outrun his enemies and gain the advantage of heights and strongholds beyond the reach of those foes. For David, this would have been fulfilled so literally in the days of his battles in the hills and mountains of Judea.

David likewise attributes his strength and skill in war to divine enabling. The word translated "steel" (5154) in the AV is more probably "copper" or "bronze". Whether this is the bending, to breaking point, of David's own bow, or whether it is the breaking of the bow of the enemy, is difficult to determine, but, either way, it is gratitude to Jehovah for necessary strength. Then, for the third time in the Psalm, David uses the word "shield" (4043). "Buckler", in vv. 2 and 30, is the same word. Jehovah was not only his strength but also his protection, and the right hand of God upheld him. He exclaims, "Thy gentleness (6037) hath made me great". This strangely beautiful expression has been variously interpreted. Perowne is worth quoting at length. "Jehovah's wonderful condescension (by which he was taken from the sheepfolds to be king) made him great; Jehovah made room for him to stand, and subdued those that rose up against him. Thy graciousness, lit. 'meekness', 'lowliness', a very remarkable word as applied to God, and just one of those links connecting the Divine with the human, which in the Old Testament so strikingly foreshadow an incarnation". How graciously and gently does Jehovah stoop to meet the need of his servants in every age.

Jehovah too, had enlarged the place of David's steps, and had given him a sure foothold in his many conflicts. No doubt David had experienced this literally and physically among the cliffs of the Judaean wilderness. With God's help his feet did not slip and with confidence he had pursued and routed his enemies and destroyed them. His victories were complete. The enemies were vanquished, disabled and wounded so as not to rise again. And yet again David ascribes the glory to God, and says again, as in v.32, that it was He who had girded him with the necessary strength to subdue those that had risen up against him. God had given them into his hand. They had hated him and he had destroyed them. His enemies had none to help them, as he had. They cried, but there was none to hear.

Even Jehovah would not answer when they cried to Him. They were the enemies of His servant and His anointed, and He would not save them. Did they, as some suggest, cry to their own gods first? Did they call to their idols? Did they, when that was futile, then cry to Jehovah? He would not hear. It was not a sincere recognition of Him but a selfish cry out of their fear, and He would not move to deliver them. Instead, they would become as fine dust in the wind. They would be blown away helplessly in the conflict. They would fall, beaten, in the streets. Plumer remarks, "Like several other verses of this Psalm, this never had its complete fulfilment in David. It points to Christ".

David is delivered from them all. He speaks of "the people" and "the heathen". Are these the enemy within and without? From all their strivings Jehovah has delivered him and exalted him. Nations and strangers acknowledge his headship. They bow to him and serve him. They submit to him and obey him. His fame reaches out beyond the boundaries of Israel. Before his triumph his enemies faded away, emerging from their stronghold in fear and trembling. What hiding place is of any value when Jehovah is against them? Once again Plumer says, "This cannot have its complete fulfilment except in Christ". All is, indeed, so similar to that millennial Psalm 72 which envisages the ultimate triumph and enthronement of Messiah, and His universal rule.

Verses 46-50: The Epilogue

David exults, and exclaims "The Lord liveth!". If the supposition at v.41 that the heathen had cried to their lifeless gods and found no help is correct, then this is the joyous confidence of the believer, that Jehovah lives. He only has immortality (1 Tim 6.16). It is fitting then, that He, the living God, should be blessed and exalted, adored and praised. How does David delight to use the personal pronoun, and speak of, *my* rock, *my* salvation. The God who dwells in light unapproachable deigns to be, to David, and to every saint, "The God of my salvation". For the third time in the Psalm, in the AV, the Psalmist speaks of Jehovah as his rock (vv.2, 31, 46). There are two different words in the original but both rightly translated "rock". The first, in v.2, is a stronghold (5553). The remaining two signify strength (6697). The living Jehovah was David's strength and his rock-fortress.

It was this God, this mighty El (410) who had wrought salvation for David. He had avenged David of his enemies. He had subdued them and delivered David, and had lifted His servant up above the men of violence who had opposed and oppressed him. Therefore, it seemed but a right and proper thing, that David should render due thanks. This thanksgiving, and this singing of praises, however, should not be heard in the assembly of the people only, in ritual ceremony. David desires that the praise should be heard among the nations. The sounds of adoration which began in Jerusalem would reverberate into the lands of the heathen (1471). The GOYIM would hear the praise of Jehovah in foreign parts.

David was God's king. Jehovah had been faithful to His anointed and had delivered him from the enemies David mentions so often in the Psalm. The shepherd boy from Bethlehem had been anointed in 1 Samuel 16.13, but Jehovah's delight in David and His choice of him was but a foreshadowing of a greater than David. "To his seed for evermore". Again we must look beyond David to One greater than Solomon, to David's greater Son, born in the same Bethlehem of the seed of David and with unchallengeable rights to the throne. He will yet subdue every enemy and reign supreme as God's anointed

PSALM 19

Introduction

The title of the Psalm indicates that this is another Psalm of David, and yet another of those fifty-five Psalms which are committed to the care of the Chief Musician. The Chief Musician was the Precentor, or Master of Music, who superintended the service of song in the temple ceremonies. This Psalm would therefore be added to that special collection of his for continuing usage by the worshippers in the temple. The Psalm is a contrast, but a companion and complement, to Psalm 8. One is a contemplation of the moon and the stars of the sky at night. This Psalm is a consideration of the same heavens in the daytime, when the sun is shining in his strength. In both Psalms the glory of God is being told out in the wonders of creation. David the shepherd boy must often have lain in the fields of Bethlehem admiring the expanse of the heavens above him while the flock quietly grazed or rested around him. How much may be learned from the Book of Nature! Here, in His creation, those invisible things of God are clearly seen, even His eternal power and Godhead (Rom 1.20). The boy from the Bethlehem sheepcotes knew more than many a philosopher.

There is, in this Psalm, a progressive revelation of God. It is God making Himself known to men in a threefold way. The skies, the Scriptures, and the Saviour will together reveal the greatness, the grandeur, and the grace of God. It is His desire that men should know Him, and accordingly He will reveal Himself to those who have the will to know.

Verses 1-6 present that revelation of God in the skies. This revelation proves that God is, and it shows to men His power and might and magnificence, but does not particularly reveal His character. Verses 7-11 deal with various aspects of the Scriptures wherein those who read may now discover the character of One who is righteous, holy, and pure. Such knowledge will, of necessity, also discover to the reader his own sinfulness and need, but will lead him to a revelation of God as his strength and redeemer. This revelation of a Saviour is the grand culmination of the Psalm in verses 12-14.

Verses 1-6: God Revealed in the Skies

The pages of the Book of Nature are many. Earth, sky and sea; sun, moon and stars; oceans, rivers and lakes; mountains, valleys and hills; flowers, fruits and trees; birds, tiny insects and giant mammals. All are expositions of the magnificence of the Creator, but here David is concerned chiefly with the heavens. The heavens have so often been God's chosen venue for the revelation of His glory. The shining heavens declare His glory in creation. The singing heavens declared His glory at the incarnation. The darkened heavens declared His glory at the crucifixion. The opened heavens declared His glory at the ascension of the risen Christ. The fiery heavens will one day declare His glory in awful retribution on those who obey not the gospel. The firmament, the great expanse of those heavens, shows forth His glory at all times. It is the revelation of His handywork. "Handywork" (4639) must not be understood in the way in which the term is commonly used. It is rather "hand-work". Indeed the word may be translated "needlework", as if to suggest that the Creator has embroidered the heavens with the beauty and splendour of the heavenly bodies. As that other Psalm has it, "the work of thy fingers" (8.3).

The revelation of God in the skies knows no restrictions or boundaries. Neither time nor distance nor language is any barrier to Him. As day follows day, and night follows night, day and night continuing endlessly, without pause or interruption, so the glorious declaration goes on and on. It is a timeless testimony to the glory of God, offering to every willing mind a knowledge of the Creator.

This testimony is neither restricted by, nor dependent upon, speech or language. This has been variously translated and explained. Some will retain the AV text, and, of course, it is true, that wherever men are, and whatever language they may speak, the declaration of the heavens may be understood. There is no speech or language where their voice is not heard. Others, probably more accurately, like JND prefer to understand the verse to say that there is no speech, there is no language, there is no audible word, and yet without these the message goes forth. The splendour of a sunrise, the after-glow of a glorious sunset, these, in every part of the world, are the silent preachers of God's glory, inaudible witnesses to His majesty. Perowne quotes the lovely words of Addison -

"What though in solemn silence all
Move round this dark terrestrial ball,
In reason's ear they all rejoice,
And utter forth a glorious voice".

There is no geographical boundary to the witness of the heavens. No measuring line can determine any limits to the scope and sphere of their testimony. Their line (6957) is gone out through all the earth and their unspoken word to the extremities of the globe. The golden sun travels the length and breadth of the skies ceaselessly and tirelessly. Out of his tent he arises in glory at the dawning, and, having traversed the expanse in splendour, he returns to his pavilion in glory in the evening hour. He comes forth with joy and gladness like a bridegroom. He appears as a valiant champion to run the race and later return in glory. Believers of a later day than David's will see in this a lovely foreshadowing of Him who came forth in glory from the womb of the virgin, who sojourned in sinless splendour among men for thirty-three years and then returned to the heavens in the same unsullied glory with which He came forth. The sun travels the circuit unceasingly, constantly witnessing to the glory of its Creator, dispensing warmth impartially to all men of whatever land or language.

Verses 7-11: God Revealed in the Scriptures

David now introduces the great name of Jehovah. This is important. The Book of Nature reveals God (EL - 410) the God of power and might (v.1). The Scriptures reveal Jehovah (3068), the one true God, ever existing, self-sufficient. The Psalmist employs the holy name seven times in the Psalm, six of which are to be found in this section. Six times he speaks of the sacred Scriptures in association with Jehovah. He tells what the Scriptures are, what they do, and what their effect is on the hearts of the hearers. In all of this the reader may learn the character of Jehovah. Here he may learn the will of God and the heart of man. Note the variety of terms by which the Scriptures are presented in the Psalm. David calls them, the law of Jehovah, the testimony of Jehovah, the statutes of Jehovah, the commandment of Jehovah, the fear of Jehovah, and the judgments of Jehovah. This is an inspired way of emphasising the several facets of God's Word. It is touching to remember that David's Bible was relatively small. He must have had the Pentateuch, the five Books of Moses. Did he have the Book of Job? Was that all? He certainly had much less of the divine Word than believers of this present day, and yet, how precious it was to him.

The law of Jehovah is perfect (8549). It is complete and entire. There is no discrepancy or error. It is healthful and wholesome. It has neither spot nor blemish. For those who will obey it, it will effect conversion. It will bring a man to confront himself in his need and then turn to God in repentance, to be restored to what God intended man to be.

The testimony of Jehovah is sure (539). It is a faithful word. It is to be believed with assurance. It will give wisdom to the simple (6612). That man who, in child-like simplicity, is humble enough to receive the guidance of its testimony will be granted that wisdom of which Paul writes; "...the holy scriptures, which are able to make thee wise unto salvation" (2 Tim 3.15).

The statutes of Jehovah are right (3477). His precepts are righteous. They offer right directions and advice and they are opposed to the crookedness of man. They are upright and true and they can fill the responsive heart with joy and gladness.

The commandment of Jehovah is pure (1249). Here is sincerity, clean, clear, unalloyed and unadulterated. "The sincere milk of the word," writes Peter (1 Pet 2.2). It will enlighten the eyes, giving clear vision of spiritual realities, illuminating the darkened mind.

The fear (3374) of Jehovah is clean (2889). This word is used elsewhere of physical, moral, and ceremonial cleanness. The Scriptures are associated here with their effect upon the obedient heart. They will produce a reverential fear of God, an awe of divine Persons, and a consequent purity of life. Such purity will endure when the corrupt things of the world have decayed and perished.

The judgments (4941) of Jehovah are true and righteous altogether. The judicial decisions and decrees of the Lord as revealed in His Word are truth. They are founded upon that justice and equity and righteousness which is His own abiding character.

Notice how that character is revealed in the Psalmist's admiration of the law, and observe, too, the progression of blessing which Jehovah dispenses to those who love His law. There is conversion, assurance and wisdom. There is joy, purity and knowledge. There is holiness, truth and righteousness. These reveal the kind of God that He is, but yet there is more.

To the believing heart the preciousness of the sacred Scriptures is beyond description. David speaks of gold and honey. There is richness and sweetness, and the Psalmist has an increasing appreciation of both. Gold, fine gold, much fine gold. How precious is this Word to the believer. Sweeter also than honey and the honeycomb. The gold is refined gold without dross, and it is in plenty. The honey is as that honey dripping from the comb in all its sweet purity. But what is all this if a man does not hear and heed its message? David recognises the solemn warnings of the law, enlightening a man as to his own need and to Jehovah's provision. He sees, too, that for the keeping of these precepts there is great reward. There is great gain in the keeping of God's law. Jehovah then has revealed His character in His Word. It is for man to acknowledge that revelation and to respond obediently.

Verses 12-14: God Revealed in the Saviour

"By the law is the knowledge of sin". So Paul writes in Romans 3.20 and this we learn experimentally in this Psalm. The law exposes a man, lays him bare, and judges him. Sin in all its forms is made known to the exercised soul until the same Word draws the man in penitence and weakness to look for a Saviour, crying, like the Apostle, "O wretched man that I am!" (Rom 7.24). David speaks of sins as errors (7691), as secret (5641) faults, and as presumptuous (2086) sins. In whatever form they may be discovered or described, sins are offensive to the holiness that has been mirrored in the previous section of the Psalm and the penitent will look for pardon.

The word translated "errors" is found only here. It indicates a failing and is akin to those sins of ignorance which are dealt with particularly in Leviticus 4. There are sins which are committed unintentionally and unwittingly, but they are sins nonetheless. Indeed, do they not rather reveal the awful depravity of the human heart, if a man can sin and not even be aware, or recognise, that he is sinning? "Who can understand his errors?", cries the Psalmist. The question is rhetorical and does not call for an answer. No man can understand or assess either the degree or the enormity of those sins which have been committed in ignorance. Sometimes they may come to light and be regretted and repented of, but some will never be known in a lifetime. It is important to remember that they are indeed sins nevertheless, and just as foul as sin in any other form.

Other sins are known to the sinner, but concealed. They may be committed in secret and hidden away from the eyes of family and friends. But this is foolish. "All things are naked and opened unto the eyes of him with whom we have to do" (Heb 4.13), as David learned to his cost. Concealed and secret they may be as far as others are concerned, but they are there, lurking in the life and in the conscience, known to God and demanding judgment. And may it also be true, that, if sins are harboured in secrecy for too long, and not confessed, they may eventually be lost in the forgetfulness of the sinner himself? "Cleanse thou me", should be the early prayer of the offender.

It is contrary to human nature to desire to be restrained, but this is just what David now asks for. He is Jehovah's servant, therefore Jehovah is his Lord. He prays to be kept back, to be preserved, and to be prevented from a most grievous form of sinning. Presumptuous sins are the sins of proud, arrogant, insolent men and David can detect an awful irony. Presumptuous sins are committed by men who boast that they are unrestrained, doing as they please, when they please. It is not so. Such sins will soon master the man. He will become a slave to them. There will be bondage. They will have the dominion and will rule over the proud sinner. That man has a great advantage who knows the Saviour for "sin shall not have dominion over you" (Rom 6.14). So delivered from the power of sin, the believer will live uprightly, his life complete for God. The alternative is fearful.

Observe the awful potential progression of evil. From sins of ignorance to secret faults to presumptuous sins and to the great transgression. This may mean, if read without the article, "much transgression". However, it may anticipate that the sinner, continually unrepentant, may become apostate. Apostasy is a great transgression. It is an abandonment of all the truth that a man has ever learned. It is wilful rejection of all that God in grace has revealed of Himself and of salvation. Judas is the classic apostate. How much he knew, but he persisted in a hypocritical secrecy, hiding from his fellows his covetous intent, until at last he sold himself and the Saviour. It was the great transgression, for which there was no pardon.

The Psalm concludes with a touching prayer. How often in the Scriptures are heart and mouth mentioned together. "My heart...my tongue," says the Psalmist in Psalm 45.1. "Confess with thy mouth...believe in thine heart," says the apostle in Romans 10.9, And, "With the heart man believeth...and with the mouth confession is made" (Rom 10.10). "For of the abundance of the heart his mouth speaketh", said the Saviour (Lk 6.45). Heart and mouth must be in harmony, and David desires that the words of his mouth and the meditation of his heart should be in accord, and be acceptable in the sight of his God.

The final address to God in the Psalm employs three Divine Titles. "O Jehovah, my rock, and my redeemer". For the seventh time in the Psalm David uses the name Jehovah. He then repeats that lovely title which he has used before, especially in the previous Psalm 18, "My Rock". But then, the closing word in the Psalm is that title found only once more in Scripture as used in an individual personal way: "My Redeemer". Only David and Job exclaim, in that manner, "My Redeemer" (Job 19.25). Jehovah had revealed Himself to them as a Redeemer from sorrow and from sin in all its forms. He has made Himself known. There is a Saviour for every obedient soul.

There is, therefore, a message in the skies, in the Scriptures, and in the Saviour. It is for man to look and listen and learn, and the principle is, as announced by the Lord Jesus Himself, that, "If any man will...he shall know" (Jn 7.17).

PSALM 20

Introduction

It is impossible to say in what special circumstances this Psalm was composed, or, indeed, if it was written for any particular event at all. It may well have been intended to be sung by the congregation on any of those many occasions when David and succeeding kings were in trouble and in need of prayer. That it was purposed for public worship is evident in that it has been dedicated to the Chief Musician. The inscription tells us also that it was a Psalm of David and there is no reason to doubt the Davidic authorship. The fact that the king is spoken of in the third person has led some to think that the Psalm was not written by David but by some unknown person in his honour. However, it is quite reasonable to believe that David composed the Psalm in this form to be included in the liturgy of the nation as a poetical prayer for the king in times of trouble. Here are the longings and desires of David's own heart for himself produced in Psalm form for the nation to sing on his behalf, and on behalf of those kings who would follow him.

The Psalm is in several parts. The opening section, verses 1-5, is the prayer of the people for the king, perhaps to be chanted by the Levites on their behalf. Verses 6-8 are a response to the congregational petition, singing of confidence in Jehovah to give the king victory over his enemies. Verse 9 is the final brief prayer of the people for the salvation of the king and for his encouragement as he hears them call to Jehovah for him.

Verses 1-5: Prayer for the King

The prayer and desire of the people for their king is a compilation of short and direct requests. To the king they say, "The Lord hear thee, defend thee, help thee, strengthen thee, remember thee, accept thee, give thee". Though they appear to be addressing the king, they are, in fact, petitioning Jehovah on his behalf. Note that their appeal is to Jehovah. It is the awesome name of the eternally existing all-sufficient One, but, almost at once, they have cause to remember that He is the God of Jacob. In Jehovah there is all power and might to deliver their king in the day of trouble, and in the God of Jacob there is grace that will hear them. There may well be a remembrance of Jacob's words in Genesis 35.3, where the patriarch says, "God, who answered me in the day of my distress, and was with me in the way which I went". By "the name" is meant that character by which God has revealed Himself, and the manner in which He revealed Himself to Jacob seemed so suitable and so applicable to David in his trouble. Jacob had his days of trouble. David, too, had many such days. There were days of distress both with the patriarch and with the king. The God of Jacob was a merciful God, a God of all grace, and faithful, and the prayer of the Psalm is that He would minister to David as He had ministered to Jacob.

The opening petition is that Jehovah would hear and defend (7682). The word "defend" means to protect by setting on a high place. It is the thought of a high tower, inaccessible and secure, beyond the reach of the enemy. This divine help and protection would come from the sanctuary. David did not have the privilege of such a temple as that of Solomon his son, but he did have a sanctuary, where, behind curtains on Mount Zion, dwelt the holy Ark of the Covenant, and with it, in symbol, the very presence of Jehovah. David desired sanctuary help, that from the divine presence in Zion there might come to him the strengthening that he needed to face his many foes. The believer today similarly prays that from the heavenly sanctuary, from the throne, there might be granted enabling grace to help in time of need (Heb 4.16).

If much is being asked of God for the king, the people now pray that Jehovah will remember what David has offered to Him. Will Jehovah call to mind the many oblations that the king has brought to Him? "Offerings" (4503) is the word MINCHA, as in the meat offering of Leviticus 2. "Burnt sacrifice"(5930) is OLA, from which the word "holocaust" is derived. These are not sacrifices for sin. They are gifts and approach offerings. They are presents and tributes offered in appreciation to Jehovah from a willing and grateful heart. They were not compulsory offerings, but were offered freely as worship. Will Jehovah graciously remember these and grant a token of His acceptance of them and accordingly bless His servant the king?

There follows a "Selah" (5542). It indicates a solemn interlude. There is a fitting silence for reflection on what has been said. These are great things which are being asked for the king, and it is well for the suppliants to pause, to meditate, and to wait on the Lord.

The prayer now resumes. May Jehovah grant to the king the desires of his heart and bring to fulfilment his purposes and plans. David had, of course, learned a great principle, which he enunciates in his Psalm 37.4. "Delight thyself also in the Lord; and he shall give thee the desires of thine heart". Jehovah delights to respond to those who delight in Him. The prayer now is that the king's plans and counsel relative to the battle may be blessed of God and wrought out as the king has purposed. If David's counsel as a warrior-king is of God, then victory is assured. The praying people ask that that counsel might be fulfilled (4390), that it might be brought to fruition, to completion, and that the purpose of it might be accomplished.

It is now anticipated that victory will indeed be granted, and the people will triumph in the triumph of their king. They will exult and share together in the jubilation which inevitably follows victory. Notice that it is not now "in the name of the God of Jacob", but "in the name of our God". It is good when saints can appropriate to themselves what the Lord has been to others. This is now an experimental knowledge of the God of Jacob. It is not just historical, or theological, or theoretical, but practical. The God of Jacob is their God and will answer them in their day of trouble as He answered Jacob in days of old. In the name of their God they will set up their banners in joy. The banner was an essential part of military equipment. Banners and standards were raised in open declaration of war when an army marched into battle. They were unfurled in defiance even when defeat seemed near. But they were raised in triumph when the battle was won, to be flown from every high hill, from every dome and turret and tower. "We will set up our banners", they cry in joyful hope of victory, and pray again that Jehovah in His might will fulfil all the petitions of their king.

Verses 6-8: The Response

There is a difference of opinion among commentators as to whether this is the response of the king himself, or that of an officiating priest or Levite. Some think that the king was responding to the prayer of the people with a glad assurance. He was, after all, the Lord's anointed (1 Sam 16.13). Had not Jehovah chosen him from among all the sons of Jesse, and would Jehovah fail him in battle? "Now know I", the king might be saying. It is not presumptuous for those who trust in Jehovah to say, "I know". So did Paul write, and John also, saying again and again, "We know; we know". It is not fleshly complacency or arrogance. It is the language of simple trust in the Word of Him who cannot lie.

Others, however, understand this response to be that of a priest or Levite, speaking concerning the king. The assumption then is that as the offerings were being presented on the king's behalf the Psalm may have been sung while the ritual was taking place. Whether this response is that of the king or of a priest does not affect the confident spirit of it. Jehovah would deliver His anointed. He would hear him from His holy heaven. Jehovah had indeed an earthly sanctuary, but the singers looked for an answer from His dwelling place in the heaven of His holiness. From there He would send to His anointed the saving strength of His right hand. The right hand is the symbol of might and power, and in this David could safely trust. "They that wait upon the Lord shall renew their strength" (Is 40.31).

Indeed, who, knowing Jehovah, would trust in human strength? David's foes might trust in the abundance of their chariots and horses but David must trust in Him who is now called, "The Lord our God". This is Jehovah (3068) our Elohim (430). What a majestic title is this! Jehovah the eternal is our Elohim the mighty. Who would not trust in Him! As that other Psalm agrees, "It is better to trust in the Lord than to put confidence in man. It is better to trust in the Lord than to put confidence in princes" (118.8-9). David had learned this at an early age. He was but a lad, a stripling, when he challenged Goliath, crying across the valley, "I come to thee in the name of the Lord of hosts, the God of the armies of Israel, whom thou hast defied. This day will the Lord deliver thee into mine hand" (1 Sam 17.45-46). And as it was with the giant of Gath, so would it be with his enemies now, "They are brought down and fallen". But David and his people would stand, triumphant. The battle is the Lord's!

Verse 9: The Final Petition

The concluding prayer is but a summary of all that has already been requested. "Save, Lord". This last clause of the Psalm is difficult and there are variations of interpretation. Are the people desiring that the king might indeed hear them as they call? That for his encouragement he might hear the united cry of his people on his behalf? "Let the king hear us when we call". It is always comforting to the saints to hear that others are interceding for them. Some, however, as Perowne, will understand the people to be saying, "Jehovah, save the king! May He (Jehovah) answer us when we cry (unto Him)". This is in agreement with the comment of Dr Cohen who says, "The ancient versions divide the verse into two equal halves: 'Lord, save the king; and may He answer us'". This is similar to the "God save the king" of 2 Samuel 16.16. Yet again, others, as Delitzsch, will see the king in v.9 to be Jehovah, and so, "Let the king (Jehovah) hear us when we call. This, however, tends to confuse, since the king is obviously David the anointed of v.6. Perhaps the suggestion of Perowne is the most acceptable, and nearest to current understanding of the text.

So ends the short Psalm which is the prayer of the congregation on behalf of the king. The people invoke Jehovah to hear and help, to defend and deliver, to strengthen and save, to remember the king and so rejoice their hearts. The Psalm is not usually reckoned among those that are termed "Messianic", but it is not at all difficult to catch glimpses of Messiah in it and to anticipate His future triumph and glory.

PSALM 21

Introduction

This Psalm is an obvious companion to the preceding Psalm 20. If, as has been suggested, the previous Psalm is a prayer for the king on his way to battle, then Psalm 21 is a song of thanksgiving for victory granted. With those fifty-four other Psalms dedicated to the Chief Musician, this Psalm is also committed to that Master of Song and Music, to be used in the congregational liturgy of temple worship. Being a Psalm of David, it was therefore composed a millennium before Christ, but the exact date cannot be fixed since it contains nothing which can relate it to any specific event in David's life or reign. It must be pointed out that, although the Psalm, like many others, is not usually reckoned with those which are called "Messianic", it is impossible not to catch glimpses in it of that greater Son of David, the Lord Jesus Christ, the Messiah. Much of the language, the triumph, the glory and majesty, of the Psalm will only be realised fully in Him who is the true King of Israel.

The thirteen verses may be divided almost equally into two parts. Verses 1-7 are retrospective. They are the king's thanksgiving for the blessing of Jehovah upon him. The remaining verses 8-13 anticipate that the Lord will continue to subdue the king's enemies so that He, Jehovah, will be exalted.

Verses 1-7: The Joy of Victories Granted

The prayer of the preceding Psalm had asked for strength and salvation for the king in his day of trouble. That prayer had been heard and answered and now the king rejoices in the strength of the Lord and in the salvation which has been afforded him. That prayer had also asked that the desire of the king's heart might be granted to him, and this too has been given him. He rejoices that the request of his lips and the thoughts of his heart have not been denied him, and it is an occasion for a "Selah". It is a suitable time to pause, to reflect, to be silent in wonder and lift up the heart in worship for what Jehovah has wrought for the king.

The old word "preventest" (6923) of v.3, is an interesting word. It means "to precede; to go before; to meet; to anticipate; to confront". Jehovah had indeed anticipated the need of His servant and had gone before and met him for his deliverance and his prosperity. Jehovah had blessings of such goodness (2896) in mind and in preparation for the king even before his prayer had been uttered. It is rather like that other promise of Jehovah to saints of a blessed day yet future, "Before they call, I will answer; and while they are yet speaking, I will hear" (Is 65.24).

Jehovah had crowned the king with a crown of pure gold, and here is one of those lovely foreshadowings of the Son of Man, who, in that very last reference to Him in Scripture as Son of Man, is seen with a golden crown on His head (Rev 14.14). That holy head which was once adorned with a crown of thorns will one day be crowned with pure gold like the king of Psalm 21. "Pure gold" (6337), is but one word in the Hebrew original. It is gold refined. There is no dross. The crown of the Lord's anointed is pure preciousness unalloyed. It is not necessary, however, to see here a literal crown, or any reference to David's actual coronation, as in 2 Samuel 5.3-5 or 1 Chronicles 11.1-9. It simply indicates that Jehovah had conferred upon him a regal dignity and majesty consistent with the triumphs granted to him.

"Long live the king!" is a familiar exclamation. So the king of the Psalm has asked life, and Jehovah has granted length of days for ever (5769) and ever (5703). These two words are different, but similar, indicating perpetuity and futurity. Of course this, in its fullness, can only be true of Him of whom it is said that He lives "after the power of an endless life" (Heb 7.16), but David will rejoice in a long and triumphant reign and in such blessing his glorying will be great. He did indeed live to a good old age and died in peace. Honour and majesty had been laid upon him. He had been richly blessed, and, before the face of Jehovah who had so blessed him, he could be glad with a rejoicing which was abundant and overflowing, an exceeding gladness indeed. Of David's greater Son it is written, "He shall bear the glory" (Zech 6.13). King David's honour and majesty are a fitting, though faint, picture of that coming glory of Messiah in the millennial day.

David's joy was born in trust. Monarch and warrior though he was, he had a child-like trust in Jehovah. It was a confidence that gave him hope and made him bold and rendered him safe. The Most High (5945) had dealt with him in lovingkindness. This is Jehovah Elyon, the God of Melchizedek and of Abram long before David (Gen 14.18-22). That man cannot be moved whose trust is in the Most High. This is the firm assurance of many a Psalm and it is the message of all Holy Scripture.

Verses 8-13: The Assurance of Victories Anticipated

There are two things which give David confidence. First, the memory of past deliverances must engender hope for the future. But second, and even more than this, is the realisation that the king's enemies are God's enemies also. Did they hate David? They hated David's Lord too. Jehovah, therefore, would find them out. He would expose them and confront them. He would encounter and engage them and there would be no hiding place for them. Notice the repetition of "shall find out". There can be no doubting that the right hand of Jehovah will expose those who are His enemies and the enemies of His people, and their end will be fearful. There will be a fiery oven (8574). The word is sometimes rendered "furnace". It is an awful doom, like the judgment of Sodom and Gomorrah (Gen 19.28) when the smoke of their destruction went up as the smoke of a furnace. It is like that coming judgment of those of whom it is written that "the smoke of their torment ascendeth up for ever and ever" (Rev 14.11).

It is interesting to observe that the word "anger" (6440) in v.9 is exactly the same as the word "countenance" in v.6. The thought seems to be that Jehovah is showing His face, He is appearing, He is making His presence known. To David, the revealing of that countenance brings joy and gladness, but to the wicked it is a revelation of anger and wrath. They shall, when Jehovah shows Himself, be swallowed up in an inescapable judgment, devoured in divine vengeance. Their judgment is far reaching too, for their fruit (6529), a synonym for their offspring, and called also "their seed", will be destroyed likewise. This must indicate those children who inherit and follow the wicked ways of their fathers. For these there can be no place among the sons of men, and the Lord will accordingly remove them from the earth.

Jehovah, and Jehovah alone, can foreknow the intentions of a man. He can detect and determine just exactly what a man is imagining in his heart. As a man's intended actions might be recognised by other men by his physical, outward, movements, so Jehovah can know motives and designs which are as yet hidden. He can discern the thoughts and intents of the heart (Heb 4.12). The intended evil, however, is not always realised. The mischievous device (4209) of which the Psalmist speaks, is a wicked purpose, a lewd and evil plot which is at times frustrated. It may come to nothing. In defeat they turn their back. They flee in a hasty retreat from an angry God whose arrows are ready to be released against them. Jehovah is against "the face of them". Here again, and for the third time in the Psalm, this word is employed. In v.6 the countenance of God shines upon His servant. In v.9 that countenance is revealed in anger against the enemy. In v.12 Jehovah prepares His arrows against the face of those who oppose Him. They turn the shoulder in flight, and, in their retreat, become a target for the arrows of the Almighty.

The Psalm concludes in a crescendo of praise, a doxology so like the opening verse. It sings of the strength and power of Jehovah. His saints will sing and praise as He is exalted. It is a celebration of divine victory over the king's enemies. The might of Jehovah has prevailed and His people must praise. Even when it seems, in the darkest hour, that evil has triumphed, the believer can know with assurance that the ultimate triumph is the Lord's. As the Saviour Himself said, "Verily, verily, I say unto you, That ye shall weep and lament, but the world shall rejoice: and ye shall be sorrowful, but your sorrow shall be turned into joy...and your joy no man taketh from you" (Jn 16.20, 22).

PSALM 22

Introduction

Psalm 22 is the fourth of those Psalms which are specifically called "Messianic". For an explanation of this term see Note 5 in the general Introduction to this Commentary. It is also the first of a delightful trilogy of Psalms in which the Psalmist moves from suffering in Psalm 22, through shepherd care in Psalm 23, to future glory in Psalm 24. These are, respectively, the Psalms of the Saviour, the Shepherd, and the Sovereign. Or, as is often said, the Psalms of the Cross, the Crook, and the Crown. The two sections of this Psalm are an exposition of those words of Peter as he writes of "The sufferings of Christ, and the glory that should follow"(1 Pet 1.11). The first part of the Psalm, verses 1-21, is a Sob. The second part, verses 22-31, is a Song. The reader is on holy ground and must come in the utmost reverence, with unshod feet, to learn the thoughts and feelings of the Prince of Sufferers, the Man of Sorrows.

There is no reason to question the Davidic authorship. The date must therefore be agreed at around 1050BC, but it is not possible to associate the Psalm with any particular event or circumstance in David's life. Does he write beyond his own experience? Is he not one of those OT prophets in whom the Spirit of Christ was speaking, and speaking of things not fully understood by the prophets themselves? There are some who suppose that David has written out of the depths of his own sorrow, but has, by inspiration, written of the deeper sufferings of Christ. Those who wish to consider this in depth might consult Plumer who has treated the question most thoroughly and at great length. In his very detailed summing up he writes, "There is no part of this Psalm which may not be applied to Messiah. Many parts of it are expressly applied to Christ in the New Testament, Matthew 27.46; Mark 15.34. In the same chapter of Matthew, v.35, and in John 19.24, the evangelists show that v.18 of this Psalm was fulfilled at the crucifixion. Matthew also tells that v.8 of this Psalm contains the very words of taunt and bitterness used by Christ's murderers (27.43). The whole history of the crucifixion shows the fulfilment of that clause in v.16, 'They pierced my hands and my feet'. Now crucifixion was not a Jewish but a Roman punishment. Paul in Hebrews 2.12, arguing on the humanity and sufferings of Christ, expressly applies to Him the whole of v.22. Immediately on His resurrection Christ calls the disciples, 'My brethren' (Mt 28.10; Jn 20.17), in fulfilment of the twenty-second verse of this Psalm. Indeed it would be hard to frame any argument proving any prophecy directly and exclusively Messianic, if this is not so".

The title of the Psalm has words familiar and unfamiliar. It is, with those fifty-four other Psalms, dedicated to the Chief Musician, the Precentor, the Master of Temple Song, and it is a Psalm of David. The unfamiliar are those Hebrew words, "Aijeleth Shahar". As to the meaning of these strange words there is no problem. The difficulty arises in seeking to understand their import and their relevance to the content of the Psalm. "Aijeleth" (365) is rightly rendered "hind" in Proverbs 5.19 and in Jeremiah 14.5. "Shahar" (7837) is rendered "morning" in Genesis 19.15, Psalm 139.9 and Song of Solomon 6.10. There is no doubt that the words mean "The Hind of the Morning", or, as some prefer, "The Hind of the Dawn".

But how then does this apply to the Psalm? Was it a title of some piece of morning music used in the service of the tabernacle or temple? Or was it the name of a musical instrument for which the Psalmist is stating a preference for use in the singing of his Psalm? We cannot know with certainty. Many devout readers, lovers of the Lord Jesus, will have no difficulty in seeing here a tender description of Him who, gentle and meek, was pursued by enemies from the dawning of His earthly life at Bethlehem until eventually they slew Him at Calvary. The gentle hind appears to be almost defenceless. It does not retaliate or engage in battle. It is a fitting symbol of Him of whom it is written that He, "when he was reviled, reviled not again; when he suffered, he threatened not" (1 Pet 2.23). In the early morning hours, before the animal creation has properly awakened, the hind may be seen drinking and feeding. It is indeed "the hind of the dawn". But when the beasts of prey have aroused themselves then the hind will be hunted, its only defence being a keen sense of danger and a fleetness of foot. So it was with the Lord Jesus, Herod cruelly seeking His life in those morning hours of His holy infancy, and, after that, enemies following Him relentlessly with evil intent until His death at Golgotha in the prime of sinless manhood. This Psalm, then, may be clearly seen to be an account of the sufferings of the Messiah and of the vindication and glory that follow. It is an inspired record of His death by crucifixion, composed over one thousand years before His incarnation, with an accompanying meditation upon His present and future exaltation.

Verses 1-21: The Sob

The Psalm begins with a cry from the depths of a suffering which can neither be comprehended nor expounded. It is a cry of abandonment, of desertion, of utter loneliness - "Eloi, Eloi, lama sabachthani?". Is this the only occurrence, in all of Holy Scripture, of the repeated "My God, my God"? What mystery is this? The sinless One is forsaken by the Holy One. Who can understand it? Judas may betray Him. Peter may deny Him. But, "My God, my God, why hast thou forsaken me?". However, this is not a cry of despair, or of complaint, or of impatience, or of arrogance. It is the cry of a willing, voluntary sin-bearer and substitute, who has assumed and accepted accountability for the sins of others and is now paying the price in deepest suffering. His God is far from helping Him, apparently unheeding the loud crying. Like the scapegoat in the land of forgetfulness, laden with the iniquities of the people, so does the Saviour cry alone upon the cross (Lev 16.22). There is none to hear Him or to come to His salvation. It is a wilderness of sorrow. The groanings of the sufferer are compared to the lion's roar. In the case of the Psalmist this may have been literally true, but not so with the Lord Jesus. With Him there was no such audible roaring during His hours of suffering, but nevertheless there must have been wrung from His heart, unheard by men, the sad and solemn cries of One in the intensity of indescribable anguish.

His cries continue. He calls to men, and to His God and Father, in the daytime and in the night season. They crucified the Saviour at the third hour, nine o'clock in the morning. For three hours he hung suffering under the burning Jerusalem sun. At the sixth hour, noonday, there fell an unnatural, supernatural, darkness which persisted until the ninth hour, three o'clock in the afternoon (Mk 15.25, 33). These were His daytime and His night season. For six hours, in the light and in the darkness, He endured the pain with none to help. His cries ascended to a silent heaven and dissolved in the darkness. There was no one to hear or to help the abandoned One. Forsaken! Alone! A sin-bearer on the behalf of others, Himself sinlessly perfect. There was no answer from God to the cry of desolation. "Thou hearest not".

It is, however, a consolation for every sufferer in the darkest hour to remember that God is holy. In His holiness, whatever the circumstances of His saints on earth, He is to be praised. Did Job grasp this, when, from the depths of his sorrow he cried, "Blessed be the name of the Lord" (Job 1.21)? Job's friends might not understand. Even his wife criticised him and gave ill advice. But Job looked up from his grief and blessed the Lord. In the case of the holy sufferer seen prophetically in this Psalm, it is holiness which demands the forsaking of the sin-bearer. He who sits in holiness, enthroned amid the praises of Israel, cannot look upon sin. Messiah, in His sinlessness, voluntarily and vicariously takes the place of sinners and is accordingly forsaken.

He remembers the patriarchs, Abraham, Isaac and Jacob; Moses, Joshua, Samuel and others. They trusted, they cried, and were delivered. They trusted and were not confounded (954). They were not disappointed. They had no reason to be ashamed about their trusting, for their God heard them and delivered them. Notice how David twice says, "They trusted", "They trusted", but between these he says, "They cried". There was an intensity and an earnestness with their trust. It was expressed in cries. They trusted with fervour. They cried in confident hope, and Jehovah had heard, and delivered.

"But I..."! O the sadness of this. The pronoun "I" is emphatic. "*I* am a worm" (8438). This is neither nature nor character, but expresses the human weakness of One who is utterly despised and rejected. The worm, in its helplessness, is trodden underfoot by men, despised and defenceless. But there is more yet. As F.W. Grant comments, "Gone down to a depth far below that of any man whatever. The word "worm" (TOLAAT) applies especially to the coccus from which the scarlet dye of the tabernacle was obtained, of course by its death: in that way, how significant of the One before us! But only as suffering under the judgment of sin could this be true of Him: indeed the word is used (Is 1.18) for the crimson red colour of sin, and that of a heinous kind; and thus the application is still clearer: He was made sin for us, He who knew no sin, that we might be made the righteousness of God in Him (2 Cor 5.21)". His people must bow their heads in deepest reverence, and view with wonder and worship that which they cannot comprehend.

Those are sad words in John 1.10-11 which tell us that "the world knew him not", and that "his own received him not". Jesus lived unrecognised in the world that He had made, and His own people, Israel, to whom He had been sent, despised Him. In His closing hours men laughed at His suffering. The Gospels record the literal fulfilment of these verses at Calvary. "They that passed by reviled him, wagging their heads...Likewise also the chief priests mocking him, with the scribes and elders" (Mt 27.39, 41). It was the reproach of men indeed. He was "despised of the people". Did they know, these mockers, how accurately they were fulfilling their own Psalm? They said, "He trusted in God; let him deliver him now, if he will have him" (Mt 27.43). They laughed Him to scorn and shook their heads, pouting with their lips as they taunted Him. These were gestures of contempt and of ridicule. They laughed in their derision of Him, ignorant of the truth of what they were saying, that Jehovah delighted in Him. They derided Him in whom Jehovah delighted. O the perversity of man!

But the holy sufferer continues to trust. His had ever been a life of dependence and trust and His trust would not be shaken now by the tauntings of wicked men. He had trusted (1556) His God since infancy. He had rolled Himself in dependence upon Jehovah all His life long, and though men might scoff and deride, still He would trust in the God who had taken Him out of the womb and caused Him to hope (982) since that day of His entry into the world.

In v.11 there is a plaintive appeal which is repeated in v.19. "Be not far from me". To the plea of v.11 is added the sad lament, "There is none to help", and to that of v.19 is added the call, "Haste thee to help me". Between these two verses lies that description of the sufferings of the Crucified, so accurate in the details as to appear more like a record of the past than a prediction of the future. Here is inspiration indeed, for it must always be remembered that death by crucifixion was a Roman invention, not Jewish. "Trouble is near", the sufferer cries. Why should Jehovah remain distant when trouble is near?

The tormentors are described as bulls and dogs, fiercely encompassing their victim. "Strong bulls of Bashan" encircle Him. Bashan was a most fertile country east of Jordan, famous for its rich pasture-land and therefore for its superior flocks and herds. The rams of Bashan are mentioned as early as Deuteronomy 32.14. In Amos 4.1 the cattle of Bashan are used symbolically of the leaders of the nation, and doubtless the same symbolism is employed here. The proud and arrogant scribes and Pharisees, with the priests and the doctors of the law, surrounded the lone sufferer in the palace of the High Priest on that dark night of His unjust trial. Caiaphas was a Sadducee, but Pharisees, Sadducees, and Herodians were united on that night in their opposition to the Blessed One. They gaped upon Him as they beset Him around. They raged upon Him like a ravening roaring lion in their ferocity, until He felt like water poured out, drained with the suffering and the strain of a long night. His heart, like wax in the intense heat, was melted within Him as He was taken from prison and from judgment to the place of execution (Is 53.8).

The cruel extending of the arms in crucifixion, and the fixing of the hands and feet with nails, caused dislocation of the bones. The hours of pain upon the cross brought great physical weakness. The strength of the Crucified was dried up. He likens it to a potsherd (2789), a broken piece of earthenware, lying on the floor of the oven, in the unremitting heat of the furnace, until every drop of moisture has been drained from it. If, and when, it might be touched, it would crumble to dust. So did He feel in His weakness, brought into the dust of death. It was such an One who cried, "I thirst" (Jn 19.28), His tongue cleaving to His jaws.

When the bulls of Bashan, the leaders of the nation, had finished with Him in that early morning hour, after the night of mockery and derision, they had handed Him over to the Gentiles. The dogs of Rome had then compassed Him in Pilate's judgment hall. There they had scourged Him, and spat on Him, stripping Him of His garments, and crowning Him with a wreath of thorns. Like a pack of dogs they had surrounded Him on the way to Golgotha. How lonely He must have been in that congregation of wicked men which enclosed Him as they pierced His hands and His feet. Bereft of His garments, His bones were exposed to their gaze. Heartlessly, callously, shamelessly, they stared upon Him, and wantonly gambled for His clothing at the foot of His cross. Four gambling soldiers divided His outer garments among them, then cast lots for the seamless inner robe which must not be spoiled by rending. The heart of man was truly revealed in the shades of Calvary.

Thus ends, in the Psalm, the story of the physical sufferings of the Messiah, with the renewed plea, "Be not thou far from me, O Lord: O my strength, haste thee to help me". He lifts His eyes away from His tormentors. He looks to heaven and to His God. "Help me! Save me! Deliver my soul!" He appeals for deliverance from the paw of the dog, from the mouth of the lion, and from the horns of the unicorns (7214). In such symbolic language He describes His enemies. The unicorn was probably the wild buffalo, the aurochs, to the antlers of which the victim was sometimes bound, to be left at the mercy of a stampeding herd. So had the herd, the multitude, been stampeded into clamouring for His death. "Crucify him! Crucify him!", they had cried in the early morning. Bulls and dogs had encompassed Him. The lion had raged upon Him. Even the common people had been against Him. But Jehovah will hear Him now, and deliver His only One from them all. "It is finished". "Thou hast heard me". The sob has ceased. "'Tis past, the dark and dreary night". The suffering must now be followed by the glory.

Verses 22-31: The Song

There is now a most marked transition from the sob to the song, from gloom to glory, from the storm to the calm. Messiah speaks of "my brethren". How early after His resurrection did He announce this holy relationship. "Go to my brethren, and say unto them, I ascend unto my Father, and your Father; and to my God, and your God" (Jn 20.17). Observe that the Saviour does not say directly, either here or elsewhere, "Our Father". His personal relationship with the Father is unique, but nevertheless a new relationship has now been established for those who are associated with Him. "He is not ashamed to call them brethren" (Heb 2.11). It has been dearly bought, this relationship, by the sufferings earlier described in the Psalm. Now, in the midst of His brethren, He will declare Jehovah's name and lead the praise of His saints. He who had been encompassed by the assembly of the wicked is now surrounded by a great congregation of those who love Him, and He is their precentor as they unite in praise of Jehovah. He is no longer alone. The great company of the redeemed gather around Him in His glory. He is pre-eminent, supreme, declaring the heart and character of Jehovah to them, and delighting in their song of praise. Once before He had joined in song with those who loved Him, but then it was a small remnant company in the quiet privacy of the Upper Room (Mt 26.30). Now the company is vast, if not innumerable, and He glorious in the midst.

Four times in five verses (22-26) the word "praise" is repeated. There is an almost universal summons for others to join in the praise. The God of Jacob is the God of grace. The God of Israel is the God of salvation and of glory. Let the seed of Jacob therefore, and the seed of Israel, praise Him. Doubtless there is always a remnant within, in true and loyal devotion to Jehovah; let these that fear the Lord praise Him. Some, however, will see this expression, "Ye that fear the Lord", as being rather an extended call to include all who feared Jehovah, whether Israelites or not. Many there must have been who, although Gentile, feared God and were known as "God-fearers", as Cornelius in Acts 10.1-2. Thus the term may not be descriptive just of an inner circle or remnant of the faithful in Israel, but may look beyond the favoured nation, and wider. There is good reason for this call to praise. Jehovah has not despised nor abhorred the affliction of the afflicted One. Jehovah may indeed, in His holiness, have hidden His face for a while from the holy Sin-Bearer, but the Saviour's cry has been heard and the face of Jehovah now shines on Him in resurrection. With strong crying and tears He had called unto Him who was able to save Him out of death, and He was heard for His piety (Heb 5.7). God has raised Him out from among the dead, and the great congregation must praise. Jehovah is not only the object of that praise but the very source of it also. "My praise shall be from thee". Or, as in the RV, "Of thee cometh my praise". It is, as Paul writes in Romans 11.36, "For of him, and through him, and to him, are all things: to whom be glory for ever". He is the source, the channel, and the object, of the praises of His people. He gives them not only the reason for praise but also the very ability to praise.

In vv. 25-26 there is, as others have observed, a reference to the peace offering of Leviticus 3. That offering was a thank-offering which accompanied vows. This may of course be the personal exercise of the Psalmist himself, and yet it is Messianic. The peace offering was shared by many. Jehovah had His portion on the altar. The priests had their portion. The offerer enjoyed his portion also, and it was eaten with his family and friends in the enjoyment and fellowship of the thanksgiving which had been rendered or the vow which had been made. The flesh of the sacrifice of a peace offering which accompanied a vow was eaten on the same day on which it was offered, or on the morrow. (Lev 7.16). There was an immediate fellowshipping in the joy of the occasion. So it is with Christ. He will hasten to share with His people the fruits of Calvary. Today and tomorrow they shall feast upon the provision made by His offering of Himself. The meek shall eat and be satisfied. In such sacred matters there is no room for pride. It is the meek (6035), the humble, who enjoy with the Saviour that which has been accomplished in His sacrifice, and those who seek Him shall share with Him. As F.W. Grant so beautifully comments, "Messiah's vows furnish forth, indeed, a royal banquet upon which, in communion, the humble feed to fullest satisfaction. 'Your heart shall live for aye' becomes thus an assurance full of blessing". If however, the RV, RSV or JPS renderings are accepted, then this phrase may be a benediction or a blessing, "May your heart live forever". It is a desire for an undying affection and devotion, and an endless energy in praise.

The Psalmist now looks beyond. He anticipates a future age when not only Israel but all the kindreds of the nations will unite in the worship of Jehovah. The remotest parts of the earth will recall the triumph of the Messiah; they will remember His person and His work and bow to His claims, praising accordingly. It envisages that day promised to Messiah in the second Psalm, "Ask of me, and I shall give thee the heathen for thine inheritance, and the uttermost parts of the earth for thy possession". It is the word of Revelation 11.15, "The kingdoms of this world are become the kingdoms of our Lord, and of his Christ". This is millennial glory, and, glorious though it is, it is but the ante-chamber to that eternal state when God shall be all in all and be the theme and the object of universal adoration and homage. There will be a recognition by all of Jehovah's sovereignty in the universe. He will be the governor, the ruler, supreme and unchallenged.

The closing verses of the Psalm are difficult, and have been variously interpreted. "They that be fat upon earth", and, "They that go down to the dust", are obviously to be contrasted in some way. There may be a contrast between rich and poor, between those who are nourished and prosperous and those who are in the dust in material poverty. There may also be a contrast between the proud and the humble, the self-sufficient and the dependent. Kirkpatrick has the following note, "Others suppose that the contrast intended is not between rich and poor, but between the living and the dead. 'Earth's fat ones' are those in the full vigour of life: *all they that have gone down into the dust* are the dead. Quick and dead bow in homage before the universal sovereign. (Compare Phil 2.10)". But whatever the difficulty and whatever interpretation be accepted, the problems must not rob the reader of the basic premise. There is no doubt that a contrast of some sort is intended to indicate that all men will one day acknowledge the rule of Jehovah and His Anointed. The living and the dying, the mighty and the meek, the rich and the poor, the great and the small, shall all bow before Him and worship. All are mortal. All are going down to the dust. What are any apart from Him? No man can keep alive his own soul.

In the prophecy of Daniel it was predicted that Messiah would be cut off and would have nothing (Dan 9.26, JND). In Isaiah's prophecy it was similarly predicted that He would be cut off out of the land of the living (Is 53.8). Who then can point to the generation of a Messiah so cut off? But Isaiah continues, "He shall see his seed". So does this Psalm confirm, "A seed shall serve him". There will be a generation for His glory. Indeed there is a generation even now which will declare His righteousness unto a generation yet to be born. From generation to generation, through an age of grace into a day of millennial glory, and into the Day of God, the praises will reverberate, never dying, never ceasing, and all because "He hath done this". It is finished! The work is done, and done perfectly. All is accomplished by Him who cried at the beginning of the Psalm, "My God, my God, why hast thou forsaken me?". Who can know the depths of His suffering? Who can tell the height of His glory? The purpose of God is fulfilled in Him, the Messiah, the Anointed, and the Man of Sorrows is now the Man in the Glory.

To quote Kirkpatrick again, "The song of praise, begun by the Psalmist, is taken up by Israel; all the nations of the earth swell the chorus; and the strain echoes on through all the ages. So gloriously ends the Psalm which began in the darkest sorrow. It is the history of the individual, of Israel, of the Church, of the world".

PSALM 23

Introduction

It has been said of Psalm 23 that "the world could spare many a large book better than this sunny little Psalm. It has dried many tears and supplied the mould into which many hearts have poured their peaceful faith. In a pastoral community such as Israel was, a faithful shepherd was the personification of tender care and unwearying watchfulness, and men gratefully applied the term to God as the Provider and Protector of His flock" (A. Cohen).

It is often pointed out that, in the preceding Psalm 22, the Messiah is seen as the good shepherd, giving His life for the sheep. Here, in Psalm 23, He is the great shepherd of the sheep, brought again from the dead by the God of peace (Heb 13.20). This little shepherd song has been translated and paraphrased and arranged for singing in a myriad of languages. It is a Psalm so full of comfort and assurance, and provision and promise, that for some three thousand years saints of every age have been singing it on every occasion. In days of prosperity believers read this Psalm, but in days of adversity they sing it too. Whether mourning or rejoicing, whether sick or sad, in delight or in depression, in joy or in sorrow, in triumph or in tragedy, it seems that there is always something in the Psalm for every vicissitude of life. Whether in green pastures of tender grass, or beside the waters of quietness, or in the dark valley of the shadow of death, the believer is assured of shepherd care. This is the pearl of Psalms, with a lustre all its own. It has been likened to the nightingale among birds, small, plain, and homely, but soaring high and singing sweetly (Spurgeon).

It is a Psalm of David. There is no title, nor any link with any one particular event in David's life, but it is easy to picture the shepherd boy in the fields of Bethlehem in the midst of the flock, watching, caring, tending the sheep and lambs. In his own care for his sheep David sees reflected the care of Jehovah for His flock, and in this way the Psalm is written out of personal experience.

Like the first Psalm, Psalm 23 has but six verses, and these are readily and naturally divided into two equal sections with three verses in each. Verses 1-3 sing of the tender and gentle care of the Divine Shepherd for His sheep. Verses 4-6 look forward with assurance and see that care and comfort continuing through the valley of the shadow of death into the everlasting joy of the house of the Lord. Some have imagined a change of metaphor after v.4, from sheep and pasture to guests at a banquet, where the shepherd now becomes a host, but it is not necessary to see such a change, as will be shown in the commentary.

Verses 1-3: Provision and Protection

The Psalm opens with an exclamation rather than with a statement. "Jehovah - my shepherd!" Note that "is" has been supplied in italics in our English translation. The remaining verses of the Psalm are then but an exposition or amplification of this exclamation. Jehovah is often spoken of as a shepherd, perhaps the earliest such references being those of Jacob in Genesis 48.15 and 49.24. Jacob speaks of "the God which fed me all my life long". Literally, and beautifully, it is "the God who shepherded me". In Psalm 80.1 Jehovah is called "The Shepherd of Israel", and in Psalm 74.1 His people are called the sheep of His pasture, which figure is often used in the Psalms. Israel is His flock and He is their shepherd, leading and guiding them in their varied national experiences. Not only David and Asaph and the Psalmists, but the prophets too use the same lovely imagery. Isaiah says, "He shall feed his flock like a shepherd: he shall gather the lambs with his arm, and carry them in his bosom, and shall gently lead those that are with young"(Is 40.11), with which can be compared Micah 7.14. Then, in John 10, the Saviour speaks of Himself as "the shepherd of the sheep" and "the good shepherd" (vv. 2, 11, 14). But for many saints the great word in Psalm 23.1 is that little pronoun "my". This makes Jehovah's shepherd ministry so very personal. To be able to say "my Shepherd", and to hear Him respond and say "My sheep"(Jn 10.27), is very precious. "I am His", said another, "and He is mine" (Song 6.3). There is a link so tender and yet so strong.

The "I shall not want" of v.1 has suggested to many readers the great title Jehovah Jireh, first used by Abraham in Genesis 22.14. This may mean "The Lord will see", or, "The Lord will provide", but, on comparing vv. 8 and 14 of Genesis 22, perhaps there is, in the title, a combination of both of these thoughts. Jehovah Jireh both sees and provides. So it was with Abraham on that day, and so it was with the nation of Israel in their journeyings. Compare those lovely testimonies with Jehovah's care for them in Deuteronomy 2.7; 8.7-10. The personal pronoun "I" makes this gracious provision so very individual. He who sees and knows the varied needs of His people will always suitably provide just what will meet their need at any time, whether collectively or personally.

The Psalmist now recognises two particular aspects of the need of saints in every age - food and rest, pasture and quietness. Jehovah sees His flock, ofttimes weary, thirsty, hungry, and He leads the sheep to tender grass and quiet waters. When the heat of the sun is oppressive He makes His flock to rest at noon in the cool meadows (Song 1.7). "Still waters" must not, of course, be thought of as placid or stagnant waters. These are waters of restfulness where the sheep may be refreshed in quietness. Observe, too, that the Eastern shepherd "leads" his flock. There is no harsh driving of the sheep, as is common in other cultures. "He leadeth me", says David. When it is remembered that this was a land greatly parched, with but two rainy seasons in the year, a thirsty land where green pastures were not found in abundance, this is pleasant indeed. So does the believer find himself in the wilderness of a world where there is nothing for his soul unless Jehovah leads.

The theme of "leading" recurs in v.3, but the two words, which are each translated "leadeth" in the AV, are different. In the first, in v.2, "leadeth" (5095) has the thought of guiding towards a particular goal. This goal, of course, is the peaceful scene depicted by the pastures of tender grass and the waters of quietness. In v.3, "leadeth" (5148) may rather convey the thought of guidance along the way, leading in the straight paths of righteous living. Jehovah would have His people walk in righteousness. He guides along that way, and, if one should stray, He graciously restores the wanderer. "He restoreth (7725) my soul", the Psalmist sings. He restores, revives, refreshes, recovers, the erring one, and this for His name's sake. The honour of His name is paramount and must be upheld in the godly lives of His people walking in straight paths, and so does He lead and guide and restore them along the way. It is for His glory.

Verses 4-6: Divine Care and Companionship

In the lives of the saints there may indeed be quiet waters and green pastures, but there is also the valley of the shadow. The Bedouin shepherd of the East is familiar with the fierce gorges, the ravines and wadis so deep that the sun never shines into their dark depths. David as a shepherd boy would have been thoroughly acquainted with such valleys as he led the sheep from pasture to pasture. But what, to the believer today, is the valley of the shadow of death? Is it the actual experience of dying? Many think so, and it has been a comfort to many a saint in the final weakness, to know the presence of the Lord in those last hours. It is a consolation also to know that it is not just "in" the valley, but "through" the valley, that the good Shepherd is with His sheep, and that the valley eventually opens into the light of a better life. It may be however, that the valley of the shadow of death is not just dying. All saints have their dark days and gloomy valley experiences. The very world through which we walk daily is a veritable valley constantly shaded by death and dying. Maybe it is in living, not dying, that we walk through the valley of the shadow of death. But as Plumer writes, "Why may we not unite these views? Paul says he was *in deaths oft*, because he suffered things which commonly lead to death. The darkness in our way through life is often a fit emblem of the gloom of a dying hour. It is probable that by *shadow of death* we are to understand all that is dark in life and in death". Whichever be the thought, there is comfort in this assurance, "Thou art with me", says the Psalmist. "Lo, I am with you alway", is the promise of the good Shepherd to His flock. (Mt 28.20).

David takes comfort from the rod and the staff of his Shepherd. He was familiar with these. The rod was for the defence of the sheep from marauding predators. The staff was for guidance and for support. Thy rod (7626) and Thy staff (4938). The words are different, but this may simply be a dual way of describing the single shepherd's crook, which as a rod defended the sheep from attackers, but could also support the animal by being passed under its body to stay it in slippery places in the slopes of the valley. Some commentators feel, though, that these were separate items, the customary shepherd staff and the shorter rod or club for defence. The chief comfort, however, is that He is there with rod and staff to care for His flock, and, that being so, the believer may safely say, "I will fear no evil" (7451). No mischief or wickedness can hurt the sheep while the Shepherd is there. The valley may be deep and dark and dangerous, and the journey through may be difficult, but the comfort of His presence, who is the Shepherd of His sheep, will stay His flock in every trying hour until the valley is passed and the better brighter land has been attained.

As mentioned in the introduction, many expositors feel that here in v.5, with the prepared table, the anointing oil, and the cup running over, the imagery changes. To quote Plumer again, "With the fourth verse the figure of a shepherd is dropped. Then that of a kind and rich host, exercising a large hospitality, is introduced. The imagery is drawn from the customs of oriental nations". If this view is accepted then the figure of shepherd and sheep and pasture land is exchanged for that of host and guests and banqueting house. But such an abrupt change in the imagery of this little shepherd song may be unnatural and unnecessary, as A.G. Clarke and Phillip Keller point out. Keller, a shepherd himself, writes, "In thinking about this statement it is well to bear in mind that the sheep are approaching the high mountain country of the summer ranges. These are known as alplands or tablelands so much sought after by sheepmen. In some of the finest sheep country of the world...the high plateaux of the sheep ranges are always referred to as *mesas* - the Spanish word for *tables*". Clarke, commenting on v.5, is worth quoting in full; "To find a good and safe feeding-place for the sheep often calls for the highest skill and heroism on the part of the shepherd. He must study the nature of the grass, note the presence or absence of poisonous plants and reptiles, search out the lairs of predatory animals, stopping up their dens with stones, and if necessary, attacking and destroying the animals themselves. At the close of the day the shepherd stands at the door of the fold 'rodding the sheep', i.e. controlling them with his rod, and not only counting them as they pass in, but closely examining the condition of each sheep. Using olive oil and cedar tar, he anoints wounds, scratches, and bruises, and refreshes the worn and weary by making them drink out of a large two-handled cup, brimming with water from cisterns provided for the purpose". It is easy to see here God's abundant provision for His people. The gracious ministry of His Spirit, so often symbolised by the anointing oil, the refreshment of His Word, symbolised by the water, and all this in overflowing measure, and in the very presence of enemies in an adverse and hostile world.

There is great assurance and confidence as David exclaims, "Surely!". This is like the NT "Verily". The believer may rest safely on Jehovah's promise and provision and protection. Some versions, as well as the Newberry Bible margin, prefer "only" goodness and mercy, instead of "surely" goodness and mercy. But both are true. There is a certainty about this, that only loving-kindness, grace, mercy, favour, and divine tenderness, only goodness and mercy will follow the saint all through life. David knew that enemies had followed him, and were probably still following him, but, with the divine presence, he would safely reach Jehovah's dwelling place and abide there continually and for ever.

So does this little Psalm trace the pathway of the sheep and the care of the good Shepherd. Green pastures, still waters, straight paths, the dark valley, rod and staff, the prepared table, the anointed head, the overflowing cup, goodness and mercy, and the house of the Lord for ever. How sweet to be able to say, "The Lord is my shepherd"!

PSALM 24

Introduction

There is general, if not total, agreement that the historical background to Psalm 24 is in 2 Samuel 6 and 1 Chronicles 15, and that it was composed for the joyous occasion of the return of the Ark of the Covenant from its long exile. For many years the Ark had been out of its rightful place. It had been taken by the Philistines in the days of Eli in 1 Samuel 4. For seven months the Philistines had held it captive, moving it from city to city, but it plagued them in every place, and eventually they sent it on a cart drawn by cattle to Bethshemesh. The men of Bethshemesh handled it irreverently, and consequent upon Jehovah's severe judgment on them they pleaded with the men of Kirjath-Jearim to take it from them. For twenty years the Ark was sheltered in the house of one Abinadab in Kirjath-Jearim until, at last, David had an exercise to bring it back, to a home prepared for it behind curtains on Mount Zion. Sadly, David also transported the Ark on a cart, as the Philistines had done. This was not God's way. It had to be carried by priests and Levites, as David should have known. When the oxen stumbled, a man named Uzzah put out his hand to steady the Ark and God smote him. David was displeased, and would not proceed with the bringing of the Ark to Zion, but carried it aside into the house of Obed-edom. For three months the Ark continued there, and the Lord blessed Obed-edom and his household. It was the news of this blessing on Obed-edom which then encouraged David to go again for the Ark. This time it was borne on the shoulders of sanctified Levites in the appointed way, and with much gladness. Accompanied by sacrificing and singing and dancing and the sound of trumpets, the procession made its triumphal way to Mount Zion where the Ark was placed in the tent which David had prepared for it. The holy Ark, with its cherubim of glory, had found a resting place. It was indeed an historic and memorable day and the sentiments of this Psalm seem so eminently suited to the joy of the occasion.

The Psalm is undoubtedly David's. The LXX adds to the superscription the words, "On the first day after the Sabbath", which is, of course, the first day of the week. From the Jewish *Kiddush* and

Tamid and other Rabbinical writings, and confirmed by Alfred Edersheim in his *The Temple, Its Ministry and Services*, it is known that this was the Psalm appointed to be recited or chanted on the first day of the week at the morning sacrifice in the temple liturgy. In keeping with the opening verses of the Psalm, this celebrated the beginning of the creation of the world as in Genesis 1.1-2, but, according to tradition, it is also believed that the ascent of the Ark to Mount Zion, as just described, took place on the day after the Sabbath. For the New Testament believer this has great significance.

Very many commentators believe that Psalm 24 anticipates the resurrection and the ascension of the risen Messiah into exaltation in glory. Spurgeon speaks eloquently for such when he writes, "The eye of the Psalmist looked, however, beyond the typical up going of the Ark, to the sublime ascension of the King of glory. We will call it The Song of the Ascension". The Psalm may indeed portray, symbolically, an interesting picture of the ascension of Christ, but this is not the prophetic or true interpretation. The Psalm is earthly. It is millennial. It has to do with the return of the long rejected King to be accorded His rightful place in the millennial metropolis. Everything in the Psalm agrees with this, as will be seen in the commentary.

The Psalm is written in what is known as an antiphonal style. This means that there are two parties or choruses involved in the singing, each responding to the other in an orderly way almost like an echo. This will be easily observed in the opening verses. One chorus will sing, "The earth is the Lord's, and the fulness thereof". The antiphonal response is an echo of this same truth in the words, "The world, and they that dwell therein". This continues with, "For he hath founded it upon the seas", to which the response is, in similar vein, "And established it upon the floods". So the same style of poetry is maintained throughout the whole Psalm, as will be seen.

The ten verses of the Psalm are divided into two parts by the "Selah" at the end of verse 6, but another division may also be noted at the end of verse 2.

Verses 1-2: The Procession Begins

What a triumphal and joyful day it must have been! The sacred Ark was returning after so many years. King David himself led the procession. There followed the choirs of singers, the minstrels with their psalteries, harps, and cymbals, cornets and trumpets (1 Chr 15.28). The priests and Levites carried the Ark on their shoulders according to the word of the Lord (1 Chr 15.14-15), and the jubilant throngs, the thousands of Israel, would join in the shouts of praise. The Psalm commences with an ascription of praise to Jehovah as the Creator. He might indeed be, in a special way, the Lord God of Israel (1 Chr 15.14), but He had universal and creatorial rights which were greater than either the nation, or the land, of Israel.

The earth (776) and the world (8398) are His. The earth which He created is His, with all its fulness. Its fields, its fruits, and its harvests, its mines and its hidden treasures all belong to Him. He is, in the words of Melchizedek, "the most high God, possessor of heaven and earth" (Gen 14.19). He is Lord of the universe. The world is His too, those habitable regions where men and creatures dwell. Men may argue over title deeds and lands and property, but Jehovah is the sovereign Lord and the sole proprietor of all. Men may be in revolt and rebellion against Him but the claims of the Creator remain, the world and they that dwell therein are His by sovereign right.

There follows the basis for this right of ownership. "For he hath founded it upon the seas", sings one choir. "And established it upon the floods", echoes the other. In mighty power the Creator has ordered the oceans and seas (Gen 1.6-9). He has divided and gathered the waters and used them as a foundation for His earth. He has established, prepared, and settled His created earth upon the floods. "Where wast thou", He asks of Job, "when I laid the foundations of the earth?...who shut up the sea with doors...And said, Hitherto shalt thou come, but no further: and here shall thy proud waves be stayed?" (Job 38.4, 8, 11). These opening verses would be chanted repeatedly as the procession moved along and until it arrived at the foot of Mount Zion. This concludes the first movement of the Psalm.

Verses 3-6: Who Shall Ascend? Who Shall Stand?

There is, in the Psalm, a holy hill, and soon, on that holy hill there would be a holy house, the abode of Jehovah. Not everyone has the moral fitness to ascend that hill or stand in that holy place, and so the questions. The great company now pauses at the slopes of Zion and the questions are chanted, "Who shall ascend into the hill of the Lord? or who shall stand in his holy place?" "Lord" (3068), is Jehovah. For the second time in the Psalm the awful name is employed. The earth is the Lord's, and therefore Mount Zion is His. It is the mountain of Jehovah. Who is able to stand there, in the mountain of His holiness? (Ps 48.1). The answer is direct and plain. Holiness is the glory of the house of God and must therefore be the character of those who would enter. Clean hands and a pure heart signify outward and inward purity. This is reminiscent of the requirements in the Levitical offerings, fulfilled in Him who was the true Lamb of God, "Without blemish and without spot" (1 Pet 1.19). These are the positive moral virtues; the negatives are these, that there must be no vanity nor pride, and no falsehood in deceitful swearing. Notice again the inward and outward aspect of character.

Such is the character of those whom Jehovah blesses, but perhaps the blessing envisaged here is that special blessing of admittance to His presence. For such a man, too, the God of his salvation would grant righteousness and vindication, divine approval and acceptance of the life that has pleased Him. It must never be forgotten that all of this is fulfilled in perfection in that One of whom Jehovah could say, "In whom I am well pleased".

There is indeed a generation, a race of men in every age, who seek after Jehovah and His glory. The accompanying phrase, "That seek thy face, O Jacob", has occasioned problems of interpretation. Some think that it ought to read, "That seek thy face, O God of Jacob". This is the sense of the rendering of the LXX and several other versions. Plumer writes, "This gives a good sense", but he adds, "The great objection to reading *God of Jacob* is that the Hebrew text of collated MSS. does not sufficiently authorise it". Perhaps the understanding may be this, that those who seek after God will seek the face of His people. Recall what God in grace did for Jacob, blessing him and making him Israel, a prince with God. Will a man seek after God? Let him seek out God's people, and learn from them what kind of God He is. How particularly applicable this would have been to Gentile seekers. Go to Jacob, to Israel, and learn there just who and what the God of Jacob is.

The now familiar "Selah" brings this section to a close. Was there now a cessation of the singing and a musical interlude rising to a crescendo as the procession approached the gates of Zion?

Verses 7-10: The King of Glory

The final movement in the Psalm is composed of a challenge, a question, and an answer, each of which is repeated with but a slight change in the wording. Five times in four verses in this section the title "King of glory" occurs, and this is the only place in Holy Scripture where the title is to be found. This uniqueness, therefore, gives a special importance to these verses and indeed to the whole Psalm. Since the Psalm is Messianic in character, the King of glory is the Messiah, the Christ. In the immediate context, the entry of the Ark into its tabernacle is really the entry of Jehovah Himself into His sanctuary. This is in accord with 2 Samuel 6.2 - "the ark of God, whose name is called by the name of the Lord of hosts that dwelleth between the cherubims". The presence of the Ark was to Israel the symbol presence of Jehovah, hence the tragedy of those years when the Ark was in captivity and exile, and the unbounded joy of the nation when now the Ark was returning to the sanctuary and into their midst. (See Num 10.35).

The first challenge is now issued to the ancient gates of Zion. "Lift up your heads, O ye gates". The gates of walled cities were often in three parts. Two large and main gates swung horizontally. These were opened at sunrise and closed at sunset. For the ordinary routine of the daily business of the city it was sufficient to open these two main gates. Above these gates, however, and stretching across them, there was often a third portion, perhaps rectangular, perhaps semi-circular. This was the head of the gate. Now, if it was enough to open the main gates for the daily life of the city, it was not so when a visiting dignitary was coming. To assure the noble visitor of an unstinted welcome, the head of the gates must be lifted up too, whether drawn up into the wall cavity or swung upward on its hinges. Zion must give such a royal welcome to the sacred Ark, and Jerusalem, prophetically, must likewise welcome the returning Messiah.

The gates are called "everlasting doors". The gates of Zion were ancient indeed. Jerusalem was not only the city of the Jebusites before David conquered it (1 Chr 11.4-7). It was the Salem of Melchizedek of Genesis 14.18, contemporary with Abram. Did the nation look forward also, anticipating in hope that the gates of their Zion would abide forever? So the grand procession now waited. The gates must open. The King of glory must enter.

Somewhere within the walls of the city a porter or doorkeeper, perhaps a Levite, has been positioned for the occasion. It is he who now demands, "Who is this King of glory?". The answer is chanted back by the choirs. "The Lord strong and mighty", sings one chorus. "The Lord mighty in battle", echoes the other. Prophetically this may anticipate the Messiah's conquest over His enemies as predicted in such Scriptures as Isaiah 63 in the OT and Revelation 19 in the NT. Mighty and triumphant at Megiddo, coming victorious from Edom and from Bozrah, the Messiah has a conqueror's rights to the throne.

The challenge is now repeated. Is there a holy impatience? "Lift up your heads, O ye gates; even lift them up, ye everlasting doors; and the King of glory shall come in". But yet again comes the question, "Who is this King of glory?". The answer is sent back in a united voice from the singers, "The Lord of hosts (6635), he is the King of glory". It is a divine title. It was an ancient title (1 Sam 1.3). Jehovah Sabaoth! The gates must open to Him. Jerusalem must welcome Messiah. The armies of heaven are His (Rev 19.14), the hosts of the Lord. The reader must indeed look beyond the immediate context of the bringing back of the Ark, wondrous as that was. He must see, predicted here, that glorious return of the rejected King Messiah, to take His rightful place in the Zion of a future day. Jerusalem once cast Him out. Outside its gates and in the shadow of its walls they crucified Him, but He must return to be vindicated. He who was called "The King of the Jews" both at the beginning and at the end of His life (Mt 2.2; 27.11, 37), and who was called "The King of Israel" at the commencement of His ministry (Jn 1.49), is "King of glory" and "King of kings" (Rev 19.16).

The Psalm reaches a crescendo of glory. It is crowned with another "Selah". It is time to pause, to reflect, and to lift up the voice in loud praise. Messiah's rights have been established. He has creatorial glory, moral glory, official glory, and personal glory. All this demands that He be given the place of supremacy, not only in Israel and Zion, but also in His world and in His universe. One day it will be so, and in the language of another Psalm, "Jehovah shall send the rod of thy strength out of Zion: rule thou in the midst of thine enemies" (Ps 110.2).

Spurgeon quotes one Patrick Delany of the 17th-18th century, who, writing of this Psalm, says, "How others may think upon this point, I cannot say, nor pretend to describe, but for my own part, I have no notion of hearing, or of any man's ever having seen or heard, anything so great, so solemn, so celestial, on this side the gates of heaven". Many will say, "Amen"!

PSALM 25

Introduction

This Psalm is one of several Psalms which are composed in acrostic or alphabetical style, most probably intended to assist the Hebrew reader in the committing of the text to memory. The best known of the alphabetical Psalms is Psalm 119 where, in twenty-two stanzas, each line of each stanza begins with the same letter, covering the twenty-two letters of the Hebrew alphabet in sequence. Other alphabetical Psalms are Psalms 34, 37, 111, 112 and 145. Psalm 25 has twenty-two verses or stanzas, also corresponding to the twenty-two letters of the Hebrew alphabet, but the acrostic here is somewhat irregularly constructed in that there is both repetition and omission of certain letters. The most scholarly expositors have sought, without total agreement, to explain this irregularity, but, since the alphabetical style is lost in translation in any case, perhaps the important thing is to find the mind of the Spirit in the Psalm. The very irregularity may, indeed, be reflective of the national condition, and of the state of the Psalmist's own heart, when the Psalm was composed. For those who wish to study this irregularity in more detail however, the learned Dr. Maclaren is most helpful and lucid. He writes, referring to the relevant Hebrew letters in italics, "It is acrostic, but with irregularities. As the text now stands, the second, not the first, word in v.2 begins with *Beth*; *Vav* is omitted or represented in the 'and teach me' of the *He* verse (v.5); *Qoph* is also omitted, and its place is taken by a supernumerary *Resh*, which letter has thus two verses (18, 19); and v.22 begins with *Pe*, and is outside the scheme of the Psalm, both as regards alphabetic structure and subject. The same peculiarities of deficient *Vav* and superfluous *Pe* verses reappear in another acrostic Psalm (34), in which the initial word of the last verse is, as here, 'redeem'. Possibly the two Psalms are connected". He later comments, "The irregularity in v.2, where the second, not the first, word of the verse begins with *Beth*, may be attenuated by treating the Divine name as outside the acrostic order"

There is no good reason to doubt the Davidic authorship of the Psalm, but, as with many other of David's Psalms, it is not possible to relate it positively to any particular circumstance or period in his life. Since he refers to the sins of his youth however, and to his many enemies, it may be assumed that it was composed in his later years. Some think that it may belong to the sad days of Absalom's rebellion.

The Psalm is meditative, contemplative, and penitential. It is a prayer for protection, for guidance, and for forgiveness. Perhaps the acrostic style precludes any distinct or definite order of thought in the Psalm, and a formal division is therefore difficult. It will be noted, though, that the first seven verses are written in the first person, as is the third set of seven verses, 15-21. The central seven verses, 8-14, are a contemplation of the goodness of the Lord to those who fear Him, and the final and lovely verse 22 seems to stand by itself as a heart-cry for the nation, "Redeem Israel, O God, out of all his troubles". To quote Maclaren again, he notices "the division of the verses (excluding v.22) into three sevens, the first of which is prayer, the second meditation on the Divine character and the blessings secured by covenant to them who fear Him, and the third is bent round, wreath-like, to meet the first, and is again prayer".

Verses 1-7: Personal Petitions

The very personal nature of the early petitions in the Psalm is evidenced by the frequent use of the personal pronoun. Sixteen times in seven verses the Psalmist uses the pronouns "I", "Me", "My", and "Mine". He speaks in these verses of, "My soul", "My salvation", "My youth", and "My transgressions". A paraphrased summary of his requests will indicate that he asks, "Keep me; Guard me; Guide me; Teach me; Lead me; Remember me; Forgive me". He says, "I lift up my soul to Thee"; "I trust in Thee"; "I wait on Thee". David had indeed an individual, personal, intimate relationship with Jehovah.

"Unto thee, O Lord..." (3068). Ten times in the Psalm David uses the great name Jehovah, and so personal is Jehovah to him that he can call Him "My God" (430). Jehovah, in all His eternal greatness, Elohim, in all His might and power, is the One to whom David lifts up his heart and soul in prayer and praise. "Unto thee!" The pronoun "thee" is emphatic. How different was the Psalmist to the surrounding nations. Let them lift up their eyes and their hearts to the gods of their high places in the hills, if they will, but David will lift up his soul to Jehovah. He pleads that his trust in God might be vindicated. If it were not so he would be personally ashamed (954), disappointed and confused, and his enemies would exult. His plea is that it might not be so. His trust (982), his confidence, was in a great God, and such trust must be justified in the eyes of many who hated him.

But David was not narrow and selfish in his petitions. There were others, too, who waited upon his God as he did, hoping and trusting, looking expectantly to Him in the daily cares of life. For these, also, David prays, that they might not be ashamed or disappointed in their trust. Rather does he desire that those men should be abashed who transgressed (898) without cause. The word "transgress" indicates betrayal, deceit and treacherous dealings. Let such be ashamed, he asks, using the word "ashamed" for the third time in two verses. Let them be confused, who without justification, so treat their fellows. It is to be admired in the Psalmist, that, though he pleads for himself and presents his own personal needs, yet his heart is enlarged to embrace kindred souls who trusted in the same God as he. It is good when the individual requests of a saint widen out to include the large family circle of believers.

David now returns to his own needs. "Show me thy ways…teach me thy paths". The world has always been a moral wilderness for the believer. The Psalmist would know those ways, those paths, which would be for the pleasure and the glory of Jehovah. "The paths of righteousness", he had called them in Psalm 23. "Show me" (3045), he says. "Teach me" (3925). "Make Thy ways clear to me, that I may know them and understand them, that I may be able to discriminate and distinguish, and be diligent to walk in the ways of Thy pleasing". How well David knew that there were pitfalls and snares which endanger all those who would live godly. There are quicksands of sin on every hand. He prays for guidance into those paths which were Jehovah's intended way for him. These would be a safe way through life's difficulties. Still, today, the believer prays, "Show me; teach me", and, by the ministry of the Word and the guidance of the Spirit, God graciously directs the way of those who trust Him.

It is good to be ever led in God's truth, but there is a difficulty in defining the exact meaning of "truth" in the present context of v.5. It may mean that divine attribute, the faithfulness of God, or it may mean the revelation of the will of God and His way for the believer. F.W. Grant translates, "Direct me in Thy faithfulness, and teach me", and he comments, "Faithful He must be to this purpose of His heart; and the glad soul may without weariness 'wait upon Him all the day long'". Others however, prefer to understand the "truth" here to be the revealing of the mind of God in relation to the believer's daily walk. Perhaps it may not be necessary to choose out of the apparent ambiguity, since both thoughts are precious, and both are true. The believer asks to be led in God's truth, and taught, and God in His faithfulness hears and answers such a request.

David now adds the grounds upon which he makes his request; "For thou art the God of my salvation". To whom else could he look for the guidance that he needed? He waited unceasingly, all the day, upon Jehovah. He had no other resource. Jehovah was his only hope. When David says, "On thee do I wait", does he mean that this was his state of heart at that particular time? Or that it was his habitual attitude and exercise, ever to be waiting upon God? Whichever is intended, it is good always to wait on the Lord, for they that wait upon the Lord shall renew their strength (Is 40.31). "Wait" (6960) is the same word here; looking to Him, waiting for Him, expectantly, eagerly, and trustingly. As he says in another Psalm, "Wait on the Lord: be of good courage, and he shall strengthen thine heart: wait, I say, on the Lord" (27.14).

Three times now, in two verses, David uses the word "Remember". It is in the power of Deity alone to choose not to remember. Men may forget, but men cannot choose not to remember. He who says, "Their sins and their iniquities will I remember no more" (Heb 8.12; Jer 31.34), alone has the power not to remember. It is a divine prerogative. David appeals to this, asking Jehovah not to remember the sins of his youth nor his transgressions. He acknowledges both youthful indiscretions and deliberate acts of wilful sin, and he pleads that Jehovah, in love, may not remember these. But both before and after this appeal David also asks, "Remember; Remember". He pleads the tender mercies and the lovingkindnesses of God. Compassions and mercies have ever been characteristic of God. They have been, as the Psalmist says, "ever of old". They are both ancient and everlasting. They are eternal and abiding. Since the fall of man and the entry of sin into the world, Jehovah has always been compassionate and merciful. Though men might rebel and transgress deliberately, yet there has been a divine compassion toward the sinning man. David appeals to this, that Jehovah might now forgive, in keeping with His compassionate character. He makes the appeal very personal, pleading, "remember…me". It brings to mind the plea of another, a thief and a robber, who, to the same God, only now incarnate and hanging beside him in crucifixion, cried, "Lord, remember me" (Lk 23.42). He, too, found the reality of divine compassion in the response of the Saviour. Notice that David is wholly cast upon God. "Thy mercy", he says, "thy goodness". He has no personal merit to plead, but he knows the character and the heart of the God of his salvation, and he knows that for His goodness sake Jehovah will hear and forgive. Men say, "Forgive and forget". Jehovah will forgive and choose not to remember.

Verses 8-14: From Petition to Praise

Only briefly, in the central v.11 of this section, is David occupied with himself, asking for personal forgiveness. It is a principle that thoughts of God in His greatness will inevitably eclipse thoughts of self. Having introduced the subject of the character of God and the divine attributes, he now continues to extol and magnify these attributes of goodness and righteousness, mercy and truth. In the meditation of these seven verses, the Psalmist makes much of the great name Jehovah, mentioning it five times. Jehovah is good and upright, and therefore, because He is so, He accordingly instructs them in His way. Dr Cohen writes, "The Rabbis deem this one of the great sayings of Scripture. Because God is good, He is just, and because God is just, He is good". This holy blending of goodness and righteousness persists throughout every age and in all of God's dealings with men. Observe the same in Paul's grand thesis on the gospel in the Epistle to the Romans. "Therein is the righteousness of God revealed", he writes, and then, "The goodness of God leadeth thee to repentance" (Rom

1.17; 2.4). As sinners, men have fallen short of that righteousness, but His goodness will provide a way of recovery for them and instruct them in that way.

This blessed instruction, however, is not for the proud or arrogant. The meek (6035) are the recipients of this divine guidance into holy and heavenly ways. He who said, "I am meek and lowly in heart" (Mt 11.29), is the same One who said, so early in His ministry, "Blessed are the poor in spirit" (Mt 5.3). What He was Himself, He taught to others. Meekness is humility. Jehovah rewards the humble learner with further revelation of His purpose and His truth. "Teach me thy paths", David has asked in v.4. "All the paths of the Lord are mercy and truth", he now says. These have been called "carriage tracks". They are the well-worn paths of righteousness which have been trodden by the saints of every age. Truth will guide the believer along the way. Mercy will gently bear with him when he fails. To those who are loyal and true, and who keep His Word, Jehovah will always show Himself true to them, and merciful.

For a brief moment, in v.11, David pauses in his meditation to remember his sin and to ask for pardon. Notice how again he disclaims any merit of his own. "For thy goodness' sake, O Lord", he had pleaded in v.7. "For thy name's sake, O Lord", he now prays in v.11. He appeals to the revealed character of God. His iniquity is great and demands the intervention of a great God. If pardon will be granted according to the greatness of the divine name, then that pardon will be sufficient. "He will abundantly pardon", is the promise of Isaiah 55.7.

Having, in a fleeting parenthesis, remembered his sin, David now returns to his meditation. He calls the attention of those who fear the Lord. This fear (3373) is not a slavish fear, but a due reverence for, and respect for, Jehovah. It is rather beautiful to note that what is stated by the Psalmist with regard to this in Psalm 111.10 is stated again, exactly, word for word, by the wise Solomon in Proverbs 9.10, "The fear of the Lord is the beginning of wisdom". This resultant wisdom is demonstrated here in v.12. The man who fears the Lord will always be amenable to the teaching of the Lord. This will guide him aright so that he chooses the proper path to tread. Here is a free-will to choose, but it is a will moulded by divine counsel. This is wisdom indeed, when a man knows to choose what God wills. The promise of Proverbs 3.6 is assuring, "In all thy ways acknowledge him, and he shall direct thy paths". Such a man will dwell (3885) at ease (2896). These are two interesting words. "Dwell" is the word for "lodge". "Ease" is variously translated "pleasantness; prosperity; preciousness". There is a pilgrim aspect of the believer. He is but passing through, temporarily lodging, as it were, in this world, and travelling on to another world. But he who does so in the fear of the Lord will have a pleasant lodging and a prosperous life. The children of this man, then, begin life with a great privilege and advantage, inheriting what has been gained for them by the godly life and testimony of their father. Materially, of course, the sons of those who fear the Lord often inherit an actual prosperity bequeathed to them, but, sadly, these inheritances, whether material or spiritual, are sometimes not fully appreciated, and are consequently forfeited.

A further blessing for those who fear the Lord is that they enjoy the secret (5475) of the Lord. This word "secret" implies a holy, but familiar, intercourse with Jehovah on the part of the godly. He brings them into His counsel. He confides in them. He makes His purposes known to them. Abraham was the friend of God, and Enoch walked with God, and such communion is the portion of all those who fear Him. He reveals to such a deeper and fuller knowledge of His covenant than other men would have.

Verses 15-21: Renewed Personal Petitions

David now leaves his meditation and returns to speak, in the first person again, of his own need. From praise he turns again to prayer. This section begins similarly to the first. "Unto thee, O Lord, do I lift up my soul", he has said at the commencement of the Psalm. "Mine eyes are ever toward the Lord", he says now. He gives the reason for this look of faith to Jehovah, "For he shall pluck my feet out of the net". Jehovah alone could deliver him from the entanglements and snares of life. Troubles are like a net, whether the deceitfulness of the heart within a man, or the callousness of adversaries without, or the pressures of circumstances around. There are pitfalls and traps that might imprison a man as in a net. As another has written, "What foes and snares surround me! What lusts and fears within!" (J.G. Deck). There was help in Jehovah alone and to Him only David lifts his eyes for deliverance. He pleads that mercy once more which he has already pleaded several times in the earlier section of the Psalm in vv. 6, 7 and 10. The word "mercy" (2603) of v.16 is different from the others, but very similar in meaning. He desires pity, and appeals for a gracious movement of Jehovah towards him in his afflictions. He feels desolate (3173), destitute and solitary, friendless and alone, and in his loneliness he longs for the presence of the Lord. "Turn thee unto me", he prays. Had his sins caused an estrangement? Had the face of his God been turned away from him? How he yearned for a renewed sense of the divine presence and for the smile of God to be upon him again. Without this David was lonely in a sad and awful solitude. "Mine eyes are toward Thee", he cries, "turn Thee unto me".

How sad the Psalmist felt in his condition, and how graphically he describes it. Troubles! Distresses! Affliction! Pain! O the travail of a believer who has lost the joy of salvation and the sense of God's presence. David's troubles were many. They filled his heart and he longed for relief. "O deliver me", is his plea, "Bring me out of my anguish". Perowne translates; "My heart is full of troubles: O set it at liberty". He was in straits of sorrow and pain, and he asks for divine consideration. "Look", in v.18

and "Consider" in v.19 are the same word (7200). David is asking for a double consideration. "Mine affliction", he says, "mine enemies". Behold them both, look upon them, consider them, and forgive all my sins. His affliction was real travail. His enemies were many and their hatred of him was cruel (2555). This word is very often translated "violence". It was unjust too. It was malice. As he says in other places, quoted by the rejected Messiah Himself in John 15.25, "They hated me without a cause" (Ps 35.19; 69.4). They were his oppressors without reason and the anxiety of it all filled his heart with pain. Those who refer this Psalm to the period of Absalom's rebellion see reflected here the deep grief which this must have been to David. His own son, with his own erstwhile friend and counsellor, Ahithophel, and a large part of the nation, were against him. They would stop at nothing to see him destroyed.

Observe then the repetition and the increasing intensity of David's personal pleas. "Keep me" (8104). "Deliver me". He repeats the prayer of v.2, "Let me not be ashamed". He dreads the taunts of his enemies if his trust in Jehovah should not be vindicated. How they would exult in his disappointment and confusion if his God did not help him. In spite of shortcomings and failings, and what he calls his transgressions and his great iniquity, David now speaks of integrity and uprightness. He is not, however, asserting or boasting that he possesses these virtues - he is neither innocent nor perfect. Rather does he desire them, for, even though he is conscious of failure, he still waits upon Jehovah and he knows that these are the qualities which Jehovah would desire for him. The possession of these virtues would preserve a man. Some have understood the integrity to be a single-hearted devotion to God, and the uprightness to be righteous living before men. Before God and men, David in sincerity desired to be right, and to this end he waited upon Jehovah. So ends the third section of a touching Psalm of meditation, contemplation, and penitence.

Verse 22: A Prayer for the Nation

The concluding verse of the Psalm embraces the whole nation. It may indeed have been intended as a kind of brief epilogue to make the Psalm suitable for congregational worship. As David had prayed for deliverance for himself, so now he desires the same for all Israel. Did David have troubles personally? So did Israel nationally. He prays for redemption (6299) for the people who were God's people, and his people. The prayer for the nation is addressed to God (430), to Elohim, as in vv. 2 and 5. The predominating divine name in the Psalm is Jehovah, but on these three occasions David employs the name of the great Tri-unity, the Creator of Genesis 1.1. It is a name of power and of might, and to such an One the Psalmist can appeal with confidence, whether that appeal is for himself personally or for Israel nationally. Davison says of this closing verse, "The prayer admirably harmonises with the whole spirit of the Psalm and sums up its petitions"

PSALM 26

Introduction

The title ascribes the Psalm to David, with "Psalm" in italics, on which see the note at the end of the commentary on Psalm 11. Being David's Psalm, it must therefore be dated around 1050 BC, but it is not possible to be more exact. Neither is it possible, and perhaps it is not necessary, to relate the Psalm to any special event or experience, whether personal or national. The sentiments expressed and the circumstances envisaged in the Psalm may obtain at any time for the godly of any age.

A resemblance has often been noticed between this Psalm and the preceding Psalm 25. There are the same declarations of the Psalmist's trust in Jehovah, and the same acknowledgements of Jehovah's loving-kindness and mercy. Perowne, though, observes so very beautifully, "There is, however, this marked difference between the two, that there are wanting, in this Psalm, those touching confessions of sinfulness and pleadings for forgiveness which in the other are thrice repeated. Here is only the avowal of conscious uprightness, an avowal solemnly made as in the sight of the Searcher of hearts, and deriving, no doubt, much of its intensity and almost impassioned force, from the desire, on the part of the singer, to declare his entire separation from, and aversion to, the vain and evil men by whom he is surrounded".

There is such a unity of thought and flow of language in the Psalm that a methodical division is difficult. The twelve verses, though, are comprised of six couplets, and these may again be suitably arranged in three sections, with two couplets, or four verses, in each section.

Verses 1-4: Judge me! Prove me! Try me!

Tired of the injustices of men, David appeals to Jehovah for righteous judgment. He is content and willing to be laid bare before his God. He is not pleading moral perfection, or claiming that he has never sinned, but, in spite of his human failings, he has walked in his integrity (8537). A derivative of this word is used to describe those Levitical offerings which were required to be without blemish. David may have failed, and he knew it, but he was wholly devoted in his desire to walk in accordance with the laws of God. His intentions were sincere, and in this he was blameless. This was integrity, and he pleads it before the One who knew the innermost recesses of his being. He would judge His servant righteously. David would accordingly trust without wavering. He would not be shaken in his confidence in Jehovah. Note that the word "therefore" is in italics, supplied by the translators. Whether, then, this means that he had so trusted, unwaveringly, in the past, or that he would so trust in the future, is of no account. Both were true. It had been his habit, and it would continue to be, that he should rest on the Lord and not stagger or be shaken. Plumer quotes Calvin, who, he says, unites all the clauses: "Because I have walked in mine integrity, and trusted in Jehovah, I shall not be moved".

David continues to invite divine scrutiny of his thoughts and motives. "Examine (974) me", he says. "Prove (5254) me". "Try (6884) my reins and my heart". The three words are almost interchangeable, the same English words being variously used to translate them. The first, "examine", and the third, "try", however, are especially used of the testing of metals. They signify the testing and refining of gold and other metals by the trial of fire which would detect and remove all dross. David was willing to be so tried by Jehovah. He would submit to be examined by the searching eye of God. The word translated here "prove" is that which is used in Genesis 22.1, where God tempted, or tested, Abraham. Jehovah was not "tempting", in the sense in which that word is often used, but rather "testing" the patriarch. The reins, mostly translated "kidneys" in the book of Leviticus, are used symbolically as the seat of the emotions and affections. "Reins" and "heart" are the deep inner being of a person, and together they determine a man's character and behaviour.

David's willingness to be examined and tried by Jehovah is based on this, that he knows the loving-kindness of God. With this loving-kindness ever in his sight David had been enabled to walk according to God's truth. The constant remembrance of the character of God was a deterrent to sin and an encouragement to godly living. Remembering the kindness and love of God should always be to the believer an incentive to walk in the truth. So it was with the Psalmist. He had not sat in the company of vain (7723) persons, men of falsehood who pursued worthless aims in life, empty and void. He had no desire to associate with such men. He would not be involved with them. His ideals were higher and nobler than theirs. Dissemblers (5956), hypocrites, deceitful men who disguised or concealed their true character, were not his chosen company. He would not go in and out with them. This is reminiscent of the blessed man of Psalm 1.

Verses 5-8: Hatred and Love

This second quadruplet of verses begins with, "I have hated", and ends with, "I have loved". How interesting and beautiful to observe that the same two words, "love"(157), and "hate" (8130), are used of the Messiah in Psalm 45.7. He loved righteousness and He hated wickedness. Between these avowals of his love and hate David repeatedly declares, "I will", and, "I will not". It is like a summary, a cameo, of the Psalmist's whole life and character. His attitudes to both God and men are described here. Already he has stated that he will have nothing to do with the vain men of the world, but now his thoughts of them are intensified. He hates their gatherings. They congregate, they assemble, to devise evil counsel, and David hates such wickedness. He would not sit in company with them. Notice the change of tense. Alexander writes, "The change of tense is anything rather than unmeaning. 'I have not sat with them in time past, and I will not go with them in time to come'. The form of expression is borrowed from Genesis 49.6".

There follows the double "I will". "I will wash my hands in innocency". "So will I compass thine altar". Washing, especially the washing of the hands, was a constant requirement under the old covenant. For this reason there was a laver for the cleansing of the priests before they ministered at the altar. Before eating, and before praying, a man was required to wash his hands. The well-known incident of Matthew 27.24, where Pontius Pilate publicly washed his hands and declared his innocence, illustrates that even among the nations the action was sometimes used symbolically. The expression is used figuratively here. With washed hands and in innocency, David would compass the altar. Perowne comments, "This compassing, or going round the altar, was, it would seem from this passage, a part of the ritual of Divine worship, and was performed with the accompaniment of music and singing, as may be gathered from the next verse". Modern Judaism no longer has an altar, but a similar ritual may yet be seen in Jerusalem on the eve of every Sabbath, when crowds of worshippers rotate ceremonially in a large circle of song and dance in the forecourt of the Western Wall.

David's appreciation of divine things was unbounded. He could not contain it for himself but desired to tell it around and abroad. He would publish it for others to know. The works of the Lord were wondrous. He had done marvellous things for David and for Israel, and this called for the voice of thanksgiving. It was fitting that both the Psalmist and the nation should render praise to Jehovah. Sincere praise from a worshipper with clean hands and a pure heart was better than any ritual ceremony.

Although David did not have a "temple magnifical" (1 Chr 22.5) such as that which was built later by his son Solomon, nevertheless there was in Zion a house, a tent which David had spread, wherein dwelt the holy Ark of the Covenant with its cherubim of glory (1 Chr 15.1; 16.1). This tent was neither the tabernacle of the wilderness, nor the temple of Solomon, but David loved it as the place where Jehovah's honour dwelt. It was the habitation of God, its holiness contrasting with the wickedness of the men of the world. "I have loved it", declares the man who says, "I have hated them" (v.5).

Verses 9-12: As for me!

David now prays that he might always be distinguished from sinful men. Whether in life or in death, he would be separate from them, and this is the import of the two clauses which he now uses. "Gather not my soul with sinners", he pleads, "nor my life with bloody men". He has had no fellowship with them in their evil designs and therefore asks that he might be separate from them in his end. Plumer sums it all up so aptly; "David desired that no portion of his existence, neither the general course of his temporal life, nor its solemn close, nor his existence beyond the grave, might be in common with the wicked. The reasons for such a prayer are found in all the differences of the character, pursuits, preferences, habits, aims, ends and destinies of saints and sinners. They do not think alike, feel alike, speak alike, act alike, live alike, die alike, or fare alike. David wished to be remembered, cared for, and gathered, but not with sinners".

How different were the hands of David from the hands of these men of blood. David had washed his hands in innocency. He was clean. These men had blood on their hands, and the guilt of bribery too. Bloodshed and bribery! They were unprincipled and unscrupulous men who would mock at the law and pervert the course of justice. David would have nothing of it, but would walk in simple uprightness. This is the integrity of which he has already spoken in v.1. But he knows his weakness, and he pleads again the mercy, the pity, the grace of God. His prayer for redemption (6299) is a cry for rescue, for deliverance. From his failings, from his sinful tendencies, from temptation, and from all that would grieve Jehovah, David desires to be delivered. He might plead integrity and uprightness, but he knew his own heart and his need for divine mercy. This mercy is the ground of his redemption. What he had asked for the nation in Psalm 25.22, he now asks for himself.

In the congregation of evil-doers David would have no part, but there were other congregations. He would join with the assemblies of the just, and would bless the Lord with them. He knew where he stood, on the level ground of righteousness. It was a table-land, inaccessible to the ungodly. He was safe there, in confidence, and in communion with God.

PSALM 27

Introduction

As with many other Psalms, this one is entitled simply, "*A Psalm* of David", and there is no certain connection with, or relevance to, any particular event or circumstance in his life. The LXX however, has an addition to the short title, and reads, "A Psalm of David, before he was anointed". But, even if this addition to the original Hebrew is permissible, the occasion is still unknown, since David was anointed three times (1 Sam 16.13; 2 Sam 2.4; 2 Sam 5.3). Many have tried to fix some special period of distress in the life of David, and a great variety of opinions has been offered and suggestions made, but David had many times of trouble and distress and the language of the Psalm might well have been his on numerous occasions. Perhaps it is best, then, to leave the particulars in doubt, and to see in the Psalm the character and confidence of a man who constantly waited upon Jehovah and who sang praises even when there were problems. David could speak of joy and of courage, even when enemies encompassed him and false witnesses accused him. The Psalm reveals the secret of such strength; "Wait, I say, on the Lord".

In a simple division of the fourteen verses it might be observed that verses 1-6 portray David's confidence in God and his communion with God. Verses 7-13 are a prayer for divine help in his time of trouble. The concluding verse 14 stands in solitary beauty and dignity, showing, as has been said, the secret of David's strength and courage in the face of so much persecution and cruel adversity.

Dr Cohen remarks that "In the Jewish ritual the Psalm is appointed for recital daily throughout the sixth month as preparation for the advent of the New Year and Day of Atonement".

Verses 1-6: Confidence and Communion

In v.1 of the Psalm there is to be found the only occurrence in all of Holy Scripture of the expression "my light". Light, of course, is much used of God in many other places. "Arise, shine; for thy light is come", was the word to Israel in Isaiah 60.1. "The Lord shall be a light unto me", said Micah the prophet (7.8). But here the Psalmist enjoys this character of Jehovah in a very special and personal way and exclaims, "Jehovah my light"! In the NT it is stated that God is light (1 Jn 1.5). This is not just that He gives light, or brings light, but that He *is* light. When the Saviour was born Simeon said of Him, "A light to lighten the Gentiles" (Lk 2.32). Later Jesus said of Himself, "Light is come into the world" (Jn 3.19), and, "I am the light of the world" (Jn 8.12). It was declared of John Baptist that, "he was not that Light, but was sent to bear witness of that Light. That was the true Light" (Jn 1.8-9). This is all very beautiful, but how exceedingly blessed when the individual believer can say of the Lord, "My light". This is the Psalmist's personal appreciation of the glory of God and it is precious.

Because David can so confidently affirm this, he can now also say, with equal confidence, "And my salvation". To walk in the light is salvation. If that light at first exposes a man, showing him what he is as a sinner, and discovering to him his moral unfitness for Jehovah's presence, so then does that same light reveal God to the sinner for salvation. Then, for the believer, Jehovah becomes also the strength (4581), the stronghold, of his life. Jehovah was David's refuge and fortress. Well might such a man say, "Whom shall I fear?". "Of whom shall I be afraid?". It is like the apostle's challenge in Romans 8.31, "If God be for us, who can be against us?".

With such a stronghold, such a fortress, David was safe from his many enemies. This had been his experience in the past, that when his foes came upon him they stumbled and fell. They were wicked and beastly men, these enemies, seeking to devour him. Some think of Saul, but others have noticed the correspondence with the story of Goliath in 1 Samuel 17.44, where the Philistine says to David, "I will give thy flesh unto the fowls of the air, and to the beasts of the field". It was the giant, however, who stumbled and fell, and the host of the Philistines fled. "Though an host should encamp against me, my heart shall not fear". This was not merely doctrine, or theology, or theory, with David. He had learned and proved, practically, that Jehovah was the God of his salvation, and the remembrance of past deliverances emboldened him for the future. "My heart shall not fear", he declares confidently. Even if war should be declared against him, even then, for all this, and in spite of this, he would continue to be confident. Jehovah was his light and his salvation and the stronghold of his life.

In the lovely v.4 of the Psalm, David turns from thoughts of enemies and foes and war. He had one impelling, compelling and chief desire in his life, a sincere longing for the presence of the Lord. "One thing is needful", the Saviour gently told Martha (Lk 10.42). Her sister Mary had found it, sitting at His feet, listening to His voice, in the enjoyment of His presence. David desired the same, and it was no vain idle wish; he would positively and actively seek after that which he desired. The house of the Lord had become a synonym for the presence of the Lord, and this was the Psalmist's longing, that, all the days of his life, he might enjoy that divine presence, ever beholding the beauty of the Lord. Observe the loveliness of the words which David employs. "Beauty" (5278), is "pleasantness". "Behold" (2372), is not just simple sight, it is "contemplation", "perceiving", even "looking with ecstasy". Delitzsch says that it signifies "a clinging, lingering, chained gaze". "Enquire" (1239), is "meditate", "reflect", "consider". This "one thing" that David desired was therefore three-fold. He would dwell in the presence of the Lord, and behold the beauty of the Lord, and meditate in admiring contemplation on the pleasantness of all that he had seen and heard.

As has been noted before, there was, at that time, no "temple magnifical" (1 Chr 22.5). David wanted such a temple, and prepared for it, but was not permitted to build it. It was built after his death by his son Solomon. The tabernacle which had been constructed in the wilderness had been brought into the land and was in Shiloh in the days of the Judges (Josh 18.1). In the reign of Saul it was at Nob (1 Sam 21), and later at Gibeon (1 Chr 16.39), from where Solomon eventually brought it to be laid up in the Temple (1 Kings 8.4). David may, at times, have this tabernacle in mind when he speaks of the house of the Lord. In later life he pitched a tent of curtains on Mount Zion for the Ark of the Covenant, and this would have then symbolised Jehovah's presence among the people. Sometimes, however, as here in v.4, David may be thinking of that heavenly temple, the palace where Jehovah reigned in glory. Observe the four different words which David uses to speak of Jehovah's dwelling - "house" (1004); "temple" (1964); "pavilion" (5520); "tabernacle" (168). The meanings are varied, and yet there is a commonality in that these are all dwelling places. The Psalmist's interest is in the place where Jehovah dwells. The house is the abode. The temple conveys the thought of a palace. Both pavilion and tabernacle are tents or booths. David was confident that, in the presence of Jehovah, there was security, there was refuge from his foes. Neither the tabernacle at Gibeon nor the curtain tent which was later spread on the Mount Zion, were materially imposing structures, as was Solomon's temple. But the glory of God was there. As Davison comments, "A flimsy tent may be the surest of all refuges in the desert, if reception into it means that the traveller is under the powerful protection of a Bedouin sheikh. Or, as in the latter part of this verse (v.5), a rocky fastness perfectly impregnable against enemies may be the figure employed. In either case it is the presence and favour of God which provides all that is needed. One who enjoys the intimacy of this high communion need fear neither foe nor storm". These rock fortresses were common in Judea. The Psalmist knew them well. Set safely there, a man was out of reach of the swords, spears, and arrows, of his enemies. David saw the protecting presence of God as such a refuge.

Being so protected, David could lift his head in triumph. There might be enemies all around but faith rose above them. This called for thanksgiving and praise, and the language suggests the Peace Offering of Leviticus 3. David would offer with joy and singing in gratitude for Jehovah's protection of him. Whether the tent of v.6 is the tabernacle pitched at Gibeon, or the tent spread for the Ark on Zion, is difficult to say, since, as has already been noted, the exact date of the Psalm cannot be determined with any certainty. Whichever is the case, David sought the presence of Jehovah to render his thanksgiving with shouts of jubilation. It is hardly likely, as some suggest, that the reference is to the blowing of trumpets and the sacrifices of Numbers 10.10. That would rather appear to be a national occasion whereas here in the Psalm it is David's personal exercise.

Verses 7-13: Sunshine and Shadow

There is such a very definite break at this point in the Psalm, and such a distinct change of tone, that some have suggested a dual authorship, as if two fragments had been joined together. This is an unnecessary hypothesis. As Spurgeon says, so very aptly, "The pendulum of spirituality swings from prayer to praise. The voice which in the last verse was tuned to music is here turned to crying". In the earlier part of the Psalm David has been in the sunshine, in the confidence of faith, but even the man of faith must be realistic and concede that circumstances may at times be difficult. It is not all sunshine, and David now considers the shadows. "Hear, O Lord…have mercy…answer me". Mercy and grace are almost like identical twins and hard to distinguish, so that the words are often used interchangeably. The word here translated "mercy" (2603) is just as often translated "grace". "Be gracious unto me", the Psalmist is pleading. To quote Spurgeon again, "Mercy is the hope of sinners and the refuge of saints". Whether mercy or grace, David's cry is for timely help when the storms come. He cries with his voice; he cries aloud.

The construction of v.8 is difficult. The italicised words in the AV will be noted. They have been supplied by the translators but there is little doubt that they give the sense. Without the italicised words the sentence is broken and abrupt. "Seek ye my face; my heart said unto thee, Thy face, Lord, will I seek". It is the meditation of the Psalmist's heart. It gives the echo of his heart to the heart of Jehovah. "Seek ye my face". "Thy face...will I seek". Davison is most helpful. His suggestion is that the heart is dialoguing with itself. He writes, "An inner colloquy has been going on: God's voice sounding in the heart, with its gracious invitation met by a response on the part of the Psalmist to the call which summons all God's people to follow Him". This is abounding grace, indeed, that Jehovah, in all His greatness, should desire to look upon His people. Compare the word of the Beloved to His spouse in the Song of Solomon 2.14, "Let me see thy countenance, let me hear thy voice". The believer of the present day can say, "Truly our fellowship is with the Father" (1 Jn 1.3).

Having responded so readily to Jehovah's invitation to seek His face, what a disappointment to David it would be, if the face of Jehovah should be hidden from him. He pleads as a servant (5650), a bondservant, a slave, that there should be nothing between him and the God of his salvation. But Jehovah had been his help in times past, and on this past experience David would trust. Jehovah had always been his help. He would not leave him or forsake him. Indeed even if father and mother forsook him, David knew that the Lord would never do so. Some have associated this with that occasion when David left his father and mother in Moab in 1 Samuel 22.3, 4, but it is hardly fair to say that they then forsook him. Rather we should understand this as hypothetical, that, even if those so close as father and mother should forsake him, he knew that Jehovah would not. There is a similar thought in Isaiah 49.15, where Jehovah asks, "Can a woman forget her sucking child, that she should not have compassion on the son of her womb?". "Yea", He says, "they may forget, yet will I not forget thee". The Lord would, if such loneliness should ever come, take him up (622). The Lord would gather him to Him, protectively, and shield him from harm. The same word is used for the gathering in of a harvest.

How very, very often in his Psalms does David pray, "Teach me...Lead me". It is good to be teachable, to be pliable and willing to be guided in the difficult path of testimony for God. There were crooked ways and rough ways, and David asks to be led in the right way and in a plain path. The way for which he prays is God's way. The plain (4334) path is a straight path and a level place, perhaps "an open place" where he might be safe from ambush by those who continually lay in wait for him. It is because of these enemies that he asks to be taught, and guided in the right way. David had many foes who were always ready to accuse him, to slander him, and to take advantage of him, therefore he desired guidance in a right path that there might be no justification for their cruel attacks on him. As he prays to be delivered from his enemies (6862), he now uses a more complex word to describe them and their evil intentions. They were his adversaries.

They were troublers and oppressors, hard and unyielding as flint, determined if possible to afflict him and cause him distress, both physically and morally. They were false witnesses, slanderers, who breathed out cruelty. This clause is reminiscent of Saul of Tarsus, of whom it is said that he breathed out threatenings and slaughter against the believers of his day. They are active in every age, these persecutors of God's people and God's truth. From such the Psalmist asks to be delivered.

The opening words of v.13, "I had fainted", are italicised. They have been supplied by the translators, some think correctly and helpfully, but others think needlessly. Without the italicised words the sentence is, to quote Maclaren, "an abrupt half-sentence". But this incompleteness is inspired and intentional, and gives more force to the meaning, when once understood. J.N. Darby translates, "Unless I had believed to see the goodness of Jehovah in the land of the living…!" If I had not believed? What? What then? It is unthinkable! Maclaren comments, "He breaks into an exclamation which he leaves unfinished. The omission is easy to supply. He would have been their victim but for his faith. The broken words tell of his recoil from the terrible possibility forced on him by the sight of the formidable enemies". Plumer agrees, quoting Hammond who says that it is "a figure of elegance, purposely breaking off in the midst of the speech; yet so as every man can foresee what kind of conclusion should follow". In the mind of each reader some thought has to be supplied to the incompleteness. The translators have supplied this for most, but others will prefer to leave the incomplete sentence as it is - incomplete.

The man who believes, who trusts, enjoys the goodness of the Lord. "The land of the living" appears to be a synonym for this present life. It is simply the opposite to the land of the dead.

Verse 14: Serene in the Storm

The concluding verse of the Psalm is like a jewel encased in two clasps. "Wait on the Lord" is one clasp. "Wait, I say, on the Lord", is the other. The preciousness enclosed between the two is an emboldened heart, strong and courageous, calm and serene even though in the presence of cruel and unremitting enemies. There is an interesting parallel in Isaiah 40.31, "They that wait upon the Lord shall renew their strength; they shall mount up with wings as eagles; they shall run, and not be weary; and they shall walk, and not faint". This is the third mention of the heart in the Psalm. There is a trusting heart in v.3, unafraid though surrounded by foes. There is a responsive heart in v.8, seeking the face of Jehovah. The heart is the seat and centre of a man's emotions, feelings and affections. Well it is when the heart is trusting in the Lord, responsive to the voice of the Lord, and patiently waiting on the Lord. Whether David is addressing others here, or appealing to his own heart, it is not necessary to decide or to choose. Both are relevant, and every believer will appreciate the exhortation of the trusting Psalmist.

PSALM 28

Introduction

As with so many of the Psalms attributed to David, there is no good reason for doubting his authorship of Psalm 28, but it is not possible to determine the precise occasion for which it was composed, nor any particular circumstances or events which may have prompted the writing of it. Some commentators will relate it to the time of Absalom's rebellion, others earlier, to the persecutions by Saul, but the language employed and the sentiments expressed will suit so many periods in David's life that it is perhaps unnecessary to be exact about a date of composition. Davison, commenting on the variety of suggestions which have been made, says, "It may be viewed as a great and abiding advantage - though to the historical student disappointing - that the language of the Psalm is found to suit periods and cases so different as these, together with a multitude besides in all generations". How many songs have been composed in the night by suffering saints, and many of David's Psalms rank among such. There is a close resemblance between Psalm 28 and the preceding Psalm 27, and, indeed, Psalm 26 also. There is such a similarity of vocabulary, of atmosphere, and of tone, that the three Psalms, with others, may well have been born during the same time of trouble, whenever that was.

The Psalm is constructed to a familiar pattern, the principle of strophes, or stanzas, with two verses in each. In the heart of the Psalm, however, that particular strophe runs into three verses, so that the division is as follows. Verses 1-2 are a prelude to the prayer which follows. In verses 3-5 the prayer itself is presented to Jehovah, a cry for deliverance from wicked men. Verses 6-7 anticipate that the Lord will hear and answer, and verses 8-9 widen out to embrace all of the Lord's people, and to appeal for blessing on these His inheritance.

Verses 1-2: The Prelude to the Prayer

As David had commenced Psalm 25, so he now commences this Psalm, "Unto thee will I cry, O Lord". The nations had their gods and their high places. They had their lifeless deities of wood and stone, of gold and silver, but David is emphatic, "Unto *thee* will I cry". David's God was the Rock of Ages (Is 26.4, margin), and those who trusted Him could rest safely. To the very end of his life, to his last words, the sweet Psalmist of Israel believed this. The God of Israel was the Rock of Israel (2 Sam 23.1-3), and David could call Him "My Rock" (Ps 19.14, margin) in that personal way in which he had learned to know Him. To Him, and to Him alone, would David present his petitions. "Unto *thee* will I cry, O Jehovah my rock".

Believers often speak of "a prayer-hearing and a prayer-answering" God. This was David's desire - that Jehovah would both hear him, and speak to him. It was too awful to contemplate that Jehovah should be silent, neither hearing, nor answering. It was so with the heathen, whose gods did not answer because they could not hear. Elijah mocked the prophets of Baal who vainly called upon Baal from morning until noon. "Cry aloud", Elijah taunted, "for he is a god, is he not? Either he is talking, or hunting, or travelling, or perhaps sleeping!" They continued to cry loudly, from noon until the evening, but there was neither voice nor any answer. "O Baal, hear us", they cried, but Baal was silent to them (1 Kings 18.26-29). He was deaf, and dumb. "Be not silent to me", David pleads of Jehovah. If Jehovah remained silent as if deaf to David's prayer, and did not speak to His servant in reply, then would David be any different to those who were perishing, going down hopelessly and helplessly into the pit? Life without God was not life. This clause, "them that go down into the pit", is used again by David in Psalm 143.7.

The lifting up of the hands was a familiar gesture in prayer and worship (Ps 134.2). The Saviour lifted up His hands when He called a blessing upon His own as He was leaving them (Lk 24.50). Paul exhorts the saints in 1 Timothy 2.8, saying, "I will therefore that men pray everywhere, lifting up holy hands". The lifting up of the hands signified the lifting up of the heart, and David's heart was lifted towards the holy oracle (1687), the holy of holies, the innermost shrine. It was an attitude of appeal, and David's appeal was to the sanctuary where Jehovah dwelt in awful majesty. "Hear the voice of my supplications", he prays. These supplications (8469) were earnest entreaties. The Psalmist pleads that his voice might be heard in the sanctuary and that he, in turn, might hear the voice of Jehovah in reply.

Verses 3-5: The Petition Presented

David shrinks from any association with the workers of iniquity. This "Draw me not away with the wicked" is similar to the "Gather not my soul with sinners" of Psalm 26.9. The Psalmist recoils from their present company and from their future fate. Neither in life nor in death does he want any part or complicity with them. He recognises that they are deceitful and mischievous, saying one thing and thinking another. They are workers of iniquity indeed. As Plumer says, "Where is the worker of iniquity who does not use guile, fraud, cunning, trick, artifice, intrigue, feigned words, smooth speeches? Nothing is more offensive to a pure mind than double dealing". The Psalmist would have nothing to do with it.

David asks for just retribution for the wickedness of these men. He asks that they be judged according to their evil deeds and their wicked endeavours (4611). This latter may refer to what they have actually done, or it may signify what they have imagined and invented in the depravity of their hearts and thoughts, and then produced in the works of their hands. David prays that they will be given what they deserve. Two things should be noted. First, this is not the Psalmist's private and personal desire for revenge for what these evil men have done to him. He knows the holiness of God and he knows too the rebelliousness of the wicked. They deserve retribution and they deserve it in the measure in which have sinned. He asks that it might be so. Second, note that, in what are called the Imprecatory Psalms there is language and sentiment which cannot now be used by the New Testament believer, who, while loathing the wickedness of the wicked, and knowing the inevitable punishment which awaits the unrepentant, nevertheless announces to the ungodly man the forgiveness procured at Calvary, and prays for his repentance and salvation. Some of the language of these Psalms, however, may well be used by a persecuted godly remnant after the rapture of the church. Compare the cry of the martyrs of that period as recorded in Revelation 6.9-10.

Intent on the evil workings of their own hands these men have no regard (995) for the works of the Lord or the operation of His hands. They have no intelligence or understanding of divine things. They have neither discernment or discretion in matters spiritual. Their end is destruction. Jehovah, whom they have disregarded, will destroy them. He will neither build up nor sustain what they are or what they have done. They are destined to perish and all their works with them.

Verses 6-7: The Answer Anticipated

Prayer now turns to praise. Verse 6 is the counterpart of v.2. "Hear the voice of my supplications", David had asked. "He hath heard the voice of my supplications", he now exclaims, and, "Blessed be the Lord". It is the joy of answered prayer, and this gives birth to praise. "Those who pray well, will soon praise well", Spurgeon says. David had lifted up his hands in prayer, now he lifts up his heart in praise. Jehovah was his sword and shield, his strength and his defence. Notice the Psalmist's two references to his heart in v.7. The heart that trusts is the heart that rejoices. To "trust" (982) is to have such confidence as produces a sense of security, even to the point of being carefree. David so trusted and was helped. He found safety and succour and a joy that could only be expressed in singing. He must praise for all that Jehovah has done for him, and so he raises his song. His rejoicing (5937) was such that an English translation requires the adverb "greatly" to express the import of it. David's joy was full, it was triumphant. Jehovah had heard him and he exulted.

The opening clause of v.7 is repeated at the beginning of v.8 except for a change of pronoun. "The Lord is my strength" (5797), David had declared, and now he echoes, "The Lord is their strength" (5797). What Jehovah was to the king, he would be to his people. What He was to His anointed He would be to the nation. The word "strength" (4581) is then used again in v.8, but, although similar, the words are different. This second "strength" in v.8 signifies a stronghold or fortress for the salvation, the deliverance, of His anointed. In the context, David is the Lord's anointed, but this title, "The Anointed", belongs in a special way to Christ, Messiah and Saviour.

All that Jehovah was to David was a foreshadowing of what He is to His anointed King, presently rejected by the nation and by the world, but in the purpose of God destined to rule in Zion (Ps 2.2, 6).

Verses 8-9: A Plea for the People

It is always touching to notice that David, again and again, looks away from his personal problems and embraces the whole nation in his thoughts and prayers. In spite of his own trials he can think tenderly and unselfishly of his people. In such a way the Psalm concludes, with a four-fold intercession for the nation. He pleads for them as God's people. They were God's inheritance, His possession, and the Psalmist pleads this fact as a reason why Jehovah should remember them. So he prays for them. "Save them!" "Bless them!" "Feed them!" "Lift them!" They needed a Saviour, a Benefactor, a Shepherd, a Sustainer. A Saviour would deliver them from their enemies. A Benefactor would grant them peace and prosperity. A Shepherd would guide them and guard them. A Sustainer would lift them above their troubles, support them, and carry them in safety. Only Jehovah could be all this to His people, and David accordingly commits the great national need to Him. Every believer will know that this four-fold need is just the same today as it was then. It is the recurring and universal need of saints in every age, and what Jehovah was to His people then, He is to them now.

PSALM 29

Introduction

This Psalm of David is a magnificent literary picture of an Eastern thunderstorm. Delitzsch calls it "The Psalm of the seven thunders" and Davison comments that "few finer descriptions of a storm are to be found in literature". Maclaren suggests that the picture is framed by two verses of introduction and two of conclusion, the one dealing with "glory to God in the highest", and the other with "peace on earth". The storm rises on the waters of the Mediterranean, from which westerly direction the storm usually comes to the Holy Land, and from whence the first distant thundering can be heard. It then travels across Lebanon, reverberating through the hills, breaking the giant cedars, shaking the mountains of Lebanon and causing even the majestic Hermon to tremble and leap like the antelope or young ox. The seven times repeated "voice of the Lord" is like the pealing of thunder as the storm increases in intensity, sweeping down through mountain and plain with torrential rain and flashes of forked lightning. It reaches the wilderness of Kadesh in the south, laying the forests bare, stripping the trees of their foliage and causing the hinds to calve prematurely. But Jehovah sits enthroned upon the swelling torrents, in divine control of all. At last the storm subsides into calm and the closing word in the Psalm is "Peace" (7965). It is the lovely "Shalom", and a beautiful reminder of Him who once slept in the storm and then arose to say, "Peace, be still".

The Psalm is in three obvious parts. The first two verses are a prologue or prelude, a call to adoration and worship. Verses 3-9 are the main body of the Psalm, describing the storm, with seven references, in seven verses, to the voice of the Lord. The final two verses, 10-11, with their four mentions of the great name Jehovah, are a fitting conclusion, extolling the majesty of the God of glory and His care for His people.

Verses 1-2: The Prologue - A Call to Worship

The Psalm commences with a three-fold call to ascribe glory to Jehovah. The thrice repeated "Give unto the Lord" signifies the importance and the urgency of the call and it is almost universally agreed that "the mighty" (1221; 410) who are being addressed are "the sons of the mighty". The same phrase occurs elsewhere only in Psalm 89.6 where it seems obvious that the angelic hosts are in view. The description is similar to, but not exactly the same as, "the sons of God" in Genesis 6.4; Job 1.6; 2.1; 38.7. In these latter verses God's title is the plural Elohim (430). In Psalm 89.6 and here in Psalm 29.1 it is the title El (410). The call however, must extend beyond the angels. If these sons of the mighty are called to ascribe glory to God, how much more must mortals of earth acknowledge His greatness and give Him due honour and adoration. Whether angels or men, the worshippers must be suitably attired for His august presence. There is beauty in holiness, and in this priestly dress those who approach to worship are acceptable in the sanctuary. By divine command, Israel's first high priest, Aaron, wore holy garments for glory and for beauty as he ministered in the holy place (Ex 28.2). For other references to this holy adornment see Psalm 96.9 and Psalm 110.3, and compare also 2 Chronicles 20.21. In Psalm 96 the call to worship is worded almost exactly as here in Psalm 29, with the same three-fold exhortation to "Give unto the Lord" the glory due unto His name.

Verses 3-9: The Seven Thunders

In Psalm 18.13 the voice of the Lord is likened to thunder. Here in Psalm 29 that voice of thunder is heard seven times in seven verses. Compare the seven thunders of the apocalypse in Revelation 10.3. At its first sounding the thunder is heard distantly upon the waters. The storm is approaching. The voice which resounds across the waters is the voice of the God of glory (3519). This majestic title of God is found only once more in Holy Scripture, in Acts 7.2. Even the English word "glory" is difficult to define. The Oxford Dictionary employs such words as, "honour and splendour; dignity and majesty; brightness and bliss; effulgence and beauty". These are the characteristics of the God of glory who called Abram out from the idol gods of the Chaldees. It is His voice which now thunders across the waters as the storm is about to break.

Notice the oft repeated "Jehovah" (3068). Seventeen times in the eleven verses of this short Psalm the awful name is heard. It is the inscrutable name of Him who is, and who was, and who is to come (Rev 1.4,8). It is His voice which thunders these seven times and His voice is powerful (3581) and full of majesty (1926). Might and majesty are combined in Him; strength and splendour.

The voice which echoed across the waters is now heard on the land. In ever increasing intensity the storm rages through Lebanon, snapping the great cedars. The mountain range of Lebanon, at Israel's northern border, was famed for its giant cedars. Tristram says of these cedars that they are, "a type of grandeur, might, and lofty stature...the prince of trees". But the voice of the Lord can break cedars, yea, even the cedars of Lebanon. As men often startle in fear at the sound of thunder, so do the trees and the hills leap at the sound of Jehovah's voice. Great Hermon itself is moved. "Sirion", of v.6, is an old Sidonian name for Mount Hermon according to Deuteronomy 3.9. Hermon, eternally snow-capped, symbol of strength and royal dignity, shudders in the storm as the voice of the Lord sweeps through the mountains. Trees and mountains, symbols of strength and stability, alike are startled, jumping as a frightened calf or a young wild ox would jump in fear. "Unicorn" (7214), in v.6, is the wild buffalo. The young of that species would be similar in many ways to the young bullock or calf (5695) of the same verse. Then again, lightning always adds to the fear created by thunder, and this is especially so in tropical and Eastern climates. Like flashes of forked lightning the voice of the Lord now breaks through the cloud, so that earth, sea, and sky, are all affected by the storm. Like cleft flames of fire His voice rends the storm clouds.

In v.8 the storm sweeps on, from the mountains in the north, down through the Jordan valley and the central plains to the wilderness of Kadesh in the south, stirring and scattering the desert sand. It is an authentic fact that the terror of a violent thunderstorm has been known to cause animals to bring forth their young prematurely. So it is now. The thundering of the voice of the Lord brings the pains of travail to the hinds, making them calve before their due time.

The whole creation is moved at the voice of Jehovah. He "discovereth" (2834) the forests. He strips them bare of their foliage, their flowers, their fruits, and even their branches. The wilderness is shaken. The animal creation is moved with fear. But in His temple every voice cries, "Glory!". In that palace of the heavens, from where, with clear vision, adoring hosts witness the wonder of it all, every heart and voice is lifted to ascribe glory to the Lord. The believer of the present day joins in the exultation and sings -

> O Lord my God! when I in awesome wonder
> Consider all the works Thy hands have made,
> I see the stars, I hear the mighty thunder,
> Thy power throughout the universe displayed.

Then sings my soul, my Saviour God, to Thee,
How great Thou art! How great Thou art!
(tr. Stuart K. Hine)

Verses 10-11: The Epilogue - Peace on Earth

As the storm subsides the Psalmist's eyes are lifted to behold Jehovah in His sovereignty, sitting supreme in solitary royal splendour above the deluge. Notice the two references to the seated Lord, and observe also the significance of the "flood" (3999) upon which He sits. This word "flood" is only found elsewhere in Genesis with reference to the story of that deluge of judgment in the days of Noah. If there is an intended allusion here to that great flood, and if the past tense of the RV translation is accepted - "The Lord sat as king at the flood" - then the thought is that He who presided in supremacy over that deluge of old is the same who now sits, and will forever sit, as King, in control of all things. Perowne is worth quoting in full. He writes, "The Flood, i.e. the Deluge. The word here employed occurs nowhere else, except in the story of the Flood (Gen 6-11), and therefore refers, I cannot help thinking, to that great act of judgment, and not merely to a recent inundation caused by the storm, the mountain-torrents having been swollen by the rain, and having flooded the country. This might have happened. But the selection of so peculiar a word 'flood', as well as the fact that the verb is in the past tense, '*sat* throned', makes the other more probable".

That Jehovah should sit serene and calm above the waters ought to bring comfort to His people. Just as He sat in solemn judgment over the downpour that drowned an evil world in the days of Noah, so does He sit yet, and forever, for the salvation of His own. Did He then deliver Noah and his wife, and his sons with their wives, from the flood which deluged that world? Then so will He now deliver His people and give them power to live for Him.

The Psalm concludes with a delightful benediction. Jehovah will bless His people with peace (7965). It is, as has already been observed, the lovely word "Shalom". It is peace with prosperity. It is tranquillity, serenity, and contentment. It is the very character of Jehovah Himself, who is the God of peace, and of Messiah who is the Prince of "Shalom" (Is 9.6). The storm has passed. All is calm now, and Jehovah blesses His people.

PSALM 30

Introduction

The title of this Psalm as it appears in the AV is difficult, and various explanations have been offered. There is general agreement that the title is a composite one and that perhaps the phrase, "and Song at the dedication of the house", should be seen as an interpolation or parenthesis coming between "A Psalm" and "of David", so that then the title might indicate, "A Psalm - A Song at the dedication of the house - of David", as the RV rendering. If this be correct then "of David" should be related to "A Psalm" and not to "the house". It is therefore, a Psalm of David, and was composed as a Song at the dedication of the house. The difficulty remains however, as to which house is intended, and which dedication, and when.

Some commentators associate the Psalm with the building and dedication of David's own house of cedar, built for him by Hiram king of Tyre in 2 Samuel 5.11; 7.1-2. It is pointed out that the dedicating of a new house was in accord with the law of Moses as in Deuteronomy 20.5 and that it is reasonable to assume that David so dedicated his palace of cedar, though such a dedication is not actually recorded. It is perhaps more probable that the Psalm was composed at the time of the purchase of the threshingfloor of Ornan the Jebusite on Mount Moriah, for the building by Solomon of the house "exceeding magnifical, of fame and of glory" (1 Chr 21.18-30; 22.5; 2 Chr 3.1). If it is objected that at that time there was no such house to be dedicated, it should also be noted that David does say, even as he built an altar there and offered burnt offerings and peace offerings, "This is the house of the Lord God, and this is the altar of the burnt offering for Israel" (1 Chr 22.1).

If the Psalm is considered aside from its title, it is a Psalm of thanksgiving for restoration and healing, and for deliverance from death. This again would agree with the circumstances which preceded the purchase of the threshingfloor. David had sinned in the matter of his numbering of the people. It was an act of foolishness and pride, provoked by Satan and displeasing to the Lord (1 Chr 21.1, 7). It brought a judgment upon Israel, and from Dan to Beersheba there was plague and pestilence in which many thousands died (2 Sam 24.15). Whether David was himself physically affected by the pestilence is not clear but it is easy to relate the Psalm to the eventual deliverance from the national and personal distress. It is interesting too, that, at this present day, the Psalm is part of Jewish liturgy and is recited at the Feast of Dedication (Jn 10.22), as it had been until the destruction of the temple in AD70. This feast is called CHANUKKA, Hebrew for "dedication" (2598), and is an annual celebration, instituted by the Maccabees to commemorate the purification and dedication of the temple after its desecration by Antiochus Epiphanes. The suitability and appropriateness of the Psalm to such a celebration is obvious.

This is the first time in the Psalter that a Psalm is called a song (7892). Note Paul's reference in Ephesians 5.19 to "psalms and hymns and spiritual songs". It is thought that while the Psalms were always sung with an accompaniment, the song may have been sung with voice only, but, since Psalm 30 is both a Psalm and a song, it was apparently intended to be sung either way.

A five-fold division of the twelve verses may be observed. In verses 1-3 David gives thanks to Jehovah for restoration and healing. In verses 4 and 5 he calls upon others to join with him in his thanksgiving. Verses 6-7 recall his experience in his distress, and verses 8-10 are a repetition of his earlier prayer. The Psalm concludes with two verses of praise for the answer to his prayer.

Verses 1-3: Deliverance from Death

The Psalm commences with a joyful outburst of thanksgiving and praise. Three times in three verses David cries, "O Lord; O Lord; O Lord", and in the central exclamation he says, "O Lord my God". His heart overflows in gratitude for preservation and restoration, so that he desires to "extol" (7311) Jehovah. Is there a play upon words here? Paraphrased, David says, "I will lift Thee up on High, O Lord, for Thou hast lifted me up". "I will exalt Thee, for Thou hast exalted me". Jehovah has lifted up the Psalmist from his distress. David will lift up Jehovah in praise and adoration. David seems to be ever fearful lest his enemies should find some ground for reproaching either him or his God. He is therefore grateful for his present deliverance in that his enemies have no occasion to rejoice. They would have delighted in his discomfort or distress or in any indication that Jehovah had failed him, and his death would have gladdened their hearts. But it is not so. The Lord has lifted him up (1802), drawn him out of his trouble, and he will magnify the Lord.

David had cried for help (7768). Jehovah had heard, and had healed him. The great Physician of His people had healed (7495) His servant David, as He had healed His people of old (Ex 15.26). Whether, as has been suggested, David had been personally ill during the plague in which so many died, is not clear, but, from the very gates of death, as it were, Jehovah has lifted him. From Sheol (7585), from Hades, from that grave-land abode of the dead, the Lord had delivered him. He had been rescued from among those that went down to the pit. It was akin to resurrection from the dead. "Thou hast kept me alive", he says. David had been raised up to life indeed. Notice the three-fold "Thou hast; Thou hast; Thou hast". Jehovah had been true to His servant David.

Verses 4-5: A Call to praise

It is constantly typical of David that he will have others join with him in his prayers and in his praises. This is an encouraging example of the fellowship of saints of every age, that, both in joy and in sorrow, there should be a holy companionship of kindred spirits. David calls for such fellowship now. "Ye saints of his" (2623), is an interesting description of the Lord's people, and is variously translated. "His loving ones", says one rendering (Cheyne). "His men of kindness", says another (Rotherham). Yet another prefers, "His holy ones" (Strong). All are true. The saints are holy, loving, and kind, and upon such David now calls that they should join him in praising Jehovah. Indeed, it is only those who are holy who can suitably praise Him who is "Holy, holy, holy" as both Isaiah and John saw Him in glory (Is 6.3; Rev 4.8). The remembrance of such august holiness calls for praise from the Psalmist and his friends.

There follows a touching contrast between Jehovah's anger (639) and His favour (7522). Sometimes He may be angry, but His anger is momentary. Judgment is His strange work. As Spurgeon remarks, "God puts up His rod with great readiness as soon as its work is done; He is slow to anger and swift to end it". His anger - a moment! His favour - a lifetime! In a lifetime of God's favour the grief of His judgments are but a moment for those who love Him. The simile is beautiful. Weeping is viewed as a lodger for the night, but nights come to an end, and, in the morning, joy comes in to abide. To quote Rotherham, "At eventide there cometh to lodge Weeping, - in the morning Jubilation!". For the believer grief will be turned into gladness, mourning into music, sighing into singing. Weeping is a temporary lodger and must make room for another guest - joy. The Sun of Righteousness, with healing in His wings, brings the darkest night to an end. The transience of trouble is eclipsed by the permanence of joy.

Verses 6-7: Careless Confidence

David recalls that he had had to learn the truth of v.6 by experience. Prosperity often brings problems with it. It is, of course, more pleasant than adversity, but adverse conditions tend to keep the believer constantly in dependence upon God, whereas prosperity can produce a careless ease. David learned this. In his complacency, when things were going well for him, he had said, "I shall never be moved". Nothing, he thought, could shake him. There was a carnal sense of security until trouble came.

God had been good to David. By the grace of God David had been made strong. Jehovah had established him and blessed him abundantly, and it never seemed to occur to David that he might sometime lose God's favour. He was apparently lulled into that complacency which does not need to trust. All was well. "I shall never be moved", he said. There are times, however, when Jehovah allows his saints to be in the storm that they may learn how dependent upon Him they really must be. David's trouble came when Jehovah hid His face from him. At least it is an evidence of the reality of the believer when the hiding of God's face causes him anxiety. To the unbelieving man of the world this would not be a problem at all, but to the genuine believer it is the breaking of communion and the loss of the divine presence, and this frightens him indeed. "I was troubled" (926), says David. This was deep trouble. The word signifies distress and dismay. He was afraid and alarmed, disturbed and in despair. The NT word as in John 14.1 (*5015*) suggests the agitated heaving of a restless rolling sea. Such is the state of that believing heart which has lost the joy of communion with God. Poor David! As is so often the case, his prosperity had not helped spiritually, but the hiding of Jehovah's face would restore him and bring him back to simple trust and dependence again.

Verses 8-10: A Plea for Help

In three verses David now recalls his former prayer in his time of trouble, and he then repeats that plea, asking for mercy and for help. He had cried (7121) to Jehovah. It was a call from the depths of a troubled heart. It was not an isolated cry either, but supplications oft repeated and continuing from out of his anguish. "I cried...I made supplication". Literally, "Unto Thee, Jehovah, I continued crying, yea, unto the Lord making supplication". What would it profit Jehovah if he perished, he had pleaded. If he were to go down into the pit (7845) would his dust render any praise to Jehovah? Would there be any testimony to God, or for God, out of the corruption and silence of the grave? Would there be, or could there be, any declaration of His truth from the decomposed body of His servant? How would Jehovah be advantaged by his death? This was bold but reverent reasoning on the part of the Psalmist. He had God's glory in view and he pleads this as he asks for an answer to his prayer.

Note how his appeal is to Jehovah only. "Hear, O Lord". "Lord, be thou my helper". Human aid was of no avail. In the language of another Psalm David might have said, "My help cometh from the Lord" (Ps 121.2). He prays for mercy (2603). He longs for that grace and pity, that help and succour, that God alone could give.

Verses 11-12: Girded with Gladness!

His prayer is answered. There is a sudden transition from mourning to dancing. Just as earlier the weeping is replaced by joy in v.5, so now the sadness of the troubled saint is eclipsed by the joy of answered prayer and the renewal of the sense of God's presence with him. Sackcloth is the garb of the mourner. The jubilant Psalmist has exchanged it for garments of gladness. It is, as Isaiah would say, "Beauty for ashes, the oil of joy for mourning, the garment of praise for the spirit of heaviness" (Is 61.3).

But the blessing of the saints always has the greater end in view of the glory of God. There is a constant desire in the heart of God for the worship of His grateful people. "The Father seeketh such to worship him" (Jn 4.23). He looks for the appreciation and affection of those whom He has blessed. David cannot, therefore, be silent in his renewed joy, but must sing his praise to the Lord. Any glory (3519), any honour, which David may now enjoy must return to God in adoring worship. "That my glory may sing...and not be silent".

The Psalmist's usage of divine names and titles is exemplary. "O Lord (3068) my God" (430). "O Jehovah my Elohim!" The ever-existing, self-sufficient Jehovah, and the mighty Creator Elohim are his in a most personal manner. "My God!" For as long as he lives, and ever after, David will render due praise to his God. The outpouring of his thankfulness will continue forever. He will sing praise and give thanks, and God will be glorified in it all.

PSALM 31

Introduction

This Psalm, with fifty-four others, is committed to the care of the Chief Musician, the leader of temple song, indicating that it was intended for use in public worship. See note in the introduction to Psalm 4. It is entitled "A Psalm of David", and there is no reason to question the Davidic authorship. "A beautiful Psalm", says Cheyne, "in which all the keys of the soul's music are touched". Maclaren concurs when he speaks of, "The inclusion of the whole gamut of feeling", adding that, "The Psalm is like an April day, in which sunshine and rain chase each other across the plain", and Spurgeon writes of "...this song of mingled measures with alternate strains of grief and woe".

As with many other Psalms it is not possible to know with certainty either the date or the occasion of its composition, but, to quote Spurgeon again, "It is perhaps quite as well that we have no settled season mentioned, or we might have been so busy applying it to David's case as to forget its suitability to our own".

The Psalm is somewhat difficult to divide and sub-divide, but for the purpose of an orderly meditation the following sections may be noted. In verses 1-4 there is both prayer and praise, an appreciation of God and an appeal for deliverance and guidance. In verses 5-8 there is a blending of gladness and grief, with David's remembrance of what God has done for him and what He has been to him. Verses 9-13 continue in grief, with mentions of slander and sighing. Verses 14-18 anticipate deliverance, and seem to breathe confidence in the God of whom David says, "My times are in thy hand". Verses 19-22 are full of praise for One who is great in His goodness to those who fear Him. The concluding verses 23-24 are a word of comfort, and an exhortation to courage for all the saints and faithful everywhere.

Verses 1-4: Petitions and Praises

David is ever quick to declare that his trust is in Jehovah alone. "In thee, O Lord, do I put my trust". This is a true echo of that golden Psalm 16.1; compare also Psalm 71.1. David's trust (2620), his refuge, his hope, was in the Lord only. From all the trials and vicissitudes of his troubled life he would seek refuge in Jehovah, and in Jehovah alone. "In thee!" He prays that in his trusting he might never be ashamed (954). Let not Jehovah disappoint him, let him never be confused or confounded. How disconcerted would that saint be who, after trusting in Jehovah, was left, forsaken. These were the feelings of the holy sufferer of Psalm 22.4-5 - "Our fathers trusted in thee: they trusted, and thou didst deliver them...they trusted in thee, and were not confounded". And His tormentors taunted Him, "He trusted on the Lord that he would deliver him: let him deliver him!" (v.8). David appeals to the righteousness of God. Would God, in His righteousness, abandon the soul that trusted in Him? He did, in His holiness, forsake the Sin-bearer of Psalm 22 at Golgotha, but this is different. A troubled saint may safely rely on that righteousness which ensures that the God whom he trusts will never disappoint him or desert him.

The plea that Jehovah would bow down to hear him is an acknowledgement both of God's greatness and the Psalmist's lowliness. Would Jehovah bend to him and hear him and rescue him speedily? The word "rock" occurs twice in the translation, but the original words are slightly different. "Be thou my strong (4581) rock (6697)" is, literally, "Be for me a refuge rock, a stronghold rock". As Maclaren remarks, "There is a beautiful plea, which unsympathetic critics would call illogical, when David prays, 'Be thou my strong rock...for thou art my rock'. What does he mean? He is asking, 'Be Thou to me in act, in manifestation, what Thou art in Thyself, in nature: be what I, Thy poor servant, have taken Thee to be'". Jehovah is a fortified house of refuge for those who trust Him, a house of defence. "My rock (5553) and my fortress (4686)" is, "My cliff fort", or, "My high stronghold". Trusting in Jehovah, David is out of reach of those who would persecute him. It is imperative, therefore, that he should make the Lord his sole refuge. He has no merit of his own to plead, so he cries, "For thy name's sake". He desires, as ever, the glory of God, and, with this in view, he prays, "Lead me, and guide me". Some think, however, that this is a statement rather than a petition and that David is saying, "Thou wilt lead me and guide me". But whether a statement or a prayer, it is an expression of the Psalmist's trust and confidence in Jehovah. "Lead me" (5148). "Guide me" (5095). These are shepherd words meaning to lead and gently guide with care to a watering place or to a place of rest. They are reminiscent of Psalm 23; "He leadeth me beside the still waters...he leadeth me in the paths of righteousness for his name's sake".

David uses various metaphors, and now, from that of flying for refuge to a high fortress, he prays that he might be delivered from the traps and snares which his enemies set to catch him. They were cunning, these enemies of his, and would lay their snares privily (2934). Their traps would be concealed, hidden, secreted, and, if they succeeded, David would be caught, entangled as a bird in the net of the fowler. Now David returns again to the earlier metaphor, "Thou art my strength" (4581), my stronghold, my rock refuge and my place of safety. In whatever manner it may be pictured, the Psalmist's hope for salvation from his enemies was in Jehovah. In Him alone would he trust.

Verses 5-8: Grief and Gladness

In these four verses David speaks of lying vanities, of trouble and adversities, and of the hand of the enemy, but in it all he retains his trust in

Jehovah, and, in spite of the dangers, he can be glad and rejoice. There is indeed, gladness in the grief.

The opening words of v.5 have become precious to the saints, rendered sacred by the Saviour's use of them on the cross (Lk 23.46). Many believers have followed the example of the Lord Jesus and have likewise, in the hour of death, prayed, "Father, into Thy hand I commit my spirit". David, however, is not particularly thinking here of his decease but of his then present need in his hour of trouble. In the midst of adversity he would commit himself into the hand of God for safe-keeping. "Thou hast redeemed (6299) me", he says, and the remembrance of past redemptions imparted confidence as he continued to trust. There had been former deliverances. Jehovah had rescued him before, and in the memory of this he was encouraged to commit himself always to the care of his God, whom he now calls, "O Lord God of truth". This is a majestic title, used also by Moses in Deuteronomy 32.4. He is the God of faithfulness, the God who cannot lie (Tit 1.2). There can be no reason for his saints to doubt Him or to distrust Him. There is every reason for the Psalmist, and for the saints of every age, to commit life and breath to Him in constant trust.

In sharp contrast to the Lord God of truth, there were those who observed and trusted in "lying (7723) vanities"(1892). This is a scathing indictment of those who had regard for idols and idolaters and all false gods. Idol worship was, literally, "empty nothingness". Or, as Maclaren prefers, "Nothingnesses of emptiness". Or, again, as Spurgeon, "Nothings of nonentity". How the soul recoils from this who has learned to trust in the God of truth. Note the important "But". They regard their lying vanities, "But I...", says the Psalmist, "I trust in the Lord". Indeed, he not only recoiled from the worthlessness of idol worship, it was hateful to him. Idolatry displaced and despised David's God and so idolaters were not his friends.

The remembrance of God's mercy (2617) caused David to exult. It was lovingkindness indeed, and great goodness, and he would be glad and rejoice at every thought of it. Whether this is, "I will be glad and rejoice", or, as some think, "Let me be glad and rejoice", is not very relevant. There was, and ever would be, joy in the heart of the Psalmist when he remembered God's kindness and love toward him. Jehovah had graciously considered him, regarded him, perceived his trouble and his need, and had taken note of his servant's distresses. Nor was this just a divine contemplation of David's trouble, it was intervention and help in time of need. Jehovah had not permitted David to be shut up at the mercy of the enemy, but rather had He set His servant in a large place, a broad place of freedom as in Psalm 18.19. David had cause to be glad and rejoice. The two words are so similar, a joyous duplication of the gratitude in his heart. Yet, even as he exults at thoughts of the lovingkindness of God, David thinks once again of his trouble, and there follows a renewed outpouring of his grief and its effect upon him physically. Compare Psalm 6.

Verses 9-13: Slander and Sighing

He asks for renewed mercy (2603). "Have mercy upon me, O Lord". This "mercy" is not the same as the former word of v.7. Here he asks for pity, for grace and favour. He feels his great need. "I am in trouble", he laments. His grief is revealed in his countenance and has affected him physically. Maclaren tells it all so feelingly; "The physical and mental effects of anxiety are graphically described. Sunken eyes, enfeebled soul, wasted body, are gaunt witnesses of his distress. Cares seem to him to have gnawed his very bones, so weak is he. All he can do is to sigh". So much of David's life was spent in grief, and perhaps the greatest grief was that much of his trouble was the consequence of his own iniquity, as he admits here. His enemies reproached him, and this grieved him much. But his neighbours and his acquaintances, and all who knew him, saw it too, and when they saw him they shunned him. Neighbours, acquaintances, and onlookers, alike turned away from him. He was out of favour with them all. He was a reproach to all so that they were afraid and fled from him, as if reluctant to acknowledge him lest it would incur the displeasure of others. This was hard to bear, to be so despised by so many.

Poor David. He felt as forgotten as if he were dead, and as useless as a broken vessel to be cast aside. He was like a potsherd, discarded with the refuse. Then there was the slander (1681), the whispering, the backbiting, which somehow came to his ears. He had become the butt of insult and ridicule. On every side they gathered furtively in a campaign of slander against him, spreading their evil reports and cruelly defaming him. They plotted together, took counsel against him, and "devised" (2061) to take away his life. Was it any wonder that he complained that his years were spent with sighing?

Verses 14-18: Renewed Confidence

What can the grieving Psalmist do? To whom, or to where, can he turn in his grief? This section of new hope and confidence begins with an emphatic, "But I - I trusted in thee, O Lord". He has considered all those ranged around him for his hurt, and he exclaims, "But as for me - I trust in Jehovah". This is reminiscent of the spirit and language of the shepherd boy who faced Goliath in the Valley of Elah (1 Sam 17.45-46). David turns away from them all to his only resource. "Trust" (982) is confidence, hope, dependence, boldness, even to the point of being free of care. In his afflictions David would so trust, saying, "Thou art my God" (430). The mighty Elohim was greater by far than all his enemies, so that he could safely say, "My times are in thy hand". This was hope indeed. "Sunrise at midnight", says Maclaren. It was light in the darkness for the Psalmist. David's life, like the lives of so many saints, was a series of crises. There were times of prosperity and times of adversity. There were times of sorrow and times of joy. There were times of triumph and times of tragedy. Jehovah knew them all. David's God was sovereign and could regulate the changing periods of life for His own glory. The paths of life may be perplexing, but Jehovah could deliver from the enemy and from the persecutor.

David of course must have been familiar with the priestly blessing of Numbers 6.25. Does he repeat it here? "Make thy face to shine upon thy servant", he asks. To live and walk in the light of the divine countenance is sunshine indeed. It dispels the darkness for the troubled soul and brings salvation from the cares of life. "Mercy" (2617) is as in v.7 except that here it is plural. It is like a treasury, holding inexhaustible riches greater than the need of the saints. To these resources the Psalmist appeals, desiring mercy in abundance so that, as he has already asked in v.1, he may not be ashamed before his enemies. Rather let the enemies be ashamed, let them be abashed and confused in their wickedness, and, as the voice of the Psalmist is heard calling upon God, let the voice of the enemy be silent (1826) as the grave (SH^{e}OL - 7585). He asks that the lying lips of the whispering slanderers be silenced (481). They had spoken falsehoods, and had insolently treated the righteous with contempt. In their pride and arrogance they had spoken grievous (6277) things, but there was One mightier than they who could render them dumb, and David longs for this.

Verses 19-22: The Greatness of God's Goodness

The abundance of God's goodness is likened to a treasure store. Goodness and gladness, grace and glory, prosperity and joy are laid up (6845) as treasure for those who fear Him. These good things are hidden from the sons of men, from the hostile world, and, just as the divine treasure is hidden, so, too, does He hide those who trust Him. In that storehouse of God's goodness His saints are secreted in the covert of His presence. He hides them with His other treasures in His pavilion, kept safe from the proud men of the world, with their contentious and quarrelling tongues. They are in the tender security of His embrace, a quiet and tranquil retreat from the noise and bustle of the restless society without.

The thought of it all brings forth the exclamation, "Blessed be the Lord!". Praise and adoration are in order at the remembrance of God's goodness. His lovingkindness is marvellous, and He has become to His people as a fenced city, keeping them in safety. Many, however, will prefer to read this literally; "He hath shewed me his marvellous kindness in a strong city", and will relate it historically to some of David's triumphs. Was it, then, Ziklag of 1 Samuel 30? Or was it Mahanaim of 2 Samuel 17? Or perhaps Jerusalem itself? It may be better to understand it as first suggested, that Jehovah had become to the Psalmist as a city of refuge, a safe retreat from his enemies and from the world.

David remembers his former agitation, and his fear that Jehovah had forgotten him, that the Lord was neither seeing him nor hearing him. It had been a hasty thought, that he had been "cut off from God's eyes". But Jehovah had heard. The Psalmist's haste (2648) was a moment of panic, of alarm. Jehovah sees and knows the troubles of His servants, and He hears the cry of every sincere suppliant. The plaintive voice of His servant David had reached Him. He both heard and answered.

Verses 23-24: Comfort and Courage

The Psalm concludes with an exhortation to the faithful, a call to love the Lord. It is a call to every saint and to all the saints. There is just cause for His people in every place and in every age to love Him, and David gives two reasons for such love. Jehovah both preserves (5341) and requites (7999) in accordance with His divine knowledge. He preserves the faithful. He keeps them, guards them, and watches over them. They are His and He protects them. The "proud doer", however, He will requite for his proud deeds. He will recompense what evil has been done to His people, and He will reward abundantly, plentifully. There is a divine hatred of pride, and what the wicked have done in the haughtiness of their hearts will be requited accordingly and with justice.

As the Psalmist had called upon "all ye his saints", so now he calls upon "all ye that hope in the Lord". David is really calling upon kindred spirits. This is the man who, himself, loves the Lord and who, in the midst of the most severe trials, takes courage and hopes in Jehovah. He knows from personal experience that the Lord will impart strength to those who, in courage and in patience, wait for Him, and he seems, therefore, to have the right to exhort others. Note the repeated, "All ye"; "All ye". God's people are a variety of people. They differ in background, in temperament, in personality, and in capacity of both faith and knowledge. But they are all His, and the call is to all the saints to take courage. This was the word of the Lord through Moses to Israel (Deut 31.6), and the exhortation of the Lord to Joshua (Josh 1.6). It was, too, the word of the people to Joshua as they pledged their loyalty to him (Josh 1.18). Be of good courage!

Alexander Maclaren sums it up so beautifully: "Therefore the last result of contemplating God's ways with His servants is an incentive to courage, strength, and patient waiting for the Lord".

PSALM 32

Introduction

This is so obviously a "Penitential Psalm", and it is the second of those seven which are so described. Psalm 6 is the first of these, and perhaps the best known of them is the touching Psalm 51. Other "Penitential Psalms" are Psalms 38, 102, 130 and 143.

Psalm 32 is also the first of thirteen Psalms which have the word "Maschil" in their titles. "Maschil" (4905) is derived from a root which signifies "to be wise" or "to instruct", and a "Maschil" Psalm is therefore thought to be a didactic, or reflective poem, intended for instruction. If it should be objected that there is little doctrine or theology in this particular "Maschil" Psalm, nevertheless there is instruction in righteousness (2 Tim 3.16), when one saint shares with others what he has learned by experience in the school of God. In Psalm 51 David promised that, being restored, he would teach the ways of God to others who had sinned, and here he is fulfilling that promise. The other "Maschil" Psalms are Psalms 42, 44, 45, 52-55, 74, 78, 88, 89, 142.

The Davidic authorship of this Psalm is confirmed in Romans 4.6-8, where Paul, by inspiration, attributes the Psalm to David, and there seems to be little reason to doubt that it was, like Psalm 51, occasioned by the sin of his adultery with Bathsheba, and the untimely death of Uriah as recorded in 2 Samuel 11. For many months, perhaps for a whole year, David lived in dark impenitence, until, broken down by the ministry of Nathan the prophet, he bowed in contrition before the Lord, wrote Psalm 51, and pleaded for pardon and peace. Psalm 32 describes the misery of a saint who has sinned. It tells of the serious physical and mental consequences of unconfessed and unforgiven sin and the eventual blessedness of forgiveness and restoration.

The Psalm may be divided as follows. In the two opening verses David speaks of the blessedness of pardon from sin. In verses 3-5 he recalls his own personal sad experience during those days before his restoration. This part contains a double "Selah". The section which follows, verses 6-7, also ends with a "Selah" and is an application of the Psalmist's experience to others. Verses 8-10 are the voice of God to the forgiven one, and the Psalm concludes in verse 11 with a call to the righteous to rejoice.

Verses 1-2: The Blessedness of Forgiveness

How well David knew both the misery of broken communion with God and the joy of forgiveness and pardon. The word "blessed" (835) signifies happiness. It is the opening word of the whole Psalter in Psalm 1.1. The blessedness of the first Psalm is the happiness of the man who walks apart from sin. The blessedness of Psalm 32 is the happiness of a man who has sinned and has been forgiven. Perhaps here it is more of an exclamation, "O the happiness of the man!". David's sin had been great and Jehovah's forgiveness was, accordingly and necessarily, equally great, and David rejoices. In these opening verses those three great words are brought together, sin (2401), transgression (6588), and iniquity (5771). They describe sin in all its forms. Sin is a missing of the mark, a deviation from the path of right and duty. Transgression is the rebellion of a will that refuses to be subject to laws or prohibitions. Iniquity is a perverse and depraved practising of known sin. David knew what all three were, and he knew also the sad consequences of broken communion with the Lord and a loss of the joy of God's presence. Forgiveness (5375) is like the lifting of a burden or the removal of a barrier. It was a joy to be so absolved from sin. To know that the sin was covered (3680) was to know that it was now hidden from heaven's view, and to know that the Lord would not impute (2803) the iniquity. He would not reckon it, or charge it to a man's account any more. Davidson describes it all as "The lifting of a burden; the protecting from deserved wrath; release from a justly incurred debt". This was joy indeed, but such forgiveness demanded that the sinner should come without guile, sincerely penitent, and genuinely acknowledging the failure, pleading God's mercy alone, as David indeed had done (Ps 51.1). Then, having so come, with no guile, this sincere transparency ought now to characterise the pardoned sinner living in the joy of his restoration to God. Note that it is truly possible, not only to be forgiven, but also to know it, and to have the joy of it. How blessed for the believer today to hear that lovely benediction, "Be of good cheer; thy sins be forgiven thee" (Mt 9.2).

Verses 3-5: The Distress of Impenitence

For many months after his adultery with Bathsheba and the murder of her husband Uriah, David had lived impenitent. He had broken three commandments - the tenth, the seventh, and the sixth - and had sought to silence his conscience. These were not sins of ignorance. He had sinned with full knowledge of the wrong, and it was grievous. To seek to stifle the pangs of conscience was taking its toll of him mentally and physically. He was becoming like an aged man. His bones, his strength, his bodily condition, were being affected by the disturbed state of his mind. For a man such as David, who had experienced, since boyhood days, the blessedness of the presence of Jehovah, now to lose the sense of that divine presence, and to live in the consciousness of unconfessed sin, was well nigh unbearable. His whole physical frame was being affected by it, and would be until there was confession and forgiveness and restoration. His distress was such that he groaned in it. In the privacy of his chambers he groaned in grief, and yet, for all those months, he refused to repent of the evil.

His sorrow was continuous. "All the day long", he says, "...day and night". The hand of the Lord was heavy upon him. Until there was repentance, Jehovah would give him no rest in his troubled conscience. His strength was dried up. Spurgeon writes of him, "The sap of his soul was dried, and the body through sympathy appeared to be bereft of its needful fluids. The oil was almost gone from the lamp of life, and the flame flickered as if it would soon expire". The man was in spiritual drought. David knew the desert condition of Judea in summertime. "The drought of summer", he calls it. From the middle of the month of May until the middle of October Jerusalem has so very little rain, if any at all, and the extreme heat of the July/August/September months produces a parched barrenness in which vegetation becomes withered and dried. David was so familiar with these conditions, and they seemed to illustrate his own; and all this, not only because of his sin, but because there was no acknowledgement of it and no repentance. But this must change.

Verse 5, which recalls his confession, is enclosed in two "Selahs". The minor mournful strains are to be replaced by the joyous sounding cymbals of praise. The joy of restoration is near but the pathway to it must begin with an acknowledgement of the sin. "I acknowledged my sin", David says. Literally, he made it known unto God. Not, of course, that God did not know it, but true penitence is an honest laying bare before God of what the sinner knows of his sin. It is a free and open confession of the wrong. The law of the offerings for sin required it; "He shall confess that he hath sinned in that thing" (Lev 5.5). David will now hide nothing. How very similar is the story of the Psalmist to the story of the prodigal son of Luke 15. "I said, I will confess...and thou forgavest". The penitent having done his part, Jehovah in grace does His, and forgives. "If we confess our sins, he is faithful and just to forgive us our sins" (1 Jn 1.9). David speaks of "the iniquity of my sin". The expression signifies the complicated evil manner in which he had sinned. He had coveted his neighbour's wife. He had committed adultery with her. He had contrived to conceal what he had done, and he had arranged the death of Uriah. There had been idleness, self-indulgence, lust, adultery, pretence, hypocrisy, and murder. He knew it all to be wrong, but he did it nevertheless. It was iniquitous. It was sin. It was, as he says, "the iniquity of my sin", but Jehovah forgave. How rightly is the verse enclosed in those two Selahs!

Verses 6-7: An Exhortation to Others

That teacher teaches well who teaches from experience. So it is with David. He will recount what Jehovah has done for him and will encourage others to resort to Him in times of trouble. It is said that the experience of one is the encouragement of another. He appeals to the godly (2623), to those who, as saints of God, desired holiness of life, and who would live faithful to the Lord. "For this", for this reason, because of this, he says that God is merciful and gracious and ready to forgive, as had been demonstrated in David's case. For this he appeals to every saint to resort to God while and when there is opportunity. "When thou mayest be found". Is there an implied warning here, that there is the possibility of procrastinating until it may be too late to find a place of repentance and pardon? "Seek ye the Lord while he may be found" (Is 55.6). The saint who repairs to God is safe. He is, as it were, on high ground when troubles would come like a flood of great waters. They cannot reach or overwhelm the man who trusts in Jehovah.

David has found Jehovah to be his safe retreat. "Thou art my hiding place" (5643). He had found a shelter, a covert, a refuge, in his God. He would so be preserved from trouble (6862), protected from his adversaries and from distress. He was now encompassed with songs of deliverance, encircled with strains of rejoicing for what the Lord had wrought for him. He had exchanged the groaning for singing. Having been besieged by troubles he was now compassed by mercies. Wherever he looked there were reasons for praise. The section concludes with another "Selah". It is time for meditation and for a lifting up of the heart in praise and gratitude to God.

Verses 8-10: Jehovah's Response

After the "Selah" interlude the pronoun changes. Now Jehovah is speaking to His servant and promises divine guidance, if there is willingness to obey. The voice of God teaches and the eye of God watches, and the willing saint is thus guarded and guided along the pathway of life. The promise of God is threefold. He will instruct, He will teach, He will guide (3289). This latter word signifies "counsel". Literally it is, "I will counsel thee with my eye upon thee" (RV). In a tender watchfulness Jehovah guides His saints along the way in which He would have them walk, and He desires their willingness to walk in that way.

The believer is contrasted with the horse and with the mule. They are sometimes noted for their stubborn resistance, and the saint is not to be like them. They have no understanding, and must be forcibly and physically restrained and curbed by bit and bridle. They would at times run ahead unbidden. They would at other times refuse to move at all. But that understanding (995) which is lacking in the dumb animal must not be lacking in men. The obedient saint must exercise intelligent discernment and discretion. He must listen for the divine command and be prompted along the way with the eye of God upon him. Then, guided by the Word of God and by the Spirit of God, the believer can look back and say with another, "I being in the way, the Lord led me" (Gen 24.27).

The wicked can expect many sorrows (4341). Like stubborn horses and mules they bring bruises upon themselves. Sin brings pain and suffering with it, both physically and mentally, and at the end there is the ultimate grief of the judgment of God. It is different with the man who trusts in Jehovah. That man is not, of course, immune to sorrow, but having made the Lord his refuge he is at all times encompassed by mercy (2617). He sees the loving-kindness of the Lord everywhere. To quote Albert Barnes, "He shall be surrounded with mercy, as one is surrounded by the air or by the sunlight. He shall find mercy and favour everywhere - at home, abroad; by day, by night; in society, in solitude; in sickness, in health; in life, in death; in time, in eternity. He shall walk amidst mercies; he shall die amidst mercies; he shall live in a better world in the midst of eternal mercies".

Verse 11: A Call to Joy

How glad David must have been to exchange his sorrow for the happiness of the man repentant and forgiven. He will have others share his joy with him and the Psalm concludes with a call to the righteous to join him in his rejoicing. His joy is "in the Lord", and Paul echoes David's sentiments in Philippians 4.4, "Rejoice in the Lord alway: and again I say, Rejoice". David's joy is unbounded. It is a "shout" (7442) he asks for. The word indicates a ringing cry. He would have all the righteous unite in praising, and he would have all the world to hear their shout of joy. Thus the Psalm of the pardoned penitent ends on the high note of jubilation for sins forgiven and a saint restored to the joy of the Lord.

PSALM 33

Introduction

This Psalm bears no title. In the forty-one Psalms of the First Book this is unusual, the only other exceptions being Psalms 1 and 2, which are introductory to the Psalter, and Psalm 10, which is so closely adjoined to Psalm 9. The LXX attributes it to David but there is no indication in the Psalm itself as to authorship, date of composition, or the circumstances in which it was written.

Many have remarked upon the symmetry of the Psalm. There are three verses or six lines, at the beginning, which form one strophe. Similarly, there are three verses, six lines, at the conclusion, and between these two strophes lies the main body of the Psalm. The opening strophe, verses 1-3, is a fervent call to the righteous to rejoice in the Lord and to praise Him. Verses 4-19 offer a variety of reasons for this praise and the believer's grounds for trusting. The closing strophe, verses 20-22, is the avowal of the saints that they will rejoice and trust.

Verses 1-3: Rejoice ye Righteous!

The Psalm opens with the call with which the preceding Psalm closes. Only the righteous can truly rejoice in the Lord and praise Him, and it is fitting that the righteous should do so. Praise offered by the lips of the ungodly must be hypocritical and empty, but for the upright it is comely (5000). Called by the prophet Isaiah "the garment of praise" (61.3), it becomes an ornament of beauty for the believer, adorning him with a comeliness not seen in the worldling. However much the men or women of the world may adorn the body, their sought after beauty is but worthless tinsel compared with the moral beauty of the rejoicing, praising believer. The call to rejoice (7442) is an invitation to sing aloud, to shout for joy, so that others may know. It is a repetition of the word "shout", the ringing cry of Psalm 32.11.

Old Testament saints were familiar with a variety of musical instruments, which they used both in personal and in national worship. Three of these instruments may be indicated here in v.2. There is the harp (3658), the psaltery (5035), and an instrument of ten strings (6218). It will be noticed however, that in the AV the word "and", after "psaltery", is in italics, supplied by the translators. The RV omits this conjunction, reading, "Sing praises unto him with the psaltery of ten strings", indicating that the psaltery, or lute, was the ten-stringed instrument. Whichever is correct, the instrument was but an accompaniment to the voice. Skilful playing, in itself was not the praise or worship which could only be rendered by the singing voice of the righteous, praising the Lord from the heart with the words of suitably composed Psalms.

The exhortation was to sing a new song. There are several references in Scripture to a new song, six of these being in the Psalms - 40.3; 96.1; 98.1; 144.9 and 149.1. There is also a reference in Isaiah 42.10, and two in the Book of the Revelation at 5.9 and 14.3. He who says, "Behold, I make all things new" (Rev 21.5), has put a new song into the hearts and mouths of His people, and it pleases Him that His saints should give expression to this and so praise Him. It is a song which only the righteous can sing, in the enjoyment of a new relationship with heaven and with the Lord. It is the song of the redeemed.

Verses 4-19: Reasons for Praise

The reasons for praising the Lord, which the Psalmist now gives, are manifold. Jehovah has moral glory, and creatorial glory. He also has a governmental glory in His rule over the nations, and He has a providential glory in His tender care and watchfulness over them that fear Him. All are grounds for rendering due praise. True worship is intelligent worship, based upon some appreciation of the character of God. As another has said, "Worship is the honour and adoration rendered to God for what He is in Himself, and for what He means to those who render it" (J.N. Darby). So the Psalmist will now furnish sound reasons for praise and worship. What God is, what He has done, and what He is doing, all require the praise of His people.

The first reason for praise is a remembrance of God's moral attributes. The Psalmist gathers a cluster of lovely words to describe Jehovah's character. There is righteousness and truth, justice and goodness. In His word and in His work all is marked by uprightness. Whatever He decrees, whatever He performs, all is in keeping with His perfection, all is in conformity with His moral glory. It is a first and basic reason for praising Him. Jehovah loves righteousness and justice, and in spite of the moral failings of men, the earth is full of His goodness (2617), His lovingkindness. These characteristics are true of Messiah who loved righteousness and hated wickedness (Ps 45.7).

Praise is next due to God at the remembrance of His creatorial power. His eternal power and Godhead are manifest in creation (Rom 1.20). It was by His faithful word that the heavens were made. Again and again in the Genesis account of creation we read, "And God said…and it was so", until, all completed, we read, "Thus the heavens and the earth were finished, and all the host of them" (Gen 2.1), sun, moon, and stars. The word here in the Psalm rendered "breath" (7307) is the word which is translated "Spirit" in Genesis 1.2. The earth, the heavens, and the waters were all ordered by His word. Genesis 1.10 speaks of "the gathering together of the waters", and Genesis 1.16 tells us that "he made the stars also". Well might men fear, with a reverential awe, Him who spake and it was done, who commanded and it stood fast. He could speak a world out of nothing, and the message of His creation goes out to all the world, as in Psalm 19, so that men are, as Paul says, without excuse (Rom 1.20). The Psalmist, whoever he was, was familiar with the inspired Genesis account of the creative might of Jehovah.

The writer continues to find reasons for praising God, and in pursuit of his theme he now turns from creation to history, to recount God's dealings with the nations. How early did men rebel against the Creator, but in divine sovereignty He frustrates their wicked intentions. Notice how the counsel of the heathen in v.10 is contrasted with the counsel of the Lord in v.11, and notice also that the word rendered "devices" (4284) in v.10 is exactly the same as the word "thoughts" in v.11. So the counsel of rebellious nations is brought to nought while the counsel of the Lord stands fast, and the evil thoughts of men are rendered of none effect while the thoughts of God's heart are unchanged from generation to generation. Man's counsels and devices fail. God's counsels and thoughts abide. Jehovah rules in the kingdoms of men. Well might one ask, in the language of the second Psalm, "Why do the heathen rage, and the people imagine a vain thing?".

From his consideration of the heathen, the nations in general, the Psalmist now turns to one nation in particular, the favoured nation, chosen of God. Israel was His own peculiar treasure, His inheritance from among the nations. Their God was Jehovah. In this they were to be distinguished from the surrounding nations. All around them men worshipped idols. False deities abounded, but it was different with Israel. He was their God and they were His people and they were accordingly a blessed nation. Moses, who knew them so well, could say, "Happy art thou, O Israel: who is like unto thee, O people saved by the Lord" (Deut 33.29). But from His abode in the heavens Jehovah beholds all men everywhere. He can contemplate them all and He is Lord of all. From His heavenly habitation He looks upon men in their earthly habitation and perceives all that they do. He knows the minds of men and can foresee all their intentions. He can anticipate all their planned actions. He considers (995), discerns, all their works.

Against the might of Jehovah there is no human power which can prevail. No king, with a multitude of forces, and with much strength, can successfully oppose Jehovah. Pharaoh and his hosts are testimony to this

(Ex 15.1-19). Neither cavalry nor military might will avail to deliver. The "horse", mentioned in v.17, was a symbol of earthly power, but those who would afflict God's people must learn this, that no human power is powerful enough when Jehovah is on the side of His people. His eye is constantly upon these people. He watches over them that fear Him. His saints are blessed when they hope in Him and trust in His lovingkindness. Neither sword nor famine can touch them. He can deliver them at all times, preserving them from death, keeping them alive through all adverse conditions.

Verses 20-22: Waiting! Rejoicing! Trusting!

The Psalm has been called "A Song of Deliverance", and so it concludes, on a high note of trust and joy and thanksgiving. The opening words of this final stanza are most interesting, "Our soul waiteth for the Lord". "Our soul" (5315), may of course be simply a synonym for the pronoun "we", but perhaps something more than this is intended. "Soul" signifies the heart, the emotions, the desires, the deep feelings of the inner being of a man. Is the use of the word here an indication, therefore, of the intensity of genuine longing with which the nation waited for the Lord?

This "waiteth" (2442), is an unusual word in the Psalms, found only once more in Psalm 106.13, where the contrast is touching. The word means, "to tarry for", or, "to long for". It is not "waiting upon the Lord", as in Isaiah 40.31: "They that wait upon the Lord shall renew their strength". Here in Psalm 33.20 the people are waiting for the Lord. In that only other occurrence of the word, in Psalm 106, it is recalled, with sadness, that the nation which had been redeemed and which had believed God's Word and sung His praise, soon forgot His works and "waited not" for His counsel, but ran lusting in the wilderness. The people of Psalm 33 will wait for the Lord. He was, after all, their help and their shield. It is reminiscent of the Song of Moses, "O people saved by the Lord, the shield of thy help" (Deut 33.29). To whom else could they look in times of trouble? He was their succour and their defence, and they would wait, with sincere, intense longing, for Him.

As they tarried for the Lord they rejoiced. "Our heart" (3820), is similar to, but different from, "our soul" of the previous verse. This now signifies the intelligence with which they rejoiced. It was not a sentimental feeling, this joy. It was born in the mind, in understanding and wisdom. It was the fruit of knowledge gained by their experience of the One in whose name they had trusted. In boldness and in confidence they could continue to trust and rejoice.

The Psalm closes with a touching, and earnest, if brief, prayer. According as they had hoped in the Lord, so they desired that His mercy, His lovingkindness, should be upon them. The prayer may indeed be brief, but, as Spurgeon remarks, it is a large and comprehensive appeal. They had trusted. Would Jehovah now acknowledge their trust and reward it with mercy? The promise of Isaiah 49.23 is very precious; "They shall not be ashamed that wait for me".

PSALM 34

Introduction

The title assigns this Psalm to David and associates it with that sad period in his life when, as a fugitive from the jealousy of Saul, he had fled to Nob, and thence to Gath for refuge, as recorded in 1 Samuel 21. What memories of that day in the valley of Elah must have filled the mind of David as he now carried the sword of Goliath right into the homeland of the giant. How bold was the shepherd boy who had slain Goliath of Gath, trusting alone in the Lord of Hosts, the God of the armies of Israel, but now actually fleeing to Philistine country for safety from Saul.

A problem has been imagined, in that the king of Gath was, at that time, called Achish, whereas here, in the title of the Psalm, he is called Abimelech. But there is no discrepancy. Abimelech was not a name, but a dynastic title, as Pharaoh, or Caesar, or Agag among the Amalekites, and was borne by a succession of princes. Abimelech means "my Father the King". The king's personal name was Achish.

When the servants of Achish advised the king regarding David's identity as the true king of the land (1 Sam 21.11), the one of whom the people had sung, saying that Saul had slain his thousands, and David his ten thousands, David was afraid. Commentators are divided as to whether his subsequent behaviour was right or wrong. Plumer speaks of "judicious commentators who give no opinion". David feigned madness before the king of Gath. He scratched the doors of the gate with his fingers and dribbled saliva down his beard, until Achish said, "The man is mad…have I need of mad men…shall this fellow come into my house?". David left Gath and made his escape to the cave Adullam. It would seem that Psalm 34 was thereafter composed with his experience in mind, and it may well have been written in the cave of Adullam.

This is an alphabetical Psalm, but the acrostic arrangement is not perfect. Dr Cohen explains that there is "an omission of a verse beginning with *vau* and the addition at the end, of a verse with the initial letter *pe*". Davison comments similarly, "An acrostic Psalm, the couplets in regular order beginning with the letters of the Hebrew alphabet successively; except that *Vau* is omitted and an additional couplet is found at the end, beginning with *Pe*". This addition is an adjustment for the omission and completes twenty-two verses, in keeping with twenty-two letters in the Hebrew alphabet. The reason for this irregularity is not apparent. See Section 6 of the general Introduction to the Psalms in this Commentary, and compare also the comment on the introduction to Psalm 25, the first of the alphabetical Psalms.

The only name of God employed in the Psalm is the great name Jehovah which occurs sixteen times. For comment on Jehovah see the footnote to Psalm 1 in the Commentary.

Since the historical occasion for the Psalm's composition is clearly given, it must therefore be dated around 1062 - 60BC.

A simple division of the twenty-two verses will view the first seven verses as thanksgiving for divine deliverance. The second seven verses, 8-14, present a series of admonitions, and the final eight verses, 15-22, anticipate the ultimate salvation of the righteous and the judgment of the wicked.

Verses 1-7: Thanksgiving and Praise

The opening words of the Psalm, "I will bless the Lord", are so characteristic of the Psalter. To bless the Lord is to praise Him, and this the Psalmists delighted to do constantly; but to be able to bless Him "at all times" is devotion to Him indeed. It signifies a holy resolve to praise Him whatever the circumstances, whether in joy or in sorrow. This would have been the mind of Paul who was able to say, "I have learned, in whatsoever state I am, therewith to be content. I know both how to be abased, and I know how to abound: everywhere and in all things I am instructed both to be full and to be hungry, both to abound and to suffer need" (Phil 4.11-12). I will bless the Lord at all times. "Praise" (8416) may be thanksgiving or adoration, national or personal, public or private. Here it is David's own expression of gratitude to Jehovah. The praise of God was continually in His mouth.

It was fitting that he should be constantly praising, for he gloried in the Lord. His boast (1984) was in the Lord, and it was therefore right that he should praise Him. He knew, too, that the humble, the meek and lowly of Israel, would hear his praising, and rejoice. Praise gladdens the hearts of the saints, and it was ever David's desire that others would join with him in this holy exercise. He would not magnify the Lord alone, so he called on kindred spirits to magnify the Lord with him. Together they would exalt His name. To "magnify" (1431) the Lord is to acknowledge and promote His greatness, to praise His might and His power. The gods of the heathen were not as David's God. Jehovah was great and His people must exult in that greatness. Delitzsch says that to exalt the name of Jehovah is "to place God's exalted name as high in one's heart, in word, and in deed, as it is in itself".

"I sought the Lord", David writes. When? Did he, even in the moments of his pretended insanity, lift his heart to the Lord for deliverance from the Philistines? To David, his own rather dubious method of seeking escape from Gath did not seem inconsistent with calling upon God in continuing trust. What encouragement and example is this to all saints, that, even when they have sought to effect their own deliverance, the Lord will hear their feeble cries for His help, and will graciously answer. David was indeed delivered, not only from his troubles but also from his fears. This, he knows, has been true of all those who in times of distress have looked to Jehovah. A look of faith to Jehovah cannot ever be in vain. They looked to Him and were lightened (5102). The word signifies "to shine as a lamp; to be radiant". Maclaren says it so beautifully; "Whoever turns his face to Jehovah will receive reflected brightness on his face; as when a mirror is directed sunwards, the dark surface will flash into sudden glory. Weary eyes will gleam. Faces turned to the sun are sure to be radiant". No shame or disappointment shows in the faces of those who look to Jehovah.

David now speaks of "This poor man" who cried. Is this a personal reference to himself? Or is it, as some think, a general reference to all those who, in their trials, have cried to Jehovah as he did? Either way, the import is the same. "Poor" (6041), is rendered "humble" in Psalm 9.12, "afflicted" in Psalm 18.27, and "lowly" in Proverbs 3.34. The various renderings bring out the full meaning of the word, and such was poor David in Gath. It was an earnest cry, and the Lord heard, and He who had delivered him from all his fears, saved him out of all his troubles (6869). From distress and anguish, from adversity and affliction, Jehovah will deliver those who look to Him.

There are diverse views as to the identity of "the angel of the Lord", of whom David speaks here in v.7, and again in Psalm 35.5. Some think that this is characteristic, simply meaning "angels", in the plural. A comparison has been noted with the angelic hosts sent to Jacob at Mahanaim in Gen 32.1-2. The word "encampeth" suggests to some the idea of camps of armies. Others think that the expression signifies any heavenly messenger sent for the protection of believers. Many, however, prefer to see in the words a pre-incarnate appearance of the Son of God, described in Isaiah 63.9 as "the angel of his presence", and in Joshua 5.14 as "the captain of the host of the Lord". Maclaren speaks for these latter when he says, "He is '*the* angel of God's face', the personal revealer of His presence and nature. His functions correspond to those of the Word in John's Gospel, and these, conjoined with the supremacy indicated in His name, suggest that, the Angel of the Lord, is, in fact, the everlasting Son of the Father". He continues, "The Psalmist did not know the full force of the name, but he believed that there was a Person, in an eminent and singular sense God's messenger, who would cast his protection round the devout, and bid inferior heavenly beings draw their impregnable ranks about them. Christians can tell more than he could, of the Bearer of the name. It becomes them to be all the surer of His protection".

Verses 8-14: Admonitions to the Godly

The experience of divine deliverance moves a man to appeal to others to come and share in the same joy. He who has himself tasted of the blessing of God will inevitably want others to participate in the blessing that he has found. "O taste and see...", cries the Psalmist with a certain sincere zeal, and earnestly desiring that other men should enjoy that which he enjoys. The goodness of the Lord is beyond explaining or expounding. It is greater than words. It can only be fully known by experience. "Taste and see!" Consider! Perceive! The Lord is good, and that man is a happy man, a blessed man, who trusts in Him. Experience is better than theory, and the Psalmist invites others to trust (2620), to make the Lord their refuge, and know experimentally the joy and the confidence of those whose hope is in Jehovah.

The Psalmist knows the importance and value of the fear of the Lord. "Fear" (3372) is not, of course, a slavish fear. The word denotes a reverence, a holy awe, which holds God in honour and respect. Such fear of the Lord is the beginning of knowledge (Prov 1.7), and the beginning of wisdom (Ps 111.10; Prov 9.10). Those who are His saints should always be characterised by this reverential regard for Him in whom they trust. In the midst of men, of whom it is said that there is no fear of God before their eyes (Rom 3.18; Ps 36.1), God's people must be holy. They must be true to the fact that they are indeed "saints" (6918), holy ones, set apart in the world for His pleasure and for His glory. There is, too, a blessed recompense for trusting and fearing the Lord. Like an echo of the familiar words of an earlier Psalm, David says that "there is no want to them that fear him". His personal experience was, "I shall not want" (Ps 23.1). Even young lions, he proposes, can at times suffer hunger. King of beasts though they be, with all their ability and agility, their prowess and strength, they may sometimes fail to provide for themselves. But for those who look to the Lord for their provision it is not so. They shall not want (2637), they shall not lack, any good thing. "Come, ye children", he now invites. "Children" (1121) is more often translated "sons". A relationship may indeed be intended, but it is the relationship of a teacher to younger men who are willing to learn from him, almost like a Rabbi-disciple relationship. Is David appealing to those men, likely young men, who were now gathered to him, and with him, in the cave of Adullam? He is not addressing children in terms of years, but those who are prepared to listen to him, as a pupil will listen to a teacher, as youth will listen to experience, those whom he may call "my sons", as so often occurs in the Book of Proverbs. He desires to teach them the fear of the Lord. It is the beginning of wisdom, the beginning of knowledge, and he would have them instructed in such an important matter.

Many have noted the similarity of a number of these phrases to the language of the Book of Proverbs. Does a man desire life? Does he long for days of enjoyment of good things? These are not merely desires for long life and many days, although longevity was considered a sign of God's approval and blessing. Here it is rather life as lived to the full, in the joy of the good things which accompany a life lived in the fear of God.

There now follows counsel for those who would so live in the fear of God and enjoy life. Evil speaking must be shunned. The tongue and the lips must be guarded. Deceit, lying, slander, backbiting, talebearing, reviling and railing, and such like, are not compatible with piety. The tongue is a little member, says James, but as a small helm may turn a great ship, and as a little fire may start a destructive conflagration, so it is with the tongue (Jas 3.4-6). It must be guarded by the man who fears God. The safe path for the believer is to depart from evil in all its forms and do good, to seek peace and pursue it. The godly man will prefer peace, and he may endeavour to promote it, but in difficult circumstances he may have to pursue it. He must at all times seek to create harmony among his fellows, and be at peace, too, in his own heart and conscience. He must run from the evil and run after the good, or, as the prophet says, "Cease to do evil; learn to do well (Is 1.16-17).

Verses 15-22: The Righteous and the Evil-doers

The eyes and ears of Jehovah are ever towards the righteous. He sees them and he hears them. He knows their distresses and their desires. He takes knowledge of their necessities and their wants. He turns towards those whose faces are turned towards Him (v.5). But if the eyes of the Lord are toward the righteous, His face is against those who do evil. The "face (6440) of the Lord" is a synonym for His presence and He may manifest that awful Presence in wrath against ungodliness. The face which will shine upon the believer (Num 6.26) will be set against the evildoer. He will cause the unrighteous man to be forgotten. This is similar to Psalm 9.5-6, where, concerning the enemies of the Lord it is said, "Thou hast put out their name for ever and ever...their memorial is perished with them".

When the righteous cry the Lord hears, and delivers them from their troubles, as the Psalmist had personally experienced (v.6). It has always been so, as will be remembered in the words of Jehovah concerning His ancient people in their bondage, "I have heard their groaning, and am come down to deliver them" (Acts 7.34). "I know their sorrows", He said, "behold, the cry of the children of Israel is come unto Me" (Ex 3.7, 9).

It will be noticed that the words "The righteous", at the beginning of v.17, are in italics. They have been supplied by the translators. Maclaren explains, "The verse has no subject expressed, but the supplement of the AV and RV, 'the righteous', is naturally drawn from the context and is found in the Septuagint, whether as part of the original text, or as a supplement, is unknown. The construction may, as in v.6, indicate that whoever cries to Jehovah is heard".

David was no stranger to the broken heart and the contrite spirit, and he well knew that Jehovah would not despise these. He employs exactly the same words in Psalm 51.17. There may be various reasons for the broken heart, but whatever the cause, Jehovah will tenderly regard it in His people and will minister graciously to those who are crushed in spirit and accordingly humble. He is always near to comfort and console. The saint is not immune to suffering, indeed his tribulations are many. Things which might not affect the evil man will cause sorrow to the godly man, but, as David has already avowed in v.17, the Lord delivers him out of all his afflictions.

Of the righteous it is now said, "He keepeth all his bones: not one of them is broken". The preservation of the righteous is promised by Jehovah, and it cannot be unnoticed by the believer that those who crucified the Saviour were not permitted to break His legs, as they broke the legs of the two thieves who were crucified with Him (Jn 19.36). The Evangelist tells us that the Scripture must be fulfilled that "A bone of him shall not be broken". There is doubtless a reference to the Passover lamb of Exodus 12.46, but, to quote Kirkpatrick, "This passage as well as Exodus 12.46 may have been present to the Evangelist's mind as fulfilled in Christ (Jn 19.36). The promise to the righteous man found an unexpectedly literal realisation in the passion of the perfectly Righteous One".

The wicked man will eventually be slain by the evil which he has done. Delitzsch says, "The evil which he loved and cherished shall be the hangman's power to which he falls a prey". As another Scripture says, "Whatsoever a man soweth, that shall he also reap" (Gal 6.7). Those who have hated the righteous may look forward only to desolation (816). This word is used twice in the closing two verses of the Psalm. It is sometimes rendered "guilty". Does it signify the eventual awful loneliness of the guilty man? Those who have hated, and been enemy to, the righteous, shall share in this desolation of guilt, but none of those who have sought refuge in Jehovah shall ever be desolate, for the Lord redeems (6299) them. Isaiah uses this same word when he writes "The *ransomed* of the Lord shall return, and come to Zion with songs and everlasting joy upon their heads: they shall obtain joy and gladness, and sorrow and sighing shall flee away" (Is 35.10). How gloriously is the end of the righteous contrasted with the end of the wicked.

PSALM 35

Introduction

Although the words, "A Psalm", are in italics in this title there can be no reasonable doubt that this is "A Psalm of David".

For comment on the form of the title of the Psalm, see the footnote in the commentary on Psalm 11.

There is no indication in the title as to the date, or the reason for the composition of the Psalm, but there is general agreement that it is David's and refers to the days of his persecution by Saul. David was hunted by a cruel king whose jealousy was being fuelled by men who slandered him, hoping to gain the king's favour. The relevant narratives, particularly 1 Samuel 20.1; 23.15 and 24.9-15 should be considered and compared.

The Psalm is in three principal parts. There are ten verses at the beginning of the Psalm and ten verses at the end, with eight verses between, each section being concluded with a note of thanksgiving and praise. In verses 1-10 the Psalmist pleads his innocence, invokes divine help in his cause, and ends with praise. In the eight verses which follow, 11-18, he pleads not only his personal innocence, but also the unjustness of the persecution which was rewarding his good with evil, and again he concludes with praise. In verses 19-28 he renews his appeal to Jehovah, and this section ends, not only with his own personal praise, but also with a chorus of praise from his friends who recognise the righteousness of his cause.

Verses 1-10: An Appeal for Divine Help

The opening word of the Psalm, "Plead" (7378), has been variously rendered as "Strive" (JND) and "Contend" (RSV). If the AV, "plead", is preferred then the thought is that of Jehovah as Judge, to whom David appeals for vindication. He is, of course, convinced of his personal innocence and desires the Lord to plead his case and his cause for him. He is content to leave all with the Righteous Judge to represent him before those who persecute him. Some, however, with JND, prefer that the word may mean "Strive" or "Contend", in which case David is looking to Jehovah to strive, as one in battle, with those who strive against him, to contend with the contenders. The various renderings may be harmonised by understanding that David is looking for a judicial victory over those who are his enemies unjustly. It is a courtroom battle. It must be observed that David never betrays any bitter feelings towards Saul personally, whom he always respects as the Lord's Anointed. To quote Perowne, "An enemy Saul may have been; but we never find any trace of bitterness in David's feelings towards Saul. The generous enemy whose heart smote him because he had cut off Saul's skirt, and who always recognised in Saul the Lord's anointed, would never have called down the judgments of God upon his head". It may be, then, that David has in mind those malicious men in the court who slandered him to the king, plotting his hurt, and even his death. Did these men fight against David? He appeals to Jehovah to fight against them.

"Shield" (4043) and "buckler" (6793) are at times used interchangeably. The buckler, however, was a larger type of shield with a pointed prominence in the centre of it so that it could also be used as a weapon. In the two words, therefore, there is the dual thought of defending and contending. Would Jehovah so arise for the help and the protection of the persecuted Psalmist? David pleads. Did not Stephen, in later years, see the Son of Man, standing, and rising, for the comfort of His beleaguered servant? The metaphor of the battlefield continues, and David now appeals for offensive action on the Lord's part. "Draw out also the spear". The spear was often carried in the spear-holder, as the sword in its sheath. The drawing out of the spear was anticipation of battle. Indeed some commentators regard the word "stop" (5462) as the name of yet another weapon, such as a "battle axe" (RV margin and NASV), or "javelin" (RSV and NIV), so that there are then two shields for defence and two weapons of offence, spear and battle-axe. In any case, the enemy is persecuting David and he longs to see Jehovah act against them and say to him, "I am thy salvation". "Them that persecute" is rendered by some, "Them that pursue", but the difference is minimal. David longs for the assurance of divine intervention and for his deliverance.

"Let them be confounded...let them be turned back". Such is David's prayer regarding his enemies. They sought his life and they devised his hurt and it was all unjust, so that righteousness demanded that they should be ashamed and dishonoured. They deserved to be confused and confounded and halted in their evil machinations against him. He longs to see them as helpless as chaff before the wind, but, again, as Davison writes, "The Psalmist prays that this overthrow may be complete. He uses stern and relentless language, but it is not animated by a personally vindictive spirit, as is clear from vv.12-14 and 19. It is the triumph of righteousness which he desires to see consummated, and he paints the picture of an army in retreat with the utmost force and vividness". It is indeed a picture of a complete and utter rout of the enemy, as they flee, pursued by the angel of the Lord (See note at Ps 34.7). In their haste to retreat they abandon the well-trodden roads and highways and find themselves on slippery unsafe paths made dark with overhanging branches and foliage. It is a solemn portrayal of the confusion of a defeated foe. As Spurgeon comments, "Woe, woe, woe, unto those who touch the people of God; their destruction is both swift and sure".

"Without cause", says the Psalmist. "Without cause", he repeats, and he will say it yet again in v.19. There was no valid reason for their enmity. He had not provoked them or assailed them. Their hatred of him was gratuitous, as it was also with the Saviour, the greater Son of David, who, in His last hours, on the eve of His final rejection, said, "They hated me without a cause" (Jn 15.25). David was entitled to be righteously indignant. They had laid traps and snares for him. With craft and cunning they had prepared concealed pits with hidden nets as men that hunt great game. Sometimes however, trappers have been known to be caught in the snares which they have laid for others, and this is what David now asks for his persecutors. "Let his net that he hath hid catch himself". He desires that his enemies may fall into the very destruction which they had planned for him. It is all pictorial language describing their subtle plots for his downfall, and his prayer that their unjust designs against him might be frustrated.

In the darkest hours David always found reason to rejoice. His trust in Jehovah, and the assurance of his salvation from the enemy made this joy possible. The closing verses of this second division of the Psalm are taken up with his exultation for the deliverance which he so confidently anticipates. "My soul shall be joyful", he says. "My bones shall say, Lord, who is like unto thee". In body and soul, with his whole life and being, he would rejoice in Jehovah his deliverer. Jehovah would take the part of the weak and the needy against a stronger foe. There were those who would spoil (1497) the weak. They would rob and plunder, and would do it with violence, but Jehovah delighted to deliver the afflicted poor (6041), and in the assurance of this David could rejoice and praise. The Lord would vindicate him and would grant him both moral and physical relief from his adversaries.

Verses 11-18: Evil for Good; Cruelty for Kindness

David returns to the theme of his personal innocence and the unjustness of the evil that was being plotted against him. False witnesses bore testimony against him. Their testimony was not only false (2555), it was malicious, it was unjust and unrighteous. He was being accused of things of which he knew nothing. They had charged him with plotting against King Saul, and such an accusation was far from the truth. Indeed, even when his own men had urged him to kill Saul, and when the opportunity was there to do so, with Saul at his mercy, David had refused. "Wherefore hearest thou men's words?", he had called to the king; the words of men who said, "Behold, David seeketh thy hurt" (1 Sam 24.9-10). It was false and malicious. It was treacherous. But David is not alone in the matter of false accusations. Men did the same to Jeremiah (Jer 18.18ff), to Stephen (Acts 6.13), and to the Saviour Himself (Mk 14.56).

What perhaps made the injustice even harder to bear was that David had been kind to these men who were now his adversaries. In time past he had been their friend, but the kindness which he had shown and the good which he had done was now being repaid by evil. Evil for good! It was ingratitude in the extreme. It was unwarranted, unfounded, and unjustifiable, and David feels it intensely. Their baseless hostility to him was, he says, "to the spoiling of his soul". The word which in v.12 is rendered "spoiling" (7908), is not the same as that similarly rendered in v.10. Here in v.12 the word has a certain sadness in it. It is "the bereavement of my soul", says JND. "My soul is forlorn", says the RSV. It is like the mourning of a mother who has been bereft of her children. David feels a sad loneliness, the desolation of one bereaved. He has been cruelly deprived of those whom he once befriended and he will now describe, in more detail, just what he had done for them, and how he had treated them.

When they were sick, he had sympathised with them. He had suffered with them, he had prayed and fasted for them, and he had entered personally into their sorrows. Whether literally or symbolically, he had worn sackcloth, the garment of the mourner. He had afflicted his soul as, in fasting, he had denied himself physical necessities while he sorrowed with them and for them. "My prayer returned into mine own bosom", is a difficult expression, variously understood. Some understand it to mean, "My prayer - may it return into my bosom", as if he were saying, "The prayer I offered for them is a prayer I might have offered for myself...I could wish nothing more than that the blessings I asked for them should be vouchsafed to me" (Perowne). Others, however, see in the text the attitude of an intercessor, with head bowed upon the breast. With this thought the RSV agrees, rendering it, "I prayed with head bowed upon my bosom". To quote from Spurgeon, who, in turn, quotes one Walford, "Of the many interpretations that are given of this passage, that appears to me to be the most probable which derives it from the posture of the worshipper; who standing with his head inclined downward toward his bosom turned away his attention from all external objects, and uttered his mournful and earnest requests as if they were directed to his own bosom". Whichever sense or meaning of the passage is preferred, this is clear, that David had most sincerely and genuinely prayed for these men when they were sick, and they were now his adversaries. It was indeed, evil for good.

David had so keenly felt the sorrows of those who were sick that he had behaved (1980) himself as one who had been bereaved. He had walked about in mourning, bowed and stooped in grief as if he had lost a friend, a brother, or even a mother. Yet, even as he so grieved for them, they were already gathering themselves together against him. They rejoiced (8055) with a callous merriment at his discomfort, and, unknown to him, they plotted against him in a campaign of slander. "At my stumbling they gathered in glee" (RSV). With their cruel words they tore him unceasingly. As Dr Cohen puts it, "Their libellous tongues are like the fangs of a beast of prey tearing his reputation to shreds". They were as hypocritical mockers at the feasts, he says. "Profane jesters for bread", JND renders it. It is a comparison with those unprincipled court jesters who engaged in all kinds of ribald folly just to gain the favour of the king and earn a good meal. At the king's banquets these jesters were noted for their impious vulgar mockeries. They showed their teeth in a malicious grinning as they danced around the table, and, if one was present who was not particularly liked by the king, they would make sport of him, embarrassing him with sarcastic witticisms. This, the adversaries were doing to David, and it will be remembered that the Saviour Himself was similarly treated as priests and soldiers joined together and mocked Him prior to His crucifixion.

Poor David! "How long?", he asks, almost wearily. How long would Jehovah look on without intervening? When would He come to rescue His servant from them? He speaks again of "my soul". His very life was being destroyed by these men. O that the Lord would rescue him from their destructions (7722), from the ravages they had planned for him. He had, after all, only one life; "my darling" (3173), he calls it, "my only one". Should these unjust ungrateful adversaries be permitted to ruin his one life? They were merciless, strong and fierce as young lions (3715), eager to devour him.

This section ends, as the others, on a note of praise. Although he was now with but a few faithful followers in the cave of Adullam, David could envisage a time when he would yet lead the praise in the midst of the great congregation. Jehovah would deliver and restore, and, instead of the remnant, it would be the throngs of Israel. He would then give thanks with all the people. He would exchange the grief for gladness. He would have the garment of praise for the spirit of heaviness. Jehovah would yet intervene. He knew it, and was thankful.

Verses 19-28: The Plea Renewed

David cannot forget that his enemies are his enemies wrongfully. There is not, cannot be, any just grounds for their enmity. Any alleged reasons for enmity are but pretexts, and are false. Again he states that they hated him without a cause. If there was no cause for their hatred there was surely cause for David's indignation. He pleads that they may not be allowed to rejoice (8055). But they were already rejoicing over him! It is the same word as in v.15. He speaks of them that "wink with the eye". Spurgeon says that "the winking of the eye was the low bred sign of congratulation at the ruin of their victim, and it may also have been one of their scornful gestures as they gazed upon him whom they despised". It signified contempt or derision from men mischievously gloating over the success of their evil plots. (Compare Prov 6.12-13). This was their groundless attitude to David and he prays that it may be permitted no longer.

These men were disturbers of the peace. They were troublers who could not rest if others in the land were enjoying quietness. They did not talk about peace but rather devised (2803) unrest. They cunningly calculated how they might upset the quietness of the land and if this meant deceit and falsehood, so be it. They were unscrupulous men to whom craft and cunning and treachery were a way of life. They were David's erstwhile friends, but they were only opportunists and were now his adversaries. They opened their mouth wide against him. This was probably the gesture of a malicious satisfaction over misfortune, so that when they say, "Aha, aha, our eye hath seen it", they are referring to David's apparent downfall. What they had plotted had been accomplished. David had been banished from Saul's court, and they rejoiced. There is, however, another interpretation which might be preferred. They opened their mouth wide in mock unbelief. "Aha, aha", they say, "our eye hath seen it". It was a cruel, subtle, insinuation that they had seen something wrong in David. "Aha, aha, we know, we have seen". They uttered great lies, implying that they had seen evil, where there was none. It was malicious and slanderous. But if they had seen, as they professed, so had Jehovah. "Thou hast seen", David cries. He turns the taunting language of his adversaries into the language of faith. Whatever they are suggesting about what they have seen, the eyes of the Omniscient One were ever upon His child and David did that which was right in the eyes of the Lord (1 Kings 15.5). "The eyes of the Lord are in every place, beholding the evil and the good" (Prov 15.3). David knew all this, and he knew, too, as he had so recently stated, that the eyes of the Lord were upon the righteous and His ears were open to their cry (Ps 34.15). So, if his enemies had seen, so had Jehovah, and David, in the consciousness of his innocence, could cry to Him who sees all, "Keep not silence: O Lord, be not far from me". The afflicted Psalmist longs to hear the voice of the Lord and to know the presence of the Lord.

His plea continues. With the most intelligent use of divine titles David appeals to One whom he now calls, "My God (430) and my Lord (136)". He prays for divine movement on his behalf. His God is Elohim, the Mighty One. His Lord is Adonai, Proprietor and Possessor of all, and to such an One David can look for help. O that Jehovah would take up his case and his cause and come to his judgment. That, he knew, would be righteous judgment. He would obtain from the Lord the justice which was being denied him by men. "Judge me" (8199), he appeals. "Vindicate me". "Plead my cause". "Defend me". "Decide the controversy between the enemy and me". His appeal now is to Him whom he addresses as "O Lord (3068) my God (430). The Mighty Elohim is Jehovah. David's cry is to the highest court and to the supreme Judge of all the earth, and, as Davison says, "Only a clear conscience could prompt the petition to be adjudged according to the Divine righteousness". Again he voices his dread that his enemies should continue to rejoice over him. That would indicate that they had triumphed in their evil designs. It seemed to be David's constant concern that his adversaries might have cause to rejoice. (Ps 13.4; 30.1; 35.19, 24, 26). He desired, rather, that they should be ashamed.

Notice the repeated, "Let them not say". Having asked, "Let them not rejoice", now David asks, "Let them not say to themselves, 'Aha, we have our heart's desire...we have swallowed him up'" (RSV). "It is as we would have it". "It is what we desired". They had plotted his complete destruction. They had planned to see him swallowed up in ruin. He prays they may be frustrated. Now he repeats his plea of v.4 as he prays for the confusion of those who rejoiced at his afflictions. They had magnified (1431) themselves, these enemies of his. They had promoted their own importance and had vaunted their pretended greatness. David, who desires only that Jehovah should be magnified (v.27), prays that they might be clothed with shame (1322) and dishonour (3639), disgraced and ashamed, confused and confounded.

It must have been a comfort to David that there were always those who believed in his righteousness and supported him and his cause. They would believe in his eventual vindication and in such confidence they should shout for joy and be glad. "Let them shout", he declares, "let them exult, and let them say continually, 'Let Jehovah be magnified'". Let this be their constant daily employ, to see the glory of the Lord and the judgment of His enemies. Those who believed in David would know that the Lord delighted in the prosperity (7965) of His servant. "Prosperity" is the lovely word SHALOM. How much is embraced in this word! Peace and contentment, health and welfare, tranquility and rest. Messiah is called "The Prince of Shalom" (Is 9.6). The God of peace has divine pleasure in the peace of His servants.

So does this third division of the Psalm, and the Psalm itself, end on a high note of praise. David's enemies will not, cannot, prevail. In His righteousness the Lord will order everything justly, and David, like all his servants, must speak of Him and praise Him, all the day long. "Speak" (1897), is the word "meditate", as in Psalm 1.2. Our meditation of Him shall be sweet (Ps 104.34). Unceasingly, then, now and in eternity, His saints shall sing His praise and rejoice.

PSALM 36

Introduction

This Psalm is another of those fifty-five Psalms which are committed to the care and charge of the Chief Musician. For further comment on the Chief Musician see the introduction to Psalm 4. This is a Psalm of David, and, as in the title of Psalm 18, David again describes himself as "the servant of the Lord". Only in these two Psalms do we have this particular appellation of the Psalmist in the titles, although he so speaks of himself in Psalm 35.27.

The Psalm is in two parts, verses 1-4 and verses 5-12, but perhaps three parts if the closing verses, 10-12, are considered separately as a concluding prayer. The goodness and the glory of the Lord are contrasted with the wickedness of man. "The poem begins with a characterisation of the godless, but soon turns from their sordidness to extol the goodness of God in language of striking beauty" (Dr Cohen). The servant of the Lord prays that he might be preserved from the wicked and kept in the enjoyment of the loving-kindness of the Lord.

Verses 1-4: The Wickedness of the Wicked

The opening words of the Psalm have presented a difficulty. The transgression of the wicked is speaking, declaring a message, almost like the utterance of a prophet. But to whose heart is transgression speaking? Some understand this to be the heart of the wicked man, as rendered by the RSV, "Transgression speaks to the wicked deep in his heart", meaning that transgression, personified, was whispering evil suggestions to a man's depraved nature, inciting him to sin. This thought is favoured by W.T.

Davison, and by Dr Cohen who follows an English translation of the Hebrew text by the Jewish Publication Society of America, which gives, "Transgression speaketh to the wicked, methinks - There is no fear of God before his eyes". It is more probable, however, that it is the heart of David the servant of the Lord which is intended, in which case the meaning is that, as David considers a man's sinful course, the transgression of that man tells David in his heart just what the nature of the sinner really is, with no fear of God before his eyes. "The transgression of the wicked uttereth within my heart, There is no fear of God before his eyes" (JND). To paraphrase, "His transgression tells me in my heart that he has no fear of God". What a man is, is evidenced by what he does. His evil ways tell the heart of God's servant just what the man thinks of God.

With no God to fear, the wicked man flatters (2505) himself. In his conceit he assigns to himself an excellence and importance which is due to God alone. "He had not God before his eyes in holy awe, therefore he puts himself there in unholy admiration. He who makes little of God makes much of himself" (Spurgeon). The fear of God deters a man from sin, but notice that the fear (6343) spoken of here, is not the same as "the fear (3374) of the Lord" in Psalm 34.11, or in such well-known passages as Proverbs 1.7; 9.10, and in many other verses in the Book of Proverbs. The two words are perhaps similar, but need to be distinguished. The word of the Proverbs has the thought of respect and reverence and holy awe. This word in Psalm 36.1, however, is defined by Strong as meaning "dread. terror". The natural man ought so to fear God, but, where such is lacking, that man will increase in his iniquity until his iniquity becomes hateful, nauseous, odious, both to himself and to others, and of course to God. A surfeit of the sin in which he once found his pleasure can become revolting, as when the wickedness of a wicked man becomes abhorrent even to his wicked companions. John Bunyan testifies to his shame when certain women who were accustomed to using oaths and curses, rebuked him for his foul language. How distasteful and vile it must have been, he thought, when such women as these were revolted by it.

For a second time in two consecutive verses we have a reference to iniquity, but the word of v.2 (5771), is different from this of v.3, "The words of his mouth are iniquity" (205). The former is the more usual word, signifying the depravity and perverseness of the sinner. The latter word is, as Strong says, "from an unused root, perhaps meaning properly, to pant, hence to exert oneself, usually in vain". "Vanity" and "mischief" are also in the meaning, so that the thought appears to be that this ungodly man labours strenuously and mischievously in sin and in deceit (4820), speaking lies and practising treachery and guile. He has apparently abandoned all thoughts of wisdom and good, preferring rather his evil and sinful ways. In the night hours, congenial to meditation, he devises mischief. This "mischief" (205) is the same word as "iniquity" of v.3, so that the iniquity of which he speaks is not necessarily rash or impetuous but calculated and studied. Those hours which are used by the godly for profitable meditation are used by the wicked to invent evil scheming. The man has deliberately set (3320) himself in the way which he has chosen. He has, as it were, taken his stand for evil. The way which he is treading is not the better or the good way, and he has no abhorrence of that which is wrong. He has a seared conscience which cannot discern what is bad. Such is the corruption of the man who has no fear of God, who has cast off all moral restraints and standards, and who lives for self and sin.

Verses 5-9: The Greatness and Goodness of God

The Psalmist now turns his gaze from earth to heaven. From the wickedness of wicked men he will rise to contemplate the lovingkindness and faithfulness of God. From moral darkness he will look upward to the shining of the glory. It is a delightful and refreshing contrast. "Mercy" (2617) is often rendered "lovingkindness", as indeed it is in v.7 of this same Psalm. Both thoughts are included in the word, but "mercy" seems so suitable here, considering the exceeding sinfulness of men. That Jehovah should look down from His heaven, see the degradation of earth, and yet be merciful and gracious, prompts this exclamation of the Psalmist, "Thy mercy, O Lord, is in the heavens". Well does another Psalmist write, "If thou, Lord, shouldest mark iniquities, O Lord, who shall stand?" (Ps 130.3). But His mercy is as vast as the heavens and His faithfulness boundless as the clouds. The language conveys to men the thought of the infinity, the magnitude, of these attributes of God, and all this in spite of the ingratitude of wicked men.

He is righteous too, with a righteousness that is as majestic as "the mountains of God" (RSV and RV). His righteousness is as high and as mighty as the mountains of His own creation, and His judgments are a great deep. "How unsearchable are his judgments" (Rom 11.33). Here is majesty and mystery. The limitless heavens; the immeasurable skies; the immovable hills; the fathomless deeps; all are needed to portray something of the grandeur of the great Jehovah. The believer wonders and worships. Then, in what some have thought to be an anti-climax, comes that touching expression, "O Lord, thou preservest man and beast". Why should the Psalmist so suddenly turn from such high thoughts of God, to think of man and beast? This is continuing majesty, that Jehovah in all His greatness and glory, should yet care for His creation. "The Lord is good to all" (Ps 145.9). He is the Preserver, the Saviour, of even the meanest of His creatures.

Three times in the Psalm David mentions the lovingkindness of the Lord - in vv. 7 and 10, and also in v.5, where the same word is rendered "mercy". How excellent it is. "Excellent" (3368) is elsewhere, as in Psalm 139.17, and by others here, translated "precious" (RV, RSV, JND). Jehovah's lovingkindness is more precious than the rarest jewels, more to be valued than the most prized and priceless gems. Therefore, because of this excellence, the children of men flee to the covert of His wings for refuge. There are several different Hebrew words for "man". This "children of men" (120) is ADAM. Man is but dust after all. He is of the ground, of the clay, earth-born. How insignificant and frail he is. What is he, that Thou thinkest of him? (Ps 8.4). In his human weakness, man must put his trust (2620) in God. He must fly for refuge to the protection of the Almighty just as helpless chicks will run from danger to the spread wings of the mother bird. Did not David's great-grandmother Ruth, Gentile though she was, find shelter under His wings? (Ruth 2.12). David, too, himself, found refuge there when he fled from Saul. As he says in one of his "Golden Psalms", "Yea, in the shadow of thy wings will I make my refuge, until these calamities be overpast" (Ps 57.1). How tenderly and touchingly did the Saviour also use this same beautiful figure when He lamented over the city which had rejected Him, "O Jerusalem, Jerusalem…how often would I have gathered thy children together, as a hen doth gather her brood under her wings, and ye would not!" (Lk 13.34; Mt 23.37). Some, however, see here in the Psalm, a reference to the wings of the cherubim over-shadowing the mercy seat (Heb 9.5), and it may indeed be that in the verse which follows that thought is pursued and developed.

In this connection Spurgeon quotes one Samuel Burder, who writes, "The expressions here which denote the abundance of divine blessings upon the righteous man, seem to be taken from the temple, from whence they were to issue. Under the covert of the temple, the wings of the cherubim, they were to be sheltered. The richness of the sacrifices, the streams of oil, wine, odours, etc., and the light of the golden candlestick, are all plainly referred to". In His house there is an abundance of everything. There is bread enough and to spare (Lk 15.17). His trusting people therefore are abundantly satisfied.

The word "fatness" of v.8 is an interesting word. In connection with the Levitical Offerings it is several times translated "ashes" (Ex 27.3; Lev 1.16; 4.12; 6.10; 6.11; Num 4.13). It seems to signify that a sacrifice has been offered, and it may well be, as suggested by Davison, that the abundant satisfaction referred to here is the satisfaction of those who have partaken of a sacrificial meal (see Lev 7.15). He writes that it is, "the joys of spiritual communion, under the figure of God as host receiving His worshippers in His temple and regaling them with the 'Shelamim', the peace-offerings or sacrificial meal, which symbolised the Divine favour and bounty". In the divine presence pleasures flow like a river. "Pleasures" (5730) is actually the well-known word "Eden", of Genesis 2.8, except that here it is in the plural. For those who trust Him, paradise has been restored. Like as a river went out of Eden to water the garden (Gen 2.10), so there is, for the saint, an ever-flowing stream of refreshment, both now and in eternity. A pure river of water of life flows from His throne. (Rev 22.1). "There is a river, the streams whereof shall make glad the city of God" (Ps 46.4). Here is the fountain of life. Here is the source, the wellspring, of all that the believer has. There is life and light in unfailing supply. Dwelling in that light His people enjoy the light. "If we walk in the light, as he is in the light, we have fellowship one with another" (1 Jn 1.7). Whether this is fellowship of believers with each other, or, as some prefer, a personal fellowship between the believer and his God, both are equally precious, it is the light of His presence.

Verses 10-12: The Concluding Prayer

Having contemplated such beauty, it is not to be wondered at that the Psalmist should earnestly desire it to continue. Who, having known joy and satisfaction like this, would want to lose anything of it? "O continue (4900) thy lovingkindness", he pleads. "Let it be drawn out, prolonged, to them that know Thee". He longs that it may never end, this enjoyment of the love of God. Again he mentions God's righteousness. Those who are upright, righteous, will delight in God's righteousness. Divine righteousness must ever make the sinner afraid, but the same righteousness is a constant comfort and strength to His people.

From general prayer for all saints, the Psalmist now turns to particular prayer for himself. He speaks of the foot of pride and the hand of the wicked. He knows that with foot and hand, in their arrogance and in their wickedness, they are against him. They would, if they could, trample him and drive him away from home and country. He prays it may not be allowed, and then, almost abruptly, in an anticipation of faith, he sees his prayer already answered. He seems to point the finger at them and exclaim, "There they are, fallen!". By faith he sees them cast down, unable to rise. Jehovah will deal righteously with the enemies and oppressors of His people, and when He does so, the judgment will be complete.

So does the Psalm conclude. The Psalmist has seen the wickedness of the wicked, but he has contemplated that grace and glory of which the apostle says, "Where sin abounded, grace did much more abound" (Rom 5.20), and, having been in the light of the divine presence, he prays to be delivered from those who would persecute the saints.

PSALM 37

Introduction

Psalm 37 is one of several alphabetical Psalms, on which see Section 6 of the Introductory Remarks at the beginning of the Commentary. For detailed discussion of the regular alphabetical form of Psalm 37 profitable reference may be made to Delitzsch or Maclaren. For comment on the form of the title, where the words "A Psalm" are in italics, refer to the footnote to Psalm 11 in this Commentary with the interesting remarks by Plumer.

This Psalm deals with the eventual judgment of evildoers, even though they may appear now to be prospering, and with the ultimate salvation of the righteous, even though they may now be in trials. Similar sentiments are expressed in Psalm 73, with which this Psalm should be compared, and the same perplexities are also dealt with in the Book of Job. The style of the Psalm has been likened to the Book of Proverbs and this form of writing makes a clear division of the forty verses somewhat difficult. The following suggested analysis however, may be helpful.

There are four parts to the Psalm. From verse 1 to verse 11 there is a collection of exhortations and encouragements for the righteous. In the second section, verses 12-22, the inevitable doom of the wicked is assured. There follows, in verses 23-31, the sure promises of reward for the godly, and the Psalm closes with verses 32-40 dealing with the finality of Jehovah's certain judgments.

It will be noted that the Psalm was written when David was old (v.25). He writes with the benefit of hindsight, of maturity, and of a deep, wide and varied experience, of life, of men, and of God.

Verses 1-11: Exhortations and Encouragements

The believer is neither to fret (2734), nor be envious (7065), when he considers the prosperity of evil men. This exhortation is repeated in Proverbs 24.19. It is a godly tendency to be angry with the wicked, and it is a human tendency to be jealous of the prosperous. The believer must, however, exercise care in responding or reacting to the prevailing wickedness. It does not help the godly soul to become hot or incensed with anger because of evil-doers. Such is the literal meaning of the word "fret". The believer will, of course, be righteously indignant at those who sin with impunity, but he must avoid that bitterness of soul which can result from overmuch occupation with the wickedness of wicked men. Also, when these evil men are sometimes seen to be prospering materially, it must be remembered that their prosperity will be short-lived. It is but transient and temporary. The New Testament believer has also the advantage of a much more full and complete revelation than had the saints of the Psalmist's day. David lived and wrote and sang in an age when material blessings were viewed as a sign of divine favour, and in a measure this was true. On the whole, Jehovah did so bless His people. But the perplexity arose when evil men were seen to be prospering and when good men were not so prosperous. It would then be easy to become fretful and envious that evil should apparently be rewarded and goodness be disregarded. To the Old Testament believer with limited revelation this must have been perplexing indeed.

It is folly for the saint with eternal hopes and heavenly prospects, to be jealous of a prosperity which will be so suddenly brought to an end. The wicked will fall like grass before the scythe. They will wither like the herb of the field which once was so green. That once luscious grass will become dry hay. That proud herb will fade. So shall it be with the wicked who now flourish. The believer should quietly rest in the sovereignty of God, with faith in His government, knowing that eventually all will be well for the godly, when the ungodly will perish and be as chaff blown away by the wind (Ps 1.4).

In succeeding verses the Psalmist will now occupy the reader with Jehovah Himself. To turn away from the wickedness of these evil men to a holy occupation with the Lord is the true antidote to fretting and jealousy. "Trust in the Lord", he exhorts. "Delight in the Lord", he continues. "Commit thy way to the Lord", and, "Rest in the Lord". This is the believer's safeguard, to resort always to Jehovah.

Verse 3, with all its beauty, has difficulties also, which have been variously treated by different commentators and translators. The exhortation to trust (982) is plain enough. It is to confide in Jehovah, and in that confidence to feel safe and secure, and to do good and live godly. However great may be the perplexity of watching the wicked prosper, trust in the Lord who orders everything. The latter part of the verse is understood by some to be a promise, as conveyed by the AV rendering, "So shalt thou dwell in the land, and verily thou shalt be fed". Others see a command, or an imperative, as in the JND, RV (margin), and ASV, renderings, "Dwell in the land, and feed on (his) faithfulness", or, "follow after faithfulness". Maclaren, who favours the thought of promise, nevertheless seems to combine both ideas in his final comment on the verse when he writes, "The blessed results of trust and active goodness are stable dwelling in the land and nourishment there from a faithful God. The thoughts move within the Old Testament circle, but their substance is eternally true, for they who take God for their portion have a safe abode, and feed their souls on His unalterable adherence to His promises and on the abundance flowing thence".

"Delight" (6026), in v.4, is a gentle word. It signifies the sweet satisfaction of one who feeds delicately upon dainties. What satisfaction there is in so delighting in Jehovah. Those who love Him and trust Him, delight in His character, in His titles, and in His ways. They feed on His purposes, on His Word, and on all things related to Him. To delight in the Lord will preserve the believer from the fretting and envy of v.1 of the Psalm. Perhaps, indeed, it may be said that it is only the man who delights in the Lord who can confidently trust Him. Knowing Him in all His fullness genders confidence in all that He says and does. Then, also, the desires of the heart of the man who trusts him wholly will never be contrary to the will of the Lord, and so it follows that those desires of the godly heart will be granted. The truly godly will never wish what is contrary to Jehovah.The believer is now exhorted to commit his way unto the Lord. This is to roll it upon Him in the exercise of faith and trust. It implies a submission to Him and a contentment with His guidance. It is real confidence and trust when the believer is able to commit the direction of an unknown pathway to the

Lord, to rest in the will of God and realise the promise of Proverbs 3.6, "In all thy ways acknowledge him, and he shall direct thy paths". For the trusting soul, Jehovah will bring to pass all that is necessary and good. As David says in another place, "The Lord will perfect that which concerneth me" (Ps 138.8). Jehovah, too, will vindicate the godly man and will cause his righteousness to shine as the light. The clouds will roll away and all will become clear as the noonday. The believer's judgments, the decisions he has made in his life of trust, the order and the fashion of his life of faith, will all be vindicated. Jehovah, ever true to His word, will bring it to pass.

This, though, may not appear immediately. The trusting heart must rest (1826) in the Lord and wait patiently for it. "Ye have need of patience", says another writer (Heb 10.36). This is not just an uncomplaining endurance of things, but a silent waiting before the Lord. It is so similar to the exhortation of Psalm 46.10, "Be still, and know that I am God". It is a quiet and tranquil resignation to the ways of God, accepting His will and His timing, and remaining calm in trust. In the peace of this silent waiting upon God the believer will not fret (2734). Here is a repetition of the opening word of the Psalm. Those who trust will not become obsessed with anger at the prosperity of the wicked. The ungodly man may, for a little while, prosper in the way of his own choosing, but the godly man has committed his way to the Lord. The mischievous devices, the wicked inventions, of the evildoer may bring him a temporary prosperity, but to fret about this is injurious to the soul and must be avoided. Yet again the Psalmist uses the word "fret", saying, "Fret not thyself in any wise to do evil". "Fret not thyself, it tendeth only to evil-doing" (RV). "It would be only to do evil" (JND). Such fretting, such undue smouldering in anger may, indeed, only lead to doing evil in the heat of the moment. As Davison paraphrases the passage, "Allow not thyself in what may seem to be hot indignation against unrighteousness, it leads only to unrighteousness itself in the end".

Again the Psalmist emphasises the end of the wicked. They may flourish now, but so does grass for a little while! They shall be cut off, cut down, as he has said in v.2. "But!". What a happy contrast! Those who wait upon the Lord shall inherit the earth. Those wicked men, who seemed to possess so much, shall shortly and suddenly be dispossessed of all, and the righteous shall inherit all. Whether "earth" or "land" be preferred in vv. 9 and 11 (776), does not affect the force of the promise. The prosperous wicked will lose all. The patient righteous will inherit all. Five times in the Psalm is this promise repeated. See vv. 9, 11, 22, 29 and 34.

Once more the Psalmist insists upon the transient nature of the prosperity of the wicked. "Yet a little while". Then, though diligent search be made for him, he will not be found. But the meek and the righteous who have found delight in the Lord (v.4), shall then have continuing delight in what He has provided for them. They shall enjoy an abundance of peace (7965). This is the lovely word SHALOM. It signifies peace and prosperity, and such, in abundance, will be the portion of those who have eschewed the evil ways of the world and have waited in patient trust upon Jehovah. There can be no doubt, with NT revelation, that this anticipates the millennial reign of Messiah, when, as Psalm 72.7 declares, "In his days shall the righteous flourish; and abundance of peace so long as the moon endureth".

Verses 12-22: The Doom of the Wicked

Wickedness is ever opposed to righteousness. Of Messiah Himself it is said "Thou lovest righteousness and hatest wickedness" (Ps 45.7), and so the wicked continually plot against the just. They devise and imagine with evil intent, and, animal like, they gnash at the godly with their teeth. Their wicked rage is symbolised by what has been called their "arsenal of murder" (Maclaren). Their sword is drawn and their bow is bent and their evil purpose is to destroy the poor (6041) and the needy (34), those who live in meek and humble dependence on Jehovah. They would slay those whose conversation (1870), whose manner of life, is morally upright.

Jehovah laughs! How feeble and puny are those who oppose Him and His people. It is reminiscent of Psalm 2.4. Heaven laughs in holy derision at the vain efforts of wicked men for the Lord knows that their time is short. Their day is coming, a day of reckoning and of righteous judgment, when their murderous intentions will be turned back upon them and they will perish. They have brought righteous judgment upon themselves, and Jehovah says, "Vengeance is mine, and recompense...For the day of their calamity is at hand, And the things that shall come upon them make haste" (Deut 32.35, JND). Their bows shall be broken and their own sword will pierce them. It is righteous retribution.

The rewards of righteousness are great. The few possessions of one righteous man are better than the riches of many wicked men. "Riches" (1995) in v.16 is a strange word, sometimes translated "abundance", but sometimes "tumult" or "noise". It seems to signify that the riches of wicked men have brought with them an equal measure of noisy confusion in contrast to the quiet satisfaction of the godly. Maclaren says it so well; "The poor man's little is much, because, among other reasons, he is upheld by God, and therefore needs not to cherish anxiety, which embitters the enjoyment of others". As Paul says, "Godliness with contentment is great gain" (1 Tim 6.6).

Yet again, in v.17, the wicked and the righteous are seen in contrast. The arms of the wicked shall be broken. Their might, their strength, will come to nought. Their power will be shattered in the day of reckoning, but Jehovah will always support and sustain the righteous. He will bear them up and maintain their cause.

"Upright" (8549) in v.18 is a different word from that which is rendered "upright" (3477) in v.14. There, in v.14, the word is a synonym for "righteous". Here, in v.18, it carries also the thought of being complete, wholesome or healthful. Dr Cohen, in his helpful commentary on the Psalms, pays tribute to the Jewish Publication Society of America, for what he calls, "their very beautiful English text of the Scripture", which translates "the upright" as, "them that are whole-hearted". This is beautiful indeed, that Jehovah should take notice of every day in the lives of those who whole-heartedly live for Him and for righteousness. As Dr Cohen adds, "He knows the vicissitudes which befall them day by day; He is not indifferent to their fate". When the accumulated possessions of the wicked have perished, the inheritance of the upright will yet be preserved. Their riches are abiding and eternal. Their heritage is for ever. There may be times of evil (7451), times of adversity and affliction, and there may be days of famine, but Jehovah's promise to those who love Him is that when the evil time comes they will not be confounded, and when days of famine come they will have enough and to spare. These promises were doubtless claimed and enjoyed in a material sense by the godly of an earlier dispensation, but the New Testament believer will see in them blessings of a spiritual and heavenly nature.

Yet once more is the perdition of the wicked pronounced. They shall, eventually and inevitably, be utterly destroyed. The enemies of Jehovah shall be as the fat of lambs. Following this AV rendering, the thought is generally agreed to be that they shall be consumed, and pass away in smoke just as the fat of sacrificial lambs was consumed in smoke upon the great altar. There is, however, an alternative rendering, favoured by the RV and RSV, followed by Cohen, Davison, and Maclaren, and supported by Strong, which points out that the word "fat" (3368) may correctly be rendered "excellency", "glory", or "splendour", and the word "lambs" (3733), may be rendered "pastures" or "meadows". The phrase would then read, "As the excellency, or glory, of the pastures". But whichever metaphor is preferred, the end is the same. The fat of lambs is consumed in smoke. The glory of the meadows is short-lived and withers. So is the prosperity of the wicked. It is glory now, but certain doom and withered barrenness in the day of judgment.

Again the wicked and the righteous are contrasted in one verse (v.21). The wicked borrows but does not repay. The question, "Why does he not repay?", may be answered by asking, "Why does he borrow?". The man may indeed be wicked, but the fact that he does not pay his debt is not due to dishonesty. His failure to repay is not because he will not, but because he cannot. His former prosperity has already come to nothing. He is bankrupt. This is why he borrows and this is why he does not repay. As the RSV has it, "The wicked borrows, and cannot pay back". By contrast, the righteous deals both graciously and generously with him. But how can the righteous man show such mercy and give, perhaps knowing that what he gives will never be repaid? Indeed the word "give" (5414) may not anticipate a return. The righteous man knows that he is the inheritor of all and that when the wicked are cut off he will continue to enjoy his heritage. The righteous are "blessed of him" and the wicked are "cursed of him". The righteous can well afford to be generous and give to him that would borrow, even though there may be no possibility of repayment.

Verses 23-31: The Blessings of the Godly

These verses are almost entirely concerned with the great blessings which accompany godliness. "The steps of a good man are ordered by the Lord". It will be noticed that the word "good" is in italics, indicating that it is not in the original text but has been supplied by the translators, but it can hardly be doubted that it is indeed a good man's life that is being envisaged. When a man chooses a path of righteousness and determines so to walk for God, then the goings of that man are established by the Lord. To walk such a pathway may be difficult, but Jehovah will render support and the ability to live for His glory. The phrase that follows is ambiguous. "He delighteth in his way" may mean that God delights in the man's way, or that the man delights in God's way. Both thoughts are true, but in the context it would seem to be the delight of the Lord in the good man's life, and, because of the pleasure that it brings Him, Jehovah will order that man's goings. When the winds of adversity blow and troubles come to the good man, though he may stumble and fall under the trial, the hand of the Lord will sustain him. He may be cast down, but not utterly cast down. He will be upheld in the trial. Job knew this, and Joseph, and Jonah, and David himself. Davison sums it up so aptly; "The thought throughout this quatrain is that the life of a good man viewed as a journey is one of steadfast progress, even in spite of stumbles, because God is well pleased with him and supports him throughout".

David now recounts his personal observations regarding the righteous life. He is now old, and as he looks back over the years he concludes that righteousness brings its own reward. It is a general rule that neither the righteous nor their families will ever be found in utter beggarly destitution. The righteous man is never abandoned, either by his God or by the large fellowship of other saints. Though he may have privations and problems, he will eventually be recompensed, and so can bequeath his possessions to his posterity. Conversely, it must be argued and admitted that much of the suffering in the world can be traced back to sinful and immoral living. Maclaren again; "On the whole, wrong-doing lies at the root of most of the hopeless poverty and misery of modern society. Idleness, recklessness, thriftlessness, lust, drunkenness, are the potent factors of it; and if their handiwork and that of the subtler forms of respectable godlessness and evil were to be eliminated, the sum of human wretchedness would shrink to very small dimensions".

The righteous man is characteristically merciful, and willing to lend to others. The RV expresses it very beautifully: "All the day long he dealeth graciously, and lendeth; and his seed is blessed". These observations are, of course, generalisations. There may be isolated exceptions, but the Psalmist is stating the general rule. The generosity of the good man brings blessing both to him and to his family. It is a great privilege to have righteous forebears. How often the example of their trust is the means of their children determining to follow the same path of faith.

Since the righteous life is so rewarding the Psalmist therefore repeats the injunction of Psalm 34.14, "Depart from evil, and do good". This will be attended with blessing. Continue in a life of separation from what is wrong and a devotion to that which is right, and dwell for evermore in the land which God has given you. How precious would this promise have been to the families of David's day. "Dwell" (7931), has the thought of abiding in peace and quiet, at rest in the possession of the land, to bequeath to the children a divinely given heritage.

The connecting "For" of v.28 is an important encouragement to godly living. Live righteously, is the exhortation, for Jehovah loves justice. He loves righteousness and justice in His people, and in justice He Himself will deal accordingly with both the righteous and the wicked. He will never forsake His saints, His justice assures this. They shall be preserved, both now and forever. But divine justice will be meted out to the wicked and such shall be cut off, and their seed. How often is this judgment of the wicked emphasised in the Psalm. They shall, for their wickedness, be "cut down" (v.2), "cut off" (vv. 22, 28, 34, 38), but the righteous will inherit the land and enjoy forever the Lord's provision and desire for them. The blessing of the righteous is as sure and eternal as is the judgment of the unrighteous.

As is so often the case in the Scriptures, heart and mouth are here in close association. (See Ps 45.1; Mt 12.34; Rom 10.9). When the mouth of the righteous speaketh (1897) wisdom, it is speech that has been meditated. The same verb is actually translated "meditate" in Psalm 1.2. Another says that it is to "speak musingly in the low murmur of one entranced by a sweet thought" (Cheyne). The righteous man will not speak hastily, but meditatively. As the wise man says, "Be not rash with thy mouth, and let not thine heart be hasty to utter any thing before God" (Eccl 5.2). Words which are quietly meditated will, therefore, almost certainly be words of wisdom and justice, in accord with the character of the man and of God Himself. It is a principle, too, that whatever is meditated in the heart will affect a man's life and walk. When there is love for God's Word, and when its precepts are hidden in the heart, then the steps of that man are ordered accordingly. Therefore, both a man's words and his walk, his speech and his steps, are influenced by the meditations of his heart, and when those meditations are upon the law of the Lord then his words will be wise and his steps shall not slide. His way will be resolute and steadfast.

Verses 32-40: The Finality of Jehovah's Judgments

If the character of Jehovah and His saints is that of justice, it is not so with the wicked. The wicked is ever watching (6822) the righteous. He is constantly observing, espying, looking for opportunity to slay the good man. For many faithful saints, in all ages, this has meant death literally. For others it has been an assassination of reputation. The wicked are not concerned with justice. They will watch for any event or circumstance, and will wait for a moment favourable to their wicked intention to assail the godly. But if the wicked are watching the saints, with evil motives, then Jehovah is watching also and will not leave His saints in the power of the adversary. The Lord will not abandon His people to the unjust judgments of wicked men. He cannot acquiesce in the injustices which are so often meted out to His saints. Such injustices may be tolerated for a little while, but eventually, in His own good time, the Lord will vindicate. Was it not so with Job, with Joseph, with Daniel, and with Shadrach, Meshach and Abednego? And was it not so with the Saviour Himself? How often did they seek opportunity to destroy that Blessed One? They did so eventually, but God raised Him from the dead and seated Him far above the realms of those who crucified Him. Vindication may tarry, but it will surely come. The divine promise is, "The Lord will not leave him in his hand" (v.33).

Since vindication may not be immediate, the believer is now encouraged to wait (6960) for the Lord. The word signifies to "wait eagerly", to "look expectantly", or, to "linger for". The beleaguered saint must wait for God's time, and while he waits he must walk in God's way. The promise, given so often in this and other Psalms, is repeated yet again, with the bringing together another time of those two themes, "inherit", and, "cut off". When the righteous inherit the land which Jehovah has reserved for them the wicked shall be cut off. God's judgments are sure and final, and He will deal with both saint and sinner in justice. The righteous will yet see the destruction of their enemy. Davison expresses it so well: "The prospect of seeing the overthrow of the wicked is not a matter of personal gratification, but it is held out as additional evidence of the whole theme of the Psalm. Justice shall be done on earth, and the oppressed saints shall witness its triumph".

The Psalmist now draws an illustration from his personal experience. He has earlier likened the wicked to the grass and to the green herb of the field, flourishing briefly and then cut down and withered. He now recalls that he has seen the wicked in great power, vaunting himself like a giant tree. The tree, in the illustration, is growing in its native soil. It has taken over the surrounding territory, spreading its branches and stretching its roots as if it were the proud possessor of all around. But later, when the Psalmist comes to see it, it is gone. The giant has fallen and there remains only that large space the vast barrenness of which indicates just how great the tree had been in its former glory. So it is, and so it will be, with the wicked. It is better then, to observe the perfect man, and to contemplate the moral beauty and integrity of the upright. Having seen the downfall of that giant of the forests, falling from its proud heights to the ground and to oblivion, how refreshing it is to consider the true greatness of the righteous man. He may indeed be humble and of little significance in the eyes of the world, but there is a future for that man. The word "end" (319) in v.37 may indicate either a future in his posterity, or a blessed personal future for him in eternity. Whichever is intended, his end is peace (7965). It is, yet again, the lovely word, "Shalom", as in v.11. When the arrogant wicked have perished, then the righteous man will enjoy peace and prosperity, rest and tranquillity.

The impartiality of God's judgment is now assured. The transgressors will perish together, all of them, without respect of persons. Is there a future for the righteous man? So is there a future for the wicked, but it is to be cut off. They have excluded God from their lives and from their ways. He will accordingly cut them off from all that the righteous will enjoy.

The Psalm concludes on a happy and peaceful note. The salvation of the righteous is of the Lord, and they can, with calm confidence, rely upon Him. They may indeed have their times of trouble, for they are not immune, but He is their strength (4581). He is their stronghold, their rock-fortress, their refuge, their place of safety. To Him they may run when trouble comes. In Him they may safely hide and find shelter from the storm. What delightful assurances are now given to the godly as the Psalm closes. Jehovah will help them, deliver them, and save them, and all this because they trust Him. How He delights in the trust of His people.

PSALM 38

Introduction

Psalm 38 is the third of those seven Psalms which are called "The Penitential Psalms". The language is very personal. There would seem to be no reason to doubt the Davidic authorship of this Psalm, nor to interpret it as a national song of repentance. Nor does it seem necessary to suppose that David has composed a Psalm for others who are suffering. Other "Penitential Psalms" are Psalms 6, 32, 102, 130 and 143, but perhaps the greatest example is Psalm 51. These Psalms are the poetic lament of Psalmists who, in bodily suffering, feel that their affliction has been caused by sin, and who accordingly bring these "Penitents' Prayers", coming in repentance and pleading the mercy of God toward them. Maclaren calls them, "The cries of a wounded soul".

The very close resemblance between the opening words of this Psalm and those of Psalm 6.1 will at once be noted. Delitzsch takes both of these Psalms, along with Psalms 32 and 51, to belong to that same time of David's deep suffering and ultimate penitence after his great sin in the matter of Bathsheba. David's ensuing sufferings after his sin appear to have been both mental and physical.

The title, "A Psalm of David, to bring to remembrance", has presented difficulties. Psalm 70 is entitled similarly. Some think that David feels forgotten of God and is appealing for divine remembrance. It is more probable, however, that in his severe illness, perhaps indeed thinking of death, David is reminiscing. A man at the end of life has cause to think of the past and to bring to remembrance those many vicissitudes of life through which he has passed. He will remember good times, and the bad. He will recall triumphs and tragedies, joys and sorrows. It may well be that David, in his then present sickness, is so remembering. The title in the Septuagint has, "for remembrance concerning the Sabbath-day", but this throws little light upon the intention in the title, except that it may indicate that the Psalm, though so very personal, was to be used liturgically in temple worship.

The Psalm is easily and readily divided into three parts, four if the concluding verses 21-22 are considered separately. These divisions are punctuated in verses 1, 9, 15 and 21 by direct appeals to God, who, on three of these occasions, is addressed as Jehovah - verses 1, 15 and 21 - translated "LORD" (3068) in the AV. In three verses – 9, 15 and 22 - the title Adonai is employed, rendered "Lord" (136) in the AV, but, as Strong points out, this title was often used in place of Jehovah in a Jewish display of reverence. Twice in the Psalm, in verses 15 and 21, his address is to God (430), to Elohim, the Mighty One, whom he calls "my God" in verse 15. The Psalmist's studied use of divine titles is to be observed and admired.

The suggested divisions of the Psalm are therefore as follows. In verses 1-8 the Psalmist describes his personal pain and sorrow. He looks to the Lord in verse 9 and then continues to speak of his suffering and reproach through until verse 14. In verse 15 he appeals again to Jehovah and his penitent appeal is continued until verse 20. The closing verses, 21 and 22, are a final plea for help and salvation.

Verses 1-8: Pain and Penitence

As at the commencement of this Psalm, David's fear is of the wrath (7110) and the displeasure (2534) of Jehovah. He does not deny that he has, by his sin, invoked and deserved the chastening of the Lord, and he will not rebel against this, but the word "displeasure" is a strong word, correctly rendered "hot displeasure". It signifies furious indignation and wrath, and David's grief is that he has caused such. That he should be rebuked he can accept. That he needs to be chastened he can accept also. But he dreads that the due discipline should be meted out in anger and wrath. To be punished for his sin was one thing, but to incur chastening from a God so angry was quite another thing. "O Lord", he is appealing, if it may be paraphrased, "rebuke me, chasten me, but not in this hot displeasure". It was Jehovah's prerogative to discipline his servant who had sinned, but the thought of Jehovah's heated indignation was hard to bear.

David felt both wounded and pressed down. Conviction of sin is a piercing thing, and the chastening of the Lord brings accompanying pressure. Notice however, that it is "thine" arrows and "thy" hand. David, the warrior king, had faced the arrows of many an enemy, the hand of many a foe had often been against him, and he had endured and triumphed. But this was different. These were the arrows of an offended God which were piercing him, and this was the hand of Jehovah which was pressing down upon him and crushing him. He was suffering physically, mentally and spiritually, and all because of his sin. There was no soundness (4974) in his flesh. The same word is used by the prophet to describe the sad condition of Israel in Isaiah 1.6, and that passage should be compared. But this is personal. David's physical frame succumbs to restlessness and fever under the pressure of the disciplining hand of the Lord. There is no reason to take this other than literally. His health was gone, and all because of sin which he now so deeply regretted.

David feels the sense of sin as a heavy burden. But the burden is so heavy that it goes over his head. In Eastern culture and custom burdens were often carried on the shoulders. Sometimes the burden was so heavy that it bowed the physical frame of the burdened one and fell over his head to the ground. Some commentators, though, feel that there are two metaphors here; that the sense of sin is first likened to an overwhelming flood going over the head, and then also to a burden too heavy to bear.

The Psalmist's iniquity has brought corruption which he compares to festering wounds. He sees himself in all the loathsomeness of one who has grievously and foolishly sinned. He is troubled and mourning, feeble and foolish, bowed down and broken, grieving and groaning. It is a pathetic description of the man who had subdued Philistines and Syrians, Amalekites and Ammonites, Moabites and Edomites, but who could not subdue his own passions.

Davison, commenting on vv. 5-8, writes, "In each of these four verses words are used which hardly bear literal translation, but which vividly represent aspects of physical suffering. (1) The wounds are those which are caused by severe stripes, which fester and give forth a bad odour. (2) I am bent and bowed down greatly describes the cramped and cringing attitude of one who can hardly move because of pain. (3) The central parts of the body are filled with burning, i.e. the fever of inflammation.

(4) Hence he is faint and sore bruised, more literally, 'benumbed and sore broken', the chill of approaching death is upon him".

A touching comparison may be observed with the sufferings of the holy Sin-bearer of Isaiah 53.5. In that verse, "iniquities" is the same word as that in v.4 of this Psalm. "Stripes" is the same word as "wounds" of v.5 of the Psalm. "Bruised" is almost identical to "broken" in v.8 of the Psalm. The resultant "Peace" in Isaiah 53.5 is the same word as "rest" in v.3 of the Psalm. Oh the sufferings of the Sinless One, who suffered for others at Golgotha that those who had sinned might have peace and rest.

Verses 9-14: Continuing Complaint

As the Psalmist continues to unburden his heart and lament his condition, there is a glimmer of hope in the hopelessness, and of light in the darkness. The Lord knows! All the desire (8378), the longings, of David's heart were known to Jehovah. What men could not see or know was all known to the Omniscient One. Men might not understand, but there was One who did. His groaning, his inner sighing, was understood by the Lord. For this reason there may be observed in this part of the Psalm a certain calm which was not present earlier. There is still much pain of course, but alleviated by the thought that Jehovah knows all. The heart which sighs and groans is panting (5503), throbbing, perhaps because of exhaustion. There has been much physical pain, there has been almost unbearable anguish, and it has all left the Psalmist spent, and almost blind to better things around him, but the Lord knows.

An additional sorrow is that, like Job before him, David's former friends have forsaken him. Lovers (157) and friends (7453), kith and kin, companions and neighbours, all stand aloof from him. They stand away from his sore (5061). This word is more often translated "plague". It suggests the thought of leprosy, so that there was, with his friends, not only the embarrassment of seeing his affliction but also the fear of being contaminated by it. They stand afar off, even those who are his near kinsmen and family. These, therefore, not only observe his suffering but actually increase his pain and add to his distress by shunning him.

It would be suffering enough that David should be enduring such afflictions, and be abandoned by his friends, but there is yet additional pain. There are enemies who seek his life, who would now take advantage of his helplessness. They would lay snares for him, seeking to entrap him. There is a slanderous and treacherous campaign of deceit being waged against him. Mischievous things are being whispered among those who plot his hurt. It is constant too. All the day long it continues, this scheming for his destruction.

For a little while at least, occupation with others means that David is not directly occupied with himself, but is rather looking around him. Friends have forsaken him and foes plot against him and the sum of his afflictions now drives him to the very God whom he has offended. As far as the slander is concerned, the best attitude is that he should be deaf and dumb. He must determine neither to hear nor answer their whisperings against him. Let them spread their lies if they will, but David will refuse to hear. Let them wait for some response from him, but he will not give it. There will be no reproofs in his mouth, no rebuke and no argument. David will speak to God but not to men. So it was with the Blessed Saviour, "Who, when he was reviled, reviled not again; when he suffered, he threatened not; but committed himself to him that judgeth righteously" (1 Pet 2.23).

Verses 15-20: Renewed Penitence

Once again the Psalmist lifts his eyes away from himself and from friends and foes, to look to God. Observe again, as has been noted in the introduction, his use of divine titles. In v.1 he has cried to "Jehovah". In v.9 he has used the title "Lord". Now, in v.15, in one verse, he unites both "Jehovah" and "Lord" and adds, "My God". Jehovah! Adonai! Elohim! What intensity there is in his appeal to heaven. Note that in the two concluding verses of the Psalm the three titles are combined again in his final petition. David's hope (3176), his trust and his expectancy, were in his God. "Thou wilt hear", he could say confidently. It was a confidence based upon the character of God and upon the fact that he was, as David could say in a personal way, "My God". David seemed constantly to fear that his enemies might have cause to rejoice. They would taunt and insult him if it should appear that his God had forsaken him. They would magnify themselves against him. They would boast and vaunt themselves arrogantly over him, and for this reason he pleads, "Hear me".

It will be noticed that vv. 15, 16, 17 and 18 all commence with the particle "For". As Maclaren says, "The four-fold 'For' beginning each verse from 15-18 weaves them all into a chain". They become, he adds, "a striking example of faith's logic, the ingenuity of pleading which finds encouragements in discouragements" Each time, the word introduces a reason, a progressive argument, for David's turning his face away from men to God. First, in v.15, his hope was in God. Second, in v.16, it was lest they should have cause to rejoice who were both God's enemies, and his. In v.17 he declares that he is now feeble, ready to halt (6761). In v.18 he pleads what is perhaps the most powerful reason of all, his contrition and penitence for his sin. These were the four considerations which now drew him to his God.

The word which is here rendered "halting" is rendered "adversity" in Psalm 35.15. David was limping, stumbling, because of the injustices of his enemies. This may be understood either literally, as physical weakness, or it may indicate a sense of moral feebleness, or, indeed, there may be a combination of both. His sorrow was ever with him, the mental pain and anguish of one in continual grief. But he was now willing to declare (5046) the sin which had occasioned his grief. He would tell all to the Lord, in a full and open confession, without reservation. He was sincerely and truly sorry for the sin which had grieved God and had brought such trouble to himself.

Then there was the remembrance that if he was feeble and frail, by contrast his enemies were lively and powerful. If he was weak and halting, they were vigorous and strong. They were mighty and they were active and they were many. He was alone, and lonely, they were numerous and seemed to be multiplying, and their hatred of him was without cause. It was all wrong. In the injustice of it all his adversaries rendered evil for good. They were, in fact, his enemies because he pursued that which was good. This may not mean just a following after good in a general way, though that was true enough, but it may signify a pursuing of good in relation to them. Many of those who were now his adversaries had formerly been his friends, and had been the recipients of his kindness (Ps 35.12-14). It was hard to bear, that they should reward the good that he had done to them, and for them, with evil.

Verses 21-22: The Final Plea

David's friends and neighbours had forsaken him (v.11). He pleads that Jehovah will not. To be forsaken by men was grievous, but to be forsaken by the Lord would be abandonment indeed. He prays that it may not be so. It has earlier been observed that as he employs the great title Elohim, he makes the relationship so personal when he cries, "O my God". In these closing appeals for divine help, the titles which he uses, and the form of words, indicate a certain intense earnestness. "O LORD!" "O my God!" "O Lord!" "O Jehovah!" "O my Elohim!" "O Adonai!" David needs, and needs urgently, the help of God. He pleads that the Lord will make haste with the help he so much requires.

The Psalmist's final address to God is very significant; "O Lord my salvation". It is so similar to that cry from the heart in that most touching of "Penitential Psalms", "O God, thou God of my salvation" (Ps 51.14). David's sin had brought him low. He had no personal merit to plead, but casts himself in repentance upon God. Jehovah was his salvation, whether from sin, or from his enemies, or from the depression and anxiety into which sin had sunk him. But real confession and genuine contrition bring the blessing of salvation and recovery. Delitzsch says, "True repentance has faith within itself, it despairs of itself, but not of God".

So ends this, the third of the seven "Penitential Psalms". Here is the grief of a saint who has sinned, mingled with the hope of one who still trusts in his God.

PSALM 39

Introduction

Like fifty-four other Psalms, Psalm 39 is committed to the charge and care of the Chief Musician, who in this case is named as Jeduthun. It was a great privilege to be the Leader of the Praise, the Master of Song in the national worship. The Chief Musician was the Precentor, the person to whom the Psalm was handed over and who would be duly responsible for its performance. Such was Jeduthun, who is named also in the titles of Psalms 62 and 77. In 1 Chronicles 16.7, 37 and 41 Asaph, Heman and Jeduthun are named as the three leaders of the temple choirs. Of Jeduthun personally little is known apart from this. Several men in the OT may have borne the same name, but see especially the references in 1 Chronicles 16.41, 42, and note also, in 1 Chronicles 25.1, that the sons of Jeduthun, with the sons of Asaph and Heman, were appointed by David to the service of the house of the Lord. Jeduthun was a Levite, and, as Leader of the Praise, his name is most appropriate, meaning "praising". He seems also to have been known as Ethan (1 Chr 15.16-17).

This is another Psalm of David, and there is a marked resemblance to the earlier Psalm 37. It is again the song of a sufferer, composed in the minor key with the sweet sadness of one who, in his suffering, waits upon the Lord. It has been described as an elegy, a song of mourning, of which Ewald says that it is "indisputably the most beautiful of all the elegies in the Psalter". The Psalm may belong, with others, to that sad period of Absalom's rebellion, but David had so many trying experiences in life that it well suits any time of sorrow.

The Psalm can be considered in four parts. The introductory verses 1-3 describe the circumstances under which it was composed. Verses 4-5 are a prayer, remembering the frailty and brevity of life and concluding with a "Selah". In verses 6-11 the vanity of man is enlarged upon, with a personal confession of sin. This section also ends with a "Selah". The concluding two verses, 12-13, bring a final appeal from the Psalmist that God might regard his tears, hear his prayers, spare him and strengthen him.

Verses 1-3: Silence in Sorrow

David reflects that when he was assailed by the slander and insults of his enemies, he had kept silent (compare Ps 38.13-14). He had learned that the best response to their attacks was to behave as one who did not hear them and therefore could not answer. He neither reproved them nor argued with them but remained in silence. He had determined that he would resolutely control his tongue as with a bridle, or, literally, with a muzzle (JND). "I said, I will take heed to my ways...I will keep my mouth". He speaks only to himself, within his heart, vowing that he will not sin with his tongue, with the wicked before him. He would not murmur in their presence, nor complain against them. He will guard both his ways and his words, and give his enemies no occasion to accuse him. Before them he was as one who could neither hear nor speak. He was "as a deaf man" and "as a dumb man" (Ps 38.13). There is a great similarity to Job, who likewise suffered much, but of whom it is said that, "In all this did not Job sin with his lips" (Job 2.10).

The enforced and prolonged restraint, however, stirred the sorrow within the Psalmist, for his silence was absolute. He would speak neither good or bad but remain in a complete silence which was indicative of his resignation to the will of God and his submission to the ways of God. Such self-imposed silence, such suppressed feelings as this, tended to aggravate his pain and increase his sorrow, until his heart waxed hot. His troubled thoughts and his pent-up feelings were like friction in his heart creating a heat which would soon become a flame. The fire kindled. His musings (1901) were like a whispered murmuring within him until the smouldering passion burst into flame. At last his emotions could be stifled no longer. He must find relief from this mute indignation at the wicked. He must speak. "Then spake I with my tongue".

Verses 4-5: The Silence is Broken

It is to the Psalmist's credit, and for our example, that, when he must eventually speak, he will speak to God. He breaks his silence with a prayer. There is neither criticism nor complaint in his petition, but a sincere request that he should be made conscious of his end, and of the frailty and brevity of life. "Make me to know mine end", is not a desire to know when, or how, that end may come, but rather that he should realise that there is an end, and that life is very transient. To be reminded of the brief measure of his days would be a reminder also of his frailty. How frail indeed is man, whose days are as grass (Ps 103.15). "What is your life?", says another, "It is even a vapour, that appeareth for a little time, and then vanisheth away" (Jas 4.14). And yet, the very remembrance of the brevity of life may bring comfort to the sufferer. As Paul writes, "Our light affliction, which is but for a moment, worketh for us a far more exceeding and eternal weight of glory...for the things which are seen are temporal; but the things which are not seen are eternal" (2 Cor 4.17-18). It is good then, to join with David in his prayer, "Make me to know mine end, and the measure of my days".

His days are as handbreadths (JND, RV). Each day is but the measure of four fingers, less than half a span (compare Jer 52.21 and 1 Kings 7.26). How fleeting, and therefore how frail, is man. It is the eternal Jehovah who has made man so. As David addresses the eternal he recognises that mortal man is as nothing in comparison. As another puts it, "In the sight of the Eternal man's existence shrinks into nothing" (Kirkpatrick). Jehovah is from everlasting to everlasting! What is man before him? "Mine age", the Psalmist says, "is as nothing before thee". "Age" (2465), says Strong, is from an unused root apparently meaning to glide swiftly. The duration of human life is but very brief, which means that any man, every man, man at his best, even the high-placed man (JND), is altogether vanity. However well a man may stand before other men, however firmly he may seem to be established, it is vanity when the transience of it all is remembered. Of one Blessed Man it is said, "He is altogether lovely" (Song 5.16), but He is a unique Man, and others are "altogether vanity".

It is time for a "Selah" (5542). It is a moment for pausing, for meditation, for reflection. While the music may now rise to a sweet crescendo, the heart may also be lifted up in silent and solemn contemplation.

Verses 6-11: Vanity! Vanity!

This section of the Psalm begins and ends with, and pursues throughout, the folly of human vanity. Man likes to create an image, a vain show (6754). How often the image he creates of himself is but an empty portrayal of what he vainly imagines himself to be. It is a shadow, a phantom, a semblance of his proud thoughts of his own importance. In it all he is disquieted (1993), clamouring, murmuring, even roaring, to attract attention to his vain self. Like that rich farmer of Luke 12.20 he amasses possessions, forgetting that he must leave them and not knowing who shall gather them when his own brief life is past.

Having meditated on the brevity and uncertainty of life and the deceitfulness of riches, the Psalmist now turns to the Lord. "And now, Lord", he says, "what wait I for?" In view of all this vanity of men, and remembering that his short pilgrimage will soon be over, to whom could he go but to his God? Peter expressed the same sentiments centuries later, and exclaimed, "Lord, to whom shall we go?" (Jn 6.68). Both Psalmist and Apostle knew that their only hope and sure stay was in the Lord. To Him alone they would turn from the vanities of the world. Such serious consideration of the vanity and frailty of life should deaden a man's desires for the things of the world.

David prays for deliverance from all his transgressions. Base men would reproach a man of God when they saw sin in his life. David recoiled from such reproach. They taunted him that his sufferings were an evidence of God's displeasure with him but he had remained silent while he bore their criticisms (Ps 38.13-14; 39.2). They were right, of course, these foolish men. David had no good answer for their taunting, for Jehovah was displeased with him. He says, "I opened not my mouth; because thou didst it". His confession will bring deliverance. As Davison writes, "The Psalmist desires a manifestation of God to Himself; while he acknowledges that his suffering has not been undeserved, he claims that as a true servant of God he should be vindicated in the eyes of the foolish, i.e. the careless and godless evil-doers around".

"Remove thy stroke (5061) away from me", he pleads. The chastisement of the Lord had plagued him and wounded him, but he acknowledges the transgressions which had necessitated the chastisement and now prays for respite. He feels consumed (3615), spent, exhausted, by the blow of the hand of the Lord. As he has said in another place, "Thy hand was heavy upon me" (Ps 32.4). There is a certain humility in the Psalmist's pleas, indicating that the chastisement has accomplished its intended purpose, but since the stroke is from God, only God can remove it, and to His mercy David appeals for relief.

The weakness and frailty of man is emphasised again, in that, under the hand of God, when God rebukes for iniquity, man's pretended beauty melts away. "Thou makest his beauty to consume away like a moth". The commentary by Henry and Scott sums up the variation of interpretation of this last expression. "Some make the moth to represent man, who is as easily crushed as a moth with the touch of a finger (Job 4.19). Others make it to represent the divine rebukes, which silently and insensibly waste and consume us, as the moth does the garment". The conclusion can only be that which has already been stated in v.5 - "Surely every man is vanity". Again, "Selah". Pause; reflect; meditate; contemplate; lift up the heart to God.

Verses 12-13: My Prayer; My Cry; My Tears

David's final impassioned appeal is that Jehovah might hear his cry. His prayers have been as cries to Jehovah, and they were mingled with his tears. "Hear…O Lord", he cries. "Give ear". "Hold not thy peace". He pleads his tears, desiring that Jehovah might respond to them. They were evidence of his sincerity and of his true repentance. The transience of life had taught him too that he was but a stranger and a sojourner in the world, but he sojourned with God. He was passing through, his residence here but temporary. As were the patriarchs, so was David (1 Chr 29.15). Those early men of faith confessed that they were strangers and pilgrims on the earth. They looked for a better country, a heavenly country (Heb 11.13-14). Life here was not permanent, but there was a city whose Builder and Maker was God. He had prepared that city for them, and to this they looked and travelled. David walked with God, in the way that the patriarchs had trodden, and this made all the difference living in a world where all was vanity.

He prays that he might be spared for a while. The phrase which is translated here, in the AV and RV as, "spare me"(8159), is, by JND, JPS and RSV rendered, "Look away from me". Barnes comments that "it here means, 'Look away from me', that is, 'Do not come to inflict death on me. Preserve me'. The idea is this: God seemed to have fixed his eyes on him, and to be pursuing him with the expressions of His displeasure, and the Psalmist now prays that He would 'turn away His eyes', and leave him". The JFB Commentary says, "O spare me – literally, 'look away from me; turn away (thy angry look) from me'"

David longs that his physical strength might be recovered, and his health restored, before he would pass away, when, as far as earth was concerned, he would be no more. The frailty, the vanity, the brevity, and the uncertainty of which he has written, had detached him from the world. He was a stranger in it, walking with God, and soon to leave it for another world. That would be to enter into a rest never to be disturbed.

PSALM 40

Introduction

This is the sixth of those Psalms which are termed "Messianic". That much of it applies to the Psalmist personally is not denied, but vv. 6-10 are interpreted in Hebrews 10 as a prediction of the Messiah, and indeed, apart from seeing Messiah in these verses, the Psalm cannot be properly understood.

It is a Psalm of David, and, considering its content, it is not surprising that it should be committed to the care of the Chief Musician. Although the Psalm is in the first person, its being dedicated to the Chief Musician indicates that it was intended to be used in public worship.

There is no good reason to doubt, as some do, the original unity of the Psalm. Because of the difference in tone and content between its opening and the closing stanzas, the hypothesis is sometimes suggested that it is composite, being a combination of two Psalms. In this connection it is pointed out that vv. 13-17, with a few modifications, appear again separately in the Psalter as Psalm 70. But David surely had troubles that were always with him. When Jehovah granted him deliverance from one trouble, others seemed to gather around him and loom before him. So, if the early vv. 1-5 are a thanksgiving for deliverance already granted, and the latter vv. 11-17 are a prayer for further deliverance, this need not be unusual in the troubled life of the Psalmist. Was it not so also with Paul, who wrote, "God...who delivered us...and doth deliver: in whom we trust that he will yet deliver" (2 Cor 1.9-10)?

The Psalm may be divided into three parts. Verses 1-5 are a song of thanksgiving for past deliverance and a declaration of God's goodness. The central portion, verses 6-10, describes the devotion and perfect obedience of the Messiah. The closing verses, 11-17, are a petition for continuing preservation and divine help.

Verses 1-5: The New Song

The Psalmist's patient waiting upon Jehovah has been rewarded. "I waited patiently", is a beautiful expression, somewhat difficult to translate because "waited" and "patiently" are the same word in the original Hebrew of the Psalm (6960). Literally, he says, "I waited waiting upon the Lord".

Davison writes, "Render, 'For Jehovah I waited, waited'; only thus can the emphasis of the Hebrew idiom be reproduced in English". Another writes, "Waiting, I waited" (Henry and Scott), and yet another renders it, "I waited waitingly" (Kirkpatrick).

David has waited patiently for Jehovah, and Jehovah, with all His eternal greatness, inclined (5186) unto His servant and heard his cry. That Jehovah should bend down, stoop, to hear that cry is most gracious. Perhaps, too, that bending down of the Lord is an indication that He will not miss the feeblest, faintest sigh of His people. It is good, therefore, to wait, and to wait patiently. The child of God may indeed wait with assurance, but that assurance must be blended with patience, for Jehovah does not always answer immediately. David, in his great need, did not doubt that relief would come, but, while waiting expectantly, he must continue believing, trusting, hoping and praying, patiently, until Jehovah would answer in His own time. Deliverance would come, and, for David, it did.

The figurative language which the Psalmist uses to describe his distress is reminiscent of the literal and actual experience of the imprisoned Jeremiah (Jer 38.6). Evil men had him cast into a dungeon, where there was no water, but mire into which the good prophet sank. So did David feel himself entrapped, as in a horrible (7588) pit. Only once is this word "horrible" so translated in the AV. It carries the thought of noise and tumult, of roaring and crashing. It was a pit of destruction (JND and RV margin). "The tumultuous pit", it has been called (Dr Cohen). Like Jeremiah, David sank in the mire. There was a feeling of insecurity, like one walking on a swamp, with no firm foothold, or like a traveller might feel when caught in a morass or quicksand.

Jehovah's answer to the cry of His child was four-fold. He lifted him. He set his feet upon a rock. He established his steps. He gave him a new song. So has it been with all those who trust Him. David was brought up, lifted out of the slough of despair and despondency into which his spirit had sunk. He was delivered out of the mire and given a firm foothold, as on a rock. What a change! From miry clay to solid rock! His goings, too, his steps, were now divinely established. His way would now be ordered and directed by the God who lifted him, and there was a new song on his lips. This is not the only mention of the new song. See also Psalms 33.3; 96.1; 98.1; 149.1; Isaiah 42.10, as well as Revelation 5.9 and 14.3. It is the song of the redeemed. It is, like that first recorded song in Holy Scripture, a song of triumph and of praise to Jehovah (Ex 15.1-2).

The effects of praising God can be far-reaching. The Lord Himself, of course, will have His portion in it, but others, observing the joy of a redeemed people, can be drawn by such testimony to a fear of God and to eventual trust in Him. "It is a good thing to give thanks unto the Lord, and to sing praises unto thy name, O most High" (Ps 92.1). Praising and trusting are the marks of a happy saint. The man who confides in Jehovah has no need to look to proud and arrogant men for help, neither will he trust in those who have turned aside (7750) to falsehood. Such men have fallen away from what is right. They have swerved from the path of truth. The trusting man will not follow them.

As David contemplates what Jehovah has done, he revels in the wonder of it all. Both the works and the thoughts of God have been multiplied. His works are wonderful (6381), whether in creation or in redemption. They are marvellous, surpassing human understanding. His thoughts towards His people are equally great. They cannot be reckoned up in order (6186). They can neither be counted, nor estimated, nor valued, nor set in order by mortal minds. As David writes in another place, "How precious also are thy thoughts unto me, O God! how great is the sum of them! If I should count them, they are more in number than the sand" (Ps 139.17-18). Both the works and the thoughts of God are beyond telling, they cannot be recounted or declared.

Verses 6-10: Messiah!

There can be no doubt that this section looks forward, in prophetic poetry, to the coming of the Messiah. The inspired Hebrews 10.5-7 confirms this for every believer. Four kinds of offerings are mentioned here, the details of which are in the early chapters of Leviticus, but given there in a different order from that given here in the Psalm. The first is "sacrifice" (ZEBACH - 2077), the Peace Offering. The second "offering" (MINCHA - 4503) is the Meat Offering. Then there is the Burnt Offering (OLA - 5930), and, lastly, the Sin Offering (CHATSA'A - 2401). These were the principal classes of offerings which were prescribed by God in relation to the Levitical priesthood. The sacrifice of peace offering was offered as a thanksgiving, or at the making of a vow, or sometimes just as a voluntary offering. This offering was shared by the altar, the priesthood, and the offerer. It was a fellowship offering. The meat offering was the gift to the altar of the fruits of the earth. The burnt offering was wholly for God, offered in entirety (except for the skin) upon the altar. The sin offering, in its various forms, was, of course, a shedding of blood for the forgiveness of sins. These offerings were divinely prescribed and required, but they were not desired (2654), in that they brought no delight or joy to God. What would really have brought that delight would have been a life lived in such perfection that no such offerings were ever necessary, a life wholly consecrated to God and spent for His pleasure. With man this was not possible, hence the offerings. But Messiah was coming. His perfect life, requiring no offerings, would bring to Jehovah that pleasure which He desired in man.

The lovely clause interpolated in the midst of v.6, "Mine ears hast thou opened", looks forward to One who daily enjoyed communion with Jehovah and whose ear was open morning by morning to hear the will of God (Is 50.4). The quotation of this clause in Hebrews 10.5, as "A body hast thou prepared me" is from the LXX, which accounts for the variation.

Kirkpatrick explains, "The variation of the Septuagint from the Hebrew may seem to present a serious difficulty. But the appropriateness of the quotation does not depend upon this particular clause, and the rendering of the Septuagint, whatever its origin, has in effect a sense analogous to the sense of the original. As the ear is the instrument for receiving the divine command, so the body is the instrument for fulfilling it".

"Then said I", is the language of that one unique and Blessed Man who came to do the will of God, who alone could do it perfectly, and who alone could delight to do it. "Lo, I come", He said. In the volume of the inspired scroll, the Holy Scriptures, His coming had been promised. Moses and the prophets all spoke of Him. He came with the law of God enshrined in His heart, and with the moral fitness to live out all the requirements of that law. It was His joy to do the will of God. As He loved righteousness, and lived it, so He preached it. It was not in His heart only, it was in His bold testimony to men. Righteousness was the theme of His ministry and the manner of His life. He preached it freely and fully in the great congregation, without restraint or restriction. He concealed nothing, and Jehovah knew this. There was, in the ministry of the Messiah, in accord with this Psalm, a clear declaration of the message of God. His faithfulness, His salvation, His lovingkindness and His truth had all been proclaimed. Nothing had been withheld from the great congregation which heard Him.

Verses 11-17: A Prayer for Preservation

In the measure in which these verses apply to the Psalmist personally he now asks for divine recognition and reciprocation for what he has done. Since he had not withheld a faithful ministry from the people, would Jehovah likewise not withhold His tender mercies (7356) from His servant? How much he needed that compassion and pity which only God could give. How much he himself needed to be reassured of that lovingkindness and truth which he had preached to others. As Davison puts it, "The temptation may have arisen in a comparatively corrupt society not to testify thus openly: the Psalmist has not yielded to it, and therefore with confidence he appeals to God that as he has not restrained loyal witness and utterance, 'Thou, O Jehovah, wilt not restrain Thy tender mercies from me'. The tense implies, 'Thou wilt not, wilt Thou? I am persuaded that Thy lovingkindness and truth which I have declared to others will be vouchsafed to guard me' ".

Although David had already known God's deliverance, yet, still, troubles abounded. His sky is clouded again. As the wonderful works of God had been past reckoning, so the evils (7451), the afflictions which beset him were innumerable and ever present. These troubles appear to be the consequences of his sins. They have taken hold of him (5381). They have caught up with him and overtaken him, and, in his conscience, he is bowed down under the remembrance of them. His heart and courage fail him. He can scarcely lift his head to look up, and again he cries for deliverance.

Jehovah! Jehovah! Twice in one sentence he pleads the divine name. "Be pleased, O Lord, to deliver me: make haste to help me, O Lord".

As has already been noticed, vv. 13-17 appear again in the Psalter, with slight variations, as Psalm 70. Notice also that v.14 is almost a repetition of Psalm 35.4 and 26, while vv. 15 and 16 can also be found in phrases gathered from some part of the same Psalm 35. In all of these David calls for the confounding of his enemies. They sought for his destruction. He prays for their desolation. They wished him evil and delighted in his hurt. He prays for their defeat. To their shame, they said, as they looked on him, "Aha, Aha! It was an exclamation of contempt and of malicious pleasure at his trouble.

The Psalmist turns from them, to think, in happy contrast, of those who loved the Lord as he did. "Let them rejoice", he prays. "Let them be glad". Those who love His salvation must continually desire that Jehovah should be magnified. Although poor and needy, afflicted and in constant need of help, yet David has this consolation, "The Lord thinketh upon me". The thoughts of God are ever towards His suffering saints. "My help...my deliverer!", David calls Him. "O make haste", he pleads, "make no tarrying". The need is urgent. David's final appeal is to Elohim, to the Mighty One, whom he calls, "My God" (430).

PSALM 41

Introduction

This is the last Psalm in Book 1 of the Psalter. It is the third Psalm which begins with a benediction (see Psalms 1 and 32). It is fitting that as the first Psalm in Book 1 commenced with "Blessed", so should this last Psalm in Book 1 also commence with a benediction. The Psalm is counted among those that are termed "Messianic", although only one verse in the Psalm, v. 9, has direct reference to the Messiah and is so quoted by the Lord Jesus in John 13.18.

It is a Psalm of David and seems to belong, as many other Psalms do, to the period of Absalom's rebellion. Although there is no record in the account in 2 Samuel of David having such an illness as that which is described in the Psalm, there is in v.9 an obvious reference to the treachery of Ahithophel, which seems to confirm the circumstances in which it was written. Kirkpatrick's comment is very helpful. He writes, "It is true that the narrative in 2 Samuel makes no reference to an illness such as is here described; but that narrative necessarily passes over many details. Such an illness would account for the remissness in attending to his official duties, which Absalom's words to the suitors for justice seem to imply (2 Sam 15.3). It would account also for the strange failure of David's natural courage which his flight from Jerusalem at the first outbreak of rebellion appears to indicate".

He continues, "Unnerved by sickness, in which he recognised a just punishment for his sins, David watched the growing disloyalty of his courtiers, and in particular of Ahithophel, without feeling able to strike and crush the conspiracy before it came to a head". The sickness referred to seems to have been so serious that David's enemies actually anticipated, and waited for, his death (vv. 5-8).

If the final verse 13 of the Psalm is regarded separately as a closing doxology, then the other twelve verses are arranged in four stanzas of three verses each, the central two stanzas being fused together by a common theme.

The Psalm, like those many others, is committed to the charge and care of the Chief Musician, on which see the note in the introduction to Psalm 4.

Verses 1-3: The Benediction

That man is pronounced blessed who considers the poor. "Blessed" (835) is often rendered "happy". It is cognate with the name of the tribe Asher. "Happy am I", said Leah at the birth of her son in Genesis 30.13, "for the daughters will call me blessed: and she called his name Asher" (836). To consider (7919) the poor is to understand and to give attention to, but the poor in this verse is not necessarily, or exclusively, those in material poverty. It may mean those who are weak and enfeebled in health, as David then was, and perhaps the ensuing verses would indicate that this is what is intended. There is blessing for the man who behaves considerately and wisely towards those who are afflicted. This is an OT counterpart of that beatitude of the Lord Jesus, when he said, "Blessed are the merciful: for they shall obtain mercy" (Mt 5.7). The considerate and merciful man will, perhaps, some day, be himself in need of consideration and compassion, and Jehovah has promised to deliver him in his time of trouble. The Lord will preserve him. He will watch over him, guard him, and in sickness revive him. This is Jehovah's promise. It is, as Jesus said, mercy for the merciful.

Again the word "blessed" is used, but with a slight variation. "He shall be blessed (833) upon the earth". There is the thought here, not just of a present, particular happiness, but of being led on in a pathway of blessedness, ever progressing, always advancing, in happiness, and part of that blessedness is that he will be delivered from the evil designs of his enemies. When the sorrow of a bed of illness does come, then Jehovah will support and strengthen him, and make his bed during his sickness. The metaphor may be that of a nurse, attending to the needs of the sick one, supporting the patient's head while arranging the pillows to give ease and comfort. "Underneath are the everlasting arms" (Deut 33.27).

Verses 4-9: Sin, Sickness and Sorrow

David's conscience seems to be continually heavy at the remembrance of his sins. He has long since recognised that he has sinned not only against men, but also against God, and this has not ceased to trouble him. Once again he asks for mercy, saying, "I have sinned against thee". As he cries in another place, "Against thee, thee only, have I sinned" (Ps 51.4). He appears to relate his sickness to his sin and he prays for healing. His very soul, his whole life, his inner being, are all affected. He implores that Jehovah might be merciful (2603). He needs mercy, and grace, and pity.

Added to the sorrow of his sin and his sickness, is the cruelty of David's enemies and the disloyalty of some of his friends. His enemies waited, gloating, longing for news of his death. "When shall he die?", they asked with a callous impatience. They desired his end and that his name should perish, probably meaning the extinction of his posterity. His enemies visited him, but apparently it was not unusual for kings at enmity with each other to visit in times of sickness, as seen in 2 Kings 8.29. However, there was no pity. There were hypocritical expressions of feigned sympathy. Did they perhaps express hopes that he would recover? It was all falsehood and vanity, and all the time they were plotting mischief and evil in their hearts, and then, on leaving David, they joined the whispering campaign of those who devised his hurt. It was an evil (1100) disease that afflicted him, they said. It was a thing of Belial. So had Shimei cursed David in 2 Samuel 16.5-8, casting stones at him and calling him a man of Belial. It was a term denoting wickedness and worthlessness. His sickness, they said, was the result of his wickedness, and with this thing cleaving to him he would rise no more. They waited for his decease.

But there was yet sorrow to be added to sorrow. David had these multiple sorrows of remembering his sins, and suffering his illness, and enduring the taunts of his enemies, but perhaps the hardest thing to bear was this, that his own familiar trusted friend should turn against him. This is an undoubted reference to Ahithophel (2 Sam 15.12, 31; 16.20, 23). The man who had been David's friend and counsellor betrayed him, turning to the usurper Absalom. Regarding the treachery of Ahithophel, Harold St. John makes the interesting observation. He says, "For years this man's treachery and bitter malice was a mystery to me, until one day reading the list of David's mighty men, the name of Eliam the son of Ahithophel arrested me and struck a chord of memory. Eliam was also the father of Bathsheba, so that David by his sin had dishonoured and brought shame upon the granddaughter of Ahithophel, and no wonder the old man's loyalty broke beneath the strain: it is now easy to understand his peculiarly malignant counsel in respect of David's wives (2 Sam 16.21-23), and we also know why he committed suicide when he saw his counsel despised (2 Sam 17.23): he knew the breach between himself and David was irreparable". T.E. Wilson suggests the same when he writes, "When we consider that

Ahithophel was the grandfather of Bathsheba, we can understand the motive behind his treachery".

Ahithophel, both in his treachery and in his awful fate, is a foreshadowing of Judas Iscariot. As Ahithophel betrayed David and eventually hanged himself (2 Sam 17.23), so did Judas betray Jesus and then hang himself (Mt 27.3-5). The treachery of Judas was, the Lord Jesus said, a fulfilment of Scripture (Jn 13.18). Both of these traitors had eaten bread, had fellowship at the table, with those whom they betrayed. Both had "lifted up the heel" against the friend whom they were to betray. This expression, Davison says, "may refer to violence, i.e. has struck me with all his force; or to fraud, he has raised his heel covertly to trip me up and overthrow me; the latter is the more appropriate to the context". There is a deep sadness in all of this, both in the case of David and in the betrayal of the Lord Jesus. "Mine own familiar friend" is, literally, "the man of my peace". The word here rendered "familiar" (7965) is the lovely word Shalom. What callous treachery is this, that the men of Shalom should become traitors to both David and to the Son of David, plotting the deaths of those who had so recently and for so long befriended them. The greeting "Shalom!" is, literally, "Peace be to thee". Such was the kiss with which Judas betrayed the Master, and in our Lord's last word to the traitor Jesus called him, "Friend" (Mt 26.48-50). It should be noted, however, that when the Saviour quoted v.9 in the upper room, with reference to Judas, He omitted the words, "in whom I trusted", for "he knew who should betray him" (Jn 13.11). "He knew what was in man" (Jn 2.25).

Verses 10-12; But Thou, O Jehovah...

David is glad to turn away from his sorrow, from his sickness, from his enemies, and from the traitor, to look to the Lord. "But thou!", is a comforting contrast to the enemies who opposed him and the friend who has forsaken him. Jehovah was the Unfailing One, and to Him David now looks for help. He prays again, as he has done in v.4, for mercy and for health. He desires that Jehovah might be gracious to him and raise him up. His foes wait eagerly for his death, but would the Lord raise him up that he might requite them? "Requite" (7999) is often understood to be a desire for retribution, that King David might eventually be vindicated and his enemies confounded. This, of course, may be so. However it should be noted that the word rendered "requite" is a cognate word with the earlier mentioned "Shalom". It is, in fact, SHALAM. The thought may well be that David, restored, would repay evil with good and enter into a covenant of peace with those who had been at enmity with him.

In all his sorrow, David seems to be assured that the enemy will not triumph over him, and by this he will know that Jehovah's favour is upon him. He is conscious also of his own integrity. He may indeed have sinned, and sinned grievously, but his confession and repentance indicate his heart's desire for uprightness, and Jehovah will support him in that. If his enemies have desired his death and the extinction of his name, it will not be so. The Lord will give him a place before Him for ever. His standing with Jehovah is established and assured. He will enjoy the divine presence eternally.

Verse 13: The Doxology

The "Blessed" (1288) of this closing verse of the Psalm is not the same as the "Blessed" (835) of the opening verse. There, in v.1, the thought was of the happiness of the man concerned. Here, in v.13, the word signifies an ascription of praise and adoration to Jehovah. It is akin to "blessed" (*2128*) in the NT, from which is derived the English word "eulogise" meaning "to praise or speak well of" (See Ephesians 1.3 where the word occurs three times). So will David speak well of Jehovah and attribute praise to Him whom he calls the LORD (3068) God (430) of Israel. It is a majestic title, "Jehovah, Elohim of Israel", Jehovah of the eternal present, the mighty One, blessed from everlasting to everlasting. The doxology is simple, and yet profound in the extreme.

Here, for the first time in the Psalter, is the "Amen" (543). This is a transliteration of the Hebrew AMEN. In its double form it now closes Book 1 of the Psalms. "Amen, and Amen!". "Truly, truly!". "Verily, verily!". "So be it, so be it!". It is a fitting conclusion, probably the response of the congregation in the public worship, affirming their own ascription of praise to Jehovah, as in Psalm 106.48, "Blessed be the Lord God of Israel from everlasting to everlasting: and let all the people say, Amen. Praise ye the Lord". Note the similar response of the people to David's Psalm of praise when the Ark of the Covenant was brought back from its exile to the city of David, "Blessed be the Lord God of Israel for ever and ever. And all the people said, Amen, and praised the Lord" (1 Chr 16.36).

This concludes Book 1 of the Psalms

BOOK 2

PSALM 42

Introduction

This Psalm is the first in the second Book of Psalms, which book continues up to and including Psalm 72. For comment on that part of the inscription which commits it "To the Chief Musician", see the introduction in the commentary to Psalm 4. The Psalm is also the second of thirteen "Maschil" Psalms, indicating that it is a Psalm for instruction, a Psalm to be contemplated for wisdom. The first "Maschil" Psalm is Psalm 32. Also, in the inscription, the sons of Korah are mentioned, but there is no general agreement about the preposition which links them with the Psalm. Is it "for", or "by", or "to", the sons of Korah? The singular pronouns in the Psalm may indicate one Psalmist, this being an argument against a multiple authorship of the sons of Korah. But whichever preposition may be the correct one, the important consideration is that this is a Psalm which in some way may be appreciated by the posterity of a man who, having instigated a rebellion against Moses, perished beneath the severe judgment of God (Num 16). Korah was a cousin of Moses who had joined with Dathan and Abiram in the revolt and had died in the judgment with them. He perished, with 250 men, but, as Numbers 26.11 records, "The children of Korah died not", and now his descendants are remembered in this and other Psalms. These sons of Korah are frequently mentioned in connection with the temple service, both as singers and as door-keepers (1 Chr 9.19; 26.1; 2 Chr 20.19). Heman, the first of the Masters of Song appointed by David, was a descendant of Korah. They were, as Plumer says, "A Levitical family of singers". With what dedication and gratitude they must have engaged in the holy service for which they had been preserved when their rebellious father had died.

Some think that this Psalm is David's. Plumer writes, "There is reason for regarding David as the author...It well suits the case of David in his long exile from Jerusalem in the days of Saul...The geographical position of David in his exile corresponds with that noted in v.6, the land of Jordan and of Hermon...The great weight of authority is on the side of the Davidic authorship". He then quotes some fourteen authorities, and refers to the Septuagint, Vulgate, Ethiopic and Syriac versions which all give David as the author of Psalm 43 which is so intimately connected with Psalm 42. Spurgeon remarks, rather quaintly, "It is so Davidic, it smells of the son of Jesse, it bears the marks of his style and experience in every letter". Regarding the obvious relation between Psalms 42 and 43, several Hebrew manuscripts connect them as one Psalm, but, as Dr Cohen comments, "All the Ancient Versions, however, divide them, so that the separation, if such took place, must have occurred at an early date". See also the Introduction in the commentary on Psalm 43.

Psalm 42 has been called the "Lament of an Exile". It is a plaintive cry from the heart of an exile longing for Jerusalem and for the courts of the Lord. If the Psalm is considered in conjunction with Psalm 43 it will be noticed that there are three stanzas, of almost equal size, each concluding with almost identical words in vv. 5 and 11 of Psalm 42, and v. 5 of Psalm 43.

Verses 1-5: Thirsting for God

The opening stanza throbs with a tender pathos. The Psalmist is panting, thirsting, longing, weeping, remembering, and yet hoping. He is obviously in a compulsory exile, yearning for the former days and the earlier joys of the presence of God. In almost every verse, in both this Psalm and the next, the Psalmist will invoke the great name Elohim (430). Ten times it occurs in the eleven verses of this Psalm. El (410) occurs three times, and Jehovah (3068) but once. Elohim is now to be the characteristic divine name in this second Book of Psalms, as Jehovah was in the first. While neither name is used exclusively in either book, Jehovah is prominent in the first and Elohim in the second. The mighty God, the only true God, is in control of the Psalmist's life. He will appeal to Him, he will cry to Him, and pant after Him as a thirsty hart panted after the water brook. W.M. Thomson of *The Land and the Book* says, "The sacred writers frequently mention gazelles under the various names of harts, roes, and hinds...I have seen large flocks of these panting harts gather round the water brooks in the great deserts of Central Syria, so subdued by thirst that you could approach quite near them before they fled". The Psalmist's simile is most suitable. The hart was a gentle animal, of a tender nature, a fitting image of the godly soul, and as those little creatures panted after the water brook, so did he after his God. "Hart", in the original, may be either masculine or feminine, but the verb is feminine.

His soul thirsted for Elohim, the living God. The gods of the heathen were dead gods. They were lifeless deities, unable to respond or commune. The Psalmist's God was living in Himself, "the fountain of living waters" to sustain His people (Jer 2.13). It was proper that His people should therefore appear before Him in gratitude and worship. "Appearing before God" was the expression used to describe the annual pilgrimages to Jerusalem and to the temple (Ex 23.17; Ps 84.7), but how could one in enforced exile so appear? When might he return to Jerusalem and stand again in the presence of God in holy service? When would he again enjoy the spiritual refreshment for which he panted? In those Eastern lands, where the sun scorched the earth and where water was precious, thirst was an experience common to both man and beast. The hunted hart knew very well what thirst was. The simile was perfect, for the Psalmist thirsted too, after God and the service of the house of God.

His longings were continually accompanied by weeping. Tears took the place of his daily food. Appetite was gone and as he wept the men around him taunted him saying, "Where is thy God?". In a strange way, sweet memories now added to his sorrow. He recalls the festival days, the joy and praise, the multitudes making their jubilant way to the house of God, the tabernacle on Mount Zion (2 Sam 6.17). He had been one of them, and one with them. Indeed the RV rendering of v.4 suggests that he had actually led them. He had joined his voice with theirs and had rejoiced with them. With these memories he weeps out his soul. Those days were past. Jerusalem seemed far away, with the sanctuary and the holy days. But should he despair?

The sad refrain of v.5 will be repeated in v.11 and in v.5 of Psalm 43. "Why art thou cast down, O my soul?" Is he addressing a gentle rebuke to his own soul? If the mighty Elohim really is his life and his rock, as he will soon declare, why should he be so disquieted (1993)? The word signifies, "troubled, clamorous, murmuring, mourning, even growling". Was it right that, with such a God as he had, he should he be so dejected and forlorn, so drooped in sorrow so continually? No, it must not be. He exhorts his downcast soul to hope in God whose presence is salvation. He must patiently wait and trust, for the time would come when he would yet again praise God and rejoice.

Verses 6-11: Appealing to God

The fact was, however, that, in spite of his reasonings with himself in v.5, the Psalmist continued to be cast down. Perhaps he ought not to be so dejected and dispirited, but he was. "Therefore", he says, "will I remember thee". Is he saying that in his depression he will seek for some cheer in the remembrance of his God? Will thoughts of God relieve his sorrow and lift his spirits? Or is he actually saying, as some suggest, that the very remembrance of God, as he had known Him in former happier times, was the reason for his being cast down? Those who understand it so will read "because", instead of "therefore", as in JND's footnote, resulting in, "My soul is cast down within me because I remember thee". The weight of opinion though, seems to be in favour of the common version, meaning that in his sadness the Psalmist will look for consolation in the remembrance of his God.

Memories transport him from the remoteness of his exile to Jerusalem and to Zion. He is apparently far north in the land, in view of Hermon. This would suggest the region of Dan, or Caesarea Philippi, (modern Baniyas). Since the River Jordan has its source here on the slopes of Hermon, this would explain the expression, "the land of Jordan". The two other terms, "the Hermonites", and, "the hill Mizar" require comment. This plural of Hermon and the reference to Mizar are not to be found elsewhere in Holy Scripture. "Hermonites" (2769), being in the plural, probably indicates the fact that Hermon was really a mountain range consisting of several peaks. "Mizar", meaning "a little hill", is believed to have been one of the lesser peaks of Hermon. From these hills of the north the Psalmist's thoughts would go to that holy hill of Zion (Ps 43.3), and to the house of God.

These great peaks of the Hermon range formed deep ravines and chasms through which the melting snows rushed in torrents. H.B. Tristram describes it as "a wild medley of cascades and dashing torrents". As deep called unto deep, each echoing the noise of the waterfalls, it all became like a figure of the Psalmist's sorrow. Waves of sadness and depression overwhelmed him like the breakers and billows which flowed relentlessly between the surrounding rocks and hills. Yet, even in his sad plight, the Psalmist will not lose sight of the fact that his God is in control of all. "Thy waves", he says, "thy billows". The LORD (3068) was in command.

For the first and only time in the Psalm he now uses the great name Jehovah. Day and night Jehovah would be with him in lovingkindness and mercy. He must continue to pray and to sing. Prayer and song would sustain him in his calamities. He uses the beautiful expression, "the God of my life". Whatever the trials and troubles, and he had many, Jehovah was the God of his life, in sovereign control of all that was happening to His servant.

The Psalmist alternates between trusting and doubting. Having spoken so confidently of "the God of my life" and "God my rock", he now questions God's dealings with him. Had God forgotten him? Why this oppression from the enemy and the consequent mourning? Why? Why? How often has this been the heart cry of the people of God in their sorrow? Every day the enemy taunted. Daily they tortured him, stabbing him with the question, "Where is thy God?". It was hard to bear. It was like a sword piercing him and his whole being felt the wound of it.

Again he asks himself the question, as if interrogating his own heart, as he had done in v.5. "Why art thou cast down, O my soul?" Why this disquiet, this inner tumult, this murmuring and mourning? He repeats the exhortation, "Hope (3176) thou in God". Tarry for Him. Trust Him. Wait for Him patiently and expectantly. If the enemy taunts, "Where is thy God?", then faith can answer, "My God?, He is the health of my countenance, and I shall yet praise Him".

Notice the variation in the very similar expressions of vv. 5 and 11 - "the help of his countenance" (v.5), and, "the health of my countenance" (v.11). "Help" and "health" are the same word (3444), rendered differently, but each meaning "salvation". The pronouns, however, are not the same. "His countenance" (v.5); "my countenance" (v.11). The variation is beautiful. The Psalmist looks upon the countenance of God. God looks upon the countenance of His servant. The presence of God is salvation, and the Psalmist closes in this confidence, that he shall yet be delivered from his exile and return to the holy hill to praise his God (Ps 43.3-4).

PSALM 43

Introduction

Psalm 43 has been called "The Plaint of the Exile from Zion" (J.G. Murphy). The striking resemblance of the vocabulary of Psalms 42 and 43 has led some to suppose that the two Psalms might have originally been one, but, as Spurgeon remarks, "On account of the similarity of the structure of this Psalm to that of Psalm forty-two, it has been supposed to be a fragment wrongly separated from the preceding song; but it is always dangerous to allow these theories of error in Holy Scripture, and in this instance it would be very difficult to show just cause for such an admission. Why should the Psalm have been broken? Its similarity would have secured its unity had it ever been part and parcel of the forty-second. Is it not far more likely that some in their fancied wisdom united them wrongly in the few MSS in which they are found as one? We believe the fact is that the style of the poetry was pleasant to the writer, and therefore in after life he wrote this supplemental hymn after the same manner. As an appendix it needed no title". Since there is no superscription to Psalm 43, and since the theme, the style, and the tone, are the same, there can be little doubt that this Psalm is a continuation of the former sad theme by the same exiled author. The Septuagint entitles it, "A Psalm of David".

On the connection between the two Psalms, and on the authorship, see the comments in the introduction to Psalm 42.

Of the divine names employed in the Psalm, the name "Jehovah" does not occur, but there are some seven references to Elohim (430) and one to El (410).

The Psalm is an intermingling of prayer and praise, of aspiration, anticipation, and exhortation, and, on account of its unity and brevity, it needs little in the way of division. Verses 1-3, however, are the Psalmist's plea for justice, and for deliverance from oppression. Verses 4-5 are his joyful anticipation of answered prayer and of his eventual return to Zion.

Verses 1-3: A Prayer for Justice and Deliverance

The Psalmist, so often the object of malicious slander and false accusations, prays that his case should be decided by his God. "Judge me", he asks, "plead my cause". As Plumer points out, the phrase has been variously rendered by commentators, translators, and expositors. "Judge my judgment, O God". "Give me justice, O God". "Undertake my defence". "Plead my plea". "Sustain my cause". "Plead my quarrel". Then he adds that if we wish to vary from the common version we can get nothing better than, "Conduct my controversy". Happy is that man who can with confidence leave his case to be judged by the Lord. The Psalmist knows that he is the victim of deceit and injustice, and he is content to submit his case to God and wait for divine vindication.

He speaks of an ungodly nation. This word "nation" (1471) is usually reserved for Gentiles, for the heathen, and some think that it may be so here. It is more likely however, that the Psalmist has his own nation of Israel in mind, and particularly those who were in rebellion against him. It is a sad indictment of Israel that they should be so likened to the Gentiles who knew not God. They were an "ungodly (3808, 2623) nation", literally, a people without mercy. The deceitful and unjust man to whom the Psalmist refers, may be Ahithophel in particular, but the term aptly described so many of his enemies. They were deceitful, feigning to be what they were not, pretending friendship while unjustly plotting mischief. He prays for deliverance from them.

There was good reason for the Psalmist to leave his case with God. "Thou art the God of my strength", he exclaims, but is then immediately assailed by doubts and fears in the thought that God may have cast him off. "Had God forgotten him?", he had asked in Psalm 42.9. This is stronger now. Had God cast him off (2186)? Was he a castaway, rejected? If God really was the God of his life, his rock and his strength, why should he have to go about mourning because of his adversaries?

There is now wrung from his heart an impassioned plea - "O send out thy light and thy truth: let them lead me". Is there a possible allusion here to the "Urim and Thummim" in the priestly garments of Exodus 28.30, whose names meant "Lights and Perfections", and whose particular ministry was the guidance of the people of God when the way was not clear? In his dark loneliness the Psalmist longed for light. In the face of injustices and deceit he longed for truth. These would lead the way for him and restore him to the holiness of the hill and the sanctuary which were dear to his heart. He prays for an end to his exile and a return to the beloved Zion. Notice that "tabernacles" is in the plural. It may be the Hebrew way of expressing, with a plurality, the greatness and the dignity of the sanctuary, or it may have reference to the several courts and compartments which comprised the tabernacle.

Verses 4-5: The Joy of Answered Prayer

The Psalmist exults as he anticipates returning to the altar of God. 1 Chronicles 16.37-40 indicates that while the Ark of the Covenant was on Mount Zion, the altar of burnt offering was at Gibeon. Was there, according to 1 Chronicles 16.1, an altar on Mount Zion also? The altar and the harp however, were but symbolic of the worship and praise in which the exile longed to participate. He anticipates. God was his exceeding joy, "the gladness of my joy" (JND). It would be joy unspeakable to return to Zion, to the altar and to the harp, to the divine presence, to praise again as had been his custom in happier times. The intensity and fervour of his prayer is expressed in the form of address, "O God my God".

Now, for the third time in the two Psalms, he asks himself the question, "Why art thou cast down, O my soul?" (Ps 42.5, 11; Ps 43.5). It is, as has been observed, a personal, if gentle, rebuke to his own soul. Should he be depressed like this? Should he have this turmoil in his heart, this disquiet, if his hope was in the God of his life? Now he exhorts himself again, "Hope thou in God". Trust Him and wait for Him. His presence is salvation. He would yet regard the countenance of his exiled servant and deliver him to praise Him. What a comfort for the Psalmist to be able to say, "My God". There is a personal relationship here which must have been, should have been, the foundation for continuing confidence. He would soon be given the oil of joy for mourning and the garment of praise in exchange for the spirit of heaviness (Is 61.3).

PSALM 44

Introduction

The inscription of Psalm 44 is very similar to that of Psalm 42. It is the third of the thirteen "Maschil" Psalms and is yet another Psalm committed to the charge and care of the Chief Musician. These terms signify that it is to be preserved in the collection of the Master of Song as a Psalm for wisdom and instruction, but for further comment on these parts of the title see the introductions to Psalms 4 and 32. For comment on the sons of Korah refer to the introduction to Psalm 42.

This Psalm is a national, rather than personal, lament. Apart from the few personal pronouns in vv. 4, 6 and 15, the language is all in a plurality. It is the language of the nation, of the people.

Both the identity of the author and the time of its composition are uncertain. Suggestions regarding these have been many and varied, ranging from the times of David and the monarchy, to the Maccabees, very many commentators, from Calvin to Maclaren, being in favour of this latter Maccabean period. Those interested in pursuing the matter in detail would find much help in Delitzsch who examines the questions in depth, and writes, "Many considerations are opposed to the composition of the Psalm in the time of the Maccabees". He looks at these considerations and then concludes, "Thus we are driven back to the time of David; and the question arises, whether the Psalm does not admit, with Psalm 60, with which it forms a twin couple, of being understood as the offspring of a similar situation, viz. of the events which resulted from the Syro-Ammonitish war…When David was contending with the Syrians, the Edomites came down upon the country that was denuded of troops. And from 1 Kings 11.15 it is very evident that they then caused great bloodshed". He adds, and concludes, that "The lofty self-consciousness, which finds expression in the Psalm, is after all best explained by the times of David". With this conclusion Plumer concurs, and writes, "The most probable opinion is that it was written by David or one of his contemporaries. To this there is no unanswerable objection…There is no good reason for denying that it describes a state of things existing in the lifetime of David, when there was much piety and prosperity, and yet some very painful events".

David Dickson, however, writing as early as the sixteenth century, offered the wise suggestion that, "We are not to trouble ourselves about the name of the writer, or time of writing of any part thereof; especially because God of set purpose concealeth the name, sundry times, of the writer, and the time when it was written, that we should look in every book, more to the inditer of it, than to the writer of it…for this Psalm, wanting the name of the writer, and time of the writing of it also, is looked upon by the Apostle, Romans 8.36, not only as an experience of those before us, but also as a prophecy of the martyrdom of Christians under the gospel, and as encouragement to stand constant in the faith in hottest persecutions".

The Psalm may be considered in five parts. Verses 1-3 are a rehearsal of what God had done for the nation in bringing them into the land. In verses 4-8 this remembrance promotes faith in God and due praise of His name. Verses 9-16 are a sad lament that God had forsaken His people and abandoned them to the mercy of their enemies. In verses 17-22 the nation pleads its fidelity to God. The Psalm closes with a final appeal in verses 23-26 that God should arise and come to their aid.

Verses 1-3: Memories of Former Times

Recollections of God's earlier dealings with the nation are common in the Psalms and in the Prophets. The knowledge of what He has done in the past can be both a solace and a stimulant, and here they remember God's power after the Exodus, bringing the people out of the wilderness and into Canaan. It was the mind of God that these great events should never be forgotten (Ex 10.2; Deut 6.20-23). So, in accordance with this, the Psalmist says, "We have heard…our fathers have told us". Godly fathers had instructed their children, and from generation to generation the story of it all had been handed down. The "times of old" is a reference to the conquest of Canaan. God had driven out the heathen from before them in those days and had planted (5193) them in the land. He had removed the Canaanites and other tribes from the land which He had in mind for His chosen people (Gen 15.18-21) and had established Israel. The expression "cast them out" (7971) is sometimes misunderstood. It refers here to Israel and not to the tribes of Canaan. God dispossessed those tribes and planted His people as a vine in the land. He afflicted the Canaanites with judgments but caused His people to spread out and flourish. This increase, this spreading forth, is the true meaning of "cast them out", "cast them forth". With this Psalm 80.8-11 concurs; "Thou hast brought a vine out of Egypt…and planted it. Thou preparedst room before it, and didst cause it to take deep root, and it filled the land. The hills were covered with the shadow of it, and the boughs thereof were like the goodly cedars. She sent out her boughs unto the sea, and her branches unto the river". Note that the "cast out" (1644) which occurs in Psalm 80.8 is a different word from the "cast out" of Psalm 44.2.

The Psalmist remembers, and acknowledges, that it was not by their own might or power or prowess that the people possessed the land in those early days. Of course they had to fight for possession of the inheritance, of course they had sword and bow, but it was not these which gained the victories. They were a chosen people, and Jehovah loved them. He loved them, and chose them, not because they were more in number than any people for they were the fewest of all people. He loved them just because He loved them (Deut 7.7, 8). They were in His favour (7521), and the light of His countenance, the very smile of God, was upon them. It was His right hand and His arm that gave them the victory, and the land. These were familiar but precious memories of what God had wrought for their fathers, and the Psalmist, with the people, would delight to remember them.

Verses 4-8: Faith in Present Troubles

Note the personal pronoun in v.4. According to Darby, Plumer, Perowne, Davison, and indeed the LXX, the pronoun is emphatic. "Thou thyself art my King"; "Thou, even Thou Thyself art my King"; "Thou, He, Thou [art] the Same". J.N. Darby refers the reader to Deuteronomy 32.39, where, in his translation, he has an interesting footnote. He says, "This expression, 'The Same', becomes virtually a name of God". The Psalmist acknowledges, as an individual, the Kingship of the great Elohim (430), but, though he speaks personally, yet he speaks for the nation. Human monarchs there were, but their God was King over all. Those were happier days when Israel had enjoyed a theocracy, when God alone was their King. "The Lord his God is with him, and the shout of a king is among them". So Balaam had said (Num 23.21). "Happy art thou, O Israel: who is like unto thee, O people saved by the Lord", Moses had said (Deut 33.29). Jehovah was their sword and their shield, their King in the midst of them in those days, but they had desired a king like the nations and He had given them Saul. Now the Psalmist (David the king himself?) extols the Kingship of God. If the days of the theocracy were past, at least they could recover the spirit of those days. Jehovah still lived and could command deliverances for Jacob. "Where the word of a king is, there is power" (Eccl 8.4), and He who, in grace, had done so much for Jacob was still their King and would deliver them. "Deliverances" in the plural probably signifies complete deliverance.

Through God and in the name of God they could yet conquer. At His command they could push down their enemies and tread their adversaries underfoot. To "push down" (5055) has the thought of goring or tossing into the air as oxen or bulls or other animals with horns would deal with their attackers. It means to vanquish or subdue. The Psalmist again resorts to the personal pronoun, but what he declares of himself must be true also of the nation. There is a remembrance here again of the victories won by the fathers, as described in v.3. They did not conquer by their own sword or possess the land in their own power. Alexander's paraphrase of v.6 is apt and beautiful: "What was true of my fathers is equally true of me. As they did not prevail by their own strength, neither can I hope to prevail by mine". This is exactly what the Psalmist is saying, speaking not only for himself but for his people also.

Jehovah had been faithful to them in the past. He had saved them from their adversaries. By Him their enemies had been confounded and routed. There were many who hated them, but He loved them and delighted in them (v.3) and it was fitting that that they should boast in Him. "Boast" (1984) is "glory". They had a right to glory in the God who delivered them. They would spread His renown and praise His name. All the day long they would boast, and for ever they would praise. For what they were as a nation, God alone was to be praised. The honour and the glory were all His.

The section closes with a "Selah". It is a moment for reflection, for meditation, and for lifting up the heart and voice in due recognition of their God.

Verses 9-16: The Present Lament

This new section of the Psalm commences in sad and painful contrast to the glad memories of Jehovah's former dealings with the nation as rehearsed in the earlier verses. He who, in v.7, had put their enemies to shame (954) has now put them to shame (3637). The words are different, but their meanings are very similar. They blushed in their discomfiture and confusion. They felt ashamed and rejected. The God in whom they had trusted, who had wrought such victories for them in the past, had now cast them off. He denied them His saving presence and would not go forth with them to battle. This verse occurs almost word for word in Psalm 60.10. Without His presence defeat was inevitable. He was the Captain of their salvation and if He deserted them they would most certainly fail. Defeat was always accompanied by disgrace. They had had to retreat from the enemy and the enemy had spoiled and plundered them. Many of them had died in the field of battle, slaughtered like sheep. Others would be taken captive and sold into slavery, scattered among the heathen. It was national humiliation.

It was, the Psalmist reasons, as if God had sold His own people. He had sold them for nought and had in no way been Himself enriched by the sale of them. They had been sold for a nominal price. Plumer quotes Anderson who says that it is as if they had said, "Thou hast sold us to our enemies at whatever price they would give; like a person who sells things that are useless at any price, not so much for the sake of gain as to get quit of what he considers of no value and burdensome". It was a sad occasion of reproach and scorn. The neighbours dwelling on their borders, Edom,

Ammon, Moab, and the more distant nations too, mocked and jested at their plight. They had become a byword, a proverb, among the heathen who shook their heads in derision. "What had become of this great people?", they must have scoffed and taunted.

The Psalmist now returns to the personal pronoun and speaks of "my confusion". Does he, by individualising the matter, speak for the faithful in Israel, who would feel most personally, the confusion of it all? Is it not the spirit of Daniel of a later day? That godly man speaks of "my confession" and "my sin", as he acknowledges the failures and sins of the nation (Dan 9). Shame covered the Psalmist like a garment, hiding his face like a veil. The disgrace was with him all the day, daily and continually. It was a constant thing, this humiliation, and all because of the slander, the reproach, the insults, the blasphemies, of those who were the enemies of Israel.

Verses 17-22: The Pledge of Fidelity

In spite of all that has come upon the nation, the people protest that they have not forgotten their God. They had not, at this stage in their national history, lapsed into apostasy or idolatry. There may indeed have been sins and provocations for which they could be justly punished, but they were, after all, a covenant people, and they had not dealt falsely (8266) in that. In the matter of the covenant they had not cheated. Neither in their heart, nor in their walk, had they turned away from Him or from His path for them. Nationally they had neither declined nor deviated as the covenant people that they were.

Yet they were a crushed and broken people, abandoned, as it were, in the place of dragons (8577). This is rendered "jackals" by RV, JND, and others. Some, however, retain "dragons", conveying the thought of monsters. Whichever is preferred, the metaphor seems to suggest that the land had become devastated, a wilderness scene of desolation covered with the shadow of death and darkness. If they had forgotten the name of their God, if they had been unfaithful to Him and had offered their worship to strange gods, stretching out their hand to them, would not God, in His omniscience, know this? He who knows the secrets of all hearts, would He not know if they had, in heart, turned away from Him? It was a protestation of their innocence. Indeed, they argue that it was for His sake, because of their fidelity to Him, that they suffered as they did. As Dr Cohen comments, "They protested that far from suffering because of disloyalty, they were attacked for the reason that they were God's people who kept to His appointed paths. All the more inexplicable, therefore, was their hard fate, and all the more urgently should His help come to them". There were continual martyrdoms for His sake, and, as they had said in v.11, they felt as though they were being counted as sheep for the slaughter. So does Paul liken the persecutions of believers in his day. He quotes v.22 of the Psalm directly in Romans 8.36.

Verses 23-26: "Arise O Lord!"

It is fitting that such a Psalm should close with a final earnest plea for God's help. They plead for divine aid. "Awake, why sleepest thou, O Lord?". Of course the Psalmist knew that He who keeps Israel neither slumbers nor sleeps (Ps 121.4).

This is an urgent call that God should now look upon His people, that He should arise and end this dreary season of desolation and defeat which they were enduring for His sake. The "sleeping" referred to is synonymous with the "hiding of the face". O that He would be with them, as He had been with their fathers in v.3, and lift up His countenance upon them. Again the word "forget" is used. They had not forgotten God (vv.17, 20), but had He forgotten them? Had He forgotten the affliction and the oppression which they were suffering as His people? They were bowed down to the very dust, humbled and depressed. God had cursed the serpent like this in Genesis 3.14, to cleave to the ground and eat the dust. But they were His people, His covenant people, why should it be so with them? "Arise", they plead. "Help!" "Redeem!"

Note that while the people have protested innocence and fidelity to God, nevertheless they appeal for deliverance on the ground of His mercies. "Mercies" (2617), though, is a singular word, mercy or lovingkindness. This is the sole ground upon which His people ask for His help. As J.G. Murphy comments, "*Thy mercy's sake*. This is the grand plea which God has Himself revealed to us in His Word. It implies, moreover, that the people, while pleading not guilty to the charge of idolatry, were conscious that all their hopes lay in the divine mercy".

PSALM 45

Introduction

This lovely Psalm is a wedding hymn, composed for the marriage of a king to a king's daughter. But whose marriage, and which king? As Maclaren says, "The usual bewildering variety of conjectures as to his identity meets us in commentaries". After considering some of these conjectures, he concludes, "Every king of Judah by descent and office was a living prophecy. The singer sees Messiah shining, as it were, through the shadowy form of the earthly king…pointing onwards to a greater than Solomon, in whom the 'sure mercies' promised to David should be facts at last". T.E Wilson says that Psalm 45 is "the centre and crown of the Messianic Psalms", and the Messianic interpretation of the Psalm is, of course, confirmed in Hebrews 1.8-9, which must be considered later in reference to vv. 6 and 7 of the Psalm.

The older opinion, that the king in the Psalm is Solomon, and that it may celebrate his marriage to an Egyptian princess, is perhaps the popular opinion, but the main objection to this is that Solomon was not a warrior king, as is the monarch of the Psalm. There can be no doubt that there was indeed a primary reason and original circumstances for which the Psalm was composed, but W.T. Davison, after citing the names of Solomon, Ahab, Jehoram, Jeroboam II, some Persian Monarch, a Syrian Alexander, Ptolemy Philadelphus, writes, "One proof that the historical occasion was not all-important in the mind of the Psalmist is to be found in the difficulty of determining who is intended and what period is referred to". There are sentiments expressed in this Psalm which go beyond any earthly king, and, as others have commented, "A greater than Solomon is here". Those wishing to pursue the question will find much detail in Delitzsch and also in Maclaren,

For comment on the "Chief Musician", to whose care the Psalm is committed, see the introduction in the commentary to Psalm 4. On the word "Maschil" see the introduction to Psalm 32, and on "The sons of Korah" see the introduction to Psalm 42.

Regarding the transliterated Hebrew "Shoshannim" (7799) in the title, there is no difficulty as to its meaning. It is a plural word meaning "lilies", and it appears again in the headings of Psalms 69 (in the singular) and 80. The problem arises as to the association of this with the content of the Psalm. It may have indicated some preferred melody to which the Psalm was intended to be sung, or, though less probable, some lily-shaped musical instrument on which the Psalm was to be played. T.E. Wilson's suggestion, however, is very beautiful, that lilies belonged to the springtime and Passover season, when the winter was past and summer was near. The atmosphere of Psalm 45 may, indeed, be that of a glorious springtime, both for Israel and for the world, ushering in the reign of the returning Messiah who is extolled so much in the Psalm. It anticipates a millennial summer when the King will reign, and did not the Lord Jesus say, "Consider the lilies of the field…I say unto you, That even Solomon in all his glory was not arrayed like one of these" (Mt 6.28-29).

Being a "Maschil" Psalm signifies that it has a content of instruction, wisdom and teaching, but this is very beautifully, and importantly, balanced by the reminder that it is "A Song of loves", a love song whose language is so like that of the Song of Solomon, the Song of Songs. This blending of doctrine and devotion, of intelligence and affection, is to be much desired and sought after. An imbalance will tend to produce either cold and formal academics or unsound sentimentalists.

Apart from the title, the text of the Psalm may be considered in five parts. The opening verse is a personal preface in which the Psalmist speaks briefly about himself, stating his exercise, and his intention in the Psalm. In verses 2-9 he addresses the king. These verses extol several glories of Messiah. There follows, in verses 10-12 a brief address to the Royal Bride, after which, in verses 13-15, there seems to be a similarly brief address to the gathered company. The concluding verses, 16-17, are like a benediction, a prayer for blessing upon the union.

Verse 1: The Psalmist Speaks of Himself

The Psalmist will give a good example. He wishes to speak of his feelings, but he will do it very briefly. One verse will suffice for this personal prelude to a Psalm which will exalt the Messiah. After this he will talk no more about himself. He will speak here of his heart and his tongue. As the Saviour Himself said in Matthew 12.34, "Out of the abundance of the heart the mouth speaketh". The Psalmist's heart is full to overflowing, "inditing" (7370) a good matter. "Heartless hymns are insults to heaven", says Spurgeon, but it was not so with the Psalmist. His heart was bubbling up like a fountain. It was boiling over like a cauldron. "Welling forth", says JND. It was hot, seething, stirred with a good matter, for his thoughts were of the king. The definite article is missing before "king". Its absence seems to indicate the character, the royal dignity, of the one of whom he is about to write. This is no careless composition. He has been musing, meditating, and now he will pen the thoughts which he has composed in his heart. He has so much to say. His tongue will be like the pen of a ready (4106) writer (5608), a skilful and diligent scribe with ability to record accurately things touching the king. These same words, exactly, are used to describe Ezra in Ezra 7.6. From this short introduction the Psalmist will now turn directly to address the Royal Bridegroom.

Verses 2-9: The Address to the King

The personal beauty and the integrity of the king are now the subject of this eulogy. When applied to the Messiah, there is praise of His moral, official, personal and mediatorial glories. Physical beauty was always deemed to be desirable and appropriate in a monarch (compare 1 Sam 9.2). Messiah is "Fairer than the children of men". The moral glory of Christ is a subject which has commanded volumes of writings. His sinlessness, His holiness, His impeccability, the perfections of His words and His ways, make Him uniquely beautiful, more fair than the sons of men. He cannot be compared with other men, He must be contrasted. The best of other men have failed in some respect, but, as another exclaims of Him, "He is altogether lovely" (Song 5.16).

"Grace is poured into thy lips". Men wondered at the gracious words which proceeded out of His mouth (Lk 4.22). Even His adversaries had to say, "Never man spake like this man" (Jn 7.46). It is interesting that there are only two references to grace (2580) in the whole Book of Psalms (see Ps 84.11). Strong says that it signifies preciousness and pleasantness, charm and elegance. Such was the character and the ministry of Messiah. Every grace was in Him in perfect balance and this was an indication that He enjoyed the blessing of God, and would do so eternally. It is not that God has blessed Him because of what He is, but rather that what He is is an evidence that God has blessed Him.

From the moral glory of the Messiah the Psalmist now turns to His official glory. From the gentleness and meekness of Christ he now turns to His might as a warrior. In the verses which follow, four items are associated with this official glory - His sword, His throne, His sceptre, and His anointing. These are the marks of a warrior king. He is addressed as the mighty (1368) one, with glory and majesty. "Mighty" is the Hebrew GIBBOR, and He is "El Gibbor", the mighty God, in Isaiah 9.6. The sword is a symbol of power, and, so girded, the king will ride on and prosper in the cause of the truth and meekness and righteousness which have characterised Him in His life and ministry. It is all reminiscent of Revelation 19 where also He rides in triumph and where "in righteousness he doth judge and make war" (Rev 19.11). There too He wields both sword and sceptre. The "right hand" is a further emblem of authority and power, and in the exercise of this power He will accomplish such victories as will make men afraid. "Kings shall shut their mouths at him" (Is 52.15), silent in their astonishment at His prowess. On the arrows which find the heart of the king's enemies in v.5, Davison comments, "The language here is condensed and abrupt, the second line forming a kind of parenthesis between the first and the third...First the arrows are seen hurtling through the air, then the hostile ranks are thinned as one enemy after another falls, lastly the shafts are found to have penetrated the very hearts of the king's foes" (compare Is 63.1-4).

The personal glory of the Messiah, sometimes called His essential, or eternal, or divine glory, is now introduced in v.6. This verse has been corrupted, wrongly translated, and misinterpreted, by those who endeavour to deny the deity of Christ, but Hebrews 1.8 settles the interpretation for the believer. Of God, addressing the Messiah, it is written, "Unto the Son he saith, Thy throne, O God, is for ever and ever". God, addressing His Son, calls Him "God". The Messiah is Son and the Son is God. This is one of the greatest passages establishing the deity of Christ, and it is perhaps no wonder that it has been assailed so much.

A problem arises, however, in that these words were, in the first instance, addressed to an earthly monarch. In this context, what does, "Thy throne, O God (430, Elohim), is for ever and ever", mean? Plumer says, "Strenuous efforts have been made to turn aside this passage from its obvious and inspired interpretation. But Hengstenberg well says that the non-Messianic expositors have not been able to bring forward anything grammatically tenable". Harold St. John explains, "Elohim is applied to lesser beings than God in Exodus 7.1; 21.6, and see especially Zechariah 12.8; in these cases judges etc. are seen as God's mouthpieces, but here beyond question we may, and must, give the fullest value to the word. That Messiah is God in the highest sense of the word alone gives point to the argument in Hebrews 1.8". Derek Kidner's comment is also helpful. Having observed that several versions have altered the AV rendering, and have, as he says, "sidestepped the plain sense of v.6, which is confirmed by the ancient versions and by the New Testament", he continues, "It is an example of Old Testament language bursting its banks, to demand a more than human fulfilment (as did Psalm 110.1, according to our Lord). The faithfulness of the pre-Christian Septuagint in translating these verses unaltered is very striking". The throne of the divinely appointed monarch was established in perpetuity. The Davidic dynasty will be perpetuated in the reign of Messiah.

Since there is a throne and a kingdom, it follows that there must be a sceptre, which has ever been a symbol of authority and power. Messiah's sceptre is a sceptre of righteousness. It takes character from the king Himself, who loved righteousness and hated lawlessness. His rule is for ever and ever. There will, of course, be an earthly millennial phase of His kingdom, but this is indeed a phase. The kingdom itself is an everlasting kingdom (2 Pet 1.11). His throne stands eternally.

The anointing is very beautiful. He who was a Man of Sorrows has been anointed with the oil of gladness. The writer of the Epistle to the Hebrews speaks of "the joy that was set before him" (Heb 12.2), and in this, as in all things, He has precedence and pre-eminence over His fellows. This too, is quoted in the Hebrew letter (Heb 1.9). But who are His "fellows" (2270)? Some suggest that they are angels and some think that they are former kings of Israel and Judah, but both here in the Psalm, and in Hebrews 1.9, (*3353*), the word implies a companionship, the closeness of partners. It seems more probable that the fellows intended are those believers who are so near to Him and so intimate with Him as to be called His brethren (Heb 2.11-12; Ps 22.22).

The address to the king draws to a close with a lovely reference to His mediatorial glory. In great grace toward men He has come out from the ivory palaces of His glory. The word "whereby" (4482) of v.8 signifies "stringed instruments", and is so translated by JND, RV, and most others. From the joy and the gladness of the glory, the Mediator has come out, and will return, to the accompaniment of a joyful symphony. He has worn the garments of His incarnation, fragrant with the sweetness of myrrh, the bitterness of aloes, and the healing properties of cassia. It will be noticed that the word "smell" of v.8 is in italics. It has been supplied by the translators to assist in the reading of the verse, but the thought appears to be that the garments which the Mediator wears have been, as it were, woven of these very fragrances. "All of myrrh, and aloes, and cassia". Note the myrrh at His birth and both myrrh and aloes at His burial (Mt 2.11; Jn 19.39). Fragrance characterised His entire life, from the manger to the tomb.

The verse which follows has occasioned much difficulty of interpretation in regard to the queen and the kings' daughters. "Queen" (7694) is not the usual word for queen but implies rather a queen-consort, a queen by marriage, not a queen in her own right. Harold St. John says, "The Queen is the earthly Jerusalem restored with her daughter cities". A.G. Clarke understands it similarly, and adds, "'Kings' daughters', prophetically points to representatives of the Gentile nations attendant upon the Lord of the whole earth; 'Queen'...prophetically refers to Jerusalem as representative city of the nation". F.W. Grant, in language very like this, says, "The Queen...is therefore the earthly and not the heavenly bride. The 'kings' daughters' show us, in a not unusual figure, the representatives of the nations attendant upon One who is the Lord of the whole earth". Grant makes the important observation that "to import (as some do) the polygamy of ancient times into this scene of future blessedness not only occasions moral disquietude but is contrary to Scriptural statements as to Israel's distinctive place. The 'daughter of Tyre' in the twelfth verse is in fact but one of these 'kings' daughters', and indicates their place". To summarise these points of view, the Queen is Israel and the princesses are the daughters of those kings of the earth who will eventually pay homage to Messiah.

T.E. Wilson however, views it differently, and writes, "The usual interpretation is that the bride in the Psalm is Israel, forgiven and restored in her relation to Messiah in millennial days. But the word used for 'queen' in v.9, and the prophetic outline in Revelation 19-22 concerning the marriage supper of the Lamb and the appearing in glory followed by the millennium, make that interpretation difficult, if not impossible. Israel, it is true, will have a special and intimate relationship with Messiah as an earthly people...but the bride is the Church, composed of both Jew and Gentile". Concerning the gold of Ophir (211), Strong says that it was "a land or city in southern Arabia in Solomon's trade route where gold evidently was traded for goods". It is, he adds, "characteristic of fine gold". Kirkpatrick says, "The choicest gold".

Verses 10-12: The Address to the Bride

The address to the bride opens with a strong appeal to her. "Hearken...consider...incline thine ear". She is about to begin a new chapter in life. If she is, as seems possible, a Gentile bride from a foreign country, then the appeal is very pertinent indeed. She is exhorted to forget her own people and her father's house in devotion and dedication to her royal bridegroom. Ruth the Moabitess did this, as she left family and friends in Moab to commence a new life in Israel. Rebekah too, left her home in Mesopotamia for a new life with Isaac. The same is true, morally, of all believers in the Lord Jesus, who, like Matthew, rise up, leave all, and follow Him (Lk 5.28), and who, as Paul, count all things but loss for the excellency of the knowledge of Christ Jesus their Lord (Phil 3.8). The bride must be encouraged by this, that such consecration and loyalty will have its reward. She will gain, and retain, the affection of the king, and will have the privilege, for it is a privilege, of paying homage to the royal personage who has become her Lord and Master. It will be a happy union, where each is desirous of the other and there is mutual admiration and respect.

The daughter of Tyre, representative of the city and people of Tyre, is to be present at the marriage, with a gift. Prophetically this is very beautiful, pointing to a day when Gentile nations will seek Israel and her Messiah. F.W. Grant writes, "Tyre, the queen city of commerce, whose merchants are princes, and who knows well the value of all earthly things that can be bought, is now attracted by what no riches can purchase. She is here, not with a price, but with an offering. The rich entreat for what is greater than riches. This is evidently a typical example of how the 'Desire of all nations' will be found in Christ, Tyre, as the great trafficker, being the suited power to illustrate this". To see the face of the bride and to be permitted to enjoy her company and presence will be counted a favour indeed, even by the richest of the people.

Verses 13-15: A Tribute to the Bride

In an address now to the gathered company of guests, tribute is paid to the bride in her wedding attire. She is "all glorious within", a true princess. She is a king's daughter and also a king's bride. It is fitting that she should be appropriately attired. But the meaning of this "within" is disputed. Is it within the palace, as the RV renders it? Is it in the inner apartment, that inner part of the house which belonged to the women, from which she would pass to the presence-chamber of the king? Or is it rather within herself, morally and spiritually, in her real inner self, her nature and character? Whichever is true, there is glory. Her clothing is of wrought gold, fine golden threads interlaced and interwoven with the embroidery, the coloured needlework, of her beautiful wedding garments. With her virgin companions, her attendants, her ladies-in-waiting, the bride is brought to the king.

While all of this would have been literally true in the splendour of a royal wedding, there are, of course, spiritual lessons for the New Testament believer. The Church will be suitably and gorgeously arrayed in that day of His manifestation, the day of her presentation to the world as His bride and consort, as in Revelation 19-22.

It is a day of rejoicing, called in another song, "the day of his espousals...the day of the gladness of his heart" (Song 3.11). The bridal procession will enter the king's palace with great celebration and joy, and, as the royal bride and bridegroom are brought together, to be united in marriage, there remains in the Psalm just the final benediction, a blessing upon the union.

Verses 16-17: The Benediction

The grammar of the Hebrew text, with its masculine pronouns, indicates that these closing words are addressed to the king. They are both a blessing and a prophecy. The Psalmist envisages a happy and fruitful union which would ensure the preservation and the continuance of the dynasty. The royal line would be perpetuated and the sons of the marriage would be known as princes in all the earth. Prophetically it will be a fulfilment of Isaiah 53.10, "He shall see his seed", and of that other word in the Psalms which says, "A seed shall serve him; it shall be accounted to the Lord for a generation" (Ps 22.30).

The Psalmist says, "I will make…". Is this the voice of God in the Psalm, saying, "I will"? Or is the Psalmist speaking personally, saying that by the very composition of his Psalms he would make the remembrance of the king to be preserved from generation to generation? Or are both true, the voice of Jehovah heard in the voice of the inspired poet, giving divine assurance that the royal posterity would prevail and be praised for ever and ever? Notice that "people" in this closing verse is a plural word, "peoples". Not only Israel, but unborn generations of Gentile nations shall yet bring their praise, and the renown of God's King shall be universal. The kings of the earth, once allied in revolt against Him, shall be united in praise of Him and be subject to Him (Ps 2.2; Rev 19.19). So of Messiah it is written, "He shall prolong his days, and the pleasure of the Lord shall prosper in his hand" (Is 53.10).

This lovely wedding Psalm, like so many other Psalms, is both historical and prophetical. Perowne says, "The sacred poet sees the earthly king and the human marriage before his eyes, but while he strikes his harp to celebrate these, a vision of a higher glory streams in upon him. Thus the earthly and the heavenly mingle. The Divine penetrates, hallows, goes beyond the human".

PSALM 46

Introduction

Even to those who are not familiar with all the details of it, this little Psalm has been precious to many believers because of the word of comfort and assurance at its beginning and the tender exhortation at its ending. "God is our refuge and strength, a very present help in trouble", and, "Be still, and know that I am God". It is said of Luther that in his darkest hours he used to say, "Come, let us sing the 46th Psalm, and let them do their worst" (Plumer). His famous hymn, "A mighty fortress is our God", was based upon this Psalm.

For comments on "The Chief Musician", and on "The Sons of Korah", in the superscription, see the introductions in the commentaries to Psalms 4 and 42. The word "Alamoth" (5961) in the title is akin to the English word "soprano", or "maidens", and the suggestion has been made that it was to be sung by a female choir. This has been rejected by some who say that such a female choir did not exist in the temple. "Alamoth" appears again in 1 Chronicles 15.20 where the context seems to indicate that it was a musical instrument, probably with a tone of high pitch, but in a footnote there J.N. Darby says that it means "probably the voices of young women". The triumphant theme of the Psalm does seem to require treble notes.

No author is indicated in the title, and, although there is an obvious celebration of some national victory, and many suggestions have been advanced, it cannot be known with certainty just when, or why, or by whom, the Psalm was written.

Three "Selahs" divide the Psalm into three sections or stanzas, of almost equal size, but the refrain which closes the second and third stanzas is omitted after the first. As Perowne remarks, "The first strophe does not close with the refrain, as the second (v. 7) and the third (v. 11) do...It may have been purposely omitted, in order to bring into more striking contrast the roaring waves of the troubled sea, and the gentle, peaceful flow of the brook of Siloam, in the next verse".

The first part of the Psalm, verses 1-3, sings the great truth that God is the refuge of His people. Verses 4-7 have reference to some recent deliverance and victory. The third part, verses 8-11, is more general, and anticipates a day when Jehovah will bring peace not only to Israel but also to the whole earth.

Verses 1-3: Shelter and Strength, Safety and Security

The Psalm begins with God (430), and this name of the mighty Elohim will appear seven times throughout its eleven verses. He is Jehovah in vv. 7, 8 and 11, and He is the Most High in v.4, but it is Elohim who in His might accomplishes victory for the nation and becomes both refuge and strength for those in trouble. In the AV and RV there are three references to "refuge" in the Psalm, in vv. 1, 7 and 11, and, although the meanings are similar, the word "refuge" (4268) in v.1 is different from that of vv. 7 and 11 (4869), where JND translates "high fortress". In the latter part of v.1, the JND rendering is again very beautiful; "a help in distresses, very readily found". In the troubles of life, in times of affliction and adversity, His saints have always found a refuge, a shelter, in God. A NT writer concurs when he speaks of "Grace to help in time of need" (Heb 4.16). He is always at hand with seasonable help for His people.

Spurgeon remarks upon v.2: "How fond the Psalmist is of therefores! His poetry is no poetic rapture without reason, it is as logical as a mathematical demonstration". How true this is. If Elohim, with all His might, is both shelter and strength for His saints, then how illogical and irrational is fear. "Therefore", says the Psalmist, in view of this ever-available help of God, "therefore will not we fear". Even the most violent and most calamitous events ought not to make the trusting saint afraid. Though the earth be removed or changed and its great mountain pillars be lost in the oceans, it can still be said of Jehovah, "Thou remainest...thou art the same" (Heb 1.11-12). Whether the awful chaos envisaged by the Psalmist is literal, or symbolic of great political upheavals and the collapse of all that seems to be stable on earth, is not relevant. It may indeed include the overthrow of dynasties, the fall of governments and the ruin of nations, but as Dr Cohen comments, "Secure in the stronghold of God, those within it have no cause for fear though the earth be overturned by a mighty convulsion of nature and the mountains disappear in the sea. A Hebraic way of saying: whatever may happen".

The section concludes with a "Selah", always a call for a meditative pause with a lifting up of heart and voice in reflection on great things. Here the music may cease as the voices of the worshippers swell in a crescendo of praise.

Verses 4-7: Peace Like a River

From the tumult and the roar of the troubled waters the Psalm now moves suddenly but gently to a quiet flowing stream. Verse 4 commences abruptly - "A river!" Notice that the words, "There is", are italicised, having been supplied by the translators, but this is an exclamation rather than a cold statement of fact. Maclaren says, "We might almost translate, 'Lo! A river'". This figure is employed twice in the prophecy of Isaiah (8.6; 33.21). It is a symbol of the presence of God which is the refreshment and joy, and also the defence, of His people. In a delightful silence the river waters the city with gladness, its streams and tributaries bringing joy to all. The city is Zion, the holy city where are the tabernacles of the Most High. "Tabernacles" in the plural has already occurred in Psalm 43.3. As has been noted there, the plural may be the Hebrew manner of emphasising the greatness and dignity of the tabernacle, or it may denote the several compartments of the tabernacle structure, the dwelling place of God among His people.

God is in the midst. This is His rightful place, and while He is pre-eminent in the midst of His saints, their defence is sure, they shall not be moved. For the second time in the Psalm the word "help" appears. How needy are the people of God, but He is in the midst to help, and that right early. JND translates, "At the dawn of the morning". Perowne's rendering is similar, "When the morning dawns", and the beautiful text of the Jewish Publication Society has, "At the approach of morning". The thought is, to quote Dr Cohen, "After the dark night of peril God's deliverance becomes apparent at dawn".

What assurance is this, that though kingdoms are moved, the saints shall not be moved (4131). The nations may rage (1993). They may clamour and roar in loud and boisterous tumult, but when the mighty Elohim utters His voice, the uproar melts away.

The refrain, repeated in v.11, combines, in beauty and majesty, two divine titles, and gives a two-fold basis for the confidence of the saints. "The Lord of hosts" is "The God of Jacob". Jehovah Sabaoth, God All-Sovereign, to whom belong the innumerable hosts of angels, and the armies of heaven, and sun, moon, stars and all creation, has deigned to become, and to be called, the God of Jacob. He reaches down, in great grace, from the heights of His majesty, to be the Helper of a man like Jacob. But if "Jacob" is understood as describing the nation of Israel rather than the individual, then the thought is still very beautiful, that He who in His greatness is the Lord of Hosts, in His grace cares for His chosen people. Note the AV's transliteration of this latter title in Romans 9.29 and James 5.4; "The Lord of Sabaoth". Still today the Lord of Hosts is the refuge (4869), the stronghold, the high fortress, the safe retreat, for His troubled saints.

Once more the "Selah" calls. It is again a moment for reflection, for praise on the highest note, for wonder and worship.

Verses 8-11: Peace Universal

The invitation of v.8, "Come, behold", may be a wide call to the surrounding nations rather than to Israel, but it would, of course, suitably apply to both. It is an invitation to see what God has wrought. "Desolations" (8047) does not give the full meaning here. God had wrought astonishing things in the earth, and although the word may well imply destruction and devastation, yet the emphasis seems to be on the wonders which Jehovah had performed among the nations to bring peace to His people.

To the ends of earth Jehovah has the power to effect a cessation of wars and bring peace to the troubled world. Both the bow and the spear, with the chariots, He can destroy. He will break the bow, and sunder the spear, and burn the chariots. As the prophets Isaiah and Micah both predict, the day will come when, by divine decree, men shall beat their swords into ploughshares and their spears into pruning hooks; when nation shall not lift up sword against nation, neither shall they learn war any more (Is 2.4; Mic 4.3). In that millennial day it will be true that "He maketh wars to cease unto the end of the earth". The word translated here as "chariots" (5699) is not the usual word for war-chariot. It is the same word as is found in the story of Joseph and his brethren in Genesis 45-46 and there rendered "wagons". Still, the association here in the Psalm of swords, spears, and chariots, seems to signify all the apparatus and artillery of war. F.W. Grant comments, "He will make war against war, and the very implements of it shall exist no more. Blessed display of power, which shall everywhere make Him known as God - make the nations at last perforce to realise this, and exalt Him over the whole earth". Harold St. John writes, "It is the death of war".

"Be still!" He who, in a later day than the Psalmist's, stood in a little ship in a storm on the Galilean Lake, and commanded, "Peace, be still" (Mk 4.39), is the same One who in the day of His power will similarly command the storms on earth and create a universal calm. Men must desist, they must be still and restrained, and contemplate that He is God. He will yet be exalted among the nations which for so long have rebelled and raged against Him. In that day there shall be no more rebellion. He will be everywhere exalted.

With a repetition of the refrain of v.7 the Psalm closes. Jehovah of Hosts, the God of Jacob, remains the solace and shelter of His people. His presence assures for His saints in every age both safety and security. He is their high tower, their fortress, and their sure refuge. Selah.

PSALM 47

Introduction

This delightful little Psalm should be read in conjunction with Psalms 46 and 48. With these preceding and succeeding Psalms it forms a trilogy. The same joyful theme is common throughout, singing the praise of Jehovah triumphant and supreme, a great King over all the earth. It is almost an extension and amplification of the closing words of Psalm 46, "I will be exalted among the nations, I will be exalted in the earth" (RV). Dr Cohen comments that "The Psalm is recited in the Synagogue before the sounding of the "Shofar" (ram's horn) on the New Year, a day when the liturgy dwells upon the thought of God's universal Sovereignty".

While the Psalm obviously celebrates an apparently recent national deliverance and victory, neither the author, the time nor the occasion of writing, can be known with any certainty. However, as Spurgeon writes, "Our ear has grown accustomed to the ring of David's compositions, and we are morally certain that we hear it in this Psalm. Every expert would detect here the autography of the Son of Jesse, or we are greatly mistaken". Perowne agrees that, "The older Christian expositors, for the most part, suppose it to have been written, like Psalm 24, on the occasion of the removal of the Ark to Mount Zion (2 Sam 6)", which would, of course, assign it to David, but he goes on to show that many others have suggested a variety of composers and circumstances. On the now familiar title see the introduction in the commentary to Psalms 4 and 42.

Although, as Maclaren says, "The Psalm has little of complexity in structure or thought. It is a gush of pure rapture", nevertheless it may be divided into two stanzas or strophes, with the "Selah", the musical pause, marking the end of the first strophe at v.4.

Verses 1-4: A Call to the Nations

"People" in v.1 is a plural word, "peoples", and, when in the plural, the word usually indicates the Gentile nations. Since, however, the Hebrew word is AMIM (5971), and not the word GOYIM (1471), which is the usual word to describe the nations, it may well be that this is a summons to all peoples, including Israel. Indeed, the call is, "Clap your hands, all ye people". The Psalm may indicate, prophetically, that day of glory when nations everywhere, with Israel at their head, will acknowledge God as King. The clapping of the hands was a most enthusiastic and spontaneous expression of joy. Note how, at the coronation of Joash in 2 Kings 11.12, "They made him king, and anointed him; and they clapped their hands, and said, God save the king". The clapping of the hands was accompanied by the shouting of the people. It was, as Maclaren says, "A tumult of acclaim".

Having called for praise to God (430), the mighty Elohim, the Psalmist now introduces another divine title, "The LORD Most High". This is Jehovah (3068) Elyon (5945), a majestic combination of two titles. Jehovah is the eternal, ever-existing, self-existent One, to whom the past, present, and future are but one eternal "now". The Most High is the supreme One, the high and lofty One, greater than all. He is terrible (3372). He is to be feared by His creatures, to be held in awe and reverence. He is a great King over all the earth, and not over Judaea or Israel only. His kingly rights are universal and, while the Psalm calls upon all people to confess this now, the full acknowledgement of it must wait until that day when Messiah will return in power and glory as King of Kings and Lord of Lords. Then shall every knee bow to Him and every tongue confess Him Lord.

The triumph of Jehovah is the triumph of His people. He subdues the nations under them. Different renderings of the tenses in these verses have led to different interpretations. Is it, "He subdued"; "He hath subdued"; "He subdueth"; or, "He will subdue"? The same grammatical difficulty applies to, "He shall choose". Davison says, "Without discussing the matter in detail, there are good reasons for preferring the translation of the RV margin, 'He subdueth - chooseth - loveth'; understanding that a general truth is intended, with special reference to the recent deliverance and its illustration of the broad principle of God's care for His people". This is very beautiful, somewhat like Paul's word in 2 Corinthians 1.10, where, when speaking of his trust in God he writes, "Who delivered us...and doth deliver...he will yet deliver". His love and His care for His people continue always.

The excellency (1347), or, the pride, of Jacob is this, that the nation of Israel has been loved of Jehovah and that love has provided an inheritance for His chosen people. This divine favour is the nation's boast. Are there those who would seek to rob Israel of their Promised Land? Jehovah will subdue such adversaries under their feet. He who chose the inheritance for them will preserve it for them also. The "Selah" marks the end of the first strophe.

Verses 5-9: The Call Repeated

The triumphant theme is now continued and the call to praise comes with intensified fervour. Amid the shouting of the people, Elohim has ascended. Amid the sound of the trumpet, Jehovah has gone up. It is as if God had come down to intervene and deliver His people, and now, having delivered them, He has ascended His throne, returning to His palace in glory. Whether this is Jehovah's ascension to His heavenly abode, or His entering into exaltation in Zion, does not affect the meaning. Jehovah is on high and must be praised.

The call to "sing praises" is repeated five times in vv. 6 and 7. JND translates "Sing psalms". Dr Cohen says, "The Hebrew verb is the root of *mizmor*, Psalm, and is used of vocal praise". Davison seems to be in direct variance with Cohen when he says, "The word refers to instrumental rather than vocal music"! But then he adds that it "at least implies that the singing is accompanied". Perowne writes, "The word means both *to sing* and *to play*". There seems little doubt that instruments and voices are united in a joyful rendering of suitable praise to God, King of all the earth. Such praise should be with the understanding (7919). This word is akin to "maschil", as in the title of Psalm 32 and twelve other Psalms. Praise should be with intelligence and wisdom.

God is King. Note that Israel can say, "Our King", but He is, by right, "King of all the earth". He has taken His seat and He reigns over the nations. As the King of Babylon was told in Daniel 4.17, "The most High ruleth in the kingdom of men". He sits on the throne of His holiness, in sovereignty, and the Psalm envisages the day when all men will gather to pay homage to Him. The princes of the peoples and the people of the God of Abraham will join as one people to exalt Him. The nobles of the nations unite with Israel in praise of Elohim. How eloquently does Alexander Maclaren sum it up, "The obliteration of distinction between Israel and the nations, by the incorporation of the latter, so that 'the peoples' become part of the 'people of the God of Abraham', floats before the singer's prophetic eye, as the end of God's great manifestation of Himself. The two parts of that double choir, which the preceding strophes summon to song, coalesce at last, and in grand unison send up one full-throated, universal melodious shout of praise". The shields (4043) of the earth (v.9), are the human protectors of men; they are the princes just mentioned, but they are in God's hand. They belong to Him.

The Psalm closes on a high note, which is really the whole theme of the Psalm condensed into a few words - "He is greatly exalted".

PSALM 48

Introduction

With Psalms 46 and 47, this Psalm is the third in that trilogy of Psalms which celebrate some notable victory and deliverance of the nation. No author is indicated though many commentators assume that it belongs to

David. Some rather think that it is of later date and the suggestions which are offered are many and varied, but Plumer commends Henry, who, he says, "speaks as wisely as anyone" when he says, "For aught I know, it might be penned by David, upon occasion of some eminent victory obtained in his time; yet not so calculated for that, but that it might serve any other the like occasion in after times". This is indeed a wise observation, for, by inspiration, all Scripture is designed to be profitable for all the people of God in every age (2 Tim 3.16). Saints of all times may, and do, sing this Psalm sincerely and with meaning.

The Psalm is entitled "A Song (SHIR - 7892) and Psalm (MIZMOR - 4210)". The Theological Wordbook of the Old Testament comments that it is unclear if there is any appreciable difference between *mizmor* "a psalm" and *shir* "a song", and continues, "Rabbinic interpretation...recognised *mizmor* as a psalm accompanied by instruments, and *shir mizmor* as a psalm sung by a choral group alone. Several things are clear, however, in relating these two words. One is that the noun *mizmor* appears exclusively in the Psalms and there always as a title and never in the body of a psalm. By contrast, *shir* is not confined to the Psalter and within the Psalter itself is used both as a title and in the psalm proper...*mizmor* is limited to religious song. *shir*, on the other hand, may occasionally refer to secular songs", as in Isaiah 23.15-16. Psalms 120-134, known as the "Songs of Degrees", are all designated SHIR.

The Psalm is in two sections, divided by the "Selah" at the end of verse 8, but the first section may also be suitably divided into two parts. Verses 1-3 sing the glory of Zion. Verses 4-8 recount the defeat of the enemy, while verses 9-14 call for rejoicing, and ascribe praise to God.

For comment on the "Sons of Korah", mentioned in the title, refer to the introduction to Psalm 42 in this Commentary.

Verses 1-3: The Glory of Zion

The words "great" (1419), and "greatly" (3966) with which the Psalm begins, are not cognate words. They may be translated similarly here, but they are not at all identical. The thought appears to be that the greatness, the might, and the majesty of Jehovah demands that praise of Him should be rendered exceedingly, abundantly, and in magnitude. The praise of His people should accord with the excellence of His Person. While praise might be offered acceptably by the individual saint, the reference here is undoubtedly to national worship in the temple services in Jerusalem, twice called in the Psalm, "The city of our God", and once, "The city of Jehovah of Hosts". On "the city of the great King" see the comments on v.2. The presence of God in the temple in Jerusalem had made Zion "the mountain of his holiness", and Zion had become almost a synonym for Jerusalem. For other references to the holy hill see Psalms 26 and 24.3.

There are acknowledged difficulties in v.2. The fair city is indeed beautiful. No one who has stood on the Mount of Olives and viewed

Jerusalem across the valley, shining golden in the sun, can fail to exclaim, "Beautiful for situation!". But "situation" (5131), while not erroneous, may be more accurately rendered "elevation". Jerusalem occupied a lofty site some eight hundred metres above sea level, making it visible to all the surrounding countryside. It is important to notice that pilgrims and travellers always go "up to Jerusalem", whether in Old Testament or New, whether in the Psalms, in the Prophets, in the Gospels, or in the Acts of the Apostles. The many references to the "going up" to Jerusalem make an interesting and profitable study and explain this "beautiful for elevation" clause in v.2 of the Psalm. (See 1 Kings 12.28; 2 Kings 12.17; 16.5; 2 Chr 2.16; Ezra 1.3; 7.13; Ps 122.3, 4; Mt 20.17, 18; Mk 10.32, 33; Lk 2.42; 18.31; 19.28; Jn 2.13; 5.1; 11.55; Acts 11.2; 15.2; 21.4, 12, 15; 24.11; 25.9; Gal 1.17, 18).

That Mount Zion should be the joy of the whole earth is probably prophetic, when the glory of the city in millennial splendour will radiate throughout the earth. However, if "earth" is translated "land", as seems in order, see JND (footnote), and Strong (776), then all the favoured nation throughout Eretz Israel would, at any time, rejoice in this glory, but in Lamentations 2.15 the phrase, "The joy of the whole earth", is combined with Psalm 50.2 in a sad lament over Jerusalem; "Is this the city that men call, The perfection of beauty, The joy of the whole earth?".

Difficulty now arises in the latter part of v.2 in relation to "the sides of the north". Various explanations are offered with several suggestions regarding punctuation. Perowne, Maclaren, Delitzsch, and others, deal with these suggestions at length and in detail, but the simplest and the most probable interpretation may be understood in the following paraphrase - "Beautiful in elevation, the joy of the whole land is Mount Zion, with the city of the great King on its northern aspect". "City" (7151) here, however, is not the same as "city" occurring three times in vv. 1 and 8 (5892). In v.2 the word can be rendered "citadel" so that there may be a reference to the temple rather than to the city of Jerusalem itself. As Kirkpatrick says, "If we render, *on the sides of the north is the citadel of the great King*, (it is) a description of the position of the Temple".

But as Maclaren sums up, "The main thought of this first part is independent of such minute difficulties. It is that the one thing which made Zion-Jerusalem glorious was God's presence in it. It was beautiful in its elevation; it was safely isolated from invaders by precipitous ravines, inclosing the angle of the plateau on which it stood. But it was because God dwelt there and manifested Himself there that it was 'a joy for the whole earth'. The name by which even the earthly Zion is called is 'Jehovah-Shammah', The Lord is there". God is known in her palaces for a refuge. He is the protector of His people, dwelling in the midst of them as their fortress and stronghold. Notice another reference to the "palaces" in v.13.

Verses 4-8: The Defeat of the Enemy

That puny kings of earth should array themselves against the citadel of the great King is ironical. "He that sitteth in the heavens shall laugh: The Lord shall have them in derision" (Ps 2.4). Yet their arrogance will persist, until, in Revelation 19.19, the kings of the earth make war against the King of kings and are destroyed by His sword of judgment. Here they assemble (3259), united in a formal confederation to move across the frontier to Jerusalem, but their intentions are aborted by a sight of the Holy City. "They saw!" "They were astonished!" "They were dismayed!" "They fled!". Many commentators follow Calvin in finding it all reminiscent of Caesar's "Veni, vidi, vici - I came, I saw, I conquered". But here the Emperor's boast is reversed. They came, they saw, and they retreated. Gripped with fear, and seized with pain as a travailing woman, they fled in panic. There is no detail or description of battle. Was it just that sight of Jerusalem which alarmed them, beautiful and impregnable on the hill, with Jehovah in His citadel? He who could scatter the mighty armada of Tarshish with His east wind could similarly dispose of these enemy kings. The ships of Tarshish are, to quote Dr Cohen, "A symbol of great size and strength. Tarshish (see Jonah 1.3) is usually identified with Tartessus in south-west Spain, famed as a port, and its ships renowned as the largest of that age. God swept the powerful army aside like a storm which wrecks these vessels".

What the people had heard of as happening in former times, they were now experiencing for themselves. As they had heard so now they had seen. As their fathers had rehearsed stories of God's miraculous deliverances of the nation in times past, so now they had seen with their own eyes His routing of their enemies and His preservation of the city. It was fitting of course that He should so protect Jerusalem. It was, after all, His city, "The city of our God" and "The city of Jehovah Sabaoth, the Lord of hosts". This was no ordinary city. It was the very seat of theocracy. It was the place where Jehovah had chosen to place His name. Was this present triumph a pledge to Jerusalem that God would establish her for ever? Or is this, as some think, a prayerful exclamation, "God establish her for ever"? Whichever is the meaning, this is clear, that they were witnesses of a deliverance like those of which they had heard from their fathers and there was every encouragement to believe that Jehovah would continue to preserve His own.

The section closes with the familiar "Selah". These are moments for reflection, for meditation, for pausing and for lifting up the heart and voice in gratitude to God.

Verses 9-14: The Call to Praise

"We have thought" (1819) signifies a meditation in comparisons. They had pondered what they had seen, and had compared it with what they had heard, and it all confirmed for them the lovingkindness (2617), the mercy, the goodness, of Him who dwelt in His temple in Zion. Such meditation must issue in praise, resounding to the ends of the earth in accordance with the greatness of His name. In righteousness Jehovah had displayed His mighty power in the destruction of His enemies. His right hand had moved against them and Mount Zion must rejoice. Who then are "the daughters of Judah"? Some will understand the expression literally, as referring to the maidens of the nation who were often prominent in the celebration of victories in dance and song. Others think that it is rather an appeal to the smaller towns and villages of Judah, that they should join in Jerusalem's exultation over her deliverance. Such lesser towns would have been threatened by the threat to Jerusalem, and it was but to be expected that they should share in the rejoicing. Whether literal or symbolic, this is a call for praise befitting the greatness of God and the corresponding greatness of His triumph.

There now follows an invitation to survey the city. How has Jehovah preserved it from the enemy! "Walk about Zion! Count her towers! Mark her ramparts! Consider her palaces!" The siege is over. The enemy has gone. There is freedom now to walk around the city, to see her intact and unscathed, preserved by God. This God, such a God, is our God, for ever and ever. What has happened, what He has done, what they have seen and known, they will be able to recount to posterity, for His glory. "He will be our guide even unto death", is not the full meaning of the concluding words of the Psalm. It is not just "unto death", nor even "in death", but also "over death" and "beyond death", and perhaps it may be the more easily rendered, "He will be our guide eternally".

On such a confident note the Psalm ends. Regarding a supposed textual difficulty in these closing words, William Binnie writes, "Some expositors have strangely found a difficulty in the last verse, deeming such a profession of personal faith as an inappropriate ending for a national song…To me it seems that the verse, as it stands, is admirably in harmony with the song, and is its crowning beauty. When the Lord does great things for church or nation, He means that all the faithful, however humble their station, should take courage from it, should repose in Him fresh confidence, and cling to Him with firmer hope, and say, 'This God shall be our God for ever, He will guide us even unto death'".

PSALM 49

Introduction

Dr Cohen entitles this Psalm, "Death the Leveller", and how true this is! He points out that the Psalm teaches that, "The might of wealth is limited. It cannot ward off the oncoming of death, and at its advent the rich are reduced to the same level as the poor. If that truism were kept in mind, wealth would not breed insolent pride; and in that thought the poor in their disability may hope for the ultimate triumph of right". He adds that the Psalm has been appointed for recital in a Jewish house of mourning.

On the superscription, "To the chief Musician, A Psalm for the sons of Korah", common to many Psalms, see the introductions to Psalms 4 and 42 in this Commentary. Neither the date nor the authorship can be decided with any certainty.

Unlike the previous three Psalms, there is nothing either historical or national in Psalm 49. Plumer alludes to Henry, who says, "This Psalm is a sermon. In most of the Psalms we have the penman praying or praising. Here we have him preaching...The scope and design of this discourse is to convince the men of this world of their sin and folly in setting their hearts upon the things of this world, and to persuade them to seek the things of a better world; as also to comfort the people of God, in reference to their own troubles, and the grief that arises from the prosperity of the wicked".

The Psalmist deals with a problem with which philosophers have struggled for centuries, and have never yet resolved, that is, the harmonising of a man's character with his lot in things material. Why do the wicked so often seem to prosper, and why do the upright often endure poverty? It seems to many that wealth and influence are power, to be envied, but the Psalmist will show, in Dr Cohen's words, that death is indeed the leveller. No riches can buy immunity from death. It is the common lot of rich and poor alike. As the more modern poet, Gray, has so aptly expressed it:-

> The boast of heraldry, the pomp of power,
> And all that beauty, all that wealth e'er gave,
> Await alike the inevitable hour;
> The paths of glory lead but to the grave.

The Psalm is in three parts. Verses 1-3 are a preface, an introductory summons. The remaining two parts conclude with the same words in verses12 and 20. The first of these two latter parts considers a prosperity that ends in death, and the second deals with the blessed end of the righteous poor. These features are seen in the Saviour's account of that rich man whose luxurious living ended in torment, while the beggar at his gate was carried, at death, into bliss.

Verses 1-4: A Universal Summons

This Psalm is bigger than Judaism. It opens with a call to all peoples everywhere. The word "people" (5971) is a plural word, AMIM, embracing Israel and all nations. All are called to listen, to give ear, and again the universality of the summons is emphasised, "All ye inhabitants of the world". "World" (2465), however, is an interesting and important word. It denotes the lapse of time, a fleeting age, life transient and temporary. Strong says that it is "from an unused root apparently meaning to glide swiftly". It may be translated time, age, or, duration of life. Davison writes, "The second line might be rendered 'All ye that dwell in this fleeting world'. Lessons are to be announced which concern the children of mankind as a whole".

Yet once again it is emphasised that the message of the Psalm is for all men, without distinction. "Low" (1121, 120) and "high" (1121, 376) are paraphrases of the Hebrew. The call is to "sons of ADAM" and to "sons of ISH", to men in general and men in particular, low-born and high-born. The message is for all. Some of these will be rich and some will be poor. The Psalmist will have warnings for the rich and consolations for the poor. It cannot be over-emphasised that the message of the Psalm is universal. In language reminiscent of the Books of Proverbs and Ecclesiastes the Psalmist speaks of wisdom and understanding. In the Hebrew both of these words are plural, perhaps to denote the greatness, the profundity, of what he has to say. To be able to impart this wisdom and understanding to others the Psalmist himself must listen. He will incline his ear. He will be sensitive to divine revelation, waiting patiently for a word from the Lord. That word will come to him in parable and proverb, and he will convey the dark saying which he receives, with the harp. "Dark saying" (2420) means an enigma, a difficult question. It is the Psalmist's intention to explain such in inspired lyrical compositions, so that with the accompaniment of the stringed instrument men may actually sing of those things which formerly had perplexed them. As Maclaren says, "This Psalmist presents himself as a divinely inspired teacher, who has received into purged and attentive ears, in many a whisper from God, and as the result of many an hour of silent waiting, the word which he would now proclaim on the housetops".

Verses 5-12: The Weakness of Wealth

When the Psalmist considers the futility of trusting in riches, and the foolish arrogance of those who do, he exclaims, "Wherefore should I fear in the days of evil, when the iniquity of my heels shall compass me about?". This is not his own iniquity of which he speaks. It would be irrelevant, and out of context, to speak of that here. Heels (6120) is from a primitive root (6117) which denotes "supplant; circumvent; follow at the heel; attack at the heels". The Psalmist had obviously experienced those days of adversity and affliction, when the injustices and iniquity of rich men had dogged his footsteps, compassing him about and threatening to trip him up. Why should he fear those who vainly trusted in their wealth and boasted in their riches?

Such trust in riches was folly. Riches could neither purchase life nor buy immunity from death or judgment. Not the richest of these rich men could by any means redeem a friend from death, not even one so close as a brother. No ransom price offered by man would be acceptable to God, and this proved the ultimate vanity of riches. Plumer comments, "Men may own millions, but none of them can by any means redeem his brother, nor give to God a ransom for him...It is vain to offer gold as a ransom, atonement, or expiation for the guilty soul, our own or a brother's"

There follows, in v.8, a parenthesis, before the theme of v.7 is continued in v.9. The parenthesis simply restates the fact that the redemption of the soul is more precious than to be bought with wealth. The life of the soul is of more value than money can buy. All thoughts of attempting to purchase redemption with gold must be abandoned, must be left alone, for ever. Perowne says He is "God who cannot be bribed". Today the believer rejoices to say that we "were not redeemed with corruptible things, as silver and gold...but with the precious blood of Christ, as of a lamb without blemish and without spot" (1 Pet 1.18-19).

The theme begun in v.7 is now pursued. No ransom can be given to God that man should live on and escape the pit of corruption. Death is inevitable and inescapable. "It is appointed unto men once to die" (Heb 9.27), and the appointment must be kept by all. Even wise men die, the Psalmist observes. Wise men and fools, rich men and simpletons, alike go to the grave. What then of the riches that some have amassed, and in which they trusted? "Thou fool", God said to such a man, "this night thy soul shall be required of thee: then whose shall those things be, which thou hast provided?" (Lk 12.20). All must be left! Yet a man might fondly imagine that he will live on for ever, if not in this physical life, at least in his estate which he will bequeath to others. Houses and lands he might have acquired over the years, and by these his name might indeed be perpetuated. But what will this avail him personally? Nothing! However much wealth he may have accumulated, however great his estate, however much his wisdom, he cannot for ever abide in the honour and esteem which he has enjoyed in life. He must come to his end and die as the cattle die. The Psalmist is not, of course, dealing here with the doctrine of eternal destinies, but simply with life and death as they affect all men.

Verses 13-20: The End of the Upright

The Psalmist now comes to the contrasting blessedness of the upright, but first he will echo the sentiments of the preceding verses. It is like a summing up of the contents of the earlier part of the Psalm. He dwells again on the folly of those whose hope was in their wealth. Perowne calls this, "a stupid security or presumptuous confidence, fool-hardiness". It was foolishness indeed, to trust in riches, and yet such folly may often persist in the posterity of these men, never learning, and actually approving the words and the ways of their predecessors. Notwithstanding the proven futility of the course of these rich fools, there are those who will blindly follow them, imitate them, and come to the same end. The "Selah" indicates a pause for reflection on all that has been said, and the pause is almost like a silent protest against the folly.

Together, these all move like a flock to the grave (7585). "Sheol", the grave-land, the abode of the dead, the place of no return, awaits them all. In the figure of the flock and the shepherd, death is viewed as the shepherd, and the words "shall feed" (7462) might suitably be so rendered, as in the AV. The RV maintains the figure throughout with, "They are appointed as a flock for Sheol; Death shall be their shepherd". Like a flock of sheep, without choice or reason, and sometimes in confusion, these foolish rich hasten on to the grave. What a contrast is this to the fold and the flock of the good Shepherd, who guides His sheep through the valley of the shadow of death, and leads them to the waters of quietness and to the pastures of tender grass.

The morning will come! The Psalmist may not have had the full revelation of that morning as it is now enjoyed by New Testament believers, but that there would be a morning of joy he did not doubt. "Weeping may endure for a night, but joy cometh in the morning" (Ps 30.5). That will be a glad morning of vindication, when the upright will rejoice and have the dominion. But in that glorious daybreak of deliverance for the righteous, the transient glory and strength of the unrighteous will be consumed in the grave. Once they reposed in their riches, now they have no abiding place. All that outward form and show in which they gloried is now gone for ever.

For the Psalmist and his godly companions it will be different then. "God will redeem my soul...he shall receive (3947) me". Thinking of Enoch and Elijah, Perowne renders this, "He shall take me". This word is, indeed, rendered "take" or "take away" almost eight hundred times in the AV. Another Psalm, using the same word, says, "Thou shalt guide me with thy counsel, and afterward receive me to glory" (Ps 73.24). Many believers will think of the Saviour's promise, "I will...receive you unto myself" (Jn 14.3), and of the Apostle's confirmation of this in 1 Thessalonians 4.17. He will, He must, take His ransomed home, and in that day of glory His saints will sing, "O death, where is thy sting? O grave, where is thy victory?" (1 Cor 15.55). "God will redeem my soul from the power of the grave". Yet again the "Selah" calls for a pause. If the first "Selah", in v.13, required reflection on the doom of the lost, this second "Selah" demands a joyful meditation on the glory of the redeemed.

What the Psalmist had prescribed for himself he now commends to others. "Wherefore should I fear?", he had asked in v.5. "Be not thou afraid", he exhorts in v.16. Another man might be rich, the splendour and glory of his house, his home, and his reputation may be great in the world. Remember that all this honour is transient. He can carry nothing away with him in death. When he descends into the grave his glory cannot go with him. While he lived he may have congratulated himself on his success, and men may have congratulated him also, but he must go the way of his fathers, where the unrighteous shall never see light again. The refrain of v.12 is now repeated. Foolish rich man, poor in understanding, with all his earthly honour must die like the beasts.

PSALM 50

Introduction

This is the first of twelve Psalms which are ascribed to Asaph. The other eleven are all in the third Book of Psalms and are the consecutive Psalms 73 - 83. Whether Asaph was the actual author of these Psalms, or the compiler of a collection which was to bear his name, is not clear, and neither can be proved or disproved. He may well have been the originator of the collection, to be added to by his descendants, some of whom were famed as singers during the exile and the return from Babylon (Ezra 2.41). Asaph was one of three Chief Musicians appointed by David with Heman and Ethan (or Jeduthun) to preside over the singing and the service of the great choral company of Levites (1 Chr 15.16-17 and compare 1 Chr 25.1). To him was committed the Psalm which celebrated the bringing up of the Ark to Jerusalem after its many years of exile. Asaph was the chief of those appointed on that day "to minister before the ark of the Lord, and to record, and thank and praise the Lord God of Israel" (1 Chr 16.4-7).

This Psalm has been likened to a great judicial process, a court scene in which Jehovah is both Plaintiff and Judge, and Israel the defendant. Dr Cohen entitles it, "Israel Arraigned", and this seems to sum up its message. The Psalm is in four parts, of which the first three are the principal parts, the last two verses being a brief conclusion to the whole. The first part, verses 1-6, ending with a "Selah", is a grand introduction, in which both heaven and earth are summoned to witness the judgment scene. The second part, verses 7-15, deals with the essential worthlessness of animal sacrifices in that Jehovah has no personal need of them. Verses 16-21 denounce the wicked hypocrisy of those who take God's Word on their lips but whose lives are evil. The closing strophe, verses 22-23, concludes the Psalm with a warning and a promise.

Verses 1-6: The Court Assembles

The Judge who summons the solemn assembly is introduced in a glorious combination of three divine names. As a herald might proclaim the arrival of a visiting monarch or dignitary at the opening of any human assize, announcing his presence by declaring all the monarch's titles, so does the Psalm begin with these great titles of God. He is the Mighty (410) God (430), even the LORD (3068). He is El, Elohim, Jehovah. Alexander Maclaren writes, "No English equivalents are available, and it is best to retain the Hebrew, only noting that each name is separated from the others by the accents in the original, and that to render either 'the mighty God' (AV) or 'the God of Gods' is not only against that punctuation, but destroys the completeness symbolised by the threefold designation". He continues, "Each name has its own force of meaning. El speaks of God as mighty; Elohim, as the object of religious fear; Jehovah, as the self-existent and covenant God".

In the grandeur and splendour of these titles God has spoken. The whole earth is summoned to witness the righteousness of the judgment. From the rising of the sun to the going down thereof, from sunrise to sunset, from east to west, men are called to the great assize, not to be judged, but to observe. In v.4 the heavens will be summoned also. Jehovah will have His universe to assemble to behold His judgment of the defendants. He will be vindicated. His justice will be acknowledged.

"God...hath spoken", v.1 declares. "God hath shined", says v.2. Out of Zion, His dwelling place in the sanctuary, where was the Shekinah, God had manifested Himself, raying forth in His glory. Zion is "the perfection of beauty", so called also in Lamentations 2.15. Perowne quotes the Rabbis who said, "Ten measures of beauty hath God bestowed upon the world, and nine of these fall to the lot of Jerusalem". With these sentiments Psalm 48.2 would agree. But God is shining forth here as a devouring fire accompanied by a raging tempest. These are, of course, symbols of judgment. He calls now to the heavens above, and repeats His call to the earth also, that there may be universal witness as He judges His people. For long He has kept silent, but not now. Is this to be, as some suggest, a ceremonial renewal of the covenant made at Sinai?

All having been solemnly assembled, the defendants are summoned to the bar of judgment. "Gather my saints together unto me". This is Israel, holy among the nations, chosen from among them. They were in a privileged covenant relationship with God, a covenant which had been ratified at Sinai by burnt offerings and peace offerings. They had clearly heard the reading of the book of the covenant, and had been sprinkled with the blood of the covenant (Ex 24.4-6), but privilege brings responsibility, and Jehovah now has a controversy with them. They are being called to give account to Him of their unfaithfulness. The heavens know Him. They could testify to His essentially righteous character and will now witness the righteousness of His judgment, for it is the righteous God Himself who is the Judge. He will not leave the ordering of this tribunal to delegates, whether men, angels, or archangel. He Himself, with whom the covenant was made, will judge. The "Selah" calls for a pause, in which serious reflection may be made upon the solemnity of the occasion.

Verses 7-15: The True Nature of Sacrifice

The judgment begins and the Judge will address the defendants, but there is a certain tenderness even in the judgment. "O my people...I am God, even thy God". With sadness God must testify against His own people. The God of Israel must testify against Israel. Jehovah's complaint was not that they had neglected the ceremonial law in respect of the offerings. He was not charging them with having withheld the ordained sacrifices from Him. Their burnt offerings were ever before Him, but this was not the problem. There was, with them, a complacency, even a pride, in their attendance to externals and rituals. Of what value to God were their offerings if not accompanied by true confession, contrition, worship, and thanksgiving? Did they really imagine that they were enriching the Creator by their offerings? He would take nothing from them if this was their motive. Neither from their herds, their flocks, or their folds would He accept anything, and, in any case, all were His already. The sheep and the goats, the wild beasts of the forest, the cattle upon a thousand hills, and every bird in the mountains, were all His. Jehovah was self-sufficient. He had no need of anything that they could supply. "The world is mine", He says, "and the fulness thereof". Neither the flesh of bulls nor the blood of goats were necessary to Him, as they were to the idol gods of the surrounding nations.

What then was the charge, and the complaint against His people? It must be understood, and emphasised, that there is no divine rejection here of those animal sacrifices and offerings concerning which God had given such detail as outlined in the early chapters of the Book of Leviticus. He had ordained those for a purpose. But where were the obedient lives, the thankful hearts, and the worshipful spirits, the calling upon God, which should have accompanied their offerings? This was the complaint. Externals! Ceremonials! Rituals! What would be the desired outcome of this great tribunal? Would they learn to call upon their God out of true and grateful hearts? If they would, He would deliver them and they would glorify Him. But there was a wickedness yet to be addressed.

Verses 16-21: Wicked Hypocrisy

This third part of the Psalm commences with a serious "But...". These were indeed God's people, His own people - "But!". They were a covenant people in a unique relationship with Him. They were different from the nations around, chosen out from among them. "But!" With all their profession and privilege and knowledge, He had found a certain wickedness. There was formality and hypocrisy among them, wearing a cloak of religion while they violated His laws. What right had they to boast about His statutes and engage in ritual repetition of the terms of the covenant, at the same time rejecting by their behaviour the very instructions which they were repeating? Lip and life did not agree. Their words and their ways were at variance. Did they constantly, formally, repeat those ten commandments given at Sinai? They were guilty, among other things, of breaches of the eighth, the seventh, and the ninth commandments. There was complicity with thieves, there was adultery, there was evil-speaking, slander, deceit, and lying. A man would sin against his own family, slandering his own brother. These things were grievous to Jehovah, especially from a people who outwardly espoused His laws and gloried in the covenant.

The solemn indictment of them is, "These things hast thou done", but in all of this Jehovah had kept silent. He had certainly taken notice, but had not moved in judgment against them. It was a gracious forbearance, but they misunderstood it. The goodness of God in restraining His judgment should have led them to repentance, but instead they despised it (compare Rom 2.4). They interpreted His silence as acquiescence, a condoning of their evil ways. As they themselves condoned what they knew to be wrong, so they thought that Jehovah was just like them, condoning it also. But God is not mocked. The silence is past now, and Jehovah will reprove them and set in order (6186) before their eyes, as in a formal indictment, a catalogue of the things which they have done. He will array their sins before them in an orderly way, the charges prepared as in a legal case in a court of law. It will be a divinely accurate assessment, and, as Maclaren comments, "It will be the hypocrite's turn to keep silent then, and his thought of a complaisant God like himself will perish before the stern reality".

Verses 22-23: Warning and Promise

The people are called from carelessness and forgetfulness to solemn consideration. Jehovah would not forbear for ever. If and when He moved in judgment, there would be no escape or deliverance, and punishment would be severe. He would "tear them in pieces" (2963), rending them as a lion might.

On the other hand, God would be glorified in the sacrifice of thanksgiving, "the sacrifice of praise…giving thanks to his name" (Heb 13.15). This was the offering which He would accept. Such an offering, from grateful, thankful hearts, offered in sincerity, was more to Him than all the bulls and goats sacrificed in ritual only. The Psalm closes with a promise to the man who ordered his conversation (1870), his way, the course of his life, in conformity with the will of God. Such a man would enjoy the salvation of God, and this would mean an enjoyment of God Himself. A devoted and pious life would have such blessed reward.

PSALM 51

Introduction

Psalm 51 is central, and perhaps supreme, among those seven Psalms which are termed "The Penitential Psalms". It is wet throughout with the tears of a penitent, and the superscription indicates both the author and the circumstances of its composition. The Psalm is a commentary on David's confession of sin, and the prophet Nathan's assurance of forgiveness, and the whole sad story is told in 2 Samuel 11 and 12. It is the tragic tale of the moral failure of a man who had subdued Phillistines, Syrians, Amalekites, Ammonites, Moabites, and Edomites, but who could not subdue his own passions. David, who had slain a lion, a bear, and a giant, had now been slain himself by his own unbridled lust. The nation was already singing his Psalms, but now he was sobbing out his grief.

This was not altogether a sudden lapse. It had been precipitated by prosperity, ease, self-indulgence, idleness, and sloth. While his soldiers were engaged in battle with the Ammonites and were besieging their city Rabbah, David had remained in Jerusalem in the comfort and luxury of his palace home. It was the time "when kings go forth to battle", but King David had chosen, sadly, to stay at home (2 Sam 11.1) while his troops went forth without him. The consequences were morally disastrous. There followed covetousness and adultery, pretence and hypocrisy, conspiracy and murder. He broke the tenth, the seventh, and the sixth commandments, in that order (Ex 20.17, 14, 13). He had coveted his neighbour's wife. He had committed adultery with her. He had been complicit in, and guilty of, the untimely death of her husband Uriah, a faithful subject and soldier, and a captain in David's army. It was murder indeed. Although not actually there in person, the charge against him would be, "Thou hast killed Uriah the Hittite" (2 Sam 12.9).

Several months must have passed by before Nathan the prophet confronted David with a parable. When David pronounced judgment upon the sinning man of the parable Nathan bluntly and boldly accused him, saying, "Thou art the man. Thus saith the Lord God of Israel...Wherefore hast thou despised the commandment of the Lord?...thou hast killed Uriah...and hast taken his wife to be thy wife...thou hast despised me". What would David do? Of course, being king, he might have expelled, or even executed Nathan forthwith. Instead, he acknowledged, with contrition, "I have sinned against the Lord" (2 Sam 12.1-14).

Consequent upon all this David wrote Psalm 51. It is the prayer of a penitent indeed, but notice that he commits it to the Chief Musician, the Master of Song for the nation. While this may be a very personal confession and prayer of David, nevertheless, since all men at times must confess sin, the Psalm could be sung nationally in the public service of the sanctuary. It should be read in conjunction with Psalm 32. Other "Penitential Psalms" are Psalms 6, 38, 102, 130 and 143.

The Psalm may be divided as follows. Verses 1-4 are a general confession of sin. Verses 5-12 are a more detailed prayer for pardon and restoration. Verses 13-17 anticipate the results of that pardon, and verses 18-19 are a brief concluding petition.

Verses 1-4: Sin, Transgression and Iniquity

David employs each of these words in his full and frank confession. "Sin" (2403) is a missing of the mark. "Transgression" (6588) is the uprising of a will that refuses to be subject. It is a rebellious, flagrant disobedience. "Iniquity" (5771) is a crooked, perverse wickedness. Together these words convey the enormity of his sin and require an abundance of mercy from the God against whom he has sinned. David pleads for this, using another three words with which to advance his plea. He asks for mercy (2603), for lovingkindness (2617), and for tender mercies (7356). The three are somewhat similar and yet to be distinguished. Some have noted an increasing intensity in the words. He asks for that mercy which is grace for the guilty. He desires a lovingkindness which is goodness and pity mingled with the mercy. "Tender mercies" is one word which blends mercy with compassion and tender love. Such a confession of such sin demands this magnanimity of mercy, grace, goodness, pity, and compassion.

Having used three words to describe his sin, and having employed also these three words to plead for mercy, David will similarly appeal for pardon in a three-fold way. "Wash…me and cleanse me", he says in v.2. Later, in v.7, he will ask, "Purge me", and in v.9, as in v.1, "Blot out all mine iniquities". He feels like a soiled garment, like a defiled leper, and like one whose record has been stained.

"Wash me"(3526). The word means to wash by treading out or by beating, as a woman in those days might have beaten out soiled clothing against stones to remove the stains. As Alexander Maclaren writes, "The word employed is significant, in that it probably means washing by kneading or beating, not by simple rinsing. The Psalmist is ready to submit to any painful discipline, if only he may be cleansed. 'Wash me, beat me, tread me down, hammer me with mallets, dash me against stones, do anything with me, if only these foul stains are melted from the texture of my soul'. He knew the blackness of his own sin, and groaned under it". David is willing for any chastisement, if only he might be cleansed from his sin. "Cleanse me" (2891) implies a ceremonial cleansing, as one who has been defiled with disease may be purified and pronounced physically clean. "I acknowledge my transgressions" signifies, "I know them". Plumer remarks, "A declaration that *we know our trespasses* is an *acknowledgement* of them. The verb however is in the future, *will know*, thus declaring he expected to retain a deep sense of his sin, as long as he should live. And *my sin* is *ever before me.* If the verb supplied here shall follow the tense of the parallel clause, it would be, my sin shall ever be before me, I have now and I expect always to have a painful sense of my miserable misconduct".

The words of David's confession in v.4, "Against thee, thee only have I sinned", have occasioned much difficulty for some, and have been seized upon by critics who dispute the Davidic authorship of the Psalm. They argue, with some justification, that David had sinned against Uriah, against Bathsheba, against his family, and against the nation. How then could he have said, "Against thee, thee only, have I sinned"? Of course David had done grievous wrong to Uriah and to these others, but all sin is primarily against God, a breach of divine law. If David could not have employed this term, then what sinner could? "I have sinned against the Lord", was his first word to Nathan the prophet (2 Sam 12.13). Joseph, in his temptation, recognised the same, and said to Potiphar's wife, "How then can I do this great wickedness, and sin against God?" (Gen 39.9). Maclaren again: "Surely it argues a strange ignorance of the language of a penitent soul, to suppose that such words as the Psalmist's could be spoken only in regard to sins which had no bearing at all on other men. David's deed had been a crime against Bathsheba, against Uriah, against his family and his realm; but these were not its blackest characteristics. Every crime against man is sin against God...And it is only when considered as having relation to God that crimes are darkened into sins. The Psalmist is stating a strictly true and profound thought when he declares that he has sinned 'against Thee only'...that thought has, for the time being, filled his whole horizon...A man who has never felt that all-engrossing sense of his sin as against God only has much to learn". With all this Kirkpatrick agrees when he writes, "All sin, even that by which man is most grievously injured, is, in its ultimate nature, sin against God, as a breach of His holy law".

David's full and frank confession justified God in His condemnation of the sin, and Paul quotes v.4 in Romans 3.4. Any attempt at self-justification on the part of the sinner is a challenge to divine righteousness. A refusal to acknowledge sin casts aspersion on the character of God when He pronounces sentence, but confession justifies and vindicates God in His judgment, and brings into clear light the justice and holiness which condemns the sin. "Yea", says Paul, "let God be true".

Verses 5-12: More Petitions for Pardon

There is a saying that men are "sinners by nature and by practice". With this sentiment the Psalmist agrees. He was shapen in iniquity and conceived in sin. "Shapen"(2342) signifies "to bring forth", and is so translated, twice, in Proverbs 8.24-25. It is associated with that pain and travail which attends the birth. David, as all others, was conceived and brought forth in sin. This is not, of course, the sin of his mother, but his own, inherited, sinful and corrupt nature. It is the portion of all men. There was no child born in the Garden of Eden. All are the offspring of fallen parents, born with a propensity to sin. David is not, because of this, appealing for mitigation or leniency. He is not pleading the sinfulness of his nature as an excuse for the sin which he has committed. He is simply stating a sad fact. "Iniquity" in v.5, is the same word as that in v.2. What he had done only revealed what he was. In nature, as in practice, he was indeed a sinner.

Now it is time to speak of truth and wisdom. As the former verse had opened with a "Behold", to draw attention to the awful fact of man's corrupt nature, so this succeeding v.6 will also begin with "Behold", as if to indicate a correlation with what has preceded. Man may indeed be inherently sinful, but God desires that in heart and mind, in thought and will, in the inward parts, there should be sincerity and devotion, truth and wisdom.

"Purge" (2398), is a most interesting word. It is a derivative of the word rendered "sinned" in v.4. Perowne refers to Donne, and quotes from his

Sermon on this verse, (Sermon lxii), in which he says, "The root of the word is *peccare*, to sin, for purging is a purging of peccant humours...and if in our language that were a word in use, it might be translated, Thou shalt un-sin me". The hyssop which the Psalmist mentions was a wild aromatic herb which grew freely on walls and in ruins; see 1 Kings 4.33. It was common in Egypt, in the Sinai desert, and in Israel. The earliest reference to hyssop in Scripture is in Exodus 12.22 where it was used to sprinkle the blood of the paschal lamb upon the door posts. After that it is mentioned several times in Leviticus 14 in connection with the ceremonial purification of the leper, and it is probably this that suggests its usage here in a symbolical way. David, in his sin, feels defiled as a leper. "Purge me with hyssop", he prays. He wants to be both morally and ceremonially clean before God. The last references to hyssop are in John 19.29 and Hebrews 9.19, but see also Numbers 19.18. "Wash me" probably has reference to the washing of both the person and his clothes in the purification ritual. "Whiter than snow" is a hyperbole. It is a way of saying "whiter than white", purity in the extreme, and the same thought is to be found in Isaiah 1.18.

In his grief David longs for joy and gladness. He had heard denunciation of his sin from the prophet, and now he yearns to hear of the joy that accompanies pardon. Metaphorically, his bones had been broken. The pain of a troubled conscience and the sense of God's displeasure had shattered his whole physical frame and being. He had been crushed indeed. How he would rejoice, in his brokenness, to hear the assurance of sins forgiven. He asks that God might hide His face from his sins, as if seeing them no more, and that his iniquities might be blotted out. He longs that the guilt might be erased, that his record might now be clean, and his account cleared. This is, with the same word, "blot out", a repetition of the request of v.1.

Notice, in vv. 10, 11 and 12, which follow, that there are three occurrences of the same word "spirit" (7307), the central one being a reference to the Spirit of God. Later in the Psalm, in v.17, David will speak of a broken spirit, but now, having asked for inward renewal, for a pure heart, he prays for a right (3559) spirit. The word signifies a steadfast spirit, firm in purpose, prepared and determined to walk in a right way. He dreads losing the presence of God completely in his life, for only the sense of the divine presence could maintain him in the purity for which he now longs. So now he prays, "Take not thy holy spirit from me". Is he remembering what happened to his royal predecessor Saul, as recorded in 1 Samuel 16.14, "But the Spirit of the Lord departed from Saul"? Such a prayer, of course, could not now be offered intelligently by the New Testament believer. David, with fellow saints of his dispensation, did not enjoy the fullness of the blessing of an indwelling Spirit, residing permanently within. That blessing was not given until the ascension and glorification of the Lord Jesus (Jn 7.39). If the expression "thy holy spirit" of v.11, should be rendered "the spirit of thy holiness" (as JND), this does not affect the thought that David is indeed speaking of the Holy Spirit of God. The free spirit, of which he speaks in v.12, is a willing spirit, ever inclined towards divine things. The word "free" (5081) is sometimes rendered "prince" or "noble". It is a noble and princely thing indeed, to serve God freely with a willing heart. Such willingness to do His will and walk in His ways is a corollary of salvation. David had lost the joy of salvation because of his sin. Now he longs that it might be restored and that he might be upheld by that free and willing spirit.

Verses 13-17: The Grand Results of Forgiveness

There are, as the writer of the Epistle to the Hebrews says, "Things that accompany salvation" (Heb 6.9). Of some of these things the Psalmist now speaks. "Then", he says, "will I teach transgressors thy ways". "Then", when the joy of salvation has been restored to him, and when again he is in the enjoyment of communion with God, then, will he teach transgressors. The transgressor will become a teacher! He who himself has transgressed so seriously, who knows the grief and the pain of departure from God, he, restored, can now so ably instruct others in the ways of God. Who better can persuade others than one who knows, experimentally, the consequences of the path which they are treading. David will now labour for the conversion (7725), the restoration and recovery, of those who are sinning. His own personal restoration will influence theirs.

David, although forgiven, is yet carrying in his conscience, the heavy burden of his crime. He had killed Uriah (2 Sam 12.9). It was murder. It was, as he says, bloodguiltiness. He appeals to the God of his salvation and vows that, being delivered, he will sing of God's righteousness. As Kirkpatrick writes, "God's righteousness, i.e. His faithfulness to His character and covenant, is exhibited in the pardon of the penitent not less than in the judgment of the impenitent. 'If we confess our sins, he is faithful and righteous to forgive us our sins, and to cleanse us from all unrighteousness' (1 Jn 1.9)".

For too long David's lips had been sealed by his wrongdoing. How could he have praised God while unrepentant, harbouring unconfessed sin in his heart. But now, forgiven, restored, his lips would be opened again to sing. With the joy of salvation restored to him there would be testimony to men and renewed praise to God. This was true and acceptable sacrifice. It was not slain beasts which brought pleasure to God, but devotion and worship from contrite and thankful hearts. A broken spirit was more acceptable to God than a burnt offering. This does not, of course, set aside the Levitical requirement for sacrifice and offering, but simply emphasises that such offerings, if not accompanied by confession, contrition, and sincerity of heart and mind, were but valueless externals and empty ritual. Compare Psalm 50.7-14 and see the notes there in this Commentary.

Verses 18-19: Concluding Petition

These closing verses of the Psalm have been emphasised by many who deny its Davidic authorship. It is argued that these verses indicate a later period for the Psalm, either during or after the Exile, when Jerusalem was in ruins. Others, while accepting David as the author of the main body of the Psalm, maintain that these concluding verses are a liturgical addition by some priest of that Exile period, but it is not necessary to doubt the pen of David in any part of the Psalm. "Build thou the walls of Jerusalem" need not imply a city in ruins. In David's day the wall of the city was not yet complete. That was left to Solomon (1 Kings 3.1). In any case, the word rendered "build" (1129), may well be a prayer that existing walls might be established and maintained. Spurgeon's citation from James Anderson is worth giving at length. He quotes, "Some few learned Jewish interpreters, while they assign the Psalm to the occasion mentioned in the title, conjecture that the 18th and 19th verses were added by some Jewish bard, in the time of the Babylonish captivity. This opinion is also held by Venema, Green, Street, French, and Skinner. [*Many other names might be added – Author.*] There does not, however, seem to be any sufficient ground for referring the poem, either in whole or in part, to that period. Neither the walls of Jerusalem, nor the buildings of Zion, as the royal palace and the magnificent structure of the temple, which we know David had already contemplated for the worship of God (2 Sam 7.1, etc.), were completed during his reign. This was only effected under the reign of his son Solomon, (1 Kings 3.1). The prayer, then, in the 18th verse might have a particular reference to the completion of these buildings, and especially to the rearing of the temple, in which sacrifices of unprecedented magnitude were to be offered. David's fears might easily suggest to him that his crimes might prevent the building of the temple, which God had promised should be erected (2 Sam 7.13)".

David's concluding desire is that, in His good pleasure, the Lord might bring it all to pass, and find His pleasure, too, in the offerings of His people. Note the use of the two words "burnt offering" (5930) and "whole (3632) burnt offering". The former is OLA, signifying the offering ascending in smoke. The latter is KALIL, emphasising the offering utterly consumed upon the altar. In such sacrifices, offered upon His altar by a willing and devoted people, God would indeed find delight.

PSALM 52

Introduction

The dark background to this Psalm can be found in 1 Samuel 21 and 22. As the title indicates, it was composed on the occasion of David's betrayal to Saul by one Doeg the Edomite. David was a fugitive from Saul. He had fled to Nob, and to Ahimilech the priest there, asking for food and for weapons. He was observed by Doeg and afterwards admitted that he had a premonition that day that Doeg would tell Saul (1 Sam 22.22). He was right. Doeg not only betrayed David, but also occasioned the murder of eighty-five priests of Nob, himself being actively and personally involved in the massacre. It is sadly interesting to remember that Herod the Great, who sought the life of the infant Jesus, the Son of David, and who was responsible too for a massacre, the slaughter of the innocents in Matthew 2.16, was also an Edomite.

A great many commentators doubt the relevance of the Psalm to its title, suggesting that some of the language does not apply to Doeg, but rather, perhaps, to King Saul. Some will see both Saul and Doeg in its denunciations of evil-doers. Yet others think that it is a judgment of wicked men in general, prompted by the remembrance of Doeg's treachery and of what he did to David and to the priests of Nob. It is not necessary, however, to see anything in the Psalm other than a sad poetic commentary on the cowardice and wickedness of that man. There is nothing in the Psalm which may not apply to Doeg.

This Psalm is one of thirteen "Maschil" Psalms, of which Psalm 32 is the first. For an explanation of "Maschil", and a list of the other "Maschil" Psalms, see the introduction to that Psalm in this Commentary.

Like those fifty-four other Psalms, already often referred to in the Commentary, this one is committed to the charge and the care of the Chief Musician, the Master of the service of song in the national worship.

Two "Selahs" divide the Psalm, though not equally. In verses 1-3 the wicked man is addressed and described. In verses 4-5 God's judgment of him is assured. Verses 6-9 anticipate the ultimate vindication and triumph of the righteous.

Verses 1-3: An Address to the Wicked Man

To commit wickedness would be sufficient evil, but to glory in it, and to boast about it, and to praise oneself and celebrate the evil, is manifestly worse. Such is the implication in the word "boastest" (1984). "Mischief" (7451) may not, to modern Western thought and culture, convey the full meaning of this word. It is not trivial. It is unalloyed, malignant, malicious evil. It is a wickedness which plots harm and hurt to others. It is, as Strong says, "vicious in disposition". Such was the character of Doeg the Edomite. Now, although he was chief over Saul's herdsmen, and in that sense was "mighty" (1368), it is possible that the address, "O mighty man", may be spoken in irony. "Mighty? - he was a coward, cunningly and subtly informing on David only to gain favour with Saul. Mighty man indeed! "He does evil", says Murphy in his commentary, "not by the strong arm, but by the babbling tongue; and yet he boasts as if it were a brave achievement, and he a mighty man".

But why? To what purpose is this pride in evil? Such boasting is short-sighted. It will come to an end, while the goodness (2617), the lovingkindness, of God, endures in perpetuity. Note the importance of the divine title which the Psalmist uses here. "God" (410) is El, the Mighty One! See the significance. "O mighty man", why this boasting? The goodness of the truly Mighty One continues ever, when earthly glory has faded and gone. This opening verse is like a summary of the theme of the Psalm, its two parts corresponding to the contrast in the Psalm between man's wickedness and God's lovingkindness.

Doeg devised (2803) his mischief. It was not a sudden impulse. It was a carefully calculated, cunningly thought out plan. "Mischiefs" (1942) in v.2 is not the same word as that so translated in v.1. The meaning is similar, however, and the RV translates it as, "very wickedness". Doeg's tongue was sharp as a razor, whetted for the occasion and working deceit. He loved evil rather than good and preferred lies rather than righteousness. If it be objected that Doeg in fact told the truth when he informed on David's whereabouts, yet, as Kirkpatrick writes, "His tongue was a deceitful tongue, because although the facts he reported were true, he helped to confirm Saul in a false and cruel suspicion...his story was told with malicious intent and fatal result".

The "Selah" suggests a pause, perhaps that readers and singers alike may reverently contemplate what has been said, and join in the Psalmist's abhorrence of the wickedness of wicked men.

Verses 4-5: The Certainty of Divine Judgment

The Psalmist continues to upbraid the man with the deceitful tongue who loved devouring words. "Devouring" (1105) signifies "swallowing". Compare Psalm 35.25 and Psalm 53.4 for a similar thought, which appears to mean that such words swallowed up or engulfed an innocent person. God, however, the Mighty El, would most assuredly destroy such deceitful and wicked men, with a judgment which was eternal. It would be forever. God would break the man down, and take him up, and root him out, not only from his dwelling but also from the land of the living. This doom of the wicked man is portrayed in these several figures. To quote Alexander, "No exact translation can convey the full force of the verbs in this verse...The first denotes properly the act of pulling down or demolishing a house (Lev 14.45)...The second verb, in every other place where it occurs, has reference to the handling and carrying of fire or coals. See Proverbs 6.27; 25.22; Isaiah 30.14. To a Hebrew reader, therefore, it would almost necessarily suggest, not the general idea of removal merely, but the specific one of removing or taking away like fire, i.e. as coals are swept out from a hearth, or otherwise extinguished. The remaining verb adds to these figures that of violent eradication, and is well represented by its English equivalent". It is all descriptive indeed, of a judgment which is inescapable, inevitable, complete and eternal.

With the second "Selah" there is indicated another pause. Is this almost like that word in Revelation 8.1, where, after the most fearful demonstrations of divine judgment, it is said that "there was silence in heaven about the space of half an hour"? The "Selah" requires a solemn silence, perhaps to ponder afresh the awfulness of the evil and the certainty of the judgment.

Verses 6-9: The Vindication of the Righteous

Seeing this divine judgment of the wicked has a two-fold effect upon the righteous. First, it inspires fear, a fear of the Lord in a renewed confidence that God does judge wickedness. This fear is not, of course, an alarm or dread, but a reverential awe as the righteous are assured of the government of God among men. Then, the judgment also produces a holy scorn and derision for the wicked man who boasts in his wealth and comes to naught. The righteous laugh. This is not a smug malicious gloating over the calamity of the wicked. Such is expressly condemned in Scripture (Job 31.29; Prov 24.17). It is rather a righteous rejoicing in the fact that iniquity will not go unpunished, as, at the fall of Babylon in Revelation 18.20 the cry goes out, "Rejoice over her, thou heaven, and ye holy apostles and prophets!".

As they deride the wicked man the righteous say, "Lo, this is the man that made not God his strength; but trusted in the abundance of his riches, and strengthened himself in his wickedness". What folly, what utter folly, was this, to trust in such things as earthly wealth and power. The Psalmist sees himself in sharp contrast to this, exclaiming, "But as for me…" (RV). Whether he speaks personally, or representatively for all the righteous, makes no difference to the sense. The reference to the "green olive tree in the house of God", with which the Psalmist now compares himself, has been variously interpreted. To quote Kirkpatrick, "It is possible that trees grew in the Temple courts, as they grow at the present day in the Haram area, and that he compares his prosperity and security to that of the carefully tended trees planted in sacred ground. But more probably two figures are combined. He is like an evergreen olive tree, while the wicked man is rooted up: he is God's guest, enjoying His favour and protection". Perowne's suggested punctuation probably gives the sense, "I, in the house of God, am like an olive". "The Psalmist means two things", says Davison, "he is flourishing whilst his rich oppressor is desolate; he is at home, happy and safe, whilst the other, whose position seemed impregnable, is an exile and wanderer".

While the wicked man trusted in his riches, the Psalmist trusted in his God. In Him there was eternal mercy (2617), a lovingkindness in which David could trust forever, and, while he trusted, he would render thanks for ever too. He had reason to be thankful. All that he had, all that he was, and all that he enjoyed, was the Lord's doing. He had done it. It seemed only right therefore that the Psalmist should continue to trust, waiting for, hoping for, expecting, yet further manifestations of the name of his God to him. In the presence of the saints, perhaps viewed in public worship, this was pleasant and good.

PSALM 53

Introduction

With a few variations, Psalm 53 is a repeat of Psalm 14. It has been called a revision, a recension, a repetition, or a recast. The reason for this is not clear, and there is no general agreement among commentators concerning it. Spurgeon writes, "It is not a copy of the fourteenth Psalm emended and revised by a foreign hand; it is another edition by the same author, emphasised in certain parts, and rewritten for another purpose". With this conclusion Alexander agrees, saying, "That the changes were deliberately made by a later writer is improbable, because such a liberty would hardly have been taken with a Psalm of David...The only satisfactory hypothesis is, that the original author afterwards re-wrote it, with such modifications as were necessary to bring out certain points distinctly, but without any intention to supersede the use of the original composition, which therefore still retains its place in the collection. This supposition is confirmed by the titles, which ascribe both Psalms to David". He adds, rather quaintly, but helpfully, that "this kind of *retractatio* is not unknown to the practice of uninspired hymnologists". This second edition of the Psalm may well have been written to suit national conditions at a later date, but the suggestion has also been made that Psalm 14 may refer to evildoers in Israel and that in Psalm 53 the reference may be to a foreign enemy besieging Israel (Tate).

Like Psalm 14, this Psalm is committed to the Chief Musician and is also assigned to David, indicating that the sweet Psalmist intended it to be preserved for national and public worship. There are, however, two changes in the title, the words "Mahalath" and "Maschil" being added. With "Maschil" there is no difficulty. It signifies a didactic Psalm, a Psalm of wisdom and instruction. There are thirteen "Maschil" Psalms, of which Psalm 32 is the first. For further comment and for a list of the other Psalms so entitled, see the introduction to Psalm 32 in this Commentary. "Mahalath" is found only here and in the title of Psalm 88. Strong says, "meaning dubious, probably a catchword in a song giving name to tune", but almost identical forms of "Mahalath" are to be found in Exodus 15.26, Proverbs 18.14 and 2 Chronicles 21.15, where the word is translated diseases, infirmity, and sickness, respectively. (See Strong 4257 and TWOT 623, 655). The significance of the word in the title of this Psalm then may be that this is really the subject or theme of the Psalm, the moral sickness, the spiritual malady, which has infected all mankind.

For an exposition of the substance of the Psalm refer to Psalm 14 in this Commentary. It is only necessary here to deal with the variants, and little division of the Psalm is needed. Verses 1-5 are a commentary on human depravity. The closing verse 6 is a prayer, and an anticipation of a joyful future for the nation.

Verses 1-5: Moral Corruption

In the text of the Psalm perhaps the chief and most notable variant from Psalm 14 is the substitution of God (430) for LORD (3068), Elohim for Jehovah. This occurs in four instances, vv. 2, 4, 5 and 6. This Elohim is characteristic of the second Book of Psalms. The first variation in the text however, is in v.1, where "abominable works" is changed to "abominable iniquity". This seems to intensify the indictment. It is not only their conduct but their very wickedness which is abominable. It is a stronger expression to emphasise the corruption.

In v.2 the only change is that of Jehovah to Elohim, already referred to in the introduction above.

The verbs used in v.3 of each of the two Psalms to describe the apostasy, are different words, but very similar. Men have "gone aside". They have "gone back". The end result is the same, having turned away from God they are altogether become filthy.

In v.4, apart from the change in the divine name, previously noted, the only real difference with Psalm 14.4 is the omission of the word "all" before "workers of iniquity". This, of course, may be understood, and the omission of the word does not materially affect the meaning. Those who work iniquity, have they no knowledge? Devouring the people of God and refusing to call upon God is ignorance indeed and is the root cause of the ensuing depravity.

It is now, in v.5 of this Psalm, that considerable changes from Psalm 14 must be noted. Verses 5 and 6 of Psalm 14 are condensed here in an almost complete re-wording, with additions also. For comment on the interesting link between "great" and "fear" see the explanation in this Commentary at Psalm 14.5. Here, however, it is added that they were in great fear "where no fear was". This seems to imply that there had been, on the part of Israel's enemies, a self-sufficient, smug complacency. There was no fear, either of Israel or of the God of Israel, until God intervened and scattered their bones. The picture is of utter defeat with the ignominy of unburied corpses, their bones lying bleaching on the battlefield. It is a display of the power of the mighty Elohim whom they had dared to deny. This may have reference to some particular victory in a battle not identified here, or it may be metaphorical, depicting God's continual defence of His people.

These enemies had encamped (2583) against Israel. They had pitched their tents around, laying siege against them, but God, who was with the generation of the righteous (Ps 14.5), despised these enemies of His people. Had they not said, "There is no God"? He will treat such with divine contempt and put them to shame (954), confounding and confusing them.

Verse 6: Concluding Petition and Anticipation

There are only two variations in this verse from Psalm 14.7. As has previously been noted, Elohim has been substituted for Jehovah. Also, the word "salvation" is in the plural here. This probably denotes variety, intensity, completeness. The Psalmist's prayer is that God would continue, as in the past, to deliver His people. There would be victory after victory if He was with them. In this the people would rejoice and be glad. Then, whether viewed in the character of Jacob, or in the princely character of Israel, the nation would exult. For this David prayed, for salvation and joy for the nation. They were, after all, his people, and they were God's people.

PSALM 54

Introduction

Psalm 54 is a Psalm of David, committed to the charge and care of the Chief Musician, the Precentor or Master of Song in the national worship. "Neginoth" (5058) is to be found in the titles of five other Psalms (Psalms 4, 6, 55, 67 and 76) and means "stringed instruments". It appears to indicate a preference that, on these occasions, the Psalms should be sung to the accompaniment of stringed instruments rather than to the "Nehiloth", or wind instruments, the pipes or flutes, as in the title of Psalm 5. It is a "Maschil" Psalm, a Psalm of instruction and wisdom. There are thirteen "Maschil" Psalms, of which Psalm 32 is the first. Refer to the introduction to that Psalm in this Commentary for further notes and comments on these.

For the background to the Psalm, read 1 Samuel 23.19 and a similar narrative in 1 Samuel 26.1ff. David, a fugitive from Saul, and also from the men of Keilah, had fled into the Judean hills to the neighbourhood of the town of Ziph. Ziph is today identified with the ruins known as Tell Ziph, about five miles (8 kilometres) south-east of Hebron. This wilderness was a safe and congenial hiding place. It was, as George Adam Smith says, "covered with scrub and honeycombed with caves", providing strongholds for David and his men. The men of Ziph, however, betrayed David, revealing his whereabouts to Saul, who at once came to take him. This attempt was aborted by news of a Philistine raid which required Saul to return, and David resorted to En-gedi. Sometime later the Ziphites advised

Saul that David was again in their desert district. To which of these two occasions the title of the Psalm refers cannot be determined, but the language of the Psalm is such that it may well apply to either.

The seven short verses are divided into two parts by the "Selah" at the end of verse 3. In the first part of the Psalm David describes his peril and pleads for God's help. In the second part, verses 4-7, he anticipates an answer to his plea and promises thanksgiving to Jehovah.

Verses 1-3: The Psalmist's Peril and Plea

Instead of the AV, "Save me, O God", some translators and commentators, such as the LXX, JND, JPS, Maclaren, Alexander, Perowne, and Murphy, understand the Psalm to commence with the plea, "O God!". What an immediate, direct appeal to the mighty Elohim. It is followed by the earnest and urgent "save me", of a man in danger from his foes. The appeal is that God would save by His name. His name is His manifested character and David knew that character well. He knew that God was the Protector and Deliverer of His people and now, from the lips and heart of the beleaguered David the cry rises to heaven, "Save me". David is happy to appeal also to divine justice and that God should judge his cause. He is confident that he is in the right and that he is now being wronged by Saul and by the men of Ziph. "Judge me", he pleads, "by thy strength". The righteousness of God and the power of God will surely work in his favour and deliver him. Notice the poetry. "Save me"; "judge me". "By thy name"; "by thy strength".

The appeal intensifies. "O God, hear my prayer". If David knows the character of his God, and he does, then surely in the circumstances the Lord will hear these words of his mouth and vindicate him. He speaks of "strangers"(2114) and "oppressors" (6184). Maclaren says of "strangers", that this "would most naturally mean foreigners, but not necessarily so. The meaning would naturally pass into that of enemies - men who, even though of the Psalmist's own blood, behave to him in a hostile manner...though the men of Ziph belonged to the tribe of Judah, they might still be called 'strangers' ". As Strong indicates, the word may signify "estranged". These men of David's own tribe were estranged from him. They were not aliens. They were Israelites, but estranged from David and from God. The oppressors were ruthless and violent men. Strangers were against the Psalmist and violent men pursued him. They all sought his hurt, his soul, his blood, his very life. Perhaps it was all to be expected since they had no regard for God.

The "Selah" brings this first part to a close. As Spurgeon comments, "As if he said, 'Enough of this, let us pause'. He is out of breath with indignation. A sense of wrong bids him suspend the music awhile".

Verses 4-7: Assurance and Anticipation

With the exclamation "Behold", the Psalmist calls attention to God his Helper and Upholder. Observe and admire his use of divine titles. Until now, in the Psalm, he has spoken of "God" (430), the mighty Elohim. Now he will speak of the "Lord" (136), the sovereign Adonai. In v.6 he will offer praise to the "LORD" (3068) Jehovah. It is most fitting that Elohim, in his might and power, should be David's Helper. During his enforced exile he had of course many human helpers. There were six hundred men with him in the wilderness of Ziph (1 Sam 23.13). God, however, was, in a unique and special way, his Helper. The Lord, Adonai, sovereign and supreme, was his Upholder. Others there were who upheld him in his cause, but, as Dr Cohen says, "The Hebrew is idiomatic", and then, quoting Cheyne, "the sense is not that God is the support of the Psalmist among many others, but that He is so in a supreme degree, that He sums up in Himself the qualities of a class, viz., the class of helpers". Many there were who sought after David's soul, his life, but there were many also who upheld his soul, and the Lord was with them.

David was confident that the Lord would requite his enemies with the very evil which they intended for him. "Reward" (7725), as in the AV, is more often and better rendered "return". Their evil intent would rebound, it would recoil upon their own heads in just retribution. "Enemies" (8324) is an unusual word, seldom used, and different from that in v.7. Kirkpatrick suggests that it means "those who lie in wait for him, like fowlers, or a leopard for its prey". Newberry gives a marginal reading "observers", and Murphy says, "*My watchers*, who watch for an opportunity to destroy me". David asks that, in accord with truth, in keeping with divine righteousness, they should be cut off, destroyed, who had plotted to destroy him.

The glad response of a delivered David would be that he would bring his free-will offering to Jehovah. He would offer, not under compulsion or just to fulfil the accustomed ritual, but in a cheerful thanksgiving. This was the character of a particular peace offering. (Lev 7.11-13). It was an expression of real gratitude, and this David promises when he would be delivered. Jehovah's name was good and David would praise it. His deliverance would necessarily mean the destruction of his enemies and this was his desire. But, to quote Kirkpatrick again, "Such rejoicing over the fall of enemies is not of the spirit of the Gospel. But the 'salvation' for which the Psalmist prays is a temporal deliverance, which can only be effected at the expense of the implacable enemies who are seeking his life; and it will be a vindication of God's faithfulness and a proof of His righteous government at which he cannot but rejoice. The defeat of evil and the triumph of good presented themselves to the saints of the OT in this concrete form, which sometimes has a ring of personal vindictiveness about it, yet, fairly considered, is in its real motive and character elevated far above a mere thirst for revenge".

PSALM 55

Introduction

The title of this Psalm is substantially the same as the title of the preceding Psalm 54. It is, like that Psalm, committed to the care of the Chief Musician, with directions that it should be accompanied by stringed instruments (Neginoth), and, as Spurgeon remarks, "The strain is at one time mournful, and at another softly sweet. It needed the Chief Musician's best care to see that the music was expressive of the sentiment". It is a "Maschil" Psalm, and it is a Psalm of David. For more detailed comments on these terms see the introduction to Psalm 32 in this Commentary.

There appears to be no good reason for questioning, as some do, the Davidic authorship, as indicated in the superscription. There is nothing in the Psalm which can not be suitably interpreted of David, and especially of that sad period of the rebellion of Absalom, aided by the treachery of Ahithophel (2 Sam 15). It has in it, too, like Psalm 41.9, more than a thousand years before the time, a foreshadowing of the arch-traitor Judas Iscariot. But Spurgeon again: "It would be idle to fix a time, and find an occasion for this Psalm with any dogmatism. It reads like a song of the time of Absalom and Ahithophel...Altogether it seems to us to relate to that mournful era when the King was betrayed by his trusted counsellor. The spiritual eye ever and anon sees the Son of David and Judas, and the chief priests appearing and disappearing upon the glowing canvas of the Psalm".

The twenty-three verses fall naturally into three divisions, each of which may be sub-divided. It is a story of distress and despair, verses 1-8; of deceit and disappointment, verses 9-15; of desire and deliverance, verses 16-23.

Verses 1-8: Distress and Despair

In times of distress it has ever been the habit of the saints to resort to prayer. How often David had sought the face of the Lord in his difficulties. He speaks of "my prayer" (8605) and "my supplication" (8467). The first is perhaps general, while the second is more specific, seeking some particular favour from God. It is an earnest appeal that God would hear, that He would not withdraw or hide Himself from His servant in his trouble. When David repeats his plea, praying that God would attend to him and hear him, he is really pleading that God would hearken and answer. The word "hear" (6030) is , rendered "answer" more than two hundred times in the AV. The poor Psalmist in his distress is longing for a response from God to his pleadings. "I mourn in my complaint", he cries, "and make a noise". "Mourn" (7300) is from a primitive root meaning "to wander restlessly", and the noise which he makes is but a groan. Maclaren translates, "I am distracted as I muse, and must groan". JND renders it as, "I wander about in my plaint, and I moan aloud". There are times when "groanings which cannot be uttered" (Rom 8.26) are perhaps more eloquent than words. The distracted Psalmist is restless both in body and in mind, unable to settle, groaning as he broods upon his troubles and waits for an answer from his God.

He now gives the reason for, and the cause of, his groaning. He hears the voice of his enemy, no doubt slandering and reviling him. Wicked men oppressed him, heaping their iniquitous words and devices upon him. Angry men hated (7852) him, persecuted him, opposed him, in their wrath. With what a mournful vocabulary does he describe his distress. Pain and terror! Fearfulness and trembling! Horror that overwhelmed him! He was, as it were, in the valley of the shadow of death. He envied the birds and longed for the ability to fly away from it all. He thought of the dove, probably the wild rock-dove, making its home in the cleft of the rock (Song 2.14), far out of the reach of men in some precipice. How he longed for solitude, for safety and security. If he could escape to lodge in the wilderness, far away from the haunts of these wicked oppressors, then perhaps he would find rest and refuge. As Dr Cohen says, "He would gladly exchange the luxuries of the palace for a bare tent in the solitude of the desert".

There is a rather sudden and unexpected "Selah" at the end of v.7. Is the Psalmist directing a pause, a musical interlude which would express the quietness for which his heart was yearning? His life was in a storm. There was wind and tempest. He longed to hasten his escape and find shelter from it all. There was indeed distress and despair. If only God would hear, and answer.

Verses 9-15: Deceit and Disappointment

The word "destroy" (1104) with which this section commences, is, more than thirty times, rendered "swallow" in the AV. "Destroy...and divide their tongues", he pleads. Davison may have a points when he says, "The vehement prayer which bursts from the Psalmist's lips is not that the men themselves should be destroyed, but rather that their machinations may be overthrown". Alexander however, does not agree, and writes, "The object to be supplied is not *their tongue* but *themselves*". With this latter thought JND would concur, translating "Swallow them up Lord, divide their tongue". The "dividing" of their tongue is an appeal for their confusion, as other wicked men were confused at the tower of Babel (Gen 11). The Psalmist describes the evil of his enemies. He had seen violence and strife, iniquity and mischief, wickedness, deceit, and guile. "Deceit" (8496) is fraud. "Guile" (4820) is subtlety and craft. Day and night their perversion and oppression had polluted the walls and the streets of the beloved city until the king had to flee.

But perhaps worse than the open reviling from the enemy, and harder to bear, was the treachery of one who had been a friend. The greatest reproach came from one who had been his counsellor and guide, his intimate, familiar friend. Spurgeon says, "And thou, Ahithophel, art thou here? Judas, betrayest thou the Son of Man?" The reference to Ahithophel can hardly be doubted. David had trusted him and treated him as an equal. They had shared confidences. He had never been regarded as an inferior. He had been a trusted friend and companion with whom David had walked to the house of God to worship. They had walked with the throng, particularly on those great festive occasions, but Ahithophel was a special companion and there had been a pleasing converse and fellowship between them; sweet counsel indeed! How it must have pained David to say, "It was thou!" (See comments on Psalm 41.9). The cruelty and the deceit of enemies had almost been eclipsed by the treachery of an erstwhile friend. There had been both deceit and disappointment. Now, having spoken directly and personally to the betrayer, the Psalmist reverts again to his enemies. Again he prays for their destruction. Sudden death and desolation would be their deserved portion. As they had dwelt with wickedness so let them now go down alive into "sheol", into that grave-land, to be remembered no more.

Verses 16-23: Desire and Deliverance

"As for me" is a recurring expression in the Psalms. A perusal of the circumstances in which the phrase is used will be rewarding. See Psalms 5.7; 17.15; 26.11; 35.13; 41.12; 69.13; 73.2. The Psalmist avows that he will not be as his enemies. He will not meet evil with evil. He will not descend to their level, to an imitation of their subtlety and their guile. "As for me", he says, "I will call upon God". The pronoun "I" is emphatic. "*I*, on my part". Let his enemies do as they will, he will be different. He will resort for vindication to God (430). "And the LORD (3068) shall save me". Is there a significance in the Psalmist's use of two divine titles in the same sentence? Perhaps it is this, that he will call upon the mighty Elohim, and Jehovah of the covenant will save him. He will cry to God continually, evening and morning, and at noon. The Jewish day begins at sunset. Evening and morning are the day (Gen 1). "Noon" represents all that lies between the evening and the morning. It is the Psalmist's way of saying that he will call upon God unceasingly, all the day. This is not formal prayer. When he says, in v.17, "I will pray (7878), and cry aloud (1993), this is a repetition of the wording of v.2. It is complaint and groaning, and it is incessant. Yet again he asserts with confidence that God will hear him. Such, indeed, is his confidence that he can now speak of his deliverance as if it were already an accomplished fact, "He hath delivered". It is the anticipation of faith. The battle had been against him and those who beset him were many, but with his deliverance there would come peace.

In v.19 the God who would hear the Psalmist would afflict his enemies. Note that "hear" (8085), and "afflict" (6030) are from a root, implying "to answer". God would answer both David and his enemies. The prayers of David would be answered with deliverance. The wickedness of his enemies would be answered with judgment. The God who will answer both is the everlasting God who sits eternally enthroned, revealing Himself down the ages as the righteous Judge. As Spurgeon says. "All the prayers of saints and profanities of sinners are before His judgment seat, and He will see that justice is done".

Suddenly, in the midst of v.19, there appears another "Selah". It is unusual to find a "Selah" in the middle of a verse, but it does occur again in Psalm 57.3. It is a pause to reflect upon the greatness of the enthroned One and the equity of His judgments.

The expression which follows, "Because they have no changes", has been variously understood by different commentators. Some view this materially, suggesting that these men of the world have lived in uninterrupted prosperity, and that, because of this changeless undisturbed luxury in their lives, they lived complacently, with no fear of God. They had no sense of need and therefore did not regard God. There were no vicissitudes or changes of fortune in their lives to drive them to Him, and in such ease they lived godlessly. Others prefer to view the expression morally, meaning that these men continued impenitent in their sins. There was never any change of mind or heart, no pangs of conscience. They went on steadily on their chosen sinful course, with no fear of God. Whatever may be meant by "changes", the end is the same, they lacked that fear, that reverential awe of God, which was His due.

The Psalmist cannot forget the treachery of his former friend and he now reverts to speaking of him again. There had been a covenant of peace between them but Ahithophel had broken it. "Peace" (7965), is the lovely and familiar "shalom". It is both a greeting and a farewell, a salutation and a parting wish. When David had spoken of Ahithophel as "mine own familiar friend" (Ps 41.9), this word "familiar" was also the word "shalom". Ahithophel had profaned the bond of peace which was between them. Instead of the hand of friendship, he had stretched out his hands to smite as an enemy and had desecrated that happy relationship. The words of this hypocrite were smoother than butter and softer than oil, but, when the truth is known, his heart was meditating war and his words were really like unsheathed rapiers, ready to destroy. His smooth talk concealed his purpose.

Many saints carry heavy burdens, but the word here translated "burden" (3053) denotes, according to Strong, "lot (that which is given)", indicating that sometimes the burden has been laid there by God in His sovereignty. The Psalmist's exhortation, to himself and to every burdened one, is, "Cast thy burden upon the Lord". Bring to Him in trusting prayer that which He has given thee to bear. It is not said that He will remove the burden, relieving the bearer of his load, but that He will sustain the saint in his particular lot. Spurgeon's comment is very helpful, "Thy burden, or what God lays upon thee, lay thou it upon the Lord. His wisdom casts it on thee, it is thy wisdom to cast it on Him. He cast thy lot for thee, cast thy lot on Him. He gives thee thy portion of suffering, accept it with cheerful resignation, and then take it back to Him by thine assured confidence". He will never allow the righteous to be overthrown. As Peter writes, "Casting all your care upon him; for he careth for you" (1 Pet 5.7). After this tender exhortation and this sweet promise the Psalmist reverts again to the matter of his enemies and their inevitable destruction.

God will surely deal with the enemies of His people. These men are bloodthirsty and deceitful, and, as they have been violent with others, God will bring them to a violent end in a fearful and final retribution in the pit of destruction, the corruption of the grave. The death of the wicked may be premature, they "shall not live out half their days". Wicked men may not live half so long as they might have lived had it not been for their bloodthirsty and deceitful ways.

The Psalm concludes with a happy contrast to the story of the wicked, "But I will trust in thee". As Kirkpatrick says, "The same God who destroys the wicked is the object of the Psalmist's trust". God will judge and condemn the wicked, but the same God will deliver the righteous. In the course of this Psalm David has been faint, he has been betrayed and beset by enemies, he has observed deceit and violence and he has watched the wicked perish. In all this, in every circumstance of life, he has learned this, "I will trust in thee". What a wise and safe conclusion!

PSALM 56

Introduction

Here is yet another of those fifty-five Psalms which are committed to the charge and the care of the Chief Musician, probably forming a special collection of Psalms for the Master of Song.

The rather strange words in the title, "Jonath-elem-rechokim" (3128), may have been the title of a tune or melody to which the Psalm was to be sung, but literally translated they mean, "The silent dove of them that are distant, or, afar off". Alexander explains in more detail, "An enigmatic allusion to the same event (*David in Gath*) seems to be latent in the obscure phrase, *Jonath-elem-rechokim*, in which the first word means a *dove*, a favourite emblem of suffering innocence; the second means *silence*, dumbness, sometimes put for uncomplaining submission; and the third means *distant* or *remote*, agreeing with places or persons, probably the latter, in which sense it is applicable to the Philistines, as aliens in blood and religion…Thus understood, the whole is an enigmatical description of David as an innocent and uncomplaining sufferer among strangers".

This Psalm is the second of six "Michtam" Psalms, sometimes called "David's Golden Psalms". The four Psalms which follow this one, Psalms

57-60, are all "Michtam" Psalms, together with Psalm 16. For a more detailed consideration of "Michtam" see the introduction to Psalm 16 in this Commentary.

The occasion of the writing of the Psalm is stated next in the title. It was "when the Philistines took him in Gath". David had fled to Gath in fear of Saul who sought his life. It seemed a bold and desperate thing to seek refuge with the enemies of Israel, and in Gath, home of Goliath whom he had slain (1 Sam 17.23ff). It was sad that, as Davison comments, he should "esteem himself safer with the hereditary foes of Israel than with the king who ought to have been his friend and protector". Perhaps his hope was that he would not be recognised, but he was, and became a virtual prisoner in Gath. As Spurgeon says, "He was like a dove in strangers' hands". He cunningly changed his behaviour, feigned madness so that he might be supposed to be harmless, and so made his escape from Achish the king of Gath. The whole story is told in 2 Samuel 21.10ff. This Psalm expresses David's gratitude to God and his continuing confidence and trust.

The Psalm may be divided as follows. There are two stanzas, verses 1-4 and verses 5-11, ending with the same refrain, singing of praise and trust. The closing verses, 12-13, are a concluding thanksgiving.

Verses 1-4: Fear and Faith

Like Psalm 57, of which it is counted a companion, Psalm 56 commences with "Be merciful (2603) unto me, O God". It is an appeal that God might be gracious and show mercy. The reason for this present appeal of the Psalmist is that man would swallow him up. The word he employs here for "man" (582) is ENOSH. It denotes mortal man in his human frailty, but David is so conscious of his own frailty that he feels as if even frail men are about to swallow (7602) him up. They panted after him, with open mouths as it were, eager to devour him, and they were constant, unremitting in their oppression. He repeats his complaint that his enemies would swallow him up, and argues that they are many that fight against him. In the AV this appeal seems to be directed to the "most High" (4791), regarding this as the divine title. It is not, however, the "Elyon", which is the usual form of that title, as in Psalm 7.17; 9.2; 46.4; 47.2; 57.2; and elsewhere, and first appearing in Genesis 14.18. Some have thought therefore that this is not, here in Psalm 56.2, a divine title at all but that it should rather be linked with the Psalmist's enemies, as the RV rendering, "They be many that fight proudly against me", or, as Kirkpatrick, "Many are they that fight against me haughtily". Such see the word as an adverb describing how arrogantly these enemies oppress the Psalmist. It is the word rendered "loftily" in Psalm 73.8 and Plumer suggests that the probable meaning is "They fight against me from the high places of authority; both in Jerusalem and in Gath, mine enemies are in power". Whichever view is adopted, David is appealing that God would be gracious, and pity him in his afflictions.

It is not often, if ever, that David is afraid. Indeed Kirkpatrick says that

"David's sojourn in Gath is the only occasion on which he is recorded to have been afraid of man. (1 Sam 21.12; but compare Ps 18.4)". But in the day that he is afraid he vows that he will trust. Davison says, "Fear and faith may co-exist, but one must conquer". Where there is faith and trust, fear gives way to praise. David will praise God's Word and glory in it. That Word is faithful and true, and, resting upon it, he will not fear what flesh might do to him. Is this rather a question? With confidence the trusting heart may ask, "What can flesh do unto me?" (RV and JND).

Verses 5-11: Trouble and Trust

Here the Psalmist returns to his first complaint. From the mountaintop of confidence and praise he comes back to the reality of his present distress and trouble. As Weiss remarks, "The Psalmist is at one moment high in hope and confidence, and the next instant he is again plunged into a depth of lamentation". But yet again he will move towards victory and praise by trusting. These evildoers were daily misrepresenting him, wresting, distorting and twisting his words so as to accuse him, probably to Saul. All their thoughts (4284) were against him, constantly devising evil (7451), plotting mischief and trouble for him. Together they lay in wait for him, hiding themselves so as to catch him unawares as in an ambush. They marked his steps, tracking him, hunting and haunting him, seeking his very life. Do these wicked men sin with impunity? Do they imagine that by their iniquity they shall escape divine judgment? David appeals to God (430), to Elohim, that in His wrath He will cast them down. "People" (5971) is a plural word, "peoples". It is not the word usually employed to describe the Gentile nations, so that here it may envisage a judgment of all men of whatever race, who oppose God and His saints.

It must have been a great comfort to David to know that all his wanderings were known to God. Wanderings indeed! He was a fugitive in the Judean desert, in the wilderness of Ziph, hunted by the men of Keilah and by the men of Gath, hiding in hills and wadis and caves. But God could tell his every step. David must have shed many tears in those days. He asks that God would remember them, preserving them as men preserved water in a skin-bottle, every drop treasured. What a tender thought is this! Tears preserved in the memory of God! Then the metaphor changes from tears in a bottle to records in a book. Jehovah has a book of remembrance for those who fear Him (Mal 3.16). His people are His jewels, precious to Him. He will never forget the service and the sufferings of His saints, and so He knew, and remembered, every step of David the wandering fugitive.

David is now very positive, asserting, "This I know!". His enemies will one day be defeated, turned back, routed. "God is for me", he says, and he knows that his prayer for deliverance will be answered. Notice how he repeats his assurance. "I will praise...I will praise...I will not be afraid". Observe too, the emphasis which he introduces by the change in the divine title. "In God…in Jehovah…In God". In fellowship with the mighty Elohim he will praise His Word. In the same holy and happy fellowship he will praise the Word of Jehovah and he will put his trust in Elohim. Here is might and power and a faithful covenant-keeping character, and in this praise and trust in the Word of God he need not be afraid. This is, in general, a repeat of the refrain of v.4, with the change of the divine title just mentioned and the substitution of "man" for "flesh". The trusting heart will not be afraid. What can mortal "man" (ADAM - 120), in his supposed dignity, or "flesh" (BASAR - 1320) , in its human frailty, do to the saint whose trust is in Jehovah?

Verses 12-13: Concluding Thanksgiving

"Thy vows are upon me". Dr Cohen says, "The meaning is, the vows I have made to Thee are obligatory upon me to fulfil. *Vows*. Obligations assumed in the hour of distress to be discharged in the hour of relief". The praises (8426) which he promises to render are "thank-offerings". No doubt he anticipates his return to Jerusalem and to the sanctuary. So assured is he of this that he can speak in what is known as "the prophetic perfect". "Thou hast delivered". He speaks as though his complete deliverance is already an accomplished fact. He has been delivered and will be delivered. This is faith indeed, and, being delivered from death and from falling, he desires that he might, as long as he lives, walk before God, serving Him acceptably. The "light of the living" of which he speaks, may simply be a contrast to the darkness of death, but there may be more than that. Spurgeon is worth quoting in full when he writes, "That I may walk before God in the light of the living, enjoying the favour and presence of God, and finding the joy and brightness of life therein. Walking at liberty, in holy service, in sacred communion, in constant progress in holiness, enjoying the smile of heaven - this I seek after. Here is the loftiest reach of a good man's ambition, to dwell with God, to walk in righteousness before Him, to rejoice in His presence, and in the light and glory which it yields. Thus in this short Psalm, we have climbed from the ravenous jaws of the enemy into the light of Jehovah's presence, a path which only faith can tread".

PSALM 57

Introduction

This Psalm is, in many respects, a companion Psalm to the preceding Psalm 56. The structure is similar, with two divisions concluding with the same refrain, and there are certain phrases which are common to both Psalms. The tone and the spirit of the two Psalms are almost identical.

Like Psalm 56, and those many other Psalms, it is given into the charge of the Chief Musician, the Precentor and Master of Song, to be preserved for national worship.

The term "Altaschith" in the superscription occurs again in the titles of the next two Psalms and also in the title of Psalm 75. It is rendered by JND, "Destroy not", and this meaning is agreed by all. Since the Psalm is associated with Saul in the cave there may be a reference to that occasion when, for the second time, David spared Saul's life, saying to Abishai, "Destroy him not". Saul was at the mercy of David but David would not stretch forth his hand against the Lord's anointed (1 Sam 26.9). "Altaschith" may have been a particular melody to which these Psalms were to be sung.

Again, in the title, the word "Michtam" occurs. This word is found in the titles of Psalms 16 and 56-60. These Psalms are known as "David's Golden Psalms", but, for a more detailed consideration of "Michtam", refer to the Introduction to Psalm 16 in this Commentary.

There are two obvious parts in the Psalm, verses 1-5 and 6-11. Verses 5 and 11 are identical. Spurgeon says, "We have here prayer, verses 1-5, and praise, verses 6-11. The hunted one takes a long breath of prayer, and when he is fully inspired, he breathes out his soul in jubilant song". How true this is.

It should perhaps be pointed out that others, while agreeing that there are two parts to the Psalm, observe the division effected by the second "Selah" at the end of v.6, so seeing the two parts as vv. 1-6 and 7-11. Such a division however, seems to spoil the symmetry created by the two identical refrains in vv. 5 and 11.

Verses 1-5: Prayer

The first words of the Psalm are identical to the opening words of Psalm 56. David pleads for mercy. "Be merciful unto me, O God", and again he cries, "be merciful unto me". "Merciful"(2603) is "gracious". He implores the favour and pity of God in his afflictions. The particle "for" which follows seems almost to be a reasoned basis for his request - he trusted. Would God, or could God, refuse the soul that trusted in Him?

The beautiful expression "in the shadow of thy wings" is a familiar one in the Psalms. See Psalms 17.8; 36.7; 63.7 and compare Psalm 91.4. It is reminiscent of David's great-grandmother Ruth, to whom it was said, many years earlier, "The Lord God of Israel, under whose wings thou art come to trust" (Ruth 2.12). The Saviour too, in His sad lament over Jerusalem, used the same figure, saying, "How often would I have gathered thy children together, even as a hen gathereth her chickens under her wings, but ye would not" (Mt 23.37; Lk 13.34). It is the place of refuge and of comfort, and David often resorted there. This he would do now, and trust until the present calamities were past. "Overpast", may suggest the passing of a storm. He sees his afflictions like a tempest, which must inevitably subside, and until then he will find refuge "under the shadow of the wings" of His

God. Notice that "trusteth" and "refuge" in v.1 are the same word (2620). Perowne has the interesting comment: "The change of tense in the repeated use of the verb gives a force and beauty to the passage which is quite lost sight of when both are rendered as presents. The Psalmist looks back to the past and forward to the future: In Thee hath my soul found refuge; in Thee will I find refuge".

In the second verse of the Psalm David combines three titles of the God to whom he cries. He calls Him "God (430) most high" (5945), and "God" (410). These are, respectively, Elohim, Elyon, and El. This is majestic! David's God is the Mighty One, omnipotent and supreme, and He performs all things for His servant. Note that the words "all things" are italicised. They have been supplied, there being no object specified. All that the Psalmist needs, all that needs to be done, will be done, by his God. His assurance is echoed by the apostle, "My God shall supply all your need" (Phil 4.19). It has been the confidence of the saints down the ages that He who has promised will perform. He will send timely help from heaven itself. He did so for the nation in the wilderness, sending them bread daily to meet their recurring needs. David was assured that He would send deliverance for him from the taunts of those who would have swallowed him up (7602), trampling him, crushing him, thirsting for his blood. In the midst of his gratitude to God he pauses. "Selah!" As in Psalm 55.19 the "Selah" is in an unusual place, in the middle of a verse, probably to lend emphasis to what is being said. David will meditate, lifting up his heart in thankfulness. "God shall send forth his mercy and his truth", he says. Spurgeon comments, "He asked for mercy, and truth came with it. Thus evermore doth God give us more than we ask or think".

When the Psalmist now says, "My soul is among lions", some, as Delitzsch, understand this literally, as descriptive of David's wilderness environment, but it is more probable that he is referring, metaphorically, to his enemies. The ensuing statements would seem to confirm this. He speaks of the fierceness of these sons of men. Their hearts were aflame, burning with hatred towards him. Their teeth were bared, their tongues were sharp, perhaps with blasphemy and slander. He likens them to spears, arrows, and swords. There is, however, some difference of thought about the phrase, "I lie even among them". He may be expressing the danger in which he lives, lying daily amid enemies. Or, it may be an expression of confidence, saying that even though surrounded by evil men, fierce as wild beasts, yet he will lie down, even among them, in peace and safety, with trust in his God. Is it, in this sense, an echo of Psalm 4.8, "I will both lay me down in peace, and sleep: for thou, Lord, only makest me dwell in safety"?

The first part of the Psalm concludes with the chorus of praise which will be repeated in v.11. The refrain may appear abruptly, but David longs, almost impatiently now, that God will manifest Himself in glory, superior to these enemies who oppress him. "Be thou exalted", he exclaims. He desires that his God may be seen to be above the heavens and above the earth, greater than all. It is like a doxology and a prayer combined. The heart of the Psalmist is true, and his aspirations are noble. It must be admired in him, that in the midst of all his afflictions he desires not only his own deliverance but that God might be glorified in it all.

Verses 6-11: Praise

After the chorus of praise the Psalmist returns, though only momentarily, to contemplate his present situation. His enemies had prepared a net for his steps. The word "prepared" (3559) may imply a carefully planned, deliberate contrivance to set the snare which was particularly suited to trap him. To quote Spurgeon again, "As for each sort of fish, or bird, or beast, a fitting net is needed, so do the ungodly suit their net to their victim's circumstances and character with a careful craftiness of malice. Whatever David might do, and whichever way he might turn, his enemies were ready to entrap him in some way or other".

Not surprisingly, it depressed the Psalmist, even though he trusted. His soul was bowed down. The original language may imply that they, his enemies, had bowed him down. They had not only prepared a net for him, but they had dug a pit too. They were determined to snare him in some way. Faith, however, anticipates the defeat of their evil machinations, and, with assurance, he sees these wicked men fallen into their own pit. For earlier use of the same metaphor see Psalms 7.15; 9.15; 35.7-8.

With this exclamation of confidence David is now finished with his enemies in the Psalm. "Selah". Another pause, to contemplate, to lift up the heart in praise for what God has done and for what He will yet do for His saints.

"My heart is fixed…my heart is fixed". The repetition emphasises David's avowal of his firm trust in God. But is there an interesting play upon words here? The word "fixed" (3559) here in v.7, is the same word as that translated "prepared" in v.6. Had his enemies carefully and deliberately prepared a net for him? Then so had he, with equal deliberation chosen to fix his mind and heart steadfastly upon God. In spite of his afflictions he could sing and praise. He knew, in his time, the meaning of that word of the prophet of a later century than his, "Thou wilt keep him in perfect peace, whose mind is stayed on thee" (Is 26.3). These last two verbs, "sing" (7891) and "praise" (2167), are descriptive of two kinds of music, vocal and instrumental. David will employ both his voice and his harp in his praise of God.

The Psalmist now summons his glory, his lute, and his harp to awake. By his glory he probably means his very soul, and those innermost noble feelings of gratitude toward God. "I myself will awake early", he says, but JND, with the RV and Newberry margins, and others, translate, "I will (a)wake the dawn". This is very beautiful. Usually it is the dawn which awakens men, but so intense and urgent is the Psalmist's desire to render praise that he himself will awaken the morning.

He addresses Adonai, saying, "I will praise thee, O Lord (136), among the people". Adonai is the Sovereign Lord. This word is often used by Jews in a reverential way instead of the great and awful Name Jehovah. "People" in v.9, is a plural word, "peoples" (AMMIM - 5971). It is similar to, but distinct from "nations" (L^{e}OM - 3816) in the same verse. Since neither of these is GOYIM (1471), the word which denotes Gentile nations only, it is possible that the Psalmist is referring to all peoples and nations, including his own favoured nation, Israel.

Once more he sings of mercy and truth. Here is lovingkindness and truth reaching into the skies and unto the heavens. Well might all the nations of the wide world hear David's praise of this goodness of his God. This verse is almost identical with Psalm 36.5 and the doxology of v.5 is now repeated. "Be thou exalted, O God".

On this high note of praise the Psalm concludes, but note that these closing verses, 7-11, become the first five verses of Psalm 108.

PSALM 58

Introduction

This Psalm is about injustice. It is an indignant indictment and denunciation of unjust judges and wicked men, coupled with the desire, and the assurance, that they themselves would be judged and accordingly removed.

With the reference to Saul and the cave being omitted, the title is then the same as the title of the preceding Psalm 57. For further comment and explanation of "Altaschith" and "Michtam" see the introduction to Psalms 57 and 16 respectively in this Commentary. This is the fourth of the six "Michtam" Psalms, often called "David's Golden Psalms", with truths to be engraved on the mind and conscience. The remaining two of the six, follow immediately - Psalms 59 and 60.

The Psalm was born, of course, out of David's persecutions, probably in the same period as indicated in Psalm 57, when he was a fugitive from Saul, but, though it was his own personal experience, it is inscribed "To the Chief Musician", showing that it was intended for permanent and public use by the temple choirs.

There are three parts in the Psalm. The corruption of which the Psalmist complains is described in verses 1-5. In verses 6-9 he prays for the judgment of the evil. The concluding verses 10-11 sing his assurance and joy in anticipation of the triumph of righteousness and justice.

Verses 1-5: The Corruption

It is universally agreed that the opening words of the Psalm are obscure. The word which by the AV is rendered "congregation" (482) is the word ELEM, and is found elsewhere only once, in the title of Psalm 56, "Jonath-*elem*-rechokim". In this context, refer to the introduction to Psalm 56 in this Commentary. Apart from those who argue a textual corruption it is agreed by all others that the word is ELEM and means "silence". J.N. Darby will therefore translate, "Is righteousness indeed silent?". The RV rendering is similar: "Do ye indeed in silence speak righteousness?". In Mr Darby's translation there are in fact, three questions addressed to these unjust judges. "Is righteousness indeed silent? Do ye speak of it? Do ye judge with equity, ye sons of men?" Alexander is most explanatory when he writes, "The interrogation, *are ye indeed*, expresses wonder, as at something scarcely credible. Can it be so? Is it possible? Are you really silent, you whose very office is to speak for God and at the sins of men?".

Sadly, the nation's judges were corrupt, refusing to pronounce proper judgment. How fittingly does the Psalmist address them as "sons of men" as if to remind them that, in spite of the powerful positions which they held, they were but weak men, and that there was a higher tribunal before which they themselves would be judged. Probably these were arrogant men, boasting in their high office as judges, but maintaining an unjust silence when it came to dispensing true justice. David is, in the Psalm, judging the judges! There was no judicial equity.

"Yea!" There was further indictment! The injustice which they meted out was actually planned in their hearts. It was coldly calculated, premeditated, and then administered carefully, with craft, cunning, and cruelty. After deliberating, they weighed out violence. Scales are the universal symbol of justice and equity, but these men dispensed violent injustice with heart and hand.

There is, of course, a depravity which is common to all men. How early in life does this depravity reveal itself. The child does not need to be taught to tell lies. It goes that way from infancy, speaking lies when it cannot really speak, practising deceptions before it has vocabulary or language! "From the womb", says the Psalmist, "as soon as they be born". It is an early evidence of a fallen nature, alienated from God. "All we like sheep have gone astray" - it is universal. "We have turned every one to his own way" - it is individual (Is 53.6). Some men will nurture this ingrained lawlessness and will practise iniquity. Some will seek grace to be different, turning to God for mercy and forgiveness.

The behaviour of these men was as venom, like the poison of a serpent. Two words are used here to denote the serpent. The first, "serpent" (5175), is the word used to describe the serpent which deceived Eve and introduced the poison of sin into the stream of human life (Gen 3.1). The second, "adder" (6620), may be the asp, the cobra, or the viper. These all are symbols of cunning and cruelty, and such are the wicked men whom

David describes. These men are both dumb and deaf. Having earlier charged them with an unjust silence, refusing to speak, the Psalmist now likens them to the deaf adder which refuses to hear. Craftily and stubbornly it will not listen to the voice of the charmer, no matter how skilled or how sweet the charming may be. Jeremiah 8.17 speaks of serpents and cockatrices which will not be charmed. Maclaren writes, "There can be no more striking symbol of determined disregard to the calls of patient Love and the threats of enraged Justice than that of a snake lying coiled, with its head in the centre of its motionless folds, as if its ears were stopped by its own bulk, while the enchanter plays his softest notes and speaks his strongest spells in vain. There are such men, thinks this Psalmist".

Verses 6-9: The Prayer

With v.6 there commences, under a series of metaphors, a description of the eventual destruction of the wicked. Most commentators will regard this as a prayer, but some, as Davison and Weiss, understand the tenses as futures and therefore see a prophecy rather than a prayer - "God shall…", Alexander also comments on v.7 that - "There is nothing ungrammatical, however, in retaining the strict future sense, and regarding the verse as an expression of strong confidence as to the event". But whether in prayer or in prophecy, the Psalmist is anticipating the doom of the wicked men whom he has described in the earlier verses of the Psalm. The figures which he uses are varied but so very expressive. He speaks of the breaking of the teeth of the lion, the dried up river, the broken arrow, the melting snail, the untimely birth, the scattered fire. All are figurative of the sudden but inevitable judgment of these evil men.

The teeth of the lion suggest ferocity, brutality, violence. The Psalmist envisages that Jehovah can break the teeth of the lions, rendering them harmless. David, of course, brave shepherd boy that he had been, was no stranger to lions, and as he had protected his flock from them, so now he desires that the Lord will similarly protect him from beastly men. He then sees them as a raging winter torrent, like waters flowing apace (RV). God can suddenly stem their fierce flow, leaving a dried up wadi or river bed. In yet another figure, their carefully aimed arrows God can intercept. He can cause them to fall to the ground, broken as if by an unseen hand.

The metaphors continue in v.8. The end of the wicked will be like a snail that melts (8557) or dissolves. This is, as Davison describes so graphically, "intended to indicate the gradual and imperceptible but complete disappearance of evil men and their deeds. The snail which leaves behind it a slimy track and seems to waste away as it passes, or which shrivels up in its shell under the fierce heat of the Eastern sun, furnishes a striking picture". The end of wicked men will be like an untimely birth of a woman whose child is aborted or stillborn, not ever seeing the light of the sun.

The figure employed in v.9 is that of a traveller in the desert who has gathered thorns for fuel, has kindled his fire and placed his pots or cauldrons upon it, and is in the process of cooking a meal. Suddenly, without warning, a whirlwind descends. It blows away his fire and scatters the fuel which he has collected, the green sticks and the burning embers alike (RV and JND). It is a picture of the divine anger which will scatter the wicked intentions of evil men. God will blow upon them in His wrath.

Verses 10-11: The Reward of the Righteous

The Psalm closes with a most solemn metaphor as David envisages the final triumph over evil. It is a fearful picture of the righteous bathing his feet in the blood of the wicked. The righteous will rejoice. They say, "Amen", acquiescing in the judgments of God, walking in triumph on the battlefield as Jehovah takes vengeance (Deut 32.41; Rom 12.19). In that day men will see that there is a reward for the righteous, fruit for righteous living, and that there is truly a God who judges in the earth. Such rejoicing over this judgment of the wicked is not, of course, a personal vengeful spirit on the part of the Psalmist. To quote Scroggie, "If it is right for God to destroy, it cannot be wrong for His servants to rejoice in what He does". In the Book of the Revelation there is constant adoring worship when Jehovah acts in vengeance and judges evil. It is His vindication. The words of the beloved John seem to sum it up as he views the destruction of great Babylon: "I heard a great voice of much people in heaven, saying Alleluia; Salvation, and glory, and honour, and power, unto the Lord our God: for true and righteous are his judgments: for he hath judged the great whore which did corrupt the earth with her fornication, and hath avenged the blood of his servants at her hand. And again they said Alleluia. And her smoke rose up for ever and ever. And the four and twenty elders and the four beasts fell down and worshipped God that sat on the throne, saying, Amen; Alleluia"(Rev 19.1-4). David and John, Psalmist and Seer, are in total agreement about it all.

PSALM 59

Introduction

Here is yet another Psalm committed to the charge and the care of the Chief Musician, indicating that it was to be preserved for national worship. Spurgeon remarks, in his customary quaint manner, "Strange that the painful events in David's life should end in enriching the repertoire of the national minstrelsy".

The term "Altaschith" (516) means "destroy not", and may have been the name of a melody or tune to which the Psalm was to be sung. It occurs four times, in the titles of Psalms 57, 58, 59 and 75. "Michtam" (4387) in the title, occurs six times, in the titles of Psalm 16 and Psalms 56-60. These are known as "David's Golden Psalms". For further, more detailed, comment on "Altaschith" see the introduction to Psalm 57, and for an explanation of "Michtam" refer to the introduction to Psalm 16.

There is no valid reason for doubting, as some do, the Davidic authorship of Psalm 59, or for questioning the circumstances in which it was composed, as stated in the title. As Alexander Maclaren in *The Life of David* writes, quoting the title, "It refers to the time 'when Saul sent, and they watched the house to kill him'. Those critics who reject this date, which they do on very weak grounds, lose themselves in a chaos of assumptions as to the occasion of the Psalm. The Chaldean invasion, the assaults in the time of Nehemiah, and the era of the Maccabees, are alleged with equal confidence and equal groundlessness". He goes on to quote Delitzsch, who says, "We believe that it is most advisable to adhere to the title, and most scientific to ignore these hypotheses built on nothing". The occasion referred to in the title can be read in full in 1 Samuel 19, where see especially v.11. This helps to an appreciation of the spirit of the Psalm, which now reveals the thoughts and feelings of David at that time, feelings which are not recorded in the original narrative. It might be mentioned here that the same is true with regard to the sufferings of the greater Son of David. If the four Gospels record the facts of the sufferings of Christ, it is the Psalms that reveal the feelings of the holy Sufferer, as in Psalms 16, 22, 40, 41, 69, 118.

The Psalm may be considered in four parts. In verses 1-5 the Psalmist prays for deliverance. This stanza concludes with a "Selah". Verses 6-9 give a more detailed description of his adversaries and avow that his defence is in God. In verses 10-13 he renews the appeal of the opening verses. This section also concludes with a "Selah". The final stanza, verses 14-17, states again his confidence in God, and anticipates the deliverance for which he has prayed.

Verses 1-5: A Prayer for Defence and Deliverance

David's house was surrounded by assassins. The Psalm opens abruptly, with a repeated call for divine deliverance. "Deliver me...Deliver me". He appeals on the grounds of a most personal relationship with God, saying, "O my God". David, who can say in other Psalms, "My shepherd", "My Lord", "My rock", "My redeemer", has learned a holy intimacy with the mighty Elohim, and he pleads that here. The word "defend" (7682), has a meaning which is not immediately evident in the AV. It means "to set on high". JND has, "Secure me on high from them that rise up against me". It is the thought of a high fortress, whose height gives that defence from the enemy for which David prays. It is like the high tower of Psalm 18.2 and Psalm 144.2. He would be set on high, beyond the reach of his adversaries.

David's enemies had, in many senses, a certain superiority. They were numerically and militarily stronger than he was. But morally they were inferior. They were workers of iniquity and they were men of blood, wickedly and ruthlessly thirsting for his life. They lay in wait for him, besieging his house in an ambush authorised by the jealous King Saul. They were mighty and they were many, and they were gathered against him. For what reason did they seek his life? David protests his innocence and appeals to Jehovah. He maintains that there was no transgression, there was no sin, there was no fault on his part. He had behaved himself wisely before Saul. He had done nothing either to oppose or to provoke the king. Why should they make such haste to set themselves against him? It was an injustice, and again he calls upon God to help him.

Notice David's use of divine titles. "O my God (430)"; "O LORD (3068)"; "O LORD (3068) God (430) of hosts (6635)"; "The God (430) of Israel". What a majestic cluster of divine names is here! The Psalmist's appeal is to One whom he knows as, "My Elohim"; "Jehovah"; "Jehovah Elohim Sabaoth"; "Elohim of Israel". David's God was indeed the Mighty One, the eternally existing, self sufficient One, the Lord God of Hosts, and the God of Israel. Each title was significant. The covenant-keeping Jehovah was David's own God, and He had, too, a special relationship with the chosen nation. With what confidence could David invoke such an One. Would God arise to help him? The appeal is not for personal help only, but that God, the God of Israel, would arise and judge the heathen everywhere, and show no mercy to plotters of iniquity wherever they may be found. The word "heathen" (1471) is GOYIM, the word usually employed to describe the nations, those who were not Jews, and this has presented a problem for some. Spurgeon suggests that David is referring to "the heathen among thine Israel, the false-hearted who say they are Jews and are not, but do lie". He continues however, "Let all the nations of thine enemies, and all the heathenish people at home and abroad know that Thou art upon circuit, judging and punishing". Kirkpatrick is more concise when he writes, "It is possible that, as in Psalm 7, the prayer for a judgment upon personal enemies is expanded into a prayer for a judgment upon all the enemies of Israel; and in that general judgment the treacherous Israelites who are iniquitously plotting against the Psalmist's life will meet with their due reward".

The section concludes with a "Selah". With such a consideration, at such a moment, it is well to pause, to muse upon the solemnity of divine judgment of the wicked, and to dwell in silent meditation upon the majesty of God.

Verses 6-9: The Assailants Described

The Psalmist now compares his foes to a pack of dogs, prowling in the dusk of the evening, scavenging for food. Most Oriental cities had their troops of such dogs, unowned and untamed, lean and hungry, feeding on the refuse which had been scattered in the streets during the day, howling and snarling in disappointment when they found none. Those men who came to take David, as recorded in 1 Samuel 19, were similarly frustrated, as was King Saul himself, when they discovered that their cruel designs had been thwarted. Saul had unleashed them like fierce dogs, but their prey had escaped! David was gone, helped to safety by Michal, daughter of the man who sought his life (1 Sam 19.12-16). The phrase, "round about the city", need not apply literally to David's pursuers. It may simply be a part of the metaphor of the dogs roaming the city streets. In vain they hunted for David. He was now safe, beyond their reach.

The metaphor may be continued into v.7, "Behold, they belch out with their mouth", or, as some think, David may now be reverting to speaking directly of his enemies. Cruel words poured forth from their mouths, sharp and cutting as swords. There was a certain arrogance, too, when they said, "Who...doth hear?". They slandered with impunity, as if there was no one to hear or judge their injustices. Does the question imply that God Himself had ceased to observe and intervene? Although Dr Cohen thinks the implication is that they are saying that "God will pay no heed to the cry of the man they have marked down for destruction and interfere with their designs", the former interpretation seems more acceptable. They appear convinced that they are unheard in their malicious slanderings, that God is not interested sufficiently to listen and intervene. He is, however, as David now affirms.

Jehovah is indeed listening and observing. Do they say, in defiance, "Who doth hear"? Here is a repetition of Psalm 2.4; "He that sitteth in the heavens shall laugh". Jehovah returns their scorn upon them. Do they laugh at David? David's God will laugh at them. Do they deride? God shall have them in derision, and not only these particular enemies, but the heathen (1471), the "goyim" everywhere. David knew, not only theoretically but also experimentally, that the strength which he needed was in the Lord, therefore he would wait upon Him. God was his defence (4869), his fortress, his high tower, his refuge and his safe retreat. In Him he would be sheltered from those who sought his life.

Verses 10-13: The Renewed Appeal

This third section of the Psalm opens with that lovely title of God with which the Psalm closes, "The God of my mercy". "Mercy" (2617), is "lovingkindness and goodness, favour and pity". Such was the character of the God whom the Psalmist trusted. "Prevent" (6923) is an archaism, meaning "to go before, to anticipate, or to come to meet". JND renders it, "God, whose loving-kindness will come to meet me". F.W. Grant translates it as, "My God will be before me with His mercy". Whatever troubles or trials may confront His saints, Jehovah is there before them, with loving-kindness and comfort. Notice that the words "my desire", in v.10, are in italics, having been supplied by the translators. They are not in the original text and may profitably be omitted. David is anticipating the day when he would be able to look without fear upon his enemies. He would one day gaze steadily upon them without trepidation, knowing that they were a defeated foe.

In an intensified plea for retribution he now prays, "Slay them not". David desired judgment, but not sudden death for his enemies. He wanted an exemplary judgment so that others might witness both the power of God and the inevitable destruction of the wicked. A speedy, immediate, slaying of them would not serve this purpose, he thinks. "Scatter them", he asks, "bring them down". Later in the Psalm he will pray, "Let them wander up and down". Many have noticed a similarity to the judgment of Cain in Genesis 4.12-14. They were to become monuments to divine righteousness, testimonies to Israel, lest the nation should forget God's hatred of iniquity such as theirs was. Jehovah was the shield, the protection, of His people. Observe the plurality of the pronoun, "O Lord *our* shield". What God was to David personally he would be also for the whole nation - "Our shield".

The verse which follows seems to suggest that these men were constant liars. Note that the conjunction "and" is in italics. JND and others will omit it, reading, "The sin of their mouth, the word of their lips", implying, as Alexander comments, "The word of their lips is the sin of their mouth; whatever they speak is spoken sinfully; they cannot speak without committing sin". With this interpretation Davison agrees, writing, "The first line may mean that every word of their lips is a sin, and is so taken by Cheyne, Perowne, Driver, and others". David again prays for judgment, that they might be taken in their pride, caught as by surprise even while they indulged complacently in their swearing and falsehood. Not only were they liars, but apparently they could, perversely, actually swear to the truth of what they were saying. The Psalmist prays that they might be consumed (3615) in wrath. "Consume", he pleads. "Consume", he repeats. He is asking that their slanderous and murderous career might be brought to an end, that it might be finished forever, so that both they, and men everywhere, might know that the God of Jacob rules, not only among His chosen people, but unto the ends of the earth. He has universal dominion. He is the Governor of the nations. How similar is this to the language of David the stripling when he went out to face Goliath. "Jehovah will deliver", he had exclaimed to the giant, "that all the earth may know that there is a God in Israel" (1 Sam 17.46).

It is a moment for another "Selah". It is time to pause again, to ponder the wickedness of men and meditate upon the judgment of God, and quietly consider His greatness who rules in all the earth. Muse upon that word of Daniel to the king of Babylon, "The most High ruleth in the kingdom of men" (Dan 4.17).

Verses 14-17: The God of My Mercy

Whether this final stanza opens with a prediction, a prayer, or an anticipation, is not relevant to the sentiment expressed. "At evening let them return", says the AV. "In the evening they shall return", reads JND. "And so in the evening they return", gives Grant. It is almost a repeat of v.6. Knowing the inevitably of their judgment, David is saying, paraphrased, "Will they return?". "They will return." "Well, then, let them return!" He has no fear. Like hungry barking dogs prowling the streets, searching for food but unable to find it, so it was with David's enemies. They went to his house, as the title of the Psalm indicates. They went in all arrogance with a royal mandate, seeking his life, but like dogs that found nothing, so they discovered that the prey was out of their reach. David was gone. Let them return in the evening, let them bark and howl, let them wander up and down for meat and remain unsatisfied. The Psalmist was safe, and, while, humanly speaking, some of the credit might be given to Michal his wife, yet David will, as ever, attribute his deliverance to the power and the mercy of God.

The disappointed adversaries of the Psalmist may search for him all night long, but in the morning David is singing. His God has been his defence (4869) and his refuge (4498), his high tower, his stronghold, his place of safety and his retreat from danger. Well might he sing, and sing to God his strength. How well, and how personally, had the shepherd boy got to know his God! Notice the repetition of that personal, possessive pronoun, "my", so simple, yet so profound. "My strength!" "My defence!" "My mercy!"

With these notes of triumph the Psalm concludes. There was power and strength in God, but there was loving-kindness and goodness, favour and pity and faithfulness toward His young servant, and David must sing.

PSALM 60

Introduction

That there are difficulties in the lengthy title of this Psalm cannot be denied, but when once they are resolved they do bring light to bear upon the occasion, the spirit, and the language of the Psalm. With its being ascribed to the Chief Musician there is no problem, it is so obviously a Psalm to be sung nationally, and to be preserved by that Master of Song for this purpose. The undisputed meaning of "Shushan-eduth" is "The Lily of Testimony". This may have described either the music or the musical instrument which was to be used for the occasion. "Shushan" appears in its plural form, "Shoshannim", in the title of Psalm 45 and the only other occurrence of "Eduth" is in the title of Psalm 80, where it is adjoined to "Shoshannim". The lily is an emblem of beauty or loveliness and the reference here may be either to the law as the testimony, as in Psalm 19.7, or to the witness of the people to that law, as here in Psalm 60.4. This Psalm is the sixth, and last, of the "Michtam" Psalms, which are all Psalms of David. These are frequently called "David's Golden Psalms", with the thought of engraving divine secrets and precious truth upon the hearts of God's people. For a more detailed discussion of this see the introduction to Psalm 16 in this Commentary. Psalm 16 is the first of the six "Michtam" Psalms. This last "Golden Psalm" is, as the title says, "to teach", or "to be taught", indicating that it was to be learned by heart, committed to the memory.

The historical account of the battle which is referred to in the title can be found in 2 Samuel 8.13 and 1 Chronicles 18.12. Alexander says, "The name *Aram* corresponds to *Syria* in its widest and vaguest sense, and is joined with other names to designate particular parts of that large country". He says that it "denotes the space between the Tigris and the Euphrates, corresponding to *Aram-Naharaim*, or *Syria of the Two Rivers*. The king of this country was tributary to the king of *Aram Zobah*, as appears from the account of David's second Aramean war (2 Sam 10.16, 19). J.N. Darby renders this part of the title "The Syrians of Mesopotamia and the Syrians of Zobah". Alexander adds that "The *Valley of Salt* has been identified with a valley south of the Dead Sea, on the ancient confines of Israel and Edom". In confirmation of this he cites Robinson's *Biblical Researches in Palestine*, vol. 11. p. 483, as does also Spurgeon.

The difference in the record of the number killed on that occasion, twelve thousand in the Psalm title, eighteen thousand in 2 Samuel and in 1 Chronicles, may be accounted for by understanding that, of the eighteen thousand attributed to David and Abishai in the earlier records, twelve thousand were slain by Joab. Both Joab and Abishai were David's generals, and they were worthies. Joab, apparently returning with his victorious army from another battle, marched against Edom and slew his twelve thousand in the campaign. Alexander's comment is most helpful. He writes, "Joab achieved the victory here ascribed to him, as the leader of the army, but in 1 Chronicles 18.12 it is ascribed to his brother Abishai, who probably commanded under him...and in 2 Samuel 8.13, to David himself as the sovereign whom they both represented". William Streat, quoted by Spurgeon, says of Joab and Abishai, "If the enemies were too strong, one would help the other...and of this eighteen thousand attributed to David and Abishai before, Joab slew twelve thousand of them; the memory of which service is here embalmed with a Psalm".

The Psalm may be considered in three parts. In verses 1-3 David laments that the nation has been abandoned by God. Verses 4-8 are an anticipation of victory and of better days ahead. Verses 9-12 are a concluding prayer.

Verses 1-3: The Lament

The Psalm appears to have been written in the shadow of defeat, in a time of national humiliation. Whether this defeat followed as a reversal of the success spoken of in the title, or whether David is writing in retrospect of the latter days of Saul and the early days of his own reign, is hard to determine. David had inherited a troubled kingdom, with contentions and factions within, and attacks from without. Philistines, Edomites, Moabites and Syrians had all assailed him, but God had signally blessed him and he had not only subdued his enemies but had succeeded in uniting the nation. Perhaps the lessons for God's people in the Psalm are that they must not become complacent in times of success, or despondent in times of defeat and disaster. In each and every situation they must learn to seek Him whose presence is their only strength and stay.

David knew this, and cries, "O God, thou hast cast us off, thou hast scattered us, thou hast been displeased". To be "cast off" (2186) by God was an unenviable plight indeed. The word implies a rejection with abhorrence and contempt, to be spurned as something foul. "It is strong language", says Albert Barnes, "meaning that God had seemed to treat them as if they were loathsome or offensive to Him". God had scattered them, broken them, in His displeasure. That God should be angry with them was worse by far than the enmity of Philistines or Syrians. "Displeased" is perhaps not strong enough to translate the original word (599). It was indeed anger. The concluding phrase in this verse is a prayer in the AV, "O turn thyself to us again", but some will understand it rather as an expression of faith, "Thou wilt restore us again". Whichever rendering is preferred, the sentiment is the same, they were a sad people, cast off and forsaken, needing restoration to God's favour. They desired to see His smile once again.

"The earth" (776) is a synonym for the land and the kingdom, and it trembled. Social and political upheavals are viewed here under the figure of an earthquake, when tremblings are followed by cracks and chasms and structural devastation. Spurgeon describes it graphically; "Things were as unsettled as though the solid earth had been made to quake; nothing was stable; the priests had been murdered by Saul, the worst men had been put in office, the military power had been broken by the Philistines, and the civil authority had grown despicable through insurrections and intestine contests. As the earth cracks, and opens itself in rifts during violent earthquakes, so was the kingdom rent with strife and calamity". Healing of the breaches, reparation of the fractures, was needed urgently, else the whole unstable structure might topple into ruin.

Things had gone hard with Israel, but they were still God's people, and all that had happened to them would eventually turn to their profit and good. In His sovereignty God often used the enmity of surrounding nations to discipline His people. It was chastisement, which, as Hebrews 12.11 says, is never joyous, but grievous, but afterward it yields the peaceable fruit of righteousness to those who are exercised by it. So it is with the individual, and so it was with the nation. God had shown His people hard things with the end in view that they should be a better brighter testimony for Him. In the chastisement, however, it was as though they had drunk the wine of astonishment, and they reeled, bewildered, under the effects of it.

Verses 4-8: The Anticipation of Better Days

In the midst of the trouble and depression, the Psalmist now perceives and considers the purpose of the chastisement, and the great privilege conferred upon the nation. God had given a banner to those who feared Him. It was like a ray of light and hope in the darkness. It was as if they unfurled an ensign and lifted up a standard as a rallying point for those who would unite in testimony for Him. They must gather to this banner in the cause of truth, and maintain a witness to Him among the nations.

The "Selah" indicates a reverent pause. It implies a meditation upon what has been said and upon what God has done. The music may then rise to a crescendo, and, as the standard and the music are lifted, so also the hearts of the people should be lifted in praise of God. This "Selah", however, is an interlude, an interjection. God had given a banner to those who feared Him, an ensign to be displayed in the cause of truth and for the deliverance of His beloved ones. In the midst of these sentiments the "Selah" appears. It is a holy interruption to muse upon the wonder of it all.

The word "beloved" of v.5 is a plural word, indicating His beloved ones, His people. "Save", the Psalmist exclaims, "with thy right hand". The right hand is always indicative of strength and power. David prays that God, who gave the banner to be displayed by His people, will now Himself display His power and deliver His people.

The Psalmist has confidence that deliverance will come. From v.5, the remainder of the Psalm occurs again as the second half of Psalm 108. God, in His holiness, had spoken, and David could exult. Some, however, understand this "I will rejoice" and the words which follow as being the words which God had spoken. Others rather think that these are David's words as he divides out the divinely promised inheritance. It is difficult to be dogmatic, but the thought in either case is that God has promised, and that what He has promised in His holiness must be fulfilled, so that both He and His people will rejoice.

There follow, references to Shechem, Succoth, Gilead, Manasseh, Ephraim, Judah, Moab and Edom. This is a vast territory, east and west, north and south. Shechem, of course, is in Samaria, west of the Jordan. The Valley of Succoth is the land on the east of Jordan. Notice that it was at these two places, Shechem and Succoth, that Jacob built a house, made booths for his cattle, and pitched his tent, on his return from exile, as if claiming the Promised Land for his possession (Gen 33.17-19). The territory is now surveyed again, east and west of Jordan. On the east, Gilead and the inheritance of the tribe of Manasseh, which was the most fertile Bashan. On the west were Ephraim and Judah, representatives of Israel's military and civil powers respectively. Ephraim, "the strength of mine head", has been described as a particularly war-like tribe, strong in the defence of the country (Gen 48.19). Judah, "my lawgiver", is associated with the sceptre (Gen 49.10). As W.T. Davison remarks, so interestingly, "Ephraim is the helmet on the warrior's head, and Judah the sceptre in the lawgiver's hand".

The Psalm now turns to the nations. As Canaan, the Promised Land, is the portion of God and of Israel, so the surrounding nations must also be subject. Moab is but a wash-pot, as insignificant and subservient as a foot-bath or basin, in which a slave might wash his master's feet, and, if this context is preserved, then "over Edom will I cast out my shoe" may be a picture of the master throwing his soiled sandals to his slave in preparation for the wash-pot. Philistia, the land of the Philistines in the west, must "shout aloud" (JND), in acknowledgement of the triumphs of God and of Israel. Moab in the east; Edom in the south; Philistia in the west; they must all together bow in subjection to King David and his God.

Verses 9-12: The Concluding Prayer

It would appear, however, that at this time Edom had not yet been subdued. Edom, or Idumea, was a mountainous region in the south with fortified cities such as Sela, better known as Petra, rock-hewn and deemed to be impregnable. This explains the Psalmist's questions, "Who will bring me into the strong city? Who will lead me into Edom?" The entrance to Petra is by a narrow gorge, lined on either side by lofty precipices. It was all but inaccessible. Who would, or could, make it yield to David? The answer comes in the form of another question. "Wilt not thou, O God?" The same God who had cast them off, the God who in past days had refused to go forth with their armies to battle, even He was the One, the only One, who could conquer Edom for them. "Give us help", David pleads, "for vain is the help of man". No human aid could deliver them, or grant them the victory which they sought. "Wilt not thou, O God?" Their appeal is to the mighty Elohim (430). He alone could help.

The Psalm ends on a note of confidence. Through God they could do valiantly (2428). Through Him, by Him, and with Him, their armies would have valour, strength, and power. He would crush their enemies, trample their adversaries, and cause them to triumph.

So concludes the Psalm which began in an atmosphere of sadness, almost despair. The lesson for saints of every age is that all chastisement has better things in view. The believer must look out of, and away from, every difficult circumstance into which God has allowed him to come. All has been for his good. Trust and confidence reposed in Him will always be rewarded with eventual victory.

PSALM 61

Introduction

Here is yet another Psalm committed to the care of the Chief Musician, indicating its suitability for national worship. It is ascribed to David and there is no reason to doubt the Davidic authorship. Most commentators agree that it belongs to that period of David's exile during Absalom's rebellion, perhaps when the revolt had failed and the king was anticipating a soon return to Jerusalem. Delitzsch entitles the Psalm, "Prayer and thanksgiving of an expelled king on his way back to the throne". "Neginah" (5058) in the title, corresponds to "Neginoth", as in the titles of Psalms 4, 6, 54 and 55. It means "a stringed instrument", and is to be distinguished from "Nehiloth", which means "a wind instrument". In the translations of both JND and RV the word is rendered "a stringed instrument". Unlike the occurrences in the Psalms mentioned, however, the word here in the title of Psalm 61 is singular, perhaps signifying that, although the Psalm will be sung by the congregation in the public services of the sanctuary, it is most suitable also for the private and personal devotions of an individual saint.

Like so many of the smaller Psalms, Psalm 61 has been signally blessed of God in the encouragement and comfort of His people. There is an obvious and natural division in the eight short verses, a division marked by the "Selah" at the end of verse 4. Verses 1-4 are the prayer, and verses 5-8 the thanksgiving, to which Delitzsch's title refers, as mentioned above.

Verses 1-4: The Prayer of the Exile

"Hear my cry" (7440), the Psalm begins. As Strong indicates, this is a loud ringing cry. It is a piercing cry, with an urgency and an earnestness in the word. The king's need was great and he pleads that God would not only hear but attend to his appeal. David feels as if he is calling from the end of the earth. This is not to be taken literally, of course, but if David was not in his beloved Jerusalem, then he was far away indeed. As Kirkpatrick says, so very beautifully, "Jerusalem, the dwelling place of God, is for him the centre of the earth. He measures his distance from it not by miles but by the intensity of his yearning to be there, in the place where the visible pledges of God's Presence were to be found". For every devout Old Testament saint, to be exiled from the Holy City was akin to being an outcast at the end of the earth. David's heart was overwhelmed. Troubles had swept over him, deluging him as mighty billows might sweep over the sand. He felt faint and feeble in his exile from his city, his home, and his throne.

There was but one hope for the Psalmist. "Lead me", he cries, "to the rock that is higher than I". He looks for refuge and for safety as a shipwrecked mariner might look to a high rock. But his language (see JND and RV margin), seems to suggest a rock which is not accessible unless he has help. "A rock which is too high for me". The word "lead" (5148) which he uses, signifies "to lead on; to lead forth; to bring", as if to imply that he cannot, alone and unaided, in his weakness, attain to the safe place by himself. He needs divine help. "Lead me on to the rock".

He draws comfort from the experiences of the past. The God to whom he now appeals had already, in times past, been a refuge and a strong tower to which he had fled for shelter. He pleads these former mercies as the ground for his present expectation that God will protect him from the enemy. This word "enemy" (341), though in the singular, is probably a collective noun, not describing any one person, but denoting that body of enemies who opposed him. His expectation is full of confidence. He will, he believes, abide (1481), or sojourn, for ever, in the tabernacle of God. He would dwell where God dwells. He would sojourn there, a stranger in the world but at home in the courts of the Lord. In the language of the familiar figure this would be like finding comfort and protection as chicks found covert under the shadow of the wings of the mother bird. It is a lovely illustration, used frequently in the Psalter and employed by the Lord Jesus Himself in His sad lament over Jerusalem (Mt 23.37; Lk 13.34). It is a beautiful thought, too, that similar language was used by Boaz in speaking to Ruth, who became, by grace, the great-grandmother of this David, the Psalmist and King (Ruth 2.12).

It is a fitting place for a "Selah". It is a moment to pause and to praise; to reflect and to rejoice. The Psalm is by this divided equally into its two parts.

Verses 5-8: The Thanksgiving

When David now says, "For thou, O God, hast heard my vows", it is difficult to know with any certainty whether he is speaking reflectively of past experience, or in faith expressing confidence with regard to the future. It may well signify that the rebellion has been crushed and that David is now anticipating his return to his throne. The vows to which he refers are not specified. Such vows may at times be made privately, in intimacy, and be known only to the saint and to his God. To those who feared (3373) Him, and reverenced His name, God would be true to His covenant and would grant them the promised heritage. David, in his fear of the Lord, must in this have had the assurance that the throne and the kingdom would inevitably be restored to him.

He now speaks of himself in the third person, this because he speaks not only for himself, but representatively, thinking of his kingly office and of his dynasty. "Thou wilt prolong the king's life". "Thou wilt add days to the days of the king" (JND). He anticipates that the years granted to him may be as many as the generations of posterity that will follow. He had good reason to believe this, considering the word of the Lord which had come through Nathan the prophet to him; "Thine house and thy kingdom shall be established for ever before thee: thy throne shall be established for ever" (2 Sam 7.16). He expected to abide before God for ever, and this word "abide" (3427), though it is not exactly the same word, may well correspond to the word "establish", used so often in 2 Samuel 7. The promise of God would be fulfilled. His mercy, or lovingkindness, and His truth would guard and keep and preserve the kingdom. Compare Psalm 57.3, where the same "mercy and truth" are David's guardians, in a Psalm where again David sings of finding refuge "in the shadow of thy wings".

The Psalm concludes with a song of praise and the promise of the performing of vows. Singing and serving, worship and witness, devotion and duty, are joined together in this closing verse. David has cried to God and pleaded for divine attention to his prayer. This has been granted and now there must be praise accordingly. As Spurgeon remarks, "We ought not to leap in prayer, and limp in praise"! The Psalmist's praise, and his avowal that he will fulfil his promises, are but gratitude to the One who has heard his prayer and fulfilled His promises. As God had promised, and performed, so will David praise for ever and in gratitude perform his vows perpetually, from day to day.

PSALM 62

Introduction

Another Psalm composed by David and committed by him to the care of the Chief Musician, who in this case is identified as Jeduthun, as also in the titles of Psalms 39 and 77. In 1 Chronicles 16.7, 37, 41, Jeduthun, Asaph and Heman are named as the three leaders of the temple choirs. It seems most appropriate that Jeduthun's name means "praise", and it was a high privilege to be responsible for the leading of the praise in the services of the sanctuary. He was, of course, a Levite, but little more is recorded of him except that he may also have been known as "Ethan" (See 1 Chronicles 15.16-17). The sons of Jeduthun followed in the footsteps of their father in the service of the house of God. They are named as porters or doorkeepers in 1 Chronicles 16.42.

The Hebrew word AK (389), meaning "only", occurs six times in the Psalm, though not always translated so in the AV. This is a significant key-word and the occurrences of it will be noted in the commentary. Spurgeon remarks upon this, saying, "From the sixfold use of the word AK or *only*, we have been wont to call it THE ONLY PSALM". Perowne writes, "The particle may be rendered *only*, as restrictive; or, *surely*, as affirmative. Our translators have rendered it differently in different verses of this Psalm: in v.1, truly; in vv. 2, 4-6, only; in v.9, surely".

The occasion and time of the composition of the Psalm are not known. Perhaps since David's troubles, trials and trust are common to the saints of all ages, it is not at all necessary to the enjoyment of the Psalm that the original reason for its writing should be positively identified.

There are three obvious and equal parts in the Psalm, the divisions being indicated by the "Selah" at the end of verses 4 and 8. Each of these stanzas begins with the word AK, previously mentioned, and a consistent theme of assurance and confidence prevails throughout the three parts. There is, to begin with, an expression of quiet waiting upon God. This is followed by the Psalmist's declaration of all that God means to him, coupled with an encouragement to others to trust also. It concludes with similar exhortations to trust in God and not in riches.

Verses 1-4: Trusting - In Stillness

Though lost in translation, the first word in the Psalm is "only". It is, therefore, "Only upon God doth my soul wait". The believer's trust must not, cannot, be divided. He dare not share his trust with another. He must wait only upon God. "Wait" (1747) is an interesting and beautiful word. It signifies a waiting in silence, in stillness, in repose. JND renders these opening words of the Psalm, "Upon God alone doth my soul rest peacefully". Such tranquillity is foreign to the human mind in its alienation from God, but trust in God frees from that natural disquietude, and sings, "From him cometh my salvation". Trust in God, and in God alone, can give quietness of soul.

The Psalmist now repeats this little word AK, "only"; just a particle, but so important. He says, "He only is my rock and my salvation; he is my defence (4869)". His God is his rock, his refuge, and his high fortress, his stronghold and his safe retreat. With such security, why should he not be at rest? He knows that he cannot be greatly moved. His use of the word "greatly" (7227) seems to imply that he does not expect to escape all the calamities that overtake men. There may indeed be adverse circumstances. God may, in His sovereignty and wisdom, allow certain trials to come his way, but he will not be much moved by these. They will not be ruinous. God is his salvation.

If the Psalmist is peaceful Godward, he now turns abruptly to those men who would persecute him. He had many enemies. How long would they persist in opposing him? His language seems to imply that they were many against one. "All of you", he says, "against a man!" They imagined mischief (2050) towards him, setting themselves against him, assailing him with the intent of overwhelming him. But there are varied renderings of the remaining part of v.3. If the AV is preferred then the meaning is that they would be frustrated in their evil designs, that they would be slain, broken down as a bowing wall or a tottering fence. Others, however, as JND and RV, rather understand the Psalmist as saying that they sought to slay him, regarding him as vulnerable as a wall leaning over and ready to collapse, or as weak as a tottering fence which might easily be pushed over. To quote JND in full, "How long will ye assail a man; will ye seek, all of you, to break him down as a bowing wall or a tottering fence?". If the italicised words in the AV are omitted then some of this alternative rendering will be obvious.

The Psalmist's enemies were implacable but their opposition to a man God had exalted was futile. They "only" (AK again) consulted to cast him down. God had conferred a certain dignity and excellency upon David. These adversaries conspired and counselled, they devised and determined, they purposed and plotted, as to how they might degrade him. It was all to no avail if God had exalted him, and so they must resort to falsehoods and hypocrisy. They delighted in lies, blessing outwardly but cursing inwardly.

It is time to pause. "Selah!" David's tranquillity has been temporarily disturbed as he thinks of these men and their cruel opposition to him. He must return to the stillness of his opening verse. He must lift up his heart again in quiet meditation and thanksgiving to his God.

Verses 5-8: Trusting - In Safety

In the Hebrew original, the second stanza commences, as do the first and third, with the particle "only" (AK). David exhorts his own soul, "Only wait upon God, my soul". JND's rendering is very beautiful; "Upon God alone, O my soul, rest peacefully". The Psalmist's expectation and hope was from God alone. Yet again he repeats the little word, "He *only* is my rock". He resorts in confidence to Him who is his rock, his salvation, and his defence, his high fortress and his safe retreat. In his trust he can exclaim again, "I shall not be moved".

How David delights to say, "My salvation…my salvation". His safety and security were in the hands of God. His glory, too, any honour or dignity which he enjoyed, was from God. Then there is more inspired repetition. "My rock", he had exclaimed in vv. 2 and 6. "The rock of my strength", he now says in v.7. God was his refuge, his shelter from the storms of life.

From his own personal experience of his God David now appeals to his compatriots, to the people who were God's people. "Trust in Him", he exhorts, be done with care, and confide in Him at all times. In days of adversity and in seasons of prosperity, in all the vicissitudes and events of life, keep trusting in Him. Pour out your heart to Him. Tell Him the need which already He knows. Lay bare before Him your innermost thoughts and feelings, your perplexities and problems, your joys and sorrows. "God is a refuge for us". He was David's refuge in v.7 and He is a refuge for all His people in v.8.

Here is the second "Selah", another call for a moment of reflection. "Precious pause", says Spurgeon, "Timely silence! Sheep may well lie down when such pasture is before them".

Verses 9-12: Trusting - In Satisfaction

The Psalmist is satisfied with his trust in God. In this confidence he will now show the folly of trusting in anything or anyone else. This closing stanza begins, as the others, with the word AK (only), but this is lost in translation. As Dr Cohen says, "The translation fails to reproduce the important introductory AK: nothing but vanity are men". "Only vanity" is the inspired indictment of men everywhere. Two different words for "man" are used here, as in Psalm 49.2. For "men of low degree" the word is ADAM (120), and for "men of high degree" the word is ISH (376). It matters not what kind of men, whether rich or poor, whether the aristocracy or the commonality, the learned or the illiterate, the lofty or the lowly, whether men in their dignity or men in their frailty, all by nature are only vanity, and less! Whatever his class or his status, man at his best is but vanity, and man at his worst is but a lie. When laid on the scales of the sanctuary "they go up together lighter than vanity" (JND). "In the balances they will go up; They are together lighter than vanity" (RV). They are just as a breath, registering no weight at all, and the pan of the balance in which they have been placed ascends. The wealth and influence which once distinguished some of them from their fellows is now gone. What utter futility then, to trust in man!

Were there some then, who trusted in their ability to oppress others? Did they, by violence and robbery acquire riches? Such ill-gotten gains would come to naught. They were vanity. Indeed this applied to all riches, whether obtained unjustly or honestly. Certainly the saint must not set his heart upon them. Prosperity is not to be trusted. This warning is repeated in so many Scriptures, and the Lord Jesus Himself spoke of "the deceitfulness of riches" (Mt 13.22). "The love of money is the root of all evil", Paul writes (1 Tim 6.10). "Riches certainly make themselves wings", says Solomon, "they fly away as an eagle toward heaven" (Prov 23.5). Spurgeon quotes the quaint but very expressive comments of Christopher Love (1618-1651), who says of riches, "A spark of fire may set them on flying, a thief may steal them, a wicked servant may embezzle and purloin them, a pirate or shipwreck at sea, a robber or bad debtor on land; yea, an hundred ways sets them packing. They are as the apples of Sodom, that look fair yet crumble away with the least touch - golden delusions, a mere mathematical scheme or fancy of man's brain, the semblances and empty show of good without any reality or solid consistency". How the Psalmist would have enjoyed these remarks!

God had spoken, and David had heard (8085). The word signifies that he had heard attentively, diligently, obediently. Not once only, but twice, as if echoed in a divine emphasis, God's word had assured him that power belonged to God. Why should he trust in riches? He could rest, satisfied, that all that he needed was in his God. There was not only power, but power blended with mercy, with love and with justice, which rendered impartially to every man according to his work. In such a God, and in Him only, David was content to place his trust.

PSALM 63

Introduction

"This is unquestionably one of the most beautiful and touching Psalms in the whole Psalter". With these words Perowne introduces his commentary on it. It has so often been the language of many a soul sincerely thirsting after God. Those believers, who, for various reasons, of health or otherwise, have been in a kind of exile from the gatherings of the saints, have used this Psalm to express their yearnings for that fellowship which has been denied them.

It is a Psalm of David, and it belongs, as do many of David's Psalms, to the period of Absalom's rebellion. That David was already king is proven by v.11 where he so speaks of himself in the third person. But he had been rejected, and was now a fugitive in the wilderness of Judah. The story of his flight and his banishment from his beloved Jerusalem is told in 2 Samuel 15, 16 and 17. Hengstenberg, quoted by Spurgeon, defines the wilderness of Judah, saying, "The wilderness of Judah is the whole wilderness towards the east of the tribe of Judah, bounded on the north by the tribe of Benjamin, stretching southward to the south west end of the Dead Sea; westward, to the Dead Sea and the Jordan; and eastward to the mountains of Judah". For other references to this wilderness see 2 Samuel 15.23, 28; 16.2; 17.16, 29. Notice too, an interesting parallel between the language of the Psalm and the language of that narrative, which speaks of the hunger, the thirst, and the weariness of the people in the wilderness.

The eleven verses of the Psalm may be divided as follows. In verses 1-4 the Psalmist breathes his longing for the sanctuary. In verses 5-8 he remembers former mercies, and in verses 9-11 he anticipates the eventual judgment of God upon those who sought to destroy him.

Verses 1-4: Yearning for the Sanctuary

Two different titles of God are employed in the opening words of the Psalm, a plural and a singular respectively, "O God (ELOHIM - 430)...my God (EL - 410)". Both titles express greatness, might, and power, and of this God David says, "Thou art my God". This is a comfort to every believer, that he knows God, not just theologically, but personally. Conversely, it is wondrous grace that He who is the Omnipotent deigns to be interested in, and affectionate towards, the individual saint. The phrase "early will I seek" is the translation of one word SHACHAR (7836). It implies diligence and eagerness, and the RV margin, with Rotherham, renders it "earnestly will I seek thee". Alexander says that it "implies impatience or importunate desire". The root of the word SHACHAR means "the dawn; the breaking of day". At the sunrise of each new day David eagerly sought after God. No day would dawn or pass without expressions of his longings for God and the sanctuary. His whole being, body and soul, thirsted for God. There is a parallel in Psalm 84.2, "My heart and my flesh crieth out for the living God". David was in a weary land, a dry and thirsty wilderness. This, of course, was literally true, but the language may also be figurative, describing David's personal weariness in his exile.

The Psalmist longed to see the power and the glory of his God as he had seen them formerly in the sanctuary. The two clauses which compose v.2 as in the AV and JND, are transposed in the RV and some other versions, but the general sense is little affected. David is reminiscing now. He recalls that communion with God which in past days he had enjoyed in the sanctuary, and so, in the same manner, he earnestly coveted the renewal of those former blessings. Blessings they were. The lovingkindness of God was better than life itself, in the sense that any life without Him was but a mere existence. Because of this, David would even now continue praising. While he lived, even in this weary wilderness, he would bless God, lifting up his hands in His name. This lifting up of the hands was the gesture of prayer. It signified the offering up of the heart to God in worship and praise and is used elsewhere in the Psalms, as in Psalms 28.2; 134.2; and 141.2. When the NT writer, Paul, uses the expression in 1 Timothy 2.8 it is likely that he employs it in a symbolic way, not necessarily implying the actual physical lifting up of the hands as was common in OT days.

Verses 5-8: Remembering Past Days

Memories of past mercies confirm David's confidence and his joy in the Lord. The reference to "marrow and fatness" is a symbolic way of speaking of rich food. It is possible that there may be, as some think, an allusion to the sacrifice of the peace offering, but this is not probable since it was forbidden to the people to eat the fat of any of the offerings. It is better, and simpler, to understand this as a representation of full spiritual satisfaction. As the hunger of the body is satisfied with food, so the soul of the Psalmist has been richly fed with divine provision. His soul being satisfied, then his lips will praise, and this with joy.

In the stillness of the night watches David meditates and remembers. "Night" is in italics in the AV, having been supplied by the translators. It is not so italicised in other versions, for the word "watches" (821) may be correctly translated "night-watches". There were three night watches in Israel and the Psalmist seems to be saying that throughout those watches, when the silence is conducive to meditation, then upon his bed he quietly remembers. God had been his help in the past and he would therefore rejoice. Again he uses the familiar and beautiful simile, "the shadow of thy wings". Compare Psalm 61.4. This lovely figure of the sheltering wings was used by Boaz in addressing the Psalmist's great-grandmother Ruth (Ruth 2.12).

There is a reciprocal, mutual, relationship between God and His servant. The soul of David cleaves to God, and God, with His right hand, upholds His trusting child. "My soul followeth hard after thee", says David.

"Followeth hard" (1692) implies more than just following, or pursuing. The Psalmist stays close, clinging to God, cleaving to Him in a comforting togetherness. The right hand is an accepted symbol of strength and power, and this is David's support and stay in his trial, as it is indeed the strength of every soul that trusts in David's God.

Verses 9-11: God's Judgment of the Enemy

David does not gloat maliciously over the destruction of his persecutors, but he knows that there will be, eventually, a righteous judgment upon them. God's justice demands it. He often anticipates this in his Psalms, and he does so now. The "But" with which this closing stanza commences draws attention to the contrast between the safety and security of the Psalmist and the fate of his enemies. When he enjoys the presence of God again, rejoicing in the shadow of those protecting wings, then those who opposed him will go down into the lower parts of the earth, into the nethermost parts, a synonym for "Sheol", the Hebrew equivalent of the Greek "Hades". For further comment on these, see the footnote to Psalm 6 in this Commentary.

David anticipated that his enemies would become the prey of both men and beasts. They would fall by the sword and their corpses would lie unburied, to be devoured by foxes or jackals. For those who had sought to destroy him it would be a fearful and ignominious end. Dr W.M. Thomson, in *The Land and the Book*, describes it so graphically. He writes, "They shall be a portion for foxes; by which *jackals* are meant, as I suppose. These sinister, guilty, woebegone brutes, when pressed with hunger, gather in gangs among the graves, and yell in rage, and fight like fiends over their midnight orgies; but on the battle field is their great carnival. Oh! Let me never even dream that any one dear to me has *fallen by the sword*, and lies there to be torn, and gnawed at, and dragged about by these hideous howlers". Tristram, in his *Natural History of the Bible*, says, "It is the jackal rather than the fox which preys on dead bodies, and which assembles in troops on the battle-fields, to feast upon the slain".

Another "But" introduces the closing verse of the Psalm, and this again emphasises the contrast between the future of the Psalmist and the fate of his enemies. When they will languish under divine judgment, David will joy in God. He speaks of himself in the third person, but this is significant, that he is so assured of his throne, his crown, and his kingdom, that even in exile he can call himself "the king". A day of righteous vindication was coming, when all that were true to God would have cause to glory. In the expression "every one that sweareth by him shall glory", some have taken the pronoun "him" to refer to the king, to David. But as Alexander comments, "There is, in fact, no sufficient reason for departing from the obvious construction which refers the pronoun to the nearest antecedent, *God*". The Newberry Bible supplies a capital letter to the pronoun, "Him", indicating that this was how Mr Newberry interpreted the grammar. Here, then, is an acknowledgement of God as the object of allegiance, of fear, and of trust. Those who did in this way acknowledge Him will glory when the mouths of those who spoke otherwise, and who sought to prevail by lies, are silenced.

So ends a Psalm, in which there are memories and longings, praises and anticipations, gladness and joy, but, remarkably, no petitions.

PSALM 64

Introduction

The title is simple. The Psalm is for the Chief Musician, the Master of Song, and it is a Psalm of David. The Chief Musician carried a heavy responsibility, but it was a great privilege to be the Leader of the songs and Director of the worship of the people of God.

The picture portrayed in this Psalm is a familiar one in the Psalter, and is found in so many of the Psalms of David. The opening words call it a "complaint", but the Psalmist's difficult circumstances are lightened, as they usually are, by the knowledge that God will judge his enemies, to the eventual joy of the righteous. These dual themes, the wicked machinations of evil men and the certainty of divine judgment, are, respectively, the subjects of the two parts of the Psalm.

The ten verses are divided almost naturally, verses 1-6 and verses 7-10 being two obvious stanzas.

Verses 1-6: The Malice and Mischief of the Wicked

How often in his Psalms David cries, "Hear me"; "Hear my voice"; "Hear my prayer". Here again he lifts his voice to God, but the word "prayer" (7879) as in the AV, is not the usual word for prayer. It is rather, as has been noticed in the introduction above, a complaint. So the RV and others render it, while JND reads, "Hear, O God, my voice in my plaint". David's cry is, "Hear me...preserve me...hide me". His knowledge of the enemy arouses fear in him. He knows their secret counsels, and he knows that what they plot in secret will soon break out in tumultuous rage against him. What can he do? Alexander Maclaren says so aptly, "He can *but* pray, but he *can* pray; and no man is helpless who can look up".

David compares the words of his enemies to swords and arrows. These are familiar figures, as may be seen in Psalms 11.2; 55.21; 57.4; 58.7. The slanders of these evil men would have pierced David like a sword and their bitter words were as poisoned arrows. There was, too, a mixture of cowardice and cunning. They plotted in secret and lurked in hiding places from which to shoot their arrows at him. They shot at a man who was "perfect" (8535). The word signifies integrity and innocence. He was blameless and he did not deserve their enmity. Did they indeed hide in the covert of pretended friendship, and then, suddenly, aim their arrows at him to destroy him? There was slander and malice, threats and plots, in their malicious scheming against him.

They did all this without fear. They encouraged themselves, strengthened themselves, in their evil plans, saying, "Who shall see?". They reckoned that they were unobserved, perhaps unnoticed even by God Himself, and so they sinned without thought of punishment. It cannot be known with any certainty to which period of David's life this relates but it is most probable that it belongs to the time of his early life in the court of King Saul, when envy and jealousy constantly threatened him. Perowne refers to "the plots by which others were seeking to injure David and traduce him to the king". He speaks of the thoughts which filled the mind of "the upright, honest youth, when he first became aware of the deep duplicity and treachery of the aspirants to royal favour, by whom he was surrounded".

Another metaphor is now added. Swords! Arrows! Snares! They laid hidden snares for David. In their conspiracy and treachery they searched for every and any device with which they might oppose and destroy him. The word "search" (2664), used twice in v.6, implies that they diligently sought out, thinking and devising in the depth of their inward heart and thoughts, how they might entrap him. It was evil scheming indeed, and in their vanity they imagined the success of their wicked purposes. David knew, however, that God would judge them, workers of iniquity that they were.

Verses 7-10: The Righteous Judgment of God

"But God!" So this second stanza commences, in sharp contrast to the evil doings of men. Did they think that they were unobserved? Did they vainly imagine that God would not see? Let them do what they will, "But God...". Their wickedness will recoil upon them. When they shoot their arrows at David they shoot at the upright man, they shoot at the morally innocent man, but God shall shoot at them. Suddenly, when they least expect it, the divine arrow will wound them. "So shall they make their own tongue to fall upon themselves". Their own words will be a testimony against them. What they had intended for David will come upon them instead. As in the language of other Psalms, they will be caught in their own trap, they will fall into the pit which they have made for others. Compare Psalms 7.15; 35.8; 57.6.

The RV rendering is that "they shall be made to stumble", and, "All that see them shall wag the head". They shall stumble in confusion and shame, and men will shake the head in scorn. This wagging of the head is a gesture of derision at the sufferings of others (Ps 22.7; Jer 18.16). If the AV rendering is retained, with which JND agrees, then "all that see them shall flee away" implies a similar act of derision, a turning away from them in mockery and scorn. As Spurgeon remarks, in his usual quaint way, "Who cares to go near to Herod when the worms are eating him? Or to be in the same chariot with Pharaoh when the waves roar round him? Those who crowded around a powerful persecutor, and cringed at his feet, are among the first to desert him in the day of wrath".

"And all men shall fear", says the Psalmist. There must be an intended contrast here with those who "fear not" in v.4. Without fear, without moral restraint, the enemies of the Psalmist devised their plans to destroy him. Now, at the destruction of these evil and unscrupulous schemers, "all men shall fear". Men are struck with awe, and testify that this which they have witnessed is the judgment of God. It is wisdom then to consider what God has done. The wise and prudent man will acquiesce in the righteousness of God's judgment of those wicked men who have so cruelly assailed the innocent.

How all men are affected when God moves in judgment! Evil men will stumble. Men in general will fear, declaring the judgment to be the work of God. The righteous will be glad. Their trust in God will have been vindicated. When they appeared to be few and feeble it was right to make their refuge in Him. Now they can glory. They were righteous in life and upright in heart, and it is fitting that now they should exult. In the day of victory, when the innocent are delivered, and the wicked are judged, and divine justice is displayed, then the upright in heart will glory indeed.

PSALM 65

Introduction

This Psalm of David is, like those many others, committed to the Chief Musician, but notice the addition of the word "Song" in the title. The three Psalms which follow, Psalms 66, 67 and 68, are also called "Songs", a description which first appears in the title of Psalm 30, and which is also in the title of the beautiful Psalm 45. The words "Psalm" (4210) and "Song" (7892) are very similar in meaning but need to be distinguished. It will be remembered that Paul speaks of "psalms and hymns and spiritual songs" (Eph 5.19). It is thought that a Psalm was intended to be sung with an accompaniment whereas a song was for the voice only, but when both words are used in the title then the Psalm may be rendered either way and such is the case here.

Davison entitles this Psalm "A Harvest Thanksgiving" and Dr Cohen calls it "A Harvest Hymn". It is this, but it does, however, include more than thanksgiving for the blessings of harvest, for it sings praise to God for the general display of His mighty power in nature. The seas and the mountains, the rising and the setting of the sun at morning and evening, are all tokens of His greatness and this is acknowledged to the ends of the earth. The delightful crown of the Psalm, though, is that paean of gratitude in the closing stanza. It is thanksgiving for the provision of refreshing rain for pastures and flocks, for fields and furrows, for hills and valleys. The description is of a glorious harvest scene. The Psalmist looks over the cornfields and his heart is filled with joy. Was it written to be sung at the Feast of Firstfruits? We cannot tell, but it certainly would have been appropriate for such an occasion.

There are three parts in the Psalm. The opening verses 1-4 express the blessing and privilege of approach to God. The second part, verses 5-8, sings that might and power of God seen in His creation. The closing stanza, verses 9-13, is the harvest thanksgiving itself.

Verses 1-4: Approach to God

The opening word is very beautiful, "Praise waiteth for thee, O God, in Sion". ("Sion" of the AV is "Zion" of the RV, JND, and most others). "Waiteth" (1747) is that word which implies a waiting in silence. JND renders it, "Praise waiteth for thee in silence, O God, in Zion". It is the quiet adoration of a soul in deep devotion to God. The reference to Zion may indicate congregational worship and it may be that, as Dr Cohen suggests, "The concourse of people in the Temple looks forward in reverential silence for the service of thanksgiving to begin". On such holy festive occasions vows were made in association with the offerings (Lev 7.16), and in the stillness of many a devout heart there would be the quiet determination that the vows made would be performed.

Notice the repetition of "unto thee". The God who hears the prayers, and accepts the vows, of His people Israel, would one day be acknowledged and approached by all flesh. The God of Israel is greater than Israel. Whether the Psalmist had full and clear knowledge of it or not, here is an anticipation of a coming millennial day when all flesh shall give allegiance to the mighty Elohim (430).

David is ever conscious of sin. He accuses himself and he knows that the one great obstacle to approach to God is sin. His iniquities (1697) are like a chronicle of charges against him. They prevail against him and they are too strong for him. But this is precisely the reason why he must look for forgiveness to God alone. Only He can purge his transgressions and grant the necessary pardon. He is a blessed man who is chosen by God to draw near to Him. It is an inestimable privilege to be allowed to dwell in the courts of the Lord. Goodness and holiness are the grand characteristics of His house, and it is not to be wondered at that men so blessed should say, "We shall be satisfied...". The mention of the temple, as in other of David's Psalms, is not, of course, a reference to the "temple magnifical" (1 Chr 22.5) which was built later by Solomon. The house of the Lord was called "the temple" as early as the days of Eli and the child Samuel (1 Sam 3.3). It is a synonym for the sanctuary.

Verses 5-8: The Greatness of God

The "terrible things" (3372) of which David now speaks are acts of God which cause astonishment and awe. They are things which inspire godly fear and reverence, and which demand respect and honour. In such a way God moves in defence of His people and in answer to their prayers. He answers always in righteousness too, for that is the very foundation of His moral government, both now and in that day when all flesh will acknowledge Him. He will deliver His people and vanquish their enemies, and will do it all with equity. He was to Israel, the "God of our salvation", and in that coming day He will be the confidence, the trust, of men from the ends of the earth and from the far distant seas.

Such is the might of the Creator of the universe, girded with power, that He establishes the mountains. They are settled, stable, and secure, because He has made them so. Tempestuous seas and noisy waves must obey Him. How good to remember that, incarnate, He is just the same. He stood once on the deck of a little ship, in the midst of a raging storm on the Sea of Galilee, and said, "Peace, be still". "What manner of Man is this?", His disciples asked in wonder as the waves obeyed Him and there was a great calm. To the believing heart the answer to their question is so obvious. This Man is God! "Without controversy great is the mystery of godliness: God was manifest in the flesh" (1 Tim 3.16). The Man of Galilee is the Elohim of the Psalms!

Mention of the raging seas moves the Psalmist to think also of the tumult of the people. "People" is a plural word, "peoples" (3816). It is "the tumult of the races", says F.W. Grant. He who is the God of nature is God also of the nations. The sea is often used symbolically in the Scriptures as a picture of the restless masses. "The wicked are like the troubled sea, when it cannot rest" (Is 57.20). But He who calms the waves here in Psalm 65, and who stilled the storm on the Galilean Lake, can likewise control the tumult of the peoples, until, eventually, it will be one of the beauties of that future life of the saints, that there shall be "no more sea" (Rev 21.1). While life lasts, however, and the storms rage, then He can make "the storm a calm, so that the waves thereof are still" (Ps 107.29).

"The outgoings of the morning and evening", is a poetic way of speaking of sunrise and sunset. David scans the heavens and the earth. From East to West, from Zion to the uttermost parts, the tokens of God's power are seen and men stand in awe. All men everywhere observe the path of the sun from morning until evening. Ceaselessly, tirelessly, consistently, it bears testimony to the might of Him who controls all. The daily signs of divine power move some to fear while others are inspired to rejoice. Not only the rising and setting of the sun, but those fearful natural phenomena such as earthquakes and volcanoes, tornadoes and tempests, cyclones and hurricanes, these are all in His power and under His control. It is well known that in the loneliest outposts of the inhabited earth men stand in awe at these tokens, afraid at these movements of a divine Being whom they do not know.

Verses 9-13: Harvest Thanksgiving

This earlier contemplation of the power of God has been but a preparation for the final stanza, thanksgiving to God for the harvest. As Dr Cohen says, "All that has gone before in the Psalm is a prelude to its main theme which is now stated". God, in great grace, has remembered the earth. He has visited it (6485). This is the same word as that in Psalm 8.4, "What is man…that thou visitest him?". Jehovah may be great and terrible, majestic, remote and supreme, but He deigns to remember men and He visits earth with blessing. He sends rain in its season. He waters the ground, enriching it in preparation for seedtime and harvest. "The river of God" is a poetic way of describing the descending rain. Men cannot make it. It comes alone from God, flowing down like a river. There were early and latter rains. In late autumn and in early spring they came in their due season from Him who remembered His creatures. It is a faithful fulfilment of the promise of Deuteronomy 11.14. Then again, He not only prepares the earth but He provides the seed corn.

Jehovah having prepared the earth and provided the seed, continues to bless men as they labour towards the harvest. The furrows and ridges which they have ploughed are still in need of rain. God knows this. His rain waters the furrows abundantly and smoothes the ridges between the furrows so that the water will flow. He makes the earth soft and yielding so that it will drink in the rain which He sends. He crowns the year with His goodness. There are grapes on the vines, olives and citrus fruits on the terraced hills, corn in the cultivated fields and grass in the meadows. It is as if God passes over the land in a pathway of blessing, and as He passes over He dispenses blessing along the way. He drops this blessing upon the whole land, so that even in the wilderness there are tracts of pasture, testimonies to His bounty.

These closing verses speak of joy and singing, of hills and valleys, of flocks and fruits, all sharing in the joy of the harvest. Davison's concluding remarks on the Psalm are very beautiful and worth quoting in full. He writes, "This closing description is full of graphic metaphor. Not only are the hills girded with garlands of rejoicing, but the white fleeces of the sheep seem to clothe the meadows, the sheltered vales between the hills are gaily decked with wheat, and together, or in response to one another, they shout with all their heart, 'yea, they sing'! Delitzsch says that meadows and cornfields cannot sing, and that 'the expression demands men as subject'. This is an unusually prosaic touch on the part of a spirited as well as learned commentator. But it is true that it needs men with poetic souls to hear that joyous singing, and men with devout hearts to hear the hymn which the hills and valleys raise and re-echo to God".

So the Psalm concludes with a crescendo of praise to Him of whom another Psalm says, "Thou openest thine hand, and satisfiest the desire of every living thing" (145.16).

PSALM 66

Introduction

The brief title is similar to that of Psalm 65 except that the name of David is omitted. Because of this omission different dates and authors have been suggested by a variety of commentators but many will concur with Spurgeon when he says, "We do not know who is its author, but we see no reason to doubt that David wrote it. It is in the Davidic style, and has nothing in it unsuited to his times. It is true that the "house" of God is mentioned, but the tabernacle was entitled to that designation as well as the temple". For comments on "Psalm" and "Song" see the introduction to Psalm 65 in this Commentary. The Chief Musician was the Master of Song, the Precentor, the Leader of the Praise.

This is a Psalm of thanksgiving. It has been called "A Song of Deliverance" and it is a blending of both national and personal praise. Its twenty verses are divided into five stanzas, mainly punctuated by three "Selahs". The first stanza, verses 1-4, is a call to all mankind to praise God. This ends with the first "Selah". The second, stanza, verses 5-7, gives the reason for such praise. God has manifested His power, particularly as seen in the great Exodus of the people from Egypt. Here there is another "Selah". The third part of the Psalm, verses 8-12, is a further call to recognise God's deliverance of the nation, while the fourth stanza turns from the national to the personal and in verses 13-15 the Psalmist offers his individual praise and vows. Then another "Selah". The concluding verses 16-20 are the Psalmist's own testimony to what God has done for him. As he has called upon men in verse 5 to "Come and see", so now in verse 16 he calls upon them to "Come and hear". The whole is, indeed, a song of praise and worship, of national and personal gratitude to God for His many benefits.

Verses 1-4: A Call to Praise

The opening call to praise is a universal call. While God has had particular dealings with Israel, nevertheless it behoves men everywhere to recognise His greatness and sing His praise. This will eventually be fulfilled in a millennial day, when all nations will bask in the sunshine of God's love and unite in praise of Him who will hold sway over all the earth. "Make a joyful noise" (7321) is a call to "shout aloud", and is so translated in JND and others. The word signifies a shout of triumph. It might have been employed as a war-cry or a cry of victory. Contrast the opening words of the previous Psalm 65, "Praise waiteth for thee in silence, O God" (JND). Whether with a shout or in the silence, God must be praised. The audible praise of the congregation and the silent worship of an individual adoring heart are equally acceptable to Him.

This call goes out to all lands. If the Gentile nations had not known His deliverance as Israel had, still, they knew what He had done, they had seen His mighty works and it was incumbent upon them to honour His great name. They must have known how He had subdued His enemies, and those of His people, and the acknowledgement of this must produce praise, even among the heathen. In that day of His glory, already referred to, all the earth shall worship. But the invitation to men to praise is now turned to a prophecy. "All the earth shall worship thee, and shall sing unto thee". As Davison says, "The whole earth is to be the concert-chamber and all its inhabitants the chorus; no narrower sphere will suffice to set forth the praises". Notice the repetition, "Shout...Sing...worship ...sing...sing". It is a grandly urgent and emphatic call, rising to the crescendo of the "Selah". Pause and ponder, meditate and wonder, let your praise rise up in your hearts and ascend to Him, glorious.

Verses 5-7: Come and See!

Having called upon men to join in praise of God the Psalmist will now give reasons for such praise. "Come and see", he invites. He will show men what God has done. For the second time in the Psalm he uses the word "terrible" (3372), to describe God's mighty works (see v.3). Strong defines these as "fearful acts, to inspire reverence or godly fear or awe". Remember that this call is to the nations. If only they would observe the history of God's dealings with His chosen nation Israel they would learn how great He is. The writer reminds them of the power of God manifested at the Exodus. He had turned the Red Sea into dry land, so that the people went through the flood on foot, and they rejoiced. On the banks of the Red Sea they exclaimed, "Sing unto the Lord for he hath triumphed gloriously" (Ex 15.1). By His strong arm He had delivered them from slavery. He rules by His might, and will do for ever. His eyes observe the nations and rebellion and pride and arrogance are futile. It is a fitting place for another "Selah". The heart wells up in praise as it remembers the power that emancipated an enslaved people and brought them safely across the sea.

Verses 8-12: A Further Call to Praise

As the Psalmist continues his call for praise he now employs a different word. "O bless our God", he writes. "Bless"(1288) also signifies praise, but it means, also, "to salute, to kneel before in adoration". But perhaps it is now the nation, rather than the Psalmist, which is speaking. "Our God" - the call is still reaching out to "peoples", to the nations, and the favoured nation will testify to what God has done for Israel. Their God had delivered them from death. He had not suffered their feet to be moved, He had not allowed them to stumble or fall beyond recovery. They will now speak to God, but let the nations hear what they say. God had brought them into the furnace. He had tried them as men try silver to remove the dross. Egypt was a bitter experience, as were their other confrontations afterwards with many enemies. It was all to refine them and He brought them through.

At times, however, they seemed trapped, as in a net. Trouble was often like a heavy burden laid upon them, constraining them. Sometimes they were vanquished in battle and it was like being trampled under the horses and chariots of the victors. "Thou hast caused men to ride over our heads". Dr Cohen calls it, "A picture of wounded men lying helpless on the ground while horsemen ride pitilessly over them". They had indeed known such national humiliation. It was as if they had passed through fire and water, an almost universal symbolism for dangers of all kinds. But still, He had brought them into abundance, into wealth (7310) which was like a cup full and running over. Had He not promised them a land flowing with milk and honey? He brought them into it as He had promised. It was "a good land, a land of brooks of water, of fountains and depths that spring out of valleys and hills; A land of wheat, and barley, and vines, and fig trees, and pomegranates; a land of oil olive, and honey; A land wherein thou shalt eat bread without scarceness, thou shalt not lack anything in it; a land whose stones are iron, and out of whose hills thou mayest dig brass…then shalt thou bless the Lord thy God for the good land which he hath given thee (Deut 8.7-10). O what God had done for His people! Men ought to observe this, remember this, and praise Him accordingly.

Verses 13-15: The Psalmist's Personal Praise

From this point the Psalmist speaks in the first person singular. There can be no doubt that he is now offering his own personal appreciation and thanksgiving, but some think, however, that he is speaking as a representative Israelite and that his language is really that of the nation. Perhaps both things are true. In the three verses of this stanza he mentions burnt offerings twice and the reference to vows may be an allusion to the peace offering (Lev 7.16). He speaks of rams, bullocks, and goats. As Davison remarks, "It seems hardly necessary to examine the details of Levitical ritual in order to determine the exact significance of the various sacrifices mentioned here. 'Fatlings,' 'rams,' 'goats,' 'bullocks' are mentioned generally and poetically as in Psalm 50 and Isaiah 1, and in their accumulation the clauses are intended to express ample and abundant oblation".

In some earlier distress the Psalmist had made vows. Now he would fulfil his promises and come into the house of God with his offerings. As noticed in the introduction above, the "house of God" was descriptive of the tabernacle and the tent-dwelling of the Ark before the great temple was built by Solomon. To that house and that sanctuary the Psalmist would approach with suitable sacrifices. The "incense of rams" means the fuming smoke rising from the altar, the odour of the burning sacrifice, the sweet savour. The believer today enters the sanctuary, the holiest, beyond the veil, where the Saviour sits exalted. He comes to worship, not with bullocks and goats, but with his appreciation of the once-for-all sacrifice of Christ, of which those earlier offerings were but a faint foreshadowing. Well might all the godly join to say, "Selah!".

Verses 16-20: Come and Hear!

It is the joy and privilege of every saint to testify to what God has done for him, and to rejoice to hear of God's dealings with others. "Come and hear", the Psalmist now invites, "and I will declare what he hath done for my soul". His life had been in peril. God had delivered him and now he would recount what God had done. Notice how, in his former distress he had mingled praise with his prayers. "I cried unto him with my mouth, and he was extolled with my tongue". From the same lips had come the cry of a soul in trouble, and the praise of one who trusted God for deliverance. He had prayed and praised with a consciousness of his innocence. He knew that it was a principle with God that if he regarded iniquity in his heart the Lord would not hear. To fondly contemplate evil in the heart while presuming to pray and praise was not acceptable with God. "But verily", God had heard him. This was confirmation of his integrity and vindication of his righteousness and this in itself was a cause for rejoicing.

As the Psalm closes, the Psalmist again, for the second time in the Psalm, uses the word "Blessed" (1288). It is the word of v.8, signifying to salute, to praise, to kneel before in worship. "Blessed be God!" It is a personal ascription of praise, thanksgiving that God had not turned away from him in his need, but had showed His mercy, His loving-kindness, to His servant. So concludes a Psalm which sings the praise of the nation, and the praise of the Psalmist himself. Whether national or personal, collective or individual, there is always reason to bless Him who ever cares for His people.

PSALM 67

Introduction

This short Psalm is committed to the care of the Chief Musician with certain instructions regarding its accompaniment. The word "Neginoth" (5058) which appears in the title is to be found in the titles of six Psalms, of which this is the fifth. See Psalms 4, 6, 54, 55 and 76. The word means "stringed instruments", and is so translated by the RV and JND. It indicates the desired musical instruments which are to be used as an accompaniment for the Psalm, these in preference to "Nehiloth", which signifies wind instruments such as flutes. However, when the word "Song" appears in the title also, as in Psalms 65, 66 and 68, this means that the Psalm may be rendered either with an accompaniment or with the voice only.

No name appears in the title. The Psalmist is not identified, but, as Spurgeon remarks, "No author's name is given, but he would be a bold man who should attempt to prove that David did not write it". The Psalm is a delightful blending of petition and praise, and seems to have been intended as a song of thanksgiving at some temple festival, such as the Feast of Tabernacles. There are indications that it celebrates a bountiful harvest, a token of divine blessing upon Israel and a testimony to the surrounding nations of the goodness and mercy of God.

The seven short verses hardly lend themselves to any division, nor do they require it, but it might be observed that the first three verses, like the last three, each have two thoughts, whereas the central verse 4 has three, and is a kind of pivotal verse in the Psalm. F.W. Grant comments that this verse is "the hinge upon which all turns, which is the reign of God upon earth". Notice also that the refrain with which the first three verses end is the refrain with which the last three commence. The central verse then, is enclosed between the two occurrences of this lovely chorus.

Verses 1-3: Israel and the Nations

The opening words of the Psalm are an echo of the well known priestly blessing of Numbers 6.24-26, "The Lord bless thee, and keep thee: The Lord make his face shine upon thee, and be gracious unto thee: The Lord lift up his countenance upon thee, and give thee peace". There is this difference, that in the Psalm, Elohim is used instead of Jehovah. The mercy for which the Psalmist asks might be equally, or even more appropriately, rendered "grace". Indeed the word "merciful" (2603) of v.1 in the AV, is exactly the same word as that translated "gracious" in Numbers 6.25, quoted above. The Psalmist asks, using the plural pronoun "us", and so speaking for the nation, that God might look upon them graciously, with pity, and show them favour. If God would "bless"(1288) them, this signified a divine acknowledgement of them, God speaking well and approvingly of them. When men bless God, as in Psalm 66.8, then this is the least men can do, considering the greatness and the character of God, but when God blesses men then this is grace indeed. The petition that God might cause His face to shine upon them, or toward them, is just a longing for the smile of God, a desire to be ever living in the light of His countenance.

It is not usual to find a "Selah" so early in a Psalm, but here, at the close of the first verse, it seems a fitting moment to pause and reflect. Such noble aspirations have been expressed, such holy requests have been presented, that already it is time to lift up the heart in silent but sincere meditation.

It is good to notice that the desires of the nation are not entirely selfish. The blessing of others is in view also. If the blessing of God would but fall upon Israel, then would not the nations around see the way of God with His own people and be moved to enquire after Him? Would not the prosperity of Israel be a testimony to all other peoples? The power of testimony is great. The same principle might be observed in our Lord's words to that man whom He had delivered from demon possession, "Go home to thy friends, and tell them how great things the Lord hath done for thee, and hath had compassion on thee (Mk 5.19). In the same story and context an illustration might be found of the expression "saving health" (3444). This is but one word, and it is, more than sixty times, rendered "salvation" in the AV. It may, however, be translated "health" or "welfare", and for this reason the translators have preferred "saving health". This is so evident in the salvation of the man from the tombs in Mark 5.

So now, in a beautiful refrain which is repeated in v.5, the Psalmist's vision goes beyond Israel to the peoples, the nations around. He desires the conversion of the heathen, that from them also there might be praise for the God of Israel. "Let the people(s) (5971) praise thee". The repetition of the clause then creates emphasis, as does the addition of the little word "all", and the heart-cry "O God" between the clauses. "Let the peoples praise thee, O God; let all the peoples praise thee" (JND and RV). Spurgeon's remark is characteristically quaint, but apt and beautiful. He says, "May every man bring his music, every citizen his canticle, every peasant his praise, every prince his psalm".

Verse 4: Millennial Joy

This central, pivotal verse in the Psalm anticipates the coming kingdom. This is expounded more fully in Psalm 72, in Isaiah 11, in other Scriptures of the prophets, and by John in the Revelation. One day the cry will resound through earth and heaven, "The kingdoms of this world are become the kingdoms of our Lord and of his Christ" (Rev 11.15). Monarchies and democracies have failed. Republics and dictatorships have not succeeded either. The millennial kingdom will be a theocracy, and men shall enjoy peace and prosperity, safety and security, when the Lord reigns.

Note the gladness, the singing, and the joy of the nations in this refrain. "O let it be", the Psalmist is praying. God will rule the nations righteously, and not as men have done. He will govern (5148) them, leading and guiding them as a shepherd leads his flock. He who has been the "Shepherd of Israel" (Ps 80.1) will then shepherd the nations with resultant peace and plenty. He who led Israel through the wilderness to the land of promise (Ps 78.14), will lead the nations through their wilderness of corrupt and fallen governments to the glory of His kingdom. Well did the Lord Jesus teach His disciples to pray, "Thy kingdom come" (Mt 6.10), and well does the Psalmist say again, "Selah". Pause; meditate; reflect; lift up the heart.

Verses 5-7: Concluding Thanksgiving

As has already been observed, the refrain of v.5 is a repetition of the same refrain of v.3. This is not vain repetition however. It is the expression of a heart that can scarcely contain its emotions. The Psalmist has yearned for this, that the nations should join in praise of God, and out of the fullness of those feelings he repeats his prayer, "Let the peoples...all the peoples, praise thee".

Although the word "Then", with which v.6 begins, is in italics, having been supplied by the translators, it seems to suit the context. In that coming kingdom, when all nations bow to the divine Sovereign and render due homage and praise, then shall the earth yield her increase. A faithful people will be rewarded with a fruitful earth. But Dr Cohen points out that some commentators reject the thought of a literal harvest here, suggesting rather that the fact of "all nations praising God for His moral government of the world is the highest 'product' of the whole of life on earth". In support of this interpretation he quotes Psalm 85.11, where "truth shall spring out of the earth" is viewed as the land yielding her increase. Whichever thought is accepted, the bliss and the glory of the kingdom remain.

"God, even our own God, shall bless us", the Psalmist concludes, and then he repeats, as if loathe to end his meditation, "God shall bless us!". Yet again his thoughts are projected beyond Israel and he says, "And all the ends of the earth shall fear him".

So, in this short Psalm the large heart of the Psalmist embraces all men everywhere. Blessing for Israel means blessing for all. Blest anticipation indeed, that one day both the chosen nation and all nations will rejoice in the benign reign of Israel's Messiah. Then the cry will be, "The Lord reigneth" (Ps 93.1). So, in the same anticipation, the saints love to sing -

Jesus shall reign where'er the sun
Doth his successive journeys run;
His kingdom stretch from shore to shore,
Till moons shall wax and wane no more.
Isaac Watts

PSALM 68

Introduction

The title is very similar to the titles of Psalms 65 and 66. It is a Psalm of David for the Chief Musician and it is also a song, so that it may be sung with or without an accompaniment. It is the ninth of sixteen Messianic Psalms, following Psalms 2, 8, 16, 22, 24, 40, 41 and 45. This does not mean that the Psalm is wholly Messianic but, since Paul quotes from it in Ephesians 4.8 with reference to Christ, this entitles it to a place among the other Messianic Psalms.

It has been said that Psalm 68 has more than its share of textual difficulties, and that this is caused, at least in part, by the fact that it contains many words which are not found elsewhere and whose meaning is therefore not always certain. Delitzsch remarks that "the language is so bold and so peculiarly its own, that we meet with no less than thirteen words that do not occur anywhere else".

There are other problems too. Dr Cohen says "While commentators agree in judging this Psalm one of the most magnificent of all in its forceful sweep of thought and language, they are in hopeless disagreement on the date of its composition". The dates assigned to it by the critics spread over more than a thousand years! Accepting that it is indeed a Psalm of David, as the title states, the exact circumstances of its composition are still uncertain. It may have reference to some of David's many triumphs over his enemies, or, as some think, it may have been used on the occasion of the removal of the Ark of the Covenant to Zion from the house of Obed-edom. Davison's comment is that, in spite of the difficulties and disagreements, "The Psalm stands as a monument of the invincible faith and inextinguishable hopes of Israel, and a prophecy of spiritual glories in part realised, in part yet to come". It has been used in the past as an inspiring battle hymn by Crusaders, Covenanters, and Huguenots.

One majestic feature of the Psalm is the grand array of divine names and titles which the Psalmist employs. Delitzsch remarks that "the whole cornucopia of Divine names has been poured out upon this Psalm". These will be noticed in the commentary but it might be interesting to mention here that Elohim occurs twenty-six times, while Adonai, Jehovah, Jah, Shaddai, and El, with certain combinations of these, are also to be found.

For the purpose of an orderly meditation the Psalm may be divided into six parts. Verses 1-6 are a rousing introduction in which God appears as the victorious Leader of His people, scattering His enemies and riding triumphantly upon the heavens. Verses 7-18 recount the wonders of the Exodus, the march through the wilderness, and the mighty acts which God wrought for the redeemed people so that eventually He might dwell among them. Verses 19-23 sing of God's goodness and daily care for His people. Verses 24-27 describe a festal procession to the temple, a picture of the glory of Jehovah the conqueror. Verses 28-31 anticipate that day when all kings and kingdoms, princes and peoples, will pay homage to the God of Israel. The closing verses, 32-35, call upon peoples everywhere to ascribe glory to Him. There are three "Selahs", at verses 7, 19 and 32, and the Psalm concludes with a fitting, "Blessed be God".

Verses 1-6: Let God Arise!

The opening words of the Psalm are reminiscent, if not an exact quotation, of the words of Moses in Numbers 10.35. "And it came to pass, when the ark set forward, that Moses said, Rise up, Lord, and let thine enemies be scattered; and let them that hate thee flee before thee". The pillar cloud moved, and with it the Ark moved too, and the cry, "Arise, O Lord", became the watchword of Israel. These first verses of the Psalm are a prayer that the nation's experience of former days might now be renewed, and that God might once again rise up to scatter His enemies. The prayer is threefold. "Let God arise…let his enemies be scattered…let them also that hate him flee". It is a prayer for the complete rout of those who are also described in a threefold way. They are, "his enemies...them also that hate him...the wicked". Such defeat of these enemies will not prove difficult to Jehovah. They will vanish like smoke before the wind. They will melt away as wax before the fire. How humiliating for the proud and arrogant enemies of God and of Israel, to be compared to wind and wax. However black and bitter and blinding the smoke may be, the wind will soon blow it away. However hard and unyielding the wax may appear to be, the fire will soon consume it. So will it be with the wicked at the presence of God.

"Let the wicked perish" the Psalmist prays. The wicked and the righteous, describes the heathen and Israel respectively, and there now follows another three-fold prayer. "Let the righteous be glad...let them rejoice...let them exceedingly rejoice". The joy of the righteous is emphasised with this, "Yea...exceedingly".

Joy must be expressed, and what better way than in song? The Psalmist calls for singing. "Sing unto God", he exhorts. This is again reminiscent of the Exodus, when, on the banks of the Red Sea, "Then sang Moses and the children of Israel this song unto the Lord" (Ex 15.1). Notice the correspondence of, "Unto God" - "Unto the Lord". True praise must be rendered "unto Him", praises to His name.

The word "extol" (5549) may well be understood in the usual accepted meaning of that word, but JND and RV render it, "Cast up a (high) way for him", and Strong, with many commentators, agrees that this is a possible translation. Davison, preferring "Cast up a high way", comments that "An Oriental monarch on his journeys needs such road-makers or road-menders to go before him". It is a reminder of John Baptist's ministry and his call to the people, as prophesied by Isaiah the prophet, "The voice of him that crieth in the wilderness, Prepare ye the way of the Lord, make straight in the desert a highway for our God" (Is 40.3; Mt 3.3). The phrase, "rideth upon the heavens", as in the AV, is also changed by RV and JND to read, "rideth through/in the deserts". Dr Gill concurs with this, and Spurgeon renders it, "marches through the wilderness". The explanation for the variation is this, that, while the word translated here as "heavens"(6160) in the AV does basically mean "desert, wilderness, or plain", the fine dust of those arid places is used also in Hebrew for the thin layers of cloud in the sky, and therefore of the heavens themselves. The translation "wilderness" or "desert", however, is more in keeping with the context, and is another allusion to the Exodus and to the journey that followed.

The Psalmist now introduces, in v.4, that majestic title of God, "JAH" (3050). This is a contracted, poetical form of "Jehovah". The abbreviation, however, must not be understood as a diminution, but rather as an intensification of the awful incomprehensible name. "JAH", in this transliterated form, is found only here in the AV, but it is sometimes rendered "Lord", as in Isaiah 26.4 where "The Lord Jehovah" is "Jah Jehovah". Compare also the ending of the well-known "Hallelu-*jah*". "Rejoice before Him", the Psalmist exclaims, "exult, triumph".

Although He is incomprehensibly great and glorious, yet this God of the heavens deigns to be a father of the fatherless and a judge of the widows. From the heights of His holy habitation He regards the helplessness of orphans and widows and stoops to protect them. Before the Psalter closes it will again be remembered that Jehovah "relieveth the fatherless and widow" (Ps 146.9). There now follows yet another allusion to the Exodus. Did the slavery of Egypt disturb the family life of the Hebrews? God brought them out of loneliness and solitude and set them in families again to enjoy together the affection of mothers and fathers, parents and children. Were they prisoners in that house of bondage? God was their great Redeemer and Emancipator, releasing them from their chains and servitude. The rebellious He left to dwell in a barren land, parched and devastated by the plagues.

Verses 7-18: The March to Freedom

The remembrance of the great Exodus at once demands a "Selah". Every Hebrew heart would swell with praise at the thought of what God had done in those days. As Dr Cohen comments, "The exodus from Egypt and conquest of Canaan are the roots from which the tree of Israel's history grew, and naturally provide the beginnings of the survey wherein God's dealings with His people are signally revealed". Verses 7 and 8 are a quotation from the song of Deborah in Judges 5, with but a few variations, like the change from Jehovah to Elohim. Shepherd of Israel that He was, God went before them. He led them out and led them on in the great march of the redeemed through the wilderness. "Selah!" Pause and praise; meditate and muse; remember and rejoice. Lift up the heart in gratitude. "Selah!"

The earth trembled in those momentous days. The heavens dropped rain. "The clouds poured out water...The voice of thy thunder was in the heaven: the lightnings lightened the world: the earth trembled and shook" (Ps 77.17-18). Yon Sinai itself was moved at the presence of the God of Israel (Ex 19.18). God sent plentiful, bounteous rain for His people, perhaps a figurative way of describing the provision which He made for them in the wilderness. As well as giving them water, He "rained" bread from heaven for them, sending them manna (Ex 16.4). By this miraculous provision He strengthened them in the weariness of their sojourn, confirming and assuring them that they were indeed His inheritance for whom He cared. In that wilderness the great congregation dwelt for some forty years, ever provided for by the God who had brought them out. They were poor, they had been sorely afflicted in Egypt, but they were His flock, and out of His goodness He had prepared for them all that they needed for the desert journey.

When the wilderness sojourn was over, the Lord gave the word that was to bring them into the land of promise. It must have been a great host that published the tidings concerning the entry into Canaan. There is a feminine gender here, and so the RV regards the publishers of the tidings as the women, as does the lovely text of the Jewish Publication Society - "The women that proclaim the tidings are a great host". As the silver trumpet sounded the battle note, the women would help to prepare their lords for battle, and then tarry at home, waiting to divide the spoil as so graphically described in Deborah's song (Judg 5.30), while the Kings of Canaan fled. What an important part the women of Israel have played in the history of the nation. Compare the song of Miriam in Exodus 15, the song of Deborah in Judges 5, and the singing of the women from all the cities of Israel when David slew Goliath (1 Sam 18.6-7).

The difficulties of v.13 are universally acknowledged. What can this mean; "Though ye have lien among the pots" (8240)? There are several suggestions. Some retain the word "pots" as in the AV, and see a reference to the black brick kilns of Egypt. Though they had long dwelt among these, humiliated, yet now there was tranquillity and peace prepared for them in Canaan. Some point out that bricks and stones which marked boundaries and sometimes concealed rubbish were also used to support pots in the open-air cooking and baking of the Orientals. Had they, in their slavery days, lain among these? Others, however, as RV, JND and JPS, change the word "pots" to "sheepfolds", and think that there may be a remembrance of the fact that these Hebrews had been but humble shepherds, despised by their Egyptian masters. Yet again, some think that the tense should be altered, to read, "When ye lie among the sheepfolds", describing, as Dr Cohen says, "An idyllic scene of tranquillity after the conquest of Canaan had been accomplished". Whatever the interpretation of the difficult detail is, the meaning seems to be that this redeemed people were to enjoy better days ahead in the land of promise.

"Wings of a dove covered with silver, and her feathers with yellow gold". In this beautiful symbolism, the glory of the nation's blessed future is portrayed. Israel was God's turtledove (Ps 74.19; Hos 11.11). In the comfort and joy of the peaceful days which God had in mind for her, she might be compared to a dove basking in the sunshine. The changing colours, the varied hues on the plumage, are suggestive of peace and prosperity. Silver blends with shining gold as the bright, and sometimes golden, rays of the sun reflect on the feathers of the bird.

The verse which follows, v.14, is acknowledged by all to be most obscure and difficult. Maclaren confesses, "One is inclined to say with Baethgen, at the end of his comment on the words, 'After all this, I can only confess that I do not understand the verse'". Salmon (AV), or Zalmon (RV), was a dark wooded hill near Shechem, mentioned previously in Judges 9.48. The scattering of Israel's enemies by the Almighty (7706), the all-powerful Shaddai, is likened to "snow in Salmon", and there seems to be an intended contrast between the white snow and the dark hill. Alexander remarks, "The change from war to peace is likened to the dazzling whiteness of snow in the midst of blackness or darkness". Some think that this is a picture of the enemies of Israel falling defeated in the centre of the land, their corpses to be bleached white in the sun. Yet others feel that the reference is to the spoil which would be left by the routed armies of the kings. Delitzsch says, "The hostile host disperses in all directions, and Zalmon glitters, as it were with snow, from the spoil that is dropped by those who flee". Having suggested this, Delitzsch then quotes Wetzstein, who offers a different explanation, saying, "Then fell snow on Zalmon, i.e. the mountain clothed itself in a bright garment of light in celebration of this joyous event. Anyone who has been in Palestine knows how very refreshing is the spectacle of a distant mountain top capped with snow. The beauty of this poetical figure is enhanced by the fact that Zalmon, according to its etymology, signifies a mountain range dark and dusty, either from shade, forest, or black rock". Yet again, Spurgeon writes, "The word *white* appears to be imported into the text, and by leaving it out the meaning is easy. A traveller informed the writer that on a raw and gusty day, he saw the side of what he supposed to be Mount Salmon suddenly swept bare by a gust of wind, so that the snow was driven hither and thither into the air like the down of thistles or the spray of the sea: thus did the Omnipotent One scatter all the potentates that defied Israel". Perhaps there may be a measure of truth in all of these suggestions, but what can be said with certainty is that, in some way, there is a picture of triumph and victory, and the defeat of the enemy. The symbolism, no doubt, would be well understood by the people of the Psalmist's day.

The Psalmist now tells how God had chosen Mount Zion for His abode, in preference to the many other mountains of Israel. The mountain of Bashan is doubtless the majestic Mount Hermon, with its three peaks towering above all others and looking down over Bashan. It was indeed a mountain of God's creation, but He chose the humble Zion rather than Hermon in which to dwell. The Psalmist addresses the hills. "Why leap ye, ye high hills?", he asks. To "leap" (7520), is to rise in envy, to look jealously, or, as in the RV, "Why look ye askance?". The high hills of Bashan looked down on Zion, as if wondering why God had chosen it and not them. Were they not greater than Zion? But this is the way of sovereignty. God does what He wills and none has right to question what He does or what He chooses. Jehovah desired Zion for His abode and there He would dwell.

The nations of the Psalmist's day were accustomed to measure their strength by the multitude of war chariots which they possessed. "The chariots of God", he says, "are twenty thousand, even thousands of angels". This is the AV rendering, but a marginal reading, and the rendering of all other translations, with Strong, will indicate that "angels" (8136), is a word which means "repetition". It means "thousands repeated". "Even thousands upon thousands" (RV). "Thousands upon thousands" (JND). Myriads upon myriads of chariots are His! Spurgeon's comment is characteristically quaint, "It is not easy to see where our venerable translators found these 'angels', for they are not in the text; however, as it is a blessing to entertain them unawares, we are glad to meet with them in English, even though the Hebrew knows them not; and the more so because it cannot be doubted that they constitute a right noble squadron of the myriad hosts of God". The Lord (Adonai - 136) is among them in His holiness, the holiness of Sinai itself.

If, as many think, this Psalm was sung on the occasion of that triumphal procession and the entry of the Ark of the Covenant into its dwelling place behind curtains on Mount Zion, then v.18 envisages the actual ascent of the Ark to the Mount. It was set on high, thus symbolising the enthronement of God Himself in the glory of His sanctuary. The holy Ark, which had for so long been a captive of the enemies of God and of Israel, was now at rest on Zion. It is this verse, however, and Paul's employment of it in Ephesians 4.8, which makes this Psalm Messianic. Whatever may be the meaning of the text originally, prophetically it points to the triumph of Christ, who, after His ministry, His sufferings, His death and resurrection, is now exalted in the heavens. The expression, "Thou hast led captivity captive", is a quotation from the song of Deborah in Judges 5.12. The phrase is difficult of interpretation, and there are several suggestions. It is, of course, a picture of a victorious general who delivers those who have been held captive by the enemy. "Captivity" must have this sense, rather than the thought of taking the enemies prisoners. If the enemies were intended, then "captivity" would need to be rendered "captors". It is therefore not the taking of enemy prisoners which is in view, but rather, as has been stated, the recovery of those who had been the captives of the enemy. But then, who are these?

In His death, and by His death, the Lord Jesus defeated Satan and his hosts and liberated many who were held under Satan's power. This He does by the preaching of the gospel. It is a glad message of deliverance for those who have been held prisoners but who now sing, "My chains are snapt, the bonds of sin are broken, and I am free". Many think, though, that the captivity referred to is that great body of Old Testament saints who, until the death and resurrection of Christ, were confined to "sheol", in Abraham's bosom, and that these have now been led by Him in triumph to the bliss of heaven itself. Equally great expositors have, over the years, subscribed to these various interpretations. The reader must decide!

Having ascended, the risen Christ has received gifts. Is it "for men", or "among men", or "in Man"? Or are not all true? The exalted Man, Christ Jesus, has Himself received gifts which are to be distributed among men. So He has given to His saints those things which are necessary for their edification. In great grace He also extends His blessing to the rebellious. If only men will submit and surrender to Him it will be His delight, the delight of the LORD (3050) God (430), Jah Elohim, to dwell with them and among them.

Alexander Maclaren's comment on the passage is very beautiful: "That ascent of the Ark to Zion was a type rather than a prophecy. Conflict, conquest, triumphant ascent to a lofty home, tribute, widespread submission, and access for rebels to the royal presence - all these, which the Psalmist saw as facts or hopes in their earthly form, are repeated in loftier fashion in Christ".

Verses 19-23: Jehovah's Care for His People

The Psalmist has finished with his review of the past. He now dwells upon God's present care and His future deliverances of His people, and in this short section of the Psalm there is such a variety of divine names and titles. "Blessed be the Lord", he exclaims. "Lord" (136) is Adonai. It is a title of greatness, sometimes used by Hebrews instead of Jehovah. Strong says that it is a "Lord-title, spoken in place of "Yahweh" in Jewish display of reverence". In this greatness Adonai daily cares for His own. The AV, "who daily loadeth us with benefits", is very beautiful, and with this rendering JND concurs, but the RV and others render it differently, as, "who daily beareth our burden". Even though translators differ, both thoughts are true and comforting. He does indeed daily load us with good things, and likewise He carries our burdens for us. Delitzsch says, "It is the burden or pressure of the hostile world that is meant, which the Lord day by day helps His people to bear". Davison comments, "To load with benefits is gracious; to bear another's burden implies closer sympathy; but to bear and carry the heavy-laden and suffering themselves is Divine".

This God, says the Psalmist, is "the God (EL - 410) of our salvation (3444)". He is, he repeats, "Our God", and, "the God of salvation (4190). Three times he employs this title "El". It is a singular title of greatness and power, as in that name of the Saviour, "Immanu-*el*". Note that there are two different words for salvation, but the meanings are very similar, signifying deliverances, in the plural. In the midst of these ascriptions of praise, the Psalmist inserts a "Selah", as if to say that here again the people must pause, lifting up the heart in gratitude.

The issues from death, of which the Psalmist speaks in v.20, are escape from death, and the preservation of life. They belong to Him who is now called "God (3069) the Lord (136), Jehovah our Adonai. The divine hand which tenderly sustains Israel will crush the enemy. The rather strange expression "the hairy scalp" of the enemy, is apparently a reference to the long flowing hair of which Dr Cohen says, "In ancient times warriors allowed their hair to grow long under a vow not to have it cut until they returned victorious from battle". Maclaren adds that the long hair was an emblem of strength and insolence which one is almost tempted to connect with Absalom.

In v.22 the Lord (Adonai) speaks. Notice that "my people" is in italics, having been supplied by the AV translators. Most others however, omit these words, and read, "I will bring again from Bashan, I will bring them again from the depths of the sea". In keeping with the context it seems preferable to understand this as God searching out His enemies, though they hide themselves in the hills of Bashan, or even in the depths of the sea. Bashan was a frontier province of the land of Israel, but whether there, or in the ocean depths, there would be no hiding place for the enemies of God and of Israel. He would find them, and bring them back for deserved punishment. Israel would tread in their blood and the dogs would have their portion.

Verses 24-27: The Great Festal Procession

Delitzsch says of these verses, "Israel's festival of victory is regarded as a triumphal procession of God Himself". Whether, "They have seen thy goings", refers to the immediate spectators of the grand pageant, or to men in general, is not relevant. Perhaps both are true. Observe the titles of God again. "Thy goings, O God" - Elohim (430) - the Mighty One. "Even the goings of my God" - El (410) - as in vv. 19 and 20. There is again a remembrance of Miriam and her companion damsels, who, after the crossing of the Red Sea, celebrated the great deliverance of the nation with instruments and voices, with timbrels and song and dance (Ex 15.20). "Bless ye God", is the burden of the song. It is a call to the congregations that flow from "the fountain of Israel", that from the early patriarch, the source of the nation, through the entire national stream, there might arise praise to the God who delivered them. Four tribes are mentioned as taking part in the procession. They are representative of all the tribes, north and south. There is little Benjamin, born at Bethlehem (Gen 35), youngest and smallest of all the tribes, but which supplied the first king, Saul. There are the princes of Judah, regal and royal, largest and so very prominent among the tribes. There are the princes of Zebulun and Naphtali, from whose territory Messiah Himself would come (Is 9.1; Mt 4.13-16). It is indeed a great procession.

Verses 28-31: Universal Homage to God

Israel has had to learn that every victory won must be ascribed to the power of God. God (430), the mighty Elohim, had commanded the strength by which these battles were won. Appeal must be made to Him constantly therefore, "Strengthen, O God, that which thou hast wrought for us". This is a recognition, by the Psalmist and by the nation, that divine power had enabled them in the past, and that they must rely upon the same manifestations of that power for the future.

The reference to the temple, which now follows, is not initially to the temple of Solomon, though that must be envisaged. The tent which David had prepared for the Ark was as much the dwelling place of God as the later "temple magnifical" (1 Chr 22.5). Still, there may be here a prophetic anticipation of the glory of that great house which would be the wonder of the nations, and would draw the Queen of Sheba from a distant land to see for herself the truth of what she had heard.

The call to Jehovah in v.30, to rebuke the company of spearmen, is translated by RV, JND, and most others, as a call for the rebuke of "the (wild) beast of the reeds". "Company" (2416), as in the AV, is indeed rendered "beast", more than seventy times in the same AV, while the word for "spearmen" (7070) is rendered "reed(s)" almost thirty times. The beast of the reeds here is understood by many to be the hippopotamus, or, more likely, the crocodile, and appeal is made to Job 40.21. It is believed that the beast lying "in the covert of the reeds" may be a poetical reference to Egypt, Israel's avowed enemy, strong and cunning, waiting to devour. The "bulls, with the calves" may well describe the leaders of the enemy nations and their subjects. Eventually, every enemy nation will submit, all will be subdued. All will bring their silver to Israel's God, Egypt and Ethiopia alike humbled and offering their tribute. The princes of the proud and strong Egypt must yield. Ethiopia will reach out eagerly to give allegiance, but should there be those who persist in enmity, then the offering of tribute will not be acknowledged. God will trample the proffered silver underfoot contemptuously and scatter those peoples who so delight in war.

Verses 32-35: Blessed be God!

With these words the Psalm concludes, and in these closing verses there is a call to peoples everywhere to sing His praise. "Sing...ye kingdoms of the earth". Two divine titles are employed in the call for praise. "Sing unto God" (430). "Sing praises unto the Lord" (136). Whether He is known as the mighty Elohim or the sovereign Adonai, He is worthy of the praise of all people.

The "Selah" follows. How the singer and the reader should together pause in the midst of such a meditation upon divine greatness, and the heart be lifted up in due praise and worship.

God rides upon the heavens in His supremacy just as He rides upon the desert as the leader of His people in v.4. His voice has resounded throughout the earth and the heavens. His is a mighty voice, echoing in the heaven of heavens, and it is proper that men everywhere should recognise His power. When God speaks it behoves men to hear and obey. "Ascribe ye strength unto God". Let the nations acknowledge these two things, that His excellency is known in Israel and His power in the skies. Both in earth and in heaven He is majestic, the Ruler supreme.

The final note affirms yet again His greatness. He is an awe-inspiring God whose strength has gone out from His dwelling place for the strengthening of His people Israel. He is, after all, the God of Israel and He has wrought on their behalf.

In the wonder of it all the Psalmist can only exclaim, "Blessed be God!". It is fitting that such a Psalm should end on such a high note as this. If words fail and human language is exhausted, then "Blessed be God" seems a noble tribute indeed.

PSALM 69

Introduction

Here is yet another Psalm committed to the charge and care of the Chief Musician. Like Psalms 45, 60 (in the singular) and 80, the title bears the word "Shoshannim". For comment on this refer to the introduction to Psalm 45. The word means "Lilies", a symbol of tenderness, purity, beauty, and glory. See our Lord's own reference to the glory of the lilies in Matthew 6.28. It is said that the lilies often bloomed in marsh and mire, and frequently among thorns and briers (Song 2.2). Perhaps the glory aspect may be seen in Psalm 45, while here, in Psalm 69, the emphasis is on the thorny environment in which they grew. They were also associated with the springtime, and therefore with the Passover. So they would appear to be reminders both of suffering and of glory. "Upon Shoshannim" may have indicated some particular melody, or possibly, though not probably, a lily-shaped musical instrument, but the original meaning is not clear.

Although some critics, even the respected Maclaren, dispute the Davidic authorship, as stated in the title, nevertheless the majority of conservative expositors have no difficulty in seeing both David and the Son of David in the Psalm. For many readers, Romans 11.9 will be an end of the matter, and even Delitzsch has to admit, at the end of his commentary on the Psalm, "Considering the relation of the New Testament to this Psalm, we hold fast to the Inscription, (A Psalm) of David". It might be noted that those critics who deny the Davidic authorship cannot agree upon a satisfactory alternative.

The Psalm has been called by W.T. Davison, "Prayer of the Suffering Servant of God". Dr Cohen entitles it, "Prayer of the Persecuted". Spurgeon calls it, "The Psalm of the Trespass Offering", as does T.E. Wilson. In all of these suggestions it is evident that the burden of the Psalm is suffering. "Reproach" is mentioned six times and may be regarded as a key-word in the Psalm.

Psalm 69 is quoted several times in the NT with reference to the Messiah, and it is indeed quoted by Christ Himself. These quotations will be noted in the commentary and they confirm that the Psalm is truly Messianic. This does not mean that everything in it can be related to the Messiah. There are confessions of sin in the Psalm which are the personal confessions of the writer, and there are calls for the destruction of his enemies, which things obviously have nothing to do with the impeccable Christ.

The Psalm may be divided into six parts. In the opening verses, 1-4, the Psalmist spreads out his complaint before God. In verses 5-12 he argues that his sufferings have come to him because of his zeal for God. In verses 13-18 he cries for deliverance from his troubles. In verses 19-21 he repeats the story of his sufferings, and there follows, in verses 22-28, a call for the punishment of his persecutors. In the closing stanza, verses 29-36, he anticipates divine intervention and God's blessing, both for himself and for the nation.

Verses 1-4: The Suffering Servant

The contrast between the opening words of Psalm 69 and the closing joyful words of Psalm 68 is quite remarkable. "Blessed be God", the preceding Psalm had concluded. "Save me, O God", this Psalm begins. The Psalmist is overwhelmed by his sorrows. He feels as though he is sinking, drowning, in a sea of troubles. He speaks of waters, deep waters, floods, and deep mire. The word "deep" occurring twice, is a translation of two words, different, though similar in meaning, the second being a plural word, rendered by JND, "the depths of waters". In his weariness he cries until his throat is parched and his eyes fail with weeping while he waits for an answer from God. He feels exhausted physically by his much praying.

His grief is intensified by the knowledge that his enemies hated him gratuitously, without a cause. There was no reason whatever for their hostility towards him. It was all wrong. They were many too, these enemies, and they were mighty. How true was all this of the Lord Jesus (Jn 15.25). Why should they hate Him? There was no reason. He had moved among them in a gracious ministry of preaching, teaching, and healing, yet they hated Him. Pharisees and Sadducees, priests and people, scribes and soldiers, they all rejected Him. Then, by the sacrifice of Himself, He restored that which He took not away. In the law of the guilt offerings a man was required to restore that which he had acquired unlawfully, whether by deceit or fraud or by deliberate theft (Lev 5.1-6.7). This was understandable, this restoration of stolen property, but the Saviour, in the great fulfilment of these offerings, restored that which He took not away. Man had, by his sin, robbed both God and his neighbour. Jesus, by His vicarious death, restored honour to God and happiness to men.

Verses 5-12: Zeal for God; Reproach from Men

The confession of foolishness and sin which is now expressed in v.5 is David's alone. It can have nothing to do with Him who was impeccably sinless. The blessed Lord Jesus had no ability to sin. The Psalmist knows how to confess, and he knows, too, the folly of attempting to hide sin, as Adam once did. Yet he is probably taking comfort from the fact that God alone knows the whole story of his life, with its shortcomings and failings. "O God, thou knowest", he exclaims. These enemies who hated him without a cause were ignorant of all the facts. God knew, and to God he would appeal and confess.

Notice how he employs the majestic titles of God in his appeal. "Lord (136) GOD (3069) of hosts". "O God (430) of Israel". Adonai Jehovah of hosts. O Elohim of Israel. The intelligent use of these titles was the Psalmist's appeal to the sovereignty, the supremacy, and the power of his

God, as well as His relationship with Israel. There was One infinitely greater than his enemies. He desires that the faithful among the people of God should not be confused or humiliated because of him or what was happening to him. The reproach that he was suffering was due to his zeal for God, and in language quoted in reference to Messiah in John 2.17 he says, "The zeal of thine house hath eaten me up". The reproach which he was bearing came from men who had little or no regard for God, and, as they scoffed at the things of God, so they despised His servant also.

Even the Psalmist's closest friends and family apparently could not understand, and this was sadly true also in the life and ministry of Jesus. "For neither did his brethren believe in him" (Jn 7.5). "They said, He is beside himself" (Mk 3.21). The Psalmist had become estranged to his brethren and to his mother's children. His mother's children were perhaps closer than his brethren for they were from the womb of the same mother whereas those whom he describes as "his brethren", were only sons of the same father, or even more distant. As Dr Cohen remarks, "Common motherhood was the strongest of blood ties". But if all this was true of the Psalmist, and if his face was covered in shame, nevertheless he could say, "For thy sake I have borne reproach". If his zeal for God had occasioned it, then in his love for God he could bear it. These enemies of his despised his tears and his fasting. His humiliation was like a garment of sackcloth on him and they derided him for it. They poured scorn on those exercises which were evidences of his sincerity and godliness.

"They that sit in the gate", who spoke against him, have been variously interpreted. The gate was the place where local magistrates often held court. These may be intended in contrast with the drunkards, as if to say that from the expected dignity of the judges to the ribaldry of the singing drunkards, all, alike, despised and scorned him. The gate, however, was also the common gathering place, where men assembled daily in the shade of the city wall, both to do business and to gossip (see Ruth 4.1-2; Lam 5.14). Whichever is understood, the meaning is clear enough, that men of all kinds joined in the slander of this man who lived for God.

Verses 13-18: A Cry for Deliverance

"But as for me". The Psalmist will gladly, and instinctively, turn away from men and cry to God. It was a right and acceptable time to appeal to his God. It is like that word of the NT; "Grace to help in time of need" (Heb 4.16). "Grace for seasonable help" (JND). God's mercies are a multitude. His compassions are abundant. He is ever responsive to the cries of His children in need. "Hear me (6030)", the Psalmist prays. "Answer me". A divine answer to his prayer would be in accordance with the truth of God's salvation. It would be a demonstration of both the faithfulness and the power of God. Earlier in the Psalm he had spoken of the mire, and he does so again, and, although the words are different (3121 and 2916 respectively), the meanings are similar. It is miry clay and mud, and once again the Psalmist feels as though he is sinking, overwhelmed by the reproaches which are being poured upon him. How graphically he describes his feelings. His sorrows were as deep waters; miry clay; overflowing floods; depths that would swallow him up; the pit that would shut its mouth upon him. To be buried in a pit with the only opening now closed would be a fearful plight. Again he cries, "Hear me, O Lord". "Answer me". Again he appeals to that lovingkindness and to the multitude of tender mercies, to which he has already referred.

His prayers, "Turn unto me", and, "Hide not thy face", are complementary prayers. Note that the petitions of vv. 16-18 are sevenfold. He cries -

"Hear me, O Lord"
"Turn unto me"
"Hide not thy face"
"Hear me speedily"
"Draw nigh unto my soul"
"Redeem it"
"Deliver me".

These petitions are based upon three pleas. First, God is good, kind, and merciful. Second, the Psalmist is God's servant. Third, the enemies, the adversaries, would rejoice, and would renew their reproach of him, if Jehovah did not answer,

Verses 19-21: The Story Repeated

In these three verses the Psalmist rehearses again the story of his woes. My reproach! My shame! My dishonour! Mine adversaries! He tells of his broken heart and his heaviness, his yearning for pity and for comfort. But, humanly speaking, there was none to help. Rather, as is often said, they added insult to injury, adding salt to the wound, probably treating his sorrow with mockery which he likens to "gall" (7219) and "vinegar" (2558). Gall was a bitter and poisonous plant. Vinegar was a sour, unwholesome wine. Every believer will be familiar with the application of these words to the suffering Saviour in Matthew 27.34 and John 19.28ff. Between the, "I thirst", and the, "It is finished", of the Saviour's last moments on the cross, these verses were fulfilled. They were fulfilled literally as the soldier filled a sponge with the sour wine and offered it to Him. They were also fulfilled as symbols of contempt and mockery, gall and vinegar. There was indeed a little company of women with John at His cross, who must have looked lovingly and with pity upon Him in His suffering, but from Israel at large and from the Roman soldiers, there was none to pity, none to help. The mockery and the insults continued until the end, like vinegar and bitter gall.

Verses 22-28: Punish the Persecutors!

How different are the sentiments which follow, from that gentle, "Father, forgive them; for they know not what they do", of Calvary. Yet, in God's judicial dealings with the nation which crucified Messiah, these verses are fulfilled, according to Paul's quotation of them in Romans 11.9. The Saviour Himself also predicted the desolation of v.25 when He lamented over Jerusalem in Matthew 23.38. As Alexander comments, "The general doctrine of providential retribution, far from being confined to the Old Testament, is distinctly taught in many of our Saviour's parables. See Mt 21.41, 22.7, 24.51". The "table" referred to is symbolic of prosperity and plenty, perhaps also of peace and security, implying the genial company of guests enjoying hospitality. Did they give the Psalmist gall for his meat and vinegar to drink? May they be recompensed, he prays, may they be entrapped by treachery at their own table, may they be ensnared by the unhallowed enjoyment of the very welfare which they take for granted as they despise others.

The solemn imprecations continue. He prays that they might tremble in the blindness of their unbelief and cruel treatment of him, that divine indignation might be poured upon them and the fierce anger of God take hold of them. In sharp and solemn contrast to the earlier circumstances when the jovial conversation and company of guests filled their houses, the Psalmist prays that their habitations might become desolate. "Let none dwell in their tents", may indeed imply also the ruin of their family life. As Kirkpatrick remarks, "To the Oriental no prospect was more terrible than that of the complete extermination of his family".

That these men should so persecute one who is being disciplined by God was especially callous and cruel. A man being smitten, wounded by God in divine chastisement, has suffering enough, but to add to that man's suffering by persecution of him and by vindictive gossip about him is insensitive in the extreme. Dr Cohen writes, "The heinousness of their conduct is pointed out in this verse...they vented their malice upon one whom He was chastening, and selected as the victim of their savagery a man who could not defend himself because he was under God's displeasure. They discuss those who are so smitten by God to single them out as objects of their vindictiveness"

The prayer which follows, that iniquity might be added to their iniquity, seems to suggest that these wicked men might be permitted to go on in their chosen evil course, eventually receiving just recompense for the accumulation of their sin, and being excluded from any share in the righteousness of God. It is the principle of Romans 1.27, of righteous retribution. Sin is the punishment of sin, men receiving in themselves the recompense of their error. A man must choose either sin or righteousness. If he chooses sin, then he may continue in sin, and so be barred from the enjoyment of divine righteousness. To quote Spurgeon -

"He that will not when he may,
When he would he shall have nay".

The prayer that they should be blotted out of the book of the living is admirably explained by Richard Warner, quoted by Spurgeon. He writes,

"This verse alludes to the ancient Jewish practice of recording the names of the inhabitants of every division, or tribe, of the people, in a volume somewhat similar to the *Dom-boc* of the Saxons. See Luke 2.1. The names of those who died were blotted out, or *wiped* out, and appeared no longer on the list of the living. Such a book is attributed to God in Psalm 139.16, and the *blotting out of Moses from God's book*, in Exodus 32.32, is a figurative expression for depriving him of life". Such is the Psalmist's desire regarding these evil men who persecute him – that their names may not be listed with the righteous. It must be noted that this book of the living has no connection whatever with the Lamb's book of life of Revelation 21.27, from which no name will, or can, ever be erased.

Now he will pray for himself. He is poor and afflicted and in pain. He is sorrowful and sad. For his enemies he asks destruction, for himself salvation. He appeals to the mighty Elohim, "Set me up on high". It is a desire to be placed beyond the reach of danger. What he pleads for himself is in complete and absolute contrast with what he prays for his adversaries.

Verses 29-36: Thanksgiving for Divine Intervention and Blessing

The plaintive theme of the earlier verses now gives place to a happy anticipation of divine blessing. As in many other Psalms, the sob will now give way to a song and the persecuted will praise. With praise, singing and thanksgiving, God will be magnified. To magnify (1431) is "to promote the greatness of", and this the Psalmist will now do in his thanksgiving. Of course Jehovah had asked for animal sacrifices. He had required bullocks with horns and hoofs, marks of maturity and ceremonial cleanness, and the Psalmist is not at all demeaning such offerings. But these could be offered mechanically and coldly, without the gratitude of a full heart. True devotion was better. Worship from a heart overflowing with praise of Him would please Him more than ritual offerings.

With a glad assurance the Psalmist anticipates a time of future blessing. The humble, the meek and lowly, would see this. The adversaries in their arrogance would see none of it, but the humble poor would rejoice and their sad hearts would be revived. For the third time in the Psalm the great name Jehovah is now employed. It is Jehovah who is pleased with the thanksgivings of His people in v.31. It is Jehovah who takes notice of the poor and needy in v.33. It is, too, a privilege to be a prisoner of the Lord. It is a willing bondage, to be a servant of God. If such may be insignificant in the world, and even held in contempt among men, what does that matter when they have the appreciation of a God who acknowledges their service?

The Psalm now concludes with a call for universal praise. The heavens, the earth, the seas, and all that inhabit them are summoned to praise Him. Praise Him, for He will deliver Zion. He will restore and rebuild the cities of Judah. How often has Israel been scattered and her cities razed, but her ultimate blessing is assured. The posterity of the faithful will inherit the land, and they that love His name shall dwell safely in the land which He has promised to them, and secured for them.

PSALM 70

Introduction

As has been pointed out earlier in this Commentary, Psalm 70 is a reproduction, with a few modifications, of the last five verses of Psalm 40. These verses may have been detached for liturgical reasons, to be used as a separate Psalm in temple worship. The Psalm belongs to David, who initially penned Psalm 40 and then prepared this excerpt from it, modified to suit the occasion. It is the second Psalm which is a repetition of another, Psalm 53 being a reproduction of Psalm 14.

As indicated in the title, the Psalm is intended for that collection belonging to the Chief Musician, and it also carries the interesting clause in the title, "to bring to remembrance". This phrase appears also in the title of Psalm 38 and has been variously understood. Some think that David, feeling alone and forsaken, is pleading for divine remembrance, longing that he might not be forgotten of God. Others think that he is simply engaged in personal reminiscences. Dr Cohen however, with Davison, has a more specific view of it. He writes, "*To make memorial*. Hebrew *lehazkir*, again in the heading of Psalm 38...The word is best understood in a technical sense. In connection with the meal offering the priest was commanded to make *the memorial part* (azkarah) *thereof smoke upon the altar* (Lev 2.2); it is therefore possible that the term implies that the Psalm was chanted while that part of the sacrificial act took place. That it indicates a type of Temple-chanting is to be concluded from the statement: *And he appointed certain of the Levites to minister before the ark of the LORD, and to celebrate* (lehazkir) *and to thank and praise the LORD* (1 Chr 16.4)".

The short Psalm is a cry for help, appropriately placed in the Psalter. As Spurgeon says, "It is a fit pendant to Psalm 69, and a suitable preface to Psalm 71". For a detailed consideration of its five verses refer to the remarks in this Commentary on Psalm 40.13-17. Here will be noted those variations from that Psalm.

Verses 1-5: My Help and My Deliverer!

The corresponding verses in Psalm 40 commence "Be pleased, O LORD, to deliver me", but there is an urgency introduced in the opening words of Psalm 70. However, the first "Make haste" is not in the Hebrew, but has been supplied by the translators as an early repetition of the "make haste" of the second line. The double appeal for help and deliverance is, in Psalm

40, directed to Jehovah, but here in Psalm 70 the name Jehovah is changed to Elohim in the first phrase, but retained as Jehovah in the second.

In Psalm 40.15 David prays regarding his enemies, "Let them be desolate". Here in Psalm 70.3 it is "Let them be turned back". The prayer is for a routing of those enemies who, in contempt, have said, "Aha, Aha". Some have noted that the words, "unto me", of Psalm 40.15 are omitted here, and suggest that this is to adapt the Psalm from personal to national, liturgical use. However, the same words "unto me" are included in v.5 of Psalm 70, together with the personal pronouns "I" and "my", which seems rather to invalidate this suggestion, unless implying the nation personified.

In Psalm 70.4 the Jehovah title of Psalm 40 is again changed to Elohim, but in the last line of the Psalm the usual pattern is reversed and Elohim of Psalm 40 is now changed to Jehovah. The reason for these interchanges of divine titles is difficult to determine. Might it simply be for an inspired beauty and variety in the Psalm?

PSALM 71

Introduction

"The Prayer of an Aged Saint", says Davison. "Prayer in Old Age", says Dr Cohen. "The Prayer of the Aged Believer", says Spurgeon. All are agreed that here is a Psalm from the pen of an old man who has had many trials and troubles, who is now "old and grayheaded" and in failing strength (vv. 9, 18), but whose confidence is still in his God, and who can still talk about rejoicing. What an example!

In the Hebrew the Psalm has no title, but in the LXX it has the inscription, "By David, of the sons of Jonadab, and of those who were first carried captive". If this title of the LXX is accepted then it seems to indicate that the Psalm is indeed David's, adapted by the Rechabites who were descended from Jonadab (Jer 35), and used also by those Jews who were carried captive into Babylon. In spite of many suggested hypotheses from a variety of expositors, there appears to be nothing in the Psalm which would preclude Davidic authorship.

The twenty-four verses are in the nature of a mosaic, making an orderly division somewhat difficult, but they may, however, be approached as follows. In the first four verses there is a now familiar cry for help. Verses 5-8 are a testimony to what God has done, and has been, in the past. Verses 9-13 are again a cry for help and a prayer for the confounding of the Psalmist's enemies. In verses 14-16 he reaffirms his hope and expectation that God will deliver him. In verses 17-21 he again recalls God's dealings with him from youth into old age, and in the closing verses, 22-24, he promises suitable praise for divine aid in his trials.

Verses 1-4: Deliver Me! Hear Me! Save Me!

This three-fold prayer of the second verse of the Psalm is prefaced by a cry to Jehovah. The Psalmist's trust is in the LORD (3068). He employs the great name of the eternal, ever-existing, self-sufficient Jehovah, and affirms immediately in the Psalm that his trust (2620) is there. There alone can he find the refuge, the protection, which he needs. "In Thee", he says, "let me never be ashamed in this, or put to confusion". He appeals also to the righteousness of God, indicating that he has a clear conscience and can, without reservation, cast himself upon this attribute of God. Only a man with nothing to hide could so invoke the righteousness of God for his deliverance. He prays for escape, for rescue. Would Jehovah, in all His greatness, incline His ear and stoop to hear the cry of His child? "Bow down Thine ear", he cries, "and save me".

The word rendered "strong" (6697) in the AV, "my strong habitation", is, in more than sixty other places, translated "rock". This is familiar language in the Psalms, that Jehovah might be to him a strong rock dwelling place, a safe retreat from his adversaries, and one to which he might resort at all times. Jehovah, after all, commands the salvation of His people. He gives charge for their safe keeping, for He is their rock and their fortress. This word "rock" (5553) of v.3, indicates a stronghold. It is, as the Psalmist adds, a fortress, a castle to which the saints may flee from adversity. For those who choose Jehovah for their refuge He decrees their safety and security. It is as if they flee to a rock castle fortress for protection.

So, he pleads again, rescue me. Men are wicked and unrighteous, ruthless and cruel. He prays to be delivered out of their grasp, and the One to whom he appeals he calls, with pathos, "O my God".

Verses 5-8: The Lord Jehovah, My Hope, My Trust

These verses are the personal testimony of the Psalmist as to what God has been to him throughout life. He is an old man now, but from his old age he can look back and testify to God's care of him from infancy. It was He who delivered him safely out of his mother's womb, and, since birth, has sustained and kept him. Then, when he became a youth, responsible and accountable, he had consciously put his trust in Him whom he calls "O Lord (136) GOD (3069)", O Adonai Jehovah, O Sovereign Lord. It was a trusting youth who had faced Goliath in the name of the Lord. Even then, he had already defended his flock from the lion and the bear with the help of Him whom he trusted. Jehovah had never failed him and He was therefore worthy of continual praise. What a privilege it is to know God and serve Him in the difficult days of youth. Not only David, but Samuel, Josiah, Timothy, and others of a later day, might together say, "Thou art my hope…thou art my trust from my youth". The remembrance of youthful piety can be a comfort in old age. The words of the aged Polycarp, that early Christian martyr, well illustrate this thought. When he was arraigned before the Proconsul and charged to recant, to renounce Christ and worship the Emperor, he said, with dignity, "These eighty and six years have I served Him and He hath done me no wrong, and shall I now deny Him?".

This old man of the Psalm is as a wonder to many. Life has been difficult for him at times. There have been many troubles and trials, and yet he persists unshaken in his trust in God. Men wonder that a man living as righteously as he should suffer so much and still trust in God. Some expositors have seen a comparison with the suffering Servant of Isaiah, of whom it is said, "Many were astonied at thee" (52.14). Not only did he trust, but he continued in praise daily, to the glory and honour of the God whom he trusted.

Verses 9-13: Old Age and Failing Strength

Now, in the weakness of old age, when a man's physical strength declines and he becomes so vulnerable to the attacks of enemies, both human and spiritual, the Psalmist prays, "Cast me not off…forsake me not". It is the time of old age, he pleads, and my strength is failing. Advancing years had robbed him of his earlier strength and vigour. Now, perhaps more than ever, he needed the divine presence. On a certain June 28th John Wesley wrote, "This day I enter on my eighty-sixth year. I now find I grow old. My sight is decayed, so that I cannot read small print except in a strong light. My strength is decayed, so that I walk much slower than I did some years since. My memory of names, whether of persons, or places, is decayed, till I stop a little to recollect them. What I should be afraid of, is, if I took thought for the morrow, that my body should weigh down my mind, and create either stubbornness, by the decrease of my understanding, or peevishness, by the increase of bodily infirmities. But Thou shalt answer for me, O Lord my God".

The Psalmist knew that men were watching him, and talking about him. They lay in wait for him, conspiring together as they had often done at other times during his long life. In the weakness of his advanced years they said, "God hath forsaken him: persecute and take him; for there is none to deliver him". Now was their time. They would take advantage of the infirmity of this aged man and would destroy him at last. "O God", he cries, "be not far from me". How similar is this to the prayer of the suffering One of Psalm 22. "O my God, make haste to help me", he continues, and the personal pronoun "my", now seems to add emphasis and strength to his prayer, pleading his relationship to the God to whom he cries. Did his adversaries seek his hurt? He prays that they might be ashamed, consumed, covered with reproach, dishonoured and confused. He might indeed be an old man, but if the flesh is weak, the spirit is willing, and with vigour he prays for the ignominious defeat of those who seek his life.

Verses 14-16: Hope and Praise, and Strength Renewed

With an expression which is used so often in the Psalms, the Psalmist now exclaims, "As for me" (JND). Here is the great contrast between himself and his enemies, between his future and their fate. For them, shame and dishonour; for him, continuing hope and increasing praise. He must praise "more and more...all the day", for the blessings of righteousness and salvation were innumerable. So he had sung in Psalm 40.5, "Many, O Lord my God, are thy wonderful works which thou hast done, and thy thoughts to usward: they cannot be reckoned up in order unto thee: if I would declare and speak of them, they are more than can be numbered". Such countless blessings demanded unceasing praise, and, with gratitude for God's mighty acts, the Psalmist would come into the presence of the Lord God, extolling Him in His righteousness as the only Saviour. With hope, therefore, he could anticipate salvation, and in the confidence of this he would continue to praise, even in his weakness.

Verses 17-21: From Youth to Old Age!

It is said that reminiscing is one of the signs of growing old. The Psalmist does not deny or disguise his advanced years, but rather rejoices to look back and remember, and recount yet again what God has been to him in the past. "From my youth; and hitherto", he says. He has been taught lessons during his long life. He has been in the school of God. "Thou hast taught me", he says. He must have learned so much in those early shepherd-boy days, and the lessons which he learned are revealed in his Psalms. Now, again, he pleads his old age and hoary head, and cries, "O God, forsake me not". There was another generation following. There always is. "The next generation", is the RV rendering. He longs to be preserved so that he might tell others, whether in his own generation or in the next, the story of the wondrous, marvellous, works of God. God had done great things, both for him and for the nation. He had displayed His strength and His righteousness, and these must be taught to the coming generation.

The question of v.19, "O God, who is like unto thee?", does not require an answer. The God who had done such great things had no equal among the lifeless gods of the nations. But the ways of God were at times hard to understand. "Thou, who hast shown us many and sore troubles, wilt revive us again" (JND). Is not this so clearly seen in John 11, in the story of the little family of Bethany? There was sickness, bereavement, burial, and the accompanying mourning and tears. Many and sore troubles indeed! Added to this was the sorrow that the Lord was not with them, and when they sent for Him He did not immediately come. In fact He deliberately delayed for two days. Why? Eventually He did come. "Lord, if thou hadst been here", the sorrowing sisters both said. It was difficult to see at the time, but He had greater things in mind for them than the healing of their brother Lazarus. They were to see His glory and the manifestation of His power in the resurrection of the dead one. He would bring Lazarus up from the depths of the grave and would lift the sisters out of the depths of their sorrow. He would, in His own time and for His own purpose, revive them again.

The Psalmist had learned this aspect of the character of God and he now says, "Thou wilt increase my greatness, and comfort me" (AV with JND). The RV rendering makes it a prayer: "Increase thou my greatness, and turn again and comfort me". But what greatness is this of which the Psalmist speaks? Is it the greatness of his faith, his trust, his love and faithfulness to his God? Or is it his official greatness as king in Israel? Or are all of these true? Note that he is already great in these matters. He desires an increase in his greatness. What a prayer is this, for greatness and comfort combined, and only God could grant it.

Verses 22-24: Joy and Praise!

The Psalmist promises appropriate praise to the God who will revive and comfort him. He will praise with the psaltery (3627). His harp will be an implement of praise. His musical instruments will become vessels of thanksgiving. This is not so in the worship of believers today. There was a typical significance in those early instruments, as there was also in the offerings and incenses, the holy anointing oils, the new moons, the feasts, and holy days. These were all part of the externals of the worship of Israel, but have now given place to the simplicity of the worship of the spiritual people of the New Testament church, whose place of worship is in the heavenlies. It is interesting to note, as Spurgeon remarks, and agrees, that "the whole army of Protestant divines" concurred with this, not only rejecting, but condemning, the use of these externals in christian worship. He quotes at length, in support of this, *Samuel Mather on the Types* and *John Cotton* (as early as 1585-1652), as well as a long list of great names.

The Psalmist speaks of the truth of God, as if to say that God has indeed been true and faithful in all that He had ever promised to His servants. He calls Him, in a title commonly used in Isaiah but found only three times in the Psalter, "Thou Holy One of Israel". See Psalms 78.41; 89.18.

The closing verses of the Psalm are full of great truths. There is righteousness and redemption, joy and praise. "My lips shall greatly rejoice", he declares. "My tongue also shall talk". His lips and his tongue are but expressing the emotions of his soul, his very life. He will both speak and sing of all that God has wrought for him. As for his enemies, they are ashamed and confounded. They blush in their shame as he rejoices in his deliverance from them. They had conspired and contrived to injure him, but his God had intervened to the salvation of His servant. How rightly had he asked the challenging question, "O God, who is like unto thee?".

PSALM 72

Introduction

It is quite remarkable that this lovely kingdom Psalm is not once quoted in the New Testament. It does, however, embrace many of the features of the coming kingdom of Messiah detailed in the writings of the prophets, particularly the prophecies of Isaiah, Ezekiel, Daniel and Zechariah, and the glories of that millennial reign of Messiah as predicted in Revelation 20. Without hesitation or reservation it may truly be called "Messianic".

The Psalm is either "for" Solomon (AV and JND), or "of" Solomon (RV). Translators, commentators and expositors are not agreed. The closing clause of the Psalm, "The prayers of David the son of Jesse are ended" would seem to confirm that this is indeed a prayer of David for Solomon, but Spurgeon has an interesting compromise and writes, "With some diffidence we suggest that the spirit and matter of the Psalm are David's, but that he was too near his end to pen the words, or cast them into form: Solomon, therefore, caught his dying father's song, fashioned it in goodly verse, and, without robbing his father, made the Psalm his own. It is, we conjecture, the Prayer of David, but the Psalm of Solomon". Wherever the truth lies we cannot now be certain, but, in any case, Solomon and his peaceful reign are the subject of the Psalm, and, prophetically, its burden is the coming kingdom of the Messiah. Note that Solomon's name, SH^{e}LOMOH (8010), is a derivative of SHALOM (7965), which word will occur in vv. 3 and 7, signifying peace and prosperity. Messiah is the Prince of "Shalom" in Isaiah 9.6.

Although there is a certain unity in the Psalm, nevertheless, for the purpose of study and meditation, the verses may be divided as follows. Verses 1-7 emphasise the righteous nature of the king and the kingdom. Verses 8-14 then predict universal dominion. Verses 15-17 extol the prosperity and the perpetuity of the kingdom, and verses 18-19 are a beautiful doxology. The concluding verse 20 has sometimes been called a postscript, but this must not at all minimise the importance of these final words, which seem to indicate, prophetically, that when Messiah reigns, and the whole earth is filled with His glory, David has nothing more to pray for. The prayers of David the son of Jesse are then ended! Considering this, it is very appropriate that Psalm 72 is the last Psalm of Book 2 of the Psalter.

Verses 1-7: Reigning in Righteousness

The opening verse contains the only occurrence of the name of God in the Psalm until the doxology. The prayer is addressed to the mighty Elohim (430), Himself the Supreme Ruler and Judge of men and nations. The earthly monarch is but His viceroy, His vicegerent. It is fitting that prayer for the earthly ruler should be made to the heavenly. The prayer is that the king might be granted the ability to administer his kingdom in keeping with the thoughts of God. "Give the king thy judgments, O God, and thy righteousness unto the king's son". The perfect form of government was really a theocracy, God Himself ruling in the midst of His people. The people, however, had desired a king, like the surrounding nations, and were given Saul. His reign was not satisfactory, and Saul was succeeded by David, the man after God's own heart. Solomon, the son of David, was therefore both a king, and the king's son, and if his rule was to be in accordance with the divine will then he did need divine wisdom. That this might be granted to him is the prayer of the opening verse of the Psalm.

There is some disagreement as to the tenses in the verses which follow. Some expositors accept the simple futures of the AV, RV and JND, "He shall...He shall...He shall". Others rather understand that prayer for the king is now continuing, with the requests, "Let him judge thy people with righteousness", "Let him judge the poor of the people", and, "May he save the children of the needy", as indicated in the RV margin. Perhaps the differences may be resolved by remembering that the opening verse of the Psalm is quite definitely a prayer, and, if that prayer is answered, then He shall judge righteously, He shall save the children of the needy. An answer to the opening prayer will assure the equity of the king's rule. The ideal ruler will administer justice with impartiality. This was not always so in Eastern kingdoms, where, with a corrupt despot, the poor were greatly disadvantaged, being unable to offer the bribes which were often expected. With the king of Israel this was not to be, and it will certainly not be in Messiah's kingdom. There would be righteous judgment for all.

In such a benign kingdom the mountains and hills would bring forth peace, in righteousness. Mountains and hills are the known habitat and hunting ground of bandits and robbers, but in the peaceable kingdom of Solomon, and of Messiah, all fear of such will be gone. Under a righteous ruler the kingdom also would be characterised by righteousness, even in the mountains and hills. Righteous and peace would kiss each other (Ps 85.10), and dwell happily together. It will be so when Messiah comes, for He is King of righteousness and King of peace (Heb 7.2). Jehovah Tsidkenu is the Prince of Shalom. There may be an allusion here to the fact that the hills of the land were often cultivated in terraces. In symbolic language, these hills would bring forth peace for the nation, when a righteous king was on the throne.

While the descriptions "poor" (6041) and "needy" (34) may be understood literally, yet in both cases there is the thought also of those who are abused and afflicted, this perhaps because of their lowly estate and their consequent inability to retaliate against the more affluent oppressor. The righteous king will do justice for them, he will defend them and avenge them, and crush the oppressor. He will redress wrongs and vindicate rights. It may perhaps seem strange, and somewhat incongruous, that the solemn words "...break in pieces the oppressor" should be found so early in such a beautiful Psalm, but it must be remembered that Solomon's peaceful reign began with such a judgment. Adonijah had rebelled against David; Shimei had cursed him; Joab had murdered Abner. These three must first be removed. Similarly, at the beginning of the reign of Messiah, an unholy trinity must be dealt with. The Dragon, the Beast, and the False Prophet will be judged along with other enemies and aggressors (Rev 13 and 19). Then will the way be clear for righteous rule and a kingdom of peace.

The pronoun "thee" of v.5 has occasioned some controversy. "They shall fear thee as long as the sun and moon endure". Does this refer to the king, or to God? Some will point out that the king is never elsewhere addressed in the Psalm and this therefore must be an address to God. Many expositors accordingly use a capital letter to the pronoun, "Thee", indicating that they understand it to mean God, who, because He has so blessed the nation with such a king, will be held in reverence by all. Others think that such an interpretation breaks the continuity and connection of thought in the verses, and that the address is to the king. Such point out that the word "fear" (3372) signifies reverence and awe, respect and honour, and may well describe the attitude and response of the people to a righteous ruler. Since, however, this "fear" is to be continued "as long as the sun and moon endure, throughout all generations", it would seem more appropriate to understand this of God, rather than of an earthly mortal king. Messiah though, being Himself a divine Person, will command everlasting, enduring, reverence and adoration.

How precious in Eastern lands was the rain upon the mown grass and the showers that watered the earth! How quickly would the thirsty earth respond to the refreshing rain. As Davison remarks of meadows newly mown, "Prepared to receive showers more readily. The parched roots quickly take up the refreshing moisture, and even in a few hours the brown plain will be green with verdure". So would the influence of a righteous monarch descend upon a weary nation, producing both tranquillity and prosperity. Under righteous rule, righteous men would flourish and there would be an abundance of enduring peace (7965). This is, again, the lovely word "shalom", a most versatile word defined by Strong as involving peace and prosperity, welfare and health, tranquillity and safety, contentment, quietness, and friendship, whether in human relationships or with God. What blissful conditions will prevail when the true Messiah reigns, and this, as the RV has it, "till the moon be no more"!

Verses 8-14: Universal Dominion

It must be evident, that, while this is a Psalm for Solomon, not all of it had fulfilment during Solomon's reign, and for this reason the Psalm must be Messianic. Much of it still awaits the coming of Messiah, and not least this universal aspect of the king's dominion. "He shall have dominion also from sea to sea, and from the river unto the ends of the earth". But, as

Davison says, "Geographical considerations are not to be pressed here; the phraseology is employed for dominion extending to the bounds of the habitable globe". T.E. Wilson comments similarly, "During the millennium, Jerusalem will be the world's metropolis...The land promised to Abraham in Genesis 15.18 was 'from the river of Egypt unto the great river Euphrates'. That would take in Lebanon, Syria, Iran, Iraq, and Saudi Arabia. 'From sea to sea, and from the river unto the ends of the earth' would be from the Mediterranean to the Persian Gulf and from the Nile to the Euphrates. The borders of Immanuel's land during the millennium are outlined in Ezekiel 47.13-23, but the dominion of the Messiah will take in the whole world, north, south, east, and west. All will come under His righteous but benevolent administration". As Spurgeon writes, "From Pacific to Atlantic, and from Atlantic to Pacific, He shall be Lord, and the oceans which surround each pole shall be beneath His sway".

The proud Bedouin, nomads of the desert, who have never been ruled by any man, shall bow before Him. His enemies shall prostrate themselves in the dust in submission to Him. The kings of Tarshish, probably Spain in the west, with the Mediterranean Islands, will bring presents to Him. The kings of Sheba and Seba in the south will offer their gifts too. Yea, all kings and all nations, shall give Him allegiance and be His servants.

Yet, in all His greatness, it is again confirmed that He will ever remember the poor and the needy, and indeed this concern for the poor and lowly is recognised as an aspect of His greatness. He will deliver them when they cry to Him. He will be the Helper of the helpless. Note His gracious ministry as described in these words, "He shall deliver...He shall spare...and shall save...He shall redeem". No life will be accounted cheap in such a kingdom. The blood of even the poor and the needy will be precious in the sight of the righteous benevolent monarch.

Verses 15-17: Prosperity in Perpetuity

The opening words of v.15, "And he shall live", are understood by some to refer to the poor and needy who have been spared by the king. The text of the RV would encourage this interpretation, reading, "And precious shall their blood be in his sight: and they shall live". The following words then are understood to be gifts of gratitude given to the king by those who have been delivered, "To him shall be given of the gold of Sheba". This does not seem feasible, that poor and needy souls, helped in their helplessness by the king, should be able practically to bring him the gold of Sheba. Perhaps then, the AV rendering, with JND, is to be preferred; "He shall live". This might be compared with the cry of the people at the inauguration of the monarchy in 1 Samuel 10.24, "God save the king", or, "May the king live", or, "Long live the king". With reference to the Messiah, it is a prayer, and an assurance, that the king and the kingdom will be preserved. Some will bring the gold of Sheba to Him, while others will offer prayer for Him continually. Daily, men will praise Him.

Such will be the prosperity of that glorious reign that even the earth on the bleak mountain tops will yield a harvest. The "handful" of the AV may be misleading, as if suggesting a meagre supply. The thought is rather, that if it is found on the top of the mountain, rocky and barren, colder and less fertile than the plains below, then this handful is really an abundance. So it is rendered by the RV and JND - "an abundance of corn". The rich cornfields will wave in the breeze, rustling in the wind like the great cedars of Lebanon. Then, as if to complement the richness of the harvest, men of the city will flourish too, rising populous and prosperous like the green grass and herbs of the field.

"His name shall endure for ever: his name shall be continued as long as the sun". The glorious millennial reign of Messiah is but an earthly phase of His kingdom. His kingdom is an everlasting kingdom. "Thine is the kingdom, and the power, and the glory, for ever. Amen" (Mt 6.13).

There is a mutual enjoyment of blessedness when Messiah reigns. Men shall be blessed (1288) in Him and all nations shall call Him blessed (833). The two words so translated are different. Men shall bless themselves, bless one another, salute each other, in Him. All nations shall call Him blessed. The RV distinguishes this latter word from the other by rendering it "happy". It is the joy of the Messiah as He witnesses the blessing of His subjects.

Verses 18-19: The Doxology

The Psalm concludes with a doxology, which closes, not only this Psalm, but also the second book of the Psalter. It is fitting that such a Psalm should close with such a doxology. Blessed be Jehovah Elohim, God of Israel. Great things have been asked of Him in the Psalm, but then, all that He does is wondrous, and He will grant these great things too. Again the Psalmist says, "Blessed be his glorious name for ever: and let the whole earth be filled with his glory". So be it! "Amen, and Amen!"

Verse 20: The Prayers of David the Son of Jesse are Ended

The concluding verse is brief, but most important. When Messiah, the Son of David, sits upon the throne, and the whole earth is filled with His glory, David has nothing more to pray for. Amen! to this prayer; and Amen! to all his prayers. The prayers of David the son of Jesse are ended!

This concludes Book 2 of the Psalms

BOOK 3

PSALM 73

Introduction

Psalm 73 is the first Psalm in the third book of Psalms. It is also the first of a series of eleven consecutive Psalms which are assigned to Asaph, Psalms 73-83, as is Psalm 50. Asaph was one of three Chief Musicians appointed by David to preside over the services of the singing Levites, but for further comment on Asaph refer to the introduction to Psalm 50 in this Commentary. Asaph may, or may not, have been the actual author of all the Psalms which bear his name. It is to be noted that some of his descendants were singers during the time of the exile (Ezra 2.41), and some commentators think that by these the "Asaph" collection may have been completed. Note also, however, that King Hezekiah, in 2 Chronicles 29.30, commanded the Levites to sing praise to the Lord "with the words of David, and of Asaph the seer". Asaph therefore must have been the author of some, if not all, of the twelve Psalms ascribed to him.

Dr Cohen comments that this Psalm is "the outspoken confession of a man whose faith had been sorely tested". He had seen wicked men triumphing and prospering, and he had seen righteous men suffering, and this was a problem. However, as Alexander Maclaren observes, "The perennial problem of reconciling God's moral government with observed facts is grappled with in this Psalm, as in Psalms 37 and 49. It tells how the prosperity of the godless, in apparent flat contradiction of Divine promises, had all but swept the Psalmist from his faith, and how he was led, through doubt and struggle, to closer communion with God, in which he learned, not only the evanescence of the external well-being which had so perplexed him, but the eternity of the true blessedness belonging to the godly". The abiding portion of the righteous is not necessarily earthly prosperity. There is an eternal glory awaiting in the blessed "afterward" (v.24), and a holy occupation with God Himself as the supreme joy (v.25).

The twenty-eight verses of the Psalm fall into two main divisions of equal length. Verses 1-14 tell the story of the Psalmist's occupation with the wicked and of the doubts which then assailed him. Verses 15-28 confess the sinfulness of these doubts and explain how they had been overcome. These two main parts of the Psalm may be sub-divided as follows, for the purpose of meditation and study.

The opening verse is an introduction, but is in fact a conclusion, a testimony to the grand conviction to which his experience had brought him. Verses 2-14 recall his doubting and the reasons for it, being his perplexity at the prosperity of the wicked. Verses 15-20 tell of his going into the sanctuary, and how he was given a new perspective, an ability to understand the eventual destruction and desolation of these wicked men. In verses 21-27 he confesses the foolishness of his doubts as he contemplates the future glory and contrasts this with the perdition of the ungodly. The concluding verse 28 avows his trust in the Sovereign Lord and the blessedness of drawing near to Him.

Verse 1: The Goodness of God

The opening word of the Psalm has been variously translated as "Truly"; "Surely"; "Only". Perhaps the full meaning may lie in a combination of these. The thought appears to be, "Surely God is good, truly good, and only good, to Israel". That God had been gracious and good to the nation as a whole could not be denied, but there follows a certain modification, or limitation - "...even to such as are of a clean heart". Purity of heart was, after all, an essential qualification for entering the presence of the Lord, as in Psalm 24.4, and the Lord Jesus Himself reiterated this so early in His public ministry, saying, "Blessed are the pure in heart: for they shall see God" (Mt 5.8). Within the nation there were those who were truly Israel, princes with God, and these enjoyed that goodness in a special way. There may be a reminder of that word of Romans 9.6, "They are not all Israel, which are of Israel". Not all were pure in heart, in the enjoyment of the goodness of God in a personal way.

As has been noted in the introduction, this opening verse is, in reality, a conclusion. As Perowne remarks, "The result of the conflict is stated before the conflict itself is described...He states *first*, and in the most natural way, the *final* conviction of his heart".

Verses 2-14: The Problem of the Prosperity of the Wicked

The Psalmist now acknowledges, in a most frank confession, that he had been almost turned aside as he had contemplated the prosperity of proud and lawless men. "But as for me". "The pronoun is emphatic" says Perowne, and Newberry agrees. "But I -", Maclaren renders it. Paraphrased, the Psalmist is saying, "But I, even I, with all my knowledge and privilege and piety, even I, was almost turned aside". His feet had all but slipped from the firm standing of trust in God. As he looks back he recalls how his confidence had been eroded. He remembers his perplexity and doubt as he struggled with the problem which he will now explain.

In the Jewish mind material prosperity was very often regarded as divine favour. How then should wicked men flourish in their lawlessness? It was not that all wicked men prospered, not at all, but if any did, was not this a contradiction of the belief that physical and material blessing was heaven's reward for righteous living? It was an old problem, as old as the Book of Job. "I was envious", the Psalmist confesses. These men were proud boasters. They were arrogant (RV), and in their lawlessness they seemed to be at peace. The word rendered "prosperity" (7965) in v.3 is the lovely word SHALOM. This was indeed a problem. How, or why, should ungodly arrogant men be in the enjoyment of "shalom", peace and prosperity? The poor Psalmist was stumbled, almost turned aside. However, as he will later admit, he was occupied with their present and had forgotten their future. The men whom he envied were foolish men. How foolish of him to be envious of the foolish!

He had apparently observed some of these men as they approached death. There were no bands (2784) in their death. The word does indeed mean bonds or fetters, but may also be rendered "pangs". Many of these foolish men will remain defiant even in death. They are not only foolish and godless, but careless too, presumptuous and insolent, professing no fear of death or dying. They are not bound by fear of the unknown, as other men might be. Their strength remains firm, buttressed by a false peace.

Two different Hebrew words are translated similarly in v.5, words which have already appeared together in one verse in the Psalter (Ps 8.4). "Men" (582), in the earlier part of the verse, is ENOSH, man in his frail mortality. "Men" (120), in the latter part of the verse, is ADAM, which, being the name of the first man, head of the early creation, seems to indicate man in his dignity. It matters not. Whether man in his frailty or man in his dignity, these wicked men in their arrogance do not seem to be troubled or plagued in death as other men. They wear pride as a necklace, displaying it as an ornament. They are proud of their pride! They wear violence like a robe. Maclaren describes them so aptly, "Tricked out with a necklace of pride and a robe of violence, they strutted among men, and thought themselves far above the herd". This arrogance they carried to the very death-bed.

A smug satisfaction shone in the eyes of these men. They looked out from a sense of well-being and ease. They had all that their hearts desired. The world had treated them well indeed. But they were corrupt. They were scoffers. They talked openly and brazenly about the oppression of others, speaking loftily like the high and mighty, as if there was none mightier than they. They spake against the heavens, against God. This was blasphemy, and this blasphemy they preached wherever they walked, throughout the earth.

Verse 10 which follows presents difficulties. The opening word "Therefore" should be noted. These godless men are not only prosperous, but also eloquent, and, as their proud speech is heard in the land, sadly, many Israelites must have been influenced to follow them. Was there prosperity and satisfaction? Was there eloquence to convince others that this way of life was to be desired? There undoubtedly was, "therefore", because of these factors, some of His people, God's people, were drawn after them, induced to follow their example. Those who were so influenced are now pictured drinking to the full, slaking their thirst at the stream of worldly pleasures.

"And they say…". To whom does the pronoun refer? Some believe that it refers to the original wicked men who have drawn others after them. Some rather think that it refers to those who have been influenced by these men, now seeking to ease their consciences by asking, "How doth God know?". "How can He know?". Yea, "Doth He know?". Maclaren suggests that "they" may have "a more general sense, equivalent to our own colloquial use of it for an indefinite multitude. 'They say' - that is, 'the common opinion and rumour is'".

These wicked men are prosperous. They become richer by the day. Does God really punish the evil and reward the good? The poor Psalmist had a problem and the verses which now follow may describe his feelings as he mused upon the prosperity and ease of the godless. Had he chosen clean hands and a clean heart to no purpose? What profit was there in the innocency which he had pursued? He had been plagued daily, and chastened every morning, while these proud, arrogant, godless and lawless men lived at ease and prospered. Why? Why should the innocent suffer and the guilty go free? What could he say?

Verses 15-20: The Problem Resolved and Doubts Dissolved

A sense of shame now seems to come over the Psalmist. He could not really express publicly the thoughts and feelings which he had. It would be faithless to do so. It would cause many of his fellow-saints to stumble and doubt also. The faith of some might well be undermined if such an one as he expressed the mistrust and fears which had assailed him. It was too painful to think about. When he pondered it, trying to understand, it all became wearisome and laborious. Such is the meaning of the words "too painful"(5999) in v.16.

"Until!" What a blessed change does this "until" introduce. It was all confusing and frustrating until he went into the sanctuary, into the presence of God. "Sanctuary" (v.17) is a plural word, probably indicating the several buildings of which the Temple consisted. He would resort to the quietness and holiness of the place where God dwelt, and there, in the calm, he would find the answer to his problem. Then, and there, he would be helped to understand. He must look beyond the present and think about the sad future of these prosperous but wicked men of whom he had been envious. When he stood where God stood, and viewed things from the divine standpoint, everything was different. The prosperity of these ungodly men was temporary, transient, passing. Their end was fearful to contemplate. They walked in slippery places with no firm foothold on the things that really mattered. Soon they would slide into death, destruction, desolation. All would be lost in a moment, consumed in terrors.

Soon, he knew, Adonai (136), the Sovereign Lord, would arouse Himself. Had He kept silent, allowing evil to run its course? Soon He would arise to judgment as a man awaking from sleep. The story of the wicked would become but a fleeting thing of the past, like a dream which is forgotten when one awakes. As Perowne puts it, "When God thus awakes to judgment, the image, the shadow, of the wicked passes from Him as a dream from the mind of a sleeper. He 'despises' it, as a man in his waking moments thinks lightly of some horrible dream".

Verses 21-27: The Folly of Doubting, in View of the Glory

In a sad but frank and honest confession, the Psalmist again recalls how his heart and mind had been in turmoil as he had struggled with the problem. The apparent injustice of wicked men prospering and godly men suffering had disturbed him emotionally. His heart had been grieved (2556). He had become embittered and sour. "I was pricked (8150) in my reins (3629)", he says. "Pricked" has the sense of being pierced or bitten. The "reins" are the kidneys, used symbolically to indicate the seat of the emotions and affections. The poor Psalmist had been in a state of ferment, emotionally disturbed as he had grappled with the problem as described. It was perplexing to say the least. It was frustrating, when for so long he could find no answer. Until, of course, he had taken his problem into the sanctuary.

As he looks back now he confesses how foolish and ignorant he had been. He feels as though he had sunk to the level of the dumb beast (929). This is the word "behemoth", which may, at times, indicate some particular beast, but Kirkpatrick explains, "He confesses the folly of his former impatience. He had lowered himself to the level of a beast (49.10), for what distinguishes man from the lower animals is his power of communion with God. 'Behemoth', rendered 'beast', might be taken, as in Job 40.15, to mean 'the hippopotamus', as an emblem for 'a monster of stupidity', but the more general rendering is preferable".

There follows a happy "Nevertheless". In spite of his past insecurity and doubts and fears, and the foolishness of it all, as he now sees it, the Lord had upheld him and he remains in holy fellowship with Him. God had not abandoned his child for his doubting. The sentiments of these verses are so reminiscent of Psalm 23. The Lord would restore and uphold, and guide along right paths. God had a plan for the life of His child and He would direct the steps of the godly according to His counsel. Then there is the blessed "afterward". "I will dwell in the house of the Lord for ever", that other Psalm concluded. "Afterward!" After the struggles, the doubts, and the fears! After the clouds and the darkness! After the labours and the battles and the afflictions of the journey! After the pilgrimage, the problems, and the perplexities of life! "Afterward, Thou shalt receive me to glory". O how foolish had been this envying of the wicked for their fleeting prosperity. There was an eternal glory awaiting the righteous, and God Himself would guide them there. When the ungodly perish, then, for the believer, "In thy presence is fulness of joy; at thy right hand there are pleasures for evermore" (Ps 16.11).

The Psalmist's portion was in God. Neither in heaven nor on earth was there any that he desired beside the Lord Himself. True, his heart might fail at times and his flesh might be weak, but God was the strength (6697), the abiding rock, upon which his poor heart might lean. What a contrast were those men who lived at a distance from God, estranged from Him. Such would perish. "Thou hast destroyed", states a principle that God does indeed destroy those who live in wanton unfaithfulness to Him, rejecting Him for other passing pleasures.

Verse 28: Trust in the Lord GOD

"But". How important are the "buts" of Scripture! Others may depart from God, but, "It is good for me to draw near". These others seem to have estranged themselves, deliberately and wantonly. "But", the Psalmist has learned that nearness to God was the ultimate pleasure and the great antidote for the sorrows of earth. The Psalm concludes with a repetition of that majestic title of God which has already been employed in v.20, only now it is adjoined to the great name Jehovah. "I have made the Lord (136) GOD (3069) my refuge"(RV). Adonai Jehovah, the eternal, self-existent, supreme and sovereign Ruler, was the Psalmist's refuge, his safe retreat and hiding place. He had learned, not only doctrinally, but also experimentally, that the only good and profitable thing was that he should keep near to God in simple trust. Now, after all that he himself had passed through, he could with confidence exhort others. He would tell what God had done for him. It would be his mission in life to testify to the kindness of a God who had borne with him, sustained him, and preserved him in fellowship with Him through the doubts and fears which had assailed him.

So ends a Psalm which must be a source of encouragement and comfort for those many saints who struggle with the varied perplexities of life. How such sufferers will appreciate the frankness and honesty of this writer, who tells so openly of the despair which had all but turned him aside and swallowed him up. His testimony to the ways of God with him, bringing him through the dark tunnel of fear to eventual victory, will surely be a help to many believers who see their lives and problems mirrored in his.

PSALM 74

Introduction

It is impossible to determine, with any certainty, the circumstances of the writing of this Psalm or the particular events which are described here. The greatest of commentators on the Psalms acknowledge the difficulties and are not agreed. For those who wish to pursue the question, the matter is dealt with in much detail by Delitzsch, Kirkpatrick, Plumer, Perowne,

Maclaren, and many others. Maclaren probably sums up the discussion when he writes, "Two periods only correspond to the circumstances described in this Psalm and its companion (Psalm 79) - namely, the Chaldean invasion and sack of Jerusalem, and the persecution under Antiochus Epiphanes. The general situation outlined in the Psalm fits either of these; but, of its details, some are more applicable to the former and others to the latter period". He goes on to discuss the problems with either view, and concludes by giving his personal opinion that "On the whole, the balance is in favour of the later date". This, of course, would necessitate another "Asaph" of a later date, which is possible, but not probable. However, as suggested in the introduction to Psalm 73, this "Asaph" collection may have been completed by others either during, or after, the exile, and, in this connection, the name of Habakkuk has been suggested.

Another interesting suggestion, advanced by Plumer and favoured also by Spurgeon, is that the Psalm is prophetic, predicting events which, at the time of writing, had not yet taken place. Plumer, speaking of those who regard it as being a Psalm of Asaph, singer and seer and the contemporary of David, writes, "This is perhaps correct…Those who take this view regard the Psalm as wholly prophetic. Why may it not be so? Asaph was a seer. The language of the Psalm is indeed very much in the preterite form. But this may only show the certainty of the events predicted. This view relieves the interpretation of much difficulty". He points out that, if interpreted in this prophetic way, "It is also a prediction of the siege of the city of the Jews, forty years after the ascension of Christ, by the aged Vespasian, and by his son Titus, who slew myriads of Jews and destroyed Jerusalem…If we regard the Psalm as prophetic, then there is no difficulty in supposing it was written by Asaph the seer". As Plumer points out, this view is regarded as admissible by Ainsworth, Patrick, Pool, Muis, Henry, Scott and Morison. It is also preferred and defended by Dr Gill, who probably influenced Spurgeon.

The practical value of the prophetic interpretation is that here in the Psalm is to be found instruction and help for the people of God in any age who are similarly suffering. Persecuted saints at any time may readily turn to Psalms like this to find comfort and encouragement.

In keeping with the prophetic view is the fact that this is a "Maschil" Psalm. It is the ninth of thirteen "Maschil" Psalms, of which Psalm 32 is the first. "Maschil" is from a root signifying wisdom or instruction, but for further comment refer to the introduction to Psalm 32 in this Commentary. Here, in this "Maschil of Asaph", may be found instruction for days of trouble, and perhaps particularly for Israel in the last days when Jerusalem will be ravaged and the temple desolated.

The Psalm may be divided as follows. Verses 1-3 are a plaintive appeal to God that He might remember His people in their suffering. Verses 4-9 describe in pitiful detail the sad condition of the nation and the wickedness of the enemy. Verses 10-17 renew the appeal on the grounds of God's sovereignty and power. The concluding verses, 18-23, plead with Jehovah that, for the honour of His name, He should deliver His people and deal with the enemy. The whole Psalm is an appeal, presented in this variety of ways. Similarities to Psalm 79 should be noted.

Verses 1-3: "Why, O God…Why?"

The divine name Elohim (430) is employed four times in the Psalm in vv. 1, 10, 12 and 22. It is the great name of the mighty One and it is fitting that the opening appeal of the Psalm should be to Him. "O God, why hast thou cast us off?" Such are the calamities which the nation is enduring that the only explanation seems to be that God, in His anger, had cast them off. But why? The "for ever" (5331), elsewhere translated "constantly; alway; perpetually", implies a repeated and continuing rejection of them by God. Why this divine anger? Why? Smoke and fire were symbols of wrath (Ps 18.8). One might understand this breathing out of wrath against the nations, but why against the sheep of His pasture? Israel was His flock. They were His sheep and He was their Shepherd (Ps 23.1; 79.13; 80.1). This is a familiar image of God, as old as Jacob who spoke of "the God that shepherded me" (Gen 48.15, JND). Had the great Shepherd really abandoned His sheep? It would seem, rather, that as His flock they had a right to expect His care and protection.

The Psalmist now appeals for divine remembrance of them on another basis. The people were God's people, and His alone. He had purchased them of old. He had redeemed them and they were the rod (7626), the tribe, the congregation, which He had chosen as His inheritance from among the nations. This must surely be a remembrance of the redemption from Egypt? On these grounds the Psalmist pleads. The mighty Elohim was their Shepherd, and their Redeemer. He must remember them and deliver them.

But there was a stronger appeal yet. The enemy had not only oppressed the nation, they had desecrated the very dwelling place of God among them, even Mount Zion itself. Surely He must intervene. He must lift up His feet, quicken His steps, move with haste against those who were intent upon the perpetual desolation of the sanctuary. This was wickedness indeed, whether of Chaldeans, Syrians, Romans, or whoever. They must be dealt with who would desecrate the Holy Place. "O God…remember thy congregation".

Verses 4-9: The Enemies Roar; the Synagogues Burn

There is now another implicit powerful appeal by the Psalmist when he says, "Thine enemies". He will repeat this in the closing verse of the Psalm. "Thine enemies". The enemies of Israel were the enemies of Israel's God. The congregations against which they roared were God's congregations. There seemed to be a sure reason why God should intervene. "Thy congregations; thy sanctuary; thy name". These men in their wickedness were opposed not only to God's people but also to God Himself. The adversaries of Israel and of God blasphemously erected their banners, their ensigns, in the meeting-places of the nation. The word "signs" (226), occurs twice in v.4. It is once rendered "ensigns" in the AV, RV and ASV, but this is indeed the same Hebrew word. At times the word may have a military sense, and this would be admissible here, but it may be more contextual to understand that the enemy had raised up religious, pagan, idolatrous emblems as tokens or signs of their superiority and power. So it was, literally, with Israel in the days of Antiochus Epiphanes who profaned the temple, "sacrificing on the idol altar, which was upon the altar of God", as recorded by the Maccabees, and so will it be in a day yet future when the abomination of desolation will stand in the Holy Place (Mt 24.15; Dan 9.27).

The Psalmist now likens the enemy to woodcutters. Once a man might have been recognised and admired for his skill in wielding the axe, powerfully cutting his way through the trees of a thick forest. But now? Now they were swinging their axes destructively, breaking down the beautiful carved work of palm trees and open flowers on the walls and doors of the temple. Then, in the ultimate contempt, they cast fire into the sanctuary, defiling and casting down to the ground the place of Jehovah's name.

Perowne describes it all so graphically. He says of the Psalmist, "This is his greatest grief. His country has been laid waste with fire and sword, his friends slain or carried into captivity, but there is no thought so full of pain as this, that the holy and beautiful house wherein his fathers worshipped has been plundered and desecrated by a heathen soldiery. Instead of the psalms, and hymns, and sacred anthems which once echoed within those walls, has been heard the brutal shout of the fierce invaders, roaring like lions over their prey. Heathen emblems, military and religious, have displaced the emblems of Jehovah. The magnificent carved work of the temple, such as the Cherubim, and the palms, and the pillars, with pomegranates and lily-work, have been hewn down as remorselessly as a man would cut down so much wood in the forest. And then that splendid pile, so full of sacred memories, so dear to the heart of every Israelite, has been set on fire, and left to perish in the flames. Such is the scene as it passes again before the eyes of his mind".

All this they did with deliberate determination, They said in their hearts "Let us destroy them", and in the execution of their evil intent they burned up all the synagogues in the land. It is argued by some that since there were no synagogues before the captivity, the Psalm must be post-exilic. The word rendered "synagogue" (4150), however, is often translated "congregation" as in v.4, and simply means "a place of meeting or congregating". As Dr Cohen remarks, "It seems most improbable that the pious men of Israel had nothing else than the Temple to serve their religious needs. Although the Bible has no record of them, there must have been places where they met even informally to study the sacred writings".

In the oppression and suppression they sadly lament, "We see not our signs". They had been robbed of the distinctive signs and observances of their religion. Sabbaths, sacrifices, and festivals had gone. The enemies had set up their own pagan signs (v.4), but those signs which distinguished Israel from the nations had been removed. In Exodus 31.13, 17, the Sabbath was called a sign (226). It is often pointed out that after the destruction of the second temple certain glories were missing, glories which belonged exclusively to Israel. The holy Ark was gone. There was no Shekinah, no Urim and Thummim, and no sacred fire upon the brasen altar. Well might they mourn, "We see not our signs". Where too, were the prophets, and the men who could have predicted just for how long their suffering was to continue? After Haggai, Zechariah and Malachi, the spirit of prophecy was gone too. Was there no one to enlighten and encourage? O God, how long?

Verses 10-17: An Appeal to the Power of God

The name of the mighty Elohim (430) is again invoked. "O God, how long shall the adversary reproach?" What trouble had the enemy caused, what sorrow, distress and affliction. What defiance of God and blasphemy of His name. What contempt and provocation there had been. How long can it last? Since there is no prophet to tell how long, the question is addressed directly to God. "How long, O God?". Can it go on and on for ever? Why is God so restrained? Why does He remain passive, withholding His hand, His powerful right hand from these scenes of desolation? Why will He not act to relieve His people and destroy the enemy? Is not this "the mystery of God" of Revelation 10.7, the wonder that God should for so long tolerate evil and allow men to practise their wickedness with impunity? The Psalmist pleads that God should now show His hand. He will now appeal on the grounds of what God has done for His people in times past.

In spite of all that had happened, and was happening, to them, yet the mighty Elohim was their King. Heathen kings may subjugate and oppress them, but the conviction must remain that theirs was a greater Monarch. He was supreme and sovereign. They will remember His greatness as in vv. 13-17 they now address Him in an oft repeated "Thou". It is an emphatic pronoun, as if to say, "Thou and none else!". As Maclaren says, "There is singular solemnity in the emphatic reiteration of "Thou" in these verses". He adds that "The...repetition of the word brings forcibly into view the Divine personality and former deeds which pledge God to act now. Remembrance of past wonders made present misery more bitter, but it also fanned into a flame the spark of confidence that the future would be like the past". God, who had before wrought salvation for Israel in the sight of enemy nations, would again demonstrate His power.

What memories there were to encourage! God had of old divided the Red Sea for them to deliver them from Egypt. He had crushed the heads of the monsters of the deep. These, with "leviathan", are believed to be symbolic of Egypt and the Nile. The pomp and power of Pharaoh, the proud dragon of Egypt, had been broken. The carcasses of his drowned soldiers had been washed ashore to become food for the jackals and the other beasts that peopled the wilderness. Then, in that inhospitable wilderness, God had cleft the rock for His people and had given them an abundant ever-flowing supply of water for their thirst. Such was His power that He could dry up the River Jordan to let them pass through or He could cause the waters to gush from the desert rocks.

He was, after all, the Creator of everything, and some can here see similarities with the language of Job 38-41. The argument then is that if He was indeed the Creator, it was a small thing for Him to order His creation for the salvation and the good of His people. Day and night, summer and winter, sun, moon, and stars, were all His creation and under His control. All the borders of the earth, those natural frontiers of rivers, mountains, and hills, had been ordained by Him. And now, could not He who had demonstrated such power in the past, create a limit to the sorrows of His people and cause their sufferings to cease?

Verses 18-23: Arise, O God!

In a powerful concluding appeal the Psalmist pleads that God should, for the honour of His name, rise to deliver His people. Apart from all that the enemy had done to them, they had reproached Him and had blasphemed His name. This is a repeat of v.10 but he now invokes the great name of Jehovah (3068). It was this awful name that base and foolish men were blaspheming. Before the adversary, His people were as helpless as an innocent turtledove, but they were *His* turtledove. Would He, could He, abandon them as a defenceless bird to cruel birds of prey? "Remember", he appeals in v.18. "Forget not", he pleads in v.19. God's people were but a poor and afflicted family. He could not give them over for ever to the enemy.

The people of God were a covenant people (Ex 24.8). If the nation was not always true to the covenant which had been contracted between them, yet God would be faithful. "Have respect (5027) unto the covenant", the Psalmist now asks. "Look upon it", he is asking, "behold, consider, regard it". It was as if even the dark hiding places of the land offered no real security for them. There was continuing violence and persecution even there. O that they might be saved from confusion and shame in their oppression and soon have cause to praise God's name. They were poor and needy, afflicted and helpless, they needed divine succour.

But their cause was God's cause! Since they were indeed the people of the covenant, the Psalmist could, when pleading their cause, pray, "O God, plead thine own cause". Yet again he cries, "Remember...Forget not". God must remember how these foolish (5036), base men were reproaching His name daily. He could not forget the tumult (7588), the continual roaring of these arrogant but senseless men whose blasphemies ascended continually in defiance of Him.

With the Psalmist's pleadings there is, then, the constant remembrance of what God is, and what He has done, and the confidence that He is able, in His own time and way, to intervene and deliver His people. This must surely be for the comfort of suffering saints in every age.

PSALM 75

Introduction

As with many other Psalms, it is not possible to determine a clear connection between Psalm 75 and any particular event in Israel's history. Alexander Maclaren, quotes Cheyne on Psalms 74 and 75 who speaks of them as being Maccabean, but then concludes, "It is safer, I think, to assign them at the earliest to one of the happier parts of the Persian age". Maclaren then wisely observes, "It is apparently still safer to refrain from assigning them to any precise period". This does not in any way detract from the importance of the Psalm, but rather adds to its value for later readers who will appreciate its relevance to their own circumstances. The contrast with the preceding Psalm 74 will be noticed at once. If that Psalm was a prayer for deliverance, then here is thanksgiving for answered prayer and deliverance granted. As Spurgeon says, "The cry of the last Psalm is about to be heard, and the challenge of the foes of Israel taken up by God Himself".

The Psalm is committed to the care of the Chief Musician, and the superscription has in it the term Altaschith (516), which has occurred also in the titles of Psalms 57, 58 and 59. The agreed meaning of this is "destroy not", and it is believed to have been a preferred melody to which the Psalm should be sung. There may be implicit in the term a defiance of Israel's enemies. They must not, they cannot, destroy the people who are God's people. This Psalm of Asaph is also called a Song, which may indicate that it could have been sung either with or without a musical accompaniment. It is in the title of Psalm 30 that the word "Song" first appears in a superscription in the Psalter. It will be remembered that in Ephesians 5.19 Paul speaks of "psalms and hymns and spiritual songs". T.W. Davies suggests that a Psalm is "a lyric from the point of view of the music", and a Song is "a lyric from the point of view of the matter".

The ten verses may be divided as follows. The opening verse is a brief prologue of thanksgiving, and this suitably introduces the words of God Himself in verses 2-5, which are the heart or kernel of the Psalm. Verses 6-8 are a warning to Israel's enemies concerning God's judgment. The concluding verses 9 and 10 are an epilogue of praise to the God of Jacob who deals with both the wicked and the righteous.

Verse 1: A Prelude of Praise

This whole Psalm is praise rather then petition. It opens with a double exclamation of thanksgiving to the mighty Elohim (430). "Unto thee, O God, do we give thanks, unto thee do we give thanks". The repetition, or duplication, is a reverent emphasis. There is no reluctance or hesitation in this wholehearted rendering of thanks to God, and immediately there follows the reason for this. God has been near to deliver His people. His "name" is His character, and this has been revealed by His wondrous works on their behalf. What He is has been declared by what He has done. The wonder of His works are but a reflection of the wonder of His person, and it is fitting that thanksgiving should be rendered to Him. As another Psalm says, "Praise him for his mighty acts: praise him according to his excellent greatness" (Ps 150.2).

Verses 2-5: God Speaks

These verses have been called "A majestic Divine utterance" (Maclaren). God Himself is speaking personally, proclaiming to all concerned that His judgment is at hand. In His sovereignty He will decide when the time for judgment has come. "When I shall receive the congregation", has been rendered by RV and others as, "When I shall find the set time". "When I shall receive the assembly", says JND. Perhaps the meaning may be seen in a blending of the two thoughts. He will choose the time when the people are to be assembled and He will judge uprightly (4339), with equity. God is impartial and righteous in all His judgments. He will act in accordance with truth and justice, but He Himself will decide when it is time to judge. His people may sometimes think that He delays too long. His enemies may deride and tauntingly boast that He will never intervene at all. He will, at the appointed time, move to deliver His people and vanquish the enemy. Maclaren comments that to learn this lesson "would save the oppressed from impatience and despondency and the oppressor from dreams of impunity".

Such is the strength and stability of God's righteousness that, even though earth with its society should be dissolved, divine justice and truth would remain as pillars, unshakeable and immovable. The collapse of all moral order on earth would in no way affect the divine. As Hebrews 1.11 has it, "Thou remainest!". The "Selah" demands that the reader should pause, meditate, reflect, upon the wonder of it all.

God now addresses the foolish (1984). The word implies boastful arrogance. There is a divine rebuke. "I said unto the arrogant, Deal not arrogantly" (RV). Ye fools, play not the fool. What folly indeed, to defy the Almighty! To the wicked He says, "Lift not up the horn". The horn is a symbol of strength, and the figure is probably that of a horned animal proudly and confidently tossing its head in the air. To so behave in defiance of God is utter foolishness, it is impudence and pride, and again He says, "Lift not up your horn on high". The stiff neck of which He now speaks is, in symbol, a haughty insolent attitude. Delitzsch renders it, "Speak not arrogance with a stretched out neck".

Verses 6-8: Warning to the Wicked

It is difficult to be certain as to where the personal spoken word of God concludes. As Maclaren puts it, "The exact point where the Divine oracle passes into the Psalmist's own words is doubtful". He adds that "it is best to make the break at the end of v.5, and to suppose that what follows is the singer's application of the truths which he has heard". Indeed it is here, at v.6, that the AV and JND with others indicate a new paragraph.

The word rendered "promotion" (7311) in v.6 of the AV means "exaltation". It signifies "a lifting up". There is a play upon words. Did these wicked men in their pride seek to exalt themselves, lifting up the horn of their supposed power and glory? It was folly to look to any point of the compass for such glory, whether east, west, or south. Neither from the sun-rising in the east or from the sun-setting in the west, nor from the wilderness of Sinai or Egypt in the south would exaltation come. But what is the significance of the omission of the north? Is there here a veiled exhortation that for true promotion and exaltation men should indeed look up, north, to the heights, to God Himself? It is God alone who ultimately decides and orders matters. He is judge (8199). He is the governor who can vindicate or condemn, putting down one and lifting up another. This is His prerogative, and, while the wicked man will seek to exalt himself, the godly man will leave his promotion to God.

The Psalmist now employs, for the only time in the Psalm, the great name Jehovah. "In the hand of the LORD (Jehovah - 3068) there is a cup". The judgment of God is depicted as a cup of foaming wine which the wicked will be compelled to drink. Reluctantly they must drain it to its bitter dregs. The same metaphor is used by the prophet Isaiah when he writes of "the cup of his fury" (Is 51.17), and by the Apostle John in the words of the angel: "The wine of the wrath of God...the cup of his indignation" (Rev 14.10).

Verses 9-10: The Epilogue of Praise

In happy contrast to the fate of the wicked the Psalmist now exclaims, "But I". This is equivalent to that well-known expression, used so often in the Psalms, "As for me". When wicked men languish under God's judgment, the Psalmist avows that he will testify to what God has done, and will praise Him. "I will declare", he says. He will bear his testimony in the singing of psalms to the God of Jacob. This is the covenant-keeping God of grace who lifted Jacob the supplanter and beguiler to become a "prince with

God". Such is the meaning of his new name "Israel", and the grace which lifted the patriarch has ever been available for his descendants and for the people of God everywhere.

The Psalm concludes with a final contrast between the wicked and the righteous. The horns (7161), the strength and glory, of the wicked will be cut down, but the horns of the righteous shall be exalted. There is however, a difficulty with the pronoun "I" in v.10. To whom does it refer? "The horns of the wicked also will I cut off". The explanation offered by Dr Cohen seems reasonable. He writes, "By a sudden transition, common in Hebrew, the subject may be God; but more naturally it is the Psalmist as the representative of the people, who speaks with the confidence that God is Israel's Ally in the campaign against wickedness". Alexander Maclaren, after pointing out that some commentators, to resolve the difficulty of the pronoun, have proposed to transfer the verse to the earlier part of the Psalm, regarding it as part of the Divine oracle, then says, "But it is in its right place where it stands. God's servants are His instruments in carrying out His judgments; and there is a very real sense in which all of them should seek to fight against dominant evil and to cripple the power of tyrannous godlessness".

PSALM 76

Introduction

The commentator Delitzsch introduces his commentary on this Psalm saying, "No Psalm has a greater right to follow Psalm 75 than this". He remarks upon the obvious unity of authorship, as manifested in the several similar expressions used in both Psalms, and then continues, "They form a pair: Psalm 75 prepares the way for the divine deed of judgment as imminent, which Psalm 76 celebrates as having taken place". Spurgeon concurs, "Faith in the 75th Psalm sung of victories to come, and here it sings of triumphs achieved".

Like Psalm 75, this Psalm is also attributed to Asaph, and is called, as that Psalm, both a Psalm and a Song. It has already been suggested, in the introduction to Psalm 75, that this probably indicates that the Psalm may be sung either with, or without, musical accompaniment. See also the title of Psalm 30, where the term Song is first used in a superscription. When, however, a musical accompaniment is preferred with this Psalm, then "Neginoth" (5058) is an instruction to the Chief Musician that the accompaniment should be stringed instruments, these in preference to wind instruments, such as flutes. This is the last of six occurrences of "Neginoth" in the Psalm titles. See Psalms 4, 6, 54, 55 and 67.

There is a certain unity in the Psalm which deters some commentaries from either recognising, or making, divisions in the twelve verses. There is indeed a persistent and consistent jubilation all through the Psalm for the triumphs of the God of Jacob, and, to quote Spurgeon, "We have no need to mark divisions in a song where the unity is so well preserved". Nevertheless, there does appear to be an arrangement of four stanzas of equal length. Maclaren admits the unity, saying, "The singer is absorbed in the one tremendous judgment which had delivered the dwelling-place of Jehovah. His song has but one theme - God's forth-flashing of judgment on Zion's foes. One note of thankfulness sounds at the close, but till then all is awe". But having acknowledged the unity, he then continues, "The Psalm is divided into four strophes, of three verses each. The former two describe the act; the latter two deal with its results, in an awed world and thankful praise".

The first stanza, verses 1-3, indicates the scene of the triumph. It was there, in Judah, in Israel, in Salem, in Zion. The second part, verses 4-6, sings the glory of God and the destruction of the enemy. In verses 7-9 there is a blended recognition of God's power in judgment and His salvation for the meek of the earth. The last stanza, verses 10-12, is a call to bring praises and presents to Him who ought to be feared.

There are two "Selahs", one after v.3 and the other after v.9, which are the closing verses of the first and the third stanzas.

Verses 1-3: The Scene of the Triumph

It is good to see Judah and Israel brought together in the opening verse of the Psalm. Although some, as Dr Cohen and others, insist that the names Judah and Israel are here synonyms, with no reference to the two divisions in the nation, yet there is, in the two names, a remembrance of that unhappy political division. All, however, are united in their knowledge and praise of God. In Judah He is known and His name is great in Israel. If the nations around knew Him not, He was known in Judah, and if the heathen world did not recognise the greatness of His name, still, there was appreciation of that name in Israel. By His name we are to understand His Person, Himself. Believers today may take comfort and courage from this, that in spite of sad divisions in the present testimony, yet there are true hearts everywhere, united in the knowledge and love of God, with a common desire for His glory. So it must ever have been both in Judah and in Israel.

In v.2, "Salem" (8004) is a shortened version of "Jerusalem" - Jeru-*salem*, first occurring in Genesis 14.18 as the city of King Melchizedek. It is found again in Hebrews 7.1-2 where the names of both the king and the city are employed by the Holy Spirit to portray the righteousness and the peace which come by Messiah. In both Genesis 14 and Hebrews 7 this abbreviated "Salem" form of Jerusalem may be used to emphasise the meaning, "Peace". Here, in this Psalm, the triumph of Jehovah is complete, the tumult of the previous Psalm is settled, the enemy is subdued, and peace reigns. "Zion", the name of the hill, or mount, had become a synonym for Jerusalem, especially in the prophets.

The interesting observation has been made by some commentators that in v.2 the word "tabernacle" (5520) is an unusual word, which may signify a den, a covert, or a lair, and, as Dr Cohen suggests, "It is possible that the Psalmist intends to describe God as the Lion of Judah, Who has issued forth from His lair, and seized His prey". His dwelling place was, of course, in His sanctuary on Mount Zion, the God of Israel dwelling between the cherubim (1 Sam 4.4; Ps 80.1; Is 37.16).

There, in Jerusalem His dwelling place, the destruction of the enemy was effected. This does not mean that the battle was actually or physically fought in Jerusalem, but that the city was, as it were, the divine headquarters from where the authority and power issued for the defeat of the foe. The sharp and swift arrows of the enemy were aborted and broken, and not only the fiery shafts from their bow, but every weapon, whether defensive or offensive, shield or sword, was likewise shattered, and the battle was the Lord's.

How appropriately do the Psalmists here and there insert a "Selah". It seems so fitting that there should be a pause just here, at the end of the opening stanza. It is a suitable place for an interlude, a quiet meditation upon the greatness of the triumph before the continuing ascription of praise and glory to the God of Jacob.

Verses 4-6: The Majesty and Glory of God

Verse 4 is admittedly difficult of interpretation, and a variety of explanations have been offered. Some think that the mountains of prey are the mountains of Judah, where the victory has been accomplished, in which case Jehovah is viewed as sitting supreme on the mountains of His habitation. T.W. Davies says, "Zion is obviously intended". Some commentators, though, rather understand the "mountains of prey" to be a symbol of the enemies of Israel, when the meaning will be that God in His greatness is superior to these enemies. Delitzsch favours this, saying that God is represented as towering above "the Lebanon of the hostile army of peoples". Yet others follow the RV rendering, where the preposition "on" is replaced by "from", reading, "Glorious art thou and excellent, from the mountains of prey". In this case the picture is rather like that of Isaiah 63.1, "Who is this that cometh from Edom...glorious in his apparel, travelling in the greatness of his strength". This may be the preferred interpretation, Jehovah returning as a conqueror from the mountains of prey, the scene of His triumph over the enemies of His people. The rendering of the JPS is, "Glorious art Thou and excellent, *coming down* from the mountains of prey", but Dr Cohen, who uses the JPS text exclusively in his commentary, says, "There is nothing in the text to correspond with coming down, and the verb to be supplied may be 'returning'". He suggests that it is Jehovah coming back from the hills on which He had treated the enemy host as prey. Maclaren agrees that the preposition "from" is the correct one and writes, "God comes forth as 'glorious' from the lofty heights where He sits supreme". Whatever the true meaning may be, this is clear, that Jehovah is greater in glory and excellence than all.

The enemies of Israel may have been stout-hearted (47), like powerful bulls, proud of their strength and valour, but Jehovah has spoiled them and robbed them of their might, of their weapons, and indeed of life itself, for they have "slept their sleep", the sleep of death. They have been left defeated and dead on the field of battle. Where are the men of might now? Not one of them has found sufficient strength to withstand Jehovah in the battle. Note the completeness of the victory. The arrows and the bow, the shield and the sword, the chariot and the horse, are all destroyed by the God of Jacob and the battle is won.

Verses 7-9: Judgment and Salvation

In this third stanza there is, as has been suggested in the introduction, a sight, not only of the anger of God toward the enemy, but of His provision of salvation for the humble and meek of the earth. It is a magnificent blending of truth, that the God who can be angry with the wicked can be gracious with the afflicted. This God is to be feared (3372). He is to be held in reverence and in awe. The thought of an angry God is fearful indeed, and when He is angry who can stand before Him? The question needs no answer. It was an angry God who moved against the enemies of His people. The divine sentence was pronounced upon them and when heaven spoke the earth was silent. Men were awe-stricken, the earth feared, when God defeated the proud enemy.

Yet, in His judgment of the oppressor He had this in mind, to save the meek (6035) of the earth. Towards the poor and the lowly, the afflicted and humble of His people, He would move graciously, providing for their salvation. Angry with the proud; gracious with the meek; such has ever been His character. As Mary of Nazareth sang, at a date much later than the Psalmist's, "He hath put down the mighty from their seats, and exalted them of low degree" (Lk 1.52). "Selah!"

Verses 10-12: Praise and Presents for Jehovah

The opening words of this closing stanza portray the sovereignty of God. Even the very wrath of man but provides an opportunity for God to display His glory. He shows Himself superior to those puny men who would vaunt themselves in fury against Him and His people. "Man" (120) is ADAM, man of the clay, creature of the dust. How futile for such to be angry with Jehovah! He will, in His sovereignty, allow them to vent their wrath, and then, in the circumstances which they have created, He will manifest His glory.

This is clear enough, but the second clause is difficult, "The remainder of wrath shalt thou restrain". This may mean that there comes a point when God intervenes, allowing men to dispense so much wrath and fury against Him and His people, but, no more. He will restrain the wrath of men when He chooses. JND, however, with the RV, renders this clause, "The remainder of fury wilt thou gird on Thyself", as if to suggest that God, having restrained man in his anger, will then take the residue of man's wrath and turn it to His own honour as an ornamental girdle. Maclaren has another view. He points out that the second occurrence of "wrath" in the verse is a plural, "wraths", and he writes, "Whose 'wraths' are spoken of in it? God's or man's? The change from the singular ('wrath of man') to plural ('wraths') makes it all but certain that God's fulness of 'wrath' is meant here. It is set over against the finite and puny wrath of men, as an ocean might be contrasted with a shallow pond. If so, God's girding Himself with the residue of His own wrath will mean that, after every such forth-putting of it as the Psalm has been hymning, there still remains an unexhausted store ready to flame out if need arise. It is a stern and terrible thought of God, but it is solemnly true".

In view of all that has been considered of the majesty of God, men are now summoned to pay their vows to Him. Make no empty promises, but vow, and pay, is the exhortation. Those who are "round about him" is probably a reference to His own people, those who are near to Him. He is, after all, The LORD (3068) their God (410), Jehovah their Elohim. Can there be a grander title than this or a more glorious name? He is the eternally existent, self sufficient, mighty Lord. Therefore let those who are round about Him bring presents to Him. These are gifts indicating homage and tribute, such as will be paid to Messiah in the day of His millennial glory (Ps 72.10). It is fitting that such honours should be paid to Jehovah, to Him who ought to be feared by all with a reverential awe.

The closing verse of the Psalm may seem disconnected, but it sums up the spirit of the Psalm. God can cut short the life of princes and He is to be feared by the kings of the earth. Men may oppose Him. Men may resist Him, and reject Him. But the greatest of men are but puny mortals whose breath is in His hand. Whether princes or kings, nobility or royalty, all must be subject to His divine superiority. Perhaps the prophetic ultimate of this may be seen in Revelation 6.15-17; "And the kings of the earth, and the great men, and the rich men, and the chief captains, and the mighty men, and every bondman, and every free man, hid themselves in the dens and in the rocks of the mountains; And said to the mountains and rocks, Fall on us, and hide us from the face of him that sitteth on the throne, and from the wrath of the Lamb: For the great day of his wrath is come; and who shall be able to stand?". As indeed the Psalm concludes, "He is terrible to the kings of the earth".

PSALM 77

Introduction

This is a rather sad Psalm, though it ends on a brighter note than that with which it begins. It has been called "A wail of sorrow"; "A cry of affliction". Although it may have been written in a time of national distress, yet the Psalmist has made the sorrow his own personal sorrow, and he sings accordingly. It is, again, a Psalm for the Chief Musician, who carried a heavy responsibility, and yet enjoyed a great privilege, for the ordering of the temple song and the services of the sanctuary. It is a Psalm of Asaph, of which there are twelve such, Psalm 73 being the first of eleven consecutive Asaph Psalms in Book 3 of the Psalter, the only other one being Psalm 50 in Book 2. For more detailed comment on Asaph refer to the introduction to Psalm 50 in this Commentary.

The name of Jeduthun, as in the title, appears also in the titles of Psalms 39 and 62. The Psalm may have been composed for him, or simply committed to him at the time of writing. Dr Cohen suggests that the title may indicate, "For the leader Jeduthun", or, "For the leader (to be sung in the style) of Jeduthun". Jeduthun is mentioned several times in the Books of Chronicles and may be identified with Ethan of 1 Chronicles 15.16-17. He was, with Asaph and Heman, one of the three leaders of the temple choirs, but for further comment on Jeduthun see the Introduction to Psalm 39 in this Commentary.

On the divisions in the Psalm Alexander Maclaren comments, "The Psalm falls into two parts, in the former of which (vv. 1-9) deepest gloom wraps the singer's spirit, while in the latter (vv. 10-20) the clouds break". There is, however, another division of the Psalm, occasioned by the three "Selahs" after verses 3, 9 and 15. In the first part, verses 1-3, the Psalmist describes his pleadings with God in the day of his trouble. In the second section, verses 4-9, the lament continues, deepening into almost despair that God had forgotten him. In the third part, verses 10-15, there is a happy change. He remembers who, and what, God is. He recalls the wonders God has done and how He has of old been the Redeemer of His people. The Psalm closes, verses16-20, with a graphic poetic remembrance of this redemption of the people at the time of the Exodus, and, although some commentators will not accept it, to most there does seem to be a vivid description of the miraculous passage through the Red Sea, by Him who led His people like a flock.

Verses 1-3: Pleading with God

With a sad repetition the Psalmist begins, "I cried unto God with my voice...unto God with my voice". There is an emphasis here on, "My voice...my voice". JND in his translation will mark this emphasis, giving, "My voice is unto God...my voice is unto God". According to Hebrew idiom this apparently suggests that he is crying loudly. It is an expression of his anguish. The AV rendering, "and He gave ear unto me", is not agreed by all translators. JND reads, "and he will give ear unto me", whereas Maclaren and the JPS prefer, "that He may give ear". Sometimes the whole truth in an expression is to be found in a combination of all the scholarly suggestions and preferences. The Psalmist knew, experimentally, that when he had lifted up his voice, God had heard. The assurance was therefore, that now, as he cried again, God would hear. He could, thus, hope and pray with confidence, "I would lift up my voice to God, that He may give ear to me" (Maclaren).

Note how the Psalmist speaks of the day and the night. He has had days of trouble and nights of prayer. The clause in the AV, "my sore ran in the night", is strange. "Sore" (3027) is the Hebrew YAD, and is, more than thirteen hundred times translated "hand" in the AV. It is difficult to know how, or why, the AV translators used "sore" here. "Ran" (5064) means "to be stretched out", so that there is universal agreement that the phrase should read, "My hand was stretched out in the night without ceasing". The lifting up, or stretching out, of the hands was a Hebrew attitude of prayer, as in Psalms 28.2 and 134.2. It symbolised the reaching out of the heart to God. Without ceasing the Psalmist cried to God in his distress, refusing to be comforted otherwise if God did not hear.

How personal is the singer's lament. "My voice; my trouble; my hand; my soul; my spirit". His only hope was in God, and yet, the more he remembered God, the more he was overwhelmed, since God was not yet answering. With raised voice and outstretched hand he sighed and complained as he mused and longed for divine comfort.

It is time for a "Selah". It is a moment to pause, to reflect, to think. As Spurgeon says in his own quaint but expressive way, "Pause ye awhile, and let sorrow take breath between her sighs"!

Verses 4-9: The Deepening Gloom

In this next strophe the Psalmist's lament continues. Now he can neither speak nor sleep. He feels as if God is holding open his tired eyelids, preventing sleep. He longs to sleep but he cannot. So wearied is he, but he cannot rest. He is agitated and perplexed and he cannot now articulate in prayer. Throughout the troubled night he ponders and remembers. He recalls earlier days and better times. He well remembers when he had songs in the night, not these sorrows. As Maclaren says, "The Psalmist in his sleepless vigils remembers other wakeful times, when his song filled the night with music and 'awoke the dawn'". But even the remembrance of brighter days in the past brings him no ease. He continues restless and sleepless, tossing and turning, considering and communing, searching in his mind, in all directions, for some comfort. How like many other saints he is!

Now, in his depression, a series of sad questions begins to form in his mind. Will the Lord cast off forever? Will He withdraw His favour? Will His lovingkindness cease? Will His promise fail? Will He forget to be gracious? Will He shut up His compassion? What deep, deep sorrow there must have been to have occasioned questions like these in such a man as Asaph. Of course, the answer to them all is in the negative, but in the darkening gloom it is difficult for the troubled soul to see beyond. God has not changed. He cannot abandon His child, or cease to be favourable, or forget to be gracious. His compassions fail not, His word is faithful, His mercies will never cease. He is the same today as He has ever been, and as He ever will be. "The same yesterday, and today, and forever" (Heb 13.8).

Another "Selah" calls for another pause, to consider in silent meditation what has been said. Maclaren says, very beautifully, "The Selah bids us dwell on the questions, so as to realise their gravity and prepare ourselves for their answer".

Verses 10-15: Light in the Darkness

Verse 10 is admittedly difficult. Varied renderings and interpretations have been offered, but all are agreed that the Psalmist is now, with a calmer mind, about to give a more considered view of his sad situation. "And I said", or, "Then said I". He has thought about it all and now says, with a certain resignation, "This is my infirmity". He may mean that this is his grief, and he must bear it as that which has been allocated to him by the Most High. He will remember the years of Him who is called the "Ancient of days" (Dan 7.9), and he will acknowledge the divine right of that One to deal with His people as He will. Another interesting view, however, is advanced by the JPS translation, "And I say: This is my weakness, that the right hand of the Most High could change". If this rendering is accepted, then the Psalmist is saying that the cause of all his distress is this, that he dared to imagine that God could, or would, change in His thoughts towards His people and in His purpose for them.

Again he calls upon his memory. "I will remember…surely I will remember". He will remember the works and the wonders of Jehovah. No distinction is to be drawn between works and wonders. All Jehovah's works are wondrous. To consider His works is to consider His wonders. He is "the God of Israel who only doeth wondrous things" (Ps 72.18). Well do His people sing -

"Great God of wonders, all Thy ways
Are worthy of Thyself, divine".

In v.11, the title "LORD" (3050) is "Jah", a shortened form of Jehovah, as incorporated in the well-known Hallelu-*jah*.

The Psalmist will not only remember these wonders that God had wrought of old, he will meditate upon them, muse upon them, and talk of them. He is not now occupied with himself and his circumstances. The great antidote to doubts and fears is occupation with God Himself, and this is now his exercise. He says, "Thy way, O God, is in the sanctuary (6944)", meaning, "Thy way is in holiness". All that God does is in keeping with His holiness. All His works and ways must be just and right. If, at times, His ways are past tracing, nevertheless His people must rest assured that all that He does is ultimately for His own glory and for their good. His way is always in holiness. Later in the Psalm His way is in the sea, but that is another thought.

Considering these things the Psalmist exclaims (AV rendering), "Who is so great a God (410) as our God" (430). Two different words are here translated "God". JND, RV, and others, will carefully omit the capital "G" from the first, to show the difference. That first word is the Hebrew EL, which, while it is indeed used of God Himself in the very next verse (v.14), nevertheless might at times be used to indicate idols and false gods, as it is here. But, the Psalmist is asking, "Who is so great a god as our *Elohim*?". He is the God who does wonders. No other god performs wonders as He does. Here is an obvious reference to, and perhaps indeed a quotation from, Exodus 15.11, and here begins a grand reminiscence of the Exodus from Egypt, when God made known His strength and redeemed His people from bondage with His mighty arm.

The separate mention of the sons of Jacob and Joseph is not without meaning. See also v.18 of Obadiah. Together they embrace the whole nation of Israel, both the Northern Kingdom and the Southern. This must have been, to the nation in every age, a rebuke of the unhappy division, and a reminder that when Jehovah brought them out of Egypt He brought out a whole united nation for His pleasure. For the Psalmist it must have expressed a longing for the unity of his people.

A third and final "Selah" indicates a pause preparatory to the praise of the last strophe. The five closing verses of the Psalm extol the power and the sovereignty of the Redeemer who led His people out of slavery.

Verses 16-20: Miracles at the Red Sea

It is sad that certain commentators cannot see in this section any reference to the Exodus and the passage of the Red Sea, believing that in these verses we are suddenly transported from the realm of history to that of nature. Gratefully, these are a minority among commentators. Between the references to redemption in v.15 and the leading out of the people like a flock in v.20, there is a vivid, graphic portrayal of the wonder of the Exodus. As Maclaren writes, "All this pomp of Divine appearance, with lightnings, thunders, a heaving earth, a shrinking sea, had for its end the leading of the people of God to their land, as a shepherd does his flock. The image is again an echo of Exodus 15.13. The thing intended is not merely the passage of the Red Sea, but the whole process of guidance begun there amid the darkness".

The waters of the Red Sea are here personified by the inspired poet. The waters saw the mighty Elohim, and were afraid. Not only on the surface, but to their very depths they were in pain and trembled. The clouds burst, the skies thundered, and the lightning flashed forth like arrows. The voice of God was in the thunder. The lightning lightened the world so that the earth shook, trembling (7264) as did the depths of the troubled waters (also 7264) in v.16. If it is objected that such traumatic upheavals are not recorded in Exodus, it must be remembered that this is poetry. It may not be literal, but it is intended no doubt to portray the majesty of the divine intervention which delivered Israel and brought an emancipated nation of slaves out of Egypt and through the Red Sea on their way to the Promised Land.

God led the people. He led them as a shepherd leads his flock, going before them. Jehovah trod the path through the sea before them, and then, when His people were safely over, the waters returned to their place and covered His footsteps. "His footsteps (were) not known". By the hand of Moses and Aaron, the two privileged sons of Levi, He led them. Moses the prophet, and Aaron the priest, would carry the burden of guiding this great people through the wilderness, but Jehovah was their Shepherd, and He would provide and protect.

PSALM 78

Introduction

The title of this lengthy Psalm is very brief - "Maschil of Asaph". It is the tenth of thirteen Psalms which have "Maschil" in their titles. The word implies "wisdom" or "instruction", so that the "Maschil" Psalms are sometimes referred to as didactic Psalms. They contain teaching or doctrine for the people of God. The first of these is Psalm 32, and the others are Psalms 42, 44, 45, 52-55, 74, 88, 89, 142, and, of course, Psalm 78. It need not be thought strange, or surprising, that a Psalm, which is essentially historical, should be counted instructional or doctrinal. There is much to be learned from history. Whether it is the history of Israel or the history of christian testimony, history does tend to repeat itself, and saints who follow after can be instructed and guided by the experiences of those who have gone before.

This Psalm recounts the history of Israel from the Exodus and the wilderness wanderings until the time of David. There is also, in vv. 42-51, a kind of interlude, a brief excursus back into Egypt before the Exodus to recall God's plagues upon the Egyptians preparatory to the deliverance of His people. In all that happened to Israel of old there is edification and encouragement, rebuke and comfort, for the people of God today. "For whatsoever things were written aforetime were written for our learning" (Rom 15.4).

There is an orderliness, unity and a flow of thought in the Psalm which make divisions difficult, and perhaps unnecessary, but for the purpose of the present study the following will be observed.

Verses 1-8 are a prologue. They state the Psalmist's purpose and reason for writing as he does. The large section which follows, verses 9-41, is a record of the wilderness experiences of the people, their failings and murmurings, and God's patience with them throughout. Verses 42-52 are that parenthetic section which deals with events in Egypt prior to the Exodus. From verse 53 the history of the nation is resumed, and this continues until verse 66. The remaining verses, 67-72, seem to recall the removal of the Ark and the symbol presence of Jehovah from Shiloh to Zion, from Ephraim to Judah.

Verses 1-8: Prologue; The Purpose of the Psalm

"Give ear, O my people, to my law". By inspiration the words of the Psalmist are the words of God. The Psalmist speaks, but it is God who speaks, saying "My people...my law". "Law" (8451) is the Hebrew "Torah". The Torah was that body of divine teaching, ceremonial, moral, and prophetic, in which the mind of God was made known for the ordering of His people. It was therefore not only desirable, but essential, that His people should incline their ear and give heed. To "incline the ear" suggests a leaning forward to listen expectantly and earnestly to what God has to say. This, of course, would imply a willingness to obey. The words of His mouth reveal His will and to hear those words is a high privilege, bringing heavy responsibility.

Asaph sees ancient history as a great parable. He speaks of "dark sayings" (2420), a word which signifies an enigma, a riddle, truth clothed in metaphor. Paul, of a much later day, speaks also of events in history, saying, "Which things are an allegory" (Gal 4.24). These will be appreciated by the spiritual, exercised heart, but will be unintelligible and unprofitable to the carnal mind. The Saviour Himself spoke to the multitude in the same fashion (Mt 13.10-14), pointing out this very thing, that only the genuine hearer would benefit by the parable. Asaph will "utter" (5042) these dark sayings. The word implies a bubbling up and a pouring forth as from a fountain. There was much to be said, and much to be learned, from the history of the nation, for those who sincerely wished to be taught. This is his purpose then, to teach from history lessons for saints who come after. Maclaren comments that Asaph is not a chronicler, but a teacher. He is not just an historian, he has in mind the deepening of godly fear and obedience among the people by a consideration of the favours and failings of the past.

Several times in this opening section the Psalmist makes reference to the fathers, their children, and, the generation to come. Each generation must recount these things for the succeeding one. The praises of Jehovah, His strength, and the wonders He had wrought must be told again and again. The fathers must instruct the children, so that they will arise and tell the story to their children. Adam Clarke suggests that five generations appear to be mentioned here; "1. Fathers; 2. Their children; 3. The generation to come; 4. Their children; 5. And their children" Paul followed the same example, exhorting Timothy, "The things that thou hast heard of me...the same commit thou to faithful men, who shall be able to teach others also" (2 Tim 2.2). This responsibility of fathers to teach the children is much emphasised in the Pentateuch. Deuteronomy 6.7 is an example, "And thou shalt teach them diligently unto thy children, and shalt talk of them when thou sittest in thine house, and when thou walkest by the way, and when thou liest down, and when thou risest up". God had established a testimony in the nation and it must be preserved. He had appointed His law in Israel and it must be taught to the children. It was essential that it should be transmitted from generation to generation, for three reasons; that their hope might be fixed in God, that they might never forget the works of God, and that they might keep His commandments.

Obedience to God's commandments would preserve the children from the failures of the fathers. There had been a stubborn and rebellious generation in the past which had grieved the Lord. Their hearts had not been right. They had not been steadfast for God, they had not been faithful. It was the desire of God, and of the Psalmist, that their children should be different. This is the purpose of this Maschil of Asaph.

Verses 9-41: The Wilderness Wanderings

Verse 9 is a difficult verse. Whether Asaph has some particular event or circumstances in mind, or whether he is employing Ephraim representatively of the whole nation, is not clear. The Ephraimites are introduced here as an example of that unfaithfulness of which the Psalmist has just warned the people. There was faithlessness in Ephraim, in spite of God's provision for them, and because of this faithlessness there was impotence. They were armed and carrying bows, but they kept not the covenant of God; they refused to walk in His law, they forgot His works and wonders that they had seen, and, consequently, they turned back in the day of battle. Some have seen a reference to Deuteronomy 1.42-44. If it is objected that this is later than the Exodus, that may not be relevant, since the historical retrospect does not really begin until v.12. Matthew Henry comments, "Observe the shameful cowardice of the children of Ephraim, that warlike tribe, so famed for valiant men, Joshua's tribe; the children of that tribe, though as well armed as ever, turned back when they came to face the enemy. Note, weapons of war stand men in little stead without a martial spirit, and that is gone if God be gone". There may of course be an allusion, even though a prophetic one, to the prominence of Ephraim in the later division of the kingdom, and perhaps it should also be remembered that unfaithfulness and failure was as true of Judah as it was of Ephraim. Dr Cohen says that although the denunciation of the Psalmist was true of the whole people of Israel, it was especially directed against Ephraim as a warning to the kingdom of Judah, to which he belonged. He writes, "The tribe of Ephraim, as its history reveals, lacked steadfastness; therefore its men are likened to warriors who run away in battle although well armed".

It was sad in the extreme that there should be unfaithfulness to God when it is remembered what wonders He had wrought for their deliverance from Egypt. "Marvellous things" He had done in the land of Egypt and in the field of Zoan, mentioned again in the Psalm in v.43. "Field" (7704) may signify the district, or territory, of Zoan. Zoan was an ancient city of lower Egypt and was believed to be the capital, and the home of the Pharaoh at the time of the Exodus. It is interesting that, according to Strong, Zoan means "place of departure". Here began those traumatic events which were to precipitate the departure of the Israelites from the house of bondage. This is but a passing allusion to the plagues in Egypt. The Psalmist returns to the subject and to the "field of Zoan" in v.43, but meantime will recount the story of the wilderness, commencing with the passage of the Red Sea.

God divided the sea for them. As men might cut a highway through a mountain or hill, so the Lord cut a way through the waters, making them stand in a heap until His people were passed through. It was a miraculous beginning to the wilderness story. It must indeed be told again and again to the children, as the Psalmist has said. Day and night God led them. With a pillar of cloud by day and a pillar of fire by night He guided them on their way. Then, just as He divided, or clave the sea, giving them a dry pathway, so He clave the rocks in the wilderness and gave them water. He divided the sea and He clave the rocks. Note that the word (1234) is the same for His cleaving of both sea and rocks. They drank out of the depths, or, as JND adds, "abundantly". He indeed met their need in abundance for the waters flowed out of the rock in streams, running down like rivers. Compare Exodus 17.6 and Numbers 20.8.

"Yet!" How sad is this word with which v.17 begins (RV, JND, JPS). Yet! In spite of all that He had done for them, they went on sinning against Him and provoking Him. He was the Most High, and they were in the desert. How much they needed Him, and yet they provoked Him. The word "wilderness" (6723) of v.17 in the AV is an unusual word from an unused root, meaning "parched, barren, dry". There was no natural sustenance here. They were dependent upon the Most High to provide. Yet they went on sinning against Him, provoking Him, and rebelling against Him when they ought rather to have trusted Him. How patient He was with them!

They tempted God. Although we know that "God cannot be tempted with evil" (Jas 1.13), yet they tried Him, proved Him, testing His patience by their murmuring. Ever dissatisfied in their hearts, mistrusting and distrusting, this people for whom God had done so much, seemed always to be craving more, asking meat for their carnal appetites. As Dr Cohen points out, "The presentation of the circumstances is poetical rather than historical. In fact, food was supplied (Ex 16.8, 12; Num 11.31) before water (Ex 17.6; Num 20.8)". In their lusting they spake against God. In a bitter irony they asked, "Can God furnish a table in the wilderness?". He may have smitten the rock and given them water in overflowing streams, but, "Can he give bread also? can he provide flesh for His people?". In their cruel ingratitude they were not satisfied with the manna. They lusted after the food of Egypt. Forgetting the slavery and the lash of their Egyptian taskmasters they thought only of the fish and the cucumbers, the melons and the leeks, the onions and the garlic (Num 11.5), and they despised the manna.

Jehovah heard their murmurings. He was wroth with them. He kindled a fire expressive of His anger and it consumed those that were in the uttermost parts of the camp (Num 11.1). What an awful indictment of the people is this that follows, "They believed not…and trusted not". He had given them so much reason to believe and so much ground for trust. He had, as it were, opened the very doors of heaven for them. He had rained manna down upon them. It was angels' food, the bread of the mighty, the corn of heaven. It was provision to the full but they despised it. Later they were to say, "Our soul loatheth this light bread" (Num 21.5).

Still Jehovah bore with them, though they despised Him (Num 11.20). He controlled and directed the winds for them, east wind and south wind, and rained down feathered fowl as He had rained down the manna. It was the flesh for which they had craved. They had grumbled and wept in their tents, saying, "Give us flesh", and the answer was, "The Lord will give you flesh" (Num 11.13, 18-20, 31-33). The quails fell in abundance, as the sand of the sea, in the midst of the camp and round about the camp. Jehovah gave them their desire (8378). He gave them that for which they had lusted in their covetousness and greed. But they were to pay dearly for it. "While the flesh was yet between their teeth, ere it was chewed, the wrath of the Lord was kindled against the people, and the Lord smote the people with a very great plague". There, at Kibroth-hattaavah (the graves of lust), a fearful monument to their unbelief, they buried the people that lusted (Num 11.33-34). Nothing had seemed to alienate them from their cravings and greed, so He slew the fattest, the stoutest, the lustiest of them. In righteous anger He smote down the choicest young men of the nation. Amazingly, it is recorded that "for all this they sinned still, and believed not". The water from the rocks, the manna from heaven, the quails, and even the very plague itself, were all wondrous works, but still they believed not.

The end of unbelief is both fearful and sad. "He ended their days as a breath, and their years in terror" (JPS). Unbelief would eventually bar these people from the land of promise. Their days would end in vanity, in nothingness, and their years in trouble. They would die in the wilderness of their unbelief and fail to reach the blessings which their God had for them. True, when at times He slew them, or allowed enemies to slay them, then they would inquire after Him and turn back and seek Him, apparently earnestly. Even this, though, was insincere and short-lived, and selfish in that their thought was not of Him but of their own well-being.

At such times as these they would remember that God was their Rock and the Most High God their Redeemer. Their only hope, both for salvation and security, was in Him who was both Elohim and El-Elyon. The Most High God was the God of Melchizedek, the King-Priest of Salem who had blessed their father Abram so long ago (Gen 14.18-20). Nevertheless, their professed remembrance of Him, and acknowledgement of Him, was but flattery and lies. It was only lip reverence, for their heart was not right toward Him and they were not faithful to His covenant.

"But he"! What grace is this! "But he, being full of compassion, forgave their iniquity, and destroyed them not". How often He could indeed have destroyed the whole nation. It was in His power to do so, but many a time He turned His anger away and did not give vent to His wrath (2534), His indignation and fury. In mercy He remembered their weakness. They were but flesh. They were mortal. They were like a breath which comes, and passes away, and is gone. How often they had provoked Him, grieved Him, forsaken Him, tempted Him, limited Him, and forgotten Him. They had rebelled against Him, they had tried Him, and they had dared to set bounds to the Holy One of Israel. The story of that waste wilderness and the parched desert through which He brought them is a sad story.

Verses 42-52: The Plagues in Egypt

The Psalmist now returns in thought to the redemption of the nation from Egypt. Could this people really have forgotten the wonder of their redemption from the oppressor? Forgetfulness of God and His mercy seems to be the reason for all of their sinning, so now the Psalmist takes them back in memory to that early manifestation of mercy as he sums up the story of the plagues in Egypt. He will remind them again, as he has already done in v.12, of the marvellous things which God had done in the land of Egypt, and in the district of Zoan, in preparation for their flight out of that house of bondage.

Although the first plague is here mentioned first, after this they are not arranged chronologically. God had, first of all, turned the rivers of Egypt into blood, making the waters undrinkable. Note that "rivers" and "floods" (or streams, 5140) are in the plural, indicating the Nile with its tributaries and canals. Water in the pools and the water in their vessels likewise became blood. The fish that were in the rivers died, the rivers stank, and for seven days the whole water supply of that great country was polluted. Jehovah had smitten them to secure the release of His enslaved people (Ex 7.19-25). But Pharaoh's heart was hardened.

There follows a remembrance of the plague of flies. Swarms of flies filled every house in Egypt, from the palace of Pharaoh to the houses of his servants and of all his people. They covered the ground and corrupted the land, and yet, while Egypt suffered, God protected His own people in the land of Goshen so that there were no flies upon them. This was to show them that He was Jehovah, sovereign in all the earth (Ex 8.20-24).

At this stage the second plague is mentioned, in which the land was smitten with frogs. From the rivers and ponds frogs came up in abundance. They covered the land of Egypt. They were in the houses, in the bedrooms, in the beds, in the ovens, and in the kneading troughs. Again, no one was immune. From the palace to the peasant, all were afflicted and the land stank. "That thou mayest know", said Moses to Pharaoh, "that there is none like unto the Lord our God" (Ex 8.1-14).

Locusts and caterpillars were the eighth plague. They too covered the whole land of Egypt, as the frogs had done. The land was darkened. They devoured the fruit of the trees and the herbs of the field and left no green thing (Ex 10.12-14).

Then there was hail, the seventh plague. There had been a warning, which some ignored. Such was the intensity of the hail that it destroyed their vines, broke their trees, and killed their cattle. It was mingled with fire, hot thunderbolts of lightning which slew their flocks. "Only in the land of Goshen, where the children of Israel were, was there no hail" (Ex 9.18-26).

Although the "evil angels", the messengers of woe, of v.49 may, as some think, have a specific reference to the last plague, the death of the firstborn, yet all of these plagues were messengers of evil, bringing trouble as the expressions of the wrath, the anger, and the indignation of God. In the tenth and last plague, however, Jehovah "made a way for his anger" (JND). As Dr Cohen says, "He levelled a path. He has removed every restraint from His anger so that it had full play". He did not spare.

The reference to the "pestilence" in v.50 may particularly recall the fifth plague, a grievous murrain (1698), a cattle disease which killed their horses, asses, camels, sheep and oxen. Once again, the cattle belonging to the children of Israel were unaffected (Ex 9.3-6).

Not all the plagues are specifically mentioned in the Psalm, unless they are embraced in this word "pestilence". These plagues destroyed, devoured, distressed and disabled Egypt, all for the purpose of delivering Israel from the hand of Pharaoh.

The Psalmist then mentions the final crowning judgment, the death of all the firstborn. He "smote all the firstborn in Egypt; the chief of their strength in the tabernacles of Ham" (a synonym for Egypt). JND's rendering is perhaps more explicit: "He smote all the firstborn in Egypt, the first-fruits of their vigour in the tents of Ham". All the firstborn in the land of Egypt died that night, from the firstborn of Pharaoh on the throne, even unto the firstborn of the servant girl at the mill, and the firstborn of the prisoner in the dungeon, and all the firstborn of beasts. There was a great cry in Egypt. "There was not a house where there was not one dead" (Ex 12.29-30).

Jehovah then made His own people go forth like sheep, Himself guiding them like a flock. Had Asaph's generation forgotten these wonders?

Verses 53-66: Israel's History Resumed

Having led His people out, Jehovah then led them on. For a while at least, they travelled without fear. They had been exhorted in Exodus 14.13, "Fear ye not". The Egyptian hosts that followed them were panic stricken, saying, "Let us flee", but the host of Israel went ahead safely as their enemies were swallowed up in the returning waters of the Red Sea. They journeyed on to the frontiers and into the Holy Land. "This mountain" may indicate that eventually they reached Zion, or, as some think, it may indicate the "mountain land" of Canaan, the land which Jehovah had acquired and determined for His people. He drove out the nations of that land and both the land and the tents of those nations became the property of the tribes of Israel. This nation of slaves now had an inheritance by divine allotment.

"Yet", says the AV. "But", says JND. The implication is sad. They tempted and provoked Him, the One who had delivered them. He was the Most High (ELYON - 5945). He was their God (ELOHIM - 430), and they failed Him. They kept not His testimonies, His laws. This was ingratitude in the extreme, and the children were like the fathers, rebellious, and forgetful of all that He had done for them. They turned like a deceitful bow which misses the mark and disappoints its owner.

It is almost incredible that such a people, with such a God, should turn to idolatry. High places and graven images! Plumer comments, "The *high places* were the tops of hills commonly shaded where the Canaanites had worshipped their false gods. They proved a continual snare to the Israelites. Idolatry is pleasing to the flesh. It leaves the soul to wallow in its sins. It requires no real piety to be ever so much devoted to the worship of false gods". Israel ought to have been different, but they were not. Stephen recalls their idolatry in his address to the leaders of the nation in Acts 7, just before his martyrdom. "They made a calf in those days, and offered sacrifice unto the idol, and rejoiced in the works of their own hands". They worshipped the host of heaven. They took up "the tabernacle of Moloch" (Acts 7.41-43). But God was a jealous God (Ex 20.4-5). He heard and He was wroth. The word "wroth" appears again in vv. 21 and 62, and the corresponding noun "wrath" is in v.49. It signifies a provocation to anger. God abhorred (3988) them for their idolatry. He despised them and rejected them. Idolatry was a serious matter. It implied that they had forsaken Him, so He then forsook them.

The setting up of the tabernacle at Shiloh is recorded in Joshua 18.1. It was to Shiloh that the godly Hannah came annually with her husband

Elkanah, to worship and to sacrifice (1 Sam 1.3). It was here that the young Samuel ministered with Eli the priest, but it was here, sadly, that the child was born whose name was Ichabod, "The glory is departed". The holy Ark was taken captive. Thirty thousand of their choice young men perished (1 Sam 4.10). God had forsaken them indeed. The strength and glory of Israel was gone. How great must have been the provocation when God was so wroth with His inheritance. These people were His redeemed people, His inheritance, but He gave them over to the enemy sword. Their glory was in Philistine hands. It was humiliation. Maclaren paints the picture so graphically; "Shiloh, the dwelling place of God, empty for evermore; the 'Glory' - that is, the Ark - in the enemy's hands; everywhere stiffening corpses; a pall of silence over the land; no brides and no joyous bridal chants; the very priests massacred, unlamented by their widows, who had wept so many tears already that the fountain of them was dried up, and even sorrowing love was dumb with horror and despair!".

Then, in characteristic mercy, Jehovah arose to undertake their cause. Like as a man might awake out of a deep and profound sleep, so the Lord rose to help His people. Like a mighty man who had been overcome, and yet stimulated, by reason of wine, He arose with a shout, He smote the enemy, disgracing them into retreat. He plagued the Philistines while the Ark was in their midst. There followed victories under Samuel, Saul and David. He smote the adversaries of His people, for they were His adversaries too, and He put them to everlasting reproach. They suffered, as Dr Cohen remarks, "a reverse on the battlefield from which they never recovered".

Verses 67-72: Not Shiloh in Ephraim, but Zion in Judah

Jehovah now refused (3988) the tabernacle, or tent, of Joseph. "Refused" is the same word as "abhorred" in v.59. He rejected the tent at Shiloh in the territory of Ephraim, son of Joseph. The Ark was never restored there, for, after its recovery, it was brought by David to Jerusalem. So Judah was chosen in place of Ephraim, and Mount Zion instead of Shiloh. Here, in the Zion which He loved, He built His sanctuary, glorious as the heights of heaven and stable as the earth itself.

Notice the sovereign choice of God. He "chose (977) not the tribe of Ephraim" (v.67) but the tribe of Judah. He chose David also. It is His prerogative to select or reject. David was a chosen servant. Although a king, a monarch, he was Jehovah's servant, and this was an honour. Of Abraham and Moses, of Caleb, Job and Isaiah, but more often of David than any, Jehovah says, "My servant". The word "servant" (5650) in v.70, is "bondman" or "slave". What a display of sovereignty is this! God delivers a nation of slaves, bondmen to Pharaoh. He chooses a young man from among them, makes him king, and calls him, "My bondman". He took him from the sheepfolds, a humble shepherd boy of Bethlehem. As Kirkpatrick says, "Taken from being the shepherd of Jesse's flock to be the shepherd of Jehovah's flock". As David had cared for the ewes and lambs of his father's flock, so in the integrity of his heart and with the skilfulness of his hands, he shepherded Israel. To lead and to feed were the responsibilities of every shepherd and this David did for God's people, God's inheritance.

PSALM 79

Introduction

This sad Psalm is a companion, or pendant, to Psalm 74. As with that Psalm there is much dispute as to the authorship and the time and circumstances of its composition. In its superscription it is ascribed to Asaph, but, because of its content, certain commentators will not accept that this is Asaph of the time of David. Many prefer a later date to explain the references to the invasion of the land, the defiling of the temple and the destruction of Jerusalem. To relegate the Psalm to a later date then requires another Asaph, which is but a convenient hypothesis. However, the other consideration is, as has been mentioned in the introduction to Psalm 73, that "of Asaph" may indicate an Asaph collection, completed at a date later than that of Asaph himself, the friend of David.

Dr Gill's introduction to the Psalm is both interesting and helpful. He writes, "This Psalm was not written by one Asaph who is supposed to live after the destruction of Jerusalem by the Chaldeans, or, according to some, even after the times of Antiochus, of whom there is no account, nor any certainty that there ever was such a man in those times; but by Asaph, the seer and prophet, that lived in the time of David, who, under a prophetic spirit, foresaw and foretold things that should come to pass, spoken of in this Psalm: nor is it any objection that what is here said is delivered as a history of facts, since many prophecies are delivered in this way". Isaiah 53 is, of course, an excellent example of the "prophetic past tense", where events which were still seven centuries into the future are described in a past tense, as if they had already happened:- "He was despised...he was wounded...he was bruised...he was oppressed...he was afflicted...he was numbered with the transgressors". Dr Gill then refers to the Targum, of which the IVF New Bible Dictionary says, "The word *targum* is Hebrew, although not found in the Old Testament. It means an Aramaic paraphrase, or interpretative translation of some part of the Old Testament". Dr Gill continues, "The Targum is, 'a song by the hands of Asaph concerning the destruction of the house of the sanctuary (or temple), which he said by a spirit of prophecy'".

If this prophetic view is accepted, then the Psalm may envisage either the Chaldean invasion, or the persecution in the days of Antiochus

Epiphanes, or both, or indeed the siege and destruction of Jerusalem in AD 70. No particular event being identified means, too, that troubled and persecuted saints of any age can turn to the Psalm to find expression of their sorrow, and hope for the future.

The Psalm may be divided as follows. Verses 1-4 are the Psalmist's description of the disaster which has befallen his people. Verses 5-8 are an impassioned entreaty that God might show mercy on His people and judge the oppressor. Verses 9-13 plead that, for the honour of His name and the deliverance of His flock, God should intervene in their distress.

Verses 1-4: Disaster in the Land, the City, and the Temple

The situation was indeed disastrous. The heathen (1471), the GOYIM, had invaded the land which was God's inheritance for His chosen people. Gentile intruders had dared to profane the holy land. They had defiled the holy temple too. They had destroyed Jerusalem, reducing it to heaps of rubble. Jerusalem, where Jehovah had chosen to place His name, was now in ruins. Some of this desolation did take place when the Chaldeans invaded under Nebuchadnezzar, and some in the times of the Maccabees and the Syrian invasion under Antiochus. The sacred vessels of the sanctuary were taken, the altar was polluted with the blood of heathen sacrifices, and the temple itself was burned with fire. Notice how the Psalmist pleads Israel's relationship to God. This sacrilege and the accompanying martyrdoms were not just against Israel, but against God Himself. He speaks of, "Thine inheritance...thy holy temple...thy servants...thy saints".

That the flesh of martyred saints was actually fed to the birds of the air and to the beasts of the field, in the days referred to above, is an historical fact, recorded in the Books of the Maccabees, where this Psalm is quoted freely. It is well to remember that even in those dark days, when the nation was almost utterly corrupt, still there were "saints" (2623), the CHASIDIM, pious, godly, holy ones, living for God in the midst of failure. In every age there are the faithful. As is often said, "God never leaves Himself without a witness".

The blood of these martyrs flowed like water round about Jerusalem and the crowning indignity was that the corpses were left unburied. Dr Cohen remarks, "Such treatment of the dead was regarded with the utmost horror by the Hebrews. The corpse of an executed criminal had to be given decent burial (Deut 21.23); and in Jewish law even a High Priest who was a Nazarite, and so doubly precluded from defiling himself by such contact, had the obligation of attending to the proper disposal of the dead body when there was nobody else to do so". Indeed, to be deprived of burial after death was regarded as a calamity even by the heathen themselves.

Verse 4 is almost a repetition of Psalm 44.13, on which see notes in this Commentary. Their neighbours taunted them. Canaanites in their very midst, with Edomites, Ammonites, Moabites, Philistines and Phoenicians, and perhaps the more distant nations too, mocked and derided them. These surrounding nations rejoiced in Israel's every misfortune. They added insult to injury and gloried in their plight, scorning them. It was both desolation and isolation.

Verses 5-8: A Plea for Pity

This next section of the Psalm opens with a series of questions, wrung from the heart of the Psalmist on behalf of the nation. "How long, LORD? wilt thou be angry for ever? shall thy jealousy burn like fire?". The question, "How long?", is a familiar one in the Psalms. It is an unfinished sentence which does not require to be finished. It has been the heart cry of many a sufferer, expressing the desire for relief. The cry here is addressed to Jehovah (3068). Surely the eternally existent, all-sufficient One who was their God would hear their plea, "How long, LORD?".

God was angry with them. Although their suffering was being inflicted upon them by enemies, they must have understood that it was God's displeasure with them that permitted it. He can, and did, use Gentile nations in the chastisement of His people. The heathen became the rod of His anger. But would it be for ever? Was there not an end in sight? Would there soon be deliverance? This was the anger of a jealous God. Had they not been warned, at Sinai, that He was a jealous God? Had He not demanded that He alone would be worshipped (Ex 20.5)? This claim they had disregarded, and now the anger of their God burned against them. He deplored their idolatry and He would vindicate His honour and authority against those that offended. His servants and His saints might suffer in the process, but Jehovah would maintain His honour.

The Psalmist pleads that God should now turn His wrath upon the nations that were destroying His people. There were heathen peoples who did not acknowledge Him. There were kingdoms that did not call upon His name. Should not Jehovah's anger be poured out upon them? They had devoured Jacob. This Israel had descended from Jacob, whom God in rich grace had lifted to become Israel, prince with God. Would the God of Jacob now see their plight and in that same grace deliver them? These heathen (1471), these godless "goyim", had desolated Israel's land. The habitation which God had allotted to His people had been laid waste.

Verse 8 is again reminiscent of Exodus 20.5. The "former iniquities" of the AV is rendered "the iniquities of our forefathers" by RV, JND, and others. Jehovah had warned them that He was "a jealous God, visiting the iniquity of the fathers upon the children". Did this seem unfair or unjust? It is the lament of Lamentations 5.7; "Our fathers have sinned, and are not; and we have borne their iniquities". But, as Dr Cohen remarks, "Guilt is not transmitted, but the results of wrong are". Fathers sin and children suffer. "Remember not against us the sins of our fathers". However, there is another aspect of this principle in the same Exodus 20; "Shewing mercy unto thousands of them that love me, and keep my commandments" (v.6). For this mercy the Psalmist now pleads. "Let thy tender mercies (compassions, 7356) speedily prevent us". "Prevent" (6923) is an old English word meaning "to go before". The JPS reads, "Let Thy compassions speedily come to meet us". They had been brought very low. They were reduced in circumstances, enfeebled, impoverished. Well might they cry, "How long? How long?".

Verses 9-13: Help...for Thy Name's Sake

The closing verses of the Psalm are an appeal to God's honour. "Help us...deliver us...forgive us", is the plea. They long for salvation from their sufferings but have no national merits to plead. The mighty Elohim is the God of their salvation and this is really an entreaty that God might be true to Himself and deliver them for the glory of His name. "Purge away (3722) our sins", they pray. The Hebrew word is KAPAR, atonement, with the primary meaning "to cover". It had become almost synonymous with forgiveness and pardon, and Strong also associates it with propitiation and reconciliation. It suggests the covering of a crime so that it is forgiven and forgotten. Only God can hide their sins from Him, and this they ask for His name's sake. It is high ground for such an appeal, that the honour of God and the glory of His name are at stake.

How bitter was this, that the heathen should say, mockingly, "Where is their God?". Why should they be allowed to taunt so? Moses made the same plea after the sin of the golden calf (Ex 32.12). They cry, not only to be forgiven, but also to be avenged for the shedding of the blood of God's servants by their oppressors. In almost the same language will the martyrs of a future day cry to Him, "How long, O Lord, holy and true, dost thou not judge and avenge our blood on them that dwell on the earth?" (Rev 6.10). They call for evidence of this vengeance, that in their sight, before their eyes, the heathen might learn the lesson that Israel's God is able to deliver. "In our sight", however, may also mean, as some think, "Let us see it, in our day; may it happen soon; do not defer it".

"The sighing of the prisoner" may have reference to their captivity as a nation. Israel was no stranger to bondage, but they had groaned in their Egyptian imprisonment and Jehovah had heard, and had come down, and had delivered them then. The power that delivered them from Egypt was no less now. In the greatness of that power He could again deliver and preserve His people from death. To those neighbours who had gloated over their calamities He could render sevenfold retribution. The number "seven" is a symbol of completeness or thoroughness. Recompense would be complete. "Into their bosom" is believed to be a metaphor from the practice of carrying articles in the folds of the dress. Dr Cohen writes, "The folds of the garment above the girdle are used in the East as pockets for holding articles of various kinds. May punishment overtake them so closely that it is, so to speak, carried about by them in their pockets".

Have these surrounding nations reproached Israel? Then they have reproached the Lord. To scorn and deride Him was a blasphemy which must be judged.

How tenderly, yet joyfully, does the Psalm conclude. They were His people, and they were "the sheep of His pasture". Literally, they were "the sheep of His shepherding". They were His flock and He was their Shepherd. Their deliverance would produce thanksgiving and praise. These very Psalms would ensure that that praise would resound for ever, from generation to generation. From father to son, and from age to age, the story must be told and the praise must swell in ever increasing volume.

PSALM 80

Introduction

The Psalms of Asaph continue. There is, however, some dispute as to the identity of this Asaph. Because of the content of the Psalm some commentators suggest an Asaph of a later time than the Asaph who was the friend of David. It seems unlikely that there should be two Asaphs envisaged in the same collection of Psalms, all bearing that name but "of Asaph" may mean "of the Asaphite family". The term may indicate a collection of Psalms spanning a period of time beginning with the Davidic Asaph down to a later date, but see the comments on this in the introduction to Psalm 73 in this Commentary.

Spurgeon says, "If by the Asaph of David's day, this Psalm was written in the spirit of prophecy, for it sings of times unknown to David". It is the apparent recognition of a Northern Kingdom in the Psalm that occasions the difficulty regarding date and authorship. Dr Gill's comment is, "Some take this Psalm to be of the same argument as the foregoing, and think it refers to the destruction of the Jews, the two tribes, by the Chaldeans...but there is no mention made of the temple, nor of Jerusalem, as in the preceding Psalm; and besides, why should Manasseh and Ephraim be mentioned? Wherefore others are of opinion that it has regard to the captivity of the ten tribes...but then it may be asked, why is Benjamin taken notice of, which had no concern in the affliction? This has led others to conclude that it respects some time of affliction before either of these captivities, or between them both, and it may be applied to any affliction of the people of God in any age or period of time; and no doubt was written by Asaph, or by David, and put into his hands before the distress was, under a spirit of prophecy".

While commentators dispute as to whether the Psalm supposes one or other of the captivities, Plumer quotes Merrick who makes the point that the early mention of Ephraim and Benjamin and Manasseh together supposes the tribes all yet united, at least in sympathy with each other, and that the Psalm may have been written when some foe was hovering on their borders and beginning to devastate the land. This view may be both feasible and acceptable and in keeping with the well-known Asaph being the author of the Psalm. It must be remembered though, that Asaph was a seer and that he may well have written in a spirit of prophecy (2 Chr 29.30).

For the fourth time the word "Shoshannim" appears in a Psalm title. See also Psalms 45, 60 and 69. Once it is in the singular form "Shushan", in Psalm 60, where also it is adjoined to "Eduth", as it is here in Psalm 80. As suggested in the introduction to Psalm 60 in this Commentary, the words mean, "Lilies of testimony". Lilies are emblems of beauty and purity. This may signify the beauty of the law, as the testimony, or it may mean the beauty of the testimony of God's people to that law. This, of course, is the symbolic or emblematic application of the words, but to the Chief Musician, the Master of Song, to whose care the Psalm was committed, they may have indicated either the melody, or the musical instrument, which were to be used in the singing.

A sad but lovely refrain in verses 3, 7 and 19, divides the Psalm into three unequal parts. It sings, "Turn us again, O God, and cause thy face to shine; and we shall be saved". The last part may be sub-divided, which sub-divisions will be observed in the commentary. The first part, verses 1-3, is a prayer for the restoration of God's favour to the nation, and the former prosperity. The second part, verses 4-7, is the sad but familiar, "How long?". For how long will their God be angry with them? For how much longer will their enemy neighbours laugh at them? In the final part, verses 8-19, the nation is viewed under the figure of a vine, blessed but broken, privileged but perishing, and there follows a closing prayer for revival.

Verses 1-3: Prayer for Restoration

It is a tender and passionate appeal with which the Psalm opens, "Give ear, O Shepherd of Israel". Spurgeon paraphrases, "Hear thou the bleatings of thy suffering flock". This "shepherd" figure used here of God is a familiar one in the OT. Psalm 23 is the well-known and much loved example. Isaiah too employs it, "He shall feed his flock like a shepherd" (Is 40.11). It has been carried over into the NT writings also, and indeed into christian hymnology too. Perhaps the earliest reference to it is by the aged Jacob, who, blessing the sons of Joseph, said, "The God that shepherded me all my life long...bless the lads" (Gen 48.15, JND). Again, in his blessing upon Joseph he spoke of "The shepherd, the stone of Israel" (Gen 49.24). Is it significant that, when Messiah was born, it was earthly shepherds of Bethlehem who were first among men to receive the news that He had come?

The Shepherd is the Shepherd of Israel, but the nation is now viewed as "Joseph". "Thou that leadest Joseph like a flock". Joseph was, after all, as

Spurgeon says, "That renowned son who became a second father to the tribes, and kept them alive in Egypt". It is possible too, that they were known to the Egyptians as the family of Joseph. He who shepherded Israel and who led Joseph like a flock, was, in His glory, the One who dwelt between the cherubim, a reference of course to Jehovah's presence in the Holy of Holies of the Tabernacle. "Shine forth" (3313), is the plea. Show Thyself! Send out beams of that glory which illumes the Holiest of All! When that ancient structure had first been set up, "the glory of the Lord filled the tabernacle" (Ex 40.34). The Psalmist desires that the radiance of that glory should now shine forth upon the nation in its sorrow.

There is something very touching in the mention of Ephraim, Benjamin, and Manasseh together in the same verse, almost, as it were, in one breath. They were indeed of the same family. Ephraim and Manasseh were the sons of Joseph, and Joseph with his brother Benjamin were the sons of the beloved Rachel. Sadly, they were to be separated at the division of the kingdom, but here they are united with the plea that the Shepherd of Israel might manifest His power in their salvation. It will be remembered that these three tribes marched together in the wilderness, immediately behind the holy Ark of the Covenant (Num 2.17-24; 10.21-24). They were united then, and here the prayer of Asaph brings them together again. How good to remember always that, in spite of the divisions and schisms which have rent the saints and their testimony, in the mind and purpose of God all are embraced as one.

> We would remember we are one
> With every saint that loves Thy Name;
> United to Thee on the throne,
> Our life, our hope, our Lord the same.
> (James G. Deck)

Notice that in the refrain of v.3, which will be repeated in vv. 7 and 19, the prayer is "Turn us again, O God". It is not so much an appeal that the Lord might turn to them, but that they might be turned to Him, restored. His face is ever shining, but at times His people turn away and need to be recovered to Him. "Shine" (215) in v.3 is a similar word, but different, to the word of v.1. Here it is like the breaking of day, like the kindling of a fire, like the shining of sun, moon, and stars. The prayer, "cause thy face to shine" is reminiscent of the priestly blessing of Numbers 6.24-26, and indeed the word "shine" here is exactly the same word as in that lovely benediction. The shining of the face of God is really the smile of His presence, and His presence is salvation.

Verses 4-7: How Long?

In the second strophe, as Alexander Maclaren says, "A piteous tale of suffering is wailed forth". The "How long" must not be interpreted as an irreverent impatience. It is rather a sad questioning of the circumstances into which they have been brought, and a longing for divine deliverance. The appeal is addressed to God with a majestic, if unusual, title, "O LORD (3068) God (430) of hosts (6635)". This is Jehovah Elohim of Sabaoth, a title denoting universal sovereignty. There is an almost indefinable greatness here. Jehovah, eternal and self-sufficient; Elohim so mighty; God of the hosts of heaven. To such an One does the Psalmist appeal on behalf of a suffering nation. For how long will He seem to be angry against the prayer of His people. Or, as Delitzsch says, "Angry while the people are praying".

The sorrows of the nation are now described under familiar figures. Their food and drink were tears. The bread of tears was their daily portion, and they drank tears in large measure. How long? Jehovah had allowed the nation to become a strife (4066) an object of contention, to scornful neighbours. Were they quarrelling about the acquisition of Israel's territory? Their enemies laughed contemptuously among themselves, shaking their heads in derision as they watched their plight. It is not surprising that they should cry so sadly, "How long, O Lord".

The refrain of v.3 is repeated in v.7, but with an amplified title – "O God of hosts". Again the appeal is for the shining of the face of God and the salvation which His presence and favour would bring.

Verses 8-19: The Vine out of Egypt

There are reminiscences of the wilderness all down this Psalm, and this third strophe begins with a remembrance of the Exodus and the deliverance out of Egypt. Jehovah had viewed His people as a vine, with the potential to produce fruit for His pleasure and joy. With this in mind He brought them out of the house of their bondage. He drove out nations from the land which He purposed for them, preparing room for this goodly vine of His. In this Promised Land it took deep root under His care. It filled the land. The mountains were covered with its shadow. Its branches were like cedars planted by God Himself. Her boughs reached to the sea in the west and her shoots stretched to the river in the east. From the Mediterranean to the Euphrates she spread out in glory. For a while it was all so pleasant. Joseph was indeed a fruitful bough (Gen 49.22).

In v.12, however, the picture changes. It is a pathetic contrast with the former glory. The hedges of the vineyard are destroyed. The fences are broken down, so that the vine is unprotected, exposed to the destructive elements all around. The swine from the forest ravage it. Wild beasts of the field feed on it and devour it. Has God forgotten His vine, that He should leave it so, at the mercy of cruel adversaries?

There follows a heart-cry to the God of Hosts, Elohim Sabaoth. As in the earlier refrain they had asked to be turned in restoration to Him, so now the plea is that He might turn to them. The appeal is four-fold. "Return", they plead, "look down, behold, and visit". After all, this vineyard was His. It was He who had planted the stock and it was He who had made the young plant strong for Himself. Now it was burned with fire, cut down, and perishing because His face was against them.

The renewed appeal in v.17 is very tender. "The man of thy right hand" may be an allusion to Benjamin, previously mentioned in v.2, whose name means, "The son of the right hand". There may be an immediate reference to the King who ruled in Judah at the time when the Psalm was written. But the more distant and prophetic reference is to Messiah Himself. Israel will continue to have persecutions and pogroms until that time comes when Messiah reigns. He who is even now at the right hand of God, He who is the true Son of Man, will ultimately and eventually bring peace to the troubled nation. That day will be a day of quickening, of revival, and then there will be no more going back from Him. Then will they call upon His name continually and bask contentedly in the light of His countenance.

The refrain of vv. 3 and 7 is now repeated, but notice the enlarging, the amplification, of the form of address to God each time. "Turn us again, O God" (v.3). "Turn us again, O God of hosts" (v.7). "Turn us again, O LORD God of hosts" (v.19). There is a progressive intensity in the appeal to Him who is their only resource for salvation. "Cause thy face to shine; and we shall be saved". If only He would smile upon them, that would be sufficient. As Maclaren concludes, so beautifully, "The faith that grasps all that is contained in that full-toned name already feels the light of God's face shining upon it, and is sure that its prayer for salvation is not in vain".

PSALM 81

Introduction

This is yet another Psalm committed to the charge and care of the Chief Musician, the Master of Temple Song. Another Psalm of Asaph, too, and yet another Psalm upon the Gittith. Alexander says, "In the absence of any proof to the contrary, the Asaph of this title must be assumed to be the contemporary of David". This would date the Psalm around 1050-1045BC. The word "Gittith", meaning "winepress", occurs in the titles of Psalms 8, 81 and 84. It is believed by many to have been the name of a musical instrument associated with Gath, but for a more detailed consideration of this see the introduction to Psalm 8 in this Commentary. It has been noted that the three Psalms bearing this name in their titles are all of a joyful, thanksgiving character.

Dr Cohen entitles this Psalm, "A Festival Meditation", and points out that Jewish tradition connects the Psalm with the Harvest Festival, the Feast of Tabernacles, in the seventh month of the year. Tabernacles was the happiest, most joyful occasion in Israel's calendar. Many, though, prefer to link the Psalm with the Feast of Trumpets, which was celebrated on the first day of that month. Yet again, some associate the Psalm with the Feast of the Passover. Maclaren, while admitting that there has been much discussion and diversity of opinion as to which feast is in the Psalmist's mind, and conceding that Tabernacles has been widely accepted, nevertheless writes, with a certain finality, "On the whole, the Passover is most probably the feast in question". Spurgeon comments, "Praise is called for to celebrate some memorable day, perhaps the Passover" T.W. Davies sees both Passover and Tabernacles, saying, "We have probably a hymn chanted regularly at the beginning of the Feasts of Passover and Tabernacles, both of which were inaugurated at full moon by the blowing of trumpets". Plumer remarks, perhaps very wisely, "The fact is, this ode is fit to be sung on any joyous occasion of worship in Israel".

The Psalm may be divided as follows. The first five verses are a summons to keep the Festival, with the reminder that such was ordained of God. Verses 6-10 are an account of what God had done for His people, bringing them out of Egypt, caring for them in the wilderness, and entering into covenant with them at Sinai. The concluding verses, 11-16, regret the waywardness of the people but promise blessing for obedience.

Verses 1-5: The Summons to the Festival

"Sing aloud" (7442) is a translation of one Hebrew word which signifies "to shout for joy". It suggests a ringing cry of exultation and praise. "Sing ye joyously", says JND. "Sing aloud unto God our strength". If indeed the Psalm is a Passover Psalm, then there may be a reminder here, almost an echo, of that song of redemption on the banks of the Red Sea, "I will sing unto the Lord, for he hath triumphed gloriously...the Lord is my strength and song" (Ex 15.1-2). The "joyful noise" (7321) for which the Psalmist calls, is a shout of triumph. The God of Jacob is the God of grace of whom the patriarch had such rich experience.

Delitzsch suggests, and Dr Cohen agrees, that there is actually a three-fold summons in the first three verses. Verse 1 is a general call, addressed to the whole congregation. Verse 2 is a summons to the Levites, the appointed singers and musicians in Israel. Verse 3 is directed to the priests who were entrusted with the blowing of the trumpet, the "shofar", the ram's horn.

The "psalm" (2172) of v.2 is a melody. To "take" (5375) the melody signifies to lift it, to raise the song, and there follows direction as to certain musical instruments. The timbrel was the hand-drum of the Easterns. It was made of a stretched skin with a surrounding margin of wood, and was akin to the tambourine usually played by the women. The pleasant harp was the sweet sounding lyre, and the psaltery was the lute, another form of harp. There joined with these the blowing of the "shofar", the trumpets, and Maclaren comments, "One can almost hear the tumult of joyful sounds, in which the roar of the multitude, the high-pitched notes of singers, the deeper clash of timbrels, the twanging of stringed instruments, and the hoarse blare of rams' horns, mingle in concordant discord, grateful to Eastern ears, however unmusical to ours".

The new moon of v.3 is the first day of the month, but since the trumpet here referred to is the "shofar" , Dr Cohen argues, "This cannot refer to the blowing at each new moon (Num 10.10), because on that occasion silver trumpets, and not the 'shofar', were sounded. The first day of the seventh month, however, was marked by blowing the 'shofar', and observed as a memorial proclaimed with the blast (of the 'shofar') (Lev 23.24). Since the first month, in which the Passover was celebrated, was not inaugurated in this manner, we must understand the feast-day of this Psalm as Tabernacles, at the full moon. The Festival of Tabernacles began on the fifteenth of the seventh month when the moon was full". As Dr Cohen also rightly points out, the phrase "the time appointed" (3677), of the AV, actually means, "the full moon".

The "solemn feast" (2282) referred to was one of the three pilgrimage-festivals of Israel. On the occasions of Passover/Unleavened Bread, Pentecost, and Tabernacles, every Jewish male was required to make pilgrimage to Jerusalem (Deut 16.16). This was a statute for Israel. It was a law of the God of Jacob, ordained in Joseph for a testimony for Him. Notice the triple designation of the nation – Israel, Jacob, Joseph. These are synonyms, but signify different aspects of the nation's relationship to God. On the reference to Joseph, Plumer comments, "Whatever was pleasant in the condition of the Israelites in Egypt was mainly through the influence of Joseph; for when there arose another Pharaoh, who knew not Joseph, they fell into great affliction. So that there is peculiar propriety in here using *Joseph* as a name for the nation".

The latter part of v.5 is admittedly difficult. The pronoun "he" should be understood as referring to God Himself, when He went out against Egypt prior to the emancipation of His people. The pronoun "I", occurring twice, may be the Psalmist speaking representatively for the nation at that time of the Exodus. "I heard a language…I understood not". Was the nation, after several centuries in the house of bondage, only now becoming familiar with the voice and the word of God? Was the divine language strange to them? Davies suggests, "Render: '[In Egypt] he [Israel] heard the language of One whom he knew not.' The words in brackets are probably to be supplied…The verbs should be read in the third person with the Septuagint. When God revealed Himself to His chosen people in Egypt He was largely unknown to them". Israel then began to hear God, revealed in their redemption, in a way which they had not known Him or His Word during their years of slavery. In the verses which follow God will speak, recalling to them what He had done for them, delivering them out of Egypt.

Verses 6-10: Egypt - Meribah - Sinai

Israel had borne heavy burdens in Egypt. They probably literally carried baskets of bricks and other building materials. These baskets were suspended, one at either end of a yoke which was laid upon the shoulders. "Pots" (1731) of the AV is "baskets". Jehovah had removed the burdens and delivered them from the Egyptian yoke. How the people had cried for relief from their bondage. "The children of Israel sighed by reason of the bondage, and they cried, and their cry came up unto God by reason of the bondage. And God heard their groaning" (Ex 2.23-24). Jehovah now recalls this, saying to them, "Thou calledst in trouble, and I delivered thee; I answered thee in the secret place of thunder". As Kirkpatrick says, "In the covert of the thunder-cloud God conceals and reveals Himself". At the passage of the Red Sea, "The pillar of the cloud went from before their face, and stood behind them: And it came between the camp of the Egyptians and the camp of Israel; and it was a cloud and darkness to them, but it gave light by night to these" (Ex 14.19-20).

But it was not only in Egypt that they cried and were delivered. The miracle of the waters of Meribah (Ex 17.1-7) is now singled out as an example of the patience of God with them in the wilderness. What longsuffering He displayed in spite of the ingratitude of the people He had so recently redeemed. "Meribah" means "strife". The people chided with Moses and they tempted the Lord, and still He bore with them and graciously supplied their needs continually. God proved them there. They had proved Him and found Him to be faithful, but when He proved them, sadly, they were mistrusting and distrusting, slow to believe the God whom they had proved to be faithful. How many believers can see themselves reflected in the history of this murmuring nation? Some commentators have suggested that the waters of Meribah are mentioned here particularly because of the libations of water at the Feast of Tabernacles. These libations were accompanied by prayers for the rain which was so essential for the harvest of the coming year.

The "Selah" is no doubt an indication that reader and singer alike should pause. It is a time for considered meditation upon these great matters.

Jehovah now appeals to His people, "Hear, O my people". He has something to say to them which they ought to hear. "I will testify…if thou wilt hearken". Maclaren comments so aptly, "With infinite pathos, the tone of the Divine Speaker changes from that of authority to pleading and the utterance of a yearning wish, like a sigh. 'Would that thou wouldest hearken!' That wonderful utterance of Divine wish is almost a parenthesis. It gives a moment's glimpse into the heart of God". If Israel would indeed hearken, and remember Sinai and the Exodus, they would know that their God was a jealous God who wanted them for Himself. They must be done with the worship of strange gods. He was Jehovah (3068), their Elohim (430). He had brought them out of the land of Egypt and would meet all their recurring needs. "Open thy mouth wide, and I will fill it". As young birds open wide their mouths and are fed by the mother bird, so Jehovah would feed His people. It was folly to go to strange gods when such a God as theirs could meet their every need.

Verses 11-16: Oh that My People had Hearkened!

The closing section of the Psalm begins with that sad word "But". How much Jehovah had done for them. How He had warned, and pleaded, and promised. "But!" Disobedient and obstinate, the nation would not hearken to Him. "Israel would have none of me", He laments. The RV rendering of the verse that follows is fearful: "So I let them go after the stubbornness of their heart". If they would not walk in His counsels, then He would let them walk in their own. If only they had hearkened, and walked in His ways! If only they had been as faithful to Him as He had been to them! Then He would have subdued their enemies and routed the adversaries. Their enemies were His enemies, haters of Jehovah. He would have brought them to submission and prolonged the time of their punishment. This, however, was negative, the destruction of their enemies. There was a more positive blessing for obedience and faithfulness to Him.

The Lord would have fed His obedient people with the finest of the wheat. This is, literally, the fat of wheat, the very best and richest ears of corn. Famine would have been unknown if only they had lived in faithfulness to Him. There would, too, have been "honey out of the rock" for them. Had they not been promised "a land flowing with milk and honey"? Spurgeon quotes John Duns, who writes, "Most travellers who have visited Palestine in summer have had their attention directed to the abundance of honey, which the bees of the land have stored up in the hollows of trees and in crevices of the rock. In localities where the bare rocks of the desert alone break the sameness of the scene, and all around is suggestive of desolation and death, the traveller has God's care of His chosen people vividly brought to mind, as he sees the honey which the bees had treasured up beyond his reach, trickling in shining drops down the face of the rock". Indeed, in return for their obedience, Jehovah would have provided not only necessities, but luxuries also. In a word, He would have satisfied them. "Oh that my people had hearkened!"

PSALM 82

Introduction

The title of this short Psalm is very brief, indicating simply that it is a Psalm of Asaph. There is no valid reason for doubting that this is the Asaph of the time of David, and this therefore would fix the date at around 1050-1045BC.

The Psalm is a vision of judgment. Jehovah, the supreme Judge of all the earth, takes His stand among earthly judges and upbraids them for their partiality and their injustices. Commentators disagree as to whether these are heathen judges which are arraigned, or if they might be those who carried judicial responsibility in Israel. Perhaps the indictments may well apply to both. Dr Gill says, "This Psalm was written for the use of persons in power, for the instruction of kings and princes, judges and civil magistrates". Alexander calls it, "A brief but pregnant statement of the responsibilities attached to the judicial office under the Mosaic dispensation". Many have noticed a close parallel to the scene depicted in Isaiah 3.13-14.

The eight verses of the Psalm hardly require any formal division, except that the opening two verses, ending with the "Selah", are an introduction of the great judgment scene. Verses 3-7 which follow state the charges and the warnings, and the closing verse 8 is an appeal to the Judge Supreme, to whom everything belongs, that He should arise and judge the earth.

Verses 1-2: The Judge in the Midst of the Judges

"God standeth" (5324). So the Psalm begins, but this is not the usual verb for "standing". It does not simply denote the opposite of "sitting". The divine Judge takes His stand. He assumes a position of authority. He stands in the congregation of the mighty (410). Since this is the word "El" which is so often a divine title, some, as JND, JPS, Maclaren, and the Newberry margin, prefer to render it as, "In the congregation, or assembly, of God". This indicates that it is He who has called the assembly. Men are gathered by His appointment and command for the judgment scene. It is therefore His assembly, "The assembly of God".

Others however, retain the "mighty" of the AV, as describing the powerful judges of earth who are gathered at the tribunal. Those who argue for this "mighty" rendering, point out that the word "gods" among whom Jehovah judges is the word "elohim" (430), also usually a divine title but now applied to the mighty of earth. Refer also to the Saviour's words in John 10.34, where "gods" is applied to men, a reference to v.6 of this Psalm. It may be, too, that angelic beings are included in this gathered company. See them appearing before God in Job 1.6 and 2.1. According to Strong, "elohim" may be correctly translated "rulers" or "judges", and indeed the JPS version will render it as, "In the midst of the judges He judgeth". Dr Cohen, whose commentary is based on the JPS translation, has the note, "The men who administer justice are considered to be His agents. They exercise a Godly function, and as such have His name attached to them". Alexander comments, "The idea is, that as the judges were gods to other men, so God would be a judge to them".

So often Israel and the Psalmists had cried, "How long?", but now it is Jehovah who asks the same question. "How long?" "How long will ye judge unjustly, and accept the persons of the wicked?" They were partial, and their partiality led to injustices. They did not hold the scales of justice evenly. They were corrupt, amenable to bribery and influence. Did they fear, or court, the richer men who came before them? Did they rule in favour of a man because of his person and status? It was wrong for a judge to respect persons in this manner. "Selah!" Pause.

Verses 3-7: The Indictments Detailed

Righteous judges would have defended the weak and the poor, and executed fair judgment for orphans, as for the afflicted and the needy of any status in life. A man's standing in society would not, should not, have any influence on the decisions of a righteous court. Indeed, if there was to be any respecting of persons at all, perhaps it should be to remember that the orphan has no father to protect him, and the poor and needy man likely has no friends of note to speak for him. These would be particularly dependent upon a righteous judgment. So the exhortation to the judges is to defend the poor and the fatherless, to do justice for the afflicted and needy.

Mighty and powerful as these judges were, and assumed to be learned, yet they walked in ignorance, failing to understand or practise the very basics of good judgment. They walked in moral and intellectual darkness, so that the very foundations of earthly society were disrupted by their judicial improprieties.

Jehovah addresses them once more, "I have said, Ye are gods (430)". He reminds them of their position of high authority. They should have been morally great among men. Their office as magistrates was dignified and awful. In their solemn responsibilities they were representatives of the Most High, and as children bear the likeness of the father, so should they have evidenced the characteristics of Him whom they represented. "The powers that be are ordained of God" (Rom 13.1).

Nevertheless, in spite of this conferred greatness, "Ye shall die like men", He predicts. Dr Cohen thinks that this is a reference to the death sentence pronounced upon guilty men. He writes, "As ordinary men suffer capital punishment when they incur it, so will you receive at My hands sentence of death for condemning the innocent. Far from your dignified title giving you immunity, it increases your liability". The word "men" in v.7 is ADAM (120). Plumer suggests that there may be a reference to the fall of the first man. Just as Adam fell from his dignity and his honour on account of his sin, so will these judges fall from their greatness. Even princes perish, they are reminded. High office is no protection against the righteous judgment of God when that is demanded by wrongdoing.

Verse 8: Arise, O God, Judge the Earth!

The trial of earth's judges is now over. The Psalmist appeals to God that He should arise and judge (8199) the earth. This word may be rendered "rule" or "govern". Since He, the supreme and mighty Elohim, is the

Possessor of heaven and earth (Gen 14.19), and will eventually inherit that which is His by right, so He has also the right to judge in His earth. If Israel's judges, and the judges of the nations too, have miserably failed in the execution of their judicial duties, nevertheless there is One who will not, and can not, fail. The Psalmist's appeal is to Him. "Arise…judge…for thou shalt inherit all nations". One day, in millennial glory, a Man will take possession of everything for the Almighty. In that day, "A king shall reign in righteousness, and princes shall rule in judgment" (Is 32.1), and a Man will order all things aright. Meanwhile, He waits in patience until that word of the second Psalm is fulfilled, "I shall give thee the heathen for thine inheritance, and the uttermost parts of the earth for thy possession".

PSALM 83

Introduction

This is the last of twelve Psalms which are ascribed to Asaph. Eleven of these are in the third Book of the Psalter, being the consecutive Psalms 73-83. The other, the first of Asaph's Psalms, is Psalm 50. For more detailed comment on Asaph refer to the introduction to Psalm 50 in this Commentary.

This Psalm is entitled "A Song (7892) or Psalm (4210) of Asaph". The first Psalm which is also called a song is Psalm 30. It is believed that a Psalm was always sung with a musical accompaniment, whereas a song may have been rendered with the voice only. Since, however, like Psalm 30, this Psalm is called both a Song and a Psalm, this may signify that it could be sung either with or without instrumental accompaniment. It will be remembered that in Ephesians 5.19 Paul speaks of "psalms and hymns and spiritual songs".

The Psalm is a prayer for judgment on a confederacy of nations which have united against Israel. Perhaps, as with many other Psalms, there is no need to relate it to any particular event or circumstance in the history of the nation. Many have attempted to do this and the suggestions are legion. Plumer quotes Venema on the matter, who says, maybe with some irony, "Some refer it to the times of David, some to the times of Jehoshaphat, some to the times of Jehoram, others to the times of Hezekiah, others to the return from Babylon, others to the times of Esther, and others to the times of Judas Maccabeus!". Perhaps this variety of opinion only serves to demonstrate that Israel has so often been subjected to assaults and invasions by enemy nations that the entreaty of this Psalm would have been most appropriate on more than one occasion. As Dr Cohen comments, "There is no one period in Israelite history which fully tallies with the situation outlined in the Psalm…The safest line to take is to see in the poem an amalgam of history and poetry". Maclaren suggests that, "The Psalm would then be, not the memorial of a fact, but the expression of the standing relation between Israel and the outlying heathendom". Another has said, "This Psalm can never be out of date...and to the spiritual adversaries of his soul, every private Christian may apply it at all times" (Horne).

There is a natural division in the Psalm at verse 8, created by the "Selah", but the eighteen verses may be further divided as follows. Verses 1-4 are a general cry for help and a presentation of the intentions of the enemy. From verse 5 there follows a detailed account of the nations in conspiracy against Israel, and this continues until verse 8 and the "Selah". Verses 9-15 appeal for a divine overthrow of this league of adversaries, and the closing verses, 16-18, are an expressed desire for God's glory in their defeat.

Verses 1-4: The Cry for Help

Notice the repeated "O God...O God" in the opening verse of the Psalm. The first name of God here used is Elohim (430). The second is El (410). The employment of the two names so close together is expressive of the wide appeal to the might and majesty of God that He should intervene. The prayer is three-fold, "Keep not thou silence...hold not thy peace...be not still". It is reminiscent of Isaiah 62.6-7. Is there an implication here that God had indeed been silent? If so, it was not that He could not speak. He was not like the dead deities of the heathen. But why was He silent now? O that He would arise to the cause of His people and be not still.

The appeal is now the more powerful when the Psalmist calls the enemies of Israel "thine enemies". The enemies of God's people were the enemies of God Himself. Surely He must move against them. While God was silent, these enemies made a tumult, an uproar. Their hostility was loud. Their hatred was strong. They lifted up the head in boastful confidence, as if anticipating quick success in their malicious plans to destroy Israel. It was an evil coalition of nations, who plotted with craft and cunning for the overthrow of the people of God. "Thy people", the Psalmist pleads. How can God remain passive? These were His hidden ones (6845), who were being oppressed. They were as His treasure store, hidden in His heart, in His affections, and in His counsels, for His own pleasure. It was imperative that He should protect His treasure from this conspiracy of wicked men.

Verses 5-8: The Confederacy Described

How often have nations conspired against Israel. These who now plan the destruction of the nation are unashamedly plotting such a complete extermination that the name of Israel will be removed from the annals of history so that they will be no more remembered. They are formidable foes, for they are many, and they are united, consulting together with one consent. But, pleads the Psalmist, "They are confederate against thee". This, in fact, is the weakness in their strength! To be adversaries of God's people is to fight against God. Some ten peoples are identified as playing their part in the conspiracy. How sad it is that so many of these were direct descendants of Abraham, the father of the nation whose destruction they were plotting. Others, if not directly descended, were in some way related to that same revered patriarch.

Edom is first mentioned. This is one of the names of Esau who sold his birthright to Jacob in Genesis 25.29-34. His posterity settled in mountainous country south of the Dead Sea, sometimes known as Idumea. Their capital was Bozrah but their chief city was really the almost impregnable Petra. They were inveterate enemies of Israel, the descendants of Jacob who had cheated their father Esau. They will be remembered for their refusal to allow Israel passage through their territory on the journey from Egypt to Canaan (Num 20.14-21).

The Ishmaelites are mentioned next. Ishmael was the son of Abraham, but his mother was Hagar. Hagar was an Egyptian, Sarai's handmaid and a bond-woman (Gen 16.15; Gal 4.22-23). It was promised to Hagar that her son would become a great nation (Gen 21.13-21), but there does not seem to be any promise of territory, such as there was to Isaac, and this has been a matter of controversy between Isaac and Ishmael ever since.

Next in the confederacy is Moab. The history of the Moabites is shameful from the beginning. Moab was a child of incest, the son of Lot by his eldest daughter (Gen 19.30-37). The country of Moab lay east and south-east of the Dead Sea. The Moabites were idolaters, worshipping Chemosh and Baal-peor (Num 25.1-3), and they were a constant plague upon Israel. Perhaps this very thing makes even more beautiful the story of Ruth the Moabitess, who left the gods of Moab to shelter under the wings of the God of Israel (Ruth 2.12).

The Hagarenes, called Hagarites in 1 Chronicles 5.10, 19-20, are believed by some to be descendants of Abraham by his wife Keturah (Gen 25.1). Little is known of the Hagarenes except that they dwelt east of Jordan in Gilead and were at war with Israel in the 1 Chronicles 5 passage already mentioned.

Next, Gebal were a tribe living in mountainous country in the northern part of Idumea. They may be identified with the Gibblites of Joshua 13.5.

Ammon was, as Moab, the child of Lot's incestuous relationship, but with his younger daughter (Gen 19.30-38). Like the Moabites, the Ammonites were also idolaters, worshipping Moloch, who is called "the abomination of the children of Ammon" (1 Kings 11.7). Their home was east of Jordan.

Amalek was a grandson of Esau. The Amalekites were ever bitterly hostile to Israel. "Fight with Amalek", Moses had commanded Joshua. They fought, and prevailed, and Jehovah decreed that the victory should be recorded in a book as a memorial to the triumph (Ex 17.8-14).

Philistia, from which is derived "Philistines" and "Palestine", was on the southern Mediterranean coast. The Philistines are, of course, often mentioned in Israel's history and were notorious for their hostility to the nation. They were a war-like people whose chief city was Gaza. Goliath of Gath was their champion in his day, slain by the sling and stone of David the shepherd boy of Bethlehem

These are joined with Tyre, to the north of the same Mediterranean coast. Note how they are joined again under divine judgment in Amos 1.6-10.

Assur, or Assyria (RV), is probably mentioned last of all because of its remoteness from Israel in its northern location. Asshur, father of the Assyrians, was a son of Shem (Gen 10.22). The Assyrians were the powerful and relentless foes of Israel, who eventually carried away the Northern Kingdom into captivity. Assyria was at one time a mighty empire, called by some, the "Rome of the East".

This awful coalition of enemy nations is now indicted for having helped the children of Lot, the Moabites and Ammonites already mentioned. It was a powerful but evil confederacy of peoples who were united in one thing, their opposition to, and hatred of, Israel. Would God remain in silence? Would He hold His peace? Could He be still when His beleaguered people so needed Him? The appeal continues in the next section of the Psalm. But meanwhile, "Selah"! It is time to reflect, to pause, to meditate, to think, and to quietly lift up the heart to God.

Verses 9-15: O My God...Persecute the Persecutors!

The names of several more nations and individuals are now recalled, to show that God has, in the past, dealt with the enemies of His people. The present prayer is, that as He did in the past, so He might do again, and judge the adversaries.

It has already been remarked how many of these nations were directly related to Abraham. Midian, now remembered, was the fourth son of Abraham by Keturah (Gen 25.2). The Midianites were avowed enemies of Israel, but who can forget their defeat by Gideon as recorded in ch. 7 of the Book of Judges? Indeed Oreb and Zeeb of v.11 in the Psalm were two of their celebrated princes, or generals, who were slain and beheaded when Gideon routed their armies (Judg 7.25). The Psalmist's prayer is that God may now deal with the present enemies of Israel as He dealt with the Midianites by Gideon.

The story of Sisera and Jabin is told in Judges ch. 4. Jabin was King of Canaan and Sisera was his general, the captain of his host. They were defeated at the River Kishon by Barak and Deborah, with the assistance of another courageous woman called Jael. Endor, of v.10, is not mentioned in Judges at the time of the defeat, but Endor is only four or five miles south of Mount Tabor of Judges 4.12, 14, at the foot of which the Kishon has its source in the plain of Esdraelon. The king and his general perished there and their bodies remained unburied, becoming like fertilising dung for the ground. The Psalmist longs that God might again so rout the enemies of his people. Zebah and Zalmunna, mentioned often in Judges 8.4-27, were kings of Midian who were defeated and slain by Gideon. They were also Ishmaelites. See Judges 8.24 and compare Genesis 37.28.

The common language of all of these enemies of Israel, both past and present, was, "Let us cut them off from being a nation" (v.4), and, "Let us take to ourselves the houses of God in possession" (v.12). It is a fine testimony that the tents and houses of Israel and their inherited land of Canaan, had become known as the places where God dwelt, the habitations of God. Of this evil alliance of nations the Psalmist now prays, "O my God, make them like a wheel" (1534). "Like the whirling dust" (RV). "Like a whirling thing" (JND). It is a prayer for their confusion, that they might be blown like dust in a whirlwind, routed, as T.W. Davies suggests, "Like the wheel-shaped figures made by the wind out of faded leaves". A similar expression occurs in Isaiah 17.13: "Like thistle-down (AV margin) before the whirlwind". "Stubble" (7179) of v.13 is "chaff", the empty husks of corn and barley. How often had the Psalmist seen the chaff of the threshing floors blown away by the wind. He desires the same for Israel's adversaries. He longs that the judgment of God, like a tempest, might sweep away these confederate nations, filling them with fear as men engulfed in a terrible storm. He must also have seen the wild confusion of a forest fire, burning all before it, denuding the mountains of their trees and foliage. As Dr Thomson says in *The Land and the Book*, "Thorns and briers grow luxuriantly on the mountains, and in the hot season they may often be seen all ablaze". May divine judgment so consume Israel's enemies. They have been Israel's relentless persecutors, so, he prays, "Persecute them with thy tempest".

Verses 16-18: "That men may know..."

Although the Psalmist's passionate and ardent prayer is that God may put the enemies of His people to shame, and that they should be confounded who have so oppressed Israel, yet there is another, perhaps more noble, motive in his prayer. It is "That they may seek thy name, O Lord". Plumer suggests that there are three ways of explaining these words. "1. That the Psalmist prays that these enemies may have a salutary shame, leading them to seek God in truth. This is the more obvious and easy method. 2. That the seeking of God here mentioned is a forced subjection. 3. That *they* in the last clause refers to men generally and not to the men made ashamed. The first has the fewest difficulties. Either of them gives a good sense". His suggestions are worthy of thoughtful consideration.

The prayer continues, that these enemies might be confounded. Should there be no contrition or shame, then let them be troubled for ever. Let them perish. The judgment of the unrepentant will be eternal. But again, the Psalmist does not pray vindictively, wanting only revenge. His desire is that, as men witness the judgment of God upon these powerful adversaries, they may know that He alone, whose name is JEHOVAH, is the Most High over all the earth (RV and JND). Men will be compelled to recognise His solitary greatness. They will learn, as others did, that "the most High ruleth in the kingdom of men" (Dan 4.25). They will know that He is all that His great name signifies, Eternal, Self-sufficient, Supreme and Sovereign. He is Jehovah, Most High. How good it is to recognise this now, bowing in sincere and true homage in acknowledgement of One who ever desires to be not only the God, but the Saviour, of all men.

PSALM 84

Introduction

With Psalm 83 the Psalms of Asaph are finished and there now follow more of the Korahite Psalms. Psalm 84 is often regarded as a companion of Psalm 42, which also belongs to the Korahite collection. Psalm 42 is, however, a lament of one who, in exile, has been denied the privilege of participating in the services of the temple, whereas this Psalm, expressing intense longing for the temple courts, seems to anticipate a joyous presence there at the dwelling place of Jehovah. It is a most noble Psalm, considered to be one of the sweetest in the whole Psalter.

No author is precisely identified, and consequently the date is uncertain. Dr Cohen comments, "The poem supplies no clue to the poet's identity or his history. In fact his words are more than personal; they echo the sentiments of every religious soul in every epoch". How true this is. The Psalm is committed, like fifty-four other Psalms, to the charge and the care of the Chief Musician, the Master of Temple Song, who would well understand the meaning of "upon Gittith", which is now somewhat obscure. Some commentators see a connection with Gath, whose inhabitants were known as Gittites (Josh 13.3). The "Gittith" may have been a melody or a musical instrument of Philistine origin. Others connect it rather with the Hebrew GATH, meaning a vat or winepress, and understand it as a vintage song, a Psalm to be sung at the time of the gathering in of the grape harvest. For more detailed notes on "Gittith" refer to Psalm 8. The word appears in the titles of three Psalms, 8, 81 and 84. For comment on "the sons of Korah" in the title, refer to the introduction to Psalm 42.

One of the most notable features of this lovely Psalm is the vast array of divine titles employed by the Psalmist. This reveals a most intelligent and reverent appreciation of Jehovah, which may well be coveted by believers of the present day. Three times he speaks of "Jehovah of hosts" (vv. 1, 3 and 12). The great name "Jehovah" alone, he uses twice (vv. 2 and 11). "God" in v.2 is El (410), and in other verses and combinations "God" is

Elohim (430). "Jehovah, God of hosts" is found in v.8, in which verse, also, He is "God of Jacob". The two majestic titles "Jehovah-Elohim" are compounded in v.11, and there is something beautiful in the fact that twice the Psalmist can say, with personal appreciation, "My God" (vv. 3 and 10). This is blessedness indeed, that One so mighty, so glorious, and so awful, may be invoked by the individual believer as "My King, and my God".

The twelve verses of the Psalm are divided into three equal parts by the two "Selahs" (vv. 4 and 8), and in each of these parts the word "blessed" appears (vv. 4, 5, 12). The first section, verses 1-4, expresses the Psalmist's yearning for the temple. Verses 5-8 describe the blessedness of approach to God. Verses 9-12 are a happy blending of a pilgrim's prayer and praise.

Verses 1-4: Yearning for the Courts of the Lord

Although AV, RV, and JND all agree with the opening "How amiable"(3039), others point out that the word rather indicates "lovely" or "beloved", as given in Strong's Hebrew Dictionary. As T.W. Davies says, " 'Amiable' is now used of persons, never of things". The thought either way is obvious of course. The Psalmist would extol the loveliness of Jehovah's dwelling place. But the question must be asked, "Why does he say 'tabernacles' in the plural?". There are two suggested reasons for this, both of which are well expressed by Kirkpatrick, who says, "The plural may be 'amplificative', expressive of the dignity of the Temple as the dwelling-place of God; or it may be used with reference to the various courts and buildings of which it was composed". With this latter explanation Davies agrees, saying, "The plural is used because the temple building (the house) and its courts are embraced". Here there must indeed be loveliness, for this is the dwelling-place of Jehovah of Hosts.

The Psalmist yearns with his whole being. "My soul...my heart...my flesh", he says, "cry out for the living God". He uses words implying intense desire. He is longing, pining, even fainting, as he aspires after the temple courts. "Exhausted with desire", says another commentary (Jamieson, Fausset and Brown). It is interesting that the LXX uses the same Greek word here as that by which Paul expresses his longing for the "house which is from heaven", *"earnestly desiring"* (*1971*) that habitation (2 Cor 5.2). Note the very similar language of David in Psalm 63.1. Observe, too, that it is "the living God" for whom he thirsts, as in Psalm 42.2. The nations had their gods, but they were lifeless idols. The Psalmist panted after the living God, and nothing else, no one else, would satisfy the yearnings of his heart.

Verse 3 has presented a problem in that it seems to suggest that little birds were nesting in the altars. Considering the position and the ministry of the altars, it is scarcely feasible that birds would be able, undisturbed, to build nests there and raise their young. Perhaps, some suggest, we are to understand the "altars" as a kind of synonym for the temple buildings and precincts in general. This is hardly acceptable either, since great care was taken for the constant cleansing of these sacred buildings. It is perhaps better to see the reference to the birds as a parenthesis, in which the Psalmist is comparing the rest and comfort of sparrows and swallows with his own longings. They have found houses and nesting places, and why should not he find rest at the altars of his God? The sparrow, that most worthless of birds, and the swallow, that most restless of birds, have alike found homes (Mt 8.20; Lk 9.58), and so does the heart of the Psalmist yearn to be at home where God dwells. If this reference to the birds is viewed parenthetically, then substantially the Psalmist is saying, "My heart and my flesh crieth out for the living God…even thine altars, O Lord of hosts".

The very thought of this draws out from his heart the exclamation, "Blessed are they that dwell in thy house: they will be constantly praising thee"(JND). This benediction, with the accompanying "Selah", closes the first section of the Psalm. "Blessed" (835) implies the happiness and joy of those who spend their lives in the calm of the sanctuary. It is the Hebrew equivalent of the Greek "makarios", used so often by the Lord Jesus Himself in His earliest recorded ministry in Matthew 5.3-11.

Verses 5-8: The Joy of the Divine Presence

The benediction continues, pronouncing the blessedness of the man whose strength or refuge is in the Lord. In the hearts of such are "the high ways to Zion" (RV). Three times annually pilgrims made their way to Zion, to celebrate the Feasts of Passover/Unleavened Bread, Pentecost, and Tabernacles. It may be that the Psalmist is thinking of those who looked forward to such pilgrimages to Jerusalem, travelling not by compulsion, or of necessity, but with a willing eagerness, just for the joy of being at the temple courts again. The very highways to Zion were in their hearts. Note that the words, "to Zion", in the RV are italicised, having been supplied by the translators, but they do seem necessary to complete the sense.

The journey to the temple and to the presence of God was not always easy. For some it led through the Valley of Baca. Dr Cohen writes, "This last word means the balsam-tree, which thrives in dry places. A valley thickly planted with these trees was so named and lay on the route to Jerusalem. Actually it was a waterless valley, but in the eyes of the pilgrims, religiously exalted, it was converted into a place of springs". Some dispute this literal interpretation of the valley, arguing that no such valley can be identified. These rather think that there is a spiritual or typical meaning. Both the RV and JND's alternative rendering will give "the valley of weeping", which the Lord, in grace, turns into a land of refreshing wells and pools, filled with the early rains. Perhaps the true interpretation may be found in a blending of these two ideas. There may well have been a parched and barren valley on the way to Zion, not now identifiable. Even a little rain would alleviate the barren conditions and encourage pilgrims on their way. How typical is this of believers today who, finding their way parched and barren, a valley of weeping, rejoice in a little blessing from God, falling on their path like the early rain. Franz Delitzsch must be quoted in full. He says, "The most gloomy present becomes bright to them: passing through even a terrible wilderness, they turn it into a place of springs, their joyous hope and the infinite beauty of the goal, which is worth any amount of toil and trouble, afford them enlivening comfort, refreshing, strengthening in the midst of arid steppe. Not only does their faith bring forth water out of the sand and rocks of the desert, but God also on His part lovingly anticipates their love, and rewardingly anticipates their faithfulness: a gentle rain, like that which refreshes the sown fields in the autumn, descends from above and enwraps the valley of Baca in a fulness of blessing. The arid steppe becomes resplendent with a flowery festive garment, not to outward appearance, but to them spiritually, in a manner none the less true and real. And whereas under ordinary circumstances, the strength of the traveller diminishes in proportion as he has traversed more and more of his toilsome road, with them it is the very reverse; they go from strength to strength".

From strength to strength indeed! As Sir Richard Baker comments, quoted by Spurgeon, "From strength of patience to strength of hope; from strength of hope, to strength of faith, to strength of vision; and then will be accomplished that which David speaks here; Blessed is the man whose strength is in God". The fatigues of the journey are overcome as every worshipper is strengthened to appear before God in Zion.

The Psalmist appeals to the Lord God of Hosts, whom he calls also "God of Jacob", the God of grace, kind and faithful to His people in every age. The glory of the Lord God of Hosts and the grace of the God of Jacob will be sufficient for every weary traveller to Zion. The "Selah" demands a reflection, a meditation, a pause to wonder at all that God is and all that He has done for His people.

Verses 9-12: The Pilgrim's Prayer and Praise

Praying and praising are the continual twin exercises of the people of God, and this closing section of the Psalm is a beautiful blending of both. The pilgrim may now be considered as having arrived at Jerusalem. Prayer is made for the king, the Lord's anointed. "Behold, O God our shield, and look upon the face of thine anointed". Dr Cohen remarks that although God is referred to as a shield in v.12, perhaps it is better here in v.9 to understand "our shield" as being the king himself, "thine anointed", the defender of the people. With this T.W. Davies agrees, saying, "Render, as in the RV margin, 'Behold our shield, O God'. 'Our shield' and 'thine anointed' are parallel words. The king is called a shield in Psalm 89.18, where 'our shield' and 'our king' stand in parallelism to each other". (Note that this is dependent on the RV rendering).

The pilgrim exults at being in the courts of the Lord, for one day in these sacred courts is better than a thousand elsewhere. The Psalmist considers that he would rather stand at the threshold of the house of his God than dwell in the tents of wickedness (JND). He gives his reason, "for the LORD God is a sun and shield". Although God is often spoken of as the "light" of His people, only here in the Bible is He compared to the sun. Perhaps the reason may be that among the heathen there was a great prevalence of sun-worship. Israel's living God was different. He was indeed their light, and so their sun, as He was their shield also. He would give grace and glory. Here is the second of only two references to grace in the whole Psalter. Compare Psalm 45.2 where again grace is closely associated with glory. It does not enrich Jehovah to withhold, but He will not dispense His grace and His glory indiscriminately. He delights to bless those who walk uprightly, and to them He will be lavish with His goodness.

Considering all things, how blessed is the man whose trust, whose confidence, is in Jehovah of Hosts. Alexander Maclaren says, "The Psalmist's last word translates his metaphors of dwelling in and travelling towards the house of God into their simple meaning. That trust both seeks and finds God. There has ever been but one way to His presence, and that is the way of trust".

PSALM 85

Introduction

Here is another Psalm of the sons of Korah and another Psalm committed to the care of the Chief Musician. For comments on the Chief Musician, the Leader of the Temple Liturgy, see the introduction to Psalm 4 in this Commentary. The first of the Korahite Psalms is Psalm 42, where see remarks on the significance of this expression in the titles.

There is a Jewish tradition that verses 1-7 were sung or chanted by the people and the remaining verses 8-13 by the priests or the singing Levites. This is an obvious and natural division of the thirteen verses of the Psalm. The first seven verses may be further divided as follows. Verses 1-3 recount, with gratitude, what God has already done for His people. Notice the repeated "Thou hast...Thou hast...Thou hast", some six times in these three verses. Verses 4-7 are a petition for national revival and for a return of the joy of salvation. Verses 8-13 express confidence that God will respond to the cry of His people and restore peace to them and prosperity to the land. This section does not need to be sub-divided.

Although a captivity is mentioned in the opening verse of the Psalm, it does not seem necessary to interpret this as the Babylonian exile, or to date the Psalm accordingly; it is applicable to any of the great evils which have befallen the nation of Israel over many years.

Verses 1-3: Past Mercies Recalled

Whatever the evil has been, Jehovah has now delivered His troubled people, and the opening verses of the Psalm are filled with gratitude. God had shown favour and grace, and had reversed the conditions which had prevailed. He had turned captivity into liberty. After all, the people were His and the land was His - "thy land…thy people" - and, even if at times they showed the characteristics of old Jacob, still they were His, and now He had chosen to deliver them. He had forgiven the iniquity which doubtless had been the cause of their trouble. He had covered (3680) all their sin. It was now pardoned and hidden from view so that it was seen no more. Their "iniquity" was forgiven. Their "sin" was covered. "Iniquity" (5771) is a deliberate perversion of what is right. "Sin" (2403) denotes a missing of the mark. There were sins of commission and sins of omission, but Jehovah in His grace had now pardoned all. It was the moment for a "Selah", a time to pause, to silently reflect upon His goodness to an erring people who had suffered for their unfaithfulness and had now been forgiven.

This "forgiven" (5375) of v.2 is an interesting word. It signifies a "lifting up", like the removal of a burden. So it was with Israel when Jehovah pardoned and brought them back into favour. The burden was lifted. The anger and the wrath of God were now abated. He had withdrawn from His wrath and turned away the heat of His anger. That anger had been justified by the sin of His people, but now all was forgiven and the storm was past.

Verses 4-7: Prayer for Revival

It was not sufficient for the nation, however, that their iniquity was pardoned. They desired a full restoration into the communion and confidence of God. He was the God of their salvation, and it was so desirable now that they should be in the enjoyment of that salvation and in renewed happy fellowship with Him. Would He continue to be indignant with them, even though His anger was past? Would His grief with them be prolonged from generation to generation? Would their posterity suffer because of their sinning? "Bring us back", they plead (JND). "Cause thine indignation…to cease". Jehovah had a divine right to be indignant with them. O that it might now cease.

The revival for which they entreated would be accompanied by rejoicing if it was granted. A revived and quickened nation would joy in God. It was therefore for His glory that He should revive His people. "Wilt thou not…?", they pray. With the burden of their guilt removed, the indignation of Jehovah past, and the former fellowship with Him restored, there could only be rejoicing. For this they plead, looking for a display of His mercy, His loving-kindness. "O Jehovah…grant us thy salvation". Revival added to forgiveness would for them be salvation in its fulness.

Verses 8-13: Assurance for the Future

If, as according to Jewish tradition, this part of the Psalm was sung by the priests, here indeed is a priestly recognition and confidence that Jehovah will hear the pleadings of His restored people. The priests will recognise the divine response to the entreaties of the nation and will convey that response to the people. "I will hear...he will speak". Jehovah would speak peace to them. They were His people, and they were His saints (2623). In the midst of godless nations all around them, they were the godly, His holy ones. Had He not brought them out of Egypt to be "a holy nation", His own peculiar possession from among the nations (Ex 19.5-6)? It grieved Him when they failed to be what He had desired them to be, and He would surely grant them every encouragement to return to Him in peace. With this provision, however, let them not turn back again to folly. God would do His part. Let the people do their part and not relapse into the sinning which had caused the disaster from which He had now delivered them.

The salvation of God is never distant from them that fear Him. He ever delights to meet the sincere seeking soul. The fear of God in the nation would result in glory in their land. Note that there is grace and glory, mercy and truth, righteousness and peace. These would all dwell together in the land, in mutual complacency, when the nation feared the Lord. Earth and heaven would be in happy accord. Truth would spring up and righteousness would look down. Jehovah would give what was good and necessary and the land would yield her increase in a blessed fruitfulness. All this will be fully realised for Israel when the heavenly Melchizedek reigns as King of righteousness and King of peace (Heb 7.2). Righteousness and peace will kiss each other. Shalom! (7965). Messiah will usher in a kingdom of glory and prosperity unprecedented, but the Psalmist's plea for the nation of his day is that even then, righteousness, like a herald, might go before Him, a welcome forerunner, preparing the way for divine blessing.

PSALM 86

Introduction

This Psalm is entitled "A Prayer", and the title is a true index to its contents. The JFB Commentary says, "This is a prayer in which the writer, with deep emotion, mingles petitions and praises, now urgent for help, and now elated with hope, in view of former mercies". Five Psalms have the word "prayer" in their titles, Psalms 17, 86, 90, 102 and 142. Three of these Psalms, 17, 86 and 142, are assigned to David, Psalm 90 to Moses, and Psalm 102 is entitled, "A Prayer of the afflicted". Dr Cohen calls this Psalm, "A Cry for Help". This is largely true, but there is also much praise and adoration throughout the Psalm, and constant acknowledgements of the greatness and goodness of God.

There is nothing in the Psalm to link its composition with any particular event or circumstance, and so, as with many other Psalms, it may therefore be used by saints of every age in their times of trouble. It has the character of a mosaic, an arrangement of beautiful expressions which, in many cases, may be traced in substance to various other parts of the OT, as will be noted in the commentary. This makes an orderly division of the seventeen verses difficult, if not unnecessary. The following, however, may be helpful. Verses 1-7 are, as Dr Cohen entitles the whole Psalm, a cry for help. The Psalmist, poor and needy, entreats God to hear him. Verses 8-10 extol the supremacy of the Lord among the gods of the heathen. In verses 11-13 prayer is resumed, with a request for guidance, for God's glory, and the concluding verses 14-17 are a prayer for protection from proud and violent men. There is then, prayer for help, prayer for God's glory, prayer for guidance, and prayer for protection. The Psalm is truly, as its title states, "A Prayer of David".

Verses 1-7: Prayer for Help

The Psalmist pleads that he is poor and needy, as he does also in Psalm 40.17. Will Jehovah then, in grace, incline His ear to hear him? This is not literal poverty or material need. It is rather a humble acknowledgement of dependence upon God. "Poor" (6041) might also have the thought of affliction or suffering. Such will attract the scorn of proud and arrogant men, but the poor will also be the special objects of God's mercy and grace. Note how the Psalmist appends reasons for his petitions. "Hear me…for I am poor and needy". "Preserve me…for I am holy". "Be merciful…for I cry unto thee daily". "Rejoice the soul of thy servant: for unto thee, O Lord, do I lift up my soul".

His claim that he is holy does not conflict with his stated humility. He is pleading as one who is godly, in contrast to the godless men of the surrounding nations, and his piety makes him the object of God's loving-kindness. He loves God, and he uses this as a plea that God should preserve him. How similar to the opening cry of Psalm 16, where he uses exactly the same word; "Preserve (8104) me, O God: for in thee do I put my trust". How important it was to him that in a scene of lawlessness God should preserve the godly. It is in keeping with his humility that he should now speak of himself as "thy servant". This form of speech was a Hebrew way of addressing a superior. Note how Abraham used this when speaking to the heavenly visitors in Genesis 18.3. David also used the same language in his message to Saul in 1 Samuel 20.7-8. The Psalmist uses this term again in v.4 and yet again in v.16. What a powerful plea is this that Jehovah should hear him. He is poor and needy, he is godly in a sinful scene, and he is Jehovah's servant, trusting in Him. Surely his God must bow down His ear, hear him, and preserve him.

The prayer continues to ascend daily. It was the Psalmist's constant exercise. The cry for mercy however, "Be merciful", is rather a plea for grace and favour, for such pity and kindness as might be shown to an inferior. How this would gladden his soul, if Jehovah would hear. To Him he had lifted up his soul in trust and dependence. An answer would bring joy to this poor and needy supplicant.

But there was yet another reason, and this on the divine side, why his prayer for help should be heard. The Lord was good (2896). He was kind and gracious and bountiful. He was plenteous in mercy (2617), abounding in lovingkindness and pity. This was His very nature and character. He was ever ready to forgive those who called upon Him, and He had Himself proclaimed this to Moses in Exodus 34.6-7. So, then, if the condition and character of the Psalmist was a reason for Jehovah to hear him, there was yet a more powerful reason in the nature of God Himself. A good and kind and gracious God, always ready to forgive, must surely hear the cry of His humble trusting servant in his need. So, again the Psalmist prays, "Give ear, O Jehovah...attend to the voice of my supplications". In confidence he would continue to call upon his God. In the day of his trouble to whom else could he call? He would pray in this glad assurance, "Thou wilt answer me". What inspired example and encouragement has the Psalmist left for the godly of every age. "I will call", he says. "Thou wilt answer".

Verses 8-10: Prayer for God's Glory

"Who is like unto thee, O Lord, among the gods". This was the song of Moses and the children of Israel when they crossed the Red Sea, delivered from their bondage in Egypt. That there were gods in Egypt could not be denied (Ex 12.12), but they were lifeless deities. Jehovah, the living God, was supreme. The Psalmist echoes that early song of the redeemed people, and sings, "There is none like unto thee among the gods, O Lord" (RV). Moses had repeated those sentiments in Deuteronomy ch. 3, having seen, he says, the greatness of God. The latter part of v.8 of the Psalm is so very like that same word of Moses, "What God is there in heaven or in earth, that can do according to thy works, and according to thy might?" (Deut 3.24). Jehovah was, and is, incomparable. He has no real rival. He is unique in His greatness, and this is encouragement indeed for every poor and needy supplicant like the man of this Psalm.

The Psalmist now anticipates in language which is almost Messianic. All nations shall one day come and worship Jehovah. He has made them. He has creatorial rights and the lovely JPS rendering is that they shall "prostrate themselves before Thee". His sovereignty will eventually be acknowledged by all men everywhere. This is expounded in more detail in Messianic Psalms such as Psalm 72. From sea to sea, and from the river to the ends of the earth, Jehovah will have universal dominion. The Kings of the earth will join with the Bedouin of the desert in paying homage to Him. All alike will bow the knee and all nations will serve Him (Ps 72.8-11). The Psalmist exults as he thinks of it, "They shall glorify Thy name!". He appends three reasons why all this should be. God is great! He does wondrous things! He is God alone! This again is reminiscent of what the people sang in Exodus 15.11. The Psalmist prays for, and longs for, that glory.

Verses 11-13: Prayer for Guidance

Every child of God must want to know the will of God for his life. Such desire might often be general, a sincere longing to live and walk and serve as God wills. At times the desire to know His will may be specific, relating to some particular circumstance, to some purpose in life, or to some exercise of heart. What believer has not prayed, like the converted Saul of Tarsus, "Lord, what wilt thou have me to do?" (Acts 9.6). The Psalmist is no different from other saints. "Teach me thy way, O Lord", he prays. Christians of a day much later than the Psalmist's have incorporated his prayer into their hymnology, and they sing, as he did,

"Teach me Thy way, O Lord,
Teach me Thy way".

This prayer for guidance must be accompanied by a genuine determination to obey. "Teach me thy way...I will walk in thy truth". There must be a sincere response to God's revealed will and a promise of obedience. In this matter then, the believer will require to be whole-hearted. "Unite my heart", the Psalmist prays. "Make one my heart" (JPS), completely and entirely set upon pleasing God without being distracted by other things. "I will praise thee...with my whole heart" (RV). A heart unified, at one in fearing God, will praise Him and glorify His name as long as life lasts.

Such a heart will overflow with gratitude to the Lord for His mercy, constantly remembering the deliverance from the lowest hell (7585), the lowest pit (RV). This is "sheol", on which refer to the footnote at Psalm 6 in this Commentary.

Verses 14-17: Prayer for Protection

It is a principle that those who live godly lives will suffer persecution (2 Tim 3.12). The godly Psalmist's prayer for protection begins with a passionate "O God". Proud and arrogant men had risen up against him and a company of violent men sought his soul, his very life. David had used almost the same language in Psalm 54.3. There was no fear of God with these men. They did not have God or His interests before them. It must have been with a profound sense of relief that the Psalmist turned from them to say, "But thou, O Lord". What comfort, to contrast the callous heartlessness of his enemies with the graciousness of his God. In words which are almost a quotation from Exodus 34.6 he speaks of those great attributes of the Lord: "A God full of compassion, and gracious, longsuffering, and plenteous in mercy and truth". "O turn unto me", he pleads, "and have mercy (2603) upon me". He is asking for pity, for kindness, for favour, and again his very humility becomes a claim upon God, as, praying for strength, he calls himself, "Thy servant...the son of thy handmaid". These, says Dr Cohen, are "Terms of self-humiliation used by a suppliant to arouse sympathy. The petition may also imply that, as a slave looks to his master for protection against assault, so the Psalmist turns to his Lord in this time of danger...'Son of thine handmaid' denotes a slave who is part of the household by birth with a superior claim on the master to that of a purchased slave".

His last request is for a token (226), a sign, proclaiming to those who hate him that he is in the divine favour. By this they will be ashamed and confounded, while he is helped and comforted. It is because Jehovah has helped him that his enemies are shamed. As Dr Cohen says, "A better translation is: 'that they that hate me may see and be ashamed that Thou...'. The pronoun is emphatic; the recognition that it was God, and no one else, Who has rescued him from their hands may have the effect of filling his persecutors with shame and remorse".

PSALM 87

Introduction

This Psalm (4210) of the sons of Korah is also called a Song (7892) indicating that it may be sung with, or without, a musical accompaniment. It sings the glory of Zion throughout its seven verses and there is beauty in its brevity. The Psalm has a prophetic character, anticipating the day when Zion, a synonym for Jerusalem, will be the metropolis of the universal Messianic kingdom. There is a similarity of thought and language with Psalm 46.4-7, also a Korahite Psalm and Song. There is no agreement among commentators as to the date of its composition.

Two "Selahs" divide the Psalm into two main parts, verses 1-3 and verses 4-6, and these are followed by one concluding verse. The first part extols Zion as the beloved city of God. The second part looks forward to Zion's glorious future, and the concluding verse sings the very joy of it. Oesterley writes, "The Psalmist, with his sublime outlook, envisages a time in world-history when, irrespective of nationality, men will come to themselves, and therefore to God".

Verses 1-3: Zion, City of God

The Psalm opens abruptly with the pronoun "His", for which there is no related noun, "His foundation is in the holy mountains". There is no doubt however, that the foundation referred to is Jehovah's. He has founded Zion, it is the city of God. Indeed, one of the meanings of the name

"Jerusalem" (3389) is, "Foundation of Peace". Jerusalem is associated with several mountains, Olivet, Moriah, and Zion, all of which may be viewed to advantage from Mount Scopus, an extension of Olivet. These holy mountains are shrouded with history, sharing in the sanctity of the holy city itself. So much, in both Old Testament and New Testament narrative, has happened on the slopes or in the shade of these hills, in the midst of which Jehovah chose to build His city and His temple. Another Psalm uses this theme of the mountains to teach the security of those who fear the Lord. "As the mountains are round about Jerusalem, so the Lord is round about his people from henceforth even forever" (Ps 125.2).

"The Lord loveth the gates of Zion" is a poetic way of expressing Jehovah's love for the city itself. The gates opened to the city and were, of course, an integral part of the walls which enclosed the city for its protection. The people of Israel have so often been a scattered people, dwelling in many cities other than Jerusalem. "Diaspora", or dispersion, is no strange word to the Jew. But Jerusalem has ever enjoyed a special place in the affections of Jehovah. Wherever else His people may dwell, He loves Zion more than all the habitations of Jacob.

The Psalmist now speaks to the city directly, as if addressing a person, saying, "Glorious things are spoken of thee, O city of God". Ever since its earliest mention as Salem in Genesis 14.18, Jerusalem has had a unique position in world history. "Beautiful for situation, the joy of the whole earth, is mount Zion" (Ps 48.2). This geographical centre of the land masses of earth has been the political hub of world affairs also. No city has been coveted after, fought over, besieged, destroyed, and rebuilt, as often as Jerusalem. But glorious things are predicted for it.

The "Selah" is so fitting. These very mentions of Zion, its place in the world and in the heart of God, would evoke patriotic feelings and emotions in the heart of every Jew. The "Selah" commands a reverent, silent pause, to reflect upon what has been said and to lift the heart in praise to God.

Verses 4-6: Zion, Metropolis of the World

Jehovah now speaks. This section of the Psalm has been called "The oracle of Jehovah". He will make mention, he says, of Rahab, Babylon, Philistia, Tyre, and Ethiopia, nations which were foreign to, and often opposed to, Israel and Jerusalem. There is some difference of opinion among commentators as to the meaning. Some think, as T.W. Davies, that the proper names in this verse represent the scattered Jews settled in the localities named, and that these are recognised here by Jehovah as members of the theocracy. It is more probable, however, that this is a prediction that these very nations which had once warred against Israel will one day acknowledge the rule of Jehovah and that their peoples will be enrolled as citizens of Zion. So that, whether a man was born in Babylon or Ethiopia, or elsewhere, he will be accounted in that day as if he had been born in

Zion. The Most High will order and establish the city, Himself inscribing the names of the peoples in its register.

As to the identity of these names, there is little problem. "Rahab" is a poetical name for Egypt. It means "haughty or arrogant", and was the name of a mythical sea monster to which Egypt was likened (see Is 51.9). The names of Babylon and Philistia are well-known in the history of Israel's pogroms, as are Tyre and Ethiopia. One day these erstwhile enemies of Zion will be embraced in a glorious kingdom under the rule of Messiah, "Yea, all kings shall fall down before him: all nations shall serve him" (Ps 72.11).

Verse 7: Joy in Zion

With singers, and players on instruments, men will celebrate the glory of Zion. Most other versions render this in a way similar to, "They that sing as well as they that dance"(RV); "As well the singers as the dancers"(JND); "Whether they sing or dance"(JPS). These were familiar expressions of religious fervour in the past dispensation. It will be remembered that King David danced before the Lord as the Ark of the Covenant was returned to Jerusalem (2 Sam 6.14, 16). Singing and dancing are mentioned together again in Psalm 149.3. It is interesting to note that dancing still often accompanies singing in Israel today, particularly at celebrations at the Western Wall in Jerusalem. Each Friday evening there, the Sabbath is welcomed in by song and dance. New Testament believers, following the example of the Lord Jesus and His apostles, still express their worship in song (Mt 26.30; Eph 5.19), but other outward physical expressions of emotion have now been superseded by the spiritual exercises of the heart (Col 3.16).

The theme of this song in the Psalm is, "All my springs are in thee", but what exactly is meant by "in thee"? Is this in Zion? Or in Jehovah? Or are both true? The source of all their joy, the fountain of their happiness, is in the God who dwells in Zion. So ends this brief Psalm, throbbing with glory and joy all through.

PSALM 88

Introduction

How different is this Psalm to the preceding Psalm 87. There it was all love and glory and joy. Here is the lament of one in deep distress. Dr Cohen says, "The whole of the Psalm is enshrouded in gloom". Delitzsch says, "The gloomiest of all the plaintive Psalms". The very title has a certain sadness in it. "Mahalath Leannoth" may have been the preferred melody, perhaps in the minor key, to which the Psalm was to be chanted, and this instruction is given to the Chief Musician. "Mahalath" (4257) has already occurred in the title of Psalm 53 and may mean "sickness or affliction". Of "Leannoth" (6031) Strong says that the meaning is dubious, but JND thinks it may be the plural of the word translated "wormwood", always associated with the bitterness of suffering.

This is a Korahite Psalm, called also "A Song". The JFB Commentary remarks that, "Though called a song, which usually implies joy, both the style and matter of the Psalm are very despondent; yet the appeals to God evince faith, and we may suppose that the word 'song' might be extended to such composition". It is also a "Maschil" Psalm, indicating that there is instruction here. There is something to learn even in the lament of a suffering saint. For comments on "Maschil" see the introduction to Psalm 32.

Heman the Ezrahite was a Master or Director of Temple Music. Three such leaders appointed by David in 1 Chronicles 15.17, 19, Heman, Asaph and Ethan. The meaning of "the Ezrahite" is not clear, though it is applied also to Ethan in the title of the succeeding Psalm 89.

In verses 1-9 the Psalmist describes his pitiful condition, sick and lonely, near to death and forsaken by his closest friends. In verses 10-12 he prays to be saved from death; the dead cannot praise God or see His wonders. The concluding verses 13-18 are a final pathetic and intense appeal for relief from his afflictions, which he regards as coming from the Lord.

Verses 1-9: Prayer for Pity

Depressed though he might be, the Psalmist knows that his only hope for relief is in Him whom he calls "Lord God of my salvation". He must have known the Saviour character of God in times past and to Him he now appeals for healing. Day and night he had cried. The form of words apparently suggests that he had cried in the daytime and his cry continued into the night. He longs that Jehovah might hear him, that his prayer might find its way into the presence of God. In language familiar to Psalmists he implores, "Incline thine ear unto my cry". His sorrows are many. Note the plurality; "My soul is full of troubles". His life seems to be ebbing, drawing near to the grave. This is "sheol" (7585), for comments on which see the Note on Psalm 6.5. "Sheol", or "Hades", is not only "the grave", but, as Strong's Hebrew Dictionary defines it, is "the world of the dead". JND says, "The place or state of the soul separated from the body". William Kelly calls it "the grave-land". Into this world of the dead the poor Psalmist feels he is drifting. In his extreme weakness he may be reckoned among those who are even now going down into the pit.

"Free among the dead", as in the AV of v.5, is a strange expression, somewhat changed by the RV and JND renderings - "Cast off among the dead" (RV); "Prostrate among the dead" (JND). "Set apart among the dead" is the JPS version, while the JFB commentary has, "Cut off". Whichever translation is preferred, the Psalmist's thought is evident; he is dreading death, and yet, in death he would be free from the labour and travail of life in the flesh. Is there an irony here; free – but among the dead? Spurgeon remarks, in his usual quaint way, "Unbound from all that links a man with life…a freeman of the city of the sepulchre". "The grave" (6913) of v.5, is not the same word as that in v.3, which, as has already been noted, is "sheol". This in v.5 is indeed the grave. It is the word for tomb or sepulchre. Soon, he feels, he may be numbered with those that lie in the grave, like the corpses of the slain on a battlefield, to be buried and forgotten.

The poor sufferer feels in the depths of despair. He is in the lowest pit in his deep depression. It is the valley of the shadow of death for him, as dark and lonely as "sheol" itself. The hand of God seems to be against him and the wrath of God lies hard upon him. He feels the terrible weight of this. Spurgeon quotes Thomas Goodwin, who says, "Others read, *sustains itself*, or *bears up itself upon me*, which is as if a giant should with his whole weight stay himself upon a child". Now the metaphor changes. He is in a storm, tempest-tossed, with waves and billows dashing themselves upon him and over him as great breakers might threaten a little ship at sea. Only One could speak the word, "Peace, be still", but even He seemed to have forgotten.

It may seem a strange place for a "Selah", but the Psalmist needs a pause in the telling of his afflictions. He needs some silence, and a moment to lift his head above these waves and billows that deluge him. He needs to lift up his heart, too, and to have a little relief from this sad meditation on his pitiful condition.

But he must resume his woe. He laments that his acquaintances have forsaken him. Familiar, intimate friends have withdrawn from him, and in language reminiscent of that of a leper he acknowledges that he has become an abomination to his friends. Was it the nature of his sickness? Was it that all men knew of his disease? Was it infectious? Defiling? Whatever, they stayed their distance from him, and neither could he come to them, shut up as a lone prisoner in his room. Whether for legal, social, physical, or moral reasons, they separated themselves from him and left him abandoned. This was so hard to bear since it was a chastisement from God Himself. Four times he says, "Thou hast", recognising the hand of the Lord in it all. "Thou hast laid me in the lowest pit, in darkness…thou hast afflicted me…Thou hast put away mine acquaintance…thou hast made me an abomination".

How suffering reveals itself in the eye, sooner than in any other member of the body. "Mine eye mourneth", he says. He had wept out his sorrow as he had daily called upon God, with hands stretched out as if to reach the Almighty for healing. As a little child might stretch out its hands to its mother while it cries, so did this afflicted child of God. His eyes wept, his voice cried, his hands were outstretched, and his heart broke. This was prayer indeed.

Verses 10-12: Prayer for Deliverance

The Psalmist boldly asks questions of God, all of which anticipate a negative answer. He is really giving reasons, in question form, why Jehovah should intervene and save him from death. "Wilt thou show wonders to the dead?", he asks. While he lived he had seen the wonders of God's workings among His people, but does God display His glories to the dead? Surely not; and if not, then why should he die and be deprived of those revelations of God which he had hitherto enjoyed? "Shall the dead arise and praise thee?", he continues. Do notes of praise arise from the vaults and sepulchres and tombs of the dead? Do corpses render adoration and worship? He is not, of course, thinking of the spirits of departed saints, who do render praise, but of the darkness of the grave. Why should he not be spared and continue to praise God in the land of the living. "Selah". He pauses to reflect upon his questions and upon their implications and consequences.

A third question now asks, "Shall thy lovingkindness be declared in the grave?". Can the dead bear testimony to the goodness and mercies of God? Was it not therefore better that he should be raised up, so that he could still speak for his God among men? Again, "Shall thy wonders be known in the dark?". This is akin to the first of his four questions. In the dark loneliness of the grave-land do the dead witness the wonders of the Almighty? In that land of forgetfulness what do they know, or appreciate, of His faithfulness or His righteousness? The answers to all his questions must surely be negative. It seemed to the Psalmist that it would be well for him, and for the glory of God, that he should be delivered from his affliction.

Verses 13-18: The Final Appeal

The cries of the sufferer continue daily. In the early morning hour his prayers rose to meet Jehovah. Why had the Lord hidden Himself? Why had He seemed to cast off His child. Had the Psalmist borne this sickness for many years? "From my youth up", he laments. He had been afflicted, dying as he lived, and distracted by the terrors which had reduced him to naught. Streams of divine wrath had gone over him. He felt like a drowning man, overwhelmed by the floods of fierce anger which deluged him. There was no respite. He repeats the complaint of v.8. Former loved ones and associates, familiar friends and companions, had all been forced into a dark distance from him. There was none to help or comfort.

What a sad summary of the whole Psalm is the last word. Darkness! There is no expression of hope, no ray of light, no gleam of joy. Nevertheless, as Dr Cohen remarks, "Although the note of hopefulness is not struck in the concluding verse, it may be implied in the conviction that pervades the Psalm that the sufferer is all the time in the hands of God. If He smote, He can and may heal".

PSALM 89

Introduction

Psalm 89 has been called "The Covenant Psalm". Its many references to the Davidic covenant and the mention of the Firstborn in the heart of the Psalm in v.27, make it Messianic. There is so much in the Psalm which awaits complete fulfilment in Messiah. It is the twelfth of the thirteen "Maschil" Psalms, of which Psalm 32 is the first, where see notes on the meaning of "Maschil". These are Psalms of teaching, Psalms of instruction, didactic Psalms. It is interesting to observe the variety of thought, circumstances, and sentiment expressed throughout these Maschil Psalms, indicating that not only from doctrine, but from every experience in the lives of believers, other saints may learn something of the character and the purposes of God. In the presence of some national disaster, the Psalmist here pleads with God on the grounds of the covenant made with David, and in the consciousness that God is faithful and will be true to that covenant (2 Sam 7.8-16). Ethan the Ezrahite, referred to in the title, is sometimes identified with Jeduthun, a musician in the days of David, associated with Asaph and Heman in the service of the temple music and singing (1 Chr 16.37, 41-42; 25.1). According to the ancient Jewish arrangement, Psalm 89 closes the third book of the Psalms.

The Psalm may be divided as follows. In the first four verses, concluding with the first of four "Selahs", the Psalmist recalls the Davidic covenant, and expresses his confidence in the faithfulness of God to be true to those covenant promises. Verses 5-14 are like a song of praise, extolling the power and the righteousness of Jehovah, the Lord God of hosts. In verses 15-18 the Psalmist sings the blessedness of the people who have such a God as their God. Verses 19-37 recount, in more detail, the covenant made with David, and this section ends with another "Selah". Verses 38-45 contrast the ideal, as expressed in the covenant, with the actual sad condition of the nation. This section also concludes with a "Selah". Verses 46-51 are a plea for the people, reproached by their enemies, and the final verse 52 is a closing benediction or doxology, with the double "Amen, and Amen" with which the first three Books of Psalms are concluded. See Psalms 41.13 and 72.19.

Verses 1-4: God's Covenant and Faithfulness

The Psalm begins with a note of praise, "I will sing". Whatever the failings of the people, the Psalmist can rejoice in this, that the lovingkindnesses of Jehovah can never fail. He resolves that he must sing of these mercies (2617) and testify always to the faithfulness of God. From generation to generation the story of God's goodness to His people must be recounted, remembered and appreciated. All generations must know.

"I have said", seems to express the Psalmist's personal conviction. He was fully persuaded of what he was about to say now, and had apparently said it before. He is assured that God's lovingkindness and faithfulness were firmly established in the heavens, built up eternally like some majestic palace. A.M. Toplady comments, "This house, contrary to the fate of all sublunary buildings, will never fall down, nor ever be taken down...Fire cannot injure it; storms cannot overthrow it; age cannot impair it. It stands on a rock, and is immovable as the rock on which it stands". It is built up forever.

The Psalmist's assurance is based upon the word of God. "I have made a covenant", Jehovah says, "I have sworn". In every age the believer may rest securely on the divine promise. David, with whom the covenant was made, is described in two ways, "my chosen...my servant". Is there here a foreshadowing of a greater monarch than David? "Behold my servant...mine elect, in whom my soul delighteth" (Is 42.1). One day David's greater Son will inherit the throne of His father David, and the ideal kingdom envisaged in the covenant will be ushered in in glory. He whom men despised, whom they mocked as a king, who was cut off out of the land of the living, shall see His seed and prolong His days, and be established forever. David's dynasty will be consolidated and perpetuated in the Person of Messiah, the Son of David.

It is already time for a "Selah". The reader must pause, meditating upon the greatness and the wonder of this covenant, and anticipating the glorious things which the inspired Psalmist has yet to say.

Verses 5-14: Jehovah's Attributes Recounted

"The heavens shall praise thy wonders, O Lord". This is apparently similar to the opening words of Psalm 19, "The heavens declare the glory of God", but should, nevertheless be understood differently. "The heavens" of Psalm 19 are God's creations in the sky, sun, moon and stars, evidences of His creatorial power and glory. Here, "the heavens" are rather heavenly beings, the angelic host, praising the wonders of Jehovah. "Wonders", however, is a singular word in the Hebrew text. It is the wonder of His Person, the wonder of what He is and what He does. "The congregation of the saints" as in the AV, "the assembly of the holy ones" (RV), is perhaps this vast assembly of holy angels who observe God's dealings with men and with Israel, and praise His faithfulness. And why should they not praise? Who in the skies can be compared to Jehovah? Heathen peoples often worshipped the sun and the moon, or at least saw these as representing their deities. Jehovah is supreme in the heavens. He is greater than His creation and He is pre-eminent among the sons of the mighty (410). As in Psalm 29.1 this latter expression may again refer to the angels, though it could possibly mean the gods of the heathen, as in Exodus 15.11, "Who is like unto thee, O Lord, among the gods. Whichever may be the intended meaning, both are true. Among heathen deities or among the heavenly intelligences, none are to be likened to Jehovah. He is a God greatly to be feared in the assembly of the saints, or, as in the RV, "A God very terrible in the council of the holy ones", doubtless a reference to the heavenly hosts. Jehovah is the undisputed, unchallenged, sovereign Ruler in the heavens, to be revered by all those beings who surround Him in glory. Is it to be wondered at that the Psalmist should exclaim, "O Jehovah, Elohim of hosts, who is like unto thee, the strong Jah"? (Compare RV and JND). Jah is an abbreviated form of Jehovah, not in any sense a diminution, but rather a concentration of the great name. It was the divine name used by Moses at the overthrow of Pharaoh, and, as has already been observed, the question, "Who is like unto Thee?" is also a citation from that same song of redemption at the Red Sea (Ex 15.2, 11). Jehovah's faithfulness enwraps Him like a garment, it is His girdle, round about Him.

Still the Psalmist addresses Jehovah, extolling His might. He rules the proud swelling sea, the most unstable element in creation. He stills the raging waves. He controls the waters. He did so at the great exodus of His people from Egypt, parting the Red Sea for them. Centuries later He did the same for His troubled disciples in a storm on the Sea of Galilee. He has broken Rahab (7294), a poetic name for Egypt (Ps 87.4), but probably here, in the context and according to Strong, a mythical sea monster representing the forces of chaos in the seas. Jehovah crushed His enemies, scattering their broken corpses with His strong arm. Not only the waters and the nations, but all creation is His, the heavens and the earth. It was He who founded the world and its fulness. North and south, east and west, all must acknowledge His Creatorial rights. Tabor and Hermon are the two most prominent mountains in northern Israel, and, since Tabor is west of the Jordan and Hermon east of Jordan, they may represent east and west accordingly, so that the whole land is in agreement in declaring His greatness.

The adulation continues. The Creator has an arm of might. His arm, His hand, and His right hand are all mentioned in the song at the Red Sea. They are emblems of His power in action, strong and exalted. With what praise of His attributes does this section of the Psalm conclude. Justice and judgment, mercy and truth are all His. Justice and judgment are the very foundation of His throne, the basis of divine government. Mercy and truth are His forerunners or heralds, going before His face as He intervenes in the affairs of men. Well does another Psalmist say, "O Lord my God, thou art very great; thou art clothed with honour and majesty" (Ps 104.1).

Verses 15-18: The Happiness of God's People

In this brief section of the Psalm the people of God are blessed with joy and light, with righteousness and glory, with strength and favour, and with Jehovah's defence. Blessed people indeed! Balaam knew it in his day, saying, "How goodly are thy tents, O Jacob, and thy tabernacles, O Israel...Blessed is he that blesseth thee, and cursed is he that curseth thee" (Num 24.5, 9). Moses knew it too, and said, "Happy art thou, O Israel: who is like unto thee, O people saved by the Lord" (Deut 33.29). The Psalmist says, "Blessed is the people that know the joyful sound" (8643). Dr Cohen refers to the "...Hebrew T^{e}RUA, which is employed of sounding trumpets or the SHOFAR, acclaiming a king, and the happy cries of pilgrims on the festivals. Israel has been privileged to know them all as God's people". These people are in the enjoyment of that prayer in the priestly benediction of Numbers 6.25-26, "They shall walk, O Lord, in the light of thy countenance". Daily they rejoice in the name, the revealed character, of Jehovah, and are exalted, lifted to eminence above the nations, by His righteous dealings with them. He is the glory of their strength. They have no might or strength of their own, but in His favour, in His good pleasure, their horn, symbol of power, is exalted, and they may lift their heads defiantly to their enemies. Notice how the pronouns change. Until now it has been "*they* walk...*they* rejoice...*they* be exalted...*their* strength". Now it is "*our* horn...*our* defence...*our* king". The Psalmist is proud to identify himself with this blessed people and include himself in their number. They may indeed have enemies, but Jehovah, the Holy One of Israel is their shield and their king and the Psalmist is happy to be one of them. "Happy is that people, that is in such a case: yea, happy is that people, whose God is the Lord" (Ps 144.15).

Verses 19-37: The Davidic Covenant Expounded

These verses now expound in more detail what has been said concerning the covenant with David in the first section of the Psalm. They are an amplification of God's word to David through Nathan the prophet in 2 Samuel 7.5-17. "Then", at the time of the giving of the covenant in 2 Samuel 7, "Then thou spakest in vision to thy holy one". In the RV, as in some manuscripts, this latter word is in the plural, "Thy holy ones", but there is not general agreement about this. If it is singular then it may refer to either David or Nathan. If it is plural then both may be included, and maybe Samuel too. Indeed there may be an implication that what was spoken to David personally was for the good of the people generally and of saints everywhere. None of these interpretations affects the meaning of the spoken word of God which follows.

Prior to his enthronement as king, David had already proved himself to be a mighty man. He had fought lions and bears, and Philistines too, but to be king of Israel demanded divine aid. Jehovah who had chosen him out of the people, had appointed him and anointed him to that high office, and had therefore conferred upon him the help which he needed to govern the people and confront their enemies. Jehovah had found David His servant and had consecrated him. "I took thee from the sheepcote, from following the sheep, to be ruler over my people, over Israel" (2 Sam 7.8). As priests and kings were anointed with a holy anointing oil, so had David been anointed, first by Samuel in 1 Samuel 16.13, when King Saul was yet alive, and later by the elders of Israel in 2 Samuel 5.3. It is probably to the first anointing by Samuel that the Psalmist refers. By the hand and the arm of the Lord David would be established and strengthened. The hand and the arm of the Lord have already been mentioned in v.13 as symbols of His power and might. This power would give the king power. No enemy would be allowed, as a ruthless creditor, to oppress him and exact from him. The children of wickedness would not be permitted to afflict him. These promises were in the terms of the covenant (2 Sam 7.10). Jehovah, faithful to His covenant, would beat down the king's adversaries before his face, cutting them in pieces and smiting those who hated him.

Yet again there is a reminder of God's faithfulness and mercy. These were covenanted to be with David, a pledge that, in the name of the Lord, his horn would be exalted, his power raised high over his foes, as in v.17. The authority of the king would extend over the sea and upon the rivers, a reference to the Mediterranean Sea and to the River Euphrates with its tributaries and canals. These were the ideal boundaries of the Holy Land, east and west, as in Psalms 72.8 and 80.11.

In 2 Samuel 7.14 God's promise to David concerning his son Solomon was, "I will be his father, and he shall be my son". Here, in the Psalm, God promises the same fatherly care to David himself. "He shall cry unto me, Thou art my father". It is quite remarkable however, that nowhere in Holy Scripture does David, or any other Old Testament saint, address God as "Father". This is reserved for ultimate fulfilment in David's greater Son, who, in His first recorded words in Scripture spoke of "My Father's business" (Lk 2.49), who, in His ministry in the upper room on His last evening with His disciples spoke again and again of "My Father" (Jn 14-16), and who, risen from the dead, said to Mary, "My Father and your Father (Jn 20.17). The title "firstborn" and the tribute, "highest of the kings of the earth" (RV) wait also for Him who is King of kings and Lord of lords. The words, "My God, and the rock of my salvation", are a familiar thought in the Psalter, as in Psalms 62.2, 6; 95.1. In many other Scriptures, too, this symbol of the rock is used of Jehovah.

The promises of the covenant continue. The words "forevermore" and "forever" express the enduring character of the covenant. Jehovah's mercy (2617), mentioned so often in this and other Psalms, is rather His lovingkindness. This is vouchsafed to David and to his seed. Both the covenant and the kingdom will stand fast, and his throne as the days of heaven. Literally this means that as long as the heavens endure then so will the Davidic dynasty. The promises are to David personally, to David's posterity, and to the Son of David, the Messiah, the ultimate King of Israel.

There were however, certain provisions in the covenant. Jehovah had rights. He reserved the right to punish the transgressions of the people. "If his sons forsake my law, and walk not in mine ordinances; If they profane my statutes, and keep not my commandments: Then will I visit their transgression with the rod, and their iniquity with stripes" (JND). It was reasonable and fair that, if Jehovah made such promises to the king and his seed as He had done, He should expect reciprocal behaviour from His people. If this was not forthcoming, He would judge accordingly. There would be divine retribution for their transgressions. "With the rod", Spurgeon rightly emphasises, "Not with the sword, not with death and destruction; but still with a smarting, tingling, painful rod. Saints must smart if they sin; God will see to that".

"Nevertheless!" What grace and mercy is this, that, if they failed, Jehovah would not. If they were unfaithful, He would remain faithful. In spite of their sinning, He would not completely withdraw His lovingkindness from them. He would not break His covenant nor alter His word. Once He had sworn, He would not lie. In keeping with His holiness He would perform what He had promised. His word to David therefore, was inviolable. His seed would endure forever. His throne was firm and secure, as steadfast as the sun and the moon in the heavens. Those lights in the sky were a witness. As long as they endured, so would David's throne endure. It was established forever by the word of a faithful covenant-keeping God.

Surely the "Selah" is necessary! So much has been said, and the reader needs time to think. Meditation on the righteousness, faithfulness, and loving-kindness of God, as well as upon His solemn promises and warnings, require a pause such as the "Selah" provides. Quiet reflection on these great matters must lift the heart of every saint in adoring worship.

Verses 38-45: The Ideal and the Actual

But what now has happened to the covenant? What calamity has overtaken the nation that God seems to have cast them off and abhorred them, and is wroth with the king, His anointed? Where now are those promises of an enduring kingdom? The crown has fallen from the king's head. His boundaries are broken and his strongholds are in ruin. Invaders spoil him and he has become the taunt of his neighbours who glory in his defeat. The promise was that his horn would be exalted, but now God has exalted the right hand of his adversaries instead, and his enemies rejoice. When he seeks to wield his sword its edge is turned back, useless against the foe. He cannot hold his ground in the battle. He cannot stand in adversity. Where is the former brightness of the crown? His throne, like his crown, is cast to the ground. His regal glory is gone.

The days of his youth are shortened. This does not necessarily denote an early death, but premature loss of zeal and energy and kingly authority. The prime years of life are over too soon. He is covered with shame. To which of Israel's monarchs this applies is not clear, but it is a sad contrast with the ideal conditions which were envisaged in the covenant. Adam Clarke points out that, "The four last kings of Judah reigned but a short time, and either died by the sword or in captivity. Jehoahaz reigned only three months, and was led captive to Egypt, where he died. Jehoiakim reigned only eleven years, and was tributary to the Chaldeans, who put him to death, and cast his body into the common sewer. Jehoiachin reigned three months and ten days, and was led captive to Babylon, where he continued in prison to the time of Evil-Merodach, who, though he loosed him from prison, never invested him with any power. Zedekiah, the last of all, had reigned only eleven years, when he was taken, his eyes put out, was loaded with chains, and thus carried to Babylon. Most of these kings died a violent and premature death. Thus *the days of their youth* - of their power, dignity, and life, *were shortened*". This was not at all what Jehovah had desired for His people. How different it could have been if they had been as faithful to Him as He had been to them. Another "Selah" brings this sad section to a close. Time to muse, to ponder, to consider the ideal and the actual.

Verses 46-51: A Plea for the People

The last section of the Psalm opens with the sadly familiar, "How long, Lord?". Verse 46 is almost a repetition of Psalm 79.5. Jehovah has hidden Himself from them. They have lost sight of Him and His wrath is smouldering like a fire. "How long?", they ask again. The Psalmist remembers, and seems to be asking God to remember, just how short his time is. Life is brief. The years are fleeting. He longs that there may be a recovery to better things in his lifetime. All who live must die, but to what purpose is a life lived in vanity and emptiness? No man can escape the appointed end in "sheol". All men are destined for the land of departed spirits, the "grave-land". Another "Selah"! How often does this Psalmist direct the reader to pause and think.

But how sad to live and die in the vanity of unsatisfied longing. "Lord", he asks, "where are Thy former mercies, Thy lovingkindnesses which were sworn to David?". Were not those promises made in faithfulness? Did Jehovah not swear in truth? "Remember, Lord", he pleads, "the reproach of thy servants". "Remember how I bear the reproach in my bosom. These are Thine enemies O Lord", he continues, "pursuing and taunting Thine anointed". What a foreshadowing of what they did to the Christ, the Lord's anointed, mocking Him until His last breath.

Verse 52: The Doxology

How good it is, that such a Psalm should be concluded with ascriptions of praise to the Lord. Does this not denote the triumph of faith, that even in the most difficult circumstances the godly can still say, "Blessed be the Lord for evermore"? This doxology may not belong to this Psalm alone. It is a fitting conclusion to the whole of the Third Book. Among those who advance this view are John Calvin, William Binnie, Dr Cohen, and T.W. Davies. Whichever is true, the doxology is rich in praise. "Amen, and Amen!"

This concludes Book 3 of the Psalms

BOOK 4

PSALM 90

Introduction

This is the first Psalm in the Fourth Book of Psalms. It is one of five Psalms - 17, 86, 90, 102 and 142 - which have the word "Prayer" in their titles. Three of these prayer Psalms are ascribed to David, and Psalm 142 is simply "A Prayer of the afflicted". Psalm 90 is unique among the Psalms, being the only one attributed to Moses the man of God. This very uniqueness at once commands attention. What an ancient and beautiful poem is this, bearing such likeness to the language of Moses in Deuteronomy 33, where also he is called "the man of God". Moses shares this lovely title, "man of God" with many other prophets and servants of the Lord.

Some critics have disputed the Mosaic authorship but their criticism seems unnecessary and unfounded. As Spurgeon writes, "Many attempts have been made to prove that Moses did not write this Psalm, but we remain unmoved in the conviction that he did so. The condition of Israel in the wilderness is so pre-eminently illustrative of each verse, and the turns, expressions, and words are so similar to many in the Pentateuch, that the difficulties suggested are, to our mind, light as air in comparison with the internal evidence in favour of its Mosaic origin. Moses was mighty in word as well as deed, and this Psalm we believe to be one of his weighty utterances, worthy to stand side by side with his glorious oration recorded in Deuteronomy". With this sentiment Alexander agrees wholeheartedly, saying, "The correctness of the title which ascribes the Psalm to Moses is confirmed by its unique simplicity and grandeur; its appropriateness to his times and circumstances; its resemblance to the Law in urging the connection between sin and death; its similarity of diction to the poetical portions of the Pentateuch, without the slightest trace of imitation or quotation; its marked unlikeness to the Psalms of David, and still more to those of later date; and finally, the proved impossibility of assigning it to any other age or author".

Here, then, must be the oldest of all the Psalms, sublime among the most ancient songs in Hebrew poetry. It is the prayer of an aged servant, a man of God who remembers the brevity of life and asks for the beauty and the blessing of God to be upon the people and their service, and for gladness and wisdom in that service.

The seventeen verses of the Psalm may be divided for meditation as follows. In verses 1-6 the Psalmist contrasts the eternity of God with the frailty of man and the brevity of human life. In verses 7-10 he regrets, and laments, the sins which have incurred the anger of God and brought sorrow into the life. The concluding verses 11-17 are that prayer for wisdom which has already been mentioned.

Verses 1-6: The Eternity of God and the Mortality of Man

It was these early verses of this Psalm which gave inspiration to Isaac Watts for that sublime hymn of his, considered to be one of the finest hymns in the English language, "O God, our help in ages past". The divine title "Lord" (136) with which the Psalm begins, is Adonai, the sovereign Lord, Proprietor and Owner of all things. He, in His greatness, has been the dwelling place (4583) of the generations of His people. Some prefer, "our refuge", and Isaac Watts has interpreted it as "Our shelter from the stormy blast, and our eternal home". Notice the similarity with Deuteronomy 33.27, "The eternal God is thy refuge" (4585); thy dwelling place.

There follow clear allusions to a birth; "Before the mountains were brought forth, or ever thou hadst formed the earth". The Creator must pre-date the creation. As Spurgeon writes, "Before those elder giants had struggled forth from nature's womb...the Lord was glorious and self-sufficient". Refer again to Deuteronomy 33 where v.15 speaks of the ancient mountains and the lasting hills. "From everlasting to everlasting, thou art God". What better way to express eternity? Before time was and when time shall cease, the eternal God is the dwelling-place, the refuge of His people. In awful contrast the frailty of mortal man is now described. The Creator returns him to the dust from which he came. Two Hebrew words are used for "man" in v.3. "Man" (582) is ENOSH, man in his frailty. "Men" (120) is ADAM, man of the ground, first among the creatures. This difference in the words is regarded by some as just the parallelism of Hebrew poetry, to be considered as synonyms, and of no other significance. Those who accept the divine inspiration of the Scriptures will, however, recognise an importance. Is it not this, that whatever view of man is accepted, whether man in his frailty or man in his superiority in creation, all men are mere mortals, alike destined to return to the dust from which man was created? "Dust thou art, and unto dust shalt thou return", was the sentence upon the first man after the sin in Eden (Gen 3.19).

As for God, a thousand years are to him as an evening gone, as brief as a night watch, of which, in the days of the Psalms, there were three during the night hours. Did Peter have this Psalm in mind when he wrote, "Beloved, be not ignorant of this one thing, that one day is with the Lord as a thousand years, and a thousand years as one day" (2 Pet 3.8)? "A thousand years!", says Spurgeon. "This is a long stretch of time. How much may be crowded into it - the rise and fall of empires, the glory and obliteration of dynasties, the beginning and the end of elaborate systems of human philosophy, and countless events, all important to household and individual, which elude the pens of historians. Yet this period, which might even be called the limit of modern history, and is in human language almost identical with an indefinite length of time, is to the Lord as nothing". He is, in Isaiah 57.15, "The high and lofty One that inhabiteth eternity".

The Almighty can sweep men away in a moment, as with a flood. Human life is like a sleep, like a dream, now present, now over. Men are little different to the grass of the field. In the morning it grows up and flourishes. In the evening it is cut down and withers. Tristram comments that the force of the simile is more apparent in the East, where the grass may be described as "shooting up in the early spring with the greatest luxuriance, and then as rapidly seeding and dying down, scorched and burnt up at once". So it is with man. The most successful of men, the most wealthy, the most aristocratic and proud and noble, are together destined for a return to dust.

Verses 7-10: Mortality and Sin

Man is subject to death because of sin. His mortality may be traced back to Eden. "By one man sin entered into the world, and death by sin; and so death passed upon all men, for that all have sinned" (Rom 5.12). "Sin, when it is finished, bringeth forth death" (Jas 1.15). Therefore, "It is appointed unto men once to die" (Heb 9.27). For some the summons may linger, for others the call may come soon, and, suddenly and unexpectedly, they are consumed in the anger of a God who hates sin. "Because there is wrath, beware lest he take thee away with his stroke" (Job 36.18). In His omniscience, God has cognisance of every sin. In the light of His countenance all is exposed, whether they are blatant presumptuous iniquities or sins committed in secret. Sometimes this light of His countenance means His smile and His favour, but here it is the light which reveals every sin. He sets them all before Him, with full knowledge of all.

Man's days pass away, his years come to an end and soon they are but a memory, a tale that is told. Divine wrath against sin has decreed this brevity of life and certainty of death. "Threescore years and ten" are often referred to as "the allotted span". Some think that this may not be exactly the meaning of this verse. Moses himself lived to one hundred and twenty years (Deut 34.7). Aaron was one hundred and twenty-three when he died (Num 33.39). Joshua was one hundred and ten (Josh 24.29). May the thought be, as suggested by Davies, that at the age of seventy the men of Moses' time had reached their highest point. For some, by reason of strength, that may have been eighty years. But whichever, life was so often associated with labour and sorrow, soon to pass away. Like a bird in flight, man is quickly gone.

Verses 11-17: A Prayer for Wisdom

How few they are, who, in their short lifetime, seem to appreciate the power of God's anger and wrath. How few who render to Him the fear which is His due. Like that rich but foolish farmer of Luke 12 they talk of "much goods" and "many years", and forget God. "So teach us to number our days", says the Psalmist. This is not a morbid living in fear of death, counting the days and anticipating dying. The purpose is that, considering how short the time is, it may be redeemed and the heart applied to wisdom.

This is wisdom, to buy up all the opportunities for living for God and the things of God, that none of the fleeting years be wasted.

The prayer, "Return, O Lord", is a plea that Jehovah might turn from His anger and it is followed immediately by the familiar, "How long?" "Let it repent thee concerning thy servants" is well explained by Kirkpatrick, who writes, "Compare Genesis 6.6. God's change of attitude is spoken of in Scripture after the manner of men as repenting or relenting; not of course that He can regret His course of action, or be subject to mutability of purpose". The Psalmist is imploring a change in God's dealings with the people, who, he says, are God's servants. Will Jehovah not look kindly upon His people? They are His servants.

"O satisfy us early with thy mercy", the Psalmist prays for the people. The RV rendering, with JND's footnote, and others, is, "O satisfy us in the morning". "In the morning", is a Hebrew idiom for "speedily", but there may be an allusion to the night of trouble and sorrow, a longing that the night may soon be over and the morning bring forth the lovingkindness of God. "Mercy" (2617), is lovingkindness. How this would rejoice their hearts, causing them to "sing for joy" (JND). Verse 15 is a prayer that they might have as much gladness in future days as they had sadness in days past. It is an appeal that future happiness may be proportionate to the sorrow they had endured during the days that God's anger burned against them.

The Psalm closes with desires to see God working, and that His glory might be upon them. They long to be clothed with the beauty of Jehovah their God, and, in repetition which is more for emphasis than for rhythm, they pray that He might prosper the work of their hands. Twice they make their request, "Establish thou the work of our hands...yea, the work of our hands establish thou it".

How touching, how moving, how precious to saints of every age, is this prayer of Moses the man of God.

PSALM 91

Introduction

This lovely Psalm has no title. There is, therefore, uncertainty as to its author, the date of its composition, and the circumstances in which it was written. The JFB commentary says, "David is the most probable author". Spurgeon points out that Jewish tradition considers that "when the author's name is not mentioned we may assign the Psalm to the last named writer; and, if so, this is another Psalm of Moses, the man of God". While it would not be prudent to be dogmatic, there is, in the Psalm, a close resemblance to many expressions used by Moses in Deuteronomy, and there is also, a similarity with the thought and language of Psalm 90, a Psalm of Moses. While a Davidic authorship is possible, and a Mosaic authorship probable, nevertheless, there is no certainty, and, in any case, since the Psalm is an integral part of the inspired Scriptures, the human penman is of secondary importance.

Psalm 91 is a most cheering and comforting Psalm. Aged believers, with sick and suffering saints, often request that it be read to them. It is full of encouragement and promise. The following suggested division of the Psalm may suffice for meditation and study. Verses 1-8 state the safety and security of the godly. Verses 9-13 confirm the divine protection which assures this. Verses 14-16 bring the final precious promises of the Psalm.

Verses 1-8: Safety and Security

The godly man is at home, dwelling in quietness and resting in the intimacy of the presence of God. He has discovered the greatness of God, calling Him "The Most High" (5945) and "The Almighty" (7706). These lovely titles are to be found as early as Genesis 14.19 and 17.1. How privileged was Abraham to learn these titles, first from Melchizedek and then from God Himself. El Elyon was the Most High God, the possessor of heaven and earth who could give everything to the man who refused the offer of reward from the King of Sodom. El Shaddai was the Almighty who gave a promise of the impossible to the aged Abram, changing his name to Abraham, "Father of a multitude". The covert of the Most High and the shadow of the Almighty are still the safe resort of the godly man. "Under (His) shadow" suggests the image of a mother-bird with her young sheltering beneath her wings, as again in v.4, a secret place indeed. See the same thought in Psalm 17.8 and in the words of Boaz to Ruth (Ruth 2.12).

There is richness in this great variety of divine titles, and now the Psalmist introduces another. "I will say of the LORD" (3068). This is the awful name Jehovah, which he uses again in v.9. It is the name of the ever-existent, all-sufficient One who lives in an eternal present, unaffected by past or future, "Him which is, and which was, and which is to come" (Rev 1.4). What security, then, is this, to be sheltered in the secret place of such a One. With yet another divine title the Psalmist says, "My refuge and my fortress: my God" (430). This is Elohim, name of the Mighty One. In Him the saint has found a refuge and a fortress, one in whom he can confide and trust. The metaphor has changed, but the theme remains. Not now dwelling "under the shadow", but resorting to a strong fortress, a tower of defence, safe from the assaults of the enemy.

Of the verbs which follow, "He shall deliver thee...He shall cover thee", T.W. Davies says that the tenses here are the Hebrew imperfect, "the tense (so called) of unfinished action", so that we should read, "He delivers thee...He covers thee". This of course is very beautiful, teaching that there is an ongoing, continuing care of Jehovah for His people. The saints need such care, for enemies would entrap and entangle them if they could, as a bird might be caught in the snare of the fowler. Then, too, as well as the subtle hidden snare, there is the noisome pestilence. "Noisome" (1942) is an old English translation of a word which Strong says denotes "perverse, very wicked". With such pestilence the adversaries would plague the people of God, but He is their deliverer. The metaphor of the sheltering wings is now resumed and the Psalmist says, "He shall cover thee with his feathers", or, as has already been suggested, "He covers thee with his feathers". Under the protecting wings of the Lord the believer finds refuge, while His truth is as a shield and buckler, a covering coat of mail. With the shadowing wings, the fortress, the shield, and the buckler, the saint is safe from every attack of the enemy.

These attacks come by night and by day. Dr Cohen suggests that "the language may be metaphorical and allude to secret and open antagonism". Pestilence (1698), in v.3, stalks in the night hours, seeking to produce terror in the darkness. Destruction, perhaps in various forms, would devastate at noonday. But whether by day or by night, the saint is safe. Though thousands may fall on the right hand and on the left, the believer may rest in this, that as the children of Israel were spared from the plagues that fell on Egypt, and were delivered from the judgment of that Passover night, so he is surrounded by divine protection. This does not mean that he will not ever suffer grief, or that he is immune to sorrow, but that his eventual salvation is assured. He is indeed safe, and secure. As those children of Israel stood safe on the banks of the Red Sea and saw the destruction of the pursuing enemy, so the believer will one day witness the defeat of every foe. He will, in a day of reckoning, see the meting out of divine retribution to those wicked men who had oppressed the people of God.

Verses 9-13: Divine Protection Assured

The Psalmist now repeats the great titles of the early verses. They express the Almighty character of God for the assurance of the trusting saint. Where is his refuge? Where is his trust? It is in Jehovah. Where has he chosen to rest, as in a peaceful dwelling-place? In the Most High. For such a man, who has made the Lord his refuge, there is promise of protection from distress and affliction, evil and plague. Spurgeon gives personal testimony to the faithfulness of this promise, as, during that great plague of cholera which claimed the lives of so many in London during his early ministry there, he was able to continue his visitation and ministration among those who were sick, but was himself untouched by the disease. Having read this verse he writes, "The effect upon my heart was immediate. Faith appropriated the passage as her own. I felt secure, refreshed…I went on with my visitation of the dying in a calm and peaceful spirit; I felt no fear of evil, and I suffered no harm".

Angels are ministering spirits and are sent forth in service to the heirs of salvation (Heb 1.14). They have been given charge concerning the saints, to keep them in all their ways. This is the Scripture which Satan quoted, or misquoted, during our Lord's temptation (Mt 4.6; Lk 4.10). He omitted the words "in all thy ways", temptingly suggesting a spectacular casting down from the pinnacle of the temple to prove the truth of this word and the reality of angelic ministry. Jesus answered, "Thou shalt not tempt the Lord thy God". This was not a promise of deliverance from deliberate suicidal acts such as Satan was proposing. It was an assurance of protection from tragedies along life's pathway, in the varied activities of life, "in all thy ways". Stones on the highway, lions and adders, come under the notice of guardian angels. Lions and serpents of course, may well be, as Dr Cohen suggests, "Symbols of deadly dangers, the lion representing an open attack and the serpents underhand scheming". The man of God can, with divine aid, put so many troubles beneath his feet.

Verses 14-16: Final Promises

How Jehovah appreciates the love of the saint, and rewards it. "God's love at once responds to man's love of Him" (Cohen). To those who have set their love upon Him, and because they have done so, He now gives a series of concluding promises. Notice the "I will", recurring six times. "I will deliver him; I will set him on high; I will answer him; I will be with him; I will deliver him; I will satisfy him". Jehovah always performs what He promises.

"I will deliver him" occurs twice. The trusting man will be delivered and set on high, beyond the reach of his enemies. This because he has known God's name and acknowledged Him in worship. When he calls, the Lord will hear him and answer him, and be with him in his trouble. He will not only deliver him, but honour him. He will endue him with a moral nobility among men. With length of days Jehovah will satisfy those who love Him, and then, when the long and full life is ended and eternity has begun, He will give continuing revelations of the glory of His great salvation.

So ends this lovely Psalm, full of promise, of assurance, and of love, and made rich with the majesty and greatness of divine titles.

PSALM 92

Introduction

This hymn of praise to Jehovah is both a Psalm (4210) and a Song (7892), indicating that it may be sung either with or without a musical accompaniment. It was intended for use on the Sabbath, and Jewish tradition does indeed say that its association with the day of rest was recognised in the temple, where it was chanted by the Levites every

Sabbath. Perhaps the link with the Sabbath is in v. 4-5 - "Thy work...the works of thy hands...thy works". This is a reminder of those days of creation and of that word in Genesis 2.2-3: "And on the seventh day God ended his work which he had made; and he rested on the seventh day from all his work which he had made. And God blessed the seventh day, and sanctified it: because that in it he had rested from all his work which God created and made".

The Psalm requires little in the way of division and sub-division, but for the purpose of an orderly meditation the following may be helpful. Verses 1-5 speak of the privilege of praising God and the reasons for doing so. Verses 6-11 deal with the final ruin and doom of the workers of iniquity. Verses 12-15 describe the prosperity and ultimate triumph of the righteous.

Verses 1-5: The Privilege and Pleasure of Praise

"It is a good thing to give thanks unto the Lord". The word here rendered "good" (2896) has a very wide sense, requiring a most lengthy definition in Strong's Hebrew Dictionary. He says that it may mean, among other definitions, "beautiful; better; best; bountiful; cheerful; glad; good; joyful; pleasant; precious; sweet". How descriptive are all of these of the believer's thanksgiving to God, and how much God Himself must appreciate the thankfulness of His saints. In Romans 1.21 the awful downgrade of Gentile peoples begins with this, "They glorified him not as God, neither were thankful". Thanksgiving is often accompanied by the singing of praises, and the hymns or psalms of praise composed by another often provide suitable words by which the saints might express their thankfulness. Notice the occurrence here, in a single verse, of those two divine titles which have already been observed twice in Psalm 91, "It is a good thing to give thanks unto the LORD (Jehovah - 3068); and to sing praises unto thy name O most High (Elyon - 5945)", the latter being the God of Melchizedek in Genesis 14.19. It is truly a great privilege for a mortal man, a happy blending of duty and pleasure, to be able to render thanks to the eternally self-sufficient Jehovah, and to sing praises to the name of the Most High.

In the morning and at night the Psalmist encourages praise, declaring the loving-kindness and the faithfulness of God. "No hour is too early for holy song", says Spurgeon, "no hour is too late for praise". Dr Cohen concurs, saying, "Suitable times of the day in which to direct thoughts to God, before the round of duty begins and after it has ended". It is good to begin and end the day with God, and, of course, this envisages that the intervening hours will likewise be sanctified with thoughts of Him. Three musical instruments are mentioned as aids to the Psalmist in his devotions: a ten-stringed instrument, the psaltery, and the harp. These were probably all forms of the harp, lute, or lyre. Instrumental accompaniment was of great importance in the past dispensation.

The "solemn sound" mentioned in v.3 is "Higgaion" (1902), which word appears also in Psalm 9.16. JND comments in a footnote, "Perhaps an instrument of music, or the softened tones of a harp; or 'meditation' as in Psalm 19.14". The Psalmist requests that the rendering of the desired praise should be accompanied by dulcet tones, not loud and excitable, but conducive to thoughtful meditation.

Although the Psalmist speaks personally, he probably speaks also for the nation when he gives his reason for praise, saying, "Thou, Lord, hast made me glad through thy work: I will triumph in the works of thy hands". The word translated "work" (6467) in v.4 is different from that rendered "works" (4639) also in v.4 and again in v.5. Nevertheless, both may describe the great work of creation, called in Psalm 8, "the work of thy fingers" (v.3) and "the works of thy hands" (v.6). Contemplation of the work of God calls forth praise. Whether this is the work of God in creation, or, as some think, His work in providence, each and all of His works are always a reason for praising Him. Believers today praise the greatness of God as Creator, singing -

> O Lord my God! when I in awesome wonder
> Consider all the works Thy hands have made,
> I see the stars, I hear the mighty thunder,
> Thy power throughout the universe displayed.
>
> Then sings my soul, my Saviour God, to Thee,
> How great Thou art! How great Thou art!
> (tr. Stuart K. Hine)

But not only are the works of God great, His thoughts are very deep. His purpose and His plans, both in and for creation, are fully known to Him alone, though His people may wonder and adore. His saints may contemplate, and then say, with Paul, "O the depth of the riches both of the wisdom and knowledge of God! how unsearchable are his judgments, and is ways past finding out!" (Rom 11.33). As He says in Isaiah 55.8, "My thoughts are not your thoughts". How blessed it is for the righteous, that, even in a little measure, they are permitted to enter into the thoughts of God, and worship.

Verses 6-11: The Doom of the Wicked

The brutish man is, says Dr Cohen, "One in whom animal instincts overrule the spiritual element". He is associated here with the fool, as he is also in Psalm 49.10, and in Psalm 94.8, where the Psalmist asks, "When will ye be wise?". In Proverbs 12.1 the brutish man hates being reproved. Fool, indeed, the one who despises learning. He lacks understanding and perception and is complacent in his ignorance, not knowing either the greatness of God or the awful destiny of the wicked. The workers of iniquity spring up and flourish. It may be a sudden rise to prosperity, but, like the grass and herbage of the meadow, which flourishes also, they are soon cut down. Their ascendancy is short-lived, their doom is certain, and forever.

"But thou, Lord!" How precious are these recurring contrasts between Jehovah and wicked men. "Thou...art on high for evermore" (RV, JND, JPS). He is eternally exalted when they are eternally lost. What awful folly, to live in ignorance of Him, to live like the brute or the fool, to die without Him, and be lost forever. This interjection of v.8, the central verse of the Psalm, is like a parenthetical interruption in the Psalmist's train of thought, as if he is impatient to sing the glory of God in contrast to His enemies. The main thrust of this section is resumed in v.9.

Notice again a repetition, which, though it may help the rhythm, is more for emphasis. "For, lo, thine enemies, O Lord, for, lo, thine enemies shall perish". The enemies of Jehovah are doomed. Again he calls them, "workers of iniquity" as in v.7. They shall be scattered, blown away like chaff.

Having contrasted Jehovah with these enemies, the Psalmist now contrasts himself with them. As they have been scattered, he has been exalted. In triumph over his foes, his horn, symbol of his power, has been raised in victory, like the horn of the unicorn. This "unicorn" is rendered "wild ox" by the RV and others, and "buffalo" by JND. The unicorn may have been some great ox or buffalo now unknown, and perhaps extinct. Among the ancients it was the symbol of strength and power and as such the Psalmist adopts it. In symbol also, he is anointed with fresh oil. This is not the holy anointing oil usually employed for anointing into office, but that which was used on festive occasions of rejoicing, as a token of gladness. The familiar Psalm says, "Thou anointest my head with oil" (Ps 23.5).

As he thinks of Jehovah's judgment on his enemies the Psalmist says, paraphrased, "Mine eyes have seen what I desired to see; mine ears have heard what I expected to hear". Adversaries had subtly lain in wait for him, others had risen up against him, but God had scattered them all. His joy at their judgment is not personal vindictiveness. It might indeed be a personal vindication of his faith in God, but his joy is that of a man who sees truth and righteousness triumph over evil. These men were evildoers, workers of iniquity, and he had expected that Jehovah would punish them. Such judgment was for the glory of God, and every righteous man could therefore rejoice.

Verses 12-15: The Blessing of the Righteous

In v.7 the workers of iniquity flourished, but it was transient, it was short-lived. Now the righteous flourish, as beautiful as the palm tree and as strong as the cedar of Lebanon. The wicked may be likened to the grass, but the godly are like the palm and the cedar. The palm tree is noted for its graceful stature and erectness (Song 7.7). The cedar is renowned for its strength and long life. Those godly men and women, of whom Simeon and the aged Anna are lovely examples (Lk 2.25, 36), whose lives and interests are firmly rooted in the house of the Lord, shall flourish in the things of the Lord. How like the cedar and the palm tree were those two saints in the courts of the Lord. As the promise in the Psalm, Simeon and Anna were still fruitful in old age, vigorous like trees filled with sap and still evergreen. How often they must have read this Psalm! What joy to see its promises fulfilled in their long lives.

The purpose of this blessing is to show that Jehovah is upright. There is no unrighteousness in Him. The moral and spiritual prosperity of the godly is a witness to the righteousness of God. It is with certain conviction and assurance that the Psalmist can say, "He is my rock". "And so", says Spurgeon, "we weave the end of the Psalm with its beginning...It is a good thing to sing praises unto the Lord, for 'He is my rock'".

PSALM 93

Introduction

This brief Psalm begins with majesty and ends with holiness. It has no title, no name of composer, and no mention of the circumstances in which it was born. But it is a delightful poem which sings the greatness of God throughout. That grand title Jehovah is employed five times, in keeping with the theme of glory.

The LXX does provide a superscription, "For the day before the Sabbath", and this agrees with a statement in the Jewish Talmud that the Psalm was chanted in the temple by the Levites every Friday, eve of the Sabbath.

The five short verses of the Psalm need no division. There is unity and beauty in its brevity and the reader can find consolation in contemplation, and solace in study.

Verses 1-5: Jehovah, Sovereign and Supreme

The Psalm commences with a majestic abruptness, "Jehovah reigneth!". These are the opening words of Psalms 97 and 99 also. The remainder of this Psalm is but an amplification and exposition of this great truth, that the Lord has asserted His regal rights and He reigns. Heathen deities, false gods, there may be; rebellious men and usurpers may abound in His world, but still, Jehovah reigns! How true this will be in that coming millennial day when Jesus takes the throne of His father David and rules supreme. Men had mocked His kingship when He was here. They gave Him a thorny crown, a reed for a sceptre, and a scarlet robe of mockery. They bowed the knee in feigned homage, and then lifted Him up on a cross, His only throne. One day it will be said of Him in truth, "The Lord reigneth!". Yet, even now, in spite of the turmoil of nations, and the moral and political disorder among men, Jehovah reigns! "The most High ruleth in the kingdom of men" (Dan 4.25).

As kings array themselves in royal apparel, so Jehovah has girded Himself. He has robed Himself with strength. The world is His. He has established it, so that it can not be moved without His will. His throne is established too, and has been of old. There is no beginning to His right to reign and He has ordered things since time began. In His Person, He is Himself from everlasting. This is the glorious implication in His great name "Jehovah". Past, present, and future, are all one to Him. He is eternally self-existent and self-sufficient. He is, as man conceives it, from eternity to eternity.

In a poetic, but emphatic, repetition, the Psalmist speaks of the floods, the rivers. They have lifted up their voice and their waves rise high. Whether this refers to the raging of literal waters, or, symbolically, to the nations, does not matter. Jehovah is in control of all. He rules the rivers, the oceans, and the seas, and likewise He is greater than Egypt, Assyria, or Babylon, and all those heathen peoples who had lifted up their voice against Him. Jehovah is on high, mightier than the mighty breakers of the sea. The voices of many waters are but a noise to Him. They do not, cannot, threaten Him.

The testimonies of Jehovah are sure, very sure (Ps 19.7). His laws, His commands, His precepts, are, like Himself, unchangeable and established. Because of this, holiness becomes His house forever. Evil may abound without, but sin can never be admitted to His house. "There shall in no wise enter into it anything that defileth" (Rev 21.27). The Psalm, which begins with majesty, ends with becoming holiness.

PSALM 94

Introduction

This untitled Psalm is a plea for divine judgment. In both tone and content it is in sharp contrast to the preceding and succeeding Psalms where there is an earthly acknowledgement of God's sovereignty and heaven's rule. Here again, as in other Psalms, is that enigma of the continuing triumph of the wicked. It is another example of a good man in perplexity over the prosperity and ascendancy of godless men, who, in their pride and arrogance, seem to sin with impunity. Yet there is, throughout the Psalm, the consciousness and confidence that Jehovah can, and will, in His own time, judge these workers of iniquity.

There is some difference of opinion as to whether these oppressors are foreign nations, harassing and afflicting Israel, or, as Dr Cohen prefers, "lawless Israelites dealing unjustly with their own brethren". Perhaps controversy on the matter is neither important nor relevant, for, whichever is true, evil men are oppressing God's people, and the Psalmist pleads for justice and judgment.

The Psalm may be divided as follows. In verses 1-7 the Psalmist petitions God for vengeance upon these wicked men, the oppressors of His people. In verses 8-11 he rebukes their foolish notion that Jehovah either does not see, or does not regard, their evil conduct. Verses 12-15 acknowledge that God may sometimes chasten His people, but that, even in chastisement, they are a blessed people for whom He desires only good. In verses 16-23 he renews His complaint against the evildoers, affirming his belief that only God can help, and expressing again his confidence that Jehovah, his defence and refuge, will sustain him and cut off the workers of iniquity.

Verses 1-7: A Prayer for Vengeance

Most other translations depart slightly from the AV rendering of the opening words of the Psalm and read, "O LORD, Thou God to whom vengeance belongeth". Jehovah is the God of vengeance, not in the sense of vindictiveness, but in righteous retribution. It is not possible that a righteous God could condone unrighteousness, and when the Psalmist calls for vengeance it is really a plea that God should act in accordance with His righteous character and deal with iniquity. "Vengeance", is here a plural word. Jehovah is the God of vengeances. This is the Hebrew plural of intensity, literally, "The God of great vengeance", or, "The God of much vengeance". This address to God is repeated in the same form, indicating the urgency and earnestness of the petition. It is important to note the difference between revenge and vengeance. It has been said that revenge is an act of passion, and vengeance is an act of justice. It is not revenge that the Psalmist desires, but just judgment. He is asking that Jehovah might intervene for the injustices being inflicted on his people. "Shew thyself", he cries to the God of vengeance. "Shine forth", he calls. O that God would reveal Himself for the salvation of His people. It is the cry of oppressed innocence, pleading for divine intervention and for judgment of the ruthless oppressors.

The Psalmist now invokes God with another title, "Thou judge of the earth". How reminiscent is this of Abraham's plea in Genesis 18.25, "Shall not the Judge of all the earth do right". The call that God should lift up Himself seems to suggest that He should ascend His judgment seat, and, sitting in judicial supremacy, judge the wicked. These evil men were proud and arrogant and they must be rewarded accordingly. Jehovah must lift Himself above them, greater than they, and administer righteous retribution

There follows that pathetic and familiar cry, "How long?". If these words in v.4, italicized in the AV text, are omitted, as by the RV and others, then the call rises twice to Jehovah, "LORD, how long shall the wicked, how long shall the wicked triumph?". Why should godless men triumph and godly men be oppressed? It is the perplexity of many a Psalm and many a saint. It is one of the mysteries of life that God should for so long, and so often, defer His judgment and apparently tolerate evil. It is not, of course, that He disregards the wickedness of men, but that in His sovereignty He chooses His own time to act. It is perhaps understandable, however, that, while they wait for justice, the oppressed might become impatient and distressed, crying, "How long? How long?".

The arrogance of these men is emphasized again, "They prate, they speak arrogantly" (RV). "They gush out, they speak arrogancy" (JPS). "They pour out arrogant words" (NIV). This is the word of Psalm 59.7, translated, "They belch out". Their arrogant words poured forth like a torrent and they were jubilant in their boasting. They vaunted themselves, bearing themselves loftily in their pride. "Lord, how long?"

Note how the Psalmist strengthens his appeal with the words, "thy people", and, "thine heritage". These wicked men were oppressing and crushing the people who were God's people. God's own people were being broken and afflicted. The language indicates violent and cruel treatment. They were ruthless, these men, and callous too, slaying defenceless widows and orphans. Even the stranger was not spared, and if these oppressors, or some of them, were Israelites as Dr Cohen supposes, then this was a blatant violation of the law concerning strangers in Exodus 22.21, "Thou shalt neither vex a stranger, nor oppress him: for ye were strangers in the land of Egypt".

The wicked were blind in their arrogance, protesting that Jehovah would not see and that the God of Jacob would not give heed or consider. What folly and ignorance was this, to think that the omniscient Jehovah did not see what they were doing to His people. How equally foolish it was, to think that the God of Jacob would not take note of any oppression of Israel. Jacob's God had led him, protected him, and provided for him, and these were the posterity of Jacob who were now being afflicted. How could the God of Jacob not see and consider their wickedness? Of course He saw. Of course He took note. He considered, and in His own time He would rise in judgment against them.

Verses 8-11: The Lord Knoweth!

The foolish notion of the wicked, that Jehovah either did not, or could not, see or hear what they were doing to His people, is now dealt with in greater detail. These brutish men, as lacking in perception as dumb animals, must really consider their folly. They were fools in their arrogance. When would they become wise? He who gave to others the ability to hear, could He not hear? He who gave to men the power to see, could He not see? He who had created and formed the ear and the eye for His creatures, could He not both see and hear and be fully aware of what was happening in His creation? Men must consider that the Lord has instructed the heathen by endowing them with a conscience and imparting to them a moral sense. To His own people He gave the Law (v.12), full of instruction for right living. Can He, who gives such knowledge to men, Himself be lacking in knowledge? No indeed, He not only sees and knows the behaviour of men, but He knows the very thoughts of men. He sees their wicked acts, He hears their arrogant talk, and He can read their unspoken thoughts, and He knows that they are vanity. Whether this "vanity" refers to the thoughts of men, or to the men themselves, is not relevant. These foolish but proud men are as nothing compared to the majesty of the omnipotent and omniscient Jehovah.

Verses 12-15: Chastised but Happy!

To many a man it may seem a strange thing to say, but it is real blessedness to be chastised of the Lord. To be exercised by the chastisement, and to learn by it, eventually brings gladness to the spiritual soul. The writer of the Epistle to the Hebrews concurs with this, saying, "Now no chastening for the present seemeth to be joyous, but grievous: nevertheless afterward it yieldeth the peaceable fruit of righteousness unto them which are exercised thereby" (Heb 12.11). Another Psalm agrees, "It is good for me that I have been afflicted; that I might learn thy statutes", and, "Before I was afflicted I went astray: but now I have kept thy word" (Ps 119.71, 67). If present suffering can be accepted as God's means of disciplining, then this will inevitably lead to a richer experience of God and a better understanding of His ways, and this is true happiness. "Sanctified afflictions", they have been called. That which is spoken of so often in the Psalms, and here referred to as "Thy law" (8451) is the Hebrew "Torah", the revelation of God's will for His people. "Give ear, O my people, to my law: incline your ears to the words of my mouth" (Ps 78.1).

A submissive and exercised response to divine chastening will lead to quietness and rest in the days of adversity, "the days of evil" (JND). These evil and troublous days will continue for the saint until that day comes when the wicked will have been judged and all enemies and enmity have gone forever. "Until the pit be digged for the wicked" is almost a synonym for destruction (compare Ps 7.15; 55.23; 57.6). Chastisement with the accompanying instruction ensures a spirit of rest and reassurance for the spiritual man in the evil days.

It is unthinkable that Jehovah should cast off His people or forsake His inheritance. "His people" are "His inheritance" and are too precious to Him that He should abandon them. They are His peculiar treasure and He is their Redeemer. They may fail Him and grieve Him, and He may chastise them, but He will never forsake them. Soon, the Psalmist knew, the days of adversity would be over and justice would return, bringing with it righteousness, and the upright in heart would follow after it. Spurgeon sees it as a grand and joyous procession. "The chariot of right will be drawn in triumph through our streets, and all the upright in heart shall follow it as in happy procession. A delightful hope is here expressed in poetic imagery of much beauty".

Verses 16-23: Jehovah, my Help, my Defence, my Refuge

The Psalmist now renews his complaint concerning his adversaries, evildoers and workers of iniquity. "Who will rise up for me?", he asks, "who will stand up for me?" He is looking for one who will champion his cause, but somehow he seems to know that there is no help in man. The implied answer is that God alone can help him. If Jehovah does not hear, and help, no other will hear him or answer, and he must dwell in a lonely silence. Does he mean by this that he would quickly die, that his soul "would soon have dwelt in the land of silence" (RSV), the silence of "sheol" itself? Compare Psalm 115.17: "The dead praise not the Lord, neither they that go down into silence". He may simply mean, of course, that if Jehovah does not rise up for Him and plead his cause, he would be left silent and speechless, in the shame and embarrassment of having no word to speak against his enemies.

"When I said" (559), may suggest that the poor Psalmist was actually talking inwardly, thinking and saying in his heart, "My foot slippeth". This was David's lament in Psalm 38.16, "When my foot slippeth, they magnify themselves against me". But when this Psalmist feels that he is stumbling, missing his step and falling, then, he says, "Thy mercy, O Lord, held me up". The "mercy" (149) of the Lord is His goodness, His lovingkindness, His faithfulness. It was this which upheld him in his trouble.

The thoughts of which the Psalmist now speaks in v.19 are disturbing. "Thoughts" (8312) is an unusual word, found only twice in the OT, and indicating that they were disquieting, distracting thoughts, like a multitude of cares in his mind. But into the midst of them come thoughts of comfort from the Lord. Into his anxiety comes a sense of calm, comforting and delighting his soul. "Comforts" (8575) is the same word as that in the question of Job 15.11, "Are the consolations of God small with thee?". Alternative renderings help to bring out the beauty of this lovely verse, a proven solace to saints in trouble. "In the multitude of my anxious thoughts within me thy comforts have delighted my soul" (JND). "When the cares of my heart are many, thy consolations cheer my soul" (RSV). "When my cares are many within me, Thy comforts delight my soul" (JPS). It is like that well-known and much-loved word of the Saviour, "Let not your heart be troubled" (Jn 14.1).

The Psalmist condemns, by means of a question, an unjust judiciary which he calls "the throne of iniquity", or "the seat of wickedness". Can such have fellowship with a righteous God? These unjust judges were characterised by partiality, and there was much bribery and corruption and exploitation of those who were weak and vulnerable. Their wickedness was intensified in that they actually framed laws which legalized their injustices. As Dr Cohen comments, "Under the cloak of legal enactments they work their mischievous plans. They act unjustly, although legally, because their laws are unjust". They conspired together in their wickedness, attacking the righteous and even condemning the innocent, but Jehovah was the Psalmist's stronghold, his fortress, the rock of his refuge and his defence. Expositors and translators disagree about the tense here. "The Lord *is* my defence" (AV). "The Lord *hath been* my high tower" (RV). "The Lord *has become* my stronghold" (RSV). Dr Cohen suggests, "The tense may be what grammarians call the perfect of certainty: '*will surely be*'". No doubt all of these are relevant and true.

Jehovah will deal with these men according to their iniquity. He will render righteous retribution in proportion to their evil. As they have troubled others, causing sorrow and pain, so will He bring trouble upon them. The Psalm concludes, "Yea, the Lord our God shall cut them off", and Spurgeon remarks so aptly, "Here, then, the matter ends; faith reads the present in the light of the future, and ends her song without a trembling note".

PSALM 95

Introduction

Like many other Psalms, Psalm 95 is untitled. No author's name is mentioned but the writer of the Epistle to the Hebrews quotes the Psalm as David's (Heb 4.7). Some will say that "in David" may simply be a way of describing the Psalter generally, as being "The Psalms of David". The "in David" of the AV, is, however, "through David" in the RSV, and this would seem to indicate an assigning of the Psalm to David personally. As Spurgeon comments, "It is true that this may merely signify that it is to be found in the collection known as David's Psalms; but if such were the Apostle's meaning it would have been more natural for him to have written, 'saying in the Psalms;' we therefore incline to the belief that David was the actual author of this poem".

The Psalm is in two parts, so distinct in tone and comment that some have imagined two separate Psalms brought together as one. This is unnecessary conjecture. It is a blending of invitation and admonition, of exhortation and warning. "O come", the Psalmist begins, "Let us come…O come", he continues. "Let us sing", he exhorts, "let us make a joyful noise…let us worship…let us kneel". It is an invitation to praise, and the invitation occupies verses 1-6. Verse 6 has been called "the beating heart of the Psalm". In verse 7 the Psalmist gives reasons for the call to worship, and here also the warning note begins. Verses 7-11 contain solemn warnings against disobedience and unbelief, the sins of the fathers in the wilderness. This portion is quoted twice in the Epistle to the Hebrews as a warning to Jewish readers that they too should beware of the same tendency to unbelief and hardness of heart (Heb 3.7-11; 4.7).

Verses 1-7a: The Call to Praise

There is a holy enthusiasm in the Psalmist's invitation to praise and worship. He calls for a singing (7442) to Jehovah which is really a ringing cry of joy. Twice in the opening verses he calls for a joyful noise (7321), a shout of triumph. T.W. Davies says that this "has very often the meaning of making a noise with trumpets, as was done on festive occasions". He suggests that the Psalm may be a festival song, and that "we should therefore translate here: 'Let us sound our trumpets aloud to the rock' &c. This is supported by the addition made to the same verb in the second part of the next verse, 'Let us sound our trumpets aloud with (accompanying) psalms'". There is an interesting connection in Psalm 89.15, "Blessed are the people who know the festal shout" (RSV), "the people that know the shout of joy" (JND).

Commenting on this "joyful noise", Samuel Horsely, quoted by Spurgeon, says, "The verb signifies to make a loud sound of any sort, either with voice or with instruments. In the Psalms, it generally refers to the mingled din of voices and various instruments, in the Temple services. This wide sense of the word cannot be expressed otherwise in the English language than by a periphrasis". The title of "the rock" is, of course, often used of Jehovah in the Psalms. He is a rock for refuge and for shelter, a rock to build upon or to hide in, a sure rock of salvation for His people in every age. He is like "the shadow of a great rock in a weary land" (Is 32.2). He is ever worthy of His people's praise.

Did the people really need to be reminded that Jehovah was a great God and a great King? He is "above all gods", the Psalmist declares. He is supreme. The nations had their deities of course. They were dead, lifeless gods of gold or silver, of wood or stone, and, if in some instances they were not visible and tangible, then they were mythical. Jehovah was the one true God. He was no local deity of a small and insignificant Israel. He was the Creator of the depths and the heights of the earth. Mountains and valleys, hills and dales, dry land and sea, were all the work of His hands. They were formed by His hand and were controlled in His hand. As Dr Cohen remarks, "Under Divine control is the whole universe, from its foundations in the unexplorable depths to the summit of unscalable mountains".

"O come", the Psalmist repeats. Is there a holy impatience here to bring men to God in worship and adoration? "Let us worship and bow down: let us kneel before Jehovah our maker". In v.7 he emphasises the great incentive to worship; Jehovah, our Maker, "is our God (430)". He is our Elohim and we are His people. Israel was His flock, the people of His pasture (4830), literally, His shepherding. He was the Shepherd of His people, tending them by His hand. The hand which had created the universe guided and guarded His flock. It was only but right and proper that they should bow down, bend the knee, and kneel before Him in gratitude and praise.

Verses 7b-11: The Warning

The warning against the mistakes of their forefathers is introduced abruptly, with urgency, "Today if ye will hear his voice". This "today" indicates that urgency. It is not "tomorrow", but "today". There must be no delay in responding to the voice of God. There can be no procrastination in such matters. The sheep must hear the Shepherd's voice and promptly follow in obedience. Note how the Epistle to the Hebrews confirms the inspiration of the Psalm, quoting this warning not just as the words of the Psalmist but as the words of the Holy Spirit Himself (Heb 3.7).

There is now a solemn appeal, "Harden not your heart", and a reminder of the murmurings of their fathers in the wilderness. Not long after the great exodus from Egypt they had been guilty of provocation (4808) and temptation (4531) of the Lord. Every thoughtful Israelite would know, and remember, the sad events recorded in Exodus 17 and in Numbers 20. The people had complained against Moses and against the Lord. "Even though they saw My work" (JPS, RSV), He says, "they tried Me, tempted Me, proved Me". After all that He had done for them in Egypt and at the Red Sea, they ask, "Is the Lord among us or not?" (Ex 17.7). The two words which describe these murmurings of the people, provocation and temptation, have become proper names, and are so used by RV, JND, RSV, JPS, and others, in the text of v.8. "Harden not your heart, as at Meribah , as in the day of Massah, in the wilderness". They are tragic memorials of the quarrellings and distrust of an unbelieving people for whom Jehovah had wrought so much.

What a serious warning was this, both to the readers of this Psalm and the recipients of the later Epistle to the Hebrews. For forty years Jehovah was wearied with that generation. How tenderly and patiently He had shepherded His flock, but they had grieved Him and angered Him. In their heart they had wandered from Him, and had never learned from His gracious ways with them. The Psalm ends abruptly, "I sware in my wrath that they should not enter into my rest". Perhaps the abrupt ending emphasises the solemnity of the warning. Unbelief cost their forefathers the Promised Land. The readers of the Psalm are suddenly left to consider the tragic consequences of unbelief.

PSALM 96

Introduction

With very little change, this Psalm occurs again in 1 Chronicles 16.23-33. It is a Psalm of David, composed for the occasion of the bringing back of the Ark of the Covenant to Jerusalem. The LXX entitles it "A Psalm of David", but adds, "when the house was built after the captivity". This may simply mean that a Psalm of praise like this, sung on such a joyful occasion as the return of the Ark from its long exile, was most suitable also for celebrating the return of the nation from its exile in Babylon. The earlier part of that song in 1 Chronicles 16 may be omitted here because of its almost exclusive relevance to Israel, whereas now the call for praise of Jehovah extends to the nations everywhere, probably envisaging that day when the Lord will be the Ruler of all peoples and Judge of the whole earth.

In this connection the Psalm is a fitting successor to the preceding Psalm 95. That Psalm ends with the disobedience of Israel and the grief of Jehovah over the unbelief of His people. Now He will look to Gentiles for the praise and worship which is His due. All the earth must declare His glory.

Spurgeon remarks regarding divisions of the Psalm, "We will make none, for the song is one and indivisible, a garment of praise without seam, woven from the top throughout". Nevertheless, there would appear to be four stanzas. The first three are perfectly regular, consisting of three verses each, and the fourth is of four verses.

Verses 1-3 are a hearty call to praise, "Sing…sing…sing!". The second stanza, verses 4-6, gives the reasons for such praise. The Lord is great and glorious, majestic and supreme. He is praiseworthy indeed. Verses 7-9 repeat the summons, urging men to give Him glory. The closing verses 10-13 call upon the heavens and the earth to rejoice. The Lord reigneth! Righteousness and truth will prevail.

Verses 1-3: The Call for Praise

"O sing!", is the opening joyful call of the Psalm, and this is repeated twice more. It is a new song indeed for a new age is dawning in the Psalm as the Psalmist envisages praise beyond the borders of Israel. The whole world must join in the song when Jehovah rules supreme over all the inhabitants of the earth. Every fresh revelation of God demands a new song and when the sun of righteousness arises and that millennial day breaks and Jehovah reigns universally, then, "Sing unto the Lord, all the earth", is a fitting call indeed. This is the joyous anticipation of the Psalmist. That was a glad occasion truly, when the holy Ark of the Covenant was brought back to Zion, when this Psalm was first sung. That was an equally glad celebration, when the remnant returning from Babylon began to build again a house for Jehovah. But both of these happy events are eclipsed by the joy of that day foreseen here, when the Lord will reign over all the earth and His rule will be acknowledged by nations everywhere. This is greater than Israel. This transcends national boundaries. "O sing unto the Lord, all the earth".

The continuing call to bless (1288) the name of the Lord is well summed up by T.W. Davies who writes, "Adore on bended knee". It is indeed a kneeling down before Him in tribute. "His name" is His revelation of Himself, a manifestation of His greatness, whether in word, in work, or in both. Those who respond to such revelation of Jehovah will not only bow in adoration before Him, but will daily declare to others what they have seen and heard. This is salvation, to know Him, and this must be published abroad. "Shew forth" (1319) is so similar to the NT "evangelise". It means "publish; preach; bear the tidings; announce the good news; gladden with good news" (Strong). Well have several commentators called this Psalm, "A Missionary Hymn", as the call to declare the glory of the Lord continues. "Declare (5608) His glory among the nations" (RV, JND). To declare is to recount, rehearse, and relate the glory. Tell it to all peoples, repeating again and again the wonder of His marvellous works.

All this may be, at any time, a challenge to a godly remnant of Israel, and likewise to the godly of this present age, to declare without ceasing, the wonders of redeeming grace and the greatness of the Saviour. Plumer remarks regarding the word "declare", "The corresponding word is a *book*; and the participle is often rendered a scribe, a writer (Ps 45.1). The verb is rendered, tell, show forth, declare. The variety of verbs used in Psalm 96.1-3 proves that we are to employ all proper means for making known the Saviour. One of these methods is by writing."

Verses 4-6: The Reasons for Praise

"The Lord is great (1419), and greatly (3966) to be praised". The two words "great" and "greatly", though somewhat similar in meaning, are, nevertheless, different words. Jehovah is great, inexpressibly great, high and mighty, distinguished above all. Such greatness demands correspondingly great praise, praise which is exceedingly great both in abundance and in diligence. Jehovah is to be feared (3372) above all gods. He is to be held in reverence and in awe, and with a respect which is not due to the gods of the heathen. The idol gods of the nations are nothing. The very word "idol" (457) implies "a thing of naught; of no value; good for nothing; worthless; nothingness". With what irony does the prophet write of those who trust in idols (Is 40.19-20; 45.12-19). What utter folly to bow down to wood or stone, or even to gold or silver. Jehovah is supreme above all gods. He is, after all, the Creator of the very heavens and has manifested Himself in His creation. The heavens declare His glory (Ps 19.1). Honour and majesty belong to Him alone, and strength and beauty are the inhabitants and characteristics of His dwelling place.

There are then, reasons abundant for praising Him. He is great, He is supreme, He is above all. He is the Creator. With Him are honour and majesty, strength and beauty and holiness. He is indisputably praiseworthy. Sing unto the Lord! Declare His glory!

Verses 7-9: The Summons Renewed

There is a holy urgency in the Psalmist's renewed call for praise. There is pathos, almost impatience, as he calls, "Give unto the Lord...give unto the Lord...Give unto the Lord". The threefold repetition of the call emphasises the importance of it all. Having given the reasons for ascribing praise and glory, he now urges it again. His call goes out to tribes and peoples everywhere. One day the response will be universal, "A great multitude, which no man could number, of all nations, and kindreds, and people, and tongues" will enter into millennial bliss to praise Him with the redeemed of Israel and of all ages (Rev 7.9).

The people are exhorted to ascribe glory and strength to Jehovah. Men are to acknowledge the glory that is due to Jehovah, and to pay tribute to His strength and power. This will indeed be the song of the heavens in a coming day. While an angelic host cries, "Worthy is the Lamb that was slain to receive power, and riches, and wisdom, and strength, and honour, and glory, and blessing", men throughout the universe will join in the praise with, "Blessing, and honour, and glory, and power, be unto him that sitteth upon the throne" (Rev 5.11-13). In that day the courts of the Lord will be open for all. It was not so in either of Israel's two temples, where Gentiles were restricted to a particular area. Here it appears that Gentiles will take their place alongside Israelites in the temple courts, united in one song of praise to Jehovah. All are invited to bring an offering (4503), a gift, a present, a tribute, to the Lord. These verses are an echo of Psalm 29.1-2.

True worship however, must be in holiness. "The beauty of holiness" suggests proper priestly attire. "Holy splendour", is JND's rendering of this lovely phrase. As Israel's priests wore garments for glory and for beauty (Ex 28.2, 40), so must all worshippers be morally acceptable for worship, suitably attired with becoming holiness for the service of the sanctuary. Worship is a high privilege which carries with it heavy responsibilities and great obligations. In this holy exercise men will tremble in recognition of the might and majesty of Him who is the object of their worship and praise.

Verses 10-13: The Universal Call for Joy

"The Lord reigneth!" This is the joyful message to be proclaimed to the nations. Tell it among the heathen. Is this a call to a faithful remnant of Israel, that they should announce to Gentile peoples that Jehovah has entered into the majesty of His kingship and will now reign universally? It is the gladdest news that creation has ever heard, that Jehovah has assumed the throne and has taken command of earth's affairs. For this day creation groans even now, travailing in pain until He comes whose right it is to reign (Rom 8.22). His reign will bring deliverance from the bondage of centuries of corruption, and, at last, the world (8398) will be established. A history of sin has shaken society. There have been tyrannies and dynasties, dictators and despots. Kingdoms have risen and fallen. Governments and parliaments have failed. Earthly rulers have flourished and foundered. The habitable world has been convulsed and confused. What glad news for the nations this will be, "The Lord reigneth!". He will rule with equity. He will reign in righteousness and His settled government will ensure peace and prosperity for all without distinction.

It is fitting that heaven and earth should join in the joy of it all. Heaven and earth, sea and land, will rejoice together when Jehovah reigns. The fulness of the sea and the very trees of the wood shall unite in song before Him. The Psalm concludes, "He cometh!...he cometh!". It is asserted twice. The repetition lends emphasis to the wonder and the joy of the occasion. He comes to judge (8199), to govern, to rule. It is again repeated, that He will rule in righteousness. It will be a faithful, impartial, benign rule over the peoples of all nations. "The Lord comes", as Spurgeon comments, "to be to all nations a wiser judge than Samuel, a greater champion than Samson, a mightier deliverer than Gideon". His people everywhere should even now rejoice in the anticipation of His reign.

PSALM 97

Introduction

The theme of Psalm 96 is continued in Psalm 97. So many of the sentiments of the preceding Psalm are repeated here and expanded. "The Lord reigneth" was the watchword of Psalm 96. These are the opening words of Psalm 97. This Psalm develops the truth which has been introduced in the last Psalm and tells of the effects of Jehovah's assumption of the throne. It has been composed as if in the knowledge that the Lord is already reigning. Only the wicked need fear His rule for the throne is founded upon righteousness and justice, and impartial judgment is assured for all.

The Psalm has no title and some dispute the Davidic authorship which is accepted by so many others. Spurgeon's defence of David is interesting, and characteristically quaint and to the point. He writes, "Modern critics, always intent upon ascribing the Psalms to anybody rather than to David, count themselves successful in dating this song further on than the captivity, because it contains passages similar to those which occur in the later prophets; but we venture to assert that it is quite as probable that the prophets adopted the language of David as that some unknown writer borrowed from them. One Psalm in this series is said to be "in David" [Heb 4.7], and we believe that the rest are in the same place, and by the same author. The matter is not important, and we only mention it because it seems to be the pride of certain critics to set up new theories; and there are readers who imagine this to be a sure proof of prodigious learning. We do not believe that their theories are worth the paper they are written upon". As Spurgeon says, the matter is not important. The human penman is often irrelevant and incidental in the wonder of the inspiration of the sacred writings. However, his comments on modern critics are both valid and valuable, and deserve to be noted carefully.

The twelve verses of the Psalm may be divided into three equal parts. In verses 1-3 the advent of the King is described. Verses 4-6 describe the effects of that advent upon the earth and upon nature. Verses 7-9 deal with the influence of the advent upon the idolatrous heathen and upon Israel. The concluding section, verses 10-12, brings encouragement and comfort and exhortation for the godly.

Verses 1-3: The Lord Reigneth!

The tense, and the force of these opening words may be, as preferred by many in Psalm 93.1 also, "The Lord has become King". The Psalmist brings his readers into the atmosphere of a world where Jehovah is enthroned. It is a cause for rejoicing. The earth in general and the isles in particular must be glad when the Lord reigns. It will be a restoration of Eden on a universal scale. The joy of Jehovah's rule will extend beyond the boundaries of Israel whose territory was bordered on the west by the sea. The isles (339) are the Mediterranean coastlands, those numerous islands of the sea which, in large measure, were foreign to Israel. The rule of the coming Messiah will be universal. No country or island will be outside the scope of His beneficent reign. All the earth, with its many island homes, must rejoice.

Jehovah comes in awful majesty, clothed in clouds and darkness. He reveals Himself in darkness which conceals Him! The uncovered, unveiled brightness of the glory of the essential deity would destroy men. As it was at Sinai, so it is here, His glory is mercifully shrouded in darkness (Ex 19.16-18; 20.21). Righteousness and justice are with Him. These will characterise His rule. They are the habitation (4349), the foundation, of His throne. Justice is the manifestation and outworking of righteousness in Jehovah's dealings with men. The capital city of His kingdom will be called "The city of righteousness" (Is 1.26), and His reign will be established with judgment and with justice forever (Is 9.7).

The coming King will be heralded by fire. His benign rule must be introduced with judgment to remove all that is wicked and wrong. The King will therefore be revealed in flaming fire, taking vengeance (2 Thess 1.8). He must first gather out of His kingdom all that offends, and those that do iniquity, so that only the righteous will enter in (Mt 13.40-41). Our God is a consuming fire (Heb 12.29), and His very presence will devour His enemies in the solemn day of His appearing. It will be like the burning of a furnace. Jehovah's adversaries will be as stubble, and the fire will leave neither root nor branch of them (Mal 4.1).

Verses 4-6: The Effects of His Coming

The awful description of the advent continues, depicting its effect upon the whole creation. As if a storm has broken, lightnings flash across the sky. Note the references to the "world" (8398) and the "earth" (776). The former is the habitable world, the world of men, society. The latter is the literal, physical earth, the land itself. The world is lightened and the earth trembles. All are affected at the coming of the Lord.

The mountains melt. That most solid, stable part of creation dissolves at the divine Presence. Creation bows in acknowledgement of its Creator. Like wax, which cannot resist the fire, so they must submit to Him who is the Lord of the whole earth. He has right and authority over all that He has brought into being. He has created it, and therefore can reduce it to nothing. This title of God, "Lord of the whole earth" appears first in Joshua 3.11, 13, where the Ark of the Covenant is called "The ark of the covenant of the Lord of all the earth". The import is, of course, that for Israel, about to pass over the Jordan into Canaan, their God is not a local deity like the gods of the Canaanites. He is "the Lord of the whole earth", and will give them the land which He has promised to them. The title occurs again in Micah 4.13 and twice more in Zechariah 4.14 and 6.5.

As the heavens declare the glory of God in Psalm 19.1, so here, and in Psalm 50.6, they declare (5046) His righteousness. This declaration of the heavens concerning the Creator is essentially an exposition of the greatness of His Person whereby men see (7200) His glory. Contemplation of the wonders of created things produces in the exercised soul an acknowledgement of the supreme deity. Those invisible things, even His eternal power and Godhead, are clearly seen in His creation, and, once that greatness is appreciated, idolatry becomes folly, as the Psalm will now proceed to show, and as is the case in Romans 1.20-23.

Verses 7-9: Worshippers of Idols - or of Jehovah!

How foolish are they who bow down to graven images. The Psalmist prays that they might be confounded (954), confused and ashamed. "Professing themselves to be wise, they became fools", says Paul (Rom 1.22). Foolishness indeed, to think that the glory of God might be portrayed by a lifeless image, whether of man, or bird, or beast. Yet these foolish idol worshippers boast (1984) in their pretended wisdom, glorying in what they do. They have failed to learn the lesson of the heavens, that the Creator is superior to the gods of their own making. "Worship him", is the exhortation, worship Him before whom all gods must bow, to whom all gods must yield. These "gods" "elohim" (430) would seem, in the context, to be the deities of the heathen imagination, represented by the idols. The idols are nothing. They are nonentities. The supposed deities which they represent must bow to Jehovah's supremacy. Dr Cohen quotes Cobb, who writes, "The Psalmist does not mean that he believes in the existence of heathen gods, but he uses popular language to assign them to their proper place as suppliants of God". Some commentators think however, that these "gods" or "mighty ones" are angels, and associate this with

Hebrews 1.6, and with the LXX rendering of Deuteronomy 32.43, "Let all the angels of God worship him". This, however, does not seem to suit the context.

How different to the response of the heathen is the reaction of Zion to the revelation of God. While idolaters are confounded, Zion heard, and was glad. "The daughters of Judah rejoiced". This may be an allusion to those choral bands of Hebrew maidens who, particularly after some notable victory, led the praise of the people. Miriam did so in Exodus 15.20-21, when, after the redemption of the children of Israel from Egypt, she and the women who were with her celebrated the triumph with music and song. The maidens of David's day did similarly, singing of his great victory over Goliath (1 Sam 18.6-7). See the same thought in Psalm 48.11. The nation rejoices at the judgments of Jehovah. Those who love Him, not only acquiesce in what He decides and says, but they exult, while the heathen are confused.

Jehovah is sovereign and supreme. He is Most High (5945). He is above all the earth and exalted exceedingly above all gods (430). Again, as in v.7, this is the word "elohim", but whether the reference is to heathen deities, as seems to agree with the context, or to the mighty ones of the angelic hosts, as some suggest, the glorious fact remains the same, that Jehovah is greater than all. Notice that this verse is addressed to Jehovah (3068). "Thou, LORD, art high…thou art exalted". In the midst of his meditation the Psalmist bursts forth in praise to Jehovah directly, after which he will then continue in exhortation to the people.

Verses 10-12: Exhortations and Encouragements

The Psalm now concludes with an appeal to those who love the Lord. Whether in Old Testament or New, love is the great prerequisite and basis of everything. Love to Jehovah will produce a hatred of evil. To love Him is to hate what He hates, and such love and hate are the evidences of true conversion to Him. These things were manifested in the life and ministry of Messiah Himself, who loved righteousness and hated wickedness (Ps 45.7), and His people should manifest in their lives something of His character.

Jehovah takes notice of this and preserves His saints. Such holy living is contrary to the evil world in which they live. Holiness is like a declaration of war on the iniquity of the worldling, but the Lord preserves His people in the conflict. When the wicked seem to triumph and surround the saint with evil intent, then Jehovah will deliver that saint. Preservation and deliverance are assured to those who love the Lord and who seek to live for His pleasure.

The righteous walk in the light. Light is strewn along their pathway. As seed was sown, scattered by the sower as he walked, so does Jehovah spread light along life's path for those who love Him. "The path of the just is as the shining light, that shineth more and more unto the perfect day"

(Prov 4.18). In a dark and murky world, the believer's pathway is made clear for him by the Lord. Every saint may truly say, "Thy word is a lamp unto my feet, and a light unto my path" (Ps 119.105). It is inevitable that this should produce joy in the heart of the child of God. "Blessed are the pure in heart: for they shall see God". So the Saviour said in His early ministry (Mt 5.8). The upright in heart are filled with gladness as they continually enjoy fresh glimpses of the glory of the Lord.

With an exhortation to such joy the Psalmist draws his song to a close; "Rejoice in the Lord, ye righteous". As Spurgeon remarks, "The Psalmist had bidden the earth to rejoice, and here he turns to the excellent of the earth and bids them lead the song. If all others fail to praise the Lord the godly must not. To them God is peculiarly revealed, by them He should be specially adored". How important for the saints is the maintenance of this joy. "The joy of the Lord is your strength", said Nehemiah (Neh 8.10). "Rejoice evermore", said Paul (1 Thess 5.16). "Rejoice in the Lord alway: and again I say, Rejoice" (Phil 4.4).

This joy of the believer will be blended with thanksgiving. It was an early characteristic of those who descended to idolatry and depravity, that they were not thankful (Rom 1.21). Ingratitude should never characterise those who love the Lord and rejoice in Him. Here, however, the thanksgiving is particular, it is at the remembrance of His holiness. The RV translates, "Give thanks to his holy name". Men of the world will not, can not, appreciate the holiness of God, but the saint remembers it always, and gives thanks. This holiness was so often impressed upon Israel. "He is an holy God", said Joshua to the people (Josh 24.19). "Be ye holy; for I am holy" is the injunction of the NT also (1 Pet 1.16 quoting from Lev 19.2).

So the Psalm ends. Blessed indeed is that life, where joy and gladness, light and love, thankfulness and holiness are mingled together.

PSALM 98

Introduction

The two preceding Psalms begin, "O sing unto the Lord a new song" and, "The Lord reigneth". Psalm 98 and the Psalm which follows commence respectively with exactly the same words as these, and in the same order. Here again is a summons to sing to Jehovah, and this is followed in Psalm 99 by the proclamation, "The Lord reigneth".

The Psalm has a most simple title, "A Psalm". Strictly speaking there is but one Hebrew word in the title, "Psalm" (MIZMOR - 4210). No other Psalm in the whole Psalter bears this simple inscription, so that the Jewish

Talmud calls it, "The orphan Mizmor". No author is specifically identified but it seems clear that this group of royal Psalms, 93-99, are by the same writer, and, as Plumer points out, "The Syriac, Arabic, Septuagint, Ethiopic, Vulgate, Douay, and many others, ascribe it to David". Spurgeon agrees, and, assuming, as he does, that Paul was the writer of the Epistle to the Hebrews, he says, "Paul, if we understand him aright, ascribes Psalm 95.1-11 to David, and as we believe that the same writer must have written the whole group, we ascribe this also to the son of Jesse". (See Heb 4.7).

The nine verses of this Psalm are really an extension and amplification of the opening call to praise. There are three stanzas of equal length, each dealing with some aspect of praise. Verses 1-3 are the initial summons to "sing unto the Lord". In verses 4-6 the manner and nature of the praise is described. The closing stanza, verses 7-9, indicates the ultimate universal aspect of praise to Jehovah.

Verses 1-3: The Summons to Praise

The call is for a "new" song. That song is new indeed, new on the lips of men, which sings the greatness and glory of Jehovah. Men by nature do not sing such a song. It is a privilege enjoyed only by some, to appreciate His might and His power, and to be allowed to sing to Him in gratitude for what that power has wrought. He has done marvellous things (6381), wonders. His right hand and His holy arm had wrought victories for His people Israel. Ever since that mighty arm had brought them out of Egyptian bondage, to sing to Him on the safer side of the Red Sea, there had been victory after victory. Whether this Psalm celebrates some particular triumph or not, is not of much relevance. There had been triumphs multiplied, and the remembrance of any or all of these was a cause for praise and song.

There had been revelations of His salvation, and, in keeping with His character, this was always associated with His righteousness. The holiness of His Person must ever be protected and so He saves His people righteously. His righteousness in all that He does is shown openly, transparently, in the sight of the heathen (1471). To Gentile nations the holiness of Israel's Redeemer and Lord must be manifested. He is beyond reproach in all that He does.

What a galaxy of divine attributes shines in these early verses of the Psalm! Holiness and power; righteousness and salvation; mercy and truth. In this greatness the Lord remembers His promises to the house of Israel. This is not to suggest that He ever forgets, but simply that He calls to mind those pledges to His people and He fulfils them. His lovingkindness is wedded to His faithfulness and truth, and, if sometimes the nation laments, as in the language of Zion in Isaiah 49.14, "my Lord hath forgotten me", this can never be true. His answer to His people is, "Can a woman forget her sucking child, that she should not have compassion on the son of her womb? Yea, they may forget, yet will not I forget thee" (Is 49.15).

Then, though it is Israel, the favoured nation, which is peculiarly blessed by Jehovah, the testimony of God's dealings with His people knows no boundaries. "All the ends of the earth" observe what He is doing, and in the verses which follow the call to praise will be extended far beyond the frontiers of Israel, to embrace peoples everywhere. Perhaps there is a foreshadowing here of that millennial day when, from a restored Israel, blessing will flow to all nations, and from these praise will ascend to the Lord and His Anointed (Ps 72.8, 11, 17, 19).

Verses 4-6: The Nature of the Praise

"Make a joyful noise" (7321) might be translated as one word, "Shout!". It signifies the shout of a war cry, or a joyful shout of victory in battle. There must be zeal and energy, and the sound of triumph in the praises of God's people. This is no half-hearted praise which is exhorted, but rather a whole-hearted, resounding crescendo of adulation in which all the ends of the earth are to join. It should be spontaneous too; "Break forth and sing for joy, yea, sing praises" (RV). The thought is of a bursting forth into song that cannot be contained. Like the bursting forth of a fountain of water from the parched earth, so must the song of praise break forth from the hearts of the saints. As Charles Wesley wrote –

> My heart is full of Christ, and longs
> Its glorious matter to declare,
> Of Him I make my loftier songs,
> And cannot from His praise forbear;
> My ready tongue makes haste to sing
> The glories of my heavenly King.

With Israel of old, in a past dispensation, this involved the employment of numerous musical instruments. Harps and trumpets and cornets are all mentioned here. With the harp David would have been so familiar. The trumpet would doubtless be the silver trumpet of Numbers 10. The cornet (7782) is the SHOFAR, the ram's horn, blown on festive occasions. With all of these, and with singing, those ancient people of Israel would make a loud and joyful noise as they united in praise.

Six times in the nine verses of this Psalm the great name of Jehovah is employed. Here, in v.6, He is "the LORD, the King". Before Him, and unto Him, the praises of all peoples will one day be heard, when that proclamation of the preceding and succeeding Psalms is finally realised, "The Lord reigneth".

Verses 7-9: The Universality of the Praise

This universality has already been noted in vv. 3-4. Gentile nations will observe Jehovah's doings and all the ends of the earth will witness the salvation which He has wrought for His people. The summons to praise Him now goes forth, in symbol language, to embrace sea and land, mountains and waters, floods and hills, and the inhabitants of the world everywhere. "Let the sea roar". Let its thunders unite with the chorus of the people in praise of the Creator. Let the deeps of the ocean, with all the wealth of their hidden treasures, pay tribute to Him. Let the whole habitable world (8398), with all its dwellers, join in the harmony.

"Let the floods clap their hands", like the trees of Isaiah 55.12. Perhaps the Psalmist envisages the crashing of the waves on the shore and likens this to the clapping of the ocean's hands in praise. The hills likewise unite together in the universal outburst of praise. Creation all, animate and inanimate, will exult in that day when men shall exclaim, "The Lord, the King". "The Lord reigneth!"

The closing verse points more explicitly to that day of millennial glory. "He cometh!" In language so reminiscent of Psalm 72, the Psalmist now speaks of a reign of righteousness and of equity. Jehovah will come to judge (8199), to rule, to govern His world as it has not before been governed. He will come to execute righteous judgment, and His kingdom will be characterised by impartiality and truth. The kingdoms of men have been so blighted by corruption and perversions of justice, by oppressions and cruelties, by wars and troubles. But when that cry goes forth, "The kingdoms of this world are become the kingdoms of our Lord, and of his Christ; and he shall reign for ever and ever" (Rev 11.15), then shall all be different. He will rule in righteousness and with equity. Then there will be severity without tyranny, a benign reign with no inequality.

On this note this Psalm of praise concludes. Perhaps it should be emphasised that these references to judgment have nothing to do with that final judgment of the great white throne, as described in Revelation 20. Here it is Jehovah's rule which is envisaged, His justice in the administration of His coming kingdom. Well might Israel, and the godly of every age, intelligently pray, "Thy kingdom come".

PSALM 99

Introduction

Psalm 99 continues the theme of Psalms 93 and 97, and for the fourth time in the Psalms the exclamation is heard, "The Lord reigneth". Like its companion Psalms, Psalm 99 is untitled. No author is identified, but many will again be content to recognise David, the sweet singer of Israel, in its sentiments.

There are three stanzas here, clearly marked but of unequal length. Each strophe ends with the word "holy" (vv. 3, 5 and 9). Spurgeon calls it "The Holy, Holy, Holy Psalm". Jehovah's name is holy in v.3. He Himself is holy in v.5. This thought is repeated in v.9, "The Lord our God is holy".

In the first section, verses 1-3, the greatness of Jehovah is emphasised. In His dwelling in Zion and because of the awfulness of His name He must be praised by all peoples. In verses 4-5 the righteousness of divine rule in Jacob is the theme. The concluding verses 6-9 remember former leaders of the people and Jehovah's faithfulness to them. There is then, greatness in Zion, righteous judgment in Jacob, and faithfulness in the past, all encouraging present reverence and worship.

Verses 1-3: Greatness in Zion

"The Lord reigneth!" The recognition of this great truth must cause the peoples to tremble. "Peoples" (5971) is indeed a plural word, embracing the Gentile nations. They have a right to tremble, to be disquieted and afraid, if Jehovah has been enthroned. He is, after all, the Creator who, when they heard of Him, they glorified Him not as God. In their professed heathen wisdom they became fools, and changed the glory of the uncorruptible God into images, and became idol worshippers. In their foolishness they degenerated into awful uncleanness and vile affections and served the creature rather than the Creator, until God gave them up. (Rom 1.20-25). Now, what a word is this for the idolatrous nations, "Jehovah reigneth!". Let them tremble. "Let the people tremble…let the earth be moved". "Tremble" (7264) and "moved" (5120), although different words, are very similar in meaning. Earth and its peoples everywhere must respond in fear when Jehovah reigns.

The reference to the cherubim now introduces the theme of holiness into the Psalm. The first mention of cherubim is in Genesis 3.24. The last mention is in Ezekiel 41.25. At that first mention they are at the gate of the Garden of Eden. At the last they are on the doors of the temple. Between these first and last references they are to be found chiefly in the books of Exodus, Kings, Chronicles, and Ezekiel, with two references in the Psalms (80.1 and 99.1), and one fleeting mention in Isaiah 37.16. A comparison of these various references to the cherubim will show that they are angelic representations whose ministry appears to be that of guarding the righteous character of God, whether at the gate of the garden or at the doors of the temple. In that ancient Holiest of All there was a cherub at either end of the holy Ark of Jehovah, with outstretched wings protectively overshadowing the golden mercy seat. Here, above the mercy seat and under the shadow of those wings, dwelt the Shekinah, the glory. "And there I will meet with thee", the Lord told Moses, "and I will commune with thee from above the mercy seat, from between the two cherubims" (Ex 25.22). It all radiates holiness. Again and again in the many references to them, Jehovah is viewed as Him that "sitteth between the cherubims".

There are seven occurrences of the great name Jehovah in the Psalm.

Four times this is extended as, "Jehovah our God". Here in v.2, Jehovah is great in Zion and high above all the people. Zion is the very heart of Israel, whether of the land or of the nation. It is the Throne Room of the King. But, as Dr Cohen writes, quoting Oesterley, "To say that 'here is the tone of Jewish exclusiveness' is simply to misunderstand the whole purport of the Psalm; God is here enthroned, exalted above all the peoples as Israel's God, no doubt, but also as the God of all the peoples; the tone is not one of exclusiveness, but of universalism".

Three things are said about the name of Jehovah. It is great; it is terrible; it is holy. "Let them praise". The call goes out not only to Zion but to all the peoples. When Jehovah so reveals Himself in His inscrutable majesty and holiness, it is time to praise Him, but to Hebrew commentators and Rabbis, and to devout Jews everywhere, the awful Name was a profound secret which must neither be pronounced nor written. Believers today, with a holy familiarity and intimacy, call Him, "Father", but nevertheless remember the indescribable holiness of Him who remains Jehovah. Seraphim in Isaiah 6.3 cried to each other, "Holy, holy, holy, is Jehovah of hosts". Four living creatures in Revelation 4.8 cry similarly, "Holy, holy, holy, Lord God Almighty". Every saint will join the chorus, extolling and praising the Holy One. With the word "holy", the first stanza in the Psalm concludes.

Verses 4-5: Righteousness in Jacob

The opening words of this second stanza, "The king's strength also loveth judgment", have presented a considerable problem to commentators. Is this the divine King, Jehovah, who reigns in v.1? Or is it the king of Israel at that time, David himself? Either way, the unusual expression, "The king's strength also loveth judgment", is difficult. Accepting the more commonly held view that this is the reigning king of Israel, Jehovah's vicegerent in Zion, then the thought seems to be that the monarch, although strong and powerful, does not wish to be a tyrannical despot. He would have his power blended with justice. Plumer quotes Edwards, and comments, "Probably Edwards gives the sense, although his translation is free, 'Though the king be powerful, he loveth judgment' ". This of course would be the mind of Jehovah, that His king would rule in equity and maintain righteousness and justice in Israel. Such will be true of Messiah in His millennial reign, as is predicted so beautifully in Psalm 72. "He shall judge thy people with righteousness, and thy poor with judgment". Although having undisputed sovereignty from sea to sea, yet He remembers the poor and the needy and delivers them. Equity! Justice! Righteousness! These are the desirable features in true kingship. "Jacob" is an alternative designation to "Israel", probably a reminder of the lowly beginnings of the favoured nation, and of God's grace in their election from among the nations.

So, for all His greatness and His grace, Jehovah is worthy to be extolled.

"Exalt ye the LORD (3068) our God (430)". He is Jehovah our Elohim, great and glorious. Bow before Him. Worship at His footstool. The footstool may be earth itself as in Isaiah 66.1, "Thus saith the Lord, The heaven is my throne, and the earth is my footstool". In 1 Chronicles 28.2 the footstool may be either the Ark of the Covenant, or the envisaged temple where it would dwell, as again in Psalm 132.7. Whichever of these is the thought, the main point here is that men must bow down in obeisance, in recognition of the might and majesty of Jehovah. This second stanza concludes, in the same manner the first, with the exclamation, "He is holy".

Verses 6-9: Jehovah's Faithfulness

Moses, Aaron, and Samuel are remembered as men of prayer, whose prayers the Lord heard, and answered. Although never officially ordained into priesthood like Aaron, nevertheless Moses and Samuel were of the tribe of Levi (1 Chr 6.3, 33, 34), and on at least two occasions Moses engaged in a ministry which was essentially priestly (Ex 24.4-8 and 40.20-29). Also, the word "priests" (KOHEN - 3548) has a wider sense than that which is commonly given to it. It may mean rulers, princes, or officers. These three men, prophet, priest, and prince in Israel, were great men among the nation's leaders, and Moses and Samuel are particularly mentioned in Jeremiah for the power of their intercessions, a priestly exercise. "Then said the Lord unto me, Though Moses and Samuel stood before me, yet my mind could not be toward this people" (Jer 15.1). In their day, they called upon the Lord, and He answered them.

To Moses, and to those who called upon His name, Jehovah spoke from the cloudy pillar. The cloud was an emblem of His holiness and His glory (Ex 33.9). In faithfulness to Him they kept (8104), they guarded, they observed, His testimonies (5713), His laws. Likewise they obeyed His ordinance (2716), adhering to every statute and decree which He gave them. This was their faithfulness to Him and it was rewarded by His faithfulness to them, for He answered them. Jehovah regarded the intercessions of these men on behalf of a backsliding people, and in mercy He forgave. Yet, says the Psalmist, "Thou tookest vengeance of their inventions (doings – 5949)". Though He delights to forgive, He must vindicate His holiness, and accordingly there was frequent chastisement. As Spurgeon says, in his quaint way, "He forgave the sinners, but He slew their sins". Plumer remarks, "God punished the Israelites for their wickedness, but He did not root them out as a nation".

The closing verse is an echo of v.5. "Exalt the Lord our God, and worship". If, in v.5 the call was to worship at His footstool, now the worshippers are called to His holy hill, Zion, so precious to Him; Zion, where He had placed His name; Zion, where stood the tent that sheltered the holy Ark, and where the temple "magnifical" would eventually stand as His dwelling place. "Who shall ascend into the hill of the Lord? or who shall stand in his holy place?" (Ps 24.3). Jehovah desires worshippers, but, in every age, those who approach Him must have clean hands, and a pure heart free from deceit and vanity. The reason is simple, "The Lord our God is holy". His people must be holy too. With this word the Psalm closes. First, second, and third stanzas all conclude with this solemn reminder to all saints, "He is holy".

PSALM 100

Introduction

Familiarly and affectionately known as "The Old Hundredth", this little Psalm is bursting with gladness and singing, with thanksgiving and praise. Its simple title, "A Psalm of Praise", is unique in the Psalter, for this word "Praise" (8426) is not the usual word for praise. It means, literally, "Thanksgiving". The Psalm appears to have been originally intended to accompany the bringing of thank-offerings (Lev 7.12). Indeed, the Jewish Targum renders, "A Psalm for the thank-offering", but it was never restricted to that particular purpose. It seems so suitable for a multitude of circumstances.

Here is a fitting doxology to that series of royal Psalms commencing with Psalm 93. It is a crescendo! It summarises the theme and the sentiments of the preceding seven Psalms, and lifts the people of God through the gates and into the courts of the Lord with their worship.

The Psalm has been composed for public worship, and, after centuries of use by Israel, perhaps no Psalm has been sung more often by Christians in this present day of grace than this one. Its paraphrased metrical versions have earned it universal acceptance and affection among Christians in all lands. Of these paraphrases, perhaps the best known is the Scottish version, "All people that on earth do dwell", and it is to this version, and the tune to which it is normally sung, that we owe the name "The Old Hundredth".

The five short verses need no divisions. The Psalm is one call to people everywhere to come with their thanksgiving and praise, and, while no author is indicated in the title, most commentators are happy to ascribe it to that sweet singer of Israel, David, shepherd boy and king.

Verses 1-5: "The Lord he is God...the Lord is good"

The opening clause of the Psalm, "Make a joyful noise unto the Lord", is identical with the first clause of Psalm 98.4, and, as has been observed in the commentary there, these first four words are but one word in Hebrew, "Shout!" It signifies a call for a glad shout of triumph and joy, like a shout of victory in battle. The call goes beyond the boundaries of Israel to all lands, for in every land there are evidences of God's beneficence and power.

It is but right that men and nations everywhere should join with Israel in rendering praise to Him who, four times in these five verses, is called Jehovah. As the meaning of the great name indicates, He is eternally existent, and therefore eternally self-sufficient, in His might, and it is proper that all men should praise Him for His excellent greatness (Ps 150.2).

Sincere recognition of the greatness of the Lord will result in service for Him. This will not be a servitude of fear, or of compulsion and reluctance. It will be glad service, rendered with joy and with singing. It will not be irksome to serve Him when it is remembered that all that is done *for* Him is appreciated *by* Him. Service and singing are therefore joined in happy harmony here. It is not just duty, but joy, to serve the Lord. There is a holy blend of dignity and devotion, of gladness and grace, of worship and witness, of privilege and pleasure, in serving Jehovah.

All service for Him should be rendered in the firm assurance of His greatness - "the LORD (3068) he is God (430)" - Jehovah is Elohim! This is an emphasising of that greatness. The eternally existent One is Elohim the mighty One. He is the Creator, and His saints are His people, and the sheep of His pasture. He has both creatorial and redemptive rights over all men. He is the sovereign, sole proprietor of all, Creator of men and Shepherd of His people. In this is signified that He not only creates, but provides for His creation as a shepherd would provide for his flock. Why, then, should men not praise and serve Him?

Through the several gates and into the temple courts Israel's worshippers would come with their thank-offerings. But such thanksgiving is not the privilege of Israel alone. As Maclaren says, "Israel was meant to be a sacred hearth on which a fire was kindled, that was to warm all the house. God revealed Himself *in* Israel; but *to* the world".

What rejoicing on those happy festive occasions, when multitudes of pilgrims would throng the temple courts! What a joyful noise, indeed, of united thanksgiving and praise, and of blessing the name of the Lord. This holy exercise continues with believers of the present day, who enter with their praise and worship into the heavenly sanctuary. They too, with a deep, spiritual, and intelligent appreciation of Him, unitedly render their adoration.

The brief Psalm concludes with references to His goodness, His mercy, and His truth. Plumer remarks that "as in English, 'good' is either a noun or an adjective, so in the Hebrew. The word is often rendered goodness". This may well be the thought here, that Jehovah is not only good and kind, but goodness itself. His mercy, His loving-kindness, endures forever. There is no limit to His mercy. His faithfulness is from generation to generation. Consistently, to the fathers and to their children, and to the children's children, all Israel knew that Jehovah had been faithful and true. If at times they had not been faithful to Him, yet He remained faithful to them, keeping every promise that He ever made to them. And so His people still delight to sing –

For why? the Lord our God is good,
His mercy is forever sure;
His truth at all times firmly stood,
And shall from age to age endure.
(Old Hundredth)

PSALM 101

Introduction

Dr Cohen entitles this Psalm "An Ideal Kingship". He remarks that centuries ago it was given the title "The Prince's Psalm", and both he and Dr T.W. Davies confirm that it was also known as "The Mirror for Magistrates". Plumer says that "Some old writers call this 'The Householder's Psalm'", and he adds, "A good king in his dominion ought to be like a good father and head of a family in his house. We have here the principles on which David would rule the nation".

The title "A Psalm of David", with the sentiments and desires expressed in the Psalm seem to suggest a date around 1050BC, very early in David's reign, or perhaps just immediately prior to his accession. Spurgeon's comment is, "This is just such a Psalm as the man after God's own heart would compose when he was about to become king in Israel. It is David all over, straightforward, resolute, devout; there is no trace of policy or vacillation, the Lord has appointed him to be king, and he knows it, therefore he purposes in all things to behave as becomes a monarch whom the Lord Himself has chosen".

The Psalm is a fitting successor to the series of royal Psalms just concluded. There the predominant theme was praise, but praise must be accompanied by practice, and duty must follow devotion.

The eight verses are readily divided into two sections of equal length, both dealing with the king's avowed behaviour. In verses 1-4 it is the king's vow regarding himself. In verses 5-8 it is his vow regarding his attitude to others, both godly and ungodly.

Verses 1-4: I Will Behave Myself!

Seven times in the Psalm the Psalmist vows, "I will…I will…I will". On two more occasions he says, "I will not…I will not". He is indeed making solemn vows before the Lord as to his own personal behaviour in his house and in his kingdom. Twice in the opening verse he says, "I will sing…I will sing". David was, of course, the sweet singer of Israel (2 Sam 23.1). The themes of his songs were varied, sometimes in the minor key and sometimes in loud joyful notes of praise. Here he first of all sings of those twin virtues which he desired should characterise his rule, mercy (2617) and judgment (4941), lovingkindness and justice. David had experienced both of these personally from the hand of God, and what the Lord had taught him he would show to the subjects of his realm. There must be balance, the one tempered with the other. How well the sweet Psalmist himself could have sung –

With mercy and with judgment
My web of time He wove,
And aye the dews of sorrow
Were lustred with His love.
(Anne Ross Cousin)

Justice cannot condone sin, or ignore it, but mercy can forgive. David would sing of these, and, while his people might hear and enjoy his singing, nevertheless, he says, "Unto thee, O Lord, will I sing". His song was to Jehovah.

Singing, however, is one thing, practical morality is another, and so the Psalmist's early vow is, "I will behave myself wisely in a perfect way". The JPS rendering of this is especially beautiful: "I will give heed unto the way of integrity". Another companion vow follows, "I will walk within my house with a perfect heart". The two vows are joined by a prayer for the presence and help of God, "O when wilt thou come unto me?" Vows, even though they are made with sincerity and good intention, cannot really be fulfilled in the energy of the flesh. Sadly, poor David was to learn this. Within his own house his behaviour was not always governed by wisdom, nor did it accord with integrity. Neither his heart nor his way were always marked by the perfection of which he speaks. The two words, each translated "perfect" in v.2, are different words (8549 and 8537), but they are from the same root and are therefore very similar in meaning. They each have the thought of uprightness, completeness, and even innocence. Had David continued in the enjoyment of the divine presence for which he had prayed, then perhaps he would have been spared the shame which later came upon him. How often the private lives of Eastern monarchs were tarnished by corruption and self-indulgence. David, in his heart, would have shunned this, but succumbed when out of the enjoyment of the Lord's presence (2 Sam 11; Ps 51). What a warning and salutary lesson for all saints of all ages!

His vows continue, "I will set no wicked thing before mine eyes". He seemed sincerely determined that he would not be occupied with base and worthless things, and he hated those who did turn aside to such. This was apostasy, to turn away from revealed truth and from the good things of God, to follow the unworthy ambitions of wicked men. He avers that such behaviour will not cling to him or entangle him as it had entangled others.

The froward (6141) heart of which David now speaks is a heart perverse and crooked, with twisted and distorted emotions. He desired honesty, integrity, and uprightness. These were noble motives indeed, and he wanted no familiarity with that which was otherwise. While the AV says "I will not know a wicked person", the word "person" is italicised and most other versions prefer a noun here, and, omitting the italicised word, read, "I will not know evil" (JND); "I will know no evil thing" (RV and JPS).

The six "I wills" of this first section of the Psalm represent the Psalmist's vows regarding himself. He was targeting a high moral standard, in keeping with the heavy responsibility of being king and ruler over a nation of God's people. He, the Lord's anointed, bore the great privilege of being the chosen ruler of a chosen people.

Verses 5-8: His Attitude to Others

David, as a man after God's own heart, had no time for the slandering tongue, the haughty look, or the proud heart. Slander was a common vice in the courts of kings. It was a cruel assassination of another man's character for one's own advantage. To curry favour with the king a courtier might wickedly raise false stories and innuendoes concerning another. With such slandering David resolved to deal sharply. There is apparently an old Jewish saying that a slanderer injures three persons at once - himself, his hearer, and the man who is slandered. Then there was the proud heart and the haughty look. These would be a source of discontent and strife and the king would not permit such in his court.

In contrast with these distasteful things the Psalmist's eyes were upon the faithful of the land, and these would be his chosen company in his house and his preferred attendants in his court. He would watch for those who walked in a perfect way. This is the same word as the first "perfect" in v.2. David was really looking for integrity in those who would serve him as his ministers. Those who were marked by this integrity could live with him, and serve him. Otherwise they were not welcome in his house or in his court. For deceivers and liars there was no place either. Men of this character could not be trusted and a king needed men whom he could trust. Deceitful men, therefore, would not be permitted to dwell in his house and the liar would be dismissed from the palace and out of sight of the king.

Having expressed his determination to purge his court and palace, David now turns his attention to Jerusalem itself. He would purge the city also. While he would watch for the faithful of the land, with a godly zeal he resolved that he would early destroy the wicked of the land. "Early" (1242) indicates a morning exercise. It is a plural word, "mornings". "Every morning", says JND. "Morning by morning", say the RV and JPS. It would be a daily task for the king and his faithful attendants, cleansing Jerusalem from the wickedness of evildoers. It was, after all, "The city of the Lord". It was imperative that it should be kept clean and pure for His glory.

PSALM 102

Introduction

The sad title of this Psalm encapsulates much of its theme, or at least the theme of its earlier verses. It is indeed the prayer of someone afflicted, overwhelmed with sorrow, and lamenting before the Lord. The deep sorrow is eventually relieved in its latter part by the remembrance of the eternity and glory of Jehovah.

There is no general agreement among commentators as to the identity of the Psalmist. Many understand vv.13-16 to envisage a ruined state of Jerusalem, and, because of this, they assign the Psalm to the period of the exile, reading it as the lament of a patriot longing for the restoration of the city and the nation. Some think that it may have been written as the remnant was returning with Ezra to rebuild the temple. Others see the Psalm as a most suitable link between Psalms 101 and 103, both of which are Psalms of David, and therefore they have no difficulty in regarding this Psalm as being Davidic also. Alexander remarks upon "the general Davidic character" of its composition, and of this "connecting link between the pious resolutions of Psalm 101, and the joyful acknowledgements of Psalm 103". He suggests that the Psalm "was composed in prophetic foresight of the straits to which the theocratical state should be reduced, and in which the sufferings of David, here immediately described, should, as it were, be realised anew". He points out that many of the words in the title are to be found in other Psalms of David. Perhaps the details of many Psalms, touching authorship and original circumstances, have been purposely veiled, so that saints of all ages and in all circumstances may borrow the language to express their feelings and emotions.

It is important to see that the Psalm is Messianic. Verses 25-27 are specifically quoted in Hebrews 1.10-12 with reference to Messiah, and it seems reasonable to understand that much of the loneliness and sorrow of the early verses is very applicable to the Man of Sorrows.

The Psalm is called "A Prayer" because much of it is indeed in the nature of petition. It is often called a "Penitential Psalm", as are Psalms 6, 32, 38, 51, 130, and 143, but while it contains a spirit of contrition, there is no actual reference to sin or to repentance, as might be expected in a Psalm which is truly penitential.

There are two main parts in the Psalm, the first eleven verses describing the distress of the Psalmist, and, perhaps, of the nation. The remaining seventeen verses introduce hope in the Lord, that He will hear, and deliver, for His glory. These two main parts may be subdivided as follows. Verses 1-2 are the Psalmist's introductory invocation, an impassioned appeal to Jehovah to help him in his trouble. Verses 3-11 describe his distress in graphic detail. Verses 12-22 express confidence that the Lord will indeed hear the groaning of the afflicted and arise for their salvation. Verses 23-24 are a renewal of the Psalmist's complaint, and the concluding verses

25-28 are the Messianic portion, with the nation's hope in the eternal unchanging God. Spurgeon describes the Psalm so beautifully. He writes, "The whole composition may be compared to a day which, opening with wind and rain, clears up at noon and is warm with the sun, continues fine, with intervening showers, and finally closes with a brilliant sunset".

Verses 1-2: Hear My Prayer, O Jehovah

These are the opening words of the Psalm, a plea from the heart of a man in trouble, to the heart of a God who hears the cries of His suffering people. The prayer is directed to Jehovah, "O LORD" (3068), but prayer is intensified and soon becomes a cry. As the title indicates, the afflicted one is pouring out his complaint before the LORD. Note how personal his cry is in the early verses. "My prayer...my cry...my days...my heart...my groaning...my bones". The sufferings of the nation will eventually be included in his Psalm, but they are his own sufferings first of all.

How he longs for the smile of God upon him. For his God to hide his face from him in his sorrow would add to his distress. If Jehovah would only show Himself, lifting up His countenance upon him in the day of his trouble, this would bring relief. His case is urgent too; "Answer me speedily", he implores. He had prayed, he had cried, he had called, and he yearns for the ear of God to be inclined towards him. There was no help or comfort elsewhere.

Verses 3-11: The Distress in Detail

"My days are consumed like smoke", the Psalmist now laments. There is nothing very substantial or enduring in smoke. There is only darkness and gloom, a murky vapour cloud soon to pass away. So does he feel his life to be. Like a man in a dense fog, he feels his helplessness as the days of his trouble waste away, and, like a man in a fever, his bones burn, his bodily frame affected by the pain of his distressed spirit. His heart, the seat and source of vitality and strength, is as grass that has been cut down, scorched by the sun and withered. He feels his utter weakness. He is dried up. His anxiety has robbed him of appetite so that he even forgets to eat, with the natural consequence that, as he groans, his bones cleave to his skin. His whole appearance now is that of a weary haggard man. Much of this language may be figurative. It may be hyperbolic. But there is no doubt that it is very true that suffering and sorrow affect not only the spirit of a man, but also his desire for, and his interest in, the practical things of daily life. The troubled Psalmist neglects his food, and his body suffers accordingly.

In all this he feels extreme loneliness and he mentions three birds, the pelican of the wilderness, the owl of the desert, and the sparrow of the housetop. These all seem to illustrate just how lonely he is in his trouble.

Dr Tristram in his *Natural History of the Bible*, says, "The comparison of the Psalmist of himself to the Pelican in the wilderness is suggested probably by the melancholy attitude of the bird…it sits for hours or even days with its bill resting on its breast". With this Dr Thomson, a contemporary of Tristram, agrees, writing in his *The Land and the Book* on the occasion of his visit to the marshy, lonely, Lake Hulah in Upper Galilee; "Here only have I seen the pelican of the wilderness…It was certainly the most sombre, austere bird I ever saw…David could find no more expressive type of solitude and melancholy by which to illustrate his own state".

The owl is also a picture of loneliness. As Plumer says, "The owl is never gregarious. It always seeks solitude and utters only doleful sounds". The word here rendered "desert" (2723) is a plural word and means "waste places; ruin; desolation" (Strong). JND translates it "desolate places". Again this is a most appropriate illustration of the sad condition of the Psalmist in his sorrow.

A sparrow "alone upon the housetop" is not a usual sight. These little birds are always in companies, at times congregating in countless numbers, but, to quote Dr Thomson again, he says, "When one of them has lost its mate – a matter of every-day occurrence – he will sit on the house-top alone, and lament by the hour his sad bereavement". How appropriately has the Psalmist chosen these pictures of his solitary sadness, the wilderness, the desert, and the housetop.

The poor Psalmist had many enemies, some, as he says in another Psalm, who hated him without a cause, his enemies wrongfully (Ps 69.4). These to whom he now refers reproached him all day long and were mad against him. They taunted him and used his name in cursing. Earlier in the Psalm (v.4) he had spoken of his neglect of his daily bread, but now he laments that he has eaten ashes like bread and mingled his drink with tears. Although, as has been mentioned in the introduction, there is no reference to sin in this Psalm, nevertheless this is the language of a penitent. "Ashes" are a frequent symbol of mourning, as in Isaiah 61.3. Job knew this too, when, bereft of family, property, and health, "he sat down among the ashes" (Job 2.8). Here is the Psalmist's daily food, ashes and tears. The language would seem to be figurative, though some commentators feel that they may actually envisage the man so covered with ashes in his mourning that some of them fell on his food, while his drink was also literally mingled with his tears.

He states the cause of all this sorrow, God's indignation and wrath against him. Jehovah had lifted him up, but had now cast him down. The reason for this chastisement we do not know, but it was hard to bear. It was no wonder that his adversaries taunted him. He had, for a while, been exalted, but now he was humiliated. His days are "like a lengthening shadow" (JPS), "like a lengthened-out shadow" (JND). When the shadows are long it is toward evening. Does he feel that his sun is about to set? Again he uses the expression of v.4, "I am withered like grass". The words are exactly the same, the herbage of the field cut down and scorched by the sun until withered.

So ends this section of the Psalm. In sad graphic detail the Psalmist has described his distress. The sorrow is his personal grief, but it is also the sorrow of the nation. He shares in its humiliation. However, Jehovah will not, can not, forget Zion. As Maclaren says, "Zion cannot die while Zion's God lives". The remembrance of the greatness of the Lord now brings encouragement and introduces another happier theme into the Psalm.

Verses 12-22: Hope and Confidence

Having been occupied with his mournful circumstances and misery, the Psalmist now turns to the greatness and faithfulness of his God. He rejoices that the Lord will arise for the deliverance of Zion. Jehovah will endure forever. All generations will remember Him when the memory of adversaries has faded and gone. "Zion" is a synonym for Jerusalem, and for Israel. The Lord will have compassion on His afflicted people. He will rise up for their blessing. So the Psalmist says, "But thou, O Lord". There is an obvious contrast between the sentiments of v.11 and v.12. The Psalmist views his life as in the evening shadow, his years are ebbing away. "But thou, O Jehovah!" The eternal God is his refuge, abiding always, and this thought he develops further in the closing verses of the Psalm.

The time had now arrived for Jehovah to take pity on afflicted Zion. Would the Lord look upon His servants and see their affection for the very stones and dust of Jerusalem? Was it not indeed time to come to the aid of these servants? Jerusalem has always had a magnetic and emotional attraction for the exile, even when it was in ruins. This was the song of the captives by the rivers of Babylon: "If I forget thee, O Jerusalem, let my right hand forget her cunning" (Ps 137.5). Jerusalem was to be preferred above their chiefest joy. Even in this present day, a people returning to Zion from worldwide exile, and still in sad unbelief, chant the same at the ancient Western Wall of the Temple Mount, sometimes sobbing aloud in their affection for Jerusalem.

But there was still another reason why God should act for His people. When He would reveal Himself in glory for their redemption and in answer to their prayers, then the nations of the earth with their monarchs would fear His name, and be compelled to acknowledge that He had not despised or disregarded the cries of His people. Generation after generation would tell the story of the deliverance, and render praise to Jehovah. His own glory, therefore, was involved in the salvation of Zion. Surely for this reason He must regard the prayer of the destitute.

The generation to come, and the generations which followed, would praise Him. In every new epoch in the nation's history men would tell how He had looked down from His sanctuary in the heights. They would recall and recount how He had both seen and heard. He had seen their bonds and He had heard their sighs. He had observed and He had acted. The groaning of the prisoner had reached His heavenly abode and He had come to release them, and save them from death. The story would be repeated again and again, and in Zion men would praise Him and declare His name in all its greatness. In Jerusalem men of all nations would assemble to worship. Kingdoms would acknowledge Jehovah and serve Him. The future was bright indeed.

Verses 23-24: The Lament Renewed - A Parenthesis

The Psalmist has been occupied with deliverance and with glory, and this glad theme is continued in the Messianic portion of the Psalm which commences in v.25. In a sad, but brief parenthesis, however, he reverts to his complaint. He speaks of the frailty and brevity of his life. Was it possible that he might not live to see the glory of which he had just sung? Jehovah had weakened his strength and shortened his days. How sad if he did not live to see the glory which he had foretold, and of which he was so confident. He cries passionately and tenderly, "O my God, take me not away in the midst of my days". Jehovah's years were unending. He was the eternal One. He lived on and on through all generations. Would He, who had the power of life and death, spare His servant to see the predicted glory? Soon the complaint ends and the Psalmist embarks upon a closing discourse on the glories of Messiah, a passage to be quoted centuries later by the writer of the Epistle to the Hebrews (Heb 1.10-12)

Verses 25-28: Messiah's Eternity and Glory

This closing short section extends from the creation to the millennium, indeed from eternity to eternity! In the context of the Psalm the Psalmist now extols the greatness of his God as the Creator. In Hebrews 1.10-12 however, the Spirit of God interprets this as the greatness of the Son of God, the Messiah. The passage in Hebrews is proving the superiority of the Son over angels, "Unto the Son he saith...Thou, Lord, in the beginning hast laid the foundation of the earth; and the heavens are the works of thine hands". In perfect, and inspired, agreement with John 1.3, the writer of the Epistle to the Hebrews is really saying, "All things were made by him; and without him was not anything made that was made". Such is the wondrous harmony of the Holy Scriptures - the greatness of the Psalmist's God is the greatness of the Son of God, the Messiah, the Christ. The gracious Spirit who inspired the Psalmist, inspired the apostle John too, and the unknown writer to the Hebrews also. There is complete accord.

The physical, material creation will one day perish at the will of Him who created it. The same John who wrote of it in John 1.3 predicts also the passing of it in Revelation 21.1: "And I saw a new heaven and a new earth: for the first heaven and the first earth were passed away". But God will outlast His creation. "They shall perish, but thou shalt endure". Here is an echo of v.12, "Thou shalt endure". Like a garment that has waxed old and needs to be changed, so they shall indeed be changed, but, "Thou art the same". Jehovah is the changeless One, inhabiting eternity, and this changelessness is the glory of His Son, the Messiah. "Thou remainest"

(Heb 1.11). The years of the eternal One have no end, and the Psalmist concludes on the happy note that this everlasting life is the portion of God's people too. They, as He, will continue forever. His servants and their children, and their seed after them, shall be established eternally before Him whom they have loved and served.

So, to quote Spurgeon again, "The day which opened with wind and rain finally closes with a brilliant sunset".

PSALM 103

Introduction

The brief title of this Psalm assigns it to David. There is no valid reason for doubting the Davidic authorship, and very few critics do. The Psalm is one of the best known and best loved in the Psalter, for, as Alexander says, "It is a favourite vehicle of thankful praise among the pious of all ages". Commentators vie with each other in extolling its simplicity and beauty. Plumer quotes Henry, whose first remark on the Psalm is, "This Psalm calls more for devotion than for exposition". Spurgeon agrees, saying, "There is too much in the Psalm for a thousand pens to write, it is one of those all-comprehending Scriptures which is a Bible in itself, and it might alone suffice for the hymn-book of the church".

The precise date of the composition of the Psalm cannot be determined, but it is the work of a man who is in the enjoyment and appreciation of much blessing from God, whether that be the spiritual blessing of forgiveness and pardon, or the temporal blessing of physical health. The Psalmist is very conscious, too, of the frailty of life, and all this may indicate that it belongs to David's later years. However, as has been remarked in comments on other Psalms, many of the details regarding dates and circumstances may have been divinely hidden from us so that believers of every age may borrow the language, make the Psalms their own, and use them to express their own feelings of sorrow or joy in their own times. Plumer's own comment is, "The ode suits many a condition of believers in every age. All agree that this is a poem of rare and edifying excellence"

Psalm 103 is easily divided. In verses 1-5 the Psalmist sings of personal mercies which he had himself received from God. In verses 6-19 he extols the gracious dealings of God with His people in general. In the remaining verses 20-22 he calls, not only upon himself, but also upon angels and upon the servants of God everywhere to join with him in blessing the Lord.

Verses 1-5: Praise for Personal Mercies Received

This opening call to bless the Lord is simply a call for praise. "Bless"

(1288) is the Hebrew equivalent of the Greek "eulogeo" (*2127*), which is the word from which the English "eulogise" is derived, meaning "to speak well of, to celebrate with praises". Setting the saints a good example, the Psalmist first calls upon his own soul, himself, to praise the Lord, and this he does again in the final verse. Indeed the opening clause in the Psalm is also the closing clause. These are like golden clasps in which the whole lovely jewel of the poem is enclosed. T.W. Davies says of this "Bless the Lord O my soul" that, "The self-urging to praise occurs only in these two Psalms (see Ps 103.1-2 and 22, and Ps 104.1 and 35)". The Psalmist calls upon his soul, himself, but then adds, "and all that is within me". He is invoking his whole being, body, soul, and spirit, mind and strength, all his senses and all his faculties, to praise the holy name of Jehovah. It is a call for whole-hearted fervent expression of adoration and gratitude.

After the second "Bless the Lord, O my soul" in v.2, the Psalmist then exhorts against forgetting any of the many benefits that had been bestowed upon him. It has ever been a common failing of the Lord's people to be forgetful of his mercies. Jehovah's call to redeemed Israel was, "Beware lest thou forget the Lord, which brought thee forth out of the land of Egypt, from the house of bondage" (Deut 6.12; 8.11). Alas, they often failed to remember what blessings had been lavished upon them and what deliverances had been granted. As Psalm 106.7 says, "They remembered not the multitude of thy mercies", and again in v.13 of the same Psalm, "They soon forgat his works". So have saints of succeeding ages forgotten also. The Psalmist would not forget, and now he proceeds to enumerate a few of the bounties bestowed. It is not possible for any man to count all the blessings of God, but here is a touching beginning, in which the Psalmist remembers some of the Lord's many kindnesses to him.

He begins with the spiritual - his iniquities had been forgiven. David had sad personal experience of this, as Psalm 51 reveals. In the word which follows, "Who healeth all thy diseases", he may revert to the physical. It does indeed seem to many that in these two expressions he is speaking of both spiritual and physical healing, though some commentators think he may well be referring to diseases of the soul. In support of this Plumer quotes Horne who writes, "What is pride, but lunacy; what is anger, but a fever; what is avarice, but a dropsy; what is lust, but a leprosy; what is sloth, but a dead palsy". Whichever is intended in the context, there is no doubt that God has been gracious in granting healing of the body and of the mind, and the Psalmist would not forget. "Diseases" (8463) seems to occur always in the plural, and is rendered "sicknesses" in Deuteronomy 29.22.

"Who redeemeth (1350) thy life from destruction". In a personal way David knew Jehovah as his redeemer. Indeed only David and Job use that lovely title of God, "My Redeemer" (Job 19.25; Ps 19.14). This is the Hebrew GOEL, the word for the kinsman-redeemer. Such redemption basically means deliverance, but the fact that it often involved cost and risk, and even death, implies that there is a preciousness in it. "The redemption of their soul is precious" (Ps 49.8). The Psalmist had been delivered from the penalty of his many sins and therefore from death itself. "Destruction" (7845) is sometimes translated "corruption; the pit; the grave", synonyms for death. T.W. Davies comments that the grave "is here pictured as claiming the Psalmist when he was on the point of dying: but Jehovah quashed the claim: paid, as it were, the ransom, and so brought him back to life and health".

But he was not only redeemed from destruction, he was crowned, surrounded, with lovingkindness and tender mercies. The love of God enclosed him. Divine compassions encompassed him. Jehovah had satisfied His servant with good things and even in old age (JND) his youth was renewed, like the eagle's. This appears to be a reference to the manner in which that "monarch of the air" renews its feathers, lives to a greater age than most other birds, is renowned for its strength and vigour, and is majestic in flight. Isaiah knew this too, and wrote, "They that wait upon the Lord shall renew their strength; they shall mount up with wings as eagles" (Is 40.31). So the Psalmist had such a personal experience of God that he could only call upon his soul to praise Him who had so graciously dealt with him. "Bless the Lord, O my soul".

Verses 6-19: Jehovah's Gracious Dealings with His People

Until now, the Psalmist has been speaking of the Lord's gracious dealings with him personally, but as Jehovah had dealt with him as an individual, so had he dealt with His people nationally, and, indeed, with men everywhere. All that Jehovah does is righteous, in keeping with His character. Both His doings and His judgments, His decrees and His decisions, are absolutely righteous. They must be, since He is. In that righteousness He hates oppression, will always come to the aid of the oppressed, and will judge the oppressor. He delights, too, to reveal Himself to His people. Moses had prayed, "Show me now thy way, that I may know thee" (Ex 33.13). In grace, that petition was heard and answered; "He made known his ways unto Moses". So many of these ways are recorded in the Pentateuch, as are the many wonders which God wrought for His people in their deliverance from Egypt. "He made known his ways unto Moses, his acts unto the children of Israel". These were revelations of Himself.

The sentiments and the lovely tributes which follow are almost a quotation from Exodus 34.6. Jehovah is merciful and gracious, slow to anger, and plenteous in mercy. The beauty of it all has been variously translated. "The Lord is full of compassion and gracious" (RV). "Abundant in lovingkindness" (JND). "Tenderly pitiful, rich in mercy" (Plumer). "Very compassionate and very gracious" says Davies, adding, "the adjectives are intensive in form". The greatness of His compassions and His mercies seems to defy human language, but this is how He has been toward His people. Sometimes, indeed, He had reason to be angry with them, but

He was slow to anger, and when He was angry it was not forever. He would not contend endlessly, even with a sinning people. He was neither implacable nor irreconcilable. He would not always chide or bear a grudge, as men do.

In great grace He was gentle and kind with them, in that He had not judged them harshly for their sins. The root meaning of "sins" (2399 from 2398) is "missing the mark". How often had this erring nation missed the mark. But Jehovah was forbearing and longsuffering, and had not rewarded them according to their failures. The greatness of His mercy could not be measured. It was as great as the distance between heaven and earth. Indeed, their transgressions (6588), even their rebellions, had been removed from them as far away as the East is from the West. This is infinite. A traveller journeying East will never reach the West. One travelling West will never arrive at the East. From the sunrise to the sunset the distance is immeasurable. So great is His mercy and so great is the distance to which He removes the sins of those who fear Him.

How well does the Creator know that even the choicest of His people are but dust. He knows their frame. He knows how man was formed. He remembers their humble and lowly origin, and like as a father pities his children, so Jehovah, in all His greatness, is as a Father to His people, and pities them that fear Him.

As for man (582 from 605), this is the Hebrew word ENOSH, poor mortal man in his frailty. He is as weak as the grass or the flower of the field, an echo of Psalm 90.5-6. It grows up, even flourishes for a little, but the wind passes over it and it is gone. There is an East wind, which, Tristram says in his *Natural History of the Bible*, "blowing over the desert in summer, is dry and parching, and withers up all vegetation". How different is the mercy of the Lord! It is from everlasting to everlasting like Himself. Not only the children, but also the children's children, and all those who fear Him and keep His covenant, and obey His precepts, will enjoy His blessing. This was the very promise which accompanied the giving of the law at Sinai, "Showing mercy unto thousands of them that love me, and keep my commandments" (Ex 20.6). It is to man's eternal advantage and benefit to remember and keep those precepts.

Verses 20-22: The Universal Call for Praise of Jehovah

In a brief, but majestic, concluding section, David calls upon creatures everywhere to pay tribute to Jehovah. He summons angels, heavenly hosts, and servants of God throughout the whole dominion to render praise.

Jehovah has prepared (3559), established, His throne in the heavens. The throne of God is stable and firm, secure and steadfast. It cannot be moved. "Behold, a throne was set in heaven", said the apostle of a much later day (Rev 4.2). But if the throne was in the heavens, the authority of that throne was universal. Jehovah has unlimited dominion over all. It is but right, then, that He should be praised. "Bless the Lord, ye His angels". While it is true that the word "angels" (4397) basically means "representatives", or "messengers", and may sometimes be used in this sense of men, there seems no reason to doubt that here the call is to those celestial beings who are Jehovah's constant attendants in glory. They are the mighty, excelling in strength, ever awaiting His commands, listening for His voice and delighting to do His will. This angelic praise of God would be such an example to men. These angel hosts are innumerable (Heb 12.22). Ten thousand times ten thousand, and thousands of thousands (Rev 5.11; Dan 7.10). What a chorus of praise has already begun in the heavens, and now men are exhorted to join. "Ye ministers of his, that do his pleasure". If this may, initially, refer to the angels, it must include men also since servants in all places of His dominion are summoned. Indeed "all his works" are called to bless Him. As Plumer says, "Either this is an urgent renewal of the summons to the angels to engage in blessing Jehovah; or it is an animated appeal to the sun, moon and stars to join the chorus of the universe".

The Psalm ends as it began. Having spoken so personally in the earliest verses, and having widened out his appeal to angels and men and creation everywhere, the Psalmist now returns to personal adoration again. "Bless the Lord, O my soul". Alexander writes so nicely, "The angels and heavenly bodies, with men and every other creature, are now summed up in the comprehensive phrase, all His works, i.e. all that He has made, all creatures, and invited to bless God, which invitation the Psalmist once more addresses to himself, and thus, by a beautiful transition, brings us back to the point from which we started". So might every believer exclaim, "Bless the Lord, O my soul!".

PSALM 104

Introduction

Was it from this majestic Psalm that the hymn-writer received his inspiration, who wrote –

O Lord my God! when I in awesome wonder
Consider all the works Thy hands have made,
I see the stars, I hear the mighty thunder,
Thy power throughout the universe displayed.

Then sings my soul, my Saviour God, to Thee,
How great Thou art! How great Thou art!
(tr. Stuart K. Hine)

Throughout its thirty-five verses, Psalm 104 sings the greatness of a great God. Jehovah is the Creator and the Sustainer of the universe, the unfailing

Provider for all His creatures. He cares for man and his flocks. He remembers every living thing in land, sea, and air. From the little birds among the branches to the stork in the fir trees; from the conies among the rocks to the lion-king of the jungle; from the wild asses to the mountain goats; from the creeping things on the ocean bed to the great leviathan, the sea monster sporting among the waves; He knows them all, small and great, and supplies their necessary food. He is, of course, also Lord of the angels, His ministering spirits.

The Psalm has no title, and no author is identified or indicated. Plumer comments, "Neither the Hebrew nor Chaldee have any title for this Psalm. The Syriac, Arabic, Septuagint, Ethiopic, Vulgate, Edwards, Morison, Henry and Scott, ascribe it to David". While some do not accept Davidic authorship, in a number of manuscripts the Psalm is put as a continuance of Psalm 103 which David certainly did compose. Spurgeon writes, "We have no information as to the author, but the Septuagint ascribes it to David, and we see no reason for ascribing it to any one else. His spirit, style, and manner of writing are very manifest therein, and if the Psalm must be ascribed to another, it must be to a mind remarkably similar, and we could only suggest the wise son of David – Solomon, the poet-preacher, to whose notes upon natural history in the Proverbs some of the verses bear a striking likeness". He adds, most importantly, "Whoever the human penman may have been, the exceeding glory and perfection of the Holy Spirit's own divine authorship are plain to every spiritual mind".

A quiet careful meditation on the Psalm will show that it is a beautiful poetic version of the creation-story of Genesis 1-2. This thought will be developed in the division of the Psalm observed in this commentary. Spurgeon too, employs this to give a most interesting and helpful analysis of the Psalm. Perhaps he deserves to be quoted in full as he writes, "After ascribing blessedness to the Lord the devout Psalmist sings of the light and the firmament, which were the work of the first and second days (verses 1-6). By an easy transition he describes the separation of the waters from the dry land, the formation of rain, brooks, and rivers, and the uprising of green herbs, which were the produce of the third day (verses 7-18). Then the appointment of the sun and moon to be the guardians of day and night commands the poet's admiration (verses 19-23), and so he sings the work of the fourth day. Having already alluded to many varieties of living creatures, the Psalmist proceeds from verse 24 to verse 30 to sing of the life with which the Lord was pleased to fill the air, the sea, and the land; these forms of existence were the peculiar produce of the fifth and sixth days. We may regard the closing verses (31-35) as a Sabbath meditation, hymn, and prayer. The whole lies before us as a panorama of the universe viewed by the eye of devotion".

Verses 1-6: Jehovah's Majesty in Creation

This Psalm begins and ends, like the preceding Psalm, with the Psalmist's exhortation to himself that he should bless the Lord, and immediately he embarks upon reasons for this praise. It is touching to see how he can say of Jehovah in all His inexpressible greatness, "My God". What grace already mingles with the glory, that every believing heart, while recognising such honour and majesty, can yet, in personal appreciation say, "O Jehovah my God"! This great God covers Himself with light as with a garment. Light is the robe of deity. Before the creation of sun, moon, or stars, there was light. It is the very nature of God. He is the Uncreated Light. "God is light" (1 Jn 1.5). Once again, in a day yet to come, there will be light without sun or moon. "The city had no need of the sun, neither of the moon, to shine in it: for the glory of God did lighten it, and the Lamb is the light thereof" (Rev 21.23). He dwells in light unapproachable (1 Tim 6.16). Light, which usually reveals, actually veils Him. His greatness is indescribable, incomprehensible, and inscrutable – "Thou art very great". "Let there be light", He commanded, "and there was light", and the dividing of the light from the darkness created day and night.

In those earliest days of creation Jehovah stretched out the heavens like a curtain, sheltering earth with the covering firmament. He laid the beams, the framework, of His dwelling, His chambers, in the waters above the firmament, where the clouds were His chariot, borne along by the wings of the wind. He "maketh winds his messengers", is the RV rendering of v.4, and while this is true, the Epistle to the Hebrews quotes from the LXX, and is in agreement with the AV, which says, "Who maketh his angels spirits, and his ministers a flame of fire" (Heb 1.7). The construction of this verse has been the subject of much discussion and controversy. Plumer, after considering the two translations, says, "There is no better rendering than that of the common version".

The Creator laid the foundations of the earth, He established it firmly, but in its primitive condition it was covered with the deep as with a vesture. While He was robed in light, the created earth was covered with waters as with a winding sheet until the third day. This does not refer to the flood of Genesis 7, as some suppose. Such a reference would be out of sequence, out of context, and incongruous. It is that state and condition of the earth before the dividing of the waters on the third day.

Verses 7-18: Dry Land, Springs of Water, Green Grass

The Creator's word came like a rebuke, like a voice of thunder, commanding the separation of land and water. The waters obeyed instantly. Earth and seas were now distinct, and rivers and rivulets, springs and brooks of refreshing waters ran among the hills, in the valleys. These would travel and trickle and flow at His direction and bidding. They would not, could not, pass the boundaries which He set for them. Never again, except in a coming judgment flood, would they cover the earth as they had done in its primitive state. These springs will provide drink for the beasts which are to be created. Wild asses will quench their thirst here, while birds of the air will make their homes and sing among the branches of the trees which will grow by the wadis. Jehovah will water these hills. He will send refreshing rain from the upper chambers of His dwelling, and earth will be satisfied. There will be grass for the cattle and herb for the service of man. "Herb" (6212) describes all that vegetation of the ground necessary for man's food: wheat, barley, corn, pulse, and probably the vine and the olive too. Man may indeed have to labour for these, but the Creator will give the increase and reward his labour with "bread to strengthen and wine to cheer". As Plumer says, "Wine, and oil, and bread, were the great staples of Palestine". How sad it was that so early in his history man abused and perverted that which God had intended for his good (Gen 9.21), an abuse which continues until this day. Olive oil was used for anointing and for healing, making the skin to shine.

The very trees in God's creation are satisfied. They are full of sap. The great cedars of Lebanon, mentioned so often in Scripture, and renowned for their grandeur, provide shelter for the birds. Perhaps the smaller birds are intended here, as the sparrow. They make their nests in safety and security among the cedar branches. But the larger bird is cared for also. In that equally noble tree, the evergreen fir tree, the stork builds her house. It is interesting that the Hebrew name for "stork" (CHASIDA – 2624; TWOT - 698c) signifies tenderness or lovingkindness. The stork is noted for its great affection for its young, and it may be for this reason that it has become a legendary symbol for the carrying of the newborn infant to the happy parent.

From the birds the Psalmist now returns to animals. The whole creation abounds with life, and that in great variety. How different is the wild goat to the cony, but the God who cares for sparrows and storks cares also for goats and conies. The hills provide a refuge for the fleetfooted mountain goat, a rather majestic creature moving swiftly from crevice to crag, alighting with amazing precision upon some ledge of rock, at home in the highest hills. The conies are another extreme, rock-badgers, shy and defenceless, darting among the clefts of the rocks and into their dens at the slightest suggestion of danger. Jehovah cares for all.

Verses 19-23: The Sun and the Moon

The Psalmist now passes to the events of the fourth day of creation. The Creator put two great lights in the firmament, the sun and the moon, and, in what seems to be an almost incidental comment, Moses, the inspired historian, says, "He made the stars also" (Gen 1.16)! Three reasons are given in the Genesis account for the creation of these heavenly bodies. They were set to divide the day from the night, to mark seasons, days, and years, and to give light upon the earth. They were the rulers and governors of earth's light. Although both sun and moon are referred to as "great lights", the sun is called "the greater" and the moon "the lesser" (Gen 1.14-16). The lesser light is the subordinate, and is dependent upon the greater. In the creation story the sun, the greater light, is mentioned first, and then the moon, the lesser. Here in the Psalm the moon is mentioned first, perhaps because the Jewish day began with the evening, as, for example in Genesis 1.19, "the evening and the morning were the fourth day". By the phases of the moon Israel's calendars were ordered, both civil and sacred, and so they speak of "the lunar year". By the moon the annual festivals of Israel were arranged and observed, some at the new moon and some at the full moon.

The Psalm now sings of sunset and sunrise. The greater light controls the day, and the Psalmist speaks of the day and the night in relation to the creation. But those bright orbs of the heavens move only by the direction of the Creator. The sun rises and sets at His bidding. As the sun sets and darkness falls, so many creatures of prey come to life. Beasts of the forest creep forth in search of food. The young lions roar from their jungle lairs. Yet even the lion, this strong, proud "king of beasts" is as dependent upon God as is the feeblest of all the creatures. They "seek their meat from God". As Maclaren says, "Even their roar was a kind of prayer, though they knew it not; it was God from whom they sought their food". At sunrise, nocturnal life retires to its dens as man awakes from his sleep and goes to labour until the evening. The Creator, in wisdom, has ordered evening and morning, darkness and light, night and day, to suit His creation, and He has adapted the creature to each appropriate environment.

Verses 24-30: "This Great and Wide Sea"

On the fifth and sixth days of creation God filled air, sea, and land with life. Having already spoken of the birds the Psalmist now turns to consider "this great and wide sea". Whether in retrospect or in prospect, he views the wealth and the wonder of God's creation and exclaims, "O Lord, how manifold are thy works! in wisdom thou hast made them all". As the earth is full of His riches, so, likewise, is the great sea. There are creeping things innumerable in its depths. There are living creatures small and great, abounding in its waves. Then, in an apparently incongruous comment, he says, "There go the ships!". But there is a reason for this exclamation. It is to show the vastness of the waters which are so great and so wide that man can only traverse them by means of ships of his own making. Man, with his limitations and frailty is dependent upon ships to travel this great sea. How early in his history did he learn this, when, by God's direction, he built a saving ark to rise above the deluge. The ark was constructed to a divine design, the design of Him who created the waters.

"There is that leviathan" (3382). Leviathan may well be identified with the whales, created on the fifth day in Genesis 1.21, but commentators are not agreed. There is an extended description of the appearance and habits of leviathan in Job 41. In fact, the whole of that chapter is devoted to leviathan. Strong says, "Perhaps the extinct dinosaur, plesiosaurus, exact meaning unknown". Perhaps the most that can be said with certainty is that leviathan was a giant sea monster. The mention of it here in the Psalm, sporting in the waters, is to show the power of the Creator who creates the great leviathan as well as the tiny creeping things, and who prepares an environment suited to both. All are alike dependent upon Him for their life. They all must wait upon Him for their sustenance. He gives them meat in due season. When He opens His hand they are satisfied. Should He withdraw His care they die, and return to dust. It is He who creates, sustains, and renews His whole creation, both animate and inanimate. All things are fully dependent upon Him who made them.

Verses 31-35: A Meditation, a Hymn, and a Prayer

Having recounted, in poetry, the six days of the creation story, the Psalmist now concludes with a delightful stanza which is in the spirit of that first Sabbath. "Thus the heavens and the earth were finished", says Genesis 2.1, "and all the host of them". And on the seventh day God rested. Everything was very good and Jehovah rejoiced in His works. "The glory of the Lord shall endure forever", the Psalmist writes. Many are happy enough with this AV rendering, but the RV and others prefer, "Let the glory of the Lord endure forever", and the companion prayer then is, "Let the Lord rejoice in his works". The great doxology of Revelation 4.11 sings the same thought, "Thou art worthy, O Lord, to receive glory and honour, and power: for thou hast created all things, and for thy pleasure they are and were created".

Such is the power of the Creator that earth may tremble at His look, and the mountains smoke at His touch. As Davies comments, "A mere glance from God causes earthquake: His touch turns the mountain into a volcano". Mount Sinai was "altogether on a smoke" when He descended upon it (Ex 19.18). He touches the land and it melts (Amos 9.5). The Psalmist bursts into praise. As long as he lived, as long as he had being, he would sing (7891) unto the Lord, he would sing praise (2167) to his God. The two words rendered "sing" are different. As Alexander points out, "The two verbs are those continually joined to denote vocal and instrumental praise". For confirmation of this see Psalms 21.13; 27.6; 57.7 and 68.4.

For those who recognise the greatness of the Lord, meditation is sweet (6149), acceptable and pleasing. Of course the sense given by the AV rendering is very true. "My meditation of him shall be sweet". Meditation of Him must be pleasant indeed to every believer. Both RV and JND, with others, however, translate a slightly different sense. "Let my meditation be sweet unto him" (RV). "My meditation shall be pleasant unto him" (JND). "Let my musing be sweet unto Him" (JPS). Whichever is preferred, each is true. Musing upon Him is pleasing both to the Lord and to His people. It is good for the saint to think of Him constantly, and this brings pleasure to Him too. "Let the Lord rejoice…I will rejoice" (vv. 31, 34 RV).

This is fellowship with heaven itself, to sing and praise and rejoice with the Lord as He rejoices. Compare Psalm 19.14.

The prayer for judgment on the wicked at this point may at first glance appear unconnected, irrelevant, and even incongruous, but there is a reason. The Psalmist is longing for Eden again! He petitions for a world where sin shall be no more. Sin has marred the creation which was brought into being for the pleasure of God. The prayer looks forward to that day when all that is defiled and defiling shall be removed, and when once again the whole creation shall be at peace. This will be enjoyed in the bliss of the coming millennial kingdom, but permanently, eternally, forever, in the Day of God, when God shall be all in all (2 Pet 3.12; 1 Cor 15.28).

Like the preceding Psalm, this Psalm ends as it began: "Bless...the Lord, O my soul", but there is appended, for the first time in the Psalter, that word which appears in the OT only in the Psalter, "Hallelujah", "Praise ye Jah". It is a joyful summons to praise, a Hebrew word which has been incorporated into many other languages so that it has become a universal word. The "Hallelujah Psalms", which have "Hallelujah" at the beginning, or at the end, or both, are Psalms 104-106, 111-113, 115-117, 135, 146-150. The Greek equivalent, "Alleluia", is found only in Revelation 19.1-6.

PSALM 105

Introduction

Like Psalm 78, this is an historical Psalm, and a Psalm of thanksgiving. It is a recital of God's past dealings with His people, bringing them out of Egypt, through the wilderness, and into the Promised Land. The first fifteen verses are incorporated into a Psalm which was committed by David to Asaph on the occasion of the bringing of the Ark from the house of Obededom to Mount Zion as recorded in 1 Chronicles 16.7-22 - "Then on that day David delivered first this psalm to thank the Lord into the hand of Asaph and his brethren...". Some suggest, however, that the remainder of the Psalm may have been composed and added by a later Psalmist. Such a Psalm of thanksgiving was most appropriate for the occasion mentioned. It was a reminder of God's faithfulness to His covenant, of which the Ark was a symbol. As He had in former times delivered His people, so now He had delivered the Ark. It was, at last, after many years of exile, to find a resting place on Zion. This was indeed a matter of great rejoicing and a cause for thanksgiving.

The preceding Psalm 104 was based on the opening chapters of Genesis. This Psalm begins with the later chapters of Genesis and goes on to rehearse the history of the children of Israel as recorded in Exodus and Numbers. Abraham, Isaac, Jacob, Joseph, Moses, and Aaron, the patriarchs, the prophet, and the priest, all have a place in the story, and in the Psalm. As the theme of Psalm 104 was creation, the theme of Psalm 105 is redemption. Pridham's most helpful comment is that the Psalm possesses, "not only a wonderful beauty when considered in its direct bearing upon Israel, as its primary object, but is of rich practical comfort to the believer now, as an exemplification of the perfect way of the God with whom he has to do".

In the Hebrew there is no title to the Psalm, but in the LXX, "Hallelujah" is prefixed as a title instead of being attached to the ending of Psalm 104. Whether this is the intended place or not for this particular "Hallelujah", the Psalm certainly closes with one. It was believed to be a kind of rallying call from the precentor, or by someone specially appointed, when the Psalm was about to be sung.

There are several obvious divisions in the Psalm, following chronologically the history of the children of Israel from the earliest days until their arrival in the land of promise. Verses 1-6 are an introductory summons to praise. Verses 7-15 recall Jehovah's faithfulness to the patriarchs and His promise to them of an inheritance in Canaan. In verses 16-25 the story of Joseph is retold, and God's sovereign provision for the infant nation during the years of famine. Verses 26-38 remember God's judgment upon the Egyptian oppressors and His deliverance of His people under the leadership of Moses and Aaron. Verses 39-45 are a brief summary of the wilderness journey and the eventual entry into Canaan.

Verses 1-6: The Call to Praise

Four Psalms in the Psalter commence with this "O give thanks unto the Lord". They are Psalms 105, 107, 118 and 136. In retrospect, Israel had much for which to give thanks, as these Psalms show. This thanksgiving should be manifested in several forms. There must be a calling upon His name, an acknowledgement of the character and attributes which are embraced in His holy name. This would then be accompanied by public testimony to Him, not only among His people who knew Him, but also "among the peoples". His marvellous deeds must be rehearsed to the surrounding nations as well as to Israel. Then, of course, there would be singing, "Sing unto him, sing psalms unto him". Here again are the two words of Psalm 104.33, on which, as has been noted there, Alexander says, "The two verbs are those continually joined to denote vocal and instrumental praise". Then this praising people would talk to one another about the wondrous doings of their God. Such holy converse has always been characteristic of the godly, as the prophet says, "Then they that feared the Lord spake often one to another: and the Lord hearkened and heard it" (Mal 3.16).

Once again His holy name is mentioned. Those who recognise this holy character of God, as signified by His name, can glory in it indeed. It is a privilege to be able to appreciate the true Deity, and is a cause for gladness of heart. "Let the heart of them rejoice that seek the Lord". "Seek (1875) the Lord...seek (1245) his face". The verbs of v.4 are synonyms, but not identical. Kirkpatrick comments, "Both originally referred to the outward act of visiting the sanctuary, but both come to express the inward purpose of the heart as well. So far as they can be distinguished the first denotes the attitude of loving devotion, the second that of inquiry or supplication". Perhaps the first may be said to be the approach of a worshipper and the second the approach of a petitioner. In either case, "Let the heart of them rejoice that seek (1245) the Lord".

The Psalmist continues with reasons for thanksgiving. "Remember!" Memories of what the Lord had done, for them and for their fathers, would evoke gratitude. There was indeed cause for thanksgiving. For the second time in this section of the Psalm, the Psalmist employs the word "marvellous" (6381), but rendered "wondrous" in v.2 of the AV. It is the same word. "Marvellous works" is but one word in the original Hebrew of the Psalm. It might be translated "wonders", whereas the "wonders" (4159) of v.5 is a different word, though very similar, and may have the thought of a display of power, a visible, miraculous token that God was indeed working wonders for His people. Strong says that it is "a sign, a token, in the sense of conspicuousness". It signifies Jehovah's manifest interventions for the nation. The same Hebrew word is used of the plagues in Egypt (Ex 7.3; 11.9). Of equal importance with the wonders He wrought were the words which He spoke, the judgments of His mouth. The people to whom the Psalm was committed were the seed of Abraham, the servant of God. They were, too, the children of Jacob His chosen (972). In wondrous and sovereign grace their God had made choice of Jacob. His name may mean "supplanter; beguiler", and this may indeed have been the character of the natural man, but he was elect of God, chosen to become the father of a great nation. They were a privileged people, seed of Abraham and children of Jacob. There was so much that justified the Psalmist's call, "O give thanks unto the Lord".

Verses 7-15: Jehovah, Faithful to His Covenant

Of the God of Abraham and the God of Jacob the nation could say, "He is the LORD (3068) our God (430)", or, as JND and some others prefer, perhaps adding due emphasis, "He, Jehovah, is our God". He was Jehovah All-Sufficient, and He was Elohim the Mighty, and He was their God. However, in the words of Kirkpatrick, "He stands in a special and peculiar relation to Israel the people of His choice; but He is no mere national Deity: *His judgments are in all the earth;* He exercises a universal rule over all nations as 'the Judge of all the earth' (Gen 18.25)". As the people have been exhorted to remember, so now it is said of Jehovah, "He hath remembered". Alexander comments, "There is here a kind of antithetical allusion to the exhortation in v.5. They should remember what He did, since He remembers what He promised. What He has done involves a pledge of what He will do. He has remembered (and will remember) His covenant to eternity". The expression "to a thousand generations" is originally Mosaic (Deut 7.9), and is not to be taken literally; neither is it "a thousand years", but, "a thousand generations". It signifies the endlessness, the endurance, of the faithfulness of the covenant-keeping God. It is synonymous with, and parallel to, "for ever". It is eternity!

Contrary to the interpretation of some commentators, this is not the covenant made at Sinai. That covenant was conditional. The covenant made with Abraham was unconditional, dependent only upon the faithfulness of God, as emphasised by Paul in Galatians 3. It was ratified with Abraham (Gen 17.2). It was renewed to Isaac (Gen 26.3). It was confirmed to Jacob (Gen 28.13). It was an everlasting covenant of promise for the Israel which was to spring from these patriarchs. The promise made to Abraham, Isaac, and Jacob, was intended for their descendents also. What then was this promise? Verse 11 explains, "Unto thee will I give the land of Canaan, the lot of your inheritance". So has Canaan ever since been called "The Land of Promise - The Promised Land".

It was good that the nation should always remember that all of this was God's sovereign choice and purpose. There was nothing in them to merit what He had promised. They were but a few in number when God promised that their seed should one day be innumerable as the stars, or as the sand of the seashore (Gen 22.17), and that they would inherit the land of Canaan. "Yea", says the Psalmist, "they were very few, and sojourners". They were, writes Kirkpatrick, "but an insignificant clan of protected aliens, and it seemed utterly improbable that they would ever become the owners of the land". These earliest patriarchs were wanderers in lands to which they did not belong, and which did not belong to them. As Dr Cohen says, "They resided in a land which was not theirs and were dependent upon the goodwill of the inhabitants". Abram came from Ur of the Chaldees to Haran and into Canaan. He passed through the land to Shechem and to the plain of Moreh. From there he moved to Bethel, and from Bethel he journeyed south until famine drove him into Egypt to sojourn there. From Egypt he eventually returned to Bethel again (Gen 11.31-13.3). Sojourners indeed! Strangers and pilgrims!

In all of their wanderings God protected them. He suffered no man to harm them. They were His chosen people, His anointed. He reproved kings for their sakes. This is probably a reference to Pharaoh and Abimelech in the matter of Sarai and Rebecca (Gen 12.17; 20.3, 7, 18; 26.6-11). In this same connection Abram is called a prophet (Gen 20.7), this simply indicating that he was a man to whom God had revealed Himself, and through whom He communicated His mind and will to others.

Verses 16-25: Joseph, Egypt, and Divine Preservation

The sovereignty of God can arrange famines for the fulfilment of His purpose! "He called for a famine upon the land". Bread is the staff of life, and by creating a famine Jehovah broke that upon which men leaned. He was, in His own way, working out His plans for His people. His intent was to bring them to Egypt and He sent a man before them. Joseph himself said, "God did send me before you to preserve life" (Gen 45.5). He was sold into Egypt to be a slave. He was subsequently unjustly imprisoned. He was bound with fetters and chains of iron (Gen 39.20; 40.3).

The expression, "Until the time that his word came", has been variously understood. Some think that this refers to Joseph's interpretation of the dreams of his fellow-prisoners, anticipating his own release. Others link it with Joseph's dreams in his father's house as recorded in Genesis 37.5-10, dreams which foretold his bright future. Yet others regard this as God's word, the same word which tried him, also here in v.19 of the Psalm. Whichever is the correct interpretation, Joseph's release from prison would be in God's time. When that time came the king sent and loosed him. The king, like the famine, was but a servant of sovereignty. Pharaoh, ruler of peoples, must release the slave at Jehovah's bidding. It was an honourable release, too, in which Joseph was made lord of Pharaoh's house and ruler of all his possessions. What a foreshadowing was all this of the Beloved Son who was to come, to be despised and rejected by His own people, to be condemned unjustly to death, but to be raised by the power of God and exalted to the heavens and to the throne.

Joseph, the Hebrew slave, was invested with authority to bind princes and instruct senators at his pleasure. This "binding" may be understood literally, meaning that Joseph had power to imprison princes where necessary. It may however, indicate a binding in things moral and political, compelling obedience to his every decree, controlling the greatest men in the kingdom. All this he did at his own discretion, with no necessity to consult or confer with Pharaoh.

The way having been prepared by Joseph, "Israel also came into Egypt; and Jacob sojourned in the land of Ham". Two names of Joseph's father are employed here, Israel and Jacob. These two names are seen in a most interesting connection in Genesis 45.26-28. The old name, Jacob, and the new name, Israel, may be interchangeable, but each has its significance. "Egypt" and "the land of Ham" are also convertible terms, the Egyptians being descendents of Ham. Jehovah prospered these sojourners, and greatly increased their numbers. He made them stronger than the people who were to become their adversaries and oppressors. This is expanded in Exodus 1.7 which records, "And the children of Israel were fruitful, and increased abundantly, and multiplied, and waxed exceeding mighty; and the land was filled with them". The sequel is well known. The heart of the Egyptians was turned to hate these people and to deal with them subtly, or craftily. Was even this in the purpose of God?

Undoubtedly. It was He who turned their heart. Famines, Pharaohs, and nations everywhere are in His hand for the working out of His predetermined purpose.

Verses 26-38: Moses, Aaron, and the Plagues upon Egypt

The history of this chosen people began with the call of Abram. As Stephen said, "The God of glory appeared unto our father Abraham" (Acts 7.2). The story continued in the lives of Isaac and Jacob and God's dealings with them. Then came Joseph, sent before them into Egypt for their preservation in the famine. However, a new king arose who knew not Joseph and preservation gave way to persecution. Days of prosperity were followed by days of adversity, and the people groaned under the yoke of Egyptian oppression. At a critical moment in this history came Moses and Aaron, men who, like Joseph, were prepared of God beforehand for the salvation of Israel. To quote Stephen again, speaking of the Egyptians, "The same dealt subtilly with our kindred, and evil entreated our fathers", and then he adds, "in which time Moses was born" (Acts 7.19-20). It is a high privilege for any man to be called "His servant", and in this Psalm two men are so designated. Abraham is twice referred to in this way (vv. 6 and 42) and Moses also in v.26. Moses and Aaron were chosen men, entrusted with a miraculous ministry. Through them Jehovah wrought signs and wonders among the people. In the land of Ham, in Egypt, the country of their oppressors, God used these men mightily in the fulfilment of His purpose for those who had become but a nation of slaves.

The familiar story of the plagues is now recalled, but the Psalmist does not follow the order in which they came upon the land. The ninth plague is mentioned first, "He sent darkness". It was "a darkness which may be felt" (Ex 10.21). It is not clear why the Psalmist should begin with the ninth plague but the expression which follows may be significant, "They rebelled not against his word". In the Exodus account there would appear to be a change of heart with Pharaoh after this plague so that, rather than rebelling again as formerly, he seemed to relent and permit the freedom of the slaves. Dr Cohen's comments are interesting and helpful, "The Psalmist does not follow the Exodus account of the plagues. He begins with the ninth, omits the fifth and sixth, and inverts the order of the third and fourth. Why he began with the ninth is uncertain. Ibn Ezra thinks it was because this plague broke the stubbornness of Pharaoh's ministers and even forced the king to consider releasing the Israelites (Ex 10.7ff.). It has been suggested that the Psalmist classified the plagues: the first two attacked the elements, the next three the animal life, and the two that followed the crops".

Jehovah has sovereign control over all the forces of nature. He turned the waters of the Nile, with its tributaries, their streams and canals, pools and ponds, into blood. The fish died, the polluted waters were undrinkable through all the land of Egypt (Ex 7.19-21), but after seven days of this first plague still Pharaoh's heart was hard and he refused to listen or yield.

The second plague is now recalled. "Let my people go", Jehovah demanded, "...and if thou refuse to let them go, behold, I will smite all thy borders with frogs". According to His word there were frogs everywhere. They came up from the river, into the bedrooms and upon the beds. They were in their ovens and in their kneading troughs. They invaded the chambers of the king himself, and still, even when relieved of them, Pharaoh hardened his heart against the Lord and His people (Ex 8.1-15).

The fourth and fifth plagues are referred to in v.31 of the Psalm: swarms of flies and a plague of lice. They filled the houses and covered the land, as numerous as the dust of the ground, infesting both man and beast. "This is the finger of God", the magicians said to Pharaoh, yet still his heart was hardened (Ex 8.16-32).

The seventh plague is recorded in Exodus 9.18-34. Jehovah rained hail upon the land, but it was hail mingled with fire. As David Dickson writes, "The clouds are at God's command, to send down soft rain or hard and heavy hailstones. Although fire and hailstones are very contrary in their natures, yet they can agree well in the work of God's service, when He employeth them". It was, says Moses, "very grievous" (Ex 9.24). It smote man and beast, vegetation and trees, but God again preserved His people in the midst of it all.

With the eighth plague Jehovah smote the vines and the fig trees of Egypt. He sent locusts to eat all that had been left after the hail. With the locusts came the caterpillar (3218), the cankerworm (JND and RV), which, according to Strong, may have been the young locust in the early stage of development. They devoured the fruit of the trees and the herbs, until Jehovah sent a west wind which blew them into the Red Sea. Still the heart of Pharaoh was hard, and still he refused to let the children of Israel go (Ex 10.12-20).

With the tenth and last plague Jehovah smote their firstborn (Ex 11.4-6). It was a final and fearful judgment. At midnight, death came suddenly. From the king upon the throne to the serving-girl at the mill, prisoners in the dungeon and cattle in the field, all lost their firstborn (Ex 12.29). The very strength of Egypt was destroyed in a night.

The Lord was emancipating His people, and in triumph too, for He brought them out of their bondage with silver and gold. It was, as Dr Cohen says, "Spoils in lieu of the wages for their labour which had been withheld". Jehovah so ordered it that there was not a feeble person among the tribes. None was unfit for the journey which they now faced. There was none that stumbled, or, in weariness, lagged behind as they began their departure for the Red Sea, the wilderness, and Canaan. They were free at last, and Egypt was glad when they departed.

Verses 39-45: The Wilderness Journey and the Promised Land

It was a new beginning for the nation, a renewing of their history (Ex 12.2). They set out in their newfound freedom with their loins girded, shoes on their feet, and staff in their hand, ready for the journey. But as they had known Jehovah's care for them during the years of their bondage, so they would continue to need that care on their way to Canaan. That care was indeed vouchsafed to them, and the tokens of it were soon manifested. With a cloud by day and a pillar of fire by night God provided both protection and light for them, a covering and a guide. They were, after all, His peculiar possession, and He treasured them. They were His flock, the sheep of His pasture, and He would shepherd them.

Sadly, they soon expressed discontent. So soon after their miraculous deliverance they lusted after the fleshpots and the bread of Egypt (Ex 16). They murmured against Moses and Aaron for bringing them into the wilderness, but their *murmuring* is not remembered in this Psalm, for the predominant theme here is the faithfulness of God and not the faithlessness of the people. In great grace the Psalm simply records that they "asked". God was patient with them and gave them quails, and manna, and water from the rock. He met their every need along their way. He satisfied them with the very bread of heaven, angels' food (Ps 78.25). The waters ran like a river from the stricken rock. He provided streams in the desert for them (Ex 17.1-6).

In all this Jehovah was remembering His word to Abraham. He is always true to His word and He will bring His people to the Promised Land. The exodus from Egypt was a time of joy and singing. The first song recorded in Scripture was sung on the banks of the Red Sea in Exodus 15. Moses sang, and the people sang, and Miriam sang and danced with the women. There was great rejoicing at the triumph which God had wrought. Pharaoh and his hosts, his chariots and his horses, had been drowned in the depths of the sea. "The Lord is a man of war", they sang, "glorious in power, great in His excellency, glorious in holiness, fearful in praises, doing wonders. Who is like unto Thee, O Lord, among the gods?" (Ex 15.3-11).

In fulfilment of His word, and in faithfulness to Abraham, Isaac, and Jacob, Jehovah eventually brought them into the land. He gave them the lands of the nations. He gave them "great and goodly cities" which others had built. He gave them houses which had been filled with good things by other men. He gave them wells which others had dug, and vineyards and olive trees which others had planted. His only condition was that they should keep His statutes and observe His laws. "Beware lest thou forget", He appealed to them (Deut 6.10-15). He had sworn to their fathers and He would not forget. Nor should they forget Him, who had brought them out of the house of bondage.

The Psalm concludes with a "Hallelujah", Praise ye Jah. There is always reason to praise the Lord, and now, with such a multitude of recollections of all that He was, of all that He had been, and of all that He had done, it surely was a most suitable time to render appropriate praise. So it is with all His people, at all times. Hallelujah!

PSALM 106

Introduction

Psalm 106 is the final Psalm in the fourth book of the Psalter. It has no title but there is general agreement that the author of the preceding Psalm 105 was the author of this Psalm also. There are similarities between the two Psalms, in that the sojourn of the children of Israel in the wilderness and their entry into the land are again the theme of this Psalm, as in Psalm 105. The same story is being told, but there is, however, a marked contrast. In the foregoing Psalm the emphasis of the Psalmist is on the faithfulness of God, the faithlessness of the people being, as it were, almost forgotten. Now, in Psalm 106 the emphasis is on the disloyalty, unbelief, and murmuring of the people, and many occasions of sinning are remembered and confessed. Yet, even the remembrance of grievous sins was a cause for thanksgiving because God was patient and gracious with the sinful nation, and was always true to His word concerning them. So the Psalm begins with a "Hallelujah", and, having recounted the rather sad history of those early years, the Psalmist can still conclude with another "Hallelujah".

There are three main divisions in the Psalm but the second, the central and largest section, requires to be sub-divided. The first section, verses 1-5, is a mingling of praise and prayer, expressing the Psalmist's own personal exercise before the Lord. The second division, which extends from verse 6 through until verse 46, deals with the sins and unbelief of the people at the Red Sea, in the wilderness, and in Canaan, but remembers also God's forgiveness and deliverance. These occasions of sinning may be summarised as follows. In verses 6-12 it is the provocation at the Red Sea. In verses 13-15 it is the lusting in the wilderness, and in verses 16-18 the envying of Moses and Aaron. In verses 19-23 it is idolatry, the matter of the golden calf, and in verses 24-27 the despising of the Promised Land. In verses 28-31 the iniquity of Baal-peor is remembered, and in verses 32-33 the waters of Meribah. In verses 34-46 there was disobedience even in Canaan. These events and circumstances will be considered in more detail in the commentary. The final section, verses 47-48, is a renewed prayer for salvation, and a call for thanksgiving to Him who is ever "The Lord God of Israel", no matter what the failings of the nation. An "Amen", and the accompanying "Hallelujah", bring to a conclusion, not only Psalm 106, but also, as has been noted, the seventeen Psalms of the fourth book of the Psalter.

Verses 1-5: Praise and Prayer

It is a pattern in many Psalms that the writer begins on a personal note of praise, and then calls upon the people to join him in his thanksgiving. This was, of course, the intent of the Psalms, that they should be vehicles of prayer and praise for congregational worship. It is good always to commence with praise. The "Hallelujah" is never out of place. Even though the reminiscences in the Psalm may be painful, there is reason throughout to give thanks. "O give thanks unto the Lord", says the Psalmist, "for he is good". His mercy (2617), His lovingkindness, is forever. Jehovah bestows goodness upon His people perpetually. His pity is everlasting towards them. Who can adequately tell the mighty acts of the Lord or render due praise? What man can fully rehearse the wonders that God has wrought? His mighty acts are as great in character as they are in number. As David says in another Psalm, "They cannot be reckoned up in order...they are more than can be numbered" (Ps 40.5). Human language fails to describe His works, so that His people can at times but bow in wonder and in worship, unable adequately to express appreciation of what He has done.

That man is blessed, says the Psalmist, who at all times observes justice, and maintains righteousness. This is not just occasional, but "at all times". It is good, in every circumstance of life, for a man to practise these principles of godliness. They are indeed the very character of God Himself, justice and righteousness, and to see them exemplified in His people will bring Him pleasure and win His approval. The Psalmist longs for that approval. Jehovah's favour (7522), he calls it. It is the joy of being acceptable and well-pleasing to the Lord. "Remember me, O Lord", he pleads, "with the favour that thou bearest unto thy people". His appeal is to Jehovah. When Jehovah acts towards His people in His favour, the Psalmist prays that he might personally be allowed to share in the blessing. The salvation of which He speaks is the deliverance of the people, and, as better times are anticipated for the nation, so the Psalmist's prayer is, "Remember me...visit me".

He gives three reasons for this prayer. "That I may see the good of thy chosen". This word "good" (2896) is the same as that in v.1, and while it may have the basic sense of goodness and excellence, the emphasis here may be on another shade of meaning, "prosperity", and so it is rendered by RV, RSV, JND and JPS. The Psalmist looked for the welfare, the good, of the nation, and trusted that he would have a part in the joy when the happier days arrived. These people were God's people. They were His chosen (972), His elect. Their salvation was therefore assured.

"That I may rejoice in the gladness of thy nation". How this great truth is emphasised, that the people belonged to God. "Thy chosen...thy nation...thine inheritance". It was true of Israel. It is true of believers today. They are His! Note the words "rejoice" and "gladness" in v.5. They are cognate words (8055 and 8057). The Psalmist is simply praying that he might be glad when the nation is glad, that he might rejoice when the people rejoice, that he might joy in their gladness.

"That I may glory with thine inheritance". The word "glory" (1984) is, in fact, the word "hallel", as in the familiar *Hallel*-ujah, "praise ye the Lord". "Praise" the first word of the Psalm, is the same word. Although the people had behaved badly, and this would now be confessed, a day of praising was inevitable since Jehovah would restore them. When that day came, the people would praise and the Psalmist looked forward to praising with them.

So ends this opening personal section of the Psalm, with anticipations of Jehovah's approval and pleasure, and a people rejoicing in Him. In all of this praise and pleasure the Psalmist longed to have a part, but first, he must recall, with sadness, present and past failures. Indeed, as he looked forward to sharing in the anticipated joy, so he must now join in contrition and in confession of sin. "We have sinned with our fathers".

Verses 6-12: Provocation at the Red Sea

The Psalmist, with commendable honesty and frankness, does not minimise the enormity of the sins of which the nation has been guilty. "We have sinned...we have committed iniquity, we have done wickedly". "We", he confesses, "with our fathers". Dr Cohen suggests that "More than the idea that the present generation has been as culpable as the generations of the past is intended in the phrase. It rather stresses the thought that all Israelites, both contemporary and of bygone times, are one entity and share a common responsibility". How soon after that mighty deliverance from Egypt did the fathers provoke the Lord. The sad story is recorded in Exodus 14.5-30. Jehovah had rained ten plagues upon their oppressors, most of which are remembered in Psalm 105. The redeemed multitude came out of the land of their bondage and soon arrived at the Red Sea. Meanwhile, Pharaoh was pursuing them with his chariots, his horsemen, and his army. It was when the Egyptian hosts seemed about to overtake them that the fear came and they murmured against Moses. With what hurtful sarcasm they asked, "Because there were no graves in Egypt, hast thou taken us away to die in the wilderness?". How this must have grieved the Lord.

Their situation was grave. The Egyptians were behind them and the Red Sea in front of them. They faced death. To unbelief it seemed inevitable that they should perish, but had they forgotten what wonders Jehovah had wrought in Egypt? Indeed they understood not. They remembered not. They neither gave heed nor considered what had already been accomplished on their behalf, and they provoked the Lord with their unbelief, at this, the first problem to confront them. Could not He, who had delivered them from Egypt, deliver them again? "Stand still", Moses had said, "and see the salvation of the Lord". In spite of the provocation and unbelief, Jehovah saved them for the sake of His name. He dried up the Red Sea with a word of rebuke. He led the people through the depths as though it had been dry pasture land. A wall of water stood miraculously on either side of them as they passed through to safety, following the cloudy pillar. The enemy hosts pursued but were drowned in the deluge of the returning waters. Jehovah had redeemed His people and had destroyed their enemies. Then they believed, and sang the song of their redemption on the banks of the Red Sea. Sadly, this early murmuring was but the beginning of many provocations by a people who seemed ever prone to forget what wonders God had wrought.

Verses 13-15: Lusting in the Wilderness

What sad words now follow – "They soon forgat". Jehovah had a plan and a purpose for them but they "waited not for his counsel". In their impatience they would not wait to hear of the provision He had made. Three days after they crossed the Red Sea they murmured for water (Ex 15.22), and six weeks later for food (Ex 16.1-3). It was perhaps natural that they should need food and water, but the sin was that they later "lusted exceedingly in the wilderness, and tempted God in the desert" (Num 11.4). They despised the manna and craved flesh to eat, remembering the fish which they ate freely in Egypt. They remembered too, the cucumbers, the melons, the leeks, the onions, and the garlic, but seemed to forget the whip of their taskmasters. Did they forget too, that Jehovah had promised a land flowing with milk and honey? The words "lusted" (183) and "exceedingly" (8378) are cognate, from the same root (TWOT 40), so that they may be rendered, "they lusted with lust" or, "they lusted greedily".

This despising of the manna was, however, a despising of the Lord Himself (Num 11.20). Did they lust greedily for flesh, despising His provision? Then He would give them flesh. "Jehovah will give you flesh, and ye shall eat. Ye shall not eat one day, nor two days, nor five days, neither ten days, nor twenty days, But even a whole month, until it come out at your nostrils, and it become loathsome to you" (Num 11.18-20). He sent them quails, so many that they lay two cubits deep on the ground, but even while the people chewed the flesh of the quails the Lord smote them with a very great plague. That place was called "Kibroth-hatta-avah", meaning, "The graves of lust" (Num 11.33-34).

Verses 16-18: Jealousy in the Camp

The next sin recalled by the Psalmist is that of the envy of the leadership of Moses and Aaron (Num 16). The revolt was fostered by Korah, Dathan, and Abiram. Though Korah is not identified in the Psalm, he was, nevertheless, the first to be mentioned in the conspiracy. It may be that the name of Korah is omitted out of consideration for the Korahites, who ministered in the tabernacle and temple services. Korah was a cousin of Moses, and a Levite. In league with these three men there were 250 princes of the people, men of renown. They accused Moses and Aaron of taking too much upon them and thinking themselves to be above the rest of the congregation. Moses called upon them to come to him and talk and allow the Lord to decide. They stubbornly refused. Jehovah did intervene on behalf of His appointed leaders Moses and Aaron and there was a severe judgment. It was not, as Moses said, "the common death of all men". The earth opened her mouth and swallowed them up. Korah, Dathan, and Abiram, the chief rebels, went down alive into the pit and an accompanying fire from the Lord consumed the 250 conspirators who offered incense. There is a salutary lesson here, and a solemn warning to believers about discontent with God's way and rebellion against divinely approved leadership among the saints.

Verses 19-23: Idolatry - The Golden Calf

It is almost incomprehensible that a people so privileged as Israel was should so soon turn to idolatry. Jehovah had delivered them from their slavery, and He was, even then, expressing His desire that they should make Him a sanctuary so that He might dwell among them (Ex 25.8). How early did they break His first basic commandment, "Thou shalt have no other gods before me" (Ex 20.3). Jehovah had a right to demand this from them, saying, "I am the Lord thy God which have brought thee out of the land of Egypt, out of the house of bondage", but, the Psalmist recalls, "They made a calf in Horeb, and worshipped the molten image". Horeb! Sinai! The very place where Jehovah had given such manifestations of His power. Moses never forgot this terrible sin, and he recalls the story of it in his final, lengthy address to the nation (Deut 9.8-21). They exchanged their glory, the glory of the God of Israel, for the likeness of an ox that eats grass. How foolish, and how utterly sad. Their father Abraham had been called out of idolatry by a sight of the God of glory. Were the children of that noble patriarch now going back to that form of things which their forefather had abandoned? Were they lusting, not only after the food of Egypt, but after the gods of Egypt too? "They forgat God their saviour". They forgot Him, and the great things He had done in Egypt. They danced around that molten calf singing, "These be thy gods, O Israel, which brought thee up out of the land of Egypt" (Ex 32.4, 8).

Jehovah was a jealous God (Ex 20.5), and He was righteously angry. He would have consumed them in His wrath. What wonders He had wrought in Egypt, the land of Ham, what terrible things by the Red Sea, yet now they were forsaking Him. Moses was angry too, "His anger waxed hot" (Ex 32.19). He was angry with the people and particularly angry with his brother Aaron. Three thousand people perished as a result of this sin (Ex 32.28), a sin which is laid especially to the charge of Aaron. It was, "The calf, which Aaron made" (Ex 32.35). Moses, however, angry though he was, stood in the breach, between an offended God and an offending people.

He was a mediator and an intercessor, pleading with God on their behalf, magnanimously offering himself for judgment instead of them, if only God would spare them and turn back His wrath. As Moses said, "Oh, this people have sinned a great sin, and have made them gods of gold". Jehovah did spare them any more wrath at that time, but added, "Nevertheless, in the day when I visit I will visit their sin upon them" (Ex 32.31-34). Spurgeon cites John Trapp who writes, "Although some of the Rabbins would excuse this gross idolatry of their forefathers, yet others more wise bewail them, and say that there is an ounce of this golden calf in all their present sufferings".

Verses 24-27: Despising the Promised Land

In Numbers 13 Moses sent out twelve spies, representatives of the twelve tribes, to search Canaan, the land of promise. This was at Jehovah's command, to prove to the people the beauty and the fruitfulness of the land which He had for them. The spies went out from Kadesh-barnea in the Wilderness of Paran, by the way of Hebron to the Valley of Eshcol. It was the time of first ripe grapes. For forty days these men searched the land, returning to the people with a cluster of grapes which had to be carried on a staff between two of them. There were, too, pomegranates and figs (Num 13.17-25), all evidences of a land which "floweth with milk and honey". Nevertheless, according to ten of these men, there were problems. There were walled cities there, and men of great stature, giant sons of Anak. "We are well able to overcome it", said Caleb, "let us go up at once and possess it". Joshua supported Caleb in this, while the others lamented, "We are not able...we were like grasshoppers in their sight" (Num 13.28-33). Unbelief prevailed. The people murmured in their tents. They believed not. "Yea, they despised the pleasant land". It was, indeed, a pleasant (2532) land, goodly and desirable, but they were to lose it because of their unbelief. O the sin of unbelief!

Sadly too, they not only despised this land of promise, but even spoke of electing a captain to lead them back to Egypt. Yet again Jehovah was sorely grieved with them, "How long will this people provoke me? and how long will it be ere they believe me? (Num 14.11). "I will smite them", He said, "...and disinherit them". Again Moses pleaded for them. Jehovah was longsuffering and of great mercy. "Pardon them", he appealed, and, once again, Jehovah spared them, but vowed that because of their unbelief they would never enter the land. They had forfeited all rights to it, except for Caleb and Joshua, and the little ones who had no part in the unbelief. For the rest, their carcasses would fall in the wilderness. There was, too, a far-reaching effect of their unbelief. He would scatter their seed, their descendents, among the nations. That sad word is now so familiar in the history and in the vocabulary of Israel; "diaspora", dispersion, scattered indeed, so many times since the day that they despised that pleasant land.

Verses 28-31: The Iniquity of Baal-peor

Balak, king of the Moabites, had become concerned about the increasing greatness of the children of Israel and he determined to destroy them. He called in the services of Balaam, often referred to as the false prophet, offering him great reward if he would curse Israel. After several attempts, one of these from the top of Mount Peor, which may be identified with Pisgah, Balaam found it impossible to curse those whom God had blessed. The deity worshipped by the Moabites at Peor was known as Baal of Peor. This worship was accompanied by the most corrupt and immoral practices.

The attempts to curse the people of Israel having failed, Balaam had another strategy. He taught Balak to stumble Israel by an intermingling of Israelites with Moabites. Balaam is afterwards remembered for this iniquitous advice by the NT writers Peter and Jude, as well as by Hosea the prophet, and by the Lord Himself writing to the church at Pergamos (Hos 9.10; 2 Peter 2.15; Jude v.11; Rev 2.14). But the iniquity was Israel's as much as Baalam's. They should have known better, but they joined themselves to Baal of Peor, fellowshipping in the sacrifices offered to dead idols, the lifeless gods of the heathen. They "joined themselves" (6775). This may indicate that they were initiated into the mysteries and orgies which were connected with Baal worship. They committed a fornication which was not only physical, but moral and spiritual as well, corrupting God's chosen nation and spoiling that necessary line of demarcation between them and the nations.

Yet once more they had provoked God. He sent a plague among them until the javelin of Phinehas was wielded in judgment. This stayed the plague, but not before 24,000 of the people had died. Phinehas, a son of Aaron, was blessed of God for his zeal. The tribute to him is, "He was zealous for his God", and, for his valour, his future was assured with that of his children after him (Num 25.10-13). His courageous action was counted to him for righteousness, which blessing was to continue in his generations. He was later to be involved in the slaying of Balaam (Num 31.6-8).

Verses 32-33: The Waters of Meribah

Yet once again the people angered the Lord. What a privileged people they were, and what great things Jehovah had planned for them when He brought them out of Egypt. "I bare you on eagles' wings", He had said, "and brought you unto myself. Now therefore, if ye will obey my voice indeed, and keep my covenant, then ye shall be a peculiar treasure unto me above all people...And ye shall be unto me a kingdom of priests, and an holy nation" (Ex 19.4-6). But how they had grieved Him, provoked Him, angered Him, and still He remained faithful to them in spite of all the provocation.

The waters of strife (4808) of v.32 in the Psalm, have become known as "the waters of Meribah", as in Exodus 17.7, and so the word is actually rendered in the text of JND, RV, JPS, and others. The name "Meribah" means "strife or contention". There are similarities between the two events of Exodus 17 and Numbers 20. As Spurgeon says, "The scene changes but the sin continues". In both cases there was murmuring and chiding, which was a symptom of their unbelief when simple trust in Jehovah would have honoured Him and met their need. "They angered him", says the Psalmist, and not only did they anger the Lord, but Moses, too, was sorely provoked yet another time by them.

The RV rendering is that "they were rebellious against his spirit". The JPS version is "they embittered his spirit". Some understand this as an allusion to the Spirit of God. Others see it as the spirit of Moses, provoked and embittered by the incessant grumbling of the people, and their constant blaming of him for their difficulties. Perhaps both things are true. Moses, because of them, seems to have erred in two matters. First, he called the people rebels (Num 20.10). Maybe they were indeed rebels, but it was not right for Moses to say so in his anger. "He spake unadvisedly with his lips" (v.33). Second, although not referred to in the Psalm, he smote the rock, indeed he smote it twice, when the divine instruction had been, "Speak ye unto the rock...and it shall give forth his water" (Num 20.8). Perhaps unwittingly, and certainly unintentionally, he had spoiled a beautiful type by his disobedience. The rock had already been smitten, on that former occasion in Exodus 17. It must not be smitten again. The Redeemer has been smitten once, never to suffer again. It is now sufficient that men speak to Him in their need. The type was spoiled by the angry disobedience of this otherwise meek man, wearied to breaking point by their unbelief and complaining.

"It went ill with Moses", says the Psalmist. Indeed he paid a high price for his anger and his disobedience. He forfeited the privilege of leading the people into the Promised Land, and it cost him, too, his own exclusion from it. True, he was permitted to stand on Mount Nebo and view the land, but even then he was reminded of the word of the Lord, "Thou shalt see the land before thee; but thou shalt not go thither unto the land which I give unto the children of Israel" (Deut 32.48-52).

Verses 34-46: Disobedience and its Consequence in Canaan

It might have been expected that a people so blessed of the Lord as they had been, would have been diligent now to obey Him. Already, in their wilderness journey to Canaan, they had known His unfailing protection and provision, but they had also seen His anger at their murmurings and unbelief. Yet, even now, having entered the land of promise, there was early disobedience. Jehovah had given them specific instructions concerning the Canaanites. They were to be utterly destroyed without mercy. There was to be no intermingling with them. There were to be no marriages with their sons and daughters. The images, altars, and groves of Canaan were to be burned with fire. Israel had been chosen of

God to be a special people. They must maintain separation from the heathen, and remain a people sanctified to the God who had redeemed them (Deut 7.1-6).

Regretfully, they disobeyed on all counts. They did not destroy the nations of Canaan as they had been commanded. Carnal, fleshly reasoning told them that these people could become tributaries to them, and so they spared them (Judg 1.21, 27-33). It was however, as Jehovah had warned them. It led to intermingling by marriage, to a forsaking of the God who brought them out of Egypt, and to idolatry. The idol worship of the Canaanites was, in fact, the worship of demons, associated with the abominable practice of human sacrifice. How far away had these people got, who had been delivered again and again by the hand of the Lord, that now they should be sacrificing their children to demons as the heathen did. "Why have ye done this?", Jehovah laments in Judges 2.2. The fair land was polluted with blood. The people were defiled by their own works. It was blatant infidelity. It was immoral. It was a breach of their covenant relationship with Jehovah, like a wife unfaithful to her husband.

Their disobedience was certain to bring judgment. "The wrath of the Lord (was) kindled against his people". These sad and solemn words recur frequently in the Book of Judges (see Judg 2.14, 20; 3.8). Perhaps even more sad is that word, "He abhorred his own inheritance". How they grieved Him. In chastisement He gave them into the hands of the heathen, allowing them to oppress them and rule over them. It was a heavy price for their disobedience, and yet, again and again, when they cried to Him, God delivered them. He delivered them by Othniel (Judg 3.9), by Ehud (Judg 3.15), by Shamgar (Judg 3.31). Then by Deborah and Barak (Judg 4.4-24), by Gideon (Judg 6.11-14), by Jephthah (Judg 11.6-11), by Samson (Judg 15.9-20), and later by David and others. Repeatedly they provoked the Lord, and still when they called He heard them and came to their aid. By their own iniquity they were brought low (4355), humiliated, but He saw their distress, He regarded their affliction, He heard their cries, just as He had heard their groaning in Egypt. He remembered the covenant which He had made with their fathers, and, in faithfulness to His covenant, He preserved them. They were, though so often rebellious, His covenant people, and as often as they disobeyed Him and tried Him, just as often did He deliver them out of their troubles.

He "repented according to the multitude of his mercies". As has already been observed in Psalm 90.13, this word "repent" (5162) does not mean that Jehovah changed His mind, as in the common usage of the word. The word is from a root meaning "comfort, consolation, compassion". It may mean "regret", in the sense that the death of a friend or loved one might be "deeply regretted". This is touching, that in spite of the continuing disloyalty of the people, Jehovah would console and comfort them. In the multitude of His mercies (2617), His lovingkindness and compassion for them was unfailing. He made them to be objects of pity, so that, in their humiliation, their captors at times looked upon them with a pitiful disdain, rather than see them as a threat. Compare this with that request in Solomon's prayer at the dedication of the temple (1 Kings 8.50).

Verses 47-48: Final Prayer and Thanksgiving

The sad Psalm concludes with a prayer for the salvation and preservation of the nation. The prayer is addressed to "The LORD (3068) our God (430)", Jehovah our Elohim. Although they had so sorely and so often provoked Him and grieved Him, yet still He was the Almighty, All-sufficient, Eternal Jehovah. They knew this, and the Psalmist's appeal is to Him. This is the culmination of a long confession of national sin, and the Psalmist has a noble motive in praying for national restoration. "Gather us from among the nations", he prays, "that we may give thanks...that we may praise". He is actually asking for that which Jehovah had always intended for them, that they should be kept together, distinct from the surrounding heathen nations, a people singing His praise and glorying in His great name. This may well be a prayer for recovery from many a "diaspora", a dispersion, of later days.

This Jehovah Elohim is the God of Israel. As He Himself is from everlasting to everlasting, so should His praise be also, from eternity and to eternity. As His mercy endureth for ever, so likewise should the adoration of His people know no end. If the God of Israel has blessed His people, then so should His people bless Him. Now let all the people join in a triumphant "Amen"! So be it! Hallelujah! Praise ye the LORD (3050)! Praise ye Jah! On this high note the Fourth Book of the Psalms concludes.

This concludes Book 4 of the Psalms

BOOK 5

PSALM 107

Introduction

This untitled Psalm is the first Psalm in the Fifth Book of the Psalter. Although the boundary of the Fourth and Fifth Book lies between, nevertheless there is a close affinity and connection with the two preceding Psalms 105 and 106. As Delitzsch writes, "These three anonymous Psalms form a trilogy in the strictest sense; they are a tripartite whole from the hand of one author". He adds that "The observation is an old one" and in confirmation of this latter comment he quotes from a German translation of the Psalms, *Harpffe Davids mit Teutschen Saiten bespannet,* (Harp of David strung with German Strings), which appeared in Augsburg in the year 1659. The relation of the three Psalms to each other becomes obvious with a careful comparison. They recount the history of God's dealings with the children of Israel from their redemption out of Egypt, through the wilderness journey and into the Promised Land.

Each of these Psalms, however, tells the story from a different aspect. Psalm 105 emphasises the faithfulness of God during that sojourn, with scarcely a mention of the failures of the people. Psalm 106 is a sad record of those failures, of the murmuring and unbelief of the nation, in spite of the constant care of God for them. Psalm 107 is a Psalm of thanksgiving, in which the refrain, "O that men would praise the Lord for his goodness, and for his wonderful works to the children of men!" occurs four times (vv. 8, 15, 21, 31). The recurrence of this refrain does not necessarily create an orderly division of the Psalm but it is interesting to note that each time it does appear, it is the penultimate verse in that particular section. It is always followed by a single verse which gives either the reason for praise, or an exhortation to praise. After an opening call for thanksgiving the Psalmist paints four word-pictures of the nation, showing also Jehovah's deliverance of them in a four-fold way. He first views them as travellers, lost in the desert, then as prisoners, bound in chains. He then sees them as men who are sick, near to death, and after this they are likened to mariners in a storm. The closing sections have to do with judgment and blessing, and one verse makes a final appeal to the wise. The divisions of the verses are as follows, as indicated in the texts of the RV and JND translations.

Verses 1-3 are a call from the Psalmist to the redeemed of the Lord to join him in thanksgiving. In verses 4-9 the people are seen as wanderers in the wilderness, faint with hunger, and thirsty. Verses 10-16 describe the same people as prisoners, sitting in darkness and affliction. In verses 17-22 they are regarded as sick men, drawing near to death and crying for healing. In verses 23-32 the picture is of sailors at their wits' end in a storm. Notice that in each of these cases "They cried unto the Lord in their trouble", and each time "He delivered them out of their distresses" (vv. 6, 13, 19, 28). Verses 33-42 tell of divine judgment upon the wicked and of blessing for the righteous, and the closing verse 43 simply states that the wise will give heed to these things and consider.

Verses 1-3: O Give Thanks unto the Lord

These opening words, "O give thanks (3034) unto the LORD" (3038), are a fitting sequel to the closing "Hallelujah" of Psalm 106, for these too are a call to praise, to laud Jehovah. These words are also an exact repetition of the opening words of Psalm 106, which again establishes that close connection between the Psalms which has been mentioned in the introduction. The reason for such thanksgiving is very simple, and yet profound, "He is good". This goodness is the very nature and essence of God, but manifested in goodness to His people, "Thou art good, and doest good" (Ps 119.68). "He is good!" Spurgeon quotes Andrew Bonar who asks, "Is not this the Old Testament version of 'God is love' (1 Jn 4.8)?". In "His mercy *endureth* forever", notice that the word "endureth" is italicised, indicating that it has been supplied, no doubt correctly, by the translators. Literally however, it may read, "His lovingkindness – forever!".

The Psalmist appeals to "the redeemed of the Lord" to join him in his praise of Jehovah. "Redeemed of the Lord" they certainly were. He had delivered them from Egypt's slavery and from Pharaoh's tyranny, and on that day of the great exodus from the house of bondage they had sung, "Thou in thy mercy hast led forth the people which thou hast redeemed" (Ex 15.13). Again and again throughout the wilderness journey, Jehovah had been their Redeemer from many a trouble. It was most fitting that they should share in the Psalmist's thanksgiving. In another day, yet future, men will again call them, "The holy people, The redeemed of the Lord" (Is 62.12).

Jehovah has not only brought His people out but He has led them on and gathered them together from every land. If, as many think, this Psalm belongs to a later date than David, then this is a reference to the restoration and regathering of Israel after the captivity and exile. A vital objection to this interpretation is that that restoration was not really from east, west, north, and south, but from Assyria and Babylon only. However, as J.G. Murphy suggests, "Identifying Abraham with his seed, we can see that they occupied many lands before their final settlement. Abraham was called from Ur of the Chaldees, which was east of Palestine; he entered the land of Kanaan (sic) from Padan-aram, which was north; Israel was delivered from Egypt, which lies to the west of south Palestine; and he was brought in or finally gathered from the Sinaitic peninsula or the arms of the Red Sea, which was south". This is in agreement too, with the JND and JPS renderings of v.3, which read "from the sea" instead of "from the south".

So that, when eventually Jehovah brought His redeemed people to the land of promise, He had brought them literally out of the lands of the east, of the west, of the north and of the south. Perhaps indeed there may also be a prophetic note here, a foreshadowing of that millennial day, when, from every land, Jehovah will bring His people to Zion in a great national unity. Redeemed and gathered! There was much cause for thanksgiving. This, then, is the introductory call in the Psalm for praise from the redeemed of the Lord.

Verses 4-9: Wanderers in the Wilderness

The picture is of weary travellers in a desert, hungry, thirsty, and faint with the journey. For forty years these people had wandered in the wilderness. "Wandered" is a sad word (8582). Strong says it means "To wander about; to go astray; to stagger as a drunkard". Dr Cohen writes, "*They wandered*. The verb denotes wandering about aimlessly…In English the paraphrase would be, 'travellers went astray'". The wilderness story is rehearsed in Psalms 105 and 106. They missed their way, these travellers. It was desert, with no tracks or cities or habitations, and as they had persisted in unbelief and mistrust, a journey which might have been completed in a matter of days (Deut 1.2) actually extended to four long decades of wandering. Jehovah satisfied their hunger with manna and their thirst with water from the rock. Still they forsook Him who would have been their Guide through the trackless desert to the Promised Land.

Then they cried to Him in their trouble, and He delivered them out of their distresses. When they had a will to follow He led them by the right way toward the establishment of a city of habitation, a dwelling place of His providing. This phrase "a city of habitation" is used (in the original Hebrew) in vv. 4, 7 and 36. They "looked for a city" (Heb 11.10) and He "prepared for them a city" (Heb 11.16).

The Psalmist bursts forth into praise with that refrain which, as has been noted, occurs four times in the Psalm, "Oh that men would praise the Lord for his goodness, and for his wonderful works to the children of men!". It is an exclamation! Is there an implication that men do not praise Him as and when they should? Oh that they would! "Goodness" (2617) has been variously rendered as "mercy; lovingkindness; faithfulness". The goodness of God reveals itself in these many different ways, and so it was with His people in the wilderness. Kirkpatrick makes the point that "men" is in italics, and has been incorrectly supplied by the translators. He explains, "The AV obliterates the connexion of the refrain with the doxology of v.1, and gives it a wrong turn by generalising its exhortation ('Oh that *men* would praise the Lord'). Here, and again in vv. 15, 21, 31, the subject of the verb is the men whose deliverance has just been described." Had they been weary, thirsty, and hungry? He had satisfied their longings and had filled the hungry with goodness. Oh that they would praise Him! "Goodness" (2896) in v.9 is a different word from that in the preceding verse. Here it means "good things; benefits; bounty". To quote Kirkpatrick again, "The words refer to the particular case of those who were perishing with hunger and thirst, and do not, primarily at any rate, express a general truth, as the AV suggests".

Verses 10-16: Prisoners in the Dungeon

The metaphor now changes. The wanderers in the wilderness are now viewed as prisoners in the dungeon. They sit in depressing darkness, in the shadow of death, bound in affliction and iron. The tragedy is that they have brought this upon themselves. They rebelled against the words of their God when He desired only their welfare. They despised His counsel when He would have blessed them. Note, "The words of God" (410), El, and, "The counsel of the Most High" (5945), Elyon. These are ancient titles, used by Melchizedek when blessing Abraham their forefather (Gen 14.19-20). "Blessed be Abram of El Elyon, the Most High God".

Because they rebelled, and despised Him, therefore He humbled them. He brought down their heart with travail. He subdued them with suffering and chastisement. He brought them into subjection to Him and they stumbled and fell with none to help. They were brought to an end of themselves, and then, as in v.6, "they cried unto the Lord in their trouble". He heard them. He saved them out of their distresses. He delivered them out of the darkness and the death-shade. He emancipated them, breaking the fetters that bound them. "Let them give thanks unto Jehovah for his loving-kindness"(JND). Neither gates of bronze nor bars of iron can hold His people when He chooses to deliver. He shattered the gates and sundered the bars and liberated the captives. He would always have blessed them and protected them, if only they had not rebelled against Him and despised Him. His chastisement of them had their recovery to Him in view. This was an experience repeated again and again during that wilderness journey. Now let them praise Him for His goodness.

Verses 17-22: Sick Men at the Gates of Death

Again the scene changes. The people who were seen as wanderers in the wilderness and as prisoners in the dungeon, are now regarded as men sick and lying at the very gates of death. They are the same people, their sad plight viewed from different aspects. What fools (191) they had been, perverse, despising wisdom and mocking the word of counsel. It was their own foolishness and their transgressions which had brought upon them the present affliction. Indeed, some commentators suggest that the form of the verb "afflicted" may signify "afflicted themselves", meaning that they brought sufferings upon themselves by their folly (Dr Cohen; T.W. Davies; A.F. Kirkpatrick). Their sickness was apparently God's chastisement for their iniquity, and how severely they had been smitten. They lost all appetite for food, a common symptom in those who are very sick. They lay helpless at the gates of death. Two things are implied in the expression "the gates of death". This is the very entrance to death and to the unseen world. How near to dying is a man at the gates of death. As is often said, "They were at death's door". But "gates" also imply authority and power as the "gates of brass" in v.16. The gates of a walled city had power to admit a man to the city, or bar a man from that city. The phrase is found again in Psalm 9.13, and the Saviour used a similar metaphor in Matthew 16.18.

Once again, as in vv. 6 and 13, when all human hope and help had failed, "Then they cry unto the Lord in their trouble". Does trouble bring at least this advantage with it, that it sends men to their God for help? They cried to Him in their extremity and, yet again, "he saved them out of their distresses". By His word He healed them. He snatched them from the gates of death. He saved them from destruction. Then comes the now familiar refrain of vv. 8 and 15, "Oh that men would praise the Lord for His goodness", or, as JND and others, "Let them give thanks unto Jehovah for His lovingkindness".

Note, however, that in these earlier occurrences of the refrain the verses which follow give a reason for the thanksgiving, but now the verse which follows rather amplifies the refrain; "Let them sacrifice the sacrifices of thanksgiving". These sacrifices were a form of peace offering, as in Leviticus 7.12. Such an offering was the sacrifice of a man in communion with God, a man at peace, and the very bringing of the sacrifice of thanksgiving was a declaration, a testimony, that God had signally blessed the offerer. He would bring his sacrifice with rejoicing, and, being a peace offering, a fellowship offering, others would share his joy with him.

Verses 23-32: Mariners in a Storm

Again the scene changes. Wanderers in the wilderness! Prisoners in the dungeon! Sick men at the gates of death! Now they are likened to mariners caught in a storm. It is the privilege of the sea voyager to behold the works of the Lord, to see His power in creation. As they traverse the sea in ships they must often see what other men do not see. They do business in great waters and as they travel they witness Jehovah's wonders (6381) in the deep. At first hand they see divine power controlling the billows which are beyond the power of man. The thoughtful mariner must often marvel at the excelling greatness of Him who created the great waters upon which their puny ships ply their trade. Then comes the storm! The Psalmist's description of the storm is sublime. Dr Cohen quotes Joseph Addison, who writes, "As I have made several voyages upon the sea, I have often been tossed in storms, and on that occasion have frequently reflected on the descriptions of them in ancient poems...I prefer the following description of a ship in a storm, which the Psalmist has made, before any other I have met with".

At the command of the Lord the winds blow and the waves rise and fall. With this rising and falling of the billows, the seafarers seem to be carried up into the heavens and as suddenly cast down to the depths. In fear their very souls melt within them. They lose all courage. They reel to and fro on deck, staggering like drunken men. They are at their wits' end. All their navigation skills have failed them. No wisdom of the mariner can avail in such a storm. It is then, when all else fails, that "They cried unto the Lord in their trouble". Kirkpatrick quotes a Basque proverb, "Let him who knows not how to pray go to sea!". As with the lost traveller, and the prisoner in bonds, and the sick men near to death, human helplessness drives men to God in prayer. In great grace He hears their cry. "He maketh the storm a calm, so that the waves thereof are still". How perfectly is all this illustrated in that well-known story told by Matthew, Mark, and Luke (Mt 8.23-27; Mk 4.37-41; Lk 8.22-25). The Galilean Lake was in a storm! Experienced fishermen though they were, it was too much for them, and they cried to the Master for help. When He says, "Peace, be still", then the winds and the sea must obey Him. Perowne's translation is very beautiful; "He husheth the storm to a gentle air". The fearful mariners are now glad as the waves are quietened, and "he bringeth them unto their desired haven". The Lord still calms storms in the lives of His people. Indeed, Perowne, already cited, thinks that perhaps even more than being historical, "This Psalm describes various incidents of human life, it tells of the perils which befall men, and the goodness of God in delivering them, and calls upon all who have experienced His care and protection gratefully to acknowledge them". He adds that the Psalm "is perfectly general in its character. The four (or five) groups, or pictures, are so many samples taken from the broad and varied record of human experience".

The deliverance from distress is again an occasion for thanksgiving and so the familiar refrain is repeated. "Oh that men would praise the Lord for his goodness, and for his wonderful works to the children of men". As with the earlier occurrences of the refrain, so again it is followed by an added exhortation. The praise is to be a public exaltation of the Lord, "Let them exalt him". Whether it is in the congregation of the people or in the assembly of the elders, it is public praise. "In the congregation of the people" would suggest praises in the temple, when the people would be gathered and when appropriate Psalms would be sung. "In the assembly (or seat, 4186) of the elders", refers to those meetings of the ruling council of the nation. Both people in general and rulers in particular are called upon to exalt the Lord for His goodness.

Verses 33-42: Judgment or Blessing

In His impartiality and in His providential government of Israel and of the nations, Jehovah can choose either to judge or to bless. He can turn rivers into a wilderness or He can turn a wilderness into a pool of water. He can turn watersprings into a dry thirsty land or He can turn dry ground into watersprings. For the wickedness of men He can turn a fruitful land into barrenness (4420), a plain of salt. Of course His desire would be rather to bless men, to give them a place where the hungry could dwell and be satisfied, where they could sow and plant and reap. Vineyards and fruits in plenty He would provide for them. He would multiply their harvests and increase their flocks.

At times, however, troubles may come. Such prosperity would doubtless excite the envy and hostility of neighbouring peoples and there would be attacks and oppression. As Kirkpatrick comments, "The Psalmist is following the fortunes of those whom Jehovah has blessed with prosperity. Temporary reverses may happen to them, but He will not fail them". He can pour His contempt upon princes who oppress His people. He can bring them low while He lifts His people on high, safe from the affliction. He can make the enemies wander as if lost in a wilderness, while His own dwell safely in families, and as His flock. The righteous will see what He has done, and rejoice, while the mouths of iniquitous men are closed.

Verse 43: The Wisdom of the Wise

Men who are wise should not fail to observe, and learn from, the ways of God. This Psalm demonstrates His grace and His goodness, His delight to bless and deliver His beleaguered people. Yet there is also His hatred of unbelief and disobedience, and His readiness to chastise to effect restoration. His power is seen in the Psalm too, His greatness and His glory. Wisdom will note these various manifestations and revelations of the Lord, and thereby better appreciate and understand the lovingkindness which He shows toward His people. Perowne thinks that this closing verse is in the form of a question, "Who is wise?". He compares this with that almost identical question with which the prophet Hosea closes his prophecy, "Who is wise, and he shall understand these things? prudent, and he shall know them?". Psalmist and prophet have the same desire for the Lord's people, a wisdom which gives heed to the ways of God and determines to walk in them.

PSALM 108

Introduction

This little Psalm is entitled "A Song (7892) or Psalm (4210) of David". A number of other Psalms are also called "Songs", the first of these being Psalm 30. It is believed that a "Psalm" was always sung with a musical accompaniment, whereas a "Song" might be sung with the voice only. When both terms are used in the title this may signify that the Psalm can be suitably rendered either with or without accompaniment.

This Psalm is in two parts, as often indicated in the text of the AV and most other translations, and these two parts are, with slight variations, repetitions of parts of two previous Psalms. Verses 1-5 are found in Psalm 57.7-11 and verses 6-13 are from Psalm 60.5-12. The reader may wish to refer to the commentary on these two Psalms, but, as Spurgeon quaintly and wisely comments, "We cannot find it in our hearts to dismiss this Psalm by merely referring the reader first to Psalm 57.7-11 and then to Psalm 60.5-12, though it will be seen that those two portions of Scripture are almost identical with the verses before us. It is true that most of the commentators have done so, and we are not so presumptuous as to dispute their wisdom, but we hold for ourselves that the words would not have been repeated if there had not been an object for so doing...the repetition cannot be meant merely to fill the book: there must be some intention in the arrangement of two former divine utterances in a new connection; whether we can discover that intent is another matter. It is at least ours to endeavour to do so".

It is hardly likely that David himself would have created a new Psalm by such a combination as this. To quote Delitzsch, "That a poet like David would thus compile a third out of two of his own songs is not conceivable". So there seems to be general agreement among expositors that the composition was a later arrangement for liturgical use in temple worship. There may have been some special circumstances which inspired this arrangement, which cannot now be determined, except that there is both thanksgiving and prayer in relation to confrontations with enemy nations. The Psalm would have been most appropriate for the returning exiles when under threat from their adversaries. As Kirkpatrick writes, "The old words of promise and prayer with their historical associations were adapted to new needs. Jehovah had restored His people to their home; thanksgiving for this proof of His lovingkindness and truth was their first duty: but they were exposed to the attacks of envious and malicious neighbours, and His aid was needed to maintain them in secure possession of the land".

The two parts of the Psalm provide a sufficient division of the thirteen verses. The first part, verses 1-5, is composed of praise and thanksgiving. The second part, verses 6-13, is a prayer of those in danger.

Verses 1-5: Thanksgiving and Praise

"O God, my heart is fixed". This expression occurs twice in Psalm 57.7, from which these verses are drawn. Some repetition may be vain, as the Lord Jesus Himself taught in Matthew 6.7. Such "vain repetitions" were the habit of the heathen, thinking that they would be heard by their much asking. But repetition may also be a sincere and earnest emphasis of the feelings of the heart, and so it was with David. In a changing world and in all the vicissitudes of life, his heart was steadfast. "I will sing" (7891), he exclaims, "and give praise" (2167). With voice and harp he would sing and play in praise of God. He would call upon his glory (3519) to engage in this noble exercise, meaning that all his faculties, his powers, his intellect, his dignity, his very soul, must be employed in praise of God. In Psalm 57 he had called upon his glory to awake, and now, as then, he calls upon his psaltery and harp to awake. These were perhaps two forms of harp, lute, or lyre. If this Psalm was sung by the returning exiles, how especially fitting it was for them, those whose harps had been silent for so long, hung on the willows by the rivers of Babylon in mourning (Ps 137.2). How joyously would they sing with David, "Awake, psaltery and harp"! As for David himself, "I...will awake early", he says. "I myself will awake right early", says the RV, but the marginal reading, with JND's rendering, is very beautiful, "I will awake the dawn". Usually it is the dawn which awakes men, but here it is the Psalmist who awakes the dawn with his praises.

The first notable difference from the corresponding verses in Psalm 57 now appears in v.3, where Jehovah (3068) takes the place of Adonai (136). "I will praise thee, O LORD". Adonai was, as Strong indicates, the Lord-title sometimes used instead of Jehovah in a Jewish display of reverence. The difference is noted in the AV text by the use of capitals, LORD, when the title is Jehovah, but again, this latter title would have a special significance for those who returned from Babylon. Jehovah it was, who had initially brought them out of Egypt, who had also now wrought their return from captivity and from their long exile. To Him they would give thanks among all peoples. Since the word "people" (5971) is plural here in v.3, but is not the Hebrew word "goyim" which is usually employed to describe foreign nations, the Psalmist may be using "peoples" to include his own nation among all nations. Then he mentions "nations" (3816) using yet another word. He may simply be emphasising that among people everywhere, his own people and all other people, he will praise the Lord.

David now gives his reasons for the praise which he offers. God's mercy and truth have been great. They are immeasurable, great above the heavens and reaching to the clouds. Apart from a slight change of one preposition, v.4 of the Psalm is a repeat of Psalm 57.10. There God's mercy is said to be "unto the heavens", and here it is "above the heavens". Dr Cohen quotes the Talmud which, he says, "explains the variation thus: The Divine mercy is great *above* the heavens to those who perform God's commands for their own sake, but *unto* the heavens to those who are obedient from an ulterior motive".

That God should be exalted was ever the sincere desire of David, the man after God's own heart. In spite of personal and national failures he sought always the glory of God. "Be thou exalted", he exclaims. "Exalt Thyself", Kirkpatrick prefers. In Psalm 57 this verse is a repeated refrain, as in vv. 5 and 11 there. Of course it is true that God is at all times exalted in majesty, but what the Psalmist now desires is that God should manifest Himself as the exalted One, supreme above the earth in His glory. If this is so, and it is, then this closing verse of the first section of the Psalm is a most fitting prelude to the prayer which follows. To such an One, excelling above all others in glory, the Psalmist and his people can resort with confidence, assured of His power to deliver them from their adversaries.

Verses 6-13: Prayer in Danger

As has already been noted, this second portion of Psalm 108 is a repetition, with but a few slight variations, of Psalm 60.5-12. David appeals to Jehovah for the deliverance of His beloved. "Beloved" is a plural word, "beloved ones". This is touching, that he should plead for their salvation on the grounds that they are God's beloved ones. He prays that God might hear, and answer, and manifest His right hand for them. The right hand is the emblem of power and authority. The appeal is that He who is exalted in glory above all the earth might demonstrate that power on behalf of those whom He loves. Another appeal is to the holiness of God. Being essentially holy He will always fulfil what He has promised. He has spoken, and it is impossible that He should break His word. Those whom He loves may safely rest on His promises.

There now follows, in vv. 7-9, the substance of that oracle, that word of Jehovah. There are references to the territories of Shechem, Succoth, Gilead, Manasseh, Ephraim and Judah, as well as to those adversaries of Israel, Moab, Edom and Philistia. These were representative of lands east and west of the Jordan. Perhaps Kirkpatrick summarises it well, and he is worth quoting in full. He writes, "Shechem, as a central place of importance, represents the territory west of the Jordan; Succoth, 'in the vale' (Josh 13.27) somewhere to the south of the Jabbok, between Peniel and the Jordan, represents the territory east of the Jordan. These two places in particular may be named because of their connexion with the history of Jacob, who halted first at Succoth and then at Shechem, when he returned to Canaan (Gen 33.17, 18). God will fulfil His promise to Jacob, apportioning to His people the land in which their great ancestor settled".

He continues, "Gilead and Manasseh, i.e. the land of Bashan in which half the tribe of Manasseh settled, stand for the territory east of the Jordan and the tribes settled there: Ephraim and Judah stand for the tribes west of the Jordan. God claims all as His own: therefore all can claim God's protection". As has been mentioned in the commentary on Psalm 60, Ephraim is compared to the helmet and the strength of the warrior, and Judah to the sceptre and sovereignty of the ruler and law-giver.

As for Moab, Edom, and Philistia, these proud, haughty, arrogant enemies of God's people, He will suitably humble them. Moab will be no more than a washpot, a basin in which the victorious warrior might wash his feet on his return from the battle. Edom will be like the slave to whom the warrior might throw his sandals. Over Philistia Jehovah will triumph, or, as JND and RV, "Over Philistia will I shout aloud". It is, of course, the shout of a victor.

Now the Psalmist speaks again, as representative and ruler of the people of course. "Who will bring me into the strong city? who will lead me into Edom?" This strong, fortified city is not here identified, but it may be Sela, better known as Petra, capital city of Edom. Petra was all but inaccessible, with access only by a narrow gorge bounded on either side by steep cliffs. Who was able for this? It seemed impregnable. "Wilt not thou, O God?" he pleads. Is there some misgiving here, some hesitancy on the part of the people, as to whether God will help or not? After all, He had, in former days, cast them off. He had left them on occasions, to fight for themselves, refusing to go with their armies to the battle (Ps 60.10). But would He not now go forth with the hosts of Israel? Would He not lead them out, and lead them on to victory? "Give us help from trouble", they pray, or, "Give us help against the adversary" (RV). The strongholds of these adversaries were too mighty for them, and to whom could they look for aid, except to Jehovah? Human help was vain (7723). It was worthless. They needed divine help.

How good to see the confidence with which the Psalm closes. The people have pleaded humbly for God's assistance in their danger. They have acknowledged that in times past He had indeed cast them off. They do not complain about this, for it was justified chastisement of them. Now, as their trust in Him increases they can say, "Through God we shall do valiantly" (2428). They could, through Him, have the strength and efficiency of true men of valour. Still they recognise their own weakness and inability; it must be "through God", with His help, that they conquer. "He it is", they say, "that shall tread down our enemies". The battle might be theirs, but the victory would be His.

On this note of assurance the Psalm ends. It is, altogether, a Psalm of thanksgiving, praise, and prayer, singing much of God's mercy and truth, His glory, His holiness, and His power. Believers of every age may safely trust in Him. He is ever the same God, always faithful, never changing.

PSALM 109

Introduction

Here is another Psalm dedicated to the Chief Musician, indicating that it was to be preserved for use in the liturgy of the temple. There is no reason to query, as some do, the Davidic authorship, and many think that David may have had in mind either Doeg the Edomite, or Cush the Benjamite, or even Ahithophel. None of these is identified or can be proven. The Psalm is one of a number which are referred to as "The Imprecatory Psalms", other examples of which are Psalms 58, 69, 83 and 137. By "imprecatory" is meant that these Psalms invoke vengeance and judgment upon evil-doers, and this particular Psalm does so in a most vehement manner. In the fifteen verses 6-20 there are more than twenty such calls for vengeance. This has perplexed many readers, who, with some justification, see it as opposed to the Spirit of Christ. Much has been written by many expositors in attempts either to explain or excuse the imprecations. A few commentators have even suggested that the calls for vengeance are not the prayer of the Psalmist regarding his enemies, but rather the desires of his enemies against him. This view is not at all generally accepted, but is favoured by Dr Cohen, who writes, "It has been maintained that the maledictions are not spoken by the author against his persecutors, but express the evil wishes of the latter against the man they were hounding to death. In support of this interpretation is the fact that the adversaries are in the plural, whereas the curses are directed against a person in the singular". It must be emphasised that very few expositors accept this interpretation, regarding it as being a rather strained explanation. Perhaps the greatest argument against it is that the apostles interpreted some of these imprecations as being prophetic of Judas Iscariot (Acts 1.20).

The simplest explanation seems to be that the Psalmists lived in an old dispensation, a completely different era to that of present day believers. They did not have the full revelation of God which came by Christ, and although they were, "holy men of God", who "spake under the power of the Holy Spirit" (2 Pet 1.21, JND), yet they did not enjoy the indwelling of the Spirit of God, as do Christians of the new dispensation. Notice how the spirit of that old dispensation persisted in the Jewish minds of the early disciples of Jesus when they would have called down fire from heaven to consume those who would not receive the Saviour. This they felt justified in doing since Elijah had done the same. Jesus rebuked them, saying, "Ye know not what manner of spirit ye are of" (Lk 9.54-55). How different to the Spirit of Christ who prayed, "Father, forgive them; for they know not what they do" (Lk 23.34), and to that of His martyr Stephen, who, as the stones rained upon him, kneeled down and cried, "Lord, lay not this sin to their charge" (Acts 7.60). As Delitzsch says, "These imprecations are not appropriate in the mouth of the suffering Saviour. It is not the spirit of Zion but of Sinai which here speaks out of the mouth of David, the spirit of Elias, which, according to Luke 9.55, is not the spirit of the New Testament".

It must be remembered also, that vengeance is not revenge. David is not here speaking with a personal and carnal vindictiveness, thirsting for revenge upon his adversaries. These are not the selfish emotional outbursts of a malicious man. The enemies of David were the enemies of God and of righteousness. Evildoers were rebels against God, and the Psalmist felt vindicated in calling for judgment upon such for their evil ways. His denunciations were not just against wicked men but against wickedness itself. This was virtuous righteous anger against sin and evil.

The Psalm is essentially one long prayer which may be viewed in three parts. Verses 1-5 are a prayer of the Psalmist for protection and deliverance from his adversaries. The central part, verses 6-20, is that prayer for vengeance upon the enemy, perhaps one foe in particular, with prophetic reference to Judas Iscariot, that "son of perdition". Verses 21-31 are a renewed prayer, mingled with praise, for God's help and strength for the Psalmist in his personal weakness.

Verses 1-5: Prayer for Protection

The Psalm opens with a beautiful title of God which is unique in the Psalter, and indeed found only here in all of Holy Scripture: "O God of my praise". The previous Psalm had expressed the Psalmist's determined desire to render praise to his God. "I will sing and give praise…I will praise thee, O Lord…I will sing praises unto thee". He seems entitled, therefore, to say now, "O God of my praise". God was the object of the personal adoration of the Psalmist. This is so like the prayer of the prophet Jeremiah, "Heal me, O Lord, and I shall be healed; save me and I shall be saved; for thou art my praise" (Jer 17.14), and like that word of Moses to the people in Deuteronomy 10.21, "He is thy praise, and he is thy God". To the God of his praise the Psalmist appeals, "Hold not thy peace". David's enemies were loud and vociferous. They had opened their mouths against him with deceitful words and lying tongues. Why then should David's God be silent? Why should He not speak in vindication of His servant? "Hold not thy peace", he cries. These adversaries had surrounded him with words of hatred. They had opposed him gratuitously. There was no reason or cause for their enmity. To any love which he had tried to show them they had responded with adversity. They rewarded him evil for good and hatred for love. Indeed the word "rewarded" (7760) means that they had actually "loaded him" with evil and hatred. It was all so cruel and unjust, "But", he says, "I give myself unto prayer". David's only resort was to the God of his praise. To Him he could commit his cause. Kirkpatrick also makes the interesting observation that much of the prayer was really for his adversaries. He writes, "The parallel passage in Psalm 35.13 is decidedly in favour of supposing that his prayers for them in past times are meant, and this explanation suits the context best. To these prayers he refers as the proof of his love, the good for which they are now requiting him with evil".

Verses 6-20: Prayer for Vengeance

The Psalmist now commences a lengthy call for retribution upon his enemy, to whom all reference is now made in the singular, "he; him; his". Those who think that David has one particular foe in mind have suggested Doeg, Cush, Ahithophel, Shimei, or even Saul. It is not necessary however, to see one individual here since the singular pronoun may be used in a collective sense, embracing the totality of David's enemies. What he now asks for is that as the enemy has treated him unjustly, so the same kind of judgment may be meted out to him. Let his judge be a wicked man just like himself. As Albert Barnes expresses it, "The Psalmist asks that his foe might be subjected to having a man placed over him like himself - a man regardless of justice, truth, and right, a man who would respect character and propriety no more than he had himself done. It is, in fact, a prayer that he might be punished *in the line of his offences*. It cannot be wrong that a man should be treated as he treats others". The Psalmist prays that his enemy might be put on trial before a judge as heartless as he is, and that an unscrupulous adversary might stand at his right hand in the trial. Such is the meaning of "Satan" (7854), a malicious accuser, waiting to bring charges, even though they should be false. Let him be found guilty in the judgment and be condemned, is the Psalmist's desire, and let any prayer that he makes, whether to God or to men, whether a plea for pardon or a protest of innocence, only increase his wickedness and add to his guilt. "Let his days be few; and let another take his office" (6486). How literally was this fulfilled in the case of Judas Iscariot, the man who rewarded love with treachery. His sin brought him to a premature, suicide's death, and his place in the ministry was soon filled by another man. Whether Judas himself had a wife and children is not known. The principle here is that the effects and influence of a man's sin are far-reaching, affecting his posterity. This was the warning at the giving of the law at Sinai, "I the Lord thy God am a jealous God, visiting the iniquity of the fathers upon the children unto the third and fourth generation of them that hate me" (Ex 20.5). Peter's quotation of these verses in Acts 1.20, is from the Septuagint, L.C.L. Brenton's literal translation being, "Let his days be few: and let another take his office of overseer. Let his children be orphans, and his wife a widow. Let his children wander without a dwelling-place, and beg: let them be cast out of their habitations".

The property too, of this wicked man, is forfeit. Let his creditors snatch all that he has left. Extortioners they may be, demanding exorbitant unjust repayments for what has been borrowed. Let them, as strangers, plunder his possessions, showing neither mercy, pity, or favour to his fatherless children. Indeed, let his posterity be cut off, their name forgotten by the next generation, blotted out of all records, whether human or divine. These are sad and fearful consequences of a man's wickedness which should be considered seriously by any man who persists in evil. Then also, as Perowne says, "The curse goes backward as well as forward. The whole race of the man is involved in it; root and branch he is accursed. Not the guilt of the individual only, but the guilt of all his guilty ancestors, is to be remembered and visited on his posterity...Hupfield objects that the curse on 'the fathers' is pointless, as it could no longer reach them; but if I see rightly, the object is to heighten the effect of the curse as it falls upon *the children* mentioned in v.13". But then, though their name be blotted out, let not the sins of the parents be blotted out. Let the iniquity of fathers and mother be ever remembered by Jehovah. Is there a play upon words here? He remembered not, therefore let his iniquity be remembered. This wicked man remembered not to show kindness, therefore the Lord will remember this of him, and will then erase the memory of the family from the earth. So great is the wickedness that the poor and needy are relentlessly persecuted by him, and even the broken in heart are slain. There is no mercy.

The Psalmist continues to call for just retribution. As he loved cursing, so let this wicked man be cursed. Let it come to him as he has pronounced upon others. Since he had no pleasure in blessing others, then let blessing be far from him. He can hardly complain when being dealt with according to his own rules. If malevolence and cursing was his attitude to others, so that he wore them like a habit, then let him have it completely; let it come into his very being, like water and oil in his inwards and bones. Did he indeed wear this evil character like a garment? Let it wrap itself around him, let it envelope him; let it cling to him; let it bind him like a girdle. This punishment is, as Delitzsch says, "an earned reward. The curse is the fruit of their own choice and deed". Jehovah takes notice of the manner in which wicked men treat His servant and He will reward accordingly. To speak evil of those who are the Lord's is a sin against the Lord Himself. The adversaries of God's people are the adversaries of God. To Saul of Tarsus, persecutor of the early Christians, the word of the Lord was, "Saul, Saul, why persecutest thou me?" (Acts 9.4).

Verses 21-31: Prayer with Praise

The Psalmist now turns from his enemies to his God, from the curses of his adversaries to the lovingkindness of the Lord. What relief to say, "But…thou"! The pronoun is emphatic. Well he knows what the enemy has done to him, "But do thou for me", he says, as he appeals to One whom he now addresses as "O GOD (3069) the Lord" (136). "GOD" here, is not a usual word. It is, by JND, Perowne, and others, translated "Jehovah", but it is, as Strong points out, a slight variation of "Jehovah" (3068). "Lord" (136) is Adonai, which is, again quoting Strong, "The Lord-title often used instead of Jehovah in a Jewish display of reverence". So the Psalmist is appealing to Jehovah his Adonai, "O Jehovah my Lord". With what intelligence and dignity does he address his God. He is confident in leaving his case with God, knowing that God will act in accordance with His character, His attributes of holiness and justice, "for thy name's sake". He can safely rely on the lovingkindness of the Lord to deliver him.

David feels so helpless in himself. "I am poor (6041) and needy" (34), he cries. He is afflicted and oppressed, wounded to his very heart by the malice of his adversaries. He is as a declining shadow. Delitzsch comments, "The metaphor of the shadow is as in Psalm 102.11. When the day declines, the shadow lengthens, it becomes longer and longer, till it vanishes in the universal darkness. Thus does the life of the sufferer pass away". The metaphor changes now. He feels like the locust (697), the grasshopper, homeless, helpless, and defenceless, easily frightened away, driven about, tossed up and down, shaken off as a grasshopper might be shaken off a garment. How weak he is in himself before these adversaries. His appetite has gone, and he has fasted to the point of exhaustion. His flesh has become lean for want of fatness (8081), probably a lack of oil, that essential element in the Oriental diet, and used also as an unguent for the refreshment and invigoration of the whole body. His enemies taunt him, shaking their heads in derision. "Is this the man who trusted in God?", they are probably thinking. Is this the man who lived for righteousness? They looked upon him with a kind of unfeeling pity. Poor miserable man, so weak, so vulnerable, so helpless.

"Help me!" David cries. Note again the divine titles which he employs in his renewed appeal, "O LORD (3068) my God (430)", O Jehovah my Elohim. "O save me", he prays, and once again he pleads the mercy, the loving-kindness of the Lord. He wants men to see and to know that his case and his cause are in the hand of God. His deliverance from the adversaries would be a testimony to what Jehovah could do. In himself he might be helpless against them, but they would see what the Lord had done when he was delivered out of their hands. They may curse. "Let them curse, but bless thou". As Perowne renders it, "Though they curse, yet Thou blessest", and, if God will bless him, it really matters little what men will do. He knows that they may yet arise against him with schemes of persecution, but, "When they arise", he says, "let them be ashamed; but let thy servant rejoice". There is a good measure of confidence in David's final requests in the Psalm. He seems assured that his adversaries will ultimately be clothed with shame. Indeed they will cover themselves with confusion wrapped about them like a garment. Spurgeon remarks, with characteristic quaintness, "Where sin is the underclothing, shame will soon be the outer vesture". Their shame will be visible to all.

Prayer now blends into praise in a happy conclusion to the Psalm. "I will greatly praise (3034) Jehovah…yea, I will praise (1984) him". The two words for "praise" in v.30 are different. The first has the thought of thanksgiving, the second that of boasting. David will render thanksgiving with his mouth, and will glory in the Lord among the multitude. Perhaps he is saying that both personally and privately, as well as publicly, he will boast in what the Lord has done. He gives his reasons for such glorying. The Lord will stand at the right hand of the poor and defenceless, ever ready to save him. From those who would judge and condemn his needy servant, Jehovah will deliver and vindicate him.

So ends this Psalm. There is much unpleasant but necessary reading in it, of hatred and evil, of wickedness, oppression, and persecution, as well as constant calls for judgment upon the adversary, but eventually all will be for God's glory and for the good of His beloved people.

PSALM 110

Introduction

Several interesting features contribute to the uniqueness of this lovely Psalm. It is indeed unique, not only among the Messianic Psalms, but also in the whole of the Psalter, and in the entire canon of Holy Scripture.

First, this Psalm is quoted in the NT more often than any other OT passage. It is cited in the Gospels, in the Acts of the Apostles, and in the Epistles, and the spirit of it is in the Book of the Revelation. It is referred to by the Saviour Himself, by Peter, by Paul, and by the writer of the Epistle to the Hebrews.

Second, the Psalm is essentially and solely Messianic. It is, as some scholars prefer to say, "prophetico-Messianic". There is no other primary reason for its being written. There is no other person, event, or circumstances with which it may be associated. It is pure prophetic poetry anticipating only the greatness and the glory of the Messiah who was to come, and all the NT citations prove this. There is nothing of David in this Psalm, except that he was the writer. It is all Christ.

Third, the Lord Jesus, with Peter also, confirms that David was indeed the author of the Psalm, as indicated in the brief title, "A Psalm of David". Note that word of the Lord Jesus in Matthew 22.43-44, to which further reference will be made in the commentary, as well as Peter's word in Acts 2.34, "For David...he saith himself". As Plumer remarks, "These quotations prove that David is the author of the Psalm. So clearly is this matter settled that no respectable commentator doubts it. The title, Christ, Peter, all testify to this fact". This must be emphasised, because some commentators do indeed question the Davidic authorship, and propound the great error that the Lord Jesus was not omniscient during the days of His flesh but was subject to the knowledge of the times in which he lived. Spurgeon writes, "Some critics are so fond of finding new authors for the Psalms that they dare to fly in the face of the Lord Jesus Himself".

Fourth, the Saviour confirms, if confirmation is needed, that the Psalm is divinely inspired, saying, "How then doth David in spirit call him Lord?". That Messiah should be a divine Person, one of the Godhead, was, and is, a problem to the Jew. David writes this by inspiration. David's son is David's Lord only because He is both the root and the offspring of David (Rev 22.16), and David knows this only because he is inspired of God.

There are at least seven glories of Messiah in this short Psalm. The glory of His Person is here, with the glory of His present exalted position at the right hand of God. There follows, the glory of His prospect, of ruling in the midst of His enemies. Then there is the glory of His people, and the glory of His priesthood. The glory of His power is then anticipated, and the Psalm concludes with the glory of His preeminence.

The seven short verses may be divided as follows. Verse 4 is the central key-verse of the Psalm, introducing, for the first time since the original narrative in Genesis 14, the Melchizedek priesthood. There are then three verses on either side, sometimes viewed as introductory and supplementary. Verses 1-3 consider the personal greatness of the Messiah, as already mentioned. These verses are directed to Messiah Himself. Verses 5-7 look to the future triumph of the King-Priest, and seem to be addressed to Him at whose right hand the exalted Messiah presently sits.

Verses 1-3: Messiah's Person, Present Position, and Prospect

"The LORD (3068) said unto my Lord (113)". Jehovah said unto my Adon. The word "said" (5002) signifies "an oracle". This is "the oracle of the Lord". Dr Cohen points out that, although "The Lord said" is a phrase common enough in the prophetic literature of Scripture, it occurs, in this form, only here in the Psalter. "It expresses", he adds, "a solemn declaration made upon the authority of God". It is a great privilege granted to men, that they should be permitted to hear this solemn discourse between the Father and the Son, for such it is, as the first chapter of the Epistle to the Hebrews makes abundantly clear. In Matthew 22.41-46 Jesus used this verse to confound the Pharisees. He asked them concerning Messiah, "Whose son is he?". Quite correctly they answered, "The Son of David". "How then", Jesus asks, quoting Psalm 110.1, "How then doth David in spirit call him Lord?" How can Messiah be David's Son and yet be David's Lord? To this they had no answer, but for those who recognise the deity and the eternal Sonship of Christ, there is no problem. Mark and Luke record this incident also (Mk 12.35-37; Lk 20.41-44). He is David's Lord because He is before David in His eternality. He is David's Son because, after the flesh, He comes of the seed of David (Rom 1.3; Mt 1.1). This is a most valuable and important text in defence of the deity of Christ, the great truth that Jesus is God. The difficulty for the Pharisees, and for Jews in general, is that they do not, can not, understand a plurality in the Godhead, therefore they cannot comprehend three Persons in deity, or, as men say, a Trinity. Without this understanding this verse is really unintelligible. Although David was as firm a believer as any Jew in the unity of the Godhead, yet, speaking "by the Holy Ghost" (Mk 12.36), he discerns a second Person in the deity. One divine Person addresses another, and yet the Godhead is One. Like Elizabeth the mother of John Baptist, like Mary of Magdala, and like Thomas the disciple, David says of Messiah, "My Lord".

But what is this solemn declaration, "Jehovah said unto my Lord"? The word to Messiah is, "Sit thou at my right hand". This is, of course, the seat of honour. With NT revelation this is clearly understood. Christ having come to His own, has been rejected, crucified and slain. Now He is risen from the dead and ascended into the heavens, and there Jehovah's word to Him is, "Sit thou at my right hand". Benoni, son of my sorrow, has become Benjamin, the son of my right hand (Gen 35.18)! The Man of Sorrows is now the Man in the Glory. There he will sit "until...". This little word has now spanned some two thousand years, but at the appointed time the King will be manifested in power and His enemies will be made the footstool of His feet. "Sit thou" has extended over two thousand years. "Rule thou" will last for a thousand years of millennial glory.

In that day He will wield the sceptre, a rod of iron, as prophesied in the second Psalm. By the decree of Jehovah His rule will go out from Zion. The predictions of Psalm 72 will be fulfilled as His dominion extends from sea to sea and from the river to the ends of the earth. All kings shall fall down before Him. All nations shall serve Him. Until that day He sits, "from henceforth expecting until his enemies be made his footstool" (Heb 10.13).

Messiah also has glory in His people. They are a willing (5071) people. This is a plural noun, "willingnesses". They are freewill offerings, all voluntarily yielded to Him whom they love and serve. In that day of His power they will be manifested with Him. They will appear in priestly adornment, in the beauties of holiness, and they will come forth out of the womb of the morning, just like the shimmering dew of the dawn. They have been, like the dew, conceived in the night, the night of Messiah's rejection and exile. The world has not recognised them, but the glad morning of His appearing will reveal them. As every single droplet of dew mirrors the glory of the sun in miniature, so each of these will reflect the glory of the Sun of righteousness in that day. W.E. Vine comments, "The dewdrops sparkling in the early morning sunlight, each reflect the full-circled image of the heavenly orb. So each saint will shine resplendent in the complete likeness of the Son of God". They are called His "youth". As Perowne says, "Youthful warriors in holy attire". This is not the personal youthfulness of the Messiah, but rather a collective noun describing His people in freshness and vigour. To quote Dr Cohen, "The dew falls at dawn which is poetically called its mother. It is a metaphor of freshness, and is beautifully applied to the young men of the kingdom who fill the ranks of the army".

Verse 4: Messiah's Priesthood

This is the central verse of the Psalm, a kind of climax to which the first three verses have been introductory. Jehovah has sworn, and will not repent. This indicates the utmost importance of the great revelation about to be made in this verse. The decree is absolute and unalterable. The solemn oath concerning Messiah is, "Thou art a priest for ever after the order of Melchizedek". Two offices are here combined in one Person. Messiah is to be a King-Priest, and this has not been so since Melchizedek, who was King of Salem and priest of the Most High God. When King Uzziah presumed to function as a priest he was smitten with leprosy (2 Chr 26.18-21), but Messiah will be, by divine decree, a priest upon His throne (Zech 6.13).

Only in three places in Scripture are there mentions of Melchizedek –

Genesis 14, Psalm 110, Hebrews 5-7. He may be found historically in the first Scripture, prophetically in the second, and doctrinally in the third. He is a fitting type of Him who was to come, who in His day would also be a King-Priest. Melchizedek is superior to Aaron, and his priesthood is not of the Aaronic, Levitical order. There is no record of him in Jewish genealogies. There is no account there of his birth or of his death, and no mention of his father, his mother, or his ancestry. In all this he is assimilated to the Son of God (Heb 7.3). Abraham paid tithes to him and received a blessing from him, signifying the superiority of this King-Priest, and, through Abraham, Levi also recognised the greatness of this man (Heb 7.9-10). It is interesting to note that the first recorded war in Scripture, and the first reference to Jerusalem, called Salem, are both found in the chapter which introduces Melchizedek, Genesis 14. The coming King-Priest, Messiah, will be the victor at Armageddon, scene of the last battle, and He will reign from the same Jerusalem, the Salem of Melchizedek.

Verses 5-7: Messiah's Power and Preeminence

Expositors are divided as to the meaning of v.5. "The Lord (Adonai - 136) at thy right hand". Who is "The Lord" here? Is this Jehovah at the right hand of the coming Warrior-King? Or is it Messiah, who has been seated at the right hand of Jehovah. The truth of the first is, of course, quite acceptable, that Jehovah should be at the right hand of the coming One, enabling Him and assuring the victory. It is hardly likely though, that in so short a Psalm Messiah should be at God's right hand in v.1, and Jehovah at Messiah's right hand in v.5. It seems easier to understand that, in these closing verses of the Psalm, Jehovah is being addressed, so that "The Lord at thy right hand" is the Messiah, now leaving His seat to appear in power and glory and to execute judgment. If this is the proper interpretation then there is a most important implication. "Lord" here is Adonai, and, as Perowne points out, "This form of the plural is never used except as a Divine Name. The Targum gives as the equivalent here 'the Shekinah of Jehovah'". Is this name here applied to Jehovah or to the King? If it is indeed applied to the King, then there is an implicit testimony to the deity of Christ; Messiah is Adonai, a divine Person.

The judgment of the enemies of Messiah is described in a four-fold way. He "shall strike through kings in the day of his wrath. He shall judge among the heathen, he shall fill the places with the dead bodies; he shall wound the head [singular] over many countries". The day of His power is the day of His wrath. Enemies must be dealt with before the setting up of His kingdom. Just as Solomon's peaceful reign began with the judgment of enemies, so will it be with Messiah. Solomon had to deal with Adonijah, a rebel and usurper, with Joab, who had murdered Abner and Amasa, and with Shimei, who had cursed David. These were slain by Benaiah in 1 Kings 2. Messiah's reign of peace will likewise be introduced in judgment. That evil trinity, the Devil, the Beast, and the False Prophet must be dealt with (Rev 19.20; 20.2-3). Rebel kings of the earth will be judged too, and their armies. The King of kings must reign supreme and unchallenged, therefore all these must first be removed from the scene.

He shall then judge the nations, the great event described in the Olivet discourse in Matthew 25.31-46. Men will be divided, as a shepherd divides sheep and goats. They are destined either for the joy of the kingdom or for everlasting punishment, according to what they have done with the messengers of the gospel, and with the message which they brought. The carnage of that day of His wrath will be fearful, all places filled with dead bodies, the corpses of those who have been slain in the final battle. Kings from the north, south, and east, with the armies of the west, will have converged on Israel like beasts of prey, and the Warrior-King will deal with them as described in Revelation 19.17-21. "He shall wound the head over many countries". As has been noted, the word "head" is in the singular, and may refer either to the man of sin of 2 Thessalonians 2.3-10, or, as some think, to Satan himself. Whichever is true, all enemies must be crushed.

"He shall drink of the brook in the way: therefore shall he lift up the head". This closing verse depicts the ultimate triumph and preeminence of the Messiah. The picture is of a victorious leader, perhaps still pursuing an enemy remnant, and stopping at the brook by the way to refresh himself. Then, lifting up the head, Messiah will complete the rout of His enemies and thus prepare the way for the setting up of His kingdom of peace. In all things He must have the preeminence (Col 1.18). He must reign, and He must reign supreme. So ends this delightful Psalm, pure poetic prophecy, in which Christ is the only subject.

PSALM 111

Introduction

This Psalm is the first of a trilogy of "Hallelujah" Psalms. It is a twin Psalm with Psalm 112, there being a similarity not only in structure, but also in thought and theme. These two Psalms are alphabetical, and are indeed the first Psalms to be so with strict regularity. Psalms 25, 34 and 37, are also alphabetical, but the acrostic arrangement of these is irregular. Psalms 111 and 112 in their original Hebrew form each consist of twenty-two lines. There are twenty-two letters in the Hebrew alphabet and each of these lines commences with a letter of that alphabet in perfect consecutive order. There are ten verses, each of which has two lines, except the last two, where there are three lines in each. This interesting structure may have been, to the earliest Hebrew readers, an aid to memory, but it is, of course, lost in the translation.

The Psalm is untitled. Some commentators think it is David's, but others assign it to a later date, and there is no way of proving the identity of the author. Nor is there any certainty as to the circumstances in which it was written, but because of allusions to the Exodus and to redemption, some think that it may have been sung, with other Psalms, during the time of Passover and Unleavened Bread. This does not necessarily mean that it was especially written for those occasions, but just that its theme was suitable for such.

The Psalm requires little in the way of division. Indeed the alphabetical structure makes any other division difficult. As Delitzsch says of the two Psalms 111 and 112, "Both songs are only chains of acrostic lines without any strophic grouping, and therefore cannot be divided out". However, verse 1 is an invitation to praise, with the Psalmist's own resolution that he personally will praise. Verses 2-9 give a variety of reasons for that praise, and the closing verse 10 is a commendation of those who understand, and praise accordingly.

Verse 1: Praise ye the Lord!

This opening call to praise is really a "Hallelujah". "Praise ye Jah!" It is an exclamatory introduction to the whole Psalm and, as the acrostic arrangement begins with the next line, some regard the Hallelujah as the title of the Psalm. Having invited others to join in the praise the Psalmist exclaims, without reserve, "I will praise the Lord". He desires that others will unite with him in his whole-hearted adoration. His own heart is undivided in his praise of Jehovah, whether that praise is in private or in public, in the assembly (5475) or in the congregation (5712). The first signifies a small circle of familiar friends, while the second indicates a large gathering, perhaps of a multitude. It is good that God's people should be ever ready to praise Him, in every situation.

Verses 2-9: Reasons for Praise

Every line that now follows advances a reason for praising the Lord, so that vv. 2-8 have two reasons in each verse and v.9 has three reasons. "The works of the Lord are great" (1419). All that Jehovah undertakes to do He does perfectly. His works are great both in magnitude and in magnificence, and those who delight in His works will constantly enquire, contemplate, and seek in those works fresh reasons for their praise.

The word "work" in v.3 is not just the singular of the "works" of v.2, but is a different word in the original Hebrew. The difference is difficult to define, both being translated "deeds; acts; works; things made; things done". Perhaps the Psalmist is turning from a survey of the works of God in general to some particular work which was just then engaging his thoughts. Dr Cohen thinks that the latter word has the thought of "His providence", a special work of God providing for some peculiar need of His people. Whichever is true, all that God does is "honourable and glorious" (AV), "majesty and splendour" (JND), "glory and majesty" (JPS), "honour and majesty" (Perowne). Everything, too, is righteous. His righteousness in all that He does stands as an eternal tribute to Him.

The "wonderful works" (6381) of v.4 employs a different word again. These two words are really a translation of one word, which is perhaps better rendered "wonders", as JND and others. He has made these wonders to be remembered, a memorial to His miraculous doings for His people. It will be seen how this would be appropriate for singing at Passover time. As Dr Cohen remarks, "The miracles He wrought for Israel in redeeming them from Egypt were perpetuated in the memory of the people by the institution of the Passover (Ex 12.14)". In so much of Hebrew liturgy there was a remembrance of the divine deliverance from Egypt. In all that Jehovah does He is not only righteous, but also gracious and full of compassion. There is such a marvellous blending of righteousness, and compassion, lovingkindness and mercy, in all the works of God, that it would seem almost impossible that men should forget them, and yet they do. His wonders are as a monument to His gracious dealings with His people.

With the Passover still in mind, one of the wonders which God wrought for His people coming out of Egypt was the miraculous provision of food for them in the wilderness. "He hath given meat unto them that fear him". Having fed on the roast lamb, this great company of the redeemed was soon to be a multitude of hungry people in a barren wilderness. Jehovah rained down manna for them, and when they wanted flesh to eat He gave them quails. They were His covenant people and He would be true to His covenant and provide for their every need.

The people saw the power of His works (4639). This is the word of v.2. He who had so wondrously provided for them during their wilderness sojourn would eventually bring them into the land which He had promised. What if there were enemy nations already there? He would enable Israel to dispossess them of the land which He had promised to their fathers and which He had reserved for the people of the covenant. Canaan was their heritage and He would see to it that they inherited what was theirs by divine decree. The power which wrought wonders for them in the wilderness would also bring them into the land.

The Psalmist continues to give reasons for his praise. Jehovah's works (as in vv. 2 and 6) are verity (571) and judgment (4941). All that He does is characterised by truth and faithfulness, by stability and justice. All His precepts are likewise marked by that same faithfulness. Indeed all that He says, like all that He does, is just a manifestation of His own righteous character. His Word, therefore, is to be believed and obeyed.

"They stand fast for ever and ever". Whether this refers to His commandments or to His works is not relevant. Perhaps it is to both, for both are eternal in character. They are the works and words of the eternal, unchanging God, with whom there is no variableness, neither shadow cast by turning (Jas 1.17). All is said and done in truth and uprightness. All is abidingly faithful and just.

"He sent redemption unto His people". This is an immediate and obvious reference to the great Exodus from Egypt, but it ought not to be confined to this, for again and again Jehovah delivered His people. How often were they beset by enemies stronger than they. How often were they a helpless and beleaguered people, but they cried to Him and He heard them and came to their aid, as many Psalms testify. He commanded and ordered His covenant so that everything was in accord with His faithful promises. His name is holy. It is to be revered. Men ought to stand in astonishment and awe at the mention of His name who has accomplished so much for His people.

Verse 10: Wisdom, Obedience and Praise

"The fear of the Lord is the beginning of wisdom" (compare Prov 9.10; 1.7; Job 28.28). "Beginning" (7225) is sometimes rendered "firstfruits". Such a harvest of blessing will follow if there is but a holy fear of the Lord. It will lead to wisdom and understanding, and to an observance of His precepts. This in turn will lead to praise, and His praises will never cease. How important is the fear of the Lord, then, like a fountain-head from which springs wisdom, understanding, obedience, and praise. Notice that the expression, "His commandments", is italicised, having been supplied by the translators. The words are, of course, necessary for an understanding of the text, but the emphasis is that it is not sufficient just to know His precepts. A man must "do". "A good understanding have all they that do...". God's people must have more than knowledge, they must have practical godliness. It has been said that the only truth a man really knows is that which he practises.

Kirkpatrick has a final comment. He says, "All the attributes of God which demand man's praise are, like His righteousness (v.3), eternal. Thus the Psalmist rounds off his song by returning to the thought with which he began it, and gives the reason for the 'Hallelujah' prefixed to it".

PSALM 112

Introduction

As has been observed in the introduction to Psalm 111, these two Psalms are not only companions, but twins. They are identical in size and structure, and so very alike in subject matter too. Each Psalm commences with a "Hallelujah", which may be regarded as a heading or title, after which there is a perfectly regular alphabetical arrangement. In each Psalm there are ten verses, comprised of twenty-two clauses, each of which commences with a letter of the Hebrew alphabet in consecutive order. As in Psalm 111, each of the first eight verses has two clauses and each of the last two verses has three clauses. The acrostic form may have been employed as an aid to memory for the original Hebrew readers of the Psalm, but is unavoidably lost in the translation.

There is no title to the Psalm to name or identify the author, but it is almost certain that the same Psalmist has written both of these Psalms. Many commentators assume that this was David, but some assign the Psalm to a later date and there is nothing in it to prove or disprove the one or the other.

Like Psalm 111 this Psalm needs little in the way of division or sub-division, and, indeed, if such be desired for study purposes, then this would be exactly the same as for Psalm 111. Verse 1 is introductory, proclaiming the personal happiness of the man who fears the Lord. Verses 2-9 describe the blessed effects of this, not only for himself, but for others also. In sad and solemn contrast to this blessedness is the fate of the ungodly as described in verse 10.

Verse 1: The Blessed Man

After the opening "Praise ye the Lord", the "Hallelujah", this Psalm commences where Psalm 111 has concluded, with the wisdom of fearing the Lord, and its reward. "Blessed is the man" is a familiar phrase in the Psalter, as in other parts of both Old and New Testaments. Like Psalm 112, Psalm 1 begins with this expression, but it is also seen in Psalms 32.2; 34.8; 65.4; 84.5, 12 and 94.12. It is to be found also in Proverbs 8.34; Isaiah 56.2; and Jeremiah 17.7. In the NT it is used by Paul and by James in Romans 4.8 and James 1.12. In these various Scriptures several reasons are appended for the blessedness of the man. Here it is the blessedness, or happiness, of him who fears the Lord. As is often rightly pointed out, this is not a slavish fear or dread, but rather a reverential awe which appreciates the majesty of Jehovah and delights to keep His commandments and do His will, for His pleasure. This is true happiness, and there now follows in the Psalm a discourse on the far-reaching effects of this fear of the Lord, both for the man personally, and for his house and family.

Verses 2-9: The Generation of the Righteous

The ensuing verses now introduce a problem into the Psalm in that the family and house of the blessed man seem to be associated with righteous living and with wealth and riches. It may be argued, sadly with some justification, that sometimes the children of a righteous man have behaved badly, bringing poverty to themselves as well as heartbreak to that man and dishonour to his good name. Various explanations have been offered for the problem. Some point out that the family of a righteous man will, at his decease, inherit that wealth which his prudent and industrious life has accumulated for them, and if, subsequently, this is squandered, still the words of this Psalm are true - he has bequeathed wealth and riches to his generation. Others think that the wealth referred to is not necessarily material, but rather the spiritual and moral richness which every upright man will leave to his children. Yet another interesting explanation is suggested by De Burgh, who recognises a prophecy here, and writes, "There is another alternative, and suggested by the Psalm itself – namely, a reference to a future dispensation, which has the promise of "blessedness", and "upon earth", far exceeding that of Israel in the land, though typified by it; when, as former Psalms have also said, "the meek shall inherit the earth", and this world, under altered circumstances, shall be given to a generation of the righteous". Spurgeon says that the Psalm refers to "successive generations of God-fearing men…strong and influential in society". He continues, "The true seed of the righteous are those who follow them in their virtues, even as believers are the seed of Abraham, because they imitate his faith". It may indeed be true that the children of the godly are not all mighty or prosperous, nevertheless, the fact remains that there can be no greater legacy than the spiritual, moral, and practical advantages inherited by those whose fathers have lived righteously. In this sense his personal righteousness lives on.

The righteous man, though righteous, may not escape dark days. Even for the upright there will be days of perplexity and difficulty, days of sadness and sorrow. But for him, light will arise in the darkness, a blessing not known to the ungodly. The light of the countenance of God, the very smile of heaven, will be upon him in his distress. That early benediction was, "The Lord make his face shine upon thee, and be gracious unto thee" (Num 6.25), and this is still the portion of godly men. How true is that old proverb, "The path of the just is as the shining light, that shineth more and more unto the perfect day" (Prov 4.18). The upright man is gracious and full of compassion. Note that these are the very attributes of God Himself in Psalm 111.4. The godly man is actually manifesting the character of his God. He cares for others. He deals graciously with men, ever showing mercy. He is righteous too, but his zeal for righteousness is tempered with goodness and with pity for the erring.

"A good man showeth favour, and lendeth". JND, with JPS, prefers, "It is well with the man that is gracious and lendeth". Both are true. This is the character of a good man, to be gracious, and to lend where necessary, and it is always well with such a man. As Spurgeon comments, "Providence has made him able to lend, and grace makes him willing to lend". He orders his affairs with discretion. He conducts his business judiciously and prudently. None will ever be able to accuse him of deceit or dishonesty, or even of carelessness.

The blessings of righteousness are eternal. The fortunes of the godly man do not fluctuate like those of the gambler and the cheat. The words "for ever" and "everlasting"(5769) in v.6, are the same. Both the man and his memory will abide when the worldling is gone and forgotten. Prosperity gained righteously will last. Best of all, the record of the righteous man is preserved above. "My witness is in heaven", said Job, "and my record is on high" (Job 16.19). Earthly records may be lost or destroyed, but heaven's records are permanent.

Since the godly are not immune to suffering, then it follows that from time to time there may come "evil tidings", unpleasant, distressing news. The truly blessed man is a man in the enjoyment of God's rest. He is therefore not afraid, as other men are. He finds repose in the will of God for him. His heart is fixed (3559), steadfast in trust and confidence in Jehovah. "His heart", the Psalmist repeats, "is established" (5564). It is sustained, supported, upheld, by his reliance upon God. Job again comes to mind, a man who feared God (Job 1.1). What evil tidings indeed they were that came to him, telling of the heavy loss of his sons and servants, his oxen, camels, and sheep. This good man fell on the ground and worshipped, saying, "The Lord gave, and the Lord hath taken away, blessed be the name of the Lord" (Job 1.20-21). This is the language of a man whose heart is established, trusting in the Lord.

He who rests with such confidence in God will not be afraid of his adversaries. His heart will be sustained until he is able, as is said, "to look his enemies in the face" without fear of them. Note that "his desire" is italicised, having been supplied by the translators. The words may be omitted, giving the sense as suggested. Note, also, the word "until". This does not mean that thereafter he will be afraid, but, as Plumer says, "As in Psalm 110.1, *until* does not limit the sense to the time mentioned, but *even until* then". Or, as Alexander, "*Until* does not imply that he shall then fear, but that there will then be no occasion so to do".

The godly man has been thrifty and economical in the management of his affairs, but he has not been a miserly hoarder of his wealth. He has dispersed his goods. He "scattereth abroad" (JND, JPS). He has "distributed freely" (RSV), giving generously to the poor and needy, and his generosity is suitably rewarded in that his righteousness shall be always remembered. This is a repetition of v.3, where again a good man's righteous acts live on as a lasting memorial to the man himself. His horn (7161), his strength, shall be exalted with honour, but this does have a certain effect upon the ungodly, as the closing verse of the Psalm indicates.

Verse 10: The Fate of the Ungodly

The prosperity and honour of the righteous man is, perversely, a grief to the wicked. As in v.8 he looks upon them, so now they look upon him. The word "see" is the same word (7200) in both verses. These ungodly men are not only grieved (3707), in the sense of being sad. The word is stronger than that. They are indignant, vexed, angry, full of wrath. They gnash with their teeth. Plumer says, "The phrase denotes violent rage. Sometimes it denotes impotent rage. This latter is the shade of idea here conveyed. Malignant passions, not permitted to be vented on their victims, turn with fearful power on those who indulge in them". What perversity indeed in the human heart, that a man should be angry at the success and honour of another. They melt away in their discouragement. All their hopes and selfish desires come to naught. Whatever they may have desired and obtained by evil means is but vanity and shall soon be lost for ever while the memory of the godly man will abide.

PSALM 113

Introduction

Psalm 113 is the third in a trilogy of Psalms, each of which commences with "Praise ye the Lord" or "Hallelujah". Psalm 113 also ends with a "Hallelujah". This lovely Psalm is all praise, and requires little in the way of exposition. It is particularly notable in that it is the first Psalm in that series of six, Psalms 113-118, commonly referred to as "The Egyptian Hallel", or, as the Hebrew Talmud names them, "The Hallel of Egypt", because of the reference to the great Exodus from Egypt at the beginning of Psalm 114. Dr Cohen says, "They are included in the Jewish liturgy on the New Moon, the Pilgrim Festivals, and the Feast of Dedication". Dr Edersheim writes, "The Egyptian Hallel was altogether sung on eighteen days and on one night in the year. These eighteen days were, that of the Passover sacrifice, the Feast of Pentecost, and each of the eight days of the Feasts of Tabernacles and of the Dedication of the Temple. The only night in which it was recited was that of the Paschal Supper, when it was sung by every Paschal company in their houses".

Perhaps any division of the Psalm is unnecessary, but, as De Burgh suggests, "It resolves itself into three parts, of three verses each: - the first, the call to praise; and the other two stating the grounds for it, which are twofold".

Verses 1-3: The Call to Praise

The word "praise" (HALAL - 1984*)* occurs three times in the opening verse of the Psalm, providing, as it were, a key to the its theme, and a stirring call for suitable adoration of Jehovah. This name of the Lord also occurs three times, and, as Spurgeon suggests, "The name of Jehovah is thrice used in this verse, and may by us who understand the doctrine of the Trinity in Unity be regarded as a thinly veiled allusion to that holy mystery".

The first summons is a general Hallelujah, in which Jah (3050) is used instead of Jehovah. This is a shortened, or contracted, form of the great name, a poetic abbreviation which is in no sense a diminution. This is almost an exclamation, "Hallelujah!". It behoves all God's people everywhere to praise Him at all times.

The second call is to those designated "Ye servants of the Lord". The word "servants" (5650) is "bondservants; slaves". There were, in Israel, those who were servants in a special sense, but no doubt the people of God are all willing bondmen, yielded voluntarily to Him for His glory. How readily would these "servants of the Lord" have responded to the call for praise as they remembered that once they were the bondslaves of Pharaoh! To Him who had redeemed them out of Egyptian bondage they would raise their songs of praise most heartily.

The third call gives the nature of the praise; it exalts His name. His name is His character. It is the revelation of Himself as He has made Himself known to His people. So, with their privileged knowledge of Him, a knowledge which the heathen did not possess, they would join in intelligent praise. Believers today, with a more full revelation of God in Christ, are of course, especially privileged to offer their hymns of true adoration. They worship in spirit and in truth, just as the Saviour instructed the woman of Sychar in John 4.24.

The name of the Lord is again mentioned. "Blessed" (1288) is but another form of praise. It is, as Plumer says, "heaping benedictions upon His worthy name", so that this is almost a repetition of the earlier "Praise the name of the Lord". There is to be no limit to this praise of Jehovah. "From this time forth and for evermore. From the rising of the sun unto the going down of the same the Lord's name is to be praised". This is so even today, that, as the sun traverses the heavens, there are saints somewhere, at every hour of the day, praising Him. Nevertheless, there may be a prophetic glimpse here of a day to come when the praise of Jehovah will be universal, when all men everywhere, from east to west, will unite in adoration. With this thought, compare those lovely verses of Malachi 1.11 and Isaiah 59.19.

Verses 4-6: Reasons for Praise

For those who know Him, and love Him, it is not difficult to find reasons for praising the Lord. On earth and in heaven He is supreme. He is "high above all nations, and his glory above the heavens". Whether among men on earth, or among angels in the heavens, He is preeminent. He is sovereign among nations. He can preserve them or dispose of them as He pleases. He rules in the heavens, controlling sun, moon, stars, and planets, and He is Lord of the angels who are His ministers. In glory He is above all. He is, therefore, to be praised.

"Who is like unto the Lord our God?" The question needs no answer. He is incomparable. He is alone, solitary in His greatness. In His grace too, He is great, for He dwells on high and yet condescends to take notice of His creation, whether in heaven or on earth. How great must He be, of whom it is said that He "humbleth himself" to behold the angels in heaven. When David, in another Psalm, considered that greatness, he could only exclaim, "What is man, that thou art mindful of him? and the son of man that thou visitest him?" (8.4). Here then, closely intertwined, are two reasons for praising Him – His excelling greatness and His condescending grace.

Verses 7-9: More Reasons for Praise

In His grace Jehovah reaches to help the poor and the needy. He raises them up; He lifts them. He lifts them from the dust and from the dunghill, which are, says Alexander, "common figures in all languages for a degraded social state". Commenting on the dunghill, T.W. Davies writes, "Heaps of dung and other debris...used to be in front of Oriental houses. Beggars and lepers were wont to sit on these artificial hills, soliciting by looks and gestures, if not by words, the gifts of the inmates of the houses". The sentiments of these verses might almost be quotations from the prayer of Hannah in 1 Samuel 2.8. He lifts paupers and sets them among princes! He puts men among nobles who formerly were nothing! This exaltation is, too, among "the princes of his people". This is more honourable by far than to have a place among the princes of the heathen.

There follows another reminiscence of Hannah, in that He makes the barren woman the mother of a household, a joyful mother of children. To be such was the hope of every Jewish woman, but, again, there might well be a prophetic note here, anticipating the day when poor barren Israel will be redeemed out of her desolation to a glad supremacy among the nations. (See Is 54.1 and 66.8). How appropriately therefore, does this short Psalm end, as it began, with yet another "Hallelujah!". Praise ye the Lord!

PSALM 114

Introduction

This delightful little Psalm is a poetic gem. Commentators compete with each other in their quest for language to extol its beauty. Such accolades as, "exquisite; charming; sublime; majestic; unrivalled; true poetry; elegantly composed; finest in the Psalter; surpassing beauty"; all are employed by a variety of expositors to describe this brief ode, and indeed it is worthy of them all.

There is no title, no date, and no indication as to the writer, but the Psalm does, of course, have a place of honour in the Egyptian Hallel, the series of Psalms consisting of Psalms 113-118, on which see the notes in the introduction to Psalm 113. Here, in Psalm 114, may be seen the reason why the Hallel was sung during the celebration of the Passover. The theme and purpose is to remember, poetically, that great occasion of the Exodus from Egypt of those who had been a nation of slaves in that land.

The Psalm is in two equal parts, commemorating the miracle of the Exodus in verses 1-4 and the power of the divine Presence in verses 5-8. There are, however, four stanzas, of two verses each, of which Delitzsch says, "There are four tetrastichs, which pass by with the swiftness of a bird as it were with four flappings of its wings". Of the Psalm in general he writes, "The deeds of God at the time of the Exodus are here brought together to form a picture in miniature which is as majestic as it is charming".

Verses 1-4: Coming out of Egypt

The preceding Psalm 113 has been a fitting prelude, an introductory call to praise the name of Jehovah. This Psalm is now more explicit, recalling the wonder of the Exodus, the great deliverance of Israel from centuries of Egyptian bondage. That was, of course, an historic event, marking a new beginning for the nation. As Moses was told, "This month shall be unto you the beginning of months: it shall be the first month of the year to you" (Ex 12.2). The years of slavery were to be ended. Deliverance! Emancipation! Redemption! It is not to be wondered at that there should be a regular national and family celebration of that momentous occasion, and the singing of the Hallel was an essential part of that celebration.

For four hundred years Israel had been in captivity to a people "of strange language". According to Genesis 42.23 the language of the Egyptians was unintelligible to the Hebrews, and, as Kirkpatrick suggests, "The tyranny of oppressors seemed to be aggravated by the barrier which difference of language placed between them and their victims". The slaves were the descendants of Jacob, who had become Israel (Gen 32.28), but the people of this "prince with God" had been in bondage in the land of the Pharaohs, smarting under the lash of their taskmasters. On that memorable day of the great Exodus Jehovah led His people, the house of Jacob, out of Egypt to freedom.

After the Exodus Judah was Jehovah's sanctuary and Israel His dominion. This is simply poetic parallelism, since originally Judah and Israel were one, divided only after the death of Solomon. "Israel" denoted all the tribes and "Judah" at the head, represented all. After the division, "Judah" embraced Judah and Benjamin only, and "Israel" the other ten tribes. Here, in Psalm 114, "Judah" and "Israel" are synonyms for the whole nation. In this people Jehovah found a sanctuary, a place where He would dwell, and, likewise, in them He had a dominion, a place where His rule would be acknowledged when heathen peoples were in revolt against Him. Was not this His purpose in bringing them out, that He might have in them a peculiar possession, a people who were His own people? They were to be a kingdom of priests and a holy nation, for His pleasure.

The Red Sea and the Jordan are now personified. As they witnessed their Creator drawing near at the head of His redeemed people they retreated. First the Red Sea fled, then the Jordan turned backward. They must make way for this ransomed nation. Mountains and hills joined with the sea and the river in acknowledgement of the power of the Redeemer. In the poetic language of the Psalmist, they skipped like rams and like young sheep, but at Sinai the mountains did indeed quake, quite literally and actually. Plumer quotes Calvin, who writes, "The description does not exceed the facts of the case. The sea, in rendering obedience to its Creator, sanctified His name; and Jordan, by its submission, put honour upon His power; and the mountains, by their quaking, proclaimed how they were overawed at the presence of His awful majesty". These were wonders indeed. The dividing of the Red Sea and the dividing of the River Jordan marked the beginning and the end of the journey through the wilderness from Egypt to Canaan.

Verses 5-8: The Power of His Presence

The personification of the waters continues with a series of questions to them. These are in the present tense, as the RSV rendering indicates, "What ails you, O sea, that you flee? O Jordan, that you turn back? O mountains, that you skip like rams? O hills, like lambs?". Perowne writes, "A singular animation and an almost dramatic force are given to the poem by the beautiful apostrophe in vv. 5, 6, and the effect of this is heightened in a remarkable degree by the use of the present tenses. The awe and the trembling of nature are a spectacle on which the poet is looking. The parted sea through which Israel walks as on dry land, the rushing Jordan arrested in its course, the granite cliffs of Sinai shaken to their base – he sees it all and asks in wonder what it means".

The Psalmist now widens his address from the Red Sea and the Jordan to include the whole earth, "Tremble, thou earth, at the presence of the Lord". "Tremble" (2342) signifies "pain" as of a woman in travail. Well might earth tremble, at the presence of the God of Jacob. He is Lord (113), the great Adon, Sovereign Lord and Master, Proprietor and Governor, whom all must obey. He can turn the flinty rocks into pools and fountains. He did this for Israel in the desert and He can do it again. This is not merely the record of an historic fact, but an illustration of His power and a declaration of what that power can do.

For His people today He can do the same, giving them streams in the desert. As they sojourn through a wide wilderness which has nothing of any spiritual value for them, still He can supply every need of His people, providing refreshment for them in the barren world of their pilgrimage. But might there be another prophetic glimpse here, as in other Psalms? One day, the day of His power, earth will tremble again. His presence in that day will bring warmth, healing, and nourishment to the earth, as the Sun of righteousness rises with healing in His wings (Mal 4.2).

How heartily, and with what feeling and joyful emotion, would the celebrants of the Passover sing this Hallel around their lighted supper tables!

PSALM 115

Introduction

Although some ancient versions, such as the Septuagint, Syriac, Arabic and Ethiopic, unite this Psalm with Psalm 114 to make one Psalm, this is rejected by most commentators as being an arbitrary arrangement for which there is no justification. "By these versions", De Burgh says, "this Psalm is joined to the preceding, so as of the two to make one. But without reason; as, though connected in a series, they are distinct in subject". It is important to remember however, that this Psalm does indeed belong to the Hallel, comprised of Psalms 113-118, which was sung at the Passover, and that it has, therefore, an essential link, not only with its immediate predecessor, but also with the other five Psalms of the Hallel. The identity of the Psalmist is not known. So many names have been suggested, from Moses and David to Hezekiah, with many between. All are but conjecture. There is no indication in the Psalm as to who the author really was.

Keeping the great Exodus in mind, it will be recalled that Jehovah had wrought wonders for Israel in Egypt. He had, in quite a remarkable way, manifested His power until He led the people out from their bondage. They did, of course, grieve Him in the wilderness, and even when He brought them into the Promised Land, they still provoked Him, and at times they suffered His chastisement for their unbelief, as is remembered and expounded in other Psalms, as for example, in Psalm 106.

Psalm 115 appears to belong to one of those occasions when there was, as Kirkpatrick says, "a time of national humiliation when Israel supplicates Jehovah to vindicate the honour of His name by raising His people from their degradation. Why should the heathen be allowed to mock, when Israel knows Him to be supreme and omnipotent?"

The original Hebrew form of this Psalm suggests that vv. 1-8 and vv. 16-18 were sung by the whole choir of Levites, but that each verse from 9-15 was rendered antiphonally, either by the precentor and the choir, or, as some think, by two choirs. There are other occurrences of this arrangement in the Psalms, Psalm 24 being an excellent example, and this method of singing is referred to in Ezra 3.11, where the priests and the Levites "sang together" (AV), or, "sang one to another" (JPS and ASV), or "sang responsively" (RSV and NKJV). JND says, "They sang alternately together".

Although composed by an individual Psalmist, who cherished his own hopes and fears, yet the Psalm is national rather than personal; note the pronouns "us" and "we". It is the prayer of a nation in some distressing circumstances which cannot now be identified. Nevertheless the prayer is mingled with assurance, trust, and praise, in the belief that Jehovah will again come to their relief.

Several divisions of the Psalm have been suggested by various commentators. The following should be a help in the study of the eighteen verses. Verses 1-3 are an appeal for divine aid, for God's glory. Verses 4-8 mock the impotence of the idol gods of the heathen. Verses 9-14 encourage trust in Jehovah, and verses 15-18 sing of blessing from the Creator of heaven and earth.

Verses 1-3: Help for the Nation; Glory for God

"Not unto us, O Lord, not unto us!" What an emphatic renunciation of all merits of their own, and what an intense desire for God's glory, is enshrined in these opening words of the Psalm. While without doubt the nation longed for deliverance from some present trial, yet there seems uppermost in the Psalm a jealousy for the vindication and honour of their God. This was a noble motive for their appeal, that God should be glorified. The idolatrous heathen must not be allowed to mock. They plead His mercy and His truth, or, as some prefer, His lovingkindness and His faithfulness. Mercy and truth are very often linked in the Psalms as essential attributes of God – see Psalms 25.10; 61.7; 85.10; 86.15; 89.14; 98.3. For the sake of His mercy and His truth, the appeal is that God should work mightily for the people and in vindication of His own honour.

The heathen were taunting, mocking, asking derisively, "Where is now their God?" Had God wrought for them before? Where was He now, when they needed Him? Why should the heathen be permitted to deride them like this, and speak disparagingly of their God? It was insolent of them, and v.3 brings the answer to the question of the mockers, "But our God is in the heavens: he hath done whatsoever he hath pleased". Our God is sovereign, they are protesting. He does what He wills, when He wills, how He wills, for whatever reason He wills. If at times He conceals Himself in the heavens while His people suffer, it is not that He does not have the power to help them, but that in His sovereignty He awaits His time to reveal Himself for their aid and deliverance. He will act when He pleases, for His own glory.

Verses 4-8: The Impotence of Idols

Now it is Israel's turn to mock! "Our God is in the heavens", they can say, but the gods of the heathen were useless, lifeless idols. As Kirkpatrick paraphrases, "Do the heathen taunt us? What are their own gods? Nothing but their own handiwork, destitute of ordinary human senses, though represented with organs of sense". He continues, "For similar sarcastic descriptions of idols and the contrast between them and the living God, see Isaiah 44.9, 10; Jeremiah 10.1-16; Deuteronomy 4.28; Isaiah 2.20; Habakkuk 2.18, 19". Note that this present passage, Psalm 115.4-8, is repeated in Psalm 135.15-18.

What folly is idolatry! These idols may indeed be of valuable silver or gold, but as gods they are deaf, dumb, and dead. They do not have even the life of angels or of men, much less of deity. They are inanimate lifeless images. As Plumer says, "These images are silver and gold, of no more value as gods than the mire of the streets". The idolators, in their foolishness, had made their own gods. They had created them with mouths and eyes, ears and noses, hands and feet, and throats too, but they could neither speak nor see, nor hear, nor smell, nor handle, nor walk, nor even emit an inarticulate sound from their silver throats! What ridicule was this, but it was all true. The idol could not communicate with its devotees, it could not hear the prayers that were offered to it, it could not smell the incense burned in its honour, nor respond in the slightest way to the worshippers. Idol gods were absolutely impotent, and idol worship was therefore utterly foolish. This, then, was the great sadness, that those men who made the images, and trusted in them, were just like them, lifeless and powerless, bereft of sense and reason.

Well might Israel resent the taunts of those who mocked their God. Jehovah was in the heavens, supreme and sovereign. What right had they to mock, whose gods were but useless works of their own hands, incapable of answering any prayer, and with no ability to give help in any time of need.

Verses 9-14: Jehovah! Help and Shield of His people

The Psalmist turns away from the heathen to his own nation, from idolators to those whose God is Jehovah. Three times, in three consecutive verses, he encourages trust in Jehovah. He appeals to Israel in general, to the priestly house of Aaron in particular, and to those who fear the Lord. There is pathos in his appeal. Having described the folly of idols and idolatry, he exclaims, "O Israel…O house of Aaron". This commences the antiphonal section of the Psalm, where either the precentor or the first choir would sing, "O Israel, trust thou in the Lord", and the second choir would then respond with, "He is their help and their shield". Again the first voice or voices would sing, "O house of Aaron, trust in the Lord", and the second would respond, "He is their help and their shield". The third call, "Ye that fear the Lord, trust in the Lord", brings the same response, "He is their help and their shield". This latter category, those who fear the Lord, have sometimes been understood as a faithful godly remnant within the nation. Others identify them as God-fearing Gentiles who join with Israel in the worship of Jehovah. Dr Cohen points out that this is the thought of Jewish commentators, "understanding the reference to be to the pious Gentiles who come to worship in the Temple".

He refers to 1 Kings 8.41 and Isaiah 56.6. "Help" (5828) and "shield" (4043) need little comment. Jehovah is the succourer and protector of His people. All Israel, then, should trust Him, as should the priestly family, and those God-fearing strangers who have attached themselves to the people of God.

Jehovah has been mindful of all. Though He has been silent, He has not forgotten. His people are ever precious to Him, always in His thoughts, and He will bless them. The divine response to the people's trust is, as the trust, threefold. He will bless the house of Israel; He will bless the house of Aaron; He will bless them that fear the Lord. Then, as if in an added assurance to these strangers, He says, "both small and great". Proselytes of every rank and position may enjoy the blessing of the Lord. None shall be neglected, whether high or humble. It is sufficient that they but trust Him.

This was not only a present blessing from God, but the promise of future and continuing blessing too. "The Lord shall increase you more and more". This is understood by some to be a benediction rather than a promise, as the RSV rendering, "May the Lord give you increase, you and your children". Most, however, prefer to see a divine promise, an assurance of increase more and more, both to the fathers and to their children. What comfort this must have been to those who in faithfulness celebrated the Passover, remembering the past and solemnly contemplating the future. Perhaps, as some suggest, this promise would have been very precious to that relatively small remnant which returned from exile in Babylon to resettle the land.

Verses 15-18: Jehovah! Lord of Heaven and Earth

If idols were nothing, Jehovah was everything. Israel's blessings came from One who was the Creator of heaven and earth. The heavens are His dwelling place. He has given earth to men. It was His purpose from the beginning that man should have dominion on earth, as expounded in Psalm 8. The complete fulfilment of this awaits the return of Messiah, whose future glorious reign on earth is the burden of so many Psalms.

Meantime, it is the privilege and duty of men to praise the Lord. "The dead praise not the Lord, neither any that go down into silence". This does not in any sense deny that there is an eternal life for the believer after death, nor does it question the fact that in glory now, those saints who have been called Home unite there in praising the Lord. The Psalmist is thinking and speaking of man's earthly responsibility to praise God, and in this the dead cannot join. There is a present life in which to enjoy Him and express that joy in praise of Him. From the silence of the grave no voice of praise is heard. No hymn sounds out from that lonely tomb or that granite vault. Men must praise Him now, and with this avowal the Psalmist concludes, "We will bless the Lord". The dead praise not the Lord, but we will! Not only now, he is saying, but from this time forth and for evermore, we, the living, while we live, will praise the Lord.

One final word sums it all up – "Hallelujah!". Idol worshippers do not know such a word. They do not possess such joy, nor do they have such purpose as the saints of God have. Perhaps once more there is a prophetic glimpse into the great "evermore". In that glad day of Messiah's rule the whole earth will be filled with His glory, as anticipated in Psalm 72, and all men shall say "Hallelujah!". Praise the Lord!

PSALM 116

Introduction

Perhaps the most notable feature of this Psalm, a feature which is immediately apparent, is the individualistic theme which prevails throughout its nineteen verses. This is in sharp contrast to the preceding Psalm which was rather national and congregational. There, the pronouns were "us" and "we", but here they are "I", "me" and "my". Psalm 115 was the praise of a nation. Psalm 116 is the personal thanksgiving song of one who has been delivered from some severe sickness or danger, and from death itself. The song is the Psalmist's intermingling of love and praise and vows, and promises of thanksgiving to Him who has heard and delivered him.

It must be remembered, however, that the Psalm is a continuation of the Hallel, celebrating particularly the redemption of Israel out of Egypt. Since this is so, it would have been sung congregationally, during the Feast of the Passover, as if the whole nation was singing as a redeemed individual.

Psalm 116 is anonymous, with neither title nor indication of the identity of the Psalmist. Such anonymity is not without its advantages, because then saints of every age may find language here with which to express gratitude to God for His benefits and blessings. The circumstances described here must surely be experienced by many other believers, who may freely borrow from the Psalmist's vocabulary for their thanksgiving.

The Psalm is somewhat difficult to divide, and many suggestions have been offered. The following may be helpful. In verses 1-4 the Psalmist sings of answered prayer and of love's response. Verses 5-9 recount God's gracious dealings with him in his distress. In verses 10-14 he again remembers his affliction and he resolves to pay his vows to the Lord who delivered him, and to do this publicly. Verses 15-19 repeat his determination to perform his vows and bring his thanksgiving offerings to the Temple.

Verses 1-4: Answered Prayer and Love's Response

The Psalm begins delightfully, "I love the Lord". The Psalmist will, of course, add his reasons for his love, but these opening words seem to give character to the whole Psalm. Jehovah had heard the prayer of his afflicted child who now loved Him in return. In the expression "my voice and my supplications", notice that the conjunction "and" is in italics. It has been supplied by the translators and is not in the original text. As Dr Cohen comments, "The Hebrew has no 'and', so the phrase must be translated either 'my voice (even) my supplications', or, better, 'the voice of my supplications'". The Psalmist's pleading voice was his supplication and Jehovah had inclined (5186) his ear to listen to the prayer of the sufferer. What gracious condescension was this, that Jehovah, in all His majesty and greatness, should stoop from His lofty heights, bending low to listen to His servant. Such is the significance of the word "inclined". The Psalmist appreciated such interest and care, and, because Jehovah had deigned to hear and answer his prayer, "Therefore", he says, "will I call upon him as long as I live". He had learned the lesson of a lifetime, that in every affliction there was One who would graciously take notice of his cries for help, and would come to his aid. Answers to prayer are, for every saint, encouragements to pray again.

The Psalmist recalls the seriousness of his past condition. "The sorrows of death compassed me", he says. "Sorrows" (2256) is more often rendered "cords", and with this Strong agrees, though he suggests also "pains" or "pangs". JND's translation is "the bands of death". The RSV says, "the snares of death", and the RV and the JPS give, "the cords of death". Even if the AV rendering is retained, it is evident then that the poor Psalmist in his distress felt as though he was bound by these sorrows. The pangs of approaching death were as cords entwined around him. The pains (4712) of hell (7585) took hold of him. "The anguish of Sheol", says JND. "The straits of the nether-world" (JPS). "Sheol" was the OT designation for the abode of the dead, the grave-land, the place of no return (Strong). The Psalmist was apparently gripped by the fear of it. The writer of the Epistle to the Hebrews speaks of those "who through fear of death were all their lifetime subject to bondage" (Heb 2.15). Note the play upon words here. "The pains of hell *gat hold* upon me: I *found* trouble and sorrow". "Gat hold" and "found" are the same word (4672). The pains of "sheol" found him and he found distress and anguish. His plight was sad and serious. In such an apparently hopeless condition, what could he do? He says, "Then called I upon the name of the Lord". His prayer was brief and direct, "O Lord, I beseech thee, deliver my soul". It was urgent. "O Lord, I beseech thee, save my life" (RSV). It is so like the cry of Peter, when the wind was boisterous and the waves were enveloping him, "Lord, save me!" (Mt 14.30). How many a saint in distress has cried similarly for relief.

Verses 5-9: God's Gracious Dealings Recalled

The testimony of the Psalmist, having been delivered, is that Jehovah was gracious and righteous, and then he adds, "Yea, our God is merciful" (7355). This latter word signifies somewhat more than mercy as it is commonly understood. Strong says that it means "to love deeply; to be compassionate; to have tender affection; to pity". Such is the gracious character of God, and this must surely be the testimony of all who truly know Him.

There follows another tribute to this grace of God, that though He is indeed Jehovah, majestic, supreme, self-sufficient, and eternal, He delights to be the keeper, the preserver, of the simple (6612). Plumer quotes Calvin's comment on this word, who says, "such as, being undesigning, do not possess the requisite prudence for managing their own affairs". Jehovah graciously takes notice of the naivety of such, and preserves them. Their very simplicity, in itself commends them to Him for His help. "He helped me", says the Psalmist. "I was brought low, and he saved me" (RV, JND, JPS, RSV).

Now, having addressed others, the Psalmist speaks to himself, to his own soul, "Return unto thy rest, O my soul". There is an implication in the word "return", that he had known an earlier enjoyment of rest, but that in his affliction and anguish he had lost for a while the peace that once he had. The word "rest" is, in the Hebrew, a plural word. It is the plural of intensity, untranslatable into English, denoting full, complete, and perfect rest. Edersheim writes, "The word 'rest' is in the plural, as indicating complete and entire rest, at all times, and under all circumstances". The same rest is desired for the believer today, in that lovely apostolic benediction, "Now the Lord of peace himself give you peace, always by all means" (2 Thess 3.16). The Lord had dealt bountifully with the Psalmist, and he could now return to his former rest.

Jehovah's gracious dealings with His people are always bountiful. There is nothing stinted or measured in His blessings, as the following verse now explains. The Psalmist speaks of "my soul...mine eyes...my feet". He had been saved from death, his tears had been dried, his footsteps had been steadied. From dying and weeping and stumbling he had been delivered. He had been abundantly blessed and he now had every reason to be at rest. He makes a personal, joyful resolve; "I will walk before the Lord in the land of the living". He had no dread now of the dark land of "sheol". He was in the land of the living, and he would walk as being always in the sight of God, ever conscious that He who had delivered him would continue to watch over him. Jehovah was, after all, as had just been testified, the Preserver of those who, in simplicity, trusted Him.

Verses 10-14: "I Believed...I Will Pay My Vows"

The word "believed"(539), with which this section begins, has the thought of "trusting with assurance". The Psalmist may be simply stating, like Paul in 2 Corinthians 4.13, that all that he has said is but evidence of his faith. In the most difficult and adverse circumstances he has been able to speak for God because of his trust in God. As Alexander says, "His speaking was a proof of his faith". The somewhat different renderings adopted by the RSV and JPS, however, suggest a slightly different meaning. "I kept my faith, even when I said, 'I am greatly afflicted'" (RSV). "I trusted even when I spoke: 'I am greatly afflicted'" (JPS). Dr Cohen justifies these renderings, suggesting that "his faith held firm during the time his distress was acute". Whichever view is preferred, what is obvious is that, with the Psalmist, as with Paul, faith and words were closely allied, the one revealing the other.

"I said in my haste, All men are liars". Two things require comment here. First, "haste" does not necessarily imply undue hurry. Perhaps "fear, alarm, or consternation" may be better. Second, the Psalmist does not mean that every individual man is a liar. He is referring to mankind in general and in his affliction and trouble he had learned to trust in God alone. As David had said in Psalm 60.11, "Vain is the help of man". Men may not be dependable. They may even be deceitful. They may disappoint and fail. It was vanity therefore, to rely on man.

The Psalmist now recalls again the bountiful dealings of God with him. What could he render in return? What recompense could he give to the Lord? How could he repay the benefits that had been bestowed upon him? He knows what he will do. He will lift up the cup of salvation, he would call upon the name of the Lord, and he would pay his vows, not privately, but publicly in the presence of all the people. This appears to be an allusion to the peace offering of Leviticus 7.12, which would sometimes have been a sacrifice of thanksgiving, and may also have been associated with the making of vows. The "cup of salvation" of which he speaks, may simply mean the gracious provision of the Lord for him, delivering him from his affliction and saving him from his adversaries. He would accept this gratefully. Or, as many others suggest, it may be a reference to the drink offering which was often poured upon the sacrifice. See, for example, Leviticus 23.13; Numbers 15.5; Numbers 28.7.

The Psalmist resolves to pay his vows at once, without delay. The little word "now" suggests urgency, or immediacy, to some commentators, as, for example, Spurgeon, who comments, "Good resolutions cannot be carried out too speedily; vows become debts, and debts should be paid". It should be noted however, that not all translations include the word "now" in their text. Some substitute for it the word "yea", as JND and JPS: "I will perform my vows unto the Lord, yea, before all his people". Plumer writes, "The word rendered *now* is in Genesis 12.11, rendered as here; but commonly *I pray, I beseech,* or by the optative *oh*, (Gen 18.4, 30; Ex 33.18), so that we may read the verse: 'I will pay my vows unto the Lord, (oh that I may do so) in the presence of all His people', i.e., of assembled Israel, or in the most public manner possible". Observe an exact repetition of these words in v.18, a repetition of emphasis which is not without value.

Verses 15-19: The Sacrifice of Thanksgiving

The death of His saints is a precious thing in the sight of the Lord, and for this reason He had protected the life of His servant the Psalmist. The word "precious" (3368) is elsewhere rendered "dear; costly; excellent;

honourable". As Delitzsch comments, "The death of His saints is no trifling matter with God; He does not lightly suffer it to come about". His saints (2623) are, after all, His holy ones, His faithful, pious souls in a sinful world. He will preserve them because they are precious to Him, and this care had been proven in the experience of the Psalmist. T.W. Davies writes, "Jehovah does not regard the death of His favoured ones as a thing of no importance, as trivial, as cheap: it is much thought of, and will not be allowed unless strong reasons call for it".

In genuine humility the Psalmist again expresses his gratitude to God. JND's translation is so very expressive, "Yea, Jehovah! For I am thy servant; I am thy servant, the son of thy handmaid". "Servant" (5650) is "bondman", and "handmaid" (519) is "bondwoman". He acknowledges a willing bondage to Jehovah. How feelingly they would sing this at Passover, remembering the former cruel bondage to Pharaoh! Note the repetition, the emphasis of true servitude to the Lord. Delitzsch thinks that in the expression "the son of thine handmaid", the poet is mindful of his pious mother. Alexander rather suggests that "The additional phrase, *son of Thy handmaid*, is much stronger than *Thy servant*, and describes him as a homeborn slave". With this thought Kirkpatrick concurs, writing, "The 'son of Thy handmaid' is a synonym for 'Thy servant', but denoting a closer relationship, for servants born in the house were the most trusted dependants". He refers the reader to the servants of Abraham in Genesis 14.14.

Now, in a lovely play upon words, and with a delightful intermingling of thoughts and themes, the Psalmist exclaims, "Thou hast loosed my bonds". From the bondage of affliction Jehovah had released him, and now he was a willing slave of Him who had emancipated him. This was exactly true of Israel as a whole. Bondmen they had been in Egypt, unwilling, resentful slaves of Pharaoh. Jehovah had redeemed them out of that bondage to make them His own servants, bound to Him in a servitude of love. The same is true of believers in this present day. They have been loosed from the bonds of sin and are now happy to be in a bondage of love and devotion to their Redeemer.

Again the grateful Psalmist promises to offer his sacrifice of thanksgiving, doubtless a reference to the peace offering of Leviticus 7.11-12, and, repeating the closing clause of v.13, he again avows that he will call upon the name of the Lord. As has already been noted, v.18 is an exact repetition of v.14, laying stress upon the public nature of his confession of gratitude to Jehovah. His peace offering would, of course, be shared by his family and friends, and by the priestly house too (Lev 7.33-35), so it was no private praise that he was intending. Plumer, however, suggests that in the Psalm there are various modes of expressing thanks to God in solemn acts of worship, which may be secret, social, or public, as in vv. 13, 14, 17-19. He quotes Morison, who writes, "The closet will be the first place where the heart will delight in pouring forth its lively joys; thence the feeling will extend to the family altar; and thence again it will proceed to the sanctuary of the Most High".

The Psalmist lifts his eyes to the courts of the temple. There he will offer his sacrifice of thanksgiving. How his heart is thrilled as he exclaims, "In the midst of thee, O Jerusalem". Spurgeon's comments are very beautiful: "The very thought of the beloved Zion touched his heart, and he writes as if he were addressing Jerusalem, whose name was dear to him. There would he pay his vows, in the abode of fellowship, in the very heart of Judea, in the place to which the tribes went up, the tribes of the Lord". This would have been, of course, the language and the song of those who, in the Holy City itself, annually celebrated the Passover feast in grateful remembrance of the redemption from Egypt and from bondage. But how sadly did Another address the same City of Jerusalem, and lamented, "O Jerusalem, Jerusalem...how often would I...and ye would not" (Mt 23.37).

The Psalm of thanksgiving concludes with a "Hallelujah!". Praise ye the Lord!

PSALM 117

Introduction

This little Psalm is a delightful blending of brevity and beauty. It is, as Spurgeon remarks, "very little in its letter, exceedingly large in its spirit". This is the shortest of all the Psalms, and indeed the shortest of all the chapters of Holy Scripture. It lacks nothing in importance, however, and it is remembered and quoted by Paul in his treatise to the Romans concerning the Gentiles. Having stated that "Jesus Christ was a minister of the circumcision for the truth of God...and that the Gentiles might glorify God for His mercy", he then quotes Psalm 18.49 and Psalm 117.1 in confirmation (Rom 15.10-11). J.G. Bellet writes, "This Psalm, the shortest portion of the Book of God, is quoted, and given much value to, in Romans 15. And upon this it has been profitably observed, 'it is a small portion of Scripture, and as such we might easily overlook it. But not so the Holy Ghost. He gleans up this precious little testimony which speaks of grace to the Gentiles, and presses it on our attention'". He adds, "It helps to affirm the precious truth, that 'all Scripture is given by inspiration of God'". How remarkable it is, that the same Holy Spirit who has inspired the lengthy Psalm 119, has here condensed His divine thoughts into but two verses. The Psalms may differ in length and language, as the stars differ in magnitude, but they are all, equally, like the stars, the workmanship of the same God.

Because of its brevity, it is believed that this little Psalm may have been sung as Christians today sing the doxology. Or, as some think, it may have been sung as an adjunct to another Psalm. It is all praise. Dr Cohen says, rather quaintly, "The Psalm is happily described as 'but a Hallelujah writ large in two verses' (Cobb)".

There is no title, and no indication of the composer, or of the original circumstances for which it was written. It requires no division and it needs but little comment. But it is an integral part of the Hallel, the Psalms 113-118.

Verse 1: The Universal Summons to Praise

The Psalm opens and closes with a call to praise, and the summons is repeated in the first verse, but the two words rendered "praise" are different. The first is the word HALAL (1984), which is the word in *Hallel*-ujah. The second is SHABACH (7623) rendered "laud" by JND and others. The call goes beyond the national and religious boundaries of Israel and extends to nations and peoples everywhere. "Nations" and "peoples" are both plural words, denoting Gentiles. All men are being encouraged to join in the "Hallelujahs" which God's people were already singing.

Verse 2: The Reasons for Praise

The reasons for praising Jehovah are easily expressed. His mercy, His lovingkindness, has been great towards all men. If this has been especially true for Israel, He has, nevertheless, been good to men everywhere. His truth is enduring. He is the covenant-keeping God, always true to His promises, faithful to His covenant. Mercy and truth are, again and again in the Psalms, the great characteristics of Jehovah. Men should praise Him. They ought to praise Him. They must praise Him. The brief Psalm ends as it began. "Praise ye the Lord!" "Hallelujah!"

PSALM 118

Introduction

This is the last Psalm of the Hallel, called "The Egyptian Hallel", which began with Psalm 113. These six Psalms were sung on the great festive occasions, but were especially relevant and precious at the celebration of the Passover. For more detailed comment on the Hallel, refer to the introduction to Psalm 113 in this Commentary.

This is also the last, but not the least, of those Psalms which are truly Messianic. These are Psalms 2, 8, 16, 22, 24, 40, 41, 45, 68, 69, 72, 89, 91, 102, 110 and 118. This is not to say that Messiah cannot be found foreshadowed in many other Psalms, but these sixteen Psalms cannot be properly understood or interpreted apart from Messiah. It is absolutely necessary to view Christ in them to see their complete and ultimate fulfilment and purpose. In his delightful little volume entitled *The Messianic Psalms*, T.E. Wilson presents these Psalms in a chronological order relating to the life and ministry of the Lord Jesus, dealing with His eternal Sonship, His incarnation, crucifixion, resurrection, exaltation, and future glory. This Psalm, as has been said, is the last of these lovely Messianic Psalms.

There is no title to the Psalm, and no author is identified. Plumer, however, lists the names of some fourteen respected commentators, all of whom assigned it to David. Spurgeon also believed that David was the Psalmist, and based his belief on the narrative recorded in Ezra 3.10-11, where it appears to have been sung at the laying of the foundation of the second temple "praising the Lord, after the ordinance of David King of Israel". He points out that some of the words which they sang on that occasion were the first and last words of Psalm 118, and this he regards as an indication that they sang the whole Psalm.

Psalm 118 is quoted by the Lord Jesus during His ministry, and when He sang a hymn with His disciples before leaving the Upper Room for the Mount of Olives on His last evening, it is most likely that this was the hymn, or Psalm, which they sang, for it was the closing Psalm of the Passover celebration (Mt 21.42; 23.39; 26.30). The Psalm is also quoted by Peter in Acts 4.11 and 1 Peter 2.7, and by Paul in Ephesians 2.20.

It may be of interest to mention that this was Luther's favourite Psalm. Delitzsch calls it "his noblest jewel, his defence and his treasure". Luther's own words are, "This is my Psalm, my chosen Psalm. I love them all, I love all holy Scripture, which is my consolation and my life. But this Psalm is nearest my heart, and I have a peculiar right to call it mine. It has saved me from many a pressing danger, from which nor emperor, nor kings, nor sages, nor saints, could have saved me. It is my friend, dearer to me than all the honours and power of the earth". He adds, very beautifully, "I am not jealous of my property, I would divide it with the whole world. And would to God that all men would claim the Psalm as especially theirs! It would be the most touching quarrel".

Many varied suggestions have been made as to divisions of the Psalm. The following will be observed in the commentary. Verses 1-4 call upon the faithful to magnify the Lord for His mercy. Verses 5-18 are a record of suffering, whether of the Psalmist, or of the nation, or both. Verses 19-29 predict the final deliverance by the coming of the Messiah. In verse 29 the Psalm ends exactly as it began.

Verses 1-4: "O Give Thanks"

It is a characteristic of the truly grateful heart that it will want others to share in its gratitude. Such is the desire of this Psalmist. He would give thanks himself, but calls upon his fellows to give thanks with him. He has two reasons for his thankfulness. Jehovah is good, and His mercy, His lovingkindness, is as enduring as Himself. David had earlier sung of the same "goodness and mercy" in Psalm 23.6. They would follow him all the days of his life, he sang, until he reached the house of the Lord. These were sufficient grounds for magnifying the Lord.

He calls upon three classes, or categories, of saints to join in his praise, Israel, the house of Aaron, and them that fear the Lord. These three groups have been noticed before, twice, in Psalm 115. As to the first two, there is no difficulty. His call for thanksgiving goes out first to the whole nation; "Let Israel now say". He then singles out the priesthood, the house of Aaron, who, with priestly privileges and abilities, ought to specially engage in praise of Jehovah. With regard to the third group, there is not general agreement as to who exactly is meant. Some see "them that fear the Lord" as a godly, faithful remnant within the nation, and quote Malachi 3.16. Others rather think that these are God-fearing Gentiles, those who have abandoned heathenism and, with a fear of the Lord, have attached themselves to Israel as proselytes.

Perhaps any argument is unnecessary, for the call is really universal. It is incumbent upon all men to join in praise of Him whose mercy endures for ever. Let all confess, together, unitedly, that the Lord is good and gracious, and that His lovingkindness toward them that love Him is without end.

Verses 5-18: Trial and Trust

In the sufferings described in these verses T.E. Wilson sees "an historical outline of Israel's suffering". He writes, "The history of anti-Semitism, the concerted effort to wipe out the Jew, is a long, sad, and tragic one. It is the conflict of the ages, the battle of the seeds". "This", he says, "is the teaching of Psalm 118". The suffering may, of course, be primarily the experience of the Psalmist personally, but since the Psalm is confirmed in the NT as being Messianic, the sorrows of the Psalm may indeed be the afflictions of the nation. With this view Bendor Samuel agrees, but emphasises the future sufferings of the nation as a complete fulfilment of the Psalm. In his *The Prophetic Character of the Psalms*, he writes, "Here we have a brief but graphic description of Israel's tribulation, deliverance, and conversion at the return of Christ. As a title we may write over it the words of Jeremiah 30.7, 'It is even the time of Jacob's trouble; but he shall be saved out of it'".

The Psalmist, like the suffering nation, had called upon Jehovah out of his distress, and was heard. The JPS rendering is very expressive: "Out of my straits I called upon the Lord; He answered me with great enlargement". The sufferer had been hemmed in and perplexed, but had been lifted into a large place of ease and comfort. Jehovah was on his side. There was no need to fear. What could man do to him if the Lord was for him? This verse is quoted in Hebrews 13.6 for the encouragement of persecuted

Hebrew believers of a later day. With Jehovah as his Helper the Psalmist could look without fear upon those adversaries who hated him. Indeed, he could look in triumph upon them. As Kirkpatrick points out regarding the phrase "with them that help me"; "The expression is an idiomatic one. It denotes not merely among my helpers, as one among many, but 'in the character or capacity of my helpers', 'as a host of helpers'. He sums up in Himself the qualities of a class, viz. the class of helpers".

It has been estimated that, by a count of verses, vv. 8 and 9 of the Psalm are the middle verses of the Bible. Here is the great central lesson of Holy Scripture, "It is better to trust in the Lord than to put confidence in man". It is not only good, it is better, to take refuge in Jehovah, than to put confidence in man, even if those men are princes. Men may indeed be noble, and willing, but safer refuge from affliction and trouble is to be found in the Lord than in the greatest of men.

The Psalmist has already spoken of being in straits, hemmed in by distress. He was encompassed by heathen adversaries. They swarmed about him like bees. So it has ever been with the nation of Israel, and so it will yet be in days to come. The nations of v.10, are the "goyim" (1471), the word for heathen Gentiles. There is no hope for Israel except in Jehovah. Only "in the name of the Lord" can the enemies be destroyed, and the Psalmist now affirms his confidence of that, saying, three times, "In the name of the Lord I will destroy them". It is interesting to observe that the word "destroy" (4135) is the word "circumcise". It is so translated some thirty times in the AV. These uncircumcised "goyim", enemies of the people of God, must be "cut off". If this Psalm is in fact David's, then how he must have remembered that day when he confronted the Philistine, Goliath of Gath, with the words, "Thou comest to me with a sword, and with a spear, and with a shield: but I come to thee in the name of the Lord God of hosts" (1 Sam 17.45). So, "in the name of the Lord", he would conquer now, as he did then. The enemy would be vanquished again. They would be quenched like a fire of thorns which blazed up fiercely but momentarily, and was soon reduced to ashes.

Having spoken about his enemies, the Psalmist now speaks directly to them, addressing them as an individual: "Thou hast thrust sore at me". The adversary desired and planned his fall, just as with the nation. Some interpret this as David's address to Saul, but it is better to understand it as the enemy personified, addressed in the singular, and, if the speaker is Israel, then, as Kirkpatrick comments, "The community as an individual addresses its enemies as an individual. Israel and the foe are, as it were, two warriors matched in single combat".

Jehovah was their Helper. He becomes the strength and song, and the salvation, of those who trust Him. These words are taken from the Song of Moses in Exodus 15. It is easy to see how significant they must have been for Israel as they sang the great Hallel at Passover time, for they brought to the memory of every Jew that mighty Exodus from Egypt. The implication here is that He who delivered His people out of bondage then, was still their Helper, Deliverer, and Redeemer.

From the tents or booths of the pilgrims the voice of rejoicing would sound out. The RSV translates, "Hark, glad songs of victory in the tents of the righteous". On the great festive occasions, thousands of pilgrims to the feasts pitched their tents on the hillsides around Jerusalem, and from these dwellings the joyful singing of the people would be heard. Whether Passover/Unleavened Bread, Pentecost, or Tabernacles, these were joyous occasions which brought the people together from far and near, to remember, to celebrate and commemorate, and this they did heartily with music and Psalm.

How careful the Psalmist is to ascribe all the glory to Jehovah. This was the theme of the pilgrims' songs, "The right hand of the Lord doeth valiantly. The right hand of the Lord is exalted: the right hand of the Lord doeth valiantly". Three times in two verses he sings of "the right hand of the Lord", symbol of Jehovah's strength and power. It was this, and this alone, which had accomplished, and would accomplish, victory for him personally and for Israel nationally. "I shall not die, but live", he declares. How his adversaries had desired his death, and, perhaps, in his earlier distress he may himself have thought, despondently, that he might indeed die. Now he had the assurance that he would live and give the glory of it all to Jehovah. He would recount the deeds of the Lord and testify to the faithfulness of Him who had delivered him. In a highly spiritual appraisal of all that he had suffered, he sees his afflictions as having been the chastisement of the Lord. In v.18 the words "chastened" and "sore" are translations of the same word (3256). He had suffered severe discipline. Jehovah was admonishing him, correcting and teaching him, and it had been painful, but he had not been abandoned to death. The writer of the Epistle to the Hebrews, in a day much later than the Psalmist's, wrote, "Now no chastening for the present seemeth to be joyous, but grievous: nevertheless afterward it yieldeth the peaceable fruit of righteousness unto them which are exercised thereby" (Heb 12.11). There is, in all of this, as has been noted earlier, a prophetic application to Israel's future day of tribulation, "the time of Jacob's trouble" (Jer 30.7). Then, as that same Scripture adds, "He shall be saved out of it".

Verses 19-29: Messiah! Rejected yet Victorious!

There is no doubt of course, that these verses belong primarily to the Psalmist and to Israel, but our Lord's quotation of them in Matthew 21.42, 23.39, Mark 12.10 and Luke 20.17, and the application of them to Him in Matthew 21.9 and parallel passages, make this section of the Psalm truly Messianic in character. As has been noted in the introduction above, Peter also, and Paul, interpret the Psalm in relation to Messiah. Perhaps then, while recognising the personal sentiments of the Psalmist here, it is most touching to remember that the Lord Jesus probably sang these words during His last hours with His disciples, in the Upper Room. What must have been His thoughts on that last evening?

"Open to me the gates of righteousness, that I might enter through them and give thanks to the Lord" (RSV). Alexander suggests that "this might have been intended to accompany the entrance of the priests and people into the sacred enclosure, for the purpose of laying the foundation of the temple, as when David pitched the tabernacle on Mount Zion". But it could hardly be confined to that event only. Worshippers were constantly entering the gates of Jerusalem for the purpose of praise and thanksgiving, and such language as this would have been on many lips on many occasions. See also the reference to the gates in Psalm 24.7, 9. The gates of Zion were the gates of the Lord, in that they were the portals to the place where He had chosen to place His name. The Saviour knew, however, on that last evening, that before the next evening He would suffer outside the gate. He would be rejected, with the gates of Jerusalem firmly closed against Him (Heb 13.12).

"This is the gate of the Lord; the righteous shall enter through it" (RSV, JND). Notice that it is "the righteous" who are welcomed through this "gate of the Lord". It is not only priests and Levites, but people of any rank who are righteous, and this would embrace the three groups referred to in the opening verses of the Psalm. There is, as in Psalm 24, a moral fitness for approaching the holiness of the house of the Lord. "Who shall stand in his holy place?" It is not an official status but a moral standing, "He that hath clean hands, and a pure heart; who hath not lifted up his soul unto vanity, nor sworn deceitfully" (vv.3, 4). "Who shall dwell in thy holy hill? He that walketh uprightly, and worketh righteousness" (Ps 15.1, 2). He then, the only perfectly Righteous One, in that Upper Room, and in Jerusalem, knew that so soon He would leave through the gates of the city for Golgotha, and death. Yet He could sing, "I will praise thee"!

How well the Saviour knew, while He sang, "Thou hast heard me" (v.21), that, before He would utter these same words again (Ps 22.21), He would cry from the loneliness of the cross, "Why art thou so far from helping me, and from the words of my roaring? O my God, I cry...but thou hearest not" (Ps 22.1, 2).

In Matthew 21 the chief priests and the elders of the people had questioned the right and authority of the Lord Jesus to be teaching. He answered them in parables, and then challenged them, "Did ye never read in the scriptures, The stone which the builders rejected, the same is become the head of the corner?" (v.42). This may have been, as some think, a reference to an actual happening during the building of the temple, when a stone, judged unfit to be a corner stone, was rejected by the architects and builders, but eventually sought out and employed for that very purpose. Dr Cohen calls it, "The chief corner-stone", and remarks, "Either the top stone which completes the edifice (Zech 4.7), or the large stone at the foundation which binds the two layers at right angles (Is 28.16; Jer 51.26).

On either explanation it is a stone which holds an important place in the structure". This figure of the rejected stone being elevated to a place of honour, was true of King David himself, and is also true of the nation of Israel, despised by the nations around but destined for high dignity in the administration of a future kingdom.

The true prophetic, Messianic interpretation, however, is that given by the Saviour Himself. He was the stone which they set aside as unsuited to their plans. The builders of the nation, whether chief priests, elders, or scribes, Pharisees, Sadducees, or Herodians, had no place for Him, and so they refused Him. They did not know that Jehovah would do a marvellous thing, and that He whom they despised and rejected would yet be exalted to become the chief corner-stone in a glorious "ekklesia", the church and temple of a new dispensation (Eph 2.19-21). It was Jehovah's doing alone, and it was marvellous (6381), an extraordinary wonder.

The day of celebration was always a glad day for remembering and rejoicing. Whether Passover/Unleavened Bread, Pentecost, or Tabernacles, the memorial brought precious memories of all that Jehovah had done for them. For the Lord Jesus, singing in the Upper Room on that sad last evening with His disciples, how solemnly significant were these words. "This is the day which the Lord hath made". Toward this day, and this hour, He had moved in holy submission for thirty-three wondrous years. Now it had arrived. "We will rejoice and be glad in it", the Jewish celebrants would sing heartily. For Him, the shadow of the cross loomed large over the Upper Room. Soon it would be Gethsemane, the House of Caiaphas, Pilate's Judgment Hall, Herod's Palace, and Calvary. There would be mockery and blasphemy, cruelty and pain, darkness and loneliness, thorns, nails, and spear, and yet, He must have sung this Psalm. How well the Saviour would remember that only one week earlier, both the people and the children had sung it too, crying, "Hosanna to the Son of David: Blessed is he that cometh in the name of the Lord; Hosanna in the highest" (Mt 21.9, 15). "Hosanna" is, "Save now", or, "Save, I pray". It was an acclamation coupled with a prayer for prosperity, but, sadly, they were to reject the Prince of Peace, who alone could bring the prosperity for which they prayed. Out of the house of the Lord blessings would be pronounced upon the righteous who entered in.

Still keeping in mind the little company in the Upper Room, did the Saviour then sing of light, on His way to the darkness of the cross? "God is the Lord, which hath showed us light". Jehovah, the God of the Hebrews, had dispelled the darkness of their captivity in Egypt, but the same Jehovah would forsake the holy Sin-bearer at Calvary, who, from the sixth to the ninth hour of the following day, would hang on that tree in awful darkness.

For the expression, "Bind the sacrifice with cords, even unto the horns of the altar", three interesting and possible explanations have been suggested. First, it may mean that at the point of selection the victim was bound, and then led, bound, right up to the altar of sacrifice. So it was with Jesus. They bound Him at the Garden of Gethsemane, and it would appear that they kept Him bound throughout that long night and morning, until the eventual arrival at Golgotha. Second, note that the little word "even" is in italics, having been supplied by the translators, but not in the original Hebrew text. Some think, then, that this should read, "Bind the sacrifice with cords to the horns of the altar". This view is favoured by Spurgeon who speaks of "restive bullocks (which) were bound to the altar before they were slain". The Lord Jesus was indeed "bound to the altar", not by cords or nails, but by the bonds of love for His people and devotion to the will of His Father. Perhaps the third suggestion is the most acceptable. The word rendered "cords" (5688) is not the usual word for cords. It denotes wreath-like garlands which may have been hung around the necks of victors at the games. "Interwoven foliage", says Strong. On these festive occasions, the victims were often led to the altar garlanded with decorative braiding on their way to be sacrificed. Those many things which men did to Him, intended for the Saviour's dishonour, have instead made Him glorious in the eyes of those who love Him. The cords which bound Him, the thorns which crowned Him, the scourge with which they lashed Him, the rod with which they smote Him, have all become as garlands which cause His people to admire and adore Him. So adorned, He walked to Calvary.

Notice the repeated, "My God...My God" of v.28. How feelingly would the Lord Jesus have sung these in the conscious knowledge that soon He would cry, from the pain of the cross, "My God, my God, why hast thou forsaken me?". Now, in the Upper Room, He would join in the praise, extolling and exalting Jehovah.

The Psalm ends as it began. "O give thanks unto the Lord; for he is good: for his mercy endureth for ever". May every meditation on this, the last of the Messianic Psalms, ever bring Him to mind who, on His last evening, and on many other occasions during His lifetime in Galilee, must have joined in the singing of words of which He alone knew the full meaning.

PSALM 119

Introduction

In the introduction to his commentary on this Psalm, Spurgeon writes, "I have been bewildered in the expanse of the One Hundred and Nineteenth Psalm. Its dimensions and depth alike overcame me. It spread itself out before me, like a vast, rolling prairie, to which I could see no bound...This marvellous poem seemed to me a great sea of holy teaching, moving, in its many verses, wave upon wave; altogether without an island of special and remarkable statement to break it up. I confess I hesitated to launch upon it. Other Psalms have been mere lakes, but this is the main ocean. It is a continent of sacred thought". How true!

It is well known that Psalm 119 is the most lengthy of all the Psalms and is longer than any other chapter in any other book of the Bible. Its one hundred and seventy-six verses consist of twenty-two stanzas, corresponding with the number of letters in the Hebrew alphabet. Each of these stanzas consists of eight verses, all of which begin with the same letter, and this pattern is followed through all the letters of the Hebrew alphabet consecutively, from ALEPH to TAU. The alliteration had no lyrical purpose, but may have been an aid to memorisation of the Scriptures, especially for children, who, some think, were encouraged to learn this Psalm while they learned the letters of the alphabet. Delitzsch says, "In our German version it has the appropriate inscription 'The Christian's golden A B C of the praise, love, power, and use of the Word of God'". The acrostic arrangement is, of course, lost in the translation, and, as T.W. Davies observes, "No attempt to reproduce it in other languages has approached success".

In spite of the great length of the Psalm, and its variety of thought and expression, there is, nevertheless, but one theme throughout, that of the preciousness of the Word of God as Jehovah's revelation of His mind and will, and the indispensable value of that Word as the believer's guide in life. It is perhaps a grand expansion of the latter verses of Psalm 19. With a very few exceptions the Word of God is mentioned in almost every verse in the Psalm. Perowne, with others, points out that, "in every verse but one, the 122nd , there is direct reference to the Law under some one of the ten names, supposed to allude to the Ten Commandments, (*word, saying, testimonies, way, judgment, precept, commandment, law, statute, faithfulness*, or, according to another reading, *righteousness*)". He adds, "In the 132nd verse, the word "judgment" occurs in the Hebrew". Other expositors, as Davies and Cohen, omitting "way" and "faithfulness", see only eight different key-words, and these will be noted early in the commentary

There is no title to this Psalm, nor is it assigned to a particular author. Many, however, like Spurgeon, resist any attempt to take it from David. He deplores what he calls "the fashion among modern writers, as far as possible, to take every Psalm from David", and he continues, "We believe that David wrote this Psalm. It is Davidic in tone and expression, and it tallies with David's experience in many interesting points...After long reading an author one gets to know his style, and a measure of discernment is acquired by which his composition is detected even if his name be concealed; we feel a kind of critical certainty that the hand of David is in this thing, yea, that it is altogether his own". He later adds, "If David did not write it there must have lived another believer of exactly the same order of mind as David, and he must have addicted himself to Psalmody with equal ardour, and have been an equally hearty lover of Holy Writ".

What we do know about the author is that he was a man familiar with the Word of God, by his daily study of it, by his obvious delight in it and his zeal for it. He seems to have been suffering persecution and reproach on account of his piety, but the precepts and promises of the Word are his rule of life and his comfort. He has found in the divine Word a lamp for his feet and a light for his path, and it has become to him his treasured possession, his guardian and his guide.

Some expressions in the Psalm reveal that the writer is not an old man, and yet there are other sentiments which suggest that he is not a young man either. There is, throughout the Psalm, the voice of maturity and experience, and this carries some authority as he extols the greatness and the wonder of the Law. The Psalmist's meditations are not academic or technical, they are the fruits of constant careful perusal of God's Word with a sincere desire to learn its statutes, and a willingness to obey. But these things will be noted in the commentary.

The Psalm has its own divisions, in its acrostic arrangement. It needs no others. Nor indeed does it require much exposition, for the Psalmist has stated his observations in language relatively easy to understand. There may not be any continuity or progress of thought in the Psalm, but through the whole, there is that love for the Word and a longing to know it better, which creates in the reader a kindred desire for the things of God.

ALEPH

Verses 1-8: Desires after Righteousness

This great Psalm begins, so appropriately, by remarking on the blessedness, the happiness, of those who walk uprightly. It is the opening word of the whole Psalter in Psalm 1.1, and also of the Sermon on the Mount in Matthew 5.3. Walking in the way prescribed by the Word of God brings its own happiness, and this is the theme of the Psalm throughout. With regard to the word "law" (8451), which occurs twenty-five times in the Psalm, and is the Hebrew "Torah", Dr Cohen comments that "It is inaccurately translated by 'law', which has given the wrong impression that a legal system is intended. The true meaning is 'teaching, direction,' and it connotes the whole will of God as imparted to man for his guidance". "Torah" is the first of the key-words of the Psalm, and it is followed almost immediately by the second key-word, which is "testimonies". The blessedness is repeated. How happy is the man who walks in God's ways, keeps His testimonies, and seeks God whole-heartedly.

Those who, with a whole heart, seek after God, aspire to live for His glory, and will therefore do no iniquity. This does not mean that they will ever be sinless, but that they do not deliberately practise sin. Living for God and living in sin are not compatible. Those who walk in His ways walk in the paths of righteousness and depart from iniquity. The precepts of the Lord have not been given lightly. He commands them, and those who love Him must keep them diligently.

The second part of this first stanza is addressed directly to Jehovah. "Precepts", the third key-word, is soon followed by the fourth, "statutes", and with a willing heart the Psalmist prays, "O that my ways were directed to keep thy statutes". These are noble ambitions, to obey these precepts and observe the statutes of the Lord. Then he would not be ashamed, with his eyes fixed on all the commandments of the Lord (RSV). "Commandments" is the fifth key-word, a general word for those divine regulations for holy living.

In such a condition, and perhaps only in such a condition, the believer can sincerely engage in praise and thanksgiving. With uprightness of heart, morally pure in thought, word, and deed, the Psalmist could say, "I will praise thee". Note that he confesses that he is still a learner. Will any man ever be fully conversant with all the mind of God? "When I shall have learned thy righteous judgments", he says, he vows that he will give thanks with a heart that has responded willingly to what he has learned. Of "righteous judgments" (4941), translated "ordinances" by RSV and JPS, Dr Cohen says, "*ordinances*. the sixth key-word: lit. 'judgments' which regulate a man's relationship with his neighbour, and are characterised by righteousness". The Law of God will govern every department of a man's life, his attitude toward God, toward his family and friends, and towards his fellow men everywhere. Yet again, the Psalmist declares his determined desire to observe the statutes of the Lord, and then he prays, with a certain pathos, "O forsake me not utterly". How well he knows, for he has seen it in the history of the nation, that Jehovah will indeed withdraw His presence when and where there is disobedience. This is the prayer of a man who longs to live obediently, and ever with the approval of the God of the law, the testimonies, the precepts, the statutes, the commandments, and the ordinances which he has learned, and which he knows are the mind of God for him.

BETH

Verses 9-16: Longing for Knowledge and Obedience

In the opening verse of this second stanza the Psalmist asks, and answers, an important question: "Wherewithal shall a young man cleanse his way?". The Psalmist knows the peculiar difficulties of young men, "whose passions and temptations are strong in proportion to their inexperience" (Alexander). But what of the young man who desires to keep himself pure, living for God in a sinful world? The answer is found in taking heed to the Word of God. "Word" (DABAR - 1697) is the seventh key-word, denoting generally the expressed mind and will of God. If the mind of God has been revealed in His Word, then purity of life is to be maintained by constant heed to that Word.

This whole stanza is addressed to Jehovah. Once again the importance of whole-heartedness is stressed. This has been mentioned in v.2, and now, in v.10, the Psalmist says, "With my whole heart have I sought thee". But well he knows, as every believer knows, that the human heart is prone to wander, and he prays that he might be preserved from erring, kept from straying from the divine commandments. Now he employs a different word from that of v.9, when he says in v.11, "Thy word have I hid in mine heart". "Word" (565), is now IMRA, and is, in the words of Dr Cohen, "the eighth and last key-word, a poetical variant of DABAR of v.9". It denotes the spoken Word of God, and is similar to the "Torah", the "law" of v.1. What God has said, the Psalmist has laid up in his heart as the great preservative from sin. He has hidden that Word in his heart, as a man might hide some precious object or treasure, and with that Word in his heart he will be protected from sinning against God.

"Blessed art thou, O Lord", he now exclaims, but this is not the same blessedness of the opening verses. There it was the happiness of the righteousness man. Here it is the adoration, the adulation, which is due to Jehovah. He is blessed (1288), worthy that men should bow before Him in praise and worship. Yet again, while he praises, the Psalmist pleads, "Teach me". What holy repetition there is in this Psalm! There are repeated desires to learn, to know more of the will and the ways of God, and to have a heart ready to obey. Praise is mingled with prayer, worship with wonder, and adoration with expectation that Jehovah will hear and come to the help of His child.

The Psalmist has not been reticent in speaking of these things to others. If he has hidden them in his heart, this does not mean that he has kept his knowledge to himself. He has recounted, and unashamedly declared, what he has learned, so that others too might be instructed in the ways of God. He has enjoyed his exercise too, rejoicing in the things of God as other men might rejoice in their riches. He found the joy and satisfaction in the "Torah" which others sought in the acquisition of wealth. The precepts of the Lord occupied his mind in meditation and the ways of the Lord were his continual desire. He found delight in the statutes of the Lord, and not, like others, in seeking pleasure in things material and temporal. It is in this happiness that he resolves, "I will not forget thy word".

GIMEL
Verses 17-24: Consolation in the Word

In the previous section the Psalmist has been writing as a young man who earnestly desired to know the mind of God and obey the divine precepts. Now he prays as a servant of the Lord, a pilgrim and a sojourner, a stranger in a hostile world. He is content to be a bondman of God, and as a bondman he has no personal rights or merits, but pleads, "Deal bountifully with thy servant". He appeals to the liberality of Jehovah, to grant to him that which he cannot demand. But his motives are pure. His desire is that he might live, and in his life observe the Word of the Lord.

The petition which follows has been the prayer of many a believer ever since the Psalmist penned the words. How many have borrowed his language and have also prayed, "Open thou mine eyes, that I may behold wondrous things out of thy law". The word "open" (1540) is translated "uncover" more than thirty times in the OT. He desires that the veil might be lifted, that the scales might be removed, and that he might be enabled to behold and appreciate the wonders of the Word of God. As Thomas Manton says, "The Hebrew phrase signifieth, *unveil mine eyes*. There is a double work, negative and positive. There is a taking away of the veil, and an infusion of light".

He confesses that he is a stranger in the earth, a sojourner, and then immediately adds, "Hide not thy commandments from me". His thought seems to be, paraphrased, "I am a sojourner, an alien passing through and passing on; let me know Thy will for me during this little while of my pilgrimage". Such was the intense longing which the Psalmist had after these commandments, the judgments, of the Lord, that he felt as if his heart was breaking with the yearning. It was constant too, "at all times". It was no spasmodic, fickle desire, but a continuing ardent hunger for the knowledge of the divine will as revealed in the "Torah", that body of teaching which was the mind of God for His people.

The Psalmist knew that the curse of God was upon those insolent men who despised the divine law. These were proud (2086) men, arrogant and presumptuous, who wandered with impunity from the commandments of the Lord. Such evil men despised and scorned the godly, and the Psalmist prays that their reproach and contempt might be removed (1556), rolled off from him. He pleads this on the ground that he has endeavoured always to observe the divine testimonies. If reproach has come as a result of his doing God's will, then surely the Lord would enable him to overcome. Indeed, even princely men, nobles and rulers, plotted against him, but while they conspired and consulted together, he, as the servant of the Lord meditated in the statutes of the Lord. Jehovah's testimonies were his delight and they were also his counsellors. Let the professedly wise men who reproached him do what they would, he would resort to the divine Word for guidance. While his adversaries took counsel with each other, whether Saul and his nobles, as some suggest, or whoever, the commandments of the Lord would be the Psalmist's counsellors (582). They were, in the Hebrew, "the men of his counsel", and so they are to the godly of every age.

DALETH

Verses 25-32: Longings for the Comfort of the Word

The Psalmist is depressed and the figure he uses denotes the intensity of his grief. He is bowed down, cleaving to the dust, as it were, sinking under the weight of his trouble. He longs for a quickening, a reviving of his low spirit, a renewal of his vitality, but he knows that this can come only through the divine Word (1697). Paul speaks similarly in Romans 15.4 where he says that the believer "through patience and comfort of the scriptures might have hope". The Psalmist had declared his ways to the Lord in prayer. He had made known his experiences and his need, and the Lord had heard and answered. "Teach me", he now pleads. How willingly and how often does he confess his lack of knowledge and his longing to know more of the statutes of the Lord.

Having declared his ways to the Lord, he now says, "Make me to understand the way of thy precepts". Is there an interesting play upon words here? Is the Psalmist saying, "I have recounted my ways; tell me now Thine – the way of Thy precepts."? So, if Jehovah would communicate with him, teach him, and help him to understand, he would be able to meditate upon the wonder of all that the Lord had done. Note that "wondrous works" (6381) in v.27, is exactly the same word as "wondrous things" in v.18. All that Jehovah does, and all that He says in His Word, are wonders to be discovered and explored by every meditative soul. But how very especially are these wonders precious to the soul in grief. The heart that had been breaking with longing in v.20 is now melting in sadness, but, in his heaviness, the Psalmist knows that his strength can be renewed by the Word. There are, of course, great principles here which transcend dispensations and apply to believers of all ages.

Having spoken of "the way of thy precepts", the Psalmist now speaks of another way, the way of lying, or, the way of falsehood. He prays to be kept from that way. This may simply mean lies, in the ordinary, usual sense of that word, or it may denote the false and unfaithful way taken by those who abandoned, in apostasy, the way of the Lord. This latter meaning is reinforced by the expression which follows: "I have chosen the way of faithfulness" (JND, RSV, JPS). If others, in unfaithfulness, reject the truth of God, he will cling to the "Torah", the law which reveals the mind and will of the Lord. "Grant me thy law", he prays. "Graciously favour me with its teachings". He had already made his choice. He had set the ordinances of the Lord before him. "I have stuck unto thy testimonies", he says. He would be found cleaving to them, and prays that he might never have cause to be ashamed. His plea is that the Lord would be true to him as he was true to the Lord, and that none might ever be able to taunt him, mockingly suggesting that it was futile to trust and obey as he had been doing.

Once again he speaks of "the way", saying, "I will run the way of thy commandments". This is the way of truth, the way of faithfulness, and this is the way to enlargement of heart, enabling a man to rise above circumstances, to be greater than the things which grieve him. This fourth section of the Psalm is indeed, as has been suggested, a longing for the comfort that comes alone through the Word of the Lord.

HE

Verses 33-40: Desires after Obedience and Holiness

For the third time in this Psalm the Psalmist prays, "Teach me". He makes this request nine times, spread throughout the Psalm, in vv. 12, 26, 33, 64, 66, 68, 108, 124, 135, revealing the sincere and constant desire of his heart to know more and more of the Word of God. It is interesting to note that the word "teach" (3384) is "the Hebrew verb from which the noun "Torah" is derived" (Cohen). "Torah" is the first key-word in the Psalm, rendered "law" in v.1. This the Psalmist again calls, "The way of thy statutes", and he promises to keep that which he has been taught. The expression "unto the end" (6118) is a translation of one word meaning "reward". The thought seems to be that obedience to the law of the Lord is reward in itself. There is a similar thought in Psalm 19.11, where, speaking of the judgments of the Lord, the Psalmist uses the same word, and says, "in keeping of them there is great reward". Obedience brings its own reward.

Once again he prays for understanding (995). This is another familiar word in the Psalm, occurring seven times and denoting prudence and perception, intelligence and discernment. A cognate word (7919), also translated "understanding", may be noted in v.99. The Psalmist renews his vow, that, with understanding, he will observe and keep the law (8451), the "Torah", and yet again he promises whole-heartedness in his obedience. He would have his entire being absorbed with obedience to the divine law.

In words reminiscent of Psalm 23 he now prays, "Make me to go in the path of thy commandments". This is so similar to, "He leadeth me in the paths of righteousness", in Psalm 23.3. In such a life of holiness the Psalmist found his delight (2654), his pleasure. This was the characteristic of the blessed man of Psalm 1. His delight, too, was in the law of the Lord (Ps 1.2). There is indeed a pleasure in living for God, knowing that such a life of obedience brings pleasure to Him also.

The Psalmist knows that holiness and covetousness are not compatible. He would shun covetousness, and therefore he prays, "Incline my heart unto thy testimonies". He knows, too, however, that there is a natural, human, tendency to covetousness, and this is why he prays, "Incline (5186) my heart". This word may be rendered "bend". He is willing for God to bend his will to do the divine will, so that he might be preserved from covetousness. Perowne says, "Covetousness, or, rather, 'gain unjustly acquired'...The Hebrew word can only mean *plunder, rapine, unjust gain*". Paul warns that it is the root of all evil (1 Tim 6.10). Covetousness gives birth to every kind of evil. How eloquently does Spurgeon denounce it. He writes, "It is as mean as it is miserable. It is idolatry, and so it dethrones God; it is selfishness, and so it is cruel to all in its power; it is sordid greed, and so it would sell the Lord Himself for thirty pieces of silver. It is a degrading, grovelling, hardening, deadening sin, which withers everything around it that is lovely and Christlike". Devotion to the will of

God and obedience to the Word of God are the great preservative for every saint.

Now the Psalmist prays that he may be saved from beholding vanity. Two words require comment. "Beholding" (7200) means more than merely "seeing". It implies gazing upon with approval, observing intently with a measure of enjoyment and complacency. "Vanity" (7723) is "nothingness; emptiness; worthlessness". From this the Psalmist prays to be delivered, feasting his eyes upon the unreality of the world's vain things which are nothingness compared to the merits of walking in the ways of the Lord.

As the servant of the Lord, devoted to the fear of the Lord, he now asks for confirmation of the promises of the Lord to him. "Stablish thy word unto thy servant". As the RSV renders it, "Confirm to thy servant thy promise". The greatest of the Lord's servants may at times become despondent, assailed by doubts and in need of assurance. It is for such assurance that the Psalmist now prays. Perhaps he feels that since he is devoted to the fear of the Lord he has a right to ask with reverence that the Word of the Lord might be made sure to him. The fear (3374) of the Lord has been sometimes defined as a reverential awe of the Lord. This was not a slavish fear, but a heart acknowledgement of the majesty, the greatness, and the holiness of God. This was lacking in so many other men, but the Psalmist was devoted to it.

Observe, however, that he has another fear (3025). This is a different word. There was something of which he was indeed afraid. Men around him would mock him for his piety. They would taunt him for his obedience to the law and his regard for the judgments of the Lord. These judgments were good, as he says. He desired to keep them, but there was a fear of man. The reproach for righteousness was hard to bear. It should perhaps be pointed out that some commentators view this differently, and think that the Psalmist's fear here is that he might fail in his obedience to the law and so occasion the ridicule of men who would laugh and scorn at his failure. Both things are true of course, but expositors are divided as to which particular thought is intended in the context.

The Psalmist's desire for holiness has been a sincere and genuine yearning. He has longed after the divine precepts, and prays that even now he might be quickened, revived, renewed, in his quest for righteousness. Plumer writes, "The petition is for liveliness in the knowledge and practice of holiness, according to the tenor of God's Word and by its operation on the heart". The prayer, "Quicken me", occurring twice in this section, is found nine times throughout the Psalm, and is an interesting meditation. See vv. 25, 37, 40, 88, 107, 149, 154, 156 and 159. It is always a prayer for revival.

VAU

Verses 41-48: A Prayer for Strength and Courage

As in the closing verses of the previous section, the Psalmist is again appealing for assurances from God. Albert Barnes makes an interesting observation, and writes, "This commences a new portion of the Psalm, in which each verse begins with the letter *Vau*. There are almost no words in Hebrew that begin with this letter, which is properly a conjunction, and hence in each of the verses in this section the beginning of the verse is in the original a conjunction – *vau*". Perhaps this denotes a continuing unbroken appeal for the lovingkindness and deliverance which would strengthen him in his personal trust and in his testimony for God. This section is all petitions and promises, and, as on so many other occasions, the Psalmist is careful to say, "according to thy word (565)". This expression is found eight times in the Psalm and although "word" is not always the same, nevertheless the thought is the same, that everything should be in accordance with the revealed will of God. See vv. 9, 25, 41, 58, 76, 154, 169 and 170, where the particular form of "word" is indicated in the commentary.

Strengthened by the mercy of God and the Word of God, and by the assurance of salvation, the Psalmist now feels equipped to face the scoffers. He could answer those who reproached him for his faith, whether they were heathen men of the surrounding nations, or, as was sadly possible, scornful skeptics of his own nation. With God's Word in his heart, and the assurance of his salvation he could answer their taunts and stand firm in his trust, his confidence, in the Word (1697).

He now calls that Word "the word of truth" and his prayer for strength to witness for God continues. He prays, "Take not the word of (thy) truth utterly out of my mouth". If God should indeed withhold from him the assurances for which he was asking, then this would virtually rob him of his ability to testify for God. Delitzsch, agreeing that this refers to the duty of confessing God, writes, "The meaning of the prayer is, that God may not suffer him to come to such a pass that he will be utterly unable to witness for the truth; for language dies away in the mouth of him who is unworthy of it before God". Still, the Psalmist's expectancy and hope was in the judgments of the Lord, and so, with his prayer granted, he would keep the law (8451), he would observe the "Torah", "continually for ever and ever", or, as Dr Cohen has it, "until his dying day".

The keeping of God's law, far from being bondage, is, to the Psalmist, true freedom. "I will walk at liberty", he says, "for I seek thy precepts". The JFB commentary renders, "I will walk at large". His observance of the law, his keeping of the divine precepts, brings him into a broad place, unfettered and unrestrained. As Matthew Henry comments, "The service of sin is perfect slavery; the service of God is perfect liberty. Licentiousness is bondage...conscientiousness is freedom". It is so to believers of every age. "Godliness with contentment is great gain" (1 Tim 6.6).

In the enjoyment of this liberty the Psalmist could be courageous in his testimony for God. He could witness to kings without fear or shame, as Daniel did in his day (Dan 2.15-47), as Paul did before Agrippa (Acts 26.1-

27), and as did, in later days, Martin Luther, John Knox, and others. With consciences clear before God these men boldly witnessed a good confession, and bore testimony before the monarchs of their day.

How often the Psalmist repeats his resolutions, saying, "I will...I will...I will". Now he says, "I will delight myself in thy commandments. "I have loved them", he says, but perhaps the present tense is better, "I love...". Why should he not then delight himself in the law which he loves? His love for the commandments of the Lord, and his meditation in them, cause him to lift up his hands in the attitude of prayer and worship. Here, then, is that liberty of which he has spoken. The man who diligently observes the precepts of the Lord may go out to men in testimony, and go in before God in intercession and worship. He may, with a holy freedom, speak to men about God, and speak to God about men. This is a large place indeed.

ZAIN

Verses 49-56: Renewed Comfort in God's Word

As Alexander Maclaren comments, "This section has only one verse of petition, the others being mainly avowals of adherence to the Law in the face of various trials". In keeping with this, the Psalmist here speaks as a servant. This denotes humility, obedience, and faithfulness to the divine precepts. In such a character he now pleads that the Lord will remember His Word to him. This probably has the thought of God's promises, and trust in this word of promise has brought the Psalmist comfort and hope. Kirkpatrick remarks, "As a faithful servant he ventures to claim a corresponding faithfulness from his Lord". The Psalmist is no stranger to affliction, which he mentions so often in the Psalm, but resort to the Word of the Lord has been a source of consolation to him. That Word has quickened him, has revived his drooping spirits when, in adverse circumstances, he felt downcast and discouraged.

He now mentions one particular, and familiar, source of affliction. Proud men (2086), arrogant and insolent, had mocked and scorned him. Was their derision of him due to his keeping of the law? If so, he had not swerved from adherence to that law. In spite of the ridicule of these ungodly men he had remained steadfast in his obedience to the divine Word. He had remembered Jehovah's judgments, the divine ordinances. These were, after all, greater than the men who derided him. The law was "of old" (5769). It was everlasting. It pre-dated these mockers. It existed before they did, and would abide when they had gone. In this, he says again, he had comforted himself.

As the Psalmist contemplated the wickedness of these godless men, he says, "Horror" (2152) hath taken hold upon me" (AV). This is translated "hot indignation" by the RV and RSV, and "burning indignation" by JND. Strong says, "raging heat". He was incensed at the insolence of these men who had chosen to forsake God's law. They had, by abandoning the law, rendered themselves lawless, and this created wrath in him, perhaps mingled with godly sorrow that men should so live. How different it was with him. The statutes of the Lord had become his songs. He was a pilgrim, a sojourner, just passing through, and as he journeyed he could sing. This brought the comfort and refreshment to his spirit which every pilgrim needed. Life was transient, with so many afflictions and sorrows, and it was good to have, as another ancient said, "songs in the night" (Job 35.10).

Once again the Psalmist says, "I have remembered". He had been careful to remember Jehovah's ordinances in v.52, and now, in v.55, he remembers the name, the revealed character, of Jehovah. He remembers, he says, "in the night". When the godless men who deride him were either sleeping or revelling, he was singing of Jehovah. His midnight songs were accompanied by prayer, too, in v.62. He could sing and pray, knowing that he had observed God's law and kept His precepts. This he had for his comfort and joy in the midst of his trials. This he had, and no man could take it from him. Ungodly men might mock and scorn, but they could not rob him of the consolation which was the portion of those who kept the law of the Lord.

CHETH

Verses 57-64: Devotion, even in Affliction

In the very heart of this section the Psalmist laments that lawless men have sought, as it were, to entangle him with cords. They have been relentless in their persecution, but this has not diminished his love for the Lord, nor has it deterred him in his obedience to His commandments. "Thou art my portion, O Lord", he exclaims in the opening verse of the section. With this rendering the RV and RSV agree, but others favour the translation by JND, which says, "My portion, O Jehovah...is to keep thy words". Most commentators acknowledge that either of these renderings may be correct, the difference being due to a simple variation in punctuation. Perhaps essentially there is no conflict between the two. The man who observes the words and precepts of the Lord can truly say, "The Lord is my portion". Obedience to His Word brings with it enjoyment of the Lord Himself.

The Psalmist had intreated the favour of the Lord. This word "favour" (6440), is, in the Newberry margin, rendered "face", and indeed it is so translated nearly four hundred times throughout the OT. It may also denote the thought of the divine presence, and it is as if the Psalmist is asking that the face of God might be turned towards him in grace, giving him the comfort and assurance of the presence of God with him. Perhaps the spirit of that ancient priestly blessing is here; "The Lord make his face shine upon thee...The Lord lift up his countenance upon thee" (Num 6.24-26). Both "face" and "countenance" in Numbers 6 are the same word as that translated "favour" in this verse. Yet again the writer avows his whole-heartedness. He has been sincere and diligent in his entreaties for the presence of God. "Be merciful unto me", he pleads. He longs that

Jehovah might be gracious to him, in accord with that Word (IMRA – 565) which he loves, and which he endeavours to keep.

As with every sincere and thoughtful believer, the Psalmist at times reflected on his own behaviour, and this had prompted some regulation of his pathway. Dr Cohen expresses it well when he writes, "He examined his conduct, and finding it defective, repented and returned to the path God commanded". He subjected his life to the divine law, and he did it urgently too. It is imperative that good resolutions should be carried out at once for convictions can become blurred, and even forgotten. "I made haste", he says, "and delayed not". He acted obediently and immediately.

The poor Psalmist had his share of opposition from ungodly men. These men may well have been apostates from his own nation, and this would have made it especially hard to bear. "The bands of the wicked have robbed me", he laments. The thought is that wicked men had sought to entrap him, as if wrapping cords about him. "The bands of the wicked have wrapped me round" (JND). "The cords of the wicked ensnare me" (RSV). Kirkpatrick writes, "The cords of the wicked have entangled me", and he suggests that this is "a metaphor from the snare or noose of the hunter". Compare a similar thought in v.110. But though he suffered so much from these men, he had remained faithful. "I have not forgotten thy law", he says. Indeed, far from forgetting it, the righteous judgments of the Lord were in his thoughts even at the midnight hour. It was, as Plumer says, "a time when men are commonly wrapped in slumber", and at such a time he would rise from his bed to engage in thanksgiving to God. Note, too, that this would have been an hour of very personal private devotion. In the solitude of midnight, from the privacy of his own room, the incense of his gratitude would rise to Jehovah. This was his joyful exercise while wicked men opposed him.

Those who would live godly must be careful of their company. Accordingly, the Psalmist had chosen as his companions those that feared the Lord. His associates were men of like mind as himself. Had not the opening words of the very first Psalm in the Psalter stated the same thing? "Blessed is the man that walketh not in the counsel of the ungodly, nor standeth in the way of sinners, nor sitteth in the seat of the scornful". As Paul writes, of course, it is not possible to avoid all social contact with evil men, "for then ye must needs go out of the world" (1 Cor 5.9, 10). However, choosing and preferring their company is a different matter, and the Psalmist wisely chose the fellowship of men who feared God.

In his devotion to Jehovah, the Psalmist now seems to see the love of God everywhere. The whole earth, it seemed to him, was full of the goodness and kindness of God. As Plumer says, "When the heart is duly affected by saving grace, it seems as if all nature were, for good cause, praising the Most High. Proofs of His mercy appear on every hand. The stars sing His praises. The songsters of the forest carol their notes to the glory of their Creator". Believers of the present day sing the same sentiment:

Heaven above is softer blue,
Earth around is sweeter green;
Something lives in every hue
Christless eyes have never seen.
(G. Wade Robinson)

Such noble thoughts as these now prompt the Psalmist to pray again, as he had done in v.12, "Teach me thy statutes". He longs to know more and more of his God, and of those things which would please Him in the lives of His people.

TETH

Verses 65-72: The Goodness of God

Having observed, in the closing verse of the preceding section of the Psalm, that the whole earth was full of the loving-kindness of the Lord, the Psalmist now expresses his appreciation of the goodness shown to him personally. As the servant of Jehovah, the Lord had dealt graciously with him. "According unto thy word" (DABAR – 1697) signifies that Jehovah had been true to all His promises. Once again he prays, "Teach me". With all deepening appreciation of the Lord there comes increasing desire to know Him better. The Psalmist asks for good judgment and knowledge. He wants discernment concerning the commandments which he has believed. He desires, as Dr Cohen says, "ethical insight to appreciate the moral worth of God's commandments. He has *believed* in them, knowing that since they emanate from a divine source they must be right; but he also desires to possess both understanding and knowledge of them".

The Psalmist was no stranger to suffering, but he knows that often his affliction was the chastening of the Lord. He had, at times, gone astray, he had erred, and the Lord had disciplined him. Such trials in the school of divine chastening were intended to restore him to the divine Word from which he had strayed, and in humility he recognised this. His present obedience to God's Word was the fruit of the chastisement. He harboured no bitterness at all toward the Lord for his suffering. He could see the good hand of the Lord in it all, and he exclaims, "Thou art good, and doest good". What God does is but a reflection of what He is. His acts are in accord with His nature. He does good because He is good. Perhaps it is the remembrance of this inherent goodness of God that now prompts the Psalmist to pray yet again, "Teach me thy statutes". This is the sixth time in the Psalm that he has asked, "Teach me", and he pleads the same request three times more. (See vv. 12, 26, 33, 64, 66, 68, 108, 124 and 135). His longing to know the will of God was not a fickle, transient thing, asked lightly. It was a sincere desire, oft repeated. It was a constant, continual yearning to know the way of God more perfectly.

He mentions again the proud (2086) men to whom he has already referred in vv. 21 and 51. They were presumptuous, arrogant, and insolent men. They were no friends of the godly man, but had forged falsehood against him. It was slander. They had besmeared him with lies (RSV). Their accusations were fabrications intended to besmirch his character. He knew this, but still avowed that, in spite of them, he would keep the precepts of the Lord with a whole heart. Then, while speaking of his own heart, he thinks of the hearts of these ungodly men, and says, "Their heart is as fat as grease". It is an unusual expression, the word "fat" (2954) being found only here in all of Holy Scripture. It seems to imply that they were insensitive and unfeeling, dull, without perception and incapable of being impressed or affected by spiritual values. It must have been a great comfort to the Psalmist to turn away from such, saying, "But I...". How different he was, finding his delight, his pleasure, in the law of the Lord.

Now he sees the benefits of his afflictions. It was good for him that he had suffered the chastening of the Lord. This is never pleasant at the time, but it does result in blessing for the exercised believer, as is observed in Hebrews 12.11. The law which he loved was worth more to him than untold riches. It was his guide, his comfort, his sustenance, meeting his every need. "The law of thy mouth is better unto me than thousands of gold and silver". Plumer's comment is, "When we remember that *thousands* was the largest word for number in common use among the Hebrews, the expression is as strong as it would be for one of us to say *millions*. There is force also in the omission of the noun, *pieces*, *shekels*, or *talents*. He means to say that he would not give God's Word for all the wealth of the world". Kirkpatrick says, "This is the lesson he has learned in the school of affliction – the inestimable preciousness of God's law".

JOD
Verses 73-80: Prayer for Instruction and Comfort

Recognising that he has been created by the hand of the Lord, the Psalmist now appeals that He who made him will give him understanding in His commandments. He reasons, quite correctly, that He who gave him being, who shaped him and formed him, and gave him life, could now give him also that understanding which was necessary to perceive and discern the ways and words of God. T.W. Davies suggests a helpful paraphrase, "Since Thou hast made and constituted me as I am, complete Thy work by giving me understanding of Thy law". This is not possible for the natural mind, and so the prayer. If his prayer for understanding should be granted, then the Psalmist knows that this will bring joy to those who fear the Lord. They would look on him and be glad as they see the effect of answered prayer in the life of a godly man. Observing one who has hoped in God's Word, who has prayed and been heard, will bring cheer and encouragement to all those of like mind.

Again he remembers, and refers to, his afflictions. He is not at all resentful, for he knows that all Jehovah's judgments are righteous. There has been nothing unjust in what he has suffered, for it was the faithfulness of God which had ordered it so for his good. Plumer points out that faithfulness (530) is "the cognate of the word rendered 'Amen'. It implies all truth and fidelity". Note that in almost every English translation, the remaining five verses of this *Jod* section all commence with the little word "Let". It is always the prefix to a sincere request of the Psalmist, an appeal to his God for some particular blessing.

"Let, I pray thee, thy merciful kindness be for my comfort". This needs but little comment. It is a touching appeal to the kindness and love of God, and, since it is followed by that familiar expression "according to thy word" (IMRA – 565), it is coupled with an appeal to the promise of God also. In the love of God and the Word of God the Psalmist would find comfort in his affliction. Perhaps his plea is strengthened by his description of himself as Jehovah's servant. Surely a good and kind God, ever faithful to His promise, must grant comfort to His suffering servant.

"Let thy tender mercies come unto me". "Tender mercies" (7356) is one word, sometimes rendered "compassions" or "bowels", and once "tender love". It signifies a deep love and pity toward its object, and the Psalmist desires that he might experience it. If so, he would live. This probably means more than that he would not die, but rather that he would, as might be said, "live life to the full", life lived in the delight of the law of the Lord. As the Saviour Himself said, "I am come that they might have life, and that they might have it more abundantly" (Jn 10.10).

"Let the proud be ashamed". The Psalmist truly has been plagued by these proud men. He seems to live in their very shadow and refers to them six times in this Psalm. See vv. 21, 51, 69, 78, 85, 122. As has already been noted, the word "proud" (2086) means "arrogant; insolent; presumptuous". His prayer is that they might be confounded. They had dealt perversely with him without cause. The phrase "without a cause" is the translation of one Hebrew word (8267), denoting that their dealings with him were based on deceit, falsehood, and fraud. There was no reason for the way in which they had treated him, and it was really better for him that he should meditate in the divine precepts, engaging his thoughts with these rather than with these proud men.

"Let those that fear thee turn unto me". From the proud and presumptuous he is now occupied with an entirely different company, those that fear the Lord. His prayer is that such may turn to him, be his companions and friends. Perhaps his hope is that, seeing the example of his love for God's Word and his continuance in prayer, they may want his fellowship. They are described in a two-fold way; they fear the Lord and they know His will as it is revealed in His testimonies. It is good for such to seek each other for mutual help and comfort. As in another place, "Then they that feared the Lord spake often one to another: and the Lord hearkened and heard" (Mal 3.16).

"Let my heart be sound in thy statutes". This is simply a prayer for sincerity and whole-heartedness. He prays for a heart characterised by innocence and integrity. "Blessed are the pure in heart", the Saviour taught (Mt 5.8), and it is for such a heart that the Psalmist now pleads. In such a condition he need never be ashamed. If he has asked, in v.78, that his proud adversaries might be ashamed, this would never be the lot of the man whose heart was perfectly set on living by the divine statutes. He would never be confounded as those men would who live presumptuously without God.

CAPH

Verses 81-88: Distress and Deliverance

This is the eleventh section of Psalm 119. Each of these eight verses begins with the Hebrew letter CAPH, and Spurgeon says of them, "This octave is the midnight of the Psalm, and very dark and black it is. Stars, however, shine out, and the last verse gives promise of the dawn". The Psalmist's weariness is evident from the opening verse of the section. "My soul fainteth", he laments, "mine eyes fail". "Fainteth" and "fail" are the same word (3615). He felt consumed, exhausted, languishing in his distress. He longed for relief, for comfort, but he knew that this could only come from God, and so he resorted to the Word of God, to the divine promise. In this he hoped and for this he waited. "When?", he asks. It is like the familiar "How long?" of other Psalms. For how much longer would he have to wait for deliverance?

In a rather strange expression the Psalmist now says, "I am become like a bottle in the smoke". There is general agreement among expositors that this is the skin bottle of the East, usually made of goatskin, and used for storing either water or wine. Perhaps Dr Cohen speaks for all on the meaning of the phrase, when he writes, "In the East bottles are made of skin and, when not in use, are hung up in the room which has no chimney for the escape of smoke; they become shrivelled in consequence. The Psalmist declares himself to be so affected by his trials that he is similarly shrivelled". Calvin says, "He was, as it were, parched by the continual heat of adversities". Yet, he says, and how blessed is this, that in spite of all his sorrow, he can still trust and remember the divine precepts. Although burdened with grief, he does not forget the statutes of the Lord.

Now he asks, "How many are the days of thy servant", and there are two suggestions as to what he means. The usual, majority, interpretation, which many think is the obvious one, is that he is contemplating the brevity of life. This indeed may be measured in days, not years, especially for a man so consumed with suffering as the Psalmist appears to be. Some say, however, as Plumer, that the two questions of the verse must be considered in parallel, and if so, "is not the prophet inquiring how many are to be the days of his suffering?". This does, of course, preserve a unity in the verse, since he now asks, "When wilt thou execute judgment on them that persecute me?". As Calvin puts it, "Lord, how long hast Thou determined to abandon Thy servant to the will of the ungodly? When wilt Thou set Thyself in opposition to their cruelty and outrage?".

Once again, for the fifth time in the Psalm, there is a reference to the proud (2086). These arrogant men had "digged pits" for him. They had cunningly set traps for him, trying to ensnare him. The Psalmist knew them. They were presumptuous men, who despised God's law (8451). They were in constant violation of the "Torah". This was the bent of their life and is not limited just to their digging pits for him. The "which" of the AV should be "who", as in the RV. As Davies comments, "It would be a paltry truism and off the line of thought to say that digging pits for good people is against the Divine law". Perhaps the RSV makes the meaning clear, saying, "Godless men have dug pitfalls for me, men who do not conform to thy law".

How different were these proud men to his God. All the commandments of the Lord were a testimony to His faithfulness. These men who persecuted the Psalmist were characterised by deceit, deception, and fraud. There was neither cause nor reason for their persecution of a man who delighted in the statutes of the Lord, except that they despised those commandments. There could be no negotiating with such men. As the Psalmist thought of them, and of their wrongful treatment of him, he could only look to the Lord. His cry was simple and sincere, it was brief and to the point; "Help thou me".

When he says, in the closing lament of this sad section of the Psalm, "They had almost consumed me", the word "consumed" (3615) is the same word as that rendered "fainteth" and "fail" in the opening verses of this section. But there is hope in the word "almost"! Their intended destruction of him was not complete. He had not utterly failed or been consumed. God had preserved him, and, though sorely tried, he had not forsaken the precepts of the Lord. Throughout his trials he had held fast to the Word of God and it had kept him in his sufferings. Now he prays that in loving-kindness the Lord will quicken him. It is a prayer for revival. Perhaps he needed this both physically and spiritually. If God would so revive and restore him, then, he vows, he would continue to observe the testimonies of the Lord. It is as if he is promising personally that which was so early promised nationally; "All that the Lord hath spoken we will do" (Ex 19.8). With the Lord's gracious reviving and help he would endeavour to do what the nation had failed to do. "So shall I keep the testimony of thy mouth".

LAMED

Verses 89-96: The Abiding Faithfulness of God and His Word

The Word which had been the support and stay of the Psalmist in his afflictions is for ever settled in heaven. It is firmly fixed, established, in the heavens beyond the reach of men and circumstances. It is eternal, immutable, and unalterable, abiding where God Himself abides. The faithfulness of God to His Word extends from generation to generation and His work in creation is a constant testimony to this. His Word brought the earth into existence, and so it abides. He established it and it stands fast according to His appointing who is the upholder of all things. All that He has created continues in accord with His Word. The pronoun "they", in v.91, must refer to heaven and earth. They abide because He has decreed it so. "All things were made by him" (Jn 1.3). "All things were created by him and for him...and by him all things consist" (Col 1.16-17). All things, therefore, are His servants, obedient to His Word and His will. Sun, moon, and stars move in their appointed courses, compassing their orbits with precision and power because He has ordained it so.

This faithful Word, then, had been the Psalmist's delight, and had it not been so, he feels that he would have perished in his affliction. Note that "delights" here is actually in the plural. In every trial, in every varied circumstance and vicissitude of life he had been able to enjoy the Word of God. There had been some promise of God, some encouragement, some comforting word, for every need. It is not surprising therefore, that he should say, "I will never forget thy precepts". How could he forget the words which had so often brought him consolation and revived him? There was, too, the possibility that he might need them again, in future trials. He could not afford to forget the precepts which had been his stay in suffering.

He now appeals for preservation on the grounds of his relationship with God, saying, "I am thine". He was a yielded servant of the Lord, a devoted follower who had ever sought the precepts of the Lord to obey them. He was obedient to that Word just as the universe was, desiring only to move in accord with the divine statutes. He needed preservation for he knew that wicked men lay in wait for him, eagerly watching for opportunity to destroy him. There was, he knew also, a way of escape from their evil designs. He would attend to the testimonies of the Lord, observing them, giving heed to them. This would be his salvation.

The rather strange expression, "I have seen an end of all perfection", seems to mean that in his wide and varied experience of men and the world, the Psalmist had learned that there was a limit to everything. Adam Clarke writes, "Everything of human origin has its limits and end, howsoever extensive, noble, and excellent. All arts and sciences, languages, inventions, have their respective principles, have their limits and ends; as they came from man and relate to man, they shall end with man". The word "perfection" (8502), signifying "completeness", is found only here in Holy Scripture.

In contrast to the imperfection of the greatest accomplishments of men, the Psalmist says of the Word of God, "Thy commandment is exceeding broad". The law of the Lord is so comprehensive. It does not know the narrow boundaries of men. It is wide enough to meet every need of man, spiritually, morally, emotionally, practically. As Plumer writes, "Where is the end or boundary of the Word of God? Who can ascend to the height of its excellency? who can fathom the depth of its mysteries? who can find out the comprehension of its precepts or conceive the extent of its promises? who can take the dimensions of that love of God to man which it describeth, or that love of man to God which it teacheth?...It forbids all sin. It inculcates and enforces every principle of justice, and of charity. It at once humbles and gives courage, imparts tenderness of conscience and of heart, and also makes men lion-hearted. It abounds in excellence".

MEM

Verses 97-104: Wisdom in the Word

This thirteenth octave of the Psalm begins with love and ends with hate. Love for the Word of God will produce a hatred of that which is false and vain, therefore it is incumbent upon the child of God that he cultivates a love for that Word. The section opens with an exclamation, "O how love I thy law" (8451). This was the Psalmist's love for the "Torah", that vast body of teaching, of instruction in divine things, of directives in all things moral and spiritual. It was his rule of life, and he loved it. It was his constant meditation.

The godly Psalmist had enemies and he could never forget this, but he had a wisdom which they did not have. Jehovah, by means of His Word, had imparted to His servant a wisdom which was not possessed by the worldly-wise. There is a wisdom which is from above (Jas 3.17), and which is gained only by resort to the Word of God. The commandments of the Lord were always with the Psalmist. They were enshrined in his heart. Daily meditation had rooted them in his mind and memory. They were part of his very life and being.

The expression, "I have more understanding than all my teachers", has occasioned much difficulty and controversy. Some, misunderstanding his meaning, have even accused the Psalmist of conceit. There is no conceit, when once the truth of what he is saying is understood. He is not claiming any superior knowledge to his teachers. He is not boasting that he personally knows more than they do. He is simply stating that in the "Torah", which he loves, he has more instruction than there is in the minds of any, or all, of his teachers. As Kirkpatrick says, "The Psalmist's point is not the superiority of his own stricter interpretation of the law to the laxer interpretation of his teachers, but the superiority of the law to all other sources of instruction as a fountain of wisdom and prudence and discernment". He had the law, and in the law he had more than there was in all his teachers combined. This is not conceit, but an acknowledgement of the greatness of the law. For this reason, the commandments, the testimonies of the Lord, were his meditation daily, as he has already stated.

He now turns to the ancients, the aged, the elders. The two words in vv. 99 and 100, "understanding" (7919) and "understand" (995), are different Hebrew words, but so similar in meaning that they may both be translated, as here, by the same English word. This is often the case with words which, in the original, are different, and the significance of any such differences should always be considered. It is not always possible, however, to ascertain the importance of the difference in words which can be translated similarly.

But what does the Psalmist now mean, that he understands more than the ancients? Perhaps the phrase which follows gives the explanation. He says, "Because I keep thy precepts". His thought appears to be that true understanding and discernment does not come naturally with age. A man may live long and gain little wisdom. Understanding comes with attention to the divine precepts. Those who keep the commandments of the Lord have more understanding than those who trust only in long life and experience. The JFB Commentary says, "The ancients or elders, by reason of lengthened experience and observation, were, in the East, before the days of many books, considered the repositories of knowledge. Their knowledge is natural; mine is revealed, and therefore far exceeds theirs. 'Antiquity is no help against stupidity, where it does not accord with the commandments of God' (Luther)".

Keeping the Word demands purity of life. It is not sufficient to know; there must be a corresponding holiness of walk. Knowledge is one thing; godliness is another, and the Psalmist had guarded his path accordingly. He had "refrained his feet". He walked a narrow, restricted pathway, and had forbidden his feet to tread any evil way. This is the meaning of "refrained" (3607). He so ordered his pathway that he might keep God's Word. Dr Cohen writes, "His love of God and longing to conform to His will deterred him from evil". He greatly valued the judgments of the Lord. These ordinances were his guide and guard in life. By them he was taught of God and would not depart from them. Departure from these ordinances would be disaster, for they were the communications of God to men containing everything necessary for godly living.

How sweet were these words to the Psalmist. "Yea, sweeter than honey to my mouth", he says. It is like an echo of Psalm 19.10, "More to be desired are they than gold, yea, than much fine gold: sweeter also than honey and the honeycomb". He uses again the word of v.100, saying, "Through thy precepts I get understanding" (995). They had shown him the wisdom of a holy life and had taught him to hate the ways of falsehood, deceit, and vanity. Plumer says, "The clause expresses the habit of his life...God teaches us, and we obey. We obey, and He teaches us more. We learn a little and practise that; thus we are prepared to learn and practise more".

NUN
Verses 105-112: Light for the Pathway

This lovely fourteenth section commences with one of the best known verses in the Psalm, much loved by many saints: "Thy word is a lamp unto my feet, and a light unto my path". The world is in moral darkness and men are by nature benighted. How important it is that there should be light for the godly man. The Psalmist speaks of "a lamp" (5216) and "a light" (216). The two words are different, and since there is nothing superfluous or unnecessary in the inspired language of Scripture then there must be some significance in the difference. Perhaps the answer is in the accompanying phrases, "unto my feet", and, "unto my path". The first word, "lamp", denotes the light of a candle, shedding a rather localised light around the feet. The second word, "light", is as the sun at day-break, throwing light along the pathway. Such is the versatility of the Word of God that it lets a man know where he is, and it reveals also the path ahead, showing him where he is going. "A lamp unto my feet and a light unto my path". T.W. Davies sees another interesting distinction, "God's Word gives guidance at all times: in the night it is as a lamp; in the day as the light of the sun".

The Psalmist had recognised the inestimable value of this Word for the direction of his life and he had sworn to observe it. The judgments of God's Word were righteous judgments and he solemnly vowed to keep them. He would perform his oath by his keeping of them. He would order his life by them. When he now says, "I am afflicted very much", it may well be that he is suffering because of his faithful observance of the law. Soon, in the Psalm, he will speak again of wicked men. Their shadow was always with him. They were his adversaries continually because of his piety. They sorely afflicted him because of his adherence to the righteous judgments of which he has just spoken. "Quicken me, O Lord", he prays. Downcast and discouraged at times, he needs reviving and so he cries to Him of whom another Psalm says, "He restoreth my soul" (Ps 23.3). Such restoration and comfort as he needed, would, of course, be "according to thy word". Divine help would come in accord with the promises of God.

He now asks that Jehovah might graciously accept what he brings, as "the freewill offerings of my mouth". This is a spontaneous, voluntary, presentation of thanksgiving and praise to the Lord. The writer of the Epistle to the Hebrews writes similarly, saying, "Let us offer the sacrifice of praise to God continually, that is, the fruit of our lips giving thanks to his name" (Heb 13.15). Then, immediately after offering to the Lord, he asks something from the Lord. It is, by now, a familiar request, "Teach me". Since he lives by the judgments of the Lord, he is always eager to know them better, and for this reason he makes his appeal for instruction in them again and again.

His sufferings, however, are never very far from his mind, and so severe are they that at times his very life seems to be in danger. "My soul is continually in my hand", he says, and the metaphor is a familiar one. "To take one's life in one's hand" is to hazard the life. See the same expression in Judges 12.3; 1 Samuel 19.5; Job 13.14. The thought is that to carry treasure in the hand is to expose it, so that at any moment robbers might seize it. The life of this godly man was in continual jeopardy, and yet, notwithstanding this constant danger, he did not forget the law of the Lord.

In language similar to that of v.85 he now speaks of his enemies as having "laid a snare" for him. They had, he had earlier said, "digged pits for him". They did their utmost to entrap him. Plumer writes, "What the snare was we are not informed. It may have been for his life, or for his reputation, or for his virtue. If the sense of this verse is to be controlled by that preceding, it was his life they were seeking". In all this he remained steadfast, faithful to the precepts of the Lord. He had not erred (8582) from these. He had not wandered from them. Persecution had not weakened his resolve, or seduced him away from the testimonies which he loved. These were his abiding heritage, the rejoicing of his heart. How could he give them up or depart from them? No. He had inclined his heart to perform the divine statutes, meaning that he had committed himself to the keeping of them. This he would do always, for ever, to the end. The word "end" (6118) is sometimes rendered "reward". The Psalmist may be saying that, with an eternal reward in view, he would keep the statutes of the Lord. Indeed, obedience to these statutes was reward in itself. See the same word, with the comment, in v.33 of the Psalm.

SAMECH
Verses 113-120: Safety and Security in God's Word

This section of the Psalm begins with hatred and love. The Psalmist's love for the law of the Lord is matched only by his abhorrence of those who despised that law. The word here translated "vain thoughts" (5588) signifies the ambivalent thoughts of double-minded men, and it is so rendered by JND, RV, RSV, and other versions. It denotes the cynicism of the sceptic, the man who will not whole-heartedly accept the authority of the Word of God. Such doubtings are the road to apostasy, and this was to be studiously avoided. The Psalmist loved that law which others questioned. He accepted it without reservation. An earlier section of this Psalm commenced with his exclamation, "O how love I thy law!" (v.97), and his devotion to the law shines out again and again throughout the whole Psalm.

The Psalmist had found refuge in the Lord. "My hiding-place and my shield", he exclaims. The "hiding-place" (5643) was a covert, a shelter from the storm. The same word occurs in Psalm 32.7. In God and His Word there was safety and security, and a defence from all that would assail, and so he would continue to hope and trust in the law which he loved.

With a certain indignation the Psalmist now addresses ungodly men directly. In other verses of this section he speaks about these men, but only once, in v.115, does he speak to them. There is a finality about his word to them, "Depart from me". The godly man has no desire for the company of evildoers. He has neither time nor place for them, and commands only that they leave him. Delivered from them and from their malevolent influence he can, without hindrance, keep the commandments of the Lord. Notice that the Psalmist speaks here of "my God" (430). This is Elohim, the great title used to denote the might and majesty of God. This is the only occurrence of it in this lengthy Psalm. If other double-minded men doubted God and His Word, not so the Psalmist. He would trust in the greatness of Him who, in such a personal relationship, he could call, "My God".

He knows, however, that he needs divine aid if he is to maintain his testimony for the Lord, but he knows, too, that such help is already promised in God's Word. So he prays, "Uphold me", and then immediately says, "according to thy word" (IMRA – 565). He adds, "that I may live". He has used this expression before in v.77, and, as has been noted there, this does not imply a fear of dying, or of physical death. It is rather a desire to enjoy life to the full, and this is only possible with godly living and the help of God. If this is his privilege and portion, then the Psalmist knows that he need never be ashamed, or disappointed in his hope and expectations.

"Hold thou me up" (5582) is a different word from, though very similar to, the "uphold me" (5564) of the previous verse. Both are an appeal for support and strength, and, in this present verse, a prayer for comfort too. With such divine aid the Psalmist knows that he is safe, and, being safely kept, he can continue in his respect, his godly regard, for the statutes of the Lord. As for those men who spurned those statutes, God accordingly spurned them. They erred, they went astray, they wandered deliberately from the ways of the Lord, and so He set them at naught (JND). The phrase "trodden down" (5541) of the AV, denotes "to reject; to cast aside". These godless men were characterised by deceit and falsehood, by treachery, fraud, and lies. Such a life was altogether an abandoning of the requirements of the law, the "Torah". To reject God's law was folly, for it resulted in God's rejection of them.

In a similar strain of thought the Psalmist now says, "Thou puttest away all the wicked of the earth like dross". There is an allusion to the refiner who separates the dross from the pure metal. This dross he casts aside as worthless. It is of no value whatever. So Jehovah despises those who despise His law, and He casts them away. This is righteousness of course, and the Psalmist says, "Therefore I love thy testimonies". He dreads the doom of the wicked and desires only to be of some usefulness to God. He would not be counted as dross, but rather as the precious silver, valued by the refiner.

As he thinks of the tremendous issues and consequences of a man's dealings with God, the Psalmist says, "My flesh trembleth for fear of thee…I am afraid". He stood in awe of the Almighty and was physically moved. He shuddered with the sense of the presence of God. Albert Barnes comments, "There is nothing unaccountable in this. Any man would tremble, should God manifest Himself to him as He might do; and the mind may have such an overpowering sense of the presence and majesty of God, that the body shall be agitated, lose its strength, and with the deepest alarm fall to the earth. Compare Daniel 10.8 and Revelation 1.17".

Observe, in these closing verses of this section, an interesting blending of love and fear. As Kirkpatrick says, "Reverent fear is the right complement of holy love". How true this is.

AIN

Verses 121-128: Renewed Appeal for Help, Teaching and Understanding

In this, the sixteenth section of the Psalm, each of the eight verses commences with the Hebrew letter AIN. These verses are, as T.W. Davies says, "A prayer of confidence that Jehovah will stand by His servant". The Psalmist pleads that he has done justice and righteousness, and on this ground he prays that Jehovah will not abandon him to his oppressors. He had done what was right, and on account of this he had suffered. It is inevitable of course, in an ungodly hostile world, that those who live godly should suffer persecution. This is a principle in every age. Compare Paul's experience towards the end of his life in 2 Timothy 3.12.

If David was indeed the writer of this Psalm, as many think, then perhaps, in using the phrase, "judgment and justice", he is speaking now in his judicial capacity as a ruler of men. Whereas with many other kings and despots there was injustice and corruption, he had endeavoured to do what was just and right, and in so doing he had performed that which was ordained of the Lord. Spurgeon comments, "This was a great thing for an Eastern ruler to say at any time, for these despots cared more for gain than justice. Some of them altogether neglected their duty...many more of them sold their judgments to the highest bidders by taking bribes, or regarding the persons of men. Some rulers gave neither judgment nor justice, others gave judgment without justice, but David gave judgment and justice, and saw that his sentences were carried out". With a clear conscience he could claim that he had acted righteously, and on this account he now asks that the Lord will not leave him to the mercy of those evil men who oppressed him.

As has been noted in the introduction, v.122 is the only verse in this lengthy Psalm which does not contain one of those words which describe the law, as, for example, precepts, testimonies, commandments, statutes. Indeed, since the "judgment" mentioned in v.121 is the Psalmist's own personal judgment, then it might be argued that there is no reference to the law in that verse either, although the same word "judgments" (4941) is often used in the Psalm to denote God's Word.

Three times, in four consecutive verses, the Psalmist now refers to himself as Jehovah's servant. This is not only an expression of humility, and a testimony to his faithfulness to the Lord, but it is also a powerful plea that Jehovah should stand by him. Surely the Lord must guarantee the safety of one who is His servant. "Be surety for thy servant for good", he prays. He is asking for a divine pledge for security against his oppressors, and, for the sixth time in the Psalm, he calls them "the proud" (2086). They were arrogant, insolent, and presumptuous men, and he pleads for deliverance from them. Such is the earnestness with which he has longed for this deliverance that he says, "Mine eyes fail for thy salvation". He has used this phrase before in the Psalm, in v.82, and, as Dr Cohen comments, "His sight is strained by looking out for relief which is delayed in coming". "The word of thy righteousness" is the righteous promise of God, and while he waits for salvation from his adversaries he trusts in the certainty of the promises of God.

Although the Psalmist has earlier pleaded that he had behaved righteously, and that on this account the Lord should act for him, nevertheless he now casts himself upon the mercy of God. Perhaps he is now disclaiming any human merit as he prays, "Deal with thy servant according unto thy mercy". This appeal is to the goodness, the kindness, and the love of God, and yet again he pleads the now familiar petition, "Teach me". How well he knew that all that he needed for godly living, all that was necessary for correction and comfort, and for guidance in every circumstance of life, was to be found in the statutes of the Lord. "Teach me thy statutes". Spurgeon quotes an interesting comment from William Cowper, who writes, "David had Nathan and Gad the prophets; and beside them, the ordinary Levites to teach him. He read the Word of God diligently, and did meditate in the law night and day; but he acknowledgeth all this was nothing unless God did teach him. Other teachers speak to the ear, but God speaks to the heart; so Paul preached to Lydia, but God opened her heart".

Once again, with a holy repetition, the Psalmist pleads his servant character, saying, "I am thy servant". Knowledge, though so very important, is not altogether sufficient for the man of God, and so he has a further request, "Give me understanding". Knowledge of the divine testimonies coupled with understanding, would enable him to render more perfect obedience to the Word and will of God. There is a pattern and a principle here. "Teach me...give me understanding...that I may know". This is the sincere desire and prayer of a dutiful servant. Teaching is desirable and necessary, but proper understanding of what is being taught leads to deeper knowledge and consequent obedience. Is not this exactly what the Saviour taught in John 7.17, "If any man will do his will, he shall know of the doctrine"?

Might there now be detected a note of godly impatience, as the Psalmist exclaims, "It is time for thee, Lord, to work"? Circumstances were, humanly speaking, out of control. The best endeavours of good men were of no avail. It was time for Jehovah to deal with things directly and personally. These lawless men had made void His law. Profanity, vulgarity, and immorality abounded. They had denied, and flagrantly disobeyed, the divine precepts, with their deceit and fraud, their avarice and greed, and their oppression of the godly. It was time for Jehovah to intervene.

"Therefore I love thy commandments", says the Psalmist. In a strange, paradoxical way, the fact that others made void God's law only encouraged him to love it more. If ungodly men despised the commandments, then the commandments must be good! This slighting of the Scriptures which he loved only but deepened his affection for them. To him they were better than gold, better than the purest refined gold. So he had already said in v.72, and so David had written in Psalm 19.10, "More to be desired are they than gold, yea, than much fine gold". His esteem for the precepts of the Lord was complete. Whatever they decreed, they were righteous. Concerning all things they were all right. He would obey them implicitly and he accordingly hated every false path.

PE
Verses 129-136: Light and Guidance through the Word

The Psalmist, like all godly men everywhere, never ceases to marvel at the wonder of the Word of God. This word "wonderful" (6381), in the opening verse of this seventeenth octave of the Psalm, is from the same root as the expression "wondrous things" in v.18. It is also the same word as that grand title of the Messiah in Isaiah 9.6, "His name shall be called wonderful", so that the Christ of God and the Word of God are alike "Wonderful". The testimonies of God are wonderful because they are of divine origin. Jehovah is the Author. They are inspired of Him, with no mixture of, or possibility of, the slightest error. It is not surprising, therefore, that the godly man should say, "Therefore doth my soul keep them".

"The entrance (6608) of thy words giveth light". This is the only occurrence in Scripture of this word "entrance". It signifies a doorway, an opening, or an aperture. The imagery is of light streaming through such an opening. Dickson comments, "In Palestine, houses are mostly windowless, the light entering through the doorway. Light comes through God's Word as the sun's light through an eastern door". The meaning therefore is not, primarily, the entrance of the Word of God into the minds of men, as is commonly supposed, but rather the beaming of the light of divine truth through the doorway of the inspired Word. To the mind which is open to receive light, then this is, of course, the means by which the light is imparted. Many men will not appreciate the light which is shining in and through the Word of God but to those willing to receive it in simplicity, then here is the source of true understanding.

The Psalmist was an eager and willing recipient of that light, but now the metaphor changes. With mouth opened wide he pants after the commandments of the Lord. Is this like the hart panting after the water brooks as in Psalm 42.1? Or, as Adam Clarke suggests, "A metaphor taken from an animal exhausted in the chase. He runs, open-mouthed, to take in the cooling air, the heart beating high"? Or is it the wide-open mouth of the fledgling bird expectantly looking for food from the attentive mother? Or is it, as Peter writes, like a new-born babe earnestly desiring "the sincere milk of the word" (1 Pet 2.2)? Whichever is true, the meaning is clear, the

Psalmist was a man yearning for, panting after, the commandments of the Lord.

In his longing the Psalmist prays, "Look thou upon me, and be merciful unto me". The word "look" (6437) is more often translated elsewhere in the OT as "turn", and is so rendered by the RV, RSV, JND, ASV and JPS. There is an implication here that adverse circumstances seemed to indicate the turning away of the face of God from him, and so he pleads, "Turn thou unto me". He longs that Jehovah might regard him with favour, and he reasons that this was the divine wont, for the Lord to be gracious toward those who loved the name of the Lord, as he did.

"Order my steps", he now asks. He wants guidance for life's pathway, and such guidance that every single step might be prepared and established by God. As Adam Clarke puts it, "Order my steps, make them firm, let me not walk with a halting or unsteady step". His aspiration is for a life lived according to God's Word, so that iniquity might not have dominion over him. As he has prayed for deliverance from iniquitous men, so he would have deliverance from iniquity itself. This was ambition for holiness.

Again he refers to his oppressors. "Deliver me (6299)", he prays, "redeem me; rescue me from the oppression of man". Was their oppression of him a hindrance to his leading a godly life in quietness? T.W. Davies suggests that the latter part of this verse should read, "So that I may keep Thy precepts". Freed from disturbing and disquieting influences he would be more able to live in tranquil obedience to the law which he loved. Then, in language reminiscent of the priestly blessing of Numbers 6.25, he prays, "Make thy face to shine upon thy servant". He longs for that smile of approval from God. Once more he pleads his servant relationship with Jehovah, and yet again, for the ninth time in the Psalm, he asks, "Teach me".

It is characteristic of every godly man in every age that he laments the prevailing disregard for the law of God. The Psalmist was no exception. His tears flowed freely. His eyes streamed. As Dr Cohen says, "He is overcome with sorrow at the lawlessness of the wicked". How many of the prophets wept with him, as did the apostles in their day, and as did the Saviour Himself, weeping over the city that had rejected Him (Lk 19.41). Those who love the law of the Lord will always mourn over those who do not.

TZADDI

Verses 137-144: The Righteousness of God and His Word

There is nothing difficult to understand in this eighteenth section of the Psalm. There is much godly repetition of things that have already been said, and the predominant theme is righteousness, both of Jehovah and of His law. In keeping with the acrostic arrangement of the Psalm every verse in this section commences with the same Hebrew letter TZADDI, and the first word in this portion is "righteous" (6662) which is TZADDIK. In some form or other "righteousness" occurs five times in these eight verses.

The Psalmist addresses Jehovah, saying, "Righteous art thou...upright are thy judgments". Since Jehovah Himself is righteous, it follows that all that He says and all that He does must be righteous also. He is intrinsically and essentially holy. His judgments therefore must be pure as He is. All that He has commanded, all His testimonies, have been issued in righteousness and are "very (3966) faithful (530)" This is the AV rendering, and may be better expressed by the JND and JPS translations which give "exceeding faithfulness". The righteousness and faithfulness of God's testimonies are stated also in vv. 86 and 144 of the Psalm.

In righteous anger against those men who despised God's Word the Psalmist now says, "My zeal hath consumed me". These men were his enemies, but it is not so much their oppression of him that he now laments, but rather their dishonouring of the law of the Lord. He burned with indignation for this. Their enmity of him was grief enough, but that they had forgotten, ignored, and so slighted, the Words of the Lord, was worse by far. There is a reminder here of Psalm 69.9. Horne comments, "Never could the verse be uttered, with such fulness of truth and propriety, by anyone, as by the Son of God, who had such a sense of His Father's glory, and of man's sin, as no person else ever had. And, accordingly, when his zeal had exerted itself in purging the temple, St John tells us, 'His disciples remembered that it was written, The zeal of thine house hath eaten me up'. The place where it is so written is Psalm 69.9, and the passage is exactly parallel to that before us".

The Psalmist now turns to that Word which men had forgotten. It was "very (3966) pure (6884)", he says. It was exceeding pure. It had been "tried to the uttermost" (JPS), as gold that had been tested to the limit by the refiner. There was no dross. It was all precious, well tried, and, as the servant of God, he loved it. Perhaps it was because of his known love for God's Word that he was, as he says, "small and despised". He was insignificant in the eyes of those who slighted the law of the Lord, and, because they despised it, they despised him for loving it. "Yet", he can say, "Yet do not I forget thy precepts". In spite of all that men might do or say, nothing could deter him from obeying those precepts. He would honour the Word which men dishonoured. They had forgotten (v.139), but he would not forget. Again he mentions the righteousness of God. It was an everlasting righteousness, as eternal and unchanging as God Himself, and the law of God was truth.

Trouble and anguish had taken hold of the Psalmist, sorrow and distress. It was as if they had been pursuing him and had finally apprehended him as if he was their victim. Still, notwithstanding his afflictions, the commandments of the Lord were a constant source of delight to him. Indeed, "delights" is in the plural. The divine testimonies were, he says again, "righteous for ever" (RV and JPS). He longed only for understanding of them so that he might truly live life to the full.

KOPH
Verses 145-152: Devotion, Duty, and Deliverance

These are the touching themes of this nineteenth division of the Psalm, where every verse commences with the Hebrew letter KOPH. The Psalmist engages in earnest prayer for divine aid that he might continue to keep and observe the Word of God in spite of persecution from wicked men. His prayer is a cry. "I cried with my whole heart", he says, and then repeats, "I cried unto thee". It is like the plaintive cry of a creature in pain. It is sincere and whole-hearted, denoting the earnestness with which he has pleaded. Linked with the cry is the double request, "Hear me, O Lord...save me", and these are followed by the double promise, "I will keep thy statutes...I shall keep thy testimonies". The two words here rendered "keep" in the AV are different Hebrew words (5341 and 8104), but may both be represented by, "keep; observe; guard with fidelity". This the Psalmist solemnly promises to do if Jehovah will hear and answer his cry for help.

The Psalmist's earnestness is again borne out by his use of the word "prevent" (6923) which means "to anticipate, to go before, to confront, or to forestall". He had, as it were, cheated both the dawning and the night watches. He had forestalled them, in that he was at prayer before day-break, and was meditating when other men were asleep during the night-watches. The Jews originally had three night watches, but under Roman influence they later adopted four, and these are all mentioned in Mark 13.35. The Psalmist seems to be simply saying that his prayers and meditations continued day and night. He ignored both day-break and night watches. He rose early, before dawn, and he reduced his hours of sleep in the night, so that he might engage in communion with God. He was indeed whole-hearted and earnest in his desires after God.

Again he pleads, "Hear my voice", and he appeals to the lovingkindness of the Lord. "Quicken me", he also asks. This is a prayer for restoration and revival, for deliverance from discouragement. When he now says, "according to thy judgment", the JPS version gives, "as Thou art wont", as if to indicate, as in v.132, that this was characteristic of the Lord, to deliver the godly when they cried. The Psalmist sorely needed encouragement, for there were men drawing near to him who were intent on mischief (2154). They had the most wicked and malicious designs on him. They were far removed from the law which he loved. But if the persecutors were near, the Lord was also near. They were near to destroy him, but Jehovah was near to save him, and all His commandments, including His promises, were true. They were, as Davies suggests, "full of faithfulness", and on these he could rely.

The Psalmist had not just recently come to know the testimonies of the Lord. He had known them for a long time, and from his meditations he had learned that they were as eternal and unchanging as Jehovah Himself. They were not, therefore, some temporary expediency. They were forever.

As Albert Barnes writes, "They were laid in the eternity past; they will continue in the eternity to come. They are based on eternal principles of right; they will never be changed. Such a conviction will do much to keep the soul steady and firm in the trials and uncertainties of life. Whatever may change, God's law does not change; whatever is new, that is not new; whatever will vanish away, that will remain". So this godly man could continue in his devotion and in his duty, assured of deliverance from wicked men who opposed him.

RESH

Verses 153-160: Quicken me! Quicken me! Quicken me!

This is the twentieth division of the Psalm, in which every verse commences with the Hebrew letter RESH. It is a prayer rising out of affliction, persecution, and adversity, in which, three times, the Psalmist prays for quickening, for reviving, and for restoration.

"Consider mine affliction", he begins. He is asking that Jehovah might look upon him, behold his trouble, and deliver him. With a holy boldness he pleads that he has not forgotten God's law. Will Jehovah, therefore, on this account, remember him and deliver him? Jehovah alone can vindicate him before the tribunal of wicked men who oppose him. As if he were appealing to an advocate, he asks, "Plead my cause". There is an interesting correspondence between the words "plead" (7378) and "cause" (7379). He wants the Lord to handle his case for him, and he is saying, "contend my contention for me; argue my argument; fight my fight". Alexander reads it, "Strive my strife, and redeem me". Now, for the first of three times in this section of the Psalm, the Psalmist makes the familiar request, "Quicken me". As Spurgeon says, "We had this prayer in the last section, and we shall have it again and again in this...As the soul is the centre of everything, so to be quickened is the central blessing. It means more love, more grace, more faith, more courage, more strength...God alone can give this quickening".

With regard to the men who are his persecutors and adversaries, he now says, "Salvation is far from the wicked". There is indeed, little if any hope for their salvation since they will not seek after, nor enquire into, the statutes of the Lord. They have rejected the only means of salvation when they have rejected His Word. Salvation is far from them indeed, in such a condition. But he turns from these wicked men to think again upon the Lord, and as he remembers the greatness of the tender mercies, the compassions of God, again he prays, as in v.154, "Quicken me". The quickening for which he prays these three times is always in accordance with the Word, the judgments, and the lovingkindness, of the Lord.

Sadly, he must think again about his persecutors. His adversaries are many, but he determines that they shall not deter him from obedience to the law. "I have not declined (5186) from Thy testimonies", he says. He had not swerved from them. He had walked a straight course in the paths of righteousness. These wicked men were "transgressors" (898). They were treacherous dealers in deceit and fraud, faithless men whose word could not be trusted. It grieved the Psalmist to look upon them, saddened at their disobedience to the Word of God. Note how he says, "I beheld the transgressors, and was grieved", and then says, "Consider how I love thy precepts". Notice that the two words "beheld" and "consider", are really the same Hebrew word (7200), the identity being lost in the translation. He had observed the transgressors and had been grieved. Would the Lord observe him, and take knowledge of his love for the precepts which the transgressors had despised? He considers them and Jehovah considers him, but with what a difference!

For the third time in this section he prays, "Quicken me, O Lord". See the comment on v.156. He concludes this portion by again extolling the Word of God. "From the beginning" is not just the beginning of God's revelation. The RV, JND, and others read, "The sum of thy word is truth". Dr Cohen says, "Its meaning is 'totality'; the whole of it is truth", and every one of God's righteous judgments is forever, eternal.

SCHIN

Verses 161-168: Persecution, but Praise and Peace

This is the twenty-first, the penultimate division of Psalm 119, where every verse commences with the Hebrew letter SCHIN. The section begins with persecution, but soon sings of joy and love, of peace and hope, and for all of these the Psalmist offers praise.

Persecution had come to the Psalmist from all quarters. Here he laments that even the princes of the land had persecuted him. "Princes" (8269) denotes royalty or aristocracy, or simply men in authority. The word may indicate nobles, rulers, elders, leaders, or men in high office. If David was the Psalmist, then these were either the lords of the Philistines, or nobles in the court of Saul, or those leaders of Israel who had allied themselves with Absalom against him. Whichever is true, or whoever the Psalmist may be, this persecution had come from those who ought to have known better. These were men who should have done justice. Instead, they persecuted him without a cause. There was no reason for their opposition to him, and it served no good purpose. This, of course, has been the lot of the godly down the centuries, and even the Saviour Himself could say, "They hated me without a cause" (Jn 15.25). It is to the credit of the Psalmist that, in spite of his trials, and the injustices of these ungodly men, he remained steadfast in his obedience to the law of the Lord. He stood in awe of the Word which they despised. This awe of the Word of God was not a slavish fear. Indeed it brought with it a certain joy, like the joy of a man who had found a treasure. The Psalmist compares himself to the victor in battle who rejoices over the spoil. He had found a prize, a hidden treasure in the "Torah", of which these persecutors knew nothing.

He now speaks of love and hate, of praise and peace. He loved the law of the Lord, and equally he hated falsehood. Such was his deep hatred of lying that he employs two words to express it. "I hate (8130) and abhor (8581) lying", he says. The words signify that he detested and loathed falsehood as an abominable thing to be absolutely abhorred. But he loved the law (8451), the "Torah", that great body of inspired teaching which contained all the directions and instructions necessary for godly living.

Seven times a day he praised God for the law, the righteous judgments of the Lord. This "Seven times a day" need not be understood literally. Two things are signified. He may mean that he praises frequently throughout his day, or he may mean that his praise is complete and full. Some, however, do understand this literally, and Adam Clarke comments, "We have often seen that seven was a number expressing perfection, completeness, etc., among the Hebrews; and that it is often used to signify many, or an indefinite number, see Proverbs 24.16; Leviticus 26.28. And here it may mean no more than that his soul was filled with gratitude and praise, and that he very frequently expressed his joyous and grateful feelings in this way. But Rabbi Solomon says that this is to be understood literally, for they praised God twice in the morning before reading the decalogue, and once after; twice in the evening before the same reading, and twice after; making in the whole seven times". Either way, the Psalmist's joy in the Lord and in His Word was expressed in constant praise. In Psalm 55.17 David writes, "Evening, and morning, and at noon, will I pray".

The Psalmist had learned, from experience no doubt, that there was great peace for those who loved the "Torah". "Peace" (7965) is the lovely word "Shalom". It denotes peace and quiet, tranquility and prosperity, contentment and safety. It is a most blessed condition of soul, and while a man rested in the law of the Lord, and obeyed its precepts, nothing could offend or stumble that man. Only when there was departure from, or disobedience to, the law, could there be any occasion for stumbling. Love for the law was the pledge of real peace.

The Psalmist now addresses Jehovah. He can truthfully say that his hope for salvation was in the Lord, and that he had, accordingly, obeyed His commandments. He had observed the testimonies of the Lord and he loved them greatly. Commandments, testimonies, precepts, he had observed them all. He could profess this knowing that the eye of the Lord was ever upon him. Every detail of his ways, his walk, his daily conduct, was known to Jehovah. He could not lie before the Lord who knew perfectly the manner of his life. As Dr Cohen comments, "His life is an open book which he confidently presents for God's inspection, inasmuch as he had been observant of the precepts".

TAU

Verses 169-176: Final Petitions and Praises

This is the twenty-second and closing section, of Psalm 119, in which every verse commences with the letter TAU, the last letter in the Hebrew alphabet. It is a fitting finale to the Psalm, a blending of confession and thanksgiving, prayer and praise.

In this last division of the Psalm the Psalmist twice employs the great name Jehovah in his address to God. He describes his prayer as a cry. How like the infant, who, when language is either difficult or unknown, simply sends out a cry for the making known of its need. So it is with the Psalmist. "Give me understanding", his cry is asking. This was the request of Solomon in 1 Kings 3.9, and it pleased the Lord that he should ask for this. Several times throughout this lengthy Psalm the Psalmist has repeated the same request for understanding, and perhaps this raises, for some readers, the question of repetition. There are vain repetitions of course, which were characteristic of the chantings of the heathen, and the Saviour condemned these (Mt 6.7). There is, however, a thoughtful repetition, both in prayer and in teaching, which is commendable, as indicating sincere emphasis, either in what is being asked of God, or in what is being taught to men. The Psalmist's prayer is for an understanding which was in accord with God's Word (DABAR – 1697) His prayer is in the nature of supplication (8467). It is a plea for grace and favour, and for deliverance from trials. How often he has added to his prayers, "according to thy word". The answers to prayer which he expected, would be in keeping with, and in fulfilment of, the promises of God.

Now he turns from prayer to praise. The effect of divine teaching, and of the granting of understanding to him, would be that his lips would utter praise. "Utter" (5042) is a fervent word, meaning "to pour out; to gush forth; to bubble up". It is praise out of a heart which is full and over-flowing. All true knowledge of God and His Word must result in more intelligent praise and adoration. Notice too, that, so instructed, the Psalmist will not only speak to God, but also to men, teaching them the commandments, which were all righteous. He would go in before God with his praise and worship, and then go out to men bearing testimony to the Word which he has learned. This principle still obtains for the believer of the present day. Every instructed saint may say, "My lips shall utter praise…My tongue shall speak of thy word".

Returning to prayer again the Psalmist now asks, "Let thine hand help me". The hand is the symbol of strength and power. This man knows his own personal weakness and he looks for divine aid. He pleads, almost as if he had a right to the help of God, that he had chosen the precepts which others had rejected. He had elected to observe the law in a society where so many ignored it. Would the Lord, for this reason, stretch out His hand and help him? He had longed for the salvation of Jehovah, the deliverance which only the Lord could accomplish for him, and, while he waited for the Lord to act, the law (8451) the "Torah", had been his enjoyment and his delight. He prays that his life might be spared. "Let my soul live". How often his very life seems to be in danger. If the Lord would grant him life then he would continue to praise, and he asks that the judgments of the Lord might be favourable towards him and help him.

In a rather sad and touching final verse of the Psalm, the Psalmist says,

"I have gone astray like a lost sheep; seek thy servant". While the majority of expositors read this confession as it stands, Dr Cohen makes an interesting observation, which is, in the main, supported by Delitzsch. It may be helpful to quote Dr Cohen in full. He writes, "The Hebrew accentuation supports the rendering: 'Should I go astray, like a lost sheep, seek Thy servant'. The Psalmist may be alluding to the frailty which is part of human nature, and he prays that, should he ever succumb to his weakness and err, God will speedily restore him to the fold, because His commandments are always in his mind and he longs to be obedient to them. He may, on the other hand, be using the image of a lost sheep as the symbol of forlorn helplessness and liability to attack without a protector. If he is in such a condition and at the mercy of the wicked, may God be to him like a watchful shepherd".

The last clause of the Psalm sums up much of what the Psalmist has been saying throughout its twenty-two sections, "I do not forget thy commandments". The law which he loved was an expression of the divine will, therefore loving and remembering the commandments was love for Jehovah. This, as he so often states in the Psalm, was the desire and the longing of his heart, to do the will of God, to obey the Word of God, and thereby to bring some pleasure to the heart of God. The lengthy Psalm therefore concludes on a high note. The Psalmist has left a noble example of fidelity, and of faithfulness to God and His Word, an example which may well be admired and followed by saints of every age.

THE SONGS OF DEGREES

(Psalms 120 – 134)

This little group of Psalms has been likened to a Psalter within the Psalter, and consists of fifteen Psalms - 120-134 inclusive. They are commonly called "Songs of Degrees", but by some, "Songs of Ascent", and by others, "Songs of the Going Up". The similarity between these titles is, of course apparent, but why they should be so called is not clear, and a great variety of theories has been suggested by writers both ancient and modern, and both Jewish and Christian. Readers who wish to pursue the question in depth will find it discussed at great length by Spurgeon in his *Treasury of David,* by Delitzsch in his *Commentary on the Psalms*, by Adam Clarke, J.N. Darby, Dr Cohen and most of the larger commentaries. The following comments are appended as being the explanations most usually advanced.

Many Jewish writers relate these fifteen Psalms to fifteen steps in the Temple. Dr Cohen quotes the Hebrew Mishnah, which states, "Fifteen steps led up from the Court of the Women to the Court of the Israelites, corresponding to the fifteen Songs of Ascents in the Psalms, and upon them the Levites used to sing". Another reference in the Mishnah states that, at the ceremony of the water-drawing at the Feast of Tabernacles, "The Levites were stationed upon the fifteen steps leading from the Court of the Israelites to the Court of the Women, corresponding to the fifteen Songs of Ascents in the Psalms. It was upon these that the Levites stood with their musical instruments and sang their songs". Dr Cohen comments that from such references in the Mishnah the deduction used to be drawn that the fifteen Psalms received their titles from these steps. He rightly notes, however, that, "The inference is unwarranted, because all that the Mishnah implies is the correspondence in the number, and the songs of the Levites may have been selected from other parts of the Psalter". Although some christian expositors accept this theory of the fifteen steps, such acceptance is not at all general. Luther did favour this explanation, saying that it was "the simple and plain sense"!

Another thought is that there is a musical connotation in the title, and that the "ascents" indicate an ascending lyrical construction, where both the theme and the musical notes rise as on steps throughout the series. Delitzsch accepts this, and explains it more thoroughly, saying, "Gesenius has the merit of having first discerned the true meaning of the questioned inscription, inasmuch as first in 1812, and frequently since that time, he has taught that the fifteen songs have their name from the step-like progressive rhythm of their thoughts, and that consequently the name, like the triolet (roundelay) in Western poetry, does not refer to the liturgical usage, but to the technical structure". He cites DeWette in support of this, and Calvin also concurs, saying, "The Hebrew word for degrees being derived from the word *tsalah, to ascend*, or, *go up*, I agree with those who are of the opinion that it denotes the different musical notes rising in succession".

Perhaps the most widely accepted explanation of the title is that it indicates that these Psalms were songs for the "goings up" (Newberry) to Jerusalem to attend the three great annual Festivals in the Hebrew Calendar – Passover/Unleavened Bread, Pentecost, and Tabernacles. On these three occasions it was incumbent upon every Jewish adult male to make pilgrimage to the Holy City to keep the Feasts, and the custom was for families and friends to travel together in caravan for the celebrations (compare Lk 2.41-44), always going "up" to Jerusalem from whatever part of the country they came. It is believed that these "Pilgrim Psalms", as they became known, were sung by the bands of travellers on their way to the Temple, and particularly as they eventually ascended Mount Zion. This is suggested by some passages in the Psalms themselves, as, for example, Psalm 121.1, all of Psalm 122, Psalm 132.13–16, and Psalm 134. Those must have been joyous times, when, leaving the pressures and the problems of daily life, as in Psalm 121, the pilgrims would sing their way to Jerusalem in a festive spirit, arriving in happy unity as in Psalm 133, for the worship which is described in Psalm 134.

Dr W.M. Thomson, accepting this traditional interpretation of the title "Songs of Degrees", writes, "From the customs of Orientals still prevalent, I think that such an explanation of the title may be substantially correct. Nothing is more common than to hear individuals and parties of natives, travelling together through the open country and along mountain paths, especially during the night, break out into singing their favourite songs". In his *The Land and the Book*, Dr Thomson recalls how once, travelling south from Lebanon with a large company of natives, they spontaneously began to sing. He describes how, with the moon shining in a clear sky, they kept up their chanting for a long time, and how, in the still midnight air, their voices echoed far and wide in the rocky defiles of the mountain. "Something like this", he says, "may have often rendered vocal this dreary ascent to Jerusalem. It is common in this country to travel in the night during the summer, and we know that the Hebrew pilgrims journeyed in large companies".

It must be conceded that these fifteen Psalms would have been a most suitable songbook for those journeys, and it is feasible, too, that perhaps the returning exiles from Babylon might have used them similarly, as many suggest. Edward Dennett insists, however, that while these several theories rightly coincide in making the temple the object, or goal, to which the faces of the pilgrims were turned, there has been a failure to perceive the prophetical character of these Psalms. He correctly points out that the restoration from Babylon was a shadow of a larger fulfilment for Israel, and he writes, "The last three Psalms of the series undoubtedly justify the contention that the temple, the habitation of the Mighty One of Jacob, is the longed-for end, or consummation. If, however, the prophetic interpretation of these Psalms be allowed, the temple will not be that which Solomon, or Zerubbabel, built, but that which the Man, whose name is the Branch, will build, even He who shall bear the glory, and shall sit, and rule, a priest upon His throne; that is, Christ Himself." (See Zech 6.12-15).

There is an interesting arrangement in the order of these fifteen Psalms. The central one, Psalm 127, was written by Solomon. The others are grouped around this Psalm, with seven on either side. In each group of seven, two Psalms were written by David and five are anonymous. David's Psalms are, on the one side, Psalms 122 and 124, and on the other side, Psalms 131 and 133. It has been observed that each group of seven Psalms contains the great name Jehovah twenty-four times. To many believers, this orderly arrangement of these "Pilgrim Psalms" indicates divine inspiration, as if one eternal, heavenly Mind and Author was controlling and guiding the thoughts of the Psalmists whose privilege it was to give these songs to the nation.

The "Songs of Degrees" possess a certain unity, and have a progression of thought leading up to the sanctuary in Psalm 134, but they must now be considered individually. They are all, as Davies says, "brief, bright, and beautiful"!

PSALM 120

Introduction

This first Psalm of the "Songs of Degrees" is the song of a pilgrim leaving home, commencing the journey to Jerusalem. Maclaren comments on this Psalm very beautifully, and writes, "The collection of pilgrim-songs is appropriately introduced by one expressive of the unrest arising from compulsory association with uncongenial and hostile neighbours. The Psalmist laments that his sensitive soul has been so long obliged to be a sojourner where he has heard nothing but lying and strife. Weary of these, his soul stretches her wings towards a land of rest. His feeling ill at ease amidst present surroundings stings him to take the pilgrim's staff".

Although written in the first person singular, it is, nevertheless, a national song, just as christian hymns composed in the same first person singular are often sung intelligently and heartily in collective, congregational, praise and worship. The Psalm may have been sung, as suggested, by those caravans of pilgrims leaving for the Festival celebrations in Jerusalem, and may have been equally appropriate for those exiles returning from Babylon. Either way, Jerusalem is the goal. It must have been a great joy, whether for a pilgrim journeying from afar, or for a returning exile, to leave the pressures and problems of daily life and anticipate a visit to the City and the Temple. The short Psalm requires little in the way of division, but verses 1-2 are a prayer for deliverance from lies; verses 3-4 then describe the punishment of the slanderer, and verses 5-7 are the lament of the exile.

Verses 1-2: Prayer for Deliverance

The Psalmist has been in distress. This is a strong word, indicating affliction and anguish, but in his trouble he has learned to cry to Jehovah. There are times when even the most thoughtful saints, and the kindest friends, cannot help, and the only resource for consolation is the Lord Himself. It may well be that troubles are often blessings in disguise for the exercised soul, sending him to the Lord in prayer. As the Saviour said, "Blessed are they that mourn: for they shall be comforted" (Mt 5.4). Having been in distress it must have been blessed indeed for a man to leave, say, Galilee of the Gentiles, for the refreshment of a journey to Jerusalem and the Temple in the good companionship of like-minded pilgrims.

The Psalmist's distress had been caused by "lying lips" and a "deceitful tongue". Matthew Henry suggests that this is illustrated in the experience of David, and he writes, "There were those that sought his ruin, and had almost effected it, by lying. (1) By telling lies to him…(2) By telling lies of him". The first is flattery and the second is slander, and from both of these the Psalmist had prayed to be delivered. The flatterer is a liar equally with the slanderer. Flattery smiles upon the person, offering insincere congratulations and approvals, while sometimes even plotting maliciously against that person. Slander spreads false accusations about a man, sowing doubts about his character and making cruel insinuations about him. From such lies and deceit the Psalmist prays to be delivered, and the Lord graciously heard his cry and answered.

Verses 3-4: The Punishment of the False Tongue

The deceitful tongue is now personified and addressed directly with a dual question. "What shall be given unto thee? or what shall be done unto thee?" What possible reward or profit can be gained by such malice? Surely the only recompense must be retribution. But what suitable punishment can there be for either the callousness of the slanderer or the treachery of the insincere flatterer?

As the wrongdoing, and the questions, have been two-fold, so also will be the retribution. It is likened to sharp arrows and burning coals. "Sharp arrows" suggests a punishment that is swift and sure, final and fatal. "Coals of juniper" signifies the wood of the juniper, or broom tree, regarded by the Bedouin Arabs as the best wood-fuel. It burns into charcoal and is renowned for its long retention of heat. Might this be but a feeble illustration of that fire that shall never be quenched, where all liars shall have their part (Mk 9.44, 46, 48; Rev 21.8)? As Spurgeon comments so solemnly, "Juniper coals long retain their heat, but hell burneth ever...It is better to be the victim of slander, than to be the author of it. The shafts of calumny will miss the mark, but not so the arrows of God: the coals of malice will cool, but not the fire of justice".

Verses 5-7: The Exile's Lament

Any Israelite away from Jerusalem regarded himself as an exile away from home, a stranger in a strange land. Jerusalem was the very heart of the country and the soul of the nation. Many of these pilgrims lived at a distance, and a visit to the Holy City was like coming home. The Psalmist laments concerning the people among whom he dwells. "Woe is me", he says. This is the first of seven occurrences of this phrase in the Scriptures. It is an expression of self-pity, and is found again in Isaiah 6.5; Jeremiah 4.31; 10.19; 15.10; 45.3; and Micah 7.1.

He speaks of sojourning in Mesech and dwelling in the tents of Kedar, but since there is no geographical connection between the territories of these two peoples, the Psalmist is obviously using the names symbolically. They are descriptive of the character of the hostile people among whom he lives. Mesech was a son of Japheth (Gen 10.2), whose descendants occupied the mountainous region between the Caspian Sea and the Black Sea. Kedar was the second son of Ishmael (Gen 25.13; 1 Chr 1.29), and his name later denoted the Bedouin Arabs (see Song 1.5). Both of these were known as barbarous and treacherous races. Of Ishmael it had been prophesied that, "His hand will be against every man, and every man's hand against him" (Gen 16.12). The Psalmist does not mean that he himself was actually dwelling among these, but that they were typical of the people among whom he did dwell.

For long enough, for too long, he had lived with a people who were implacable, hating peace (7965). This is the lovely word "Shalom". "I am for peace", he says. He wanted only to promote friendship with them, but all his overtures were rejected. Perhaps he offered the familiar greeting, "Shalom", but they refused his kindness and wanted only enmity and war.

Maclaren says, "The Psalm ends with a long-drawn sigh...It thus sets forth most pathetically the sense of discordance between a man and his environment, which urges the soul that feels it to seek a better home. So this is a true pilgrim-Psalm".

PSALM 121

Introduction

This is the second of the fifteen Psalms which are known as "The Songs of Degrees". Kirkpatrick calls it, "This exquisite Psalm, inspired by perfect trust in Jehovah's guardianship of His people". It was indeed such a suitable song for pilgrims going up to Jerusalem, encouraging one another as they now caught sight of the mountains which were round about the beloved city (Ps 125.2). For the Psalmist, it promised the peace which had been denied to him in the previous Psalm. For him, as for all his fellow-pilgrims, Jerusalem, the City of Peace, was the happy end of the journey, and the hills surrounding it were now in view.

The Psalm consists of four pairs of verses, which may have been adapted for antiphonal singing by different voices. One voice, either of an individual pilgrim or a group of pilgrims, would sing the first two verses, and a second voice would respond with verses 3-4. Another voice would sing verses 5-6, and yet another would answer with verses 7-8. These would probably have been chanted repeatedly, as other antiphonal Psalms, of which the clearest example may be Psalm 24.

This arrangement suggests a natural division of the Psalm for meditation and study. Jehovah is the Helper, Keeper, Protector, and Preserver of those who trust Him.

Verses 1-2: Jehovah, Helper of His People

Jerusalem is almost wholly surrounded by mountains. It lies in the shadow of Olivet, Moriah, Zion and Scopus. From a distance, the bands of pilgrims would lift up their eyes and exult at the first sight of the hills, knowing that the city itself would soon be in view. They are not only looking out, but looking up also. The question, "From whence cometh my help?", is not one of uncertainty or doubt. It is a rhetorical question, introductory to the answer which follows immediately, "My help cometh from the Lord". The suggestion has sometimes been made that the first line of the Psalm is a question also, "Shall I lift up my eyes to the hills?", implying that such a thought would be foolish, if not altogether heathenish, that help would come from the hills. This idea has very little foundation or support, and the majority of expositors understand, as has been said, that the pilgrim-Psalmist has now lifted up his eyes with joy, perhaps to catch a first glimpse of the mountains of Zion, the very precincts of Jerusalem. It will be remembered that Daniel, the exiled prophet, in the remoteness of Babylon, opened his window three times a day to pray toward Jerusalem (Dan 6.10). The Psalmist knows, and is confident, that Jehovah, Creator of heaven and earth, is his Helper, and that Jerusalem is the place in which He had chosen to place His name, and the place where His honour dwelt (Deut 26.2; Ps 26.8). His Helper is indeed Jehovah, the Eternal, not like the lifeless heathen deities. Here is the first of five occurrences of the great name Jehovah in the Psalm.

Verses 3-4: Jehovah, Keeper of Israel

How applicable this little Psalm was to the pilgrim bands travelling to Jerusalem. How precious its assurances and promises must have been. The journey to Jerusalem was an arduous one, if not hazardous, but Jehovah was their Keeper. One slip of the foot could have spelt great danger on the difficult roads, and perhaps they might have taken the promise literally, "He will not suffer thy foot to be moved". He would keep them on the way. Again, there were the dangers of the nightly encampments, but they could rest in peace knowing that their Keeper would neither slumber nor sleep. To "slumber" (5123), Strong says, is "to be drowsy". Jehovah would not sleep, nor would He slumber, in His watchfulness over His people. As Kirkpatrick writes, "Israel's watchman is not like a human sentinel, liable to be overcome by sleep upon His watch; He is not such as the heathen suppose their gods to be (1 Kings 18.27), but unceasing in His vigilance". The promise is then repeated, perhaps to bring a double assurance to the pilgrim people that their safety was with the Lord.

Verses 5-6: Jehovah, Protector and Guardian

Yet again the promise is repeated, with emphasis on the great name of their Keeper. Their Keeper was Jehovah. "Jehovah is thy keeper: Jehovah is thy shade". He was their great Protector at their right hand, and His protection of them was vouchsafed by day and by night. He would protect them from the dangers around, and likewise from the dangers above. He was their shade, shielding them from the heat of the sun by day and from the brightness of the moon by night. With the fact of sunstroke men are familiar. It was a common experience in the East during the sub-tropical summer, and may be alluded to in 2 Kings 4.18-19. While the influence of the moon may seem benign, it is from it that we derive the term "lunacy". Spurgeon's quotation from *The Biblical Treasury* may not be medically acceptable to all, but it is interesting: "In the cloudless skies of the East, where the moon shines with such exceeding clearness, its effects upon the human frame have been found most injurious...It has been proved beyond a doubt that the moon smites as well as the sun". That extract also comments that "The inhabitants of these countries are most careful in taking precautionary measures before exposing themselves to its influence. Sleeping much in the open air, they are careful to cover well their heads and faces". For Israel's pilgrim bands, Jehovah was their shade by night and by day.

Verses 7-8: Jehovah, Preserver of Pilgrims

The word "preserve" (8104) which, in the AV, occurs three times in the two final verses of the Psalm, is the same word as that which is translated "keep" in the earlier verses. It is as if the Psalmist would close with yet another emphasis on the fact that Jehovah was the Keeper, Protector, and Guardian of His people. He would preserve them from all evil. From the wickedness of wicked men He would protect His pilgrim people. They were, after all, fulfilling His will and obeying His Word in making pilgrimage to Jerusalem for the keeping of the Feasts, and He would guard them in their devotion to His express commands. "Evil" (7451) denotes "affliction; adversity; trouble; or mischief". From such Jehovah would preserve them.

This promise of preservation was unlimited. The lives and well-being of His people were precious to the Lord, and He would be their Preserver whether they were going out or coming in, whether by day or night, whether today or tomorrow, now or later, "from this time forth, and even for evermore". What a promise! As Dr Cohen comments, "This Psalm has been on the lips of countless men and women through the generations when they felt the need of help beyond that which mortals could offer".

PSALM 122

Introduction

This is the third Psalm in the series known as "The Songs of Degrees" and it is the first of these songs to be attributed to David. Samuel Cox calls this Psalm "The Song of the Arrival". He rejects the Davidic authorship, believing that the "of David" in the title was an insertion by Rabbis of a later date. He writes, "It was obviously written for the occasion, and not merely adapted to it; its author intended it to be sung as the Caravans passed through the streets of Jerusalem on their way to the Temple". Many other writers, however, are agreed that the Psalm is David's, and see no reason to query this.

The Psalm extols the compact beauty of Jerusalem and invokes peace for it, promising prosperity, too, for those who love it. It tells of the holy excitement of the pilgrim on reaching Jerusalem. It describes his sensations as he arrives at the goal of his pilgrimage and enters the precincts of the beloved city.

There are two obvious parts in the Psalm. Verses 1-5 record the pilgrim's thoughts and reflections in Jerusalem. Verses 6-9 contain prayer, and a request for prayer, for the city.

Verses 1-5: Reflections in Jerusalem

The Psalmist expresses his joy at the remembrance of the invitation to go up to Jerusalem. This is the reflection of a pilgrim who is now recalling the initial suggestion of some friends, that they should go to the house of the Lord, mentioned again in v.9. There can be no valid objection to a Davidic authorship in this thought of going up to Jerusalem. The Psalmist wrote songs for others to sing, just as christian hymn-writers have done also. He is but putting the sentiments of others into verse. As far as "the house of the Lord" is concerned, if it is objected that there was no temple in David's day, still, there was indeed a "house of the Lord" on Mount Zion.

There is some disagreement regarding the tense in the opening words of v.2. Is it, "Our feet shall stand"? Or is it, "are standing"? Or even, "have stood"? Some think that the first is correct, and that the pilgrim is anticipating his imminent entrance into the city. Others, as Samuel Cox, quoted in the introduction above, favour the second, as denoting the song of the pilgrim having now arrived and actually standing inside the city walls. Yet others understand it as the reflection of one who has already, on some earlier occasion, been to the city, and is now recalling that joy. There is another view which perhaps blends two of these, where the pilgrim is anticipating entering Jerusalem, his joy increased, as it were, by the remembrance of earlier visits; "Our feet have before stood within these gates which we are now about to enter again". Whichever of these may be the intended meaning, the basic, unchanging message is that there was a holy joy in being in Jerusalem, standing within the gates of the beloved city.

Jerusalem was compactly built. It had to be, surrounded as it was by hills and valleys which fixed its natural boundaries. The Kedron and Hinnom Valleys, the mounts Olivet, Moriah and Zion, all played their part in determining the bounds of the city. Its maze of narrow streets, its rows of closely built houses, must have greatly impressed the peasant pilgrim who had been accustomed only to rural villages and scattered dwellings. It is interesting that the word "builded" (1129) may also mean "rebuilt", or "built again", which would make the song most suitable for those pilgrims returning from exile and seeing the city reconstructed after its destruction.

Jerusalem was the city "whither the tribes go up". Some commentators, with the JPS rendering, prefer, "whither the tribes *went* up", and think that the Psalmist is remembering that this was the ancient tradition and custom of the tribes of the Lord, to make pilgrimage to the divine centre for the three great annual festivals. "Lord" (3050) is Jah, the shortened, though not diminished or diluted, form of Jehovah. The tribes went up in obedience to the testimony, or law, which had been given to the nation in Exodus 23.17 and Deuteronomy 16.16. Three times in the year they went up to Jerusalem with their thanksgiving and praise, in accordance with the testimony.

There, in Jerusalem, were set thrones of judgment. Jerusalem was the centre of the nation's civil life as well as its religious life. These thrones were judicial seats, to which a man might bring his grievances to be adjudicated. On the expression, "thrones of the house of David", Kirkpatrick suggests that, "The king appears to have been assisted in his judicial functions by members of the royal family. 'Thrones of the house of David' must mean tribunals exercising a jurisdiction corresponding to that of the royal family in ancient times".

Verses 6-9: Peace and Prosperity

Commenting on the lovely v.6 of the Psalm, Dr Cohen says, "There is a word-play in the Hebrew which cannot be reproduced in translation". But Samuel Cox explains, "In this cordial and even impassioned invocation, it is curious to find one of those puns, or plays on words, which are characteristic of Hebrew poetry. The leading words of the strophe are 'peace' and 'prosperity'. Now the Hebrew word for 'peace' is *shalom*, and the Hebrew word for 'prosperity' is *shalvah*, while the Hebrew form of 'Jerusalem', which means 'City of Peace', is Yeru-*shalaim*. So that, in effect, the poet wishes *shalom* and *shalvah* on *shalaim* – 'peace' and 'prosperity' on the City of Peace." Some think that, as the RSV and JPS translate, the latter phrase in the verse is a prayer, "May they prosper who love you". It seems indeed to be a principle, borne out by centuries of experience, and by the history of nations, that they do prosper who love and honour Jerusalem and God's ancient people.

The Psalmist himself now wishes peace and prosperity upon the city, peace within its walls and prosperity within its palaces. He addresses Jerusalem as he would address a friend, saluting it as he would a person, saying, "Peace be within thee". "Shalom!" The walls were its protection, and the palaces its residences. He prays for peace for the sake of his brethren and companions, perhaps those who were living within the city. How often it had been subjected to siege and destruction. He prays for peace for it.

But even more than his concern for his brethren and companions, the Psalmist's final thought is for the House of the Lord. As Jerusalem was the heart of the nation, so the House of the Lord was the heart of Jerusalem. He longed for its preservation, and for the sake of the House he would seek, and pray for, the good of the city.

PSALM 123

Introduction

This is the fourth of the fifteen Songs of Degrees. It is not possible to say when this Psalm was written, or by whom, since its sentiments could be those of despised Jews in many an age. The Psalm is a brief supplication, beginning in the first person singular as the prayer of the Psalmist himself, but soon, with its plural pronouns, becoming the prayer of the nation.

Hebrew scholars say that the Psalm has the distinction of having more rhyme than any other comparable passage of Scripture. This, of course, is necessarily lost in the translation, and no attempts to reproduce it have been successful. It is a rhyme of similar inflections and terminations not usual in Hebrew poetry, and whether this rhyming is accidental or by design is a matter of dispute among learned commentators.

It is touching to think that the Man of Sorrows Himself, on His many pilgrimages to Jerusalem during the days of His sojourn in Nazareth, must have joined in the singing of this little "Song of the Suppliant", as Samuel Cox calls it. He was the truly dependent Man, despised and rejected by men, and for Him the Psalm was most appropriate.

Verses 1-4: A Hymn of Prayer and Faith

The Psalmist lifts up his eyes to the heavens. The upturned eye is a familiar gesture with those who pray, and the Saviour Himself "lifted up his eyes to heaven" to address His Father in John 17.1. Delitzsch calls it "an upward glance of waiting faith". The Psalmist looks to Him who sits enthroned in the heavens as the Governor of the universe. To such an One faith can look with confidence for help in time of trouble.

Two explanations have been offered as to the meaning of v.2. These are very different, but equally beautiful. The slave looks to the hand of his master. The maid looks to the hand of her mistress. Some commentators think that these servants, faithfully observing every gesture of the hand of the master or the mistress, were able to anticipate every wish without a word being spoken. Each movement of the hand signalled a command, to be interpreted and obeyed by the watchful diligent servant. Cox favours this view, saying, "The grave, reserved Orientals, as we know, seldom speak to their attendants, at least on public occasions. They intimate their wishes and commands by a wave of the hand, by a glance of the eye, by slight movements and gestures which might escape notice were they not watched for with eager attention...Thus the Psalmist conceives of himself as waiting on God".

While this may be true, the context, with the words that follow - "Until he be gracious unto us" (JND) - probably indicates the other view, which is well presented by T.W. Davies who writes, "These servants depend on what the master hands them: so they look to his hand, just as a domestic animal will follow the hand of one who feeds it. The connexion shows that it is the hand as *giving* and not as *commanding* which is here meant". Commentators, however, just as Davies and Cox, are equally divided on these two explanations. Delitzsch, Spurgeon, Albert Barnes, favour the first; Matthew Henry, Kirkpatrick, Adam Clarke, favour the second, and great names continue to be aligned with each of the two views. The thoughtful reader must himself decide the contextual meaning, or indeed wonder, in a happy compromise, if both explanations are true.

Three times now, in swift succession, the Psalmist appeals, "Have mercy upon us". While "mercy" (2603) is retained by the RV and RSV, the JND rendering is "be gracious unto us". The word signifies both mercy and grace, pity and favour, and this plea rises from hearts which are "exceedingly filled with contempt". This expression, "exceedingly filled", is immediately repeated. The RSV rendering is helpfully explanatory; "We have had more than enough of contempt. Too long our soul has been sated with the scorn of those that are at ease, the contempt of the proud". This word "proud" (3238) is not the word which has appeared in earlier Psalms, denoting insolence and arrogance. Here it signifies oppression and violence. These persecutors, at ease in their own wanton carelessness, despised and vexed the people of God. How glad these must have been for the respite of a pilgrimage to Jerusalem.

On this sad note the Psalm concludes, and yet again it should be remembered, that, for at least twenty years, in young Manhood, the Lord Jesus must have sung these Psalms, journeying from Galilee to the Holy City at the appointed seasons to keep the Feasts. "Despised and rejected of men; a man of sorrows, and acquainted with grief", how He must have made these words His very own while the pilgrims sang together on their way to Jerusalem. Nationally, they were scorned, objects of contempt among hostile neighbours, but He personally suffered more than any others, and He alone knew just what this would eventually cost Him in physical pain.

PSALM 124

Introduction

This is the fifth of the fifteen "Songs of Degrees", and there appears to be no good reason for doubting the Davidic authorship which is indicated in the title. While there is uncertainty as to the actual dates of composition, and the original circumstances or events which prompted some Psalms, it is obvious that this Psalm was written while the remembrance of some signal deliverance was still fresh in the mind of both the Psalmist and the nation. It is, accordingly, a Psalm of thanksgiving and praise to Jehovah the Deliverer.

There is a division in the Psalm which is accepted by most translations and commentators. Verses 1-5 recall the intervention of the Lord on Israel's behalf. Verses 6-8 ascribe due praise to Him for their deliverance.

Verses 1-5: Jehovah was on our Side!

The nation had obviously escaped from some plot which had been laid for them. Looking back, they recognise that, had they been left to themselves, they would have been devoured by an angry enemy. They would have been, as they say, "swallowed up alive". It may be noticed that in the AV rendering there are many words in italics. Spurgeon acknowledges that the translators have done their best, but he suggests, in his quaint way, that "the passage perhaps had been better left in its broken grandeur, and it would then have run thus:- 'Had it not been Jehovah! He was for us, oh let Israel say! Had it not been Jehovah! He who was for us when men rose against us'. The glorious Lord became our ally; He took our part, and entered into treaty with us".

This little Psalm abounds in metaphors which are so Davidic. The enemy would have swallowed them up alive, just as the earth once opened its mouth and swallowed Korah, Dathan, and Abiram in Numbers 16. The Psalmist then speaks of wrath being "kindled" (2734), which suggests the burning of a furnace. Then he likens the anger of the enemy to a deluge, an overwhelming stream (5158), a swelling torrent which would have swept over them. He calls this flood "proud (2121) waters". This is not the same word as that last word "proud" (3238) in the previous Psalm. Here, the only occurrence of this word in the OT, it signifies that these were raging, churning, turbulent waters, and this aptly describes the wrath of the enemies of Israel. Notice the repetition, "over our soul…over our soul". This is a poetic emphasis of the great danger from which the Lord had delivered them.

Verses 6-8: Blessed be the Lord!

The Psalmist now ascribes blessing (1288), praise, to Jehovah, for His timely intervention on behalf of His people, and the changing metaphors continue. From earthquakes, burning furnaces and raging floods, the Psalmist now turns to savage beasts of prey. Their adversaries were like wild animals, baring their teeth to devour them as victims. Jehovah would not allow it, and He delivered His beleaguered people. But once again the metaphor changes. As Albert Barnes comments, "Such changes of imagery constantly occur in the Book of Psalms, and in impassioned poetry everywhere. The mind is full of a subject; numerous illustrations occur in the rapidity of thought; and the mind seizes upon one and then upon another as best suited to express the emotions of the soul. The next verse furnishes an instance of this sudden transition".

The picture now is of a helpless, defenceless little bird caught in the snare of the fowler. But the snare is broken, and, in yet another repetition, the Psalmist exclaims, "Our soul is escaped...we are escaped". Remembrance of the deliverance causes him to conclude with an expression of confidence in the Lord. From their own weakness, the saints of all ages may look up, and say like Israel, "Our help is in the name of the Lord". Was it not just a boy David who had once called out across the valley to Goliath of Gath, in defiance of the Philistines, "I come to thee in the name of the Lord of hosts, the God of the armies of Israel" (1 Sam 17.45)? The "name of the Lord" is His revealed character, the way in which He has chosen to make Himself known to men.

It was still the same for Israel, as it had been with David the shepherd boy. In themselves often weak before the strength and subtlety of their enemies, their only hope and help was in Jehovah. But then He was, after all, the Creator of heaven and earth. Such power as that which had brought the creation into being was at the disposal of those who trusted in Him. It was then, for the nation, as the Psalmist had said in that earlier song, "My help cometh from the Lord" (121.2). This little Psalm ends on a happier note than that of the preceding Psalm. Psalm 124 is, as Samuel Cox calls it, "A Song of Redemption", and it sings the praise of the Redeemer.

PSALM 125

Introduction

This little Psalm is the sixth of the "Songs of Degrees". It begins with trust and ends with peace, and there is simplicity, beauty, and brevity in its five short verses. It is a song of the safety and security of the people of God, mingled with promise and warning, and it probably requires little in the way of exposition. No author is identified, and there may have been no specific event which required its composition, but it is immediately obvious that the pilgrim bands journeying to Jerusalem must have sung it with great jubilation.

Verses 1-2 sing the blessed assurance of those who trust in Jehovah. Verses 3-5 consist of a promise, a prayer, and a warning.

Verses 1-2: The Security of the Saints

How heartily those pilgrims to Jerusalem must have joined in the singing of these opening verses. They must have revelled in the glory and beauty of their Mount Zion (Ps 48.2). Those younger men who had journeyed from country parts and were now seeing Jerusalem for the first time must especially have exulted in the experience. Mountains, being the immovable, solid part of the creation, had become a symbol of strength and stability. Those who trusted in Jehovah, confiding in Him, were like this Mount Zion, which could not be moved, but abode forever. There was a natural beauty, but also a symbolic, spiritual significance in Mount Zion.

Those who so trusted in Jehovah were as safe as Jerusalem itself. Jerusalem, surrounded by mountains, seemed unassailable. Olivet, Zion, Moriah ranged around and about it protectively, and as these mountains were round about Jerusalem, so the Lord was round about His people, and that for ever.

Verses 3-5: The Promise, the Prayer, and the Warning

The righteous are not immune to suffering and oppression. How well the Psalmist knew this. But the promise is that the rod, or sceptre, of the wicked shall not be permitted to rest forever on God's people. Dr Gill explains; "This is to be understood of a measuring rod; laid not on persons, but on lands and estates...and may signify, that though wicked men unjustly seize upon and retain the farms, possessions, and estates of good men...yet should not hold them long, or always". There is a divine reason for this. The very best of men, under severe and continuing oppression, may yield to impatient and intemperate words or actions, and behave with impropriety. Deliverance from the oppression may often save from this. Jehovah will guard His people.

The prayer of v.4 is a very simple request for divine reward for obedience. "Do good, O Lord, unto those that be good". Good behaviour springs from an uprightness of heart which observes the law of the Lord, but as for those who persist in crooked ways, they shall have their portion with all other workers of iniquity in divine judgment.

The Psalm concludes with a benediction, "Peace, Shalom, be upon Israel". Let Spurgeon have the last word. He says, "Bind the first and last verses together: Israel trusts in the Lord, Psalm 125.1, and Israel has peace, Psalm 125.5".

PSALM 126

Introduction

This delightful Psalm, the seventh of the "Songs of Degrees", is well known, much loved, and often quoted by the Lord's people. Spurgeon remarks, "This is the seventh Step, and we may therefore expect to meet with some special perfection of joy in it, nor shall we look in vain". In its six verses there is laughter and singing, gladness and joy, and even the tears at the close of the Psalm are mingled with rejoicing.

Perhaps because of the word "captivity", which occurs twice, many commentators have related the Psalm to the return from the Babylonian exile. This, of course, then requires a post-exilic date for the Psalm, and an author much later then David. There is however, little support or foundation for these conjectures, as will be seen when the word "captivity" is examined more closely in vv. 1 and 4. T.W. Davies comments helpfully on the background of the Psalm, saying, "The Psalm assumes that at some not distant period in the past Jehovah turned the tide of the nation's affairs, making the people once more happy and prosperous. But there is another change, this time for the worse, and in the present Psalm we seem to have petition and hope that Jehovah may again bless and prosper the nation". He adds, "Many have supposed that vv. 1-3 refer to the gladness which accompanied the return from Babylon, and that the distress spoken of in vv. 4-6 is that endured during the Samaritan persecutions. But there is little evidence from which we can argue with confidence".

How precious this Psalm will be, and how appropriate the words, to Israel in the future, restored to her homeland after the present long "diaspora", these two thousand years of dispersion among the nations. It must ever be remembered too, that these "Songs of Degrees" were sung by pilgrims on their way to Jerusalem for the Feasts. It is not unreasonable to feel that many of them would think, as they sang, of that great deliverance from Egypt, wrought for their fathers by Jehovah through Moses so long ago.

The Psalm may be divided as follows. Verses 1-3 are a glad reminiscence, recalling some former restoration of the nation. Verse 4 is a brief prayer in the heart of the Psalm. Verses 5-6 are a promise of joy after sorrow, rejoicing after tears.

Verses 1-3: Reminiscing!

At some time not identified, Jehovah had, as the RSV puts it, "restored the fortunes of Zion". The word "captivity" (7870) occurs in this form only here in the OT. "Captivity" (7622) in v.4 is a different word, though similar in meaning. Both words signify "restoration", so that, literally, these opening words might read, "When the Lord restored the restoration of Zion", signifying a complete return to former, happier, and more prosperous days. In Job 42.10 the phrase can have no other meaning. As Spurgeon says, " 'Turning captivity' by no means requires an actual removal into banishment to fill out the idea; rescue from any dire affliction or crushing tyranny would be fitly described as 'captivity turned'. Indeed, the passage is not applicable to captives in Babylon, for it is Zion itself which is in captivity and not a part of her citizens: the holy city was in sorrow and distress; though it could not be removed [Ps 125.1], the prosperity could be diminished. Some dark cloud lowered over the beloved capital, and its citizens prayed, 'Turn again our captivity, O Lord'".

This former restoration had obviously caused great rejoicing. They recall how they had been like men in a dream, wondering if it were true! Then, when the reality of it dawned upon them, there was delight, there was laughter and singing (7440), there were shouts of joy. Even their heathen neighbours marvelled, saying, "Jehovah hath done great things for them"! With this they wholeheartedly concurred, echoing, "Jehovah hath done great things for us; whereof we are glad". It was indeed a glad memory, a joyful reminiscence of a happy recovery to better times.

Verse 4: The Prayer

The petition is brief, but poignant, and the imagery is beautiful. In renewed distress of some kind, they now pray for another revival. How expressive is the RSV rendering of this prayer, "Restore our fortunes, O Lord, like the water-courses in the Negeb". The word translated "south" (5045) in the AV and other versions, is the Hebrew word NEGEB, or NEGEV. The Negev is that dry, arid region which lies south of Judah. The streams which irrigate the Negev dry up in summer, and then, after many months of drought, the parched wadis, the dried river beds, are flooded with sparkling, rushing torrents of water. In but a few days, these can turn the parched barrenness of that land into a green fruitful plain. This is the prayer of Zion in distress! Restore us, revive us, renew us, refresh us, just as those watercourses in the Negev transform the desert! It is such a short, but touching appeal. Jehovah has restored them on other occasions, as they have remembered. O that He might do so again!

Verses 5-6: The Promise

The promise is that they who sow in tears shall reap in joy. It was well known among them that many an Oriental husbandman sowed his seed with a heavy heart. He walked his fields carrying his seed in the folds of his robe, scattering handfuls of seed as he walked. He knew that so often the seasons were unfriendly and unpredictable. Storms or droughts might threaten his labour and toil, but even though with tears, he must nevertheless continue to sow, knowing that eventually, he who sowed with tears would reap with joy. So, year after year, season after season, the farmer would go forth weeping, bearing his precious seed, with the promise of a harvest. He would, after the work and the patient waiting, return one day from that same harvest field, bringing his sheaves with him. The weeping would be rewarded with rejoicing. Poor Israel had her share of weeping. Would her sorrow now be replaced by joy? Would Jehovah restore them again and give them showers of blessing?

But Samuel Cox has a most interesting and touching comment on this passage. He writes, "Nor, as we study this Psalm, should we forget that, among the Pilgrims who went up year by year to Jerusalem, there was One who took up the parable of the Psalm to new heights of meaning, both in His teaching and in His life. The man Christ Jesus was keeping the feast in Jerusalem – and as He went up to the city, He may have sung this very Psalm – when He addressed to His disciples the memorable words: '*Verily, verily, I say unto you, Except a corn of wheat fall into the ground and die, it abideth alone: but if it die, it bringeth forth much fruit*'...He was the Sower as well as the Seed. He went forth, weeping as He went...He would surely come again, with songs of joy, bearing the sheaves that seed had produced. It was for this joy that He endured the cross".

PSALM 127

Introduction

Another step, and another song; this is the eighth, and the central Psalm of the fifteen "Songs of Degrees". Its title bears the name of Solomon, David's son, but while the AV reads "for Solomon", other versions read, "of Solomon", so that it is not clear whether it was actually written by Solomon, or composed by David for Solomon. This does not materially affect an understanding of the Psalm since the spirit of Solomon is apparent throughout. "Solomon" (SH^{e}LOMOH - 8010), is a derivation of the lovely "shalom", meaning "peace", or "peaceable". His other name, given to him at birth by the prophet Nathan, was "Jedidiah" (3041). This means "Beloved of the Lord", and may be alluded to in v.2 of the Psalm (see 2 Sam 12.25).

In verses 1-2 the emphasis is on the pilgrim's dependence upon Jehovah and the remaining verses 3-5 deal with the pilgrim's reward in a happy family and an ordered household.

Verses 1-2: The Pilgrim's Dependence

Since the name of the wise builder of the temple is here, the opening words of the Psalm are of great importance. Solomon had wealth and wisdom, and apparently all the human resources necessary for the building of the temple, but he knew that "except the Lord build the house, they labour in vain that build it". The word "house" (1004) need not, of course, be restricted to the temple. It is a general term for any dwelling place or household, so that the injunctions and exhortations which are given are applicable not only to Solomon and his temple, but to every family man and householder.

The word "vain" (7723) occurs three times in these first two verses. It signifies "emptiness", or "worthlessness", or even "nothingness". Such is labour without the Lord. Such is human watchfulness apart from Him. Such, too, is anxious activity and toil if the Lord is not in it. They labour in vain who build without the approval and blessing of God. Those watchmen guard the city in vain who do so independently of Him, for, in spite of all their diligence and vigilance, fire or storm or the surprise assault of an enemy may overtake them. As for those who toil anxiously from early morning until late at night, as if everything depended upon them, this is vain also. Such ceaseless, restless bustle and care is not God's plan or intention for His people. To those who trust Him, who are His beloved ones, He would give refreshing sleep, rest from their labours. However, as Kirkpatrick observes, "It is hardly necessary to say that no sanction of idleness or deprecation of industry is here expressed or implied. What the Psalmist rebukes is the anxious spirit of those who toil restlessly as though they could ensure success by their own efforts, forgetting that God's blessing is needed to prosper those efforts, and that He is ever ready to give that blessing to those who trust Him".

Verses 3-5: The Pilgrim's Reward

It was perhaps the desire and ambition of every Hebrew to have a joyful household, a family of children in a happy home. Such a blessing would be an inheritance from the Lord. He could order either fruitfulness or barrenness, and if He granted children to a man, this was reward indeed for trusting Him. The word rendered "children" (1121) in vv. 3 and 4 is more often translated "sons", but "the fruit of the womb" in v.3 is a general term, implying sons and daughters alike.

Sons, born to a man in his youth, would be a special blessing to him in his old age. They would be for his protection, like arrows in the hand of a mighty man or warrior. The metaphor of the arrows and the archer continues as the Psalmist says, "Happy is the man that hath his quiver full of them". A family of sons would be the parent's defence and succour in later years, so that the more sons a man had, the more he felt blessed of the Lord, especially in view of the fact that Hebrews lived under the constant threat of enemies. What weight, too, would a large family of sons give to a man's negotiations with his adversaries at the city gate. The gate (8179) of the city was the public meeting place, where disputes were settled and justice was administered. With the support of numerous sons, a man need not be disconcerted or ashamed in such circumstances. He would be regarded with respect as a man of influence and standing in the community. Delitzsch says, "Unjust judges, malicious accusers, and false witnesses retire shy and faint-hearted before a family so capable of defending itself".

Again it should always be remembered that these Psalms were sung by the pilgrims journeying to Jerusalem. How happy was that man who, with his family, would make his way to Zion for the Feasts of the Lord. It must have been a pleasing sight, to see an older man, accompanied by his sons, on obedient pilgrimage to the Holy City to celebrate Passover/Unleavened Bread, Pentecost, or the Feast of Tabernacles.

PSALM 128

Introduction

This is the ninth Psalm of the "Songs of Degrees". It is very general in its character, and therefore does not require any discussion as to a particular reason for its composition. No author is identified, but he was obviously a family man who appreciated the blessings of a happy household. Luther called this Psalm, "A Marriage Song", and it does indeed describe a contented home and family. It is a companion, or supplement, to Psalm 127. That Psalm spoke of the vanity of building a house without the help and the presence of the Lord. This Psalm envisages the ideal household, ordered in the fear of the Lord, with the promised blessings of prosperity and peace.

The Psalm is in two equal parts, each of which emphasises the word "blessed". In the original Hebrew however, these are two different words, and this difference will be noted in the commentary. The first part, verses 1-3, deals with the blessing and tranquility which come with the fear of the Lord. In the second part, verses 4-6, the fear of the Lord is mentioned again, and a divine benediction is pronounced upon the man who fears Him.

Verses 1-3: The Promises

Like the very first Psalm in the Psalter, this Psalm begins with a pronouncement of blessing, and in both places this blessing is dependent upon a godly walk. The man who fears the Lord walks in the ways of the Lord to please Him, and this in turn calls down the blessing of the Lord upon Him. The word "blessed" (835) means "happy", indeed some say, "very happy". It is the word with which the previous Psalm ends, and it is there translated "happy" in the AV and in most other versions. The God-fearing man will enjoy the labour of his hands. God will bless his diligence and industry, and allow him to benefit from the fruit of his toil.

The Psalmist employs two metaphors to describe the domestic happiness of this man and his household. His wife is likened to a fruitful vine, and his children to olive plants around his table. The expression "by the sides of thy house" is sometimes interpreted as indicating the vine plant attached for support to the wall of the house. The word "sides" (3411), however, may mean the inner quarters or recesses of the house, where, customarily, the women's apartments were located. JND's rendering is, "the inner part of thy house". Kirkpatrick says, "the innermost chambers". The figure of the vine suggests a precious and joyful fruitfulness, although dependence and need for support may be implied also. The wife in such a happy well-ordered family will be a faithful housekeeper, adorning the home of the godly man. His children around his table are likened to olive plants. The olive tree is an evergreen, the emblem of vitality. Perowne says, "vigorous, healthy, joyous life". Dr W. M. Thomson in his *The Land and the Book* has a very lovely comment. He writes, "Follow me into the grove and I will show you what may have suggested the comparison. Here we have hit upon a beautiful illustration. This aged and decayed tree is surrounded, as you see, by several young and thrifty shoots, which spring from the root of the venerable parent. They seem to uphold, protect, and embrace it, we may even fancy that they now bear that load of fruit which would otherwise be demanded of the feeble parent". Such are the children of this blessed God-fearing man, children full of life and full of promise, sitting obediently and respectfully around his table.

Verses 4-6: The Benediction

As has been noticed, this second section of the Psalm also stresses the word "blessed" (1288), but this is a different word from that of the earlier verses. This word means "saluted; praised; congratulated". The word occurs in vv. 4 and 5, and may signify first that the man will be praised by his immediate household and friends, especially by the family around his table. By his godly living he has commanded the respect of all those who know him. They salute him for his uprightness and obedience to the law. The second occurrence of the word, in v.5, indicates that Jehovah will praise him too. The man has feared Jehovah, and has lived accordingly, and the Lord will honour him for it. Out of Zion, the Jerusalem to which the pilgrims were ascending, the very dwelling place of Jehovah, this blessing would come. Both in his home and in the house of the Lord his godliness is acknowledged and praised. This is blessing indeed.

The Psalm concludes with a brief prayer, for the man, for Jerusalem, for his posterity, and for the nation. The RSV rendering perhaps makes this clearer, reading, "The Lord bless you from Zion! May you see the prosperity of Jerusalem all the days of your life! May you see your children's children! Peace be upon Israel!". This is a delightful prayer and benediction to end a lovely Psalm. It is a prayer for blessing for the godly man and for the good of Jerusalem, and a request for longevity for him that he might have the joy of seeing his grandchildren. The final "shalom", is a salutation of peace for Israel.

PSALM 129

Introduction

This is the tenth Psalm of the "Songs of Degrees", and readers will note a similarity with the fifth of these songs, Psalm 124. There is, in both of these Psalms, a remembrance of days of oppression and of Jehovah's deliverance.

There is no necessity to relate this Psalm to any particular persecution of the nation, for, as they say, "Many a time have they afflicted me". No author is identified, but the likeness between the sentiments and the style of these two Psalms is strongly in favour of the same author for both, namely David.

The Psalm is in two parts. Verses 1-4 recall the former afflictions and describe them, and the deliverance from them, with illustrations from rural life and rustic scenes with which the pilgrims from the country would have been so familiar. Verses 5-8 are imprecatory, calling down vengeance upon the persecutors, again with metaphors from life in country parts.

Although much of the Psalm is written in the first person singular, it is not necessary to understand the experiences as being those of the Psalmist personally. It is more likely that this is the language of the nation personified.

Verses 1-4: Israel Oppressed but Delivered

The opening clause is almost at once repeated. This is not needless or superfluous repetition, but rather a poetic way of expressing the intensity of feeling as the afflictions are remembered. "Many a time have they afflicted me from my youth". Their sufferings had been sore and prolonged since the beginning of their national life in Egypt. Those were the days of her youth, as in Hosea 11.1 and Jeremiah 2.2, but the affliction and bondage under Pharaoh were only the beginning. As Samuel Cox says, "They had to strive with the power of Egypt, with the Desert clans, with the military races that held possession of Canaan and its southern borders. And since then, there had been a long succession of conflicts". Many of the pilgrims in later years would know so well that all this culminated with the oppression by the Chaldeans and the Assyrians, and the captivities of Israel and Judah. Nevertheless, in spite of all these pogroms, Jehovah had preserved them, and now, on their happy way to Jerusalem, they could sing, "Yet they have not prevailed against me". They knew, as they had said in Psalm 124, that Jehovah had been on their side.

These pilgrims from the country would have been familiar with the ploughman, the plough, and the furrows, and this imagery is now employed to describe the sore afflictions of the nation. Their cruel adversaries had lashed them. Their strokes had been like the long furrows which mercilessly tore up the soil, lacerating the back of the helpless earth. It is touching to compare this with Isaiah 50.6, and to remember that He who must have often joined in the singing of this Psalm with the pilgrims who journeyed to Jerusalem, Himself gave His back to the smiters and was cruelly scourged by the Romans. What must His feelings have been as He sang these words and anticipated Gabbatha? What must His agony have been as He endured the scourging and suffered the lash? How His people adore Him and say with deepest gratitude, "With his stripes we are healed" (Is 53.5).

Jehovah, in His righteousness, saw the afflictions of Israel and delivered them. He redeemed them from the bondage of Egypt. He saved them out of succeeding oppressions and adversities. Those pilgrims of later years would remember, too, that eventually they were released from Babylonian and Assyrian captivity also. There may be another illustration from rural life here, for many commentators think that the cords which are mentioned are the bonds which yoked the oxen to the plough. This indeed is the meaning in Job 39.10, where the same word is used (5688). Here in the Psalm, "the cords of the wicked" are a figure for the subjection, the yoke of servitude, into which other nations had, at times, brought the people of God. The Lord had snapped these bonds. He had cut them asunder and freed His people, and the pilgrims rejoiced.

Verses 5-8: The Prayer for Vengeance

It must always be remembered that the imprecatory spirit of the old dispensation does not prevail with believers today. The prayer of the Blessed One whose back they scourged and whose hands they pierced, was, "Father, forgive them". The prayer of His earliest martyr was, "Lord, lay not this sin to their charge" (Acts 7.60). Saints of that former age called for retribution and vengeance, but Calvary and the advent of the Holy Spirit have made a difference for present-day believers.

These oppressors hated Israel. Let them be ashamed! Let them be confounded! Let them retreat in confusion! The Psalmist prays that they might be as the grass upon the housetops. Rural people would recognise the imagery immediately. On the flat mud and straw roof of the peasant's house, the grass or corn would often spring up. But there was no depth of soil and soon the blades would wither in the heat of the Eastern sun. It was fruitless and worthless, and, as the Psalmist thinks of the enemies of Israel as the withering grass, he thinks of another familiar scene.

He now envisages a pleasant harvest field, beautifully described in the second chapter of the Book of Ruth. The reapers are gracefully swinging the scythe. The labourers follow, gathering the corn into their arms, folding it to their bosoms and binding it into sheaves. The gleaners come behind, gathering the handfuls which have been left on purpose for them. Samuel Cox comments, "The passers-by stop to look on at the bright, busy scene, and, in the courteous and pious Eastern fashion, they greet the reapers with the salutation, 'The blessing of Jehovah be upon you!' And the reapers, glad to pause, straighten themselves from their work amid the sheaves, look up and shout back, 'We bless you in the name of Jehovah!'" So it was when Boaz came from Bethlehem to his harvest field. He said to the reapers, "The Lord be with you!", and they answered, "The Lord bless thee".

It was a happy and tranquil harvest scene, but, in contrast, the Psalmist saw the enemies of Israel as grass withering on the housetops. "So let them be!", is his prayer. They have hated and harassed Israel. They have subjected the people of God to oppression and bondage. May Jehovah in His righteousness mete out retribution to them accordingly. Let them wither like the grass on the roof.

PSALM 130

Introduction

This Psalm is the eleventh of the fifteen "Songs of Degrees". It is also one of those seven which are called "Penitential Psalms". The other "Penitential Psalms" are Psalms 6, 32, 38, 51, 102 and 143. The term means, of course, that these are the prayers of a penitent, and perhaps the greatest example of such penitence is that of David in Psalm 51. This Psalm commences with pronouns in the first person singular, and the Psalmist may indeed be expressing personal penitence for some departure from the Lord. However, his references to Israel in vv. 7 and 8 may indicate that he is speaking representatively and on behalf of the nation, and that this is national repentance rather than personal. Whether personal or national, the penitence is sincere, and there are great principles here for every repentant soul looking for pardon.

The Psalm may be considered in two equal parts. In verses 1-4 the Psalmist cries out of the depths, praying that he might be heard and pardoned. In verses 5-8 he pleads his sincerity and encourages Israel to hope and trust in the Lord. In preparation for the Feasts, the godly pilgrims singing this Psalm on the way to Jerusalem would confess shortcomings and failures, waiting on Him who was plenteous in mercy.

Verses 1-4: The Cry from the Depths

The Psalmist is overwhelmed by thoughts of some sin, or sinful condition, or by some sorrow which is not here defined or developed. He is obviously in distress, and from out of his deep conviction he can only but cry to the Lord. He has cried from out of the floods which have deluged him. His cry is that of humble confession, but will Jehovah hear him? Twice in v.2 he mentions his voice, invoking the Lord that He might indeed hear him, that He might be attentive to him. The supplications (8469) of which he speaks are earnest entreaties, the pleadings of one looking to God alone for favour. His prayer was a supplicating cry.

The Psalmist knows that if the Lord should mark iniquities, taking account of them to demand punishment of them, none could stand before Him. The question, "O Lord, who shall stand?", is rhetorical. It is simply an emphatic way of saying that none could stand. No man could maintain or prove his innocence. All must be found guilty and be accordingly condemned. In the NT the early chapters of the Epistle to the Romans are an exposition of the inexcusable guilt and inevitable judgment of all men. "But…!". How blessedly welcome is this "But". There is forgiveness! It is possible! Jehovah is rich in mercy and in wisdom. He has the prerogative to forgive and He has the power of pardon. Punishment and judgment will never produce love for God, but He forgives men so that, in turn, forgiven men might fear Him.

Verses 5-8: Plenteous Redemption

The penitent Psalmist waits (6960) for the Lord. He looks eagerly for an answer to his cry from the depths. Has Jehovah heard? There is a mingling of patience and confidence, of assurance and hope. There is promise in God's Word, and in this promise the penitent can rest. He waits and watches with the earnestness and patience of the watchman who looks for the dawn. Most commentators interpret this as the military sentinel longing for the dawn, when he will be released from his duty. Kirkpatrick however, quotes the Jewish Targum, which renders this, "My soul waits for Jehovah, more than the keepers of the morning-watch which they keep in order to offer the morning sacrifice". Kirkpatrick adds, "…understanding the allusion to be to the custom that one of the Levites who kept the night watch in the Temple was appointed to watch for the moment of the dawn, at which the daily sacrifice was to be offered". This thought would certainly be in keeping with the tenor of this "Penitential Psalm", since the sacrifice would be a token and assurance of divine forgiveness. The Psalmist repeats that he waits and watches more than those who watch for the morning.

With a personal hope in Jehovah and His Word, the Psalmist now exhorts the nation to hope also. "Let Israel hope in the Lord". He gives sound and solid reasons for his exhortations. There is mercy (2617) with the Lord. There is lovingkindness, goodness, and pity. Trust Him! With Him there is plenteous redemption. There is redemption in abundance, redemptive grace and power which can never be exhausted. The Psalmist concludes on a most assured and definite note, "He shall redeem Israel from all his iniquities". It should be observed that "he" is emphatic. He, and He alone, can redeem. Notice too that it is from "all" iniquities. His forgiveness is neither partial nor stinted. It is complete. What a blessing is this for the penitent, whether Psalmist or nation. The iniquities which might have been marked for judgment are gone, blotted out, pardoned, forgiven, and all so that men might love and fear Him who is their Redeemer.

PSALM 131

Introduction

This little Psalm is the twelfth of the fifteen "Songs of Degrees". It is one of the shortest Psalms, but not any less important or profound than the longest. It bears the name of David, and, as Spurgeon remarks, "It is both by David and of David: he is the author and the subject of it, and many incidents of his life may be employed to illustrate it". The Psalm breathes humility throughout, which is, of course, most appropriate after the experience of forgiveness in Psalm 130. Such humility, such absence of pride, was so desirable in the pilgrims going up to the Feasts, to the sanctuary soon to be reached in Psalm 134. Although possessed of certain authority and superiority and great wealth in his kingship, yet, as a man, David displayed an admirable meekness, as will be seen in the commentary. The three short verses require no division.

Verses 1-3: The Humble Mind

David is not boasting of his meekness. He is not proud of his humility! Note that his appeal is to Jehovah, not to men. This is genuine humility which can say to Jehovah, "Lord, my heart is not haughty". He, who knows all things, knows the true condition of every heart, and it is therefore an honest spirit which can appeal directly to Him. It is the spirit of Him who said, "I am meek and lowly in heart" (Mt 11.29). Neither the Psalmist's heart nor his eyes were lifted up. He had no rich or conceited opinions about himself, nor had he any designs or aspirations after greatness. His sights were not set ambitiously on great things for himself. There was a contentment with this man, which did not covet things which were out of reach, things which he knew were too high and too wonderful for him. He was content with what he had, and with what he knew. "Godliness with contentment is great gain" (1 Tim 6.6).

This humble spirit of David is beautifully commented upon by Delitzsch, who writes, "He did not push himself forward, but suffered himself to be drawn forth out of seclusion. He did not take possession of the throne violently, but, after Samuel has anointed him, he willingly and patiently traverses the long, thorny, circuitous way of deep abasement, until he receives from God's hand that which God's promise had assured to him...He left it entirely to God to remove Saul and Ishbosheth. He let Shimei curse. He left Jerusalem before Absalom. Submission to God's guidance, resignation to His dispensations, contentment with that which was allotted to him, are the distinguishing traits of his noble character".

The Psalmist's contentment is likened to that of "a weaned child with its (his) mother" (JND and RV), or "upon his mother" (JFB). Note that the child is completely weaned. It is envisaged that the weaning process, sometimes painful and difficult, is now over, and the child can lie peacefully on its mother's breast without the pining that used to be, in the days when it constantly yearned for its mother's milk. David was similarly content. He was quieted and calm. He could rest in the Lord. Perhaps the humility of the little one is signified here also, and, characterised by such contentment and humility, the Psalmist's soul was at rest. He had no eager yearnings after the things which many other men coveted. So it is with every spiritual soul. In the enjoyment of the things of the Lord the heart is weaned from the world. Just as the weaned child has lost its earlier longings for its mother's milk, so the godly lose the desire for those things which once attracted them. There is a holy tranquility and peace when resting in the Lord.

Again, as in Psalm 130.7, the Psalmist exhorts the nation to hope in the Lord. The man who is himself at peace will encourage others to the same, and this joy of the Psalmist is attained by simple trust in Jehovah. As the JFB Commentary says, "Hope in the Lord is the antidote of haughty thoughts". Such childlike trust in Jehovah is, in itself, an acknowledgement of no confidence in self. It is a renouncing of self in all its aspects. It is a quiet, lowly, waiting upon God for the meeting of every spiritual and temporal need. Having arrived at this peaceable state himself, David now desires the same for Israel. What blessedness this would be for those pilgrims to Zion, to arrive at their goal in the sweet contentment of trust in Jehovah.

PSALM 132

Introduction

This is the thirteenth, and the most lengthy, of the fifteen "Songs of Degrees". The theme of the Psalm is obvious, but the identity of the author is obscure. Some think that David is the Psalmist; some think Solomon because the words of vv. 8-10 are so similar to the words with which Solomon concluded his prayer at the dedication of the temple (2 Chr 6.41-42). But David's son might well have borrowed these words from this Psalm, written earlier, for, as Dr Gill points out, "he sometimes did recite the words of his father" (Prov 4.4-5). The dual theme of the Psalm is the prayer, offered with the confidence of the nation, that Jehovah must remember the faithful endeavours of His servant David with regard to the Ark of the Covenant, and be gracious to them. Psalm 132 is unique in that it is the only Psalm in the Psalter to contain any direct reference to the Ark of the Lord, though there may be an allusion to it in Psalm 78.61.

There is a natural division in the Psalm, so that in verses 1-10 the people address Jehovah in prayer, with a plea that He should remember His covenant with David. In the second section, verses 11-18, Jehovah responds to that prayer, renewing His promises to David and to the nation.

The Hebrew form of the poetry of the Psalm apparently suggests that it was to be sung antiphonally, that is, some singers responding in song to the chants of others. There is, however, no general agreement as the details of this antiphonal arrangement, which, in any case, is lost in the translation, except that the second part of the Psalm is an obvious reply to the first part.

It is easy to envisage the enthusiasm of the singing pilgrims on their way to Zion as they remembered both David and Solomon, and recalled the return of the Ark from captivity and the later building of the "temple magnifical".

Verses 1-10: Lord, Remember David

So the Psalm begins, with the prayer that the Lord might remember David and his afflictions. These are not the general sufferings of David, but rather, as Dr Gill says, "His toil and labour of mind, his great anxiety about building a house for God; the pains he took in finding out a place for it, in drawing the pattern of it, in making preparations for it, and in the charges he gave his son concerning it". In 1 Chronicles 22.14 David refers to his "trouble"(6040), his afflictions, as he made preparations for the temple which he was not permitted to build. There is probably no historical reference to any specific oath or vow which David made, to build a house for God, but the intensity of his desire to do so is well known, and is the subject of a whole chapter - 2 Samuel 7.

His vow is made to "The Mighty One of Jacob" (JND, RV, RSV). "God" is in italics, having been supplied by the AV translators. He is "The Mighty One of Jacob". This title of God, occurring again in v.5, is found elsewhere only in Genesis 49.24. David vowed to the God of the patriarch, who, in Genesis 28.20, at Bethel, the house of God, had also "vowed a vow" to Jehovah, and whom God had honoured.

The essence of David's vow was that he would neither rest nor sleep until he found a place for the Lord, a Bethel for the Mighty God of Jacob. This means, of course, for the Ark, as explained in 1 Chronicles 15.1, the Ark being a symbol of the divine Presence. David's conscience was not at ease that he should have a tent and a bed, a palace and a resting place, while the Ark of the Lord had no permanent home.

The thrilling story of the recovery of the ark from Kirjath-jearim is now recalled. There had been many years of exile since its capture by the Philistines in the days of Eli and young Samuel (1 Sam 4.17). The mention of Ephratah has created problems for some, for "Ephratah" was the ancient name of Bethlehem, and the Ark was never there. What then does this mean, "We heard of it at Ephratah: we found it in the fields of the wood"? To resolve the problem some have imagined a wider meaning for "Ephratah", suggesting that it may have denoted other districts also, and therefore the district of Kirjath-jearim. There is, however, no proof of this, and perhaps J.A. Alexander has the correct, but simple, solution, when he writes: "The only explanation, equally agreeable to usage and the context, is that which makes Ephratah the ancient name Bethlehem (Gen 48.7), here mentioned as the place where David spent his youth, and where he used to hear of the Ark, although he never saw it till long afterwards, when he found it in the fields of Kirjath-jearim, which name means Forest Town, or City of the Woods (Compare 1 Sam 7.1 with 2 Sam 6.3-4)". But what does this mean, "We found it"? Had the whereabouts of the Ark been forgotten? Was it necessary to instigate a search for it? Or is the Psalmist simply saying that David heard of it as a youth in Bethlehem but did not see it until he was king, when he recovered it from the house of Abinadab in Kirjath-jearim?

Whichever of these latter thoughts is correct, the joy of the pilgrim bands must have been full, singing as they went up to Jerusalem, "We will go...we will worship". With what eager anticipation they must have journeyed towards the very dwelling place of Jehovah, to kneel in worship at His footstool, His sanctuary. They call to Him, "Arise, O Lord, into thy rest; thou, and the ark of thy strength". The Ark, symbol of His strength and power, had found a resting place, and to that place of Jehovah's rest in Zion the pilgrims were now travelling. His priests would voice the people's praise and lead their worship while the saints raised their shouts of joy. The priests would be clothed in their holy vestments, but more important was it that they should be suitably attired, morally, with righteousness.

As this first section closes, there is another reference to David. "For thy servant David's sake turn not away the face of thine anointed". To "turn away the face" of a petitioner meant to reject him, to disappoint him with a refusal. This prayer asks that God might show favour towards the Davidic dynasty, the anointed king, in accordance with His Word. It is a plea for a divine remembrance of the covenant with David, the promises of God to David and to his seed after him regarding the preservation and continuance of David's throne and kingdom (2 Sam 7). Nor must it be forgotten that this covenant would be fulfilled in the greater Son of David, the Messiah, the Lord Jesus, who will one day sit upon the throne of His father David in a peaceful and universal reign.

Verses 11-18: Jehovah's Response to the Prayer

If David swore unto Jehovah in v.2, so now Jehovah has sworn to David. It was indeed a solemn covenant between the Lord and His anointed. The Lord has sworn in truth. He who cannot lie, the faithful God, will ever be true to His Word. He will not turn back from His purpose or His promise; "Of the fruit of thy body will I set upon thy throne". Note that Peter quotes this on the day of Pentecost with reference to Christ (Acts 2.30). It must be remembered, however, that this particular promise had conditions attached - see 2 Samuel 7.14 and 1 Kings 8.25. Jehovah demanded, and had a right to demand, that the sons of David should keep His covenant and obey His law. If they did not keep His Word they could not claim His promise. Failure to obey His Word and walk in His ways explains the sad state of Israel today, and at many other times. For so long there has been no king or kingdom, and no throne. This is however, but a suspension of the promise, not an abandonment or abrogation of it, and, when Israel shall once again be repentant and obedient, then, in that day, Messiah, the Son of David, will occupy the throne in fulfilment of the covenant.

The Lord cannot forsake Zion. Both the place and the people are His by divine choice. Here He will dwell. Here He will rest. Twice it is affirmed that He desired (183) it. This is a strong word, indicating intense longing. When His people are obedient and the throne is established, then He will bless His people abundantly with material and spiritual blessings. The poor will have bread in plenty. The priests will be clothed with salvation, and the saints will raise their shouts of joy. Notice the parallel with the attire of the priests and the shouts of the saints in v.9. What has been a prayer in that verse is now a realised fact in v.16.

There is now a promise of a "horn" and a "lamp" for David, in v.17. The horn will bud (6779). It will spring forth. The horn is a symbol of strength, and is constantly employed in this symbolic way in the Books of Daniel and Revelation. The might of the Davidic dynasty shall one day be seen again, springing forth from depression to dignity, from days of gloom to national glory. The lamp will shine again, dispelling the darkness of the sad history. This will all be fulfilled ultimately in Him who is the Arm of the Lord and the Light of the world, God's Anointed.

When the priests of Israel are clothed with righteousness and with salvation, how different it will be for the enemies of the Lord's Anointed. They shall be clothed with shame. For them the end will be confusion, but of the king it is said, "Upon himself shall his crown flourish". There are two thoughts in this crown (5145). First, it may be the conventional diadem of the monarch, and the word "flourish" (6692) can mean "to shine or sparkle". It may thus be a glittering crown, an emblem of royalty, of kingship. On the other hand, some think that the words "crown" and "flourish" together denote the crown of a conqueror, a wreath of oak leaves or laurel, with which the victors at the games were garlanded. Perhaps there is no need to choose dogmatically between these two views, for the great Son of David will be both monarch and victor. The King of Glory is the Lord strong and mighty, the Lord mighty in battle, potentate and conqueror (Ps 24). He who wore the crown of thorns, actually wore, on that sad day of His crucifixion, a victor's crown (Gk. "stephanos" - *4735*), but He will appear as King of kings, and of that day John, in Revelation 19.12, writes, "on his head were many crowns" (Gk. "diadema" - *1238*).

So there is a dual encouragement in this Psalm for pilgrims of all ages. The privilege of prayer and the preciousness of the divine promises are always at the disposal of the saints. Jehovah waits to hear the petitions of the saints and He delights to fulfil His promises to them. This is the double theme of Psalm 132.

PSALM 133

Introduction

This delightful little Psalm is the fourteenth, the penultimate Psalm, of the fifteen "Songs of Degrees". It is a Psalm of David, who, in three short verses, extols the pleasantness and the preciousness of the unity of brethren. How much disunity poor David had seen in his day. There had been both national and domestic discord, quarrelling in the court and in the family. With what grief he must have often remembered the rebellion of his son Absalom, and the subsequent strife among the tribes (2 Sam 19.9). Perhaps all this only served to emphasise just how desirable harmony really was. For the pilgrims approaching Jerusalem and the sanctuary, unity was an indispensable prerequisite for true worship. How could acceptable worship be offered from brethren living in disunity? That must have been a beautiful sight indeed, the happy and holy fellowship of those pilgrims, who, three times in the year, journeyed to Jerusalem for the great Festivals. There must have been many joyous reunions on those occasions, for those who lived in distant country parts of Galilee and Judea and who met each other only at the Feasts. The unity among them must have been pleasant to behold.

The lessons of this little Psalm are both appropriate and relevant to saints today, for the unity which is envisaged is an essential condition for those who would worship together in spirit and in truth. The conditions described here are a necessary and happy prelude to the sanctuary service of Psalm 134, which is the topmost step of these "Songs of Degrees". As Edward Dennett says, "So intimately are these two Psalms connected, that it will be profitable to consider them together".

Verses 1-3: Brotherly Love

The Psalm commences with "Behold!". Is the Psalmist calling men to contemplate a wonder too rarely seen? Brethren dwelling together in unity! Is it a call to see these bands of pilgrims who have journeyed many miles in happy unison from their rural homes to Jerusalem? Such a sight! It is, he says, "How good and how pleasant". Some things may be good but not pleasant, as bitter medicine to a child. Other things may be pleasant but not good, as certain pleasures of the world. But the unity of brethren dwelling together is both good and pleasant. Notice that it is "dwelling" together. This is not just an outward show of unity in a casual acquaintance, but unity though living together in the same abode, as brothers in one family or household. Constant closeness may easily engender friction, but unity in such circumstances is good and pleasant. So with believers today, dwelling together in local church fellowship, how desirable it is that they should dwell together in unity of mind and motive. This is the true "philadelphia", of which the Epistle to the Hebrews says, "Let *brotherly love* continue" (Heb 13.1). Unity was so real with those earliest Christians, of whom it is said that "all that believed were together, and had all things common" (Acts 2.44). Perhaps the prevailing hostility of the world and of the authorities only served to cement the bond between them. Enemies without actually made it so necessary that there should be harmony within.

In a future day, the unity of Israel will become a glad reality. Jehovah says, "I…will gather them on every side, and bring them into their own land: And I will make them one nation in the land upon the mountains of Israel; and one king shall be king to them all: and they shall be no more two nations, neither shall they be divided into two kingdoms any more at all" (Ezek 37.21-22). What a happy day for the nation! Meanwhile, the preservation of unity is the joy, and the responsibility, of present day believers (Eph 4.3).

The Psalmist, ever a master of metaphor, now employs two figures of speech to portray the preciousness of the unity of brethren. He speaks of the fragrant anointing oil on the head of Aaron, and the refreshing dew from Mount Hermon. The holy oil with which Aaron was anointed at his consecration into the priesthood was a sweet-smelling compound of myrrh, cinnamon, calamus, and cassia, in olive oil. It was an unique composition, never to be imitated, and to be used only for the anointing of the High Priest and the vessels of the tabernacle (Ex 30.22-33). It was therefore very precious, just like the unity of brethren. This oil was poured upon Aaron's head (Lev 8.12). It ran down upon his beard and on to his priestly garments, but there are two interpretations of "the skirts of his garments". Commentators are almost equally divided as to the meaning of the word "skirts" (6310), which is sometimes translated "hole", or "collar", as in Job 30.18. Some accept the common rendering of "skirts", meaning the bottom, or lower, hem of the garment. JND gives "hem". Others understand the word to mean, as Dr Gill says, "Not the extremity of (the garments), as our version inclines to; for not so great a quantity of oil was poured upon him…but the upper part of his garment, the top of his coat, on which the beard lay; the neck or collar of it; the hole in which his head went through when it was put on, about which there was a band, that it might not be rent (Ex 28.32; 39.23)". Those who understand the word to mean, as Dennett says, "The lowermost borders of his priestly robe", point out that the untrimmed beard of the High Priest would likely have been very long, and, the word "garments" is in the plural, whereas the hole referred to was in one garment only. It would be sad however, if such technical niceties of interpretation were to rob the reader of the sense of the passage. Whichever view is taken, the truth is the same, that both Aaron and his robes were fragrant with a sweet and precious odour which was a symbol of the unity of brethren.

The second metaphor portrays the unity of brethren like the dew of Hermon upon the mountains of Zion. The italicised words of the AV should be omitted, so as to read, "As the dew of Hermon that descended upon the mountains of Zion". Again there are two interpretations of this. Some say that Hermon is too far removed from Zion for the dew of Hermon to be carried there. These understand the metaphor to mean simply that the dew at Zion is as beneficial as the heavy dew of Mount Hermon. Most however, agree with Delitzsch, who writes, "Nowhere in the whole country is so heavy a dew perceptible as in the districts near to Hermon. To this dew the poet likens brotherly love...An abundant dew, when warm days have preceded, might very well be diverted to Jerusalem by the operation of the cold current of air sweeping down from the north over Hermon". This majestic mount is eternally capped with snow and this creates the heavy dew, filled with freshness for the lower mountains of Zion. Such is the value and power of brethren in unity. It is, as Kirkpatrick says, "refreshing, quickening, invigorating". There, where brethren live in peace and harmony, the Lord commands the blessing, even "life for evermore", an expression found elsewhere in the OT only in Daniel 12.2. How infinitely precious and pleasant then, and prosperous too, is this unity of brethren. From such united companies of believers the glad tidings of the gospel can go forth effectively, offering eternal life to the hearers.

PSALM 134

Introduction

This is the fifteenth, and final Psalm, of the "Songs of Degrees". Samuel Cox calls it, "A Song of the Night Watch". No author is identified, but many think that it is, like the preceding one, a Psalm of David. It is a sanctuary Psalm. The pilgrims have reached Jerusalem. By night, as by day, there were priests and Levites who watched over the sacred precincts, guarding against any possible profaning of the holy places. This Psalm commences with a salutation to those on the night watch, concerning whom Perowne in his commentary gives much detail as to their duties. This greeting occupies the first two verses and the third verse is the reply of the priests to the people. The voice may be that of pilgrims departing at sunset from the evening worship, or, as some think, it may be the call of those pilgrims who have just arrived at the temple after their long journey. Adam Clarke, however, thinks that this may have been the charge of the High Priest himself to those who were commencing the night watch, and that the reply is the prayer of the priests and Levites for the High Priest who was now going to his rest. Yet others suggest that this may have been a ritual charge from those who were being relieved, to those who were now taking over their duties. Whichever is the case, the meaning and the beauty of the Psalm is not affected. It is indeed a Psalm of the sanctuary, a Psalm of worship. Notice the several occurrences in the Psalm of the great name "Jehovah". Perhaps it is in keeping with the sanctuary atmosphere of the Psalm that the writer uses this grand title of God five times in three short verses. The Psalm needs little exposition, but it may be profitable to observe the two parts; in verses 1-2, the greeting to the priests, and in verse 3 the priestly response. There is a salutation and a benediction.

Verses 1-2: The Salutation

The Psalm commences with a call to the servants of the Lord. Priests and Levites alike are His servants. Every believer today is a willing bondman to the Saviour, a servant of the Lord. Every saint in this present dispensation is also a priest, with all those attendant priestly privileges and responsibilities. To all, then, the exhortation comes, "Bless ye the Lord, all ye servants of the Lord". This word "bless" (1288) means "to salute or praise", and, as has been noted before, is the equivalent of that NT word from which comes the English "eulogise", meaning "to speak well of". The servants of Jehovah will readily respond and speak well of Jehovah, whom they serve.

Throughout the night their ministry continued. There was always much to do in sanctuary service, even during the hours of darkness. The wine and the oil, the frankincense and the shewbread, had to be prepared. Patrols must guard the courts. It seems likely, too, that the service of praise continued throughout the night. For the New Testament believer, paradoxically, today is really a night, the night of the Saviour's rejection, and the service of the sanctuary continues in worship and witness for Him.

It was traditional for the priests of the old dispensation to lift up their hands in prayer and worship. This signified the lifting up of their hearts to God. Paul doubtless had this in mind when, speaking to Timothy about prayer, he writes of, "lifting up holy hands, without wrath and doubting" (1 Tim 2.8).

Verse 3: The Benediction

Those who bless the Lord will also bless His people. "Bless ye the Lord" is the charge. "The Lord bless thee" is the response. Note that this was so true in the case of Simeon as recorded in Luke 2. "Then took he him up in his arms, and blessed God" (v.28). "And Simeon blessed them" (v.34). It is a principle that he who speaks well of God speaks well of God's people. The blessing in this Psalm is from Jehovah. Here is the fifth occurrence of the great name. He is the Creator of heaven and earth, with all power, right, might, and ability, to bless His saints. The blessing comes out of Zion, His dwelling place, home of the "Shekinah", the glory. It seems so appropriate that the closing word of the fifteen "Songs of Degrees" should be "Zion", this Zion, to which, from so many and varied rural parts of the Land, they had come, with expectations and anticipations, to worship at the Feasts. Some, no doubt, were coming for the first time. What excitement, what joy, must have filled their hearts.

Conclusion

Samuel Cox sums these Songs up so beautifully. He must be quoted in full, as he speaks of - "Psalms which were specially designed for the use of the Pilgrims, and which, therefore, could never be so appropriately sung as when the Caravans were on their way to the Feasts, or were returning from them".

He writes, "Thus, for example, we have the Psalm in which, as the Pilgrims started on their journey, they prayed that during their absence from home they and theirs might be kept in peace and delivered from the strife of tongues (Ps 120). We have the Psalm in which, as they caught their first glimpse of the holy mountain, they lifted up their eyes to the Lord, and besought Him to be their Keeper, and to bless them in their going out and their coming in (Ps 121). We have the Psalm in which, on their safe arrival within the gates, they saluted the City, rejoicing that their feet were in its streets, and praying that peace might be within its walls and prosperity within its palaces (Ps 122). We have the Psalm in which, having reached the Temple, they lifted up their eyes to Him that sat enthroned in heaven, as the slave bends his eyes to the hand of his master, or the maiden to the hand of her mistress, and implored God to be gracious unto them (Ps 123). We have the Psalm in which they recounted the history of the Ark of the Covenant, and prayed that, after so many wanderings, it might rest forever on the hill of Zion (Ps 132). We have the Psalm in which they sang the praises of the Sanctuary, in whose courts they felt that they were of one heart and one mind, and found how good and how pleasant it was for brethren to dwell together as brethren (Ps 133)".

In conclusion he says, "And now that we have arrived at the last of the series, with what should we expect the Book to close? Surely, after hearing the Song of the starting Caravan, Songs for the different stages of the journey, Songs of the City and the Ark and the Sanctuary, we can only expect to hear a Song of Farewell, a final greeting to the House in which they had met God, and had tasted the blessedness of communion with Him and with each other. And this natural expectation is fulfilled in Psalm 134".

It should be mentioned that Cox interprets Psalm 134, as he intimates here, as the parting Song of the Pilgrims just as they leave Jerusalem for home.

PSALM 135

Introduction

Several commentators have likened this Psalm to a mosaic since it seems to be composed of so many expressions which are found in other Psalms or in the writings of the prophets. Whether this Psalmist has drawn from others, or others have borrowed from him, is not agreed. However, as Spurgeon comments, "The whole Psalm is a compound of many choice extracts, and yet it has all the continuity and freshness of an original poem". Its great theme is praise, indicated by the "Hallelujahs" with which it begins and ends. A number of reasons are advanced by the Psalmist for the praise for which he calls, and the Psalm is almost like an extension of the preceding Psalm 134, which was also an exhortation to praise.

The following divisions are apparent, and are followed in the commentary. Verses 1-4 are the initial summons to praise, concluding with the first reasons for that praise. In verses 5-7 the Psalmist extols the supremacy, the sovereignty, and the omnipotence of Jehovah. Verses 8-12 are a remembrance of the power that redeemed Israel from Egypt and gave them the Promised Land. Verses 13-14 tell of Jehovah's unchanging care for His people, and, in sharp contrast to this, verses 15-18 describe the folly of idols and of idolaters. The last section, verses 19-21, is a renewed call to praise, concluding with another "Hallelujah!".

Verses 1-4: Praise! Praise! Praise!

So the Psalm begins, with a three-fold summons to praise in the opening verse. The first occurrence of "praise" (1984) is really incorporated in a "Hallelujah", and is so translated by the JND and JPS versions. Plumer points out that several ancient versions regard this "Hallelujah" as the title of the Psalm. In perfect keeping with these three references to "praise", there are also three mentions of the great name "Jehovah". The call goes out to the servants of Jehovah, to those who stand and minister in the courts of the house of the Lord, both priests and Levites. It is the privilege and duty of the servants of Jehovah to praise the name of Jehovah. Note the two references to the "name" of the Lord. This signifies His revelation of Himself, and, according to their appreciation of His revealed character, His people praise the Lord with intelligence and devotion.

If reasons are needed for praise, then the Psalmist gives them. The Lord is good. That alone is sufficient cause for praise. Then, the singing of praises is pleasant (5273). This lovely word is found six times in the Psalter, once translated "pleasures" (Ps 16.11). See also Psalms 16.6; 81.2; 133.1 and 147.1. It is indeed, as Strong's definition indicates, a delightful, agreeable, sweet pleasure to sing praises to Jehovah. But there is yet another reason for praise. The nation was Jehovah's own peculiar treasure. In His sovereignty He had chosen Jacob, and had changed his name to

Israel. He had made the supplanter a prince with God, and from him there had arisen the nation which bore his name. The expression "peculiar treasure" is one Hebrew word (5459) signifying that they were especially precious to the Lord. It is the word rendered "jewels" in Malachi 3.17. Israel then, was distinct and separate among the nations. As Deuteronomy 7.6 states, they were a holy nation, chosen of God to be a special people for Him. It was fitting that they should praise, and praise, and praise again.

Verses 5-7: Jehovah Supreme and Sovereign

Having said that the Lord is good, the Psalmist now adds, "I know that the Lord is great". The pronoun is emphatic in the Hebrew, "*I* know". Whatever other men may say or think, the Psalmist knows, positively, assuredly, personally and experientially, that Jehovah is great. How great? "Our Lord is above all gods", he says. Later in the Psalm he speaks in more detail about the impotence of the gods of the heathen, but just now he is interested in the supremacy of Jehovah over all.

This greatness is proven by demonstrations of divine power. Jehovah is omnipotent, and, in sovereignty, He does what He wills, when He wills, how He wills, for His own pleasure. There are no boundaries or barriers to His might. He moves in the heavens, on the earth, in the seas, and in the ocean depths. From the ends of the earth, from the extreme horizons, He causes the vapour clouds to ascend. They are His creation. He produces the lightnings which accompany the rainstorms. As T.W. Davies comments, "It was always a mystery to the ancients that fire and water seemed to come from the sky together, though the rain was not heated nor the fire extinguished". The heathen may wonder at such phenomena, but the Psalmist knows that "whatsoever the Lord pleased, that did he". Compare Psalm 115.3. Jehovah then brings the wind out of His storehouses and all the forces of nature are at His command. Supreme and sovereign indeed! Well might the Psalmist say, "I know that the Lord is great".

Verses 8-12: Jehovah, Redeemer of Israel

The power of Jehovah has not only been displayed in creation, but also in redemption. The power that brought all created things into existence had wrought deliverance for Israel and also given them a heritage. In the well-known story of the Exodus, Jehovah smote all the firstborn of Egypt, both of man and beast (Ex 12-13). The Psalmist briefly addresses Egypt, saying that, "He sent signs and wonders into the midst of thee, O Egypt" (RV). These were preparatory to that final plague, the slaying of the firstborn, and were predicted by Jehovah in Exodus 7.3. They were discriminatory judgments, for the children of Israel were divinely protected in them, but the Egyptians were not. Having preserved His people through the preceding plagues, the pronouncement of Jehovah concerning the firstborn was, "All the firstborn in the land of Egypt shall die, from the firstborn of Pharaoh that sitteth upon his throne, even unto the firstborn of the maidservant that is behind the mill; and all the firstborn of beasts...But against any of the children of Israel shall not a dog move his tongue, against man or beast: that ye may know how the Lord doth put a difference between the Egyptians and Israel" (Ex 11.5-7).

After the Exodus, Jehovah "smote great nations" (AV). The word "great" (7227), however, is rendered "many", by several versions (RV, RSV, JPS), and the same word is translated "many" in the AV text of Deuteronomy 7.1: "When the Lord thy God shall bring thee into the land whither thou goest to possess it, and hath cast out many nations before thee, the Hittites, and the Girgashites, and the Amorites, and the Canaanites, and the Perizzites, and the Hivites, and the Jebusites, seven nations greater and mightier than thou".

The Lord not only smote many nations for His people, but He slew mighty kings, and now the Psalmist identifies some of these kings. There was Sihon, king of the Amorites, mentioned in Numbers 21.21-29. Then there was Og, king of Bashan, who is referred to in the same chapter, and is associated with the judgment of Sihon (Num 21.33-35). Plumer comments concerning these, that "Sihon and Og are mentioned perhaps for these reasons: 1. They were at the entrance of Canaan and made the first strong opposition to the Israelites. 2. They were at the head of powerful tribes or nations. 3. These kings were of gigantic strength and stature, Deuteronomy 3.11; Amos 2.9. These were perhaps fair samples of the other kings and kingdoms encountered and vanquished". All the kingdoms of Canaan were conquered and Jehovah gave their lands as an inheritance to Israel. Note that every victory was the Lord's. It was He who redeemed. It was He who delivered. It was He who smote the nations, slew their kings, and gave their territory to His own chosen people as a heritage.

Verses 13-14: Jehovah's Concern and Care for His People

In these two verses, there are three more occurrences of the great name "Jehovah" (3068). This is the predominant divine title in this Psalm. There are some fifteen mentions of it, as well as four references to it in its contracted form "Jah" (3050). Jehovah's name endures forever. He is, after all, the God who inhabits eternity, whose name is holy (Is 57.15). His memorial, the remembrance of Him (2143), continues from generation to generation (JND), throughout all ages (RSV). How indeed could the remembrance of Him fade? He continually acted on behalf of His people, contending for them, pleading their cause, judging, and vindicating (1777). Could His care for them ever be forgotten?

In a rather strange expression, the Psalmist now says that Jehovah "will repent himself concerning His servants". The word "repent" (5162) has occasioned difficulty for some, but according to Strong it may signify "be sorry; be moved to pity; have compassion", and the RSV actually translates the phrase, "have compassion on his servants". So, then, in His concern for His servants Jehovah vindicates them and cares compassionately for them.

Verses 15-18: The Folly of Idolatry

The Psalmist now turns from the greatness of Jehovah to the impotence of heathen gods. This section of the Psalm, with very few changes, is as Psalm 115.4-8. The idols of the nations were lifeless deities. They may have been of silver or gold, but that was their only value. They were the work of men's hands. They had mouths, eyes, and ears, but they could not speak nor see nor hear. They had no breath either. They could neither respond nor correspond. What utter folly it was to trust in such. Those who did trust in them were as helpless and as foolish as the idols themselves. Those who made them, and those who confided in them, were as insensitive as the very idols to which they bowed. Dr Cohen remarks that some construe this verse as a prayer, reading, "May they that make them be like unto them". This does not affect the substantial meaning of the verse that both the makers and the devotees of the idols become like their idols. Maclaren says, so aptly, "Men make gods after their own image, and, when made, the gods make them after theirs".

Verses 19-21: A Renewed Call to Praise

The substance of this summons to praise with which the Psalm concludes, may be found again in Psalm 115.9-11 and in Psalm 118.2-4, except that here in Psalm 135 there is the addition of the house of Levi. The word "bless" (1288), occurring five times in these closing verses, means "to praise or salute". As has been remarked before in this Commentary, it is akin to the NT Greek word "eulogeo" (*2127*), from which is derived the English word "eulogise", meaning "to speak well of".

This final call is fourfold. It exhorts the house of Israel, the house of Aaron, the house of Levi, and those who fear the Lord, to bless Jehovah. This seems to indicate, first the entire nation, then the priestly family with all the Levites, many of whom were not priests, then those "God fearers" who may have been Gentiles, proselytes to Judaism. It is an all-inclusive summons to all those who are in any way associated with the favoured nation, to bless the Lord. Then, for himself the Psalmist exclaims, "Blessed be the Lord out of Zion". Jerusalem was Jehovah's dwelling place. Here He had placed His name. It was fitting that the city should be the very fountain and source of the praise which was due to Him. The Psalm closes with a "Praise ye the Lord", which is, of course, "Hallelujah".

This is both the first and last word of the Psalm. All of its lovely thoughts are, as it were, held in these two golden clasps. "Hallelujah", and, "Hallelujah".

PSALM 136

Introduction

The chief characteristic of this Psalm, so immediately apparent, is the recurrence, twenty-six times, of the refrain "for his mercy endureth for ever". These lovely words are included in every verse and have been variously translated in different versions and by different commentators. "Mercy" (2617) signifies "lovingkindness; goodness; pity". The clause is also rendered, "His lovingkindness endureth for ever" (JND), and, "His steadfast love endures for ever" (RSV). Kidner, in the Tyndale Commentary, quotes the very pleasant rendering of Gelineau; "His love has no end". The repetition of this phrase was for liturgical reasons. It was to be sung antiphonally, or responsively, either by the Levite singers or by the congregation. The words appear also in the opening verses of Psalms 106 and 107, and in the commentary on the latter Psalm it has been noted that the word "endureth" is italicised, indicating that it is a translators' addition. Without this, the clause may be understood as an exclamation, "His mercy - for ever!". Notice the same refrain occurring five times in Psalm 118, four times in the first four verses of that Psalm, and again in the closing verse 29. These are not the "vain repetitions" of which the Saviour spoke in Matthew 6.7. The repetitive style is often employed to indicate an earnest, zealous, sincere emphasis of what is being sung.

Dr Cohen and others point out that Psalm 136 is known, in Jewish tradition, as "The Great Hallel". It is all praise, for a great variety of reasons which the Psalmist enumerates.

The following division of the twenty-six verses is probably obvious, and is observed in the commentary. Verses 1-3 are an opening threefold exhortation to give thanks to the Triune God. In verses 4-9 the Psalmist raises six notes of praise to the Creator for His wondrous work in creation. Verses 10-15 recall the Exodus of the nation from Egypt and there are another six notes of praise for this. The next verses, 16-22, recount the journey through the wilderness to Canaan, and in this section there are seven reasons for praise. Two verses, 23-24, then give thanks for God's remembrance of His people, and for deliverance from their enemies. One verse, 25, sings of His gracious provision for men everywhere, and the closing verse, 26, returns to the opening theme, "O give thanks unto the God of heaven".

Verses 1-3: The Threefold Thanksgiving

Observe that in these three opening verses, in his call for thanksgiving, the Psalmist employs three names of God. The first, in v.1, is "LORD" (3068), which is Jehovah. Then, in v.2, there follows "God" (430), which is Elohim. In v.3 it is "Lord" (113), which is Adon. Perhaps those earliest

Hebrews, and indeed the Psalmist himself, could not appreciate what is now so evident to every christian reader of the Psalm, that this is a summons for thanksgiving to the Holy Trinity, that great Tri-unity of Divine Persons who, though distinct and distinguished, are yet one in essence in the Godhead. While the mystery of this plurality in the Godhead waited for further NT revelation, and may never be fully comprehended by any man, yet the believer of this privileged present day can now perceive the gracious movements of Father, Son, and Holy Spirit, in many parts of the OT. To Him who is "Holy, Holy, Holy", the saints are now exhorted to render their thanksgiving, and three reasons are incorporated into the threefold exhortation.

The first reason for this thanksgiving is that the Lord is good. This is a repeat of Psalm 135.3, "Praise the Lord; for the Lord is good". The goodness of God is a constantly recurring theme throughout the Psalms and is always a valid reason for the thanksgiving of those who know Him. "Thou art good, and doest good", says Psalm 119.68, and in another Psalm the invitation to men is, "O taste and see that the Lord is good" (Ps 34.8). "Why callest thou me good?", Jesus once asked a young man who had addressed Him as "Good Master" in Matthew 19.17. Then He added, "There is none good, but one, that is, God". Of course the Saviour was not denying that He was good, but rather, if men could have understood Him, He was claiming that He was God.

The second ground for giving thanks is that He is "the God of gods", an echo of that expression in the preceding Psalm 135.5, "Our Lord is above all gods". He was not only good, He was great too, superior to the lifeless gods of the nations. Israel's Elohim was the Mighty One, mightier than all the boasted might of the gods of the heathen. This was a reason for thanksgiving also.

The third reason for thanksgiving is similar to the second. Jehovah is not only "God of gods", but He is also "Lord of lords". He is the supreme Governor, Master, Ruler, and Proprietor, of the universe. In 1 Corinthians 8.5 Paul says, "There be gods many, and lords many", but Jehovah is greater than all and in a coming day this greatness will be invested in a Man, who is "King of kings, and Lord of lords" (Rev 19.16).

The comment of William De Burgh on these opening verses is, "Such is God in Himself. Nor is it without intention that the doxology is threefold, indicating, doubtless, like the threefold invocation of the name of the Lord in the blessing of the people (Num 6.24-26), God in Trinity, 'Father, Son, and Holy Ghost', as now fully revealed".

Verses 4-9: Praise to the Creator

Jehovah is alone in the wonder of creation. He, Himself, in solitary majesty, spoke the universe into existence. In this He has no rival, "who alone doeth wonders" (6381), and therefore His name is "Wonderful". He neither asks for, nor needs, assistance from the gods and lords of the nations. These are devoid of life and power, so He Himself, alone, has accomplished the work of creation.

Not only power was needed, however, in this great work. Wisdom also was essential, and the heavens have been arranged and ordered by divine understanding. With all this the wise man Solomon concurs, saying, in Proverbs 3.19, "The Lord by wisdom hath founded the earth; by understanding hath he established the heavens". Jeremiah, too, expresses the same thought, saying, "He hath made the earth by his power, he hath established the world by his wisdom, and hath stretched out the heavens by his discretion" (Jer 10.12).

On the expression, He "stretched out the earth above the waters", the JFB Commentary says, "Not immediately over, but raised out of and above them. He sunk the bed of the sea, that the land might be correspondingly elevated and the sea restrained by the shore". Again, as with every statement in the Psalm, the Psalmist repeats, "for his mercy endureth for ever". All that He does reveals His lovingkindness to man.

The Creator did not leave His creation in darkness. His creatures would need light, and accordingly He created the great luminaries of the heavens. They were to be the governors of the skies, ordering day and night in an unfailing rotation. Sun, moon and stars were set in the heavens to exert their benign influence over all things, animate and inanimate. By their ministry, light and darkness, day and night, heat and cold, summer and winter, would all be continually regulated. So would the comfort of the creatures be assured, as these great celestial bodies moved in obedience to the divine decree, keeping to their ordered course as directed by the power and the wisdom that had brought them into being. When the blessing of the heavenly lights is contemplated, it is easy to understand why the Psalmist says yet again, and again, that His mercy, His lovingkindness, is for ever. All that the Creator has done has been in love to man, a love that has no end.

Verses 10-15: Praise the Redeemer

Having dwelt on the wonder of creation, and having there found so many reasons for thanksgiving and praise, the Psalmist now turns to another great wonder, the deliverance of Israel from Egypt and from bondage. This section of the Psalm is quite parallel to Psalm 135.8-9. The Psalmist exhorts praise "To him that smote Egypt in their firstborn". This was the last and the greatest of the plagues. In spite of the harsh lessons of the former plagues, Pharaoh had been obstinate and stubborn, refusing to release the people. But the early word of the Lord to Moses in Exodus 4.22 had been, "And thou shalt say unto Pharaoh, Thus saith the Lord, Israel is my son, even my firstborn". The proud monarch of the Egyptians could not, with impunity, enslave Jehovah's firstborn and resist every appeal for their release. Jehovah therefore smote Egypt in the very heart, even in their firstborn. As Spurgeon remarks, "The sorrow and terror which it caused throughout the nation it is hardly possible to exaggerate...The joy and hope of every household was struck down in a moment, and each family had its own wailing".

He "brought out Israel from among them". He brought them out. He brought them all out, and whatever other pogroms may come their way, they would never again return to Egyptian bondage. Here is yet another instance of the lovingkindness that endures, and another reason for praise. Jehovah was their Redeemer from slavery. It was indeed a great wonder, this Exodus. It is estimated that more than two million people came out that night to freedom. Six hundred thousand men, with their wives and children, their flocks and herds and provisions, all left Egypt together (Ex 12.37-39). It was a strong hand and a stretched out arm that had performed this mighty work on that Passover night. When the logistics and practicalities of this are considered, it is evident that only divine power could have accomplished such a complete and orderly emigration of so many souls in one night. How right that the remembrance of this should be an integral part of "The Great Hallel", the Psalm of praise.

Having brought His people out from Egypt, Jehovah then divided the Red Sea for them. The waters obeyed their Creator and stood up in walls on either side of the pathway which the Lord designed for His people. Israel passed through the midst of the standing waters to freedom, while the hosts of the tyrant Pharaoh were drowned in the Red Sea. The pursuing Egyptians, with their horses and chariots, were deluged in the returning waters. Jehovah overthrew them. This word "overthrew" (5287) means, literally, "to shake off". Albert Barnes says that, "The word is applicable to a tree shaking off its foliage...He shook them off...He left them to perish".

Verses 16-22: Through the Wilderness to Canaan

Deliverance from Egypt was not Jehovah's entire purpose for His people. His intention was to bring them into the Promised Land, but the inhospitable wilderness lay between Egypt and Canaan. This part of the Psalm is analogous to Psalm 135.10-12. Having led them out, now the Lord led them on, until their way was barred by "great nations" (Ps 135.10) whose kings are described as great, mighty, and famous. These were men of valour, men of renown, mighty in battle. As in Psalm 135, two of these are particularly identified, Sihon, king of the Amorites, and Og, king of Bashan. These kings blocked Israel's way to Canaan, and, despite their fame and might, Jehovah smote them.

In the plan and purpose of God, the land of Sihon and Og was forfeit. He had reserved this territory for Israel His firstborn, and those who held it meantime must yield it up to Him. It was given as a divine bequest to Israel, an inheritance which would forever after be disputed by the nations. But Jehovah does what He pleases, and this land was a heritage for His chosen people. Israel was not only His firstborn, but also His servant. These who had been slaves of Pharaoh were now servants of Jehovah.

"Let my people go, that they may serve me", Jehovah had demanded of Pharaoh (Ex 9.1, 13; 10.3). Pharaoh had oppressed them. Jehovah would give them a land of their own. "His mercy endureth for ever!"

Verses 23-24: Jehovah - Deliverer of His People

It was not the greatness of the children of Israel that prompted Jehovah's gracious movements towards them. They were but a feeble people, a nation of slaves. Theirs was a low estate indeed. It could be said to them, "The Lord did not set his love upon you, nor choose you, because you were more in number than any people; for ye were the fewest of all people" (Deut 7.7). In sovereign grace He had remembered them, and had redeemed them from enemies greater than they. It was reason for thanksgiving and praise. His lovingkindness endures for ever!

Verse 25: Jehovah - Provider for All

But great as His love for Israel might be, Jehovah's gracious providence is not confined to that nation. The Psalmist speaks of "all flesh". This goes even beyond the boundaries of humanity. Another Psalm expounds it, saying, "The eyes of all wait upon thee; and thou givest them their meat in due season. Thou openest thine hand, and satisfiest the desire of every living thing" (Ps 145.15-16). Not only men, but beasts and birds also, and reptiles and fish, and even the flying and creeping insects of land, air and sea, are all dependent upon Him who cares for all. His love – for ever!

Verse 26: O Give Thanks!

"The Great Hallel" ends as it began, with a renewed appeal to grateful men to render due thanksgiving to the God of heaven. How pleasant is this, that the praise of men on earth should ascend to God in heaven. Heaven and earth in accord! All men uniting in praise, "for his mercy endureth for ever"!

PSALM 137

Introduction

How poignant and apt are Spurgeon's opening remarks in his commentary on this lovely Psalm. He writes, "This plaintive ode is one of the most charming compositions in the whole Book of Psalms for its poetic power. If it were not inspired it would nevertheless occupy a high place in poesy, especially the former portion of it, which is tender and patriotic to the highest degree". Delitzsch commends it similarly, saying, "Scarcely any Psalm is so easily impressed on the memory as this, which is so pictorial even in sound". Yet, in spite of the beauty of the Psalm, Kidner is right when he says, "Every line of it is alive with pain, whose intensity grows with each strophe to the appalling climax". Perowne writes, "What a wonderful mixture is the Psalm of soft melancholy and fiery patriotism! The hand which wrote it must have known how to smite sharply with the sword as well as how to tune the harp". With these reviews all lovers of the Psalms will agree.

The Psalm is anonymous, but must have been written by one of the returned exiles from Babylon, whose first view of Jerusalem may have prompted the imprecations of the closing verses. This would date the Psalm around 538 BC. There are two obvious parts in the Psalm. The first, verses 1-6, is a lament composed of sad memories of the exile and of the treatment of the captives there by their heartless Babylonian captors. The second part, verses 7-9, is a denunciation of Edom and Babylon, and a fearful call for vengeance against the oppressors.

Verses 1-6: Memories of the Exile

"By the rivers of Babylon, there we sat down, yea, we wept, when we remembered Zion". Those were sad days. The nation was in captivity, with little hope of recovery. It is easy to picture little groups of exiles gathering by the riverside to converse together, to think of Jerusalem, and to weep over their plight in Babylon. Babylonia had an abundant water supply, with rivers and their tributaries as well as a system of man-made canals and watercourses. There were the Euphrates, the Tigris, the Chebar, and Ulai. Note the interesting references to the Chebar in Ezekiel 1.1, 3, and to the Ulai in Daniel 8.2. The river bank appears to have been a customary place of meeting for religious Jews (Acts 16.13). Was there a soothing influence in the murmuring of the waters? Or was there a kind of sympathy with the exiles in the monotonous lapping of the streams? In the quietness of such a meeting place, away from the bustle of the city, they could sit and think, and talk of better days, and exchange reminiscences of Zion.

As they wept, they put their harps and lyres away. Strings that should have been tuned to the praise of Jehovah were silent. Harps were hung on the willows and happier days in Zion were now but a sad memory. Jerusalem had been razed and the glory of their temple was no more, the magnificent sanctuary destroyed. In such painful circumstances their captors added insult to injury, asking to hear a song. Those who wasted (8437) them required mirth of them. These were tormentors, Babylonians who came to their riverside meeting place wanting to hear one of the songs of Zion. Having reduced them to slavery and exile, having robbed them of land and home and temple, how insensitive was this, to ask them to sing a song of Zion.

The answer of the captives was pathetic. "How should we sing a song of Jehovah's upon a foreign soil?" (JND). Dr Cohen suggests that although their harps may have accompanied their dirges as they sat lamenting by the riverside, it was now, "when their captors came upon them and maliciously asked them to go on singing for the amusement of the audience, the harps were laid aside". Kirkpatrick says, "To sing the songs of Zion for the amusement of their conquerors would have been the grossest profanation of all that they held most dear", and, accordingly, they hung their harps, unstrung, on the willows. These songs belonged to the Lord, and to Temple worship. It was neither the time nor the place, exiled in Babylon, to sing for Babylonians.

Notice how the pronouns now change from "we" to "I". It seems as though every individual exile was pledged to remember Jerusalem. "If I forget thee, O Jerusalem...If I do not remember thee". To sing the sacred songs of Zion for the coarse pleasure of the enemies of Israel would be a tragedy and a travesty. Such irreverence, such sacrilege, would be tantamount to forgetting Jerusalem. Better that the right hand should forget how to string the harp, or that it should lose its dexterity for other crafts. Better that the tongue should cleave to the palate, unable to speak or sing, if Jerusalem is not preferred above the chiefest joy. Hengstenberg writes, "If I, misapplying my right hand to the playing of joyful strains on my instrument, forget thee, Jerusalem, let my right hand, as a punishment, forget the noble art...May my misemployed hand lose its capacity to play, and my tongue, misemployed in singing cheerful songs, its capacity to sing". For the believer of the present day however, Andrew Bonar has a most touching, devotional comment, saying, "O Jerusalem! Calvary, Mount of Olives, Siloam, how fragrant are ye with the Name that is above every name! '*If I forget thee, O Jerusalem*!' Can I forget where He walked so often, where He spake such gracious words, where He died? Can I forget that His feet shall stand on that 'Mount of Olives which is before Jerusalem on the east'? Can I forget that there stood the Upper Room, and there fell the showers of Pentecost?" So end the sad reminiscences of the exile returning to Zion.

Verses 7-9: Imprecations against Edom and Babylon

The sorrowful, melancholy note of the Psalm now changes as attention is turned toward the enemies of the nation. Jehovah is implored to remember the children of Edom, but JND, RSV, JPS, and others, insert the word "against", reading, "Remember, O Jehovah, against the sons of Edom". It is an invocation that Jehovah should charge them and punish them for their affliction of His people. The phrase "in the day of Jerusalem", is understood differently by commentators. Some, as Spurgeon and Barnes, think that it means that Jerusalem's day will come, that it is Jerusalem's day of restoration after all the oppression. Others, as Cohen, Fausset, and Delitzsch, understand it rather as a reference to the destruction of Jerusalem by the Chaldeans, looking back to the day when Jerusalem was destroyed, and asking for retribution.

That had been a sad and tragic event, the destruction of their Zion. It was doubly sad that there should have been such enmity from the Edomites, who were, after all, their own kith and kin, descended from Esau, brother of their father Jacob. Adam Clarke comments, "It appears that the Idumeans joined the army of Nebuchadnezzar against their brethren the Jews, and that they were main instruments in razing the walls of Jerusalem even to the ground". (See Jer 12.6; 25.14, 21; Lam 4.21-22; Ob vv. 8-14). Dr Cohen writes, "Despite the kinship of the Edomites, descended from Esau, they had proved themselves inveterate enemies of Israel, and the prophets often condemn them (Is 34.5; Jer 49.7ff; Amos 1.11 etc.). In particular, Obadiah denounces in scathing terms the heartless conduct of the Edomites when *'thou wast as one of them'*, i.e., abetting the Babylonians in the destruction of Judea". The Psalmist's appeal is that Jehovah will remember all this against them.

Not only Edom, but Babylon, too, would be laid waste. Jehovah would render to them in the measure they had meted out to His people Israel. Jehovah accordingly raised up Cyrus, King of the Medes and Persians, to effect this destruction of Babylon, which was totally ruined under the Persians. Adam Clarke points out that "after its capture by Cyrus, it could never be considered a capital city, but it appeared to follow the fortunes of its various conquerors till it was, as a city, finally destroyed".

The fierce, impassioned imprecation of the closing verse of the Psalm is not, of course, in the spirit of the New Testament gospel, but this was a nation of an old dispensation, accustomed, in times of war, to the slaughter of men, women, and children. This is really a prayer for a complete eradication of their enemies. As Babylon had committed such atrocities against Israel, so that man would be counted blessed who would play a part in the slaughter of the Babylonians. Dr Cohen comments, "Such barbarity was often perpetrated against Israel (2 Kings 8.12; Hos 10.14), and the Babylonians were guilty of it (compare Jer 51.24 with Is 13.16)". Maclaren says, in defence of this verse, "Perhaps, if some of their modern critics had been under the yoke from which this Psalmist had been delivered, they would have understood a little better how a good man of that age could rejoice that Babylon was fallen and all its race extirpated". So the Psalm concludes, with a prayer and an anticipation that the enemies of Jehovah and of Israel should be righteously rewarded.

PSALM 138

Introduction

Psalm 138 is essentially a Psalm of thanksgiving. Apart from the brief prayer in its closing phrase, it is all praise. The title attributes it to David, and it is the first of a series of eight Psalms which bear his name. Although the Septuagint adds the names of Haggai and Zechariah in the superscription, this does not in any way cast doubt on the Davidic authorship; it may simply indicate that the Psalm was adapted for liturgical use in the times of these prophets, a time of special thanksgiving for national recovery. Many expositors suggest a link between this Psalm and the promises of God to David as recorded in 2 Samuel 7. Jehovah had there, through Nathan the prophet, covenanted to him the perpetuity of his house and of his throne.

The Psalm is written in the first person singular. The thanksgiving and praise are primarily those of David himself, but soon others join in, until all the kings of the earth are uniting with Israel's king in praise of Jehovah. As will be noted in the commentary, this is prophetic, anticipating a future day which is the burden of the Messianic Psalms and other prophetic portions of the OT.

The following divisions are observed. Verses 1-3 express the personal praise of the Psalmist, and are followed by verses 4-6 which deal with the praises of the kings of the earth. The concluding verses 7-8 tell of David's confidence in the continuing care and kindness of the Lord in all times of trouble.

Verses 1-3: The Praise of the Psalmist

Although the word "praise" occurs twice in the opening verse of the Psalm in the AV, the two Hebrew words are different. The first (3034) means "to give thanks", and is so rendered by the RSV, JND, JPS, and others. The second (2167) denotes the singing of Psalms, perhaps accompanied by the harp. The thankful Psalmist employs every means of praising the Lord, and with voice and harp he does so with his whole heart. This wholeheartedness is characteristic of David, and of the Psalms in general. From its first mention in Psalm 9.1 it occurs nine times throughout the Psalter. See also Psalms 111.1; 119.2, 10, 34, 58, 69 and 145. David's praises, like his prayers, and like his obedience to the law, were all rendered with his whole heart. There was neither reservation nor hesitation in his responses to Jehovah's dealings with him.

He declares that he will sing his praises "before the gods". There is much diversity among commentators as to the meaning of "gods" (430) in v. 1. The word is "elohim", thought by some to denote the mighty ones of earth, as kings, judges, rulers. Some versions, as the Septuagint, the Vulgate, and others, render it "angels", and Adam Clarke even suggests that it indicates Jehovah Himself. He translates, "in the presence of *Elohim*", and then comments, "most probably meaning before the Ark, where were the sacred symbols of the Supreme Being". This latter suggestion is very much a minority view and perhaps the preferred meaning is that David's wholehearted praise of Jehovah is rendered in defiance of the lifeless gods of the heathen, puny deities that they were! The AV rendering "gods", is therefore most acceptable, and is in accord also with the passage already referred to, 2 Samuel 7. See, in particular, vv. 22 and 23 of that chapter, where again David speaks of the superiority of Jehovah over the gods of the nations.

The mention of the temple in v.3 of this Psalm is no impediment to a Davidic authorship. If it is argued that as yet, in David's day, there was no temple, nevertheless the same word (1964) is used as early as 1 Samuel 1.9 to describe the sanctuary where Eli ministered, and where he was later joined by the boy Samuel. Toward this house or tabernacle, David bows himself in worship, giving thanks for the lovingkindness and truth which Jehovah had shown towards him.

The strange, and rather difficult expression, "for thou hast magnified thy word above all thy name", seems to mean that Jehovah's Word is the greatest revelation of Himself that He can give to men. His "name" signifies those manifestations of Himself in the wonders He had wrought for His people, but above all these, and superior to them, is His infallible, unerring Word, His immutable promises. What He says is to be magnified even above what He does. His Word is greater than all other revelation, and, in the ultimate, that Word is Christ, who has become to men the exegesis of the very heart and character of God. This is the teaching of the early verses of John's Gospel: "In the beginning was the Word, and the Word was with God, and the Word was God...And the Word was made flesh, and dwelt among us, and we beheld his glory...No man hath seen God at any time; the only begotten Son...he hath declared him" (Jn 1.1, 14, 18). In the fullest sense, then, the Word is magnified above all other manifestations of God.

David then recalls the kindness of God to him. He had cried, and Jehovah had heard his prayer and answered him. This had greatly encouraged him. He had been strengthened in his soul knowing that God had graciously listened to his prayer. Believers often speak of a God "who hears and answers prayer". The Psalmist knew this experimentally, and the knowledge of it supported him and strengthened (7292) him. This word actually means that he was emboldened, carrying himself with pride and assurance that God had heard him. As a Father, God hears the cries of His children; as Lord, He hears the prayers of His servants. So it was with the Psalmist, and for this he worshipped.

Verses 4-6: The Praise of Kings

This expression, "the kings of the earth" is a familiar one in Holy Scripture, first appearing in 1 Kings 4.34, and afterwards occurring in the Books of Chronicles, Isaiah, Lamentations and Ezekiel. There are six references to the kings of the earth in the Psalms - 2.2; 76.12; 89.27; 102.15; 138.4; 148.11. In the NT the expression appears frequently also, being found nine times in the Book of the Revelation. So very often, when the kings of the earth are mentioned, it is to emphasise their subordination to Him who is "King of kings, and Lord of lords" (Rev 19.16). Here in the Psalm, it is a prediction that eventually they must join with King David in praise of Jehovah. The Word of God will accomplish this. How true it will be in a coming day when the kings of the earth will see the fulfilment of the promises of God in the kingdom of Messiah. Compelled to forsake the gods of their nations, "all kings shall fall down before him: all nations shall serve him" (Ps 72.11).

Of the kings of the earth it is said, "Yea, they shall sing in the ways of the Lord". "Here is a double wonder", says Spurgeon, "kings in God's ways, and kings singing there". The revelation of the greatness of His glory touches even kings. Jehovah is high, He is exalted far above all, but, though He is so high, yet He regards the lowly. From His infinite greatness He has respect for humility, but He will distance Himself from those who are proud and haughty, observing them from afar. Those kings, monarchs among men, who might imagine that they have a right to be proud, must come in lowliness to have any standing with the great Jehovah.

Verses 7-8: Confidence in God

The Psalmist is assured by former answers to prayer and by previous experiences of God's deliverance of him, that, though he walks in the midst of trouble, the Lord will recover and restore him. The word "trouble" (6869), while signifying distress and affliction, has also the thought of being in straits, being hemmed in by dangers and trials. David's confidence is that Jehovah will revive (2421) him, sustain him, and so preserve his life. Of course there were enemies. He knew their anger. He knew that their wrath was directed against him, but he knew, too, that Jehovah would stretch forth His hand against them. That right hand of power would save him from them.

In a lovely concluding verse of the Psalm, David now says, "The Lord will perfect that which concerneth me". The RSV seems to capture the sense of this, reading, "The Lord will fulfil his purpose for me". No might of any foe would be able to thwart God's purpose for His servant. Whatever Jehovah had determined for his child would be accomplished, and accomplished perfectly. The refrain, so often repeated in Psalm 118, is now the Psalmist's assurance and comfort, "Thy mercy, O Lord, endureth for ever". Jehovah's lovingkindness, His steadfast love for His own, was for ever, and no opposition of the enemies of His saints could stay that love.

Confidence in God, though, however strong, does not exclude or preclude prayer, and with a brief plea the Psalm closes, "Forsake not the works of thine own hands". David's prayer is that what the Lord had done in him, for him, and through him, for himself, for his house, for his kingdom, and for his nation, might be preserved. These were, after all, the works of God's own hands. He prays they may not be forsaken, but that all the purposes and plans of God may be completely fulfilled. Faith knows, of course, that it will be so. This is the spirit of Paul in 2 Timothy 1.12, concerning his own service for the Lord. In spite of many disappointments, and in the face of much opposition from men, he could say, "I know whom I have believed, and am persuaded that he is able to keep that which I have committed unto him against that day". David and Paul agree, "The Lord will perfect that which concerneth me". Jehovah will preserve His own work, for His own glory.

PSALM 139

Introduction

As has been mentioned several times in this Commentary, fifty-five Psalms in the Psalter are committed to the care and charge of the Chief Musician, the Director or Superintendent of Temple Song. Of this collection, Psalm 139 is the penultimate, followed only by Psalm 140. It is also the first of such Psalms since Psalm 109.

The title attributes this Psalm to David. The suggestion has been made that it may have been occasioned by some false accusations made against the Psalmist. He knows that the charges are false, and is happy to be searched by Him who has perfect knowledge of everyone and everything. There does not seem to be any good reason for rejecting the Davidic authorship. Spurgeon comments, "It bears the image and superscription of King David, and could have come from no other mint than that of the son of Jesse. Of course the critics take this composition away from David, on account of certain Aramaic expressions in it. We believe that upon the principles of criticism now in vogue it would be extremely easy to prove that Milton did not write Paradise Lost!". Plumer agrees, writing, "The Hebrew and all the ancient versions ascribe this Psalm to David...Against the Davidic authorship it is urged that there are Chaldaisms in it...but the moral arguments for David's authorship are so strong as to overwhelm any such verbal or rather literal criticism". Psalm 139 sings the attributes of Jehovah in a majestic manner. The composition has been described as "most glorious; grand; highly elevated; impressive; inimitable; unequalled". Plumer says, "Its doctrines are pure and heavenly, sublime and practical".

The twenty-four verses may be divided into four equal parts, as follows. The opening verses, 1-6, extol the omniscience of God. Verses 7-12 deal with His omnipresence. Verses 13-18 then expound His omnipotence. The concluding verses, 19-24, express the Psalmist's hatred of evil and evil men, and protest his own desire for innocency before God.

Verses 1-6: Omniscience

This attribute belongs to Jehovah exclusively. Omniscience is all knowledge – "omni-science". Not even Satan is omniscient. The Devil and demons, angels and men, may know much, but only God knows all. To this all-knowing Jehovah the Psalmist submits himself, saying, "O Lord, thou hast searched me, and known me". "Search" (2713) signifies "to explore or examine thoroughly". J.A. Alexander says that "The Hebrew word originally means 'to dig', and is applied to the search for precious metals (Job 28.3)". This is a present experience of David, searched by Jehovah, but notice that the word "me" after "known", is in italics, having been supplied by the translators. T.W. Davies argues that the pronoun is found in the ancient versions and is necessary to preserve the rhythm as well as the sense. Fausset, however, says, "There is no 'me' after 'known' in the Hebrew, therefore it is better to take the object after 'known' in a wider sense. The omission is intentional, that the believing heart of all who use this Psalm may supply the ellipsis. Thou hast known and knowest all that concerns the matter in question, as well as whether I and mine are guilty or innocent, also my exact circumstances, my needs, my sorrows, and the precise time when to relieve me".

Jehovah has complete knowledge of the entire life of every man, his sitting down and his rising up. As Plumer says, "Perfect intelligence of every posture, gesture, exercise, pursuit, state, and condition of man". But there is also a full knowledge of the inner man, his emotions and thoughts, his doubts and desires, feelings which may well be hidden from his fellow men. These thoughts are known "afar off". This may mean that, although Jehovah may seem to be distant and remote in the heavens, nevertheless He is well acquainted with the thoughts of His creatures on earth, as in Psalm 138.6. Or, as some think, it may signify that long before they enter or have been conceived in a man's mind, when they are yet "afar off", they are already known to the Lord. Whichever is the meaning here, both things are true, and both are in accord with divine omniscience. Notice also that Jehovah not only knows, but understands (995). This indicates that He knows, He observes, He considers and discerns with full intelligence, all that a man is thinking. "Thought", too, is in the singular, meaning that the entire thought-life of the person is known and understood by God. This is the truth of Hebrews 4.13, "Neither is there any creature that is not manifest in his sight: but all things are naked and opened unto the eyes of him with whom we have to do".

"Thou compassest my path and my lying down". The word rendered "compassest" (2219) is associated with the winnowing out of grain, the separation of chaff from the wheat. Jehovah can encircle a man, search out his way and his character, and separate the real and true from the false and insincere. The Psalmist speaks of "my ways" and "my lying down". Whether active or pensive, walking or resting, busy or idle, in public or in private, the Lord could trace the movements of His child, with perfect knowledge of all that he was and all that he was doing. David knew that the omniscient Jehovah was "acquainted" (5532) with, had a familiar and intimate knowledge of, all his ways. How the remembrance of this should dispel hypocrisy and insincerity in every child of God.

"There is not a word on my tongue". JND adds the little word "yet", reading, "There is not *yet* a word on my tongue". The RSV rendering agrees with this addition, and reads, "Even before a word is on my tongue". The phrase appears to mean that, knowing a man's thoughts, Jehovah therefore knows the word which is intended to make those thoughts known to others, and before a thought becomes a word on the tongue, "Lo, O Lord, thou knowest it altogether". Plumer quotes Edwards, who, he says, interprets the whole verse: "For before my words are upon my tongue, behold, Jehovah, Thou knowest the whole of them"

The expression "Thou hast beset me behind and before", in v.5, may be, as many suggest, a transition from the meditation on Jehovah's omniscience in the first part of the Psalm, to thoughts of His omnipresence in the second part. The word "beset" (6696) can be rendered "besieged", and may indeed refer to the constant presence of God, "behind and before". However, the reference to knowledge which follows immediately in v.6 seems to indicate that the Psalmist is speaking of his being "besieged" by divine knowledge, the knowledge which is omniscience. Jehovah knows what has gone before and He knows what is to follow. As Adam Clarke says, "Behold Thou, O Jehovah, knowest the whole, the hereafter and the past". The child of God is surrounded by the knowledge of God, and the hand of God is therefore ever upon him, for comfort or correction, in mercy or in chastisement. All his circumstances and all his needs are always known to God. Such knowledge, the all-knowledge, the omniscience, of the Lord, is too wonderful for the human mind. It is incomprehensible, greater than man's puny intellect, too high for his mental faculties to grasp. This, of course, is Deity inscrutable, before which men must bow in worship, even when they cannot understand.

Verses 7-12: Omnipresence

The Psalmist now comes to omnipresence, another attribute which belongs to Jehovah alone. Satan is not omnipresent. He therefore needs emissaries, demons, to further his satanic purposes. The Psalmist speaks of "thy spirit" and "thy presence", and asks, "Whither shall I go from thy Spirit? or whither shall I flee from thy presence?". This does not suggest that David desired to flee from the presence of God. It is his poetic way of saying that hiding from the divine presence is as impossible as is escape from the divine knowledge. "Spirit" and "presence" both mean God Himself, but "presence" (PANIM - 6440) is, literally, "face or countenance", and Adam Clarke makes the interesting observation, "Why do we meet with this word so frequently in the plural number, when applied to God...A Trinitarian would at once say, 'The plurality of Persons in the Godhead is intended', and who can prove that he is mistaken?".

To show the impossibility of moving beyond the reach of omnipresence David now supposes four hypothetical cases of flight. He mentions ascent to heaven, and descent into hell (Sh[e]OL - 7585), the land of departed spirits. He speaks of flying to the uttermost parts of the sea, and then of hiding in the darkness. Adam Clarke writes, "Thou art in heaven, in Thy glory; in hell, in Thy vindictive judgment; and in all parts of earth, water, space, place, or vacuity, by Thy omnipresence. Wherever I am, there Thou art; and where I cannot be, Thou art there. Thou fillest the heavens and the earth". There is no escape from the divine presence. Notice that the words "art there" are italicised. Omit them, and observe the impressive and emphatic abruptness with which the Psalmist says that wherever he may go, "Behold - thou!".

By "the wings of the morning", the Psalmist appears to mean the swiftness with which the rays of the morning sun stretch out into the dawn, suddenly dispelling the darkness. Alexander comments, "The point of comparison appears to be the incalculable velocity of light". Swift and sudden though a man's attempt to flee from God might be, yet, wherever and however he flees, Jehovah is always there, and for His child His right hand is ever ready to lead and to hold. "Yea, he loved the people; all his saints are in thy hand" (Deut 33.3).

Darkness cannot hide a man from God either. To Him, who dwells in light, the night shines as the day. Darkness and light are both alike to the omnipresent Jehovah. Neither time nor space, land or sea, heaven or hell, night or day, can conceal from Him who is eternally present everywhere. The human mind cannot comprehend either omniscience or omnipresence. These are the attributes and prerogatives of God alone, but faith, though it cannot comprehend, can apprehend, and appropriate to itself, the unfailing care of such a God as this, claiming the promises, "Lo, I am with you alway", and, "I will never leave thee, nor forsake thee" (Mt 28.20; Heb 13.5).

Verses 13-18: Omnipotence

David now considers the equally great truth of omnipotence. As omniscience is all-knowledge, omnipotence is all-power and Jehovah alone is all-powerful. To illustrate this power of the Creator, the Psalmist points out that He it is who creates the embryo, and forms the child in the womb. The word "reins" (3629) originally signified the kidneys, and is so rendered fourteen times in the Book of Leviticus alone, but it is employed by Psalmists and Prophets to symbolise the hidden, innermost being of a man, the seat of his deepest emotions and feelings, his desires and passions. In this symbolic way it can be found in the Books of Job, Proverbs, Jeremiah, Lamentations, and in several Psalms. In its Greek form ("nephros" - *3510*), it also appears symbolically in

Revelation 2.23. Jehovah therefore has divine rights to the creature. As Creator, He is the Possessor, the Owner, and the Lord, even of those secret inner parts.

The word "covered" (5526) - "Thou hast covered me in my mother's womb" - is an interesting word. Albert Barnes comments helpfully, and says, "The word here rendered 'cover' means properly to interweave, to weave, to knit together, and the literal translation would be, Thou hast 'woven' me in my mother's womb, meaning that God had put his parts together, as one who weaves cloth, or who makes a basket".

This meditation on the marvels of the human body continues in v.15, but first there is an interjection, as the Psalmist exclaims, "I will praise thee!". Even with his limited knowledge of human anatomy, he knows, "I am fearfully and wonderfully made". This is true, of course, of all that Jehovah does. His works are marvellous and wonderful, and in his heart the Psalmist knows that very well.

Now he returns to the wonder of the foetus in the womb, "made in secret, and curiously wrought (7551)". This latter phrase denotes embroidery or needlework. Such is the human form, flesh and bones, sinews and muscles, arteries, veins, and nerves, skilfully woven together by the divine hand, and all this in the silence of the womb, as secret and dark as the lowest parts of the earth. The Psalmist knew that the embryo, as yet imperfect and unformed, was known to Jehovah, since He was its Maker. The final condition and state of the body is known to Him from its conception, long before its various members are fully developed. These limbs, organs and facial features increase in strength and size daily, but He already knows the destined form of every one of them. The Omnipotent has created them!

It is a comfort to the Psalmist, as it is to every believer, that the thoughts of God are toward him. "How precious also are thy thoughts unto me, O God". These are not the Psalmist's thoughts of God, but God's thoughts of him. It is precious indeed, to remember that Jehovah thinks upon His people always. David finds solace in thinking upon the thoughts of God! They are not only precious, they are many. "How vast is the sum of them" (RSV). They are as innumerable as the sand. They are inexhaustible. By night and by day, morning and evening, God thinks of His servant. It is so when he sleeps, and it is so when he awakes. David knows that he is always in those thoughts.

Verses 19-24: The Judgment of the Wicked

In this concluding section of the Psalm David avows his righteous hatred of those who hate his God. Some have wondered at the sudden transition from such a sublime meditation on the majesty of God to such maledictions against the wicked, but the reason for this seems obvious enough. Having exulted in the greatness of the attributes of God, the Psalmist is indignant that any man should hate Him, rebel against Him, speak wickedly of Him, and take His name in vain. Yet it was so; there were indeed such men. Compare Psalm 104.35 where again there is a sudden condemnation of the wicked after a sweet meditation on the greatness of God.

Is it an assurance, with which this section of the Psalm commences, as in the AV rendering - "Surely thou wilt slay the wicked, O God"? Or is it a prayer, an aspiration, as in JND and other translations - "O that thou wouldest slay the wicked, O God"? Whichever is preferred, the Psalmist anticipates that the wicked will indeed be judged, and, meantime, he wants none of their fellowship, or intercourse with them. They were men of blood, bloodthirsty men to whom he says, "Depart from me". As Spurgeon comments, "Men who delight in cruelty and war are not fit companions for those who walk with God. David chases the men of blood from his court".

These men arrogantly and wickedly spoke against God. They insulted His glorious name, taking it in vain in blatant disregard of the third commandment. This was not only irreverence, it was blasphemy, it was profanity, and Jehovah would not hold such men guiltless (Ex 20.7). Such malicious defiance of Jehovah would not, could not, go unpunished. With righteous indignation David again protests his hatred of those who hated God. "Am not I grieved…?", he asks. "Grieved" (6962) is perhaps not strong enough to express the Psalmist's intense abhorrence of their wickedness. JND and RSV prefer the word "loathe". It was utter disgust with those who would dare rise up against God. It was nauseous. He hated them with perfect hatred. This was a consuming loathing of men whom he counted his enemies because they were the enemies of Jehovah. If they were against his God then he was against them.

As for himself, this Psalmist could say with transparency and honesty, "Search me, O God". He was content to be laid bare for divine examination. The omniscient Jehovah knew his heart and his thoughts. He was willing to be tested, to be proved, to be tried as men try gold and other precious metals. He was happy to be scrutinised, to be thoroughly searched into his innermost being. He felt that he knew his own heart and the sincerity of his desires after righteousness and the glory of God, but he says, "Search me". "Know my heart". "Try me". "Know my thoughts". If there should be in him any wicked or grievous way of which he was not aware, he wanted to know it. He wanted the better way, the good way, the way everlasting. The wicked way was the way of grief and pain, but the way everlasting was, as Plumer says so beautifully, "The one good old path trodden by pious patriarchs, prophets and saints of all ages, and leading to eternal life".

The Psalmist's foregoing treatise on the majesty of God is not, therefore, theology and doctrine only. Like all true doctrine, it has a practical bearing on the daily life and behaviour of every true lover of God. David applies it to himself, as should each saint.

PSALM 140

Introduction

Here is another Psalm assigned to David and committed to the care and charge of the Chief Musician, the Master of Temple Song. This would preserve the Psalm to be sung by succeeding generations, and by all those who suffer for righteousness sake. It is a fitting sequel to Psalm 139 where David speaks of the enemies of the Lord as being his enemies too. Poor David had many enemies. They were in the nation, in his court, and in his home. He knew what it was to be persecuted by Saul, by Doeg the Edomite, by Ahithophel and Shimei, and even by his own son Absalom. Spurgeon calls this Psalm, "The Cry of a Hunted Soul". Dr Cohen entitles it, "A Prayer for Protection", and so it is, a touching supplication for deliverance from the evil and violent men who pursued him. Maclaren says, "The familiar situation of a man ringed about by slanderous enemies, the familiar metaphors of snares and traps, the familiar venture of faith flinging itself into God's arms for refuge, the familiar prayers for retribution, are all here".

The thirteen verses may be divided as follows, the suggested divisions being punctuated in the main by the three "Selahs" at verses 3, 5 and 8. Verses 1-3 describe the malice of David's foes. Verses 4-5 are a prayer for preservation from the hands of these wicked men. Verses 6-8 continue this same theme, praying that the evil plans and intentions of these men might be thwarted. Verses 9-11 are a prayer for vengeance and the concluding verses 12-13 are an expression of confidence that Jehovah will indeed protect and deliver the righteous, and so maintain their cause.

Verses 1-3: Wicked Men Described

The Psalmist speaks of "the evil man" and "the violent man". Some commentators, as Barnes, think that these terms may indicate an individual, such as Saul or Doeg. Most, however, regard them as collective nouns, evil and violence being characteristics of the Psalmist's enemies. Perhaps the plural pronoun "they" in the second verse confirms this. David's opening prayer is two-fold, "Deliver me" (2502); "preserve me" (5431). The first is an appeal for freedom, and JND actually translates the phrase, "Free me, O Jehovah, from the evil man". The second word implies preservation by a constant defence or guard. Two different Hebrew words are used for the two occurrences of the word "man". The first is ADAM (120), and the second is ISH (376). This may simply signify that all kinds of men were hostile to the Psalmist. His enemies were from no special or particular class.

The word "mischiefs" (7451) in v.2 of the AV is more sinister than would be implied by the modern usage of this word. It here signifies evil and hurt, affliction and adversity. The enemies of David were continually banded together against him, wickedly devising harm and grief for him in their heart. Their slanderous tongues were as sharp and poisonous as those of serpents. "Serpent" (5175) is a generic term, suggesting cunning and guile. "Adder" (5919) is found only here in Scripture, but may be the "asp" (*785*) to which Paul refers in Romans 3.13, a venomous viper whose bite could be fatal. Such was the nature of the Psalmist's enemies, and the "Selah" calls for a meditative pause to consider the seriousness of it all.

Verses 4-5: Keep Me! Preserve Me!

The Psalmist's prayer for preservation continues. "Keep me", he pleads. It is a plea that Jehovah might protect him, guard him, watch over him. Notice that several words appear in v.4 which have already occurred in the opening verse of the Psalm. Once again David uses the word "preserve" which he has used in v.1, and again he employs the word "violent" (2555) which he has used in v.1 also. "Man" in this verse is ISH as in v.1, and the word now rendered "purposed" (2803) is the same as that which is earlier translated "imagine". The repetition is not vain repetition. It is an emphatic repeating of the Psalmist's fears, and of his prayers for deliverance from these evil men who were devising his overthrow.

They were proud men, these enemies. They would not easily accept the defeat of their evil designs. They were determined to succeed in their machinations against the Psalmist. Yet there may be a paradox here, proud men stooping to the mean and subtle action of setting traps for David! They were cunning in their hostility, and their treachery is depicted by snares, cords, nets and gins, this latter word simply meaning traps, perhaps especially for catching birds. The net was usually spread across the intended victim's path, concealed by grasses or leaves. When once the unsuspecting victim was caught in it then with the cord or noose the hunter pulled it together and so the entrapment was complete. David could have bravely and boldly faced an enemy in the open, as he did Goliath, but for this subtle setting of traps for him he needed divine protection. These proud men were wicked men, who would stop at nothing. "Keep me", he pleads. "Preserve me". It is again time for a pause, time to think. "Selah"!

Verses 6-8: "Thou art my God"

With this exclamation the third strophe of the Psalm begins. Jehovah was David's God! David's God was Jehovah! There is a powerful inherent appeal here. The Psalmist is not invoking some lifeless heathen deity. His God was the one true God, the Mighty One, the eternally existing, all-sufficient Jehovah. He employs this great name twice in v.6, and in a personal way he can say of Jehovah, "Thou art my God". In an impassioned plea he cries, "Give ear, O Jehovah" (JND). "Hear the voice of my supplications". This expression, "the voice of my supplications" is found only in the Psalms, where it occurs six times;

Psalms 28.2, 6; 31.22; 86.6; 130.2; 140.6. Note that it is not just, "Hear my voice". Nor is it only, "Hear my supplications". It is, "Hear the voice of my supplications", implying the pleading call of a supplicating voice to the very ear and heart of Jehovah.

David now addresses the Lord with an unusual title, saying, "O GOD the Lord", a title found elsewhere only in Psalms 109.21 and 141.8. "GOD" (3069) is a variation of Jehovah. "Lord" (136) is Adonai, which, Strong says, is "a Lord-title, used instead of Jehovah in a Jewish display of reverence". There is majesty in these divine titles, and to this Supreme One the Psalmist now appeals. He is, says David, "the strength of my salvation". How he feels his own weakness. He must lean on the Lord for salvation from the present danger. His deliverance from these scheming men who planned and plotted his overthrow was dependent on Jehovah. In past experience, Jehovah had covered his head in the day of battle. Jehovah had shielded him, screened him, in former battles, as a helmet protects a warrior. Surely He would not desert his servant now.

The Psalmist prays for divine restraint on the wicked, that their evil desires may not be realised. The hearts and hands of all men are under the control of the Lord. He can order it so that the Psalmist's foes may be frustrated in their malicious endeavours to destroy him. If their plans for his hurt are to succeed, then even this must be by the permissive will of God. David prays that it may not be so. He envisages how his enemies would gloat if their wicked schemes should prevail. How they would exalt themselves in their pride if this was allowed of God. Earnestly he pleads, "Grant not, O Lord, the desires of the wicked". The third "Selah" now indicates another pause. It is time to ponder what has been said.

Verses 9-11: A Prayer for Vengeance

Having spoken of his own head being covered protectively in the day of battle, the Psalmist now says, "As for the head of those that compass me", and he prays that they might be covered too, but in quite a different sense. The two words rendered "cover" are distinct. In v.7 it denotes a covering of the head as with a helmet (5526), but in v.9 it means "to overwhelm" (3680). David's enemies were many. They encompassed him. They besieged him. As Spurgeon says, "They hemmed him in, encircling him as hunters do their prey". His prayer is that what they had planned for him may cover them instead, that their malice might fall upon their own head, overwhelming them as they had plotted to overwhelm him. By "the mischief of their own lips", he means that their slanderous breathings against him might return upon their own head, as if by their own words they had pronounced their own sentence and framed their own unwanted reward.

In the "burning coals" and "fire" of v.10 several commentators see an allusion to the fearful doom of Sodom and Gomorrah in Genesis 19.

De Burgh makes the observation that the verse is prophetic, since such a punishment never did fall on David's enemies. He points to "the fiery judgment of the Lord's coming, and the awful sentence already pronounced against the beast and the false prophet – "these were cast alive into a lake of fire burning with brimstone" – Revelation 19.19-20". The "deep pits" (4113) referred to may be pits of water, of slime, or of clay. The word does not occur elsewhere in Scripture, and is, according to Strong, "from an unused root of uncertain meaning". The metaphor signifies a judgment from which the wicked cannot rise.

The "evil speaker" of v.11 is a slanderer, translated by JND as "the man of evil tongue", the violent man who attacks with a forked tongue, a liar who cruelly wounds others with words. David prays that such a man may never be established or feel secure on the earth, that he may not be successful or prosperous, but rather that the evil (7451), the unhappiness and pain which he has mischievously devised for others may hunt him to his ruin. Spurgeon comments, "God will not allow the specious orators of falsehood to retain the power they temporarily obtain by their deceitful speaking. They may become prominent but they cannot become permanent. They shall be disendowed and disestablished in spite of all that they can say to the contrary". In righteous retribution the hunter shall become the hunted, the huntsman pursued by his own dogs. The violent man shall be violently overthrown. It is an unchanging principle, that "whatsoever a man soweth, that shall he also reap" (Gal 6.7).

Verses 12-13: Confidence in Jehovah

The closing verses of the Psalm express the Psalmist's confidence that the Lord will maintain the cause of the afflicted. "Cause" (1779) is a legal word. It signifies that Jehovah will execute judgment for the poor and lowly in their afflictions. He will maintain their cause in any dispute or legal suit. With justice He will protect the rights of the needy. David says confidently, "I know that He will". Every slandered saint should likewise rest in this assurance, that the Lord will vindicate His maligned people. Vindication may tarry, but it is sure.

The Psalm concludes on a similarly confident note. "Surely the righteous shall give thanks unto thy name: the upright shall dwell in thy presence". Of this happy future the Psalmist has no doubts. Slandered they may have been, but Jehovah knows His people, that they are the truly righteous and upright on the earth. Whatever evil men may say of them, or do to them, they are His. He will maintain their cause during the years of their pilgrimage, and then they shall dwell in His presence. A thankful people they are now, and their thanksgiving will continue into eternity. This is the spirit of the beloved Psalm 23, "Surely goodness and mercy shall follow me all the days of my life: and I will dwell in the house of the Lord for ever".

PSALM 141

Introduction

This Psalm of David is a prayer throughout, or perhaps a series of prayers, which he trusts will rise to Jehovah as incense. The Psalm is intensely personal, as witnessed by the frequent recurrence of the personal pronoun. He speaks of "My voice; my prayer; my hands; my mouth; my lips; my heart; my head; my prayer; my words; mine eyes; my soul". It seems as if his whole being is involved in his intercession.

The Psalm is a prayer for preservation from sin and from sinners. Plumer comments that "Some refer its origin to events recorded in 1 Samuel 24; others to events recorded in 1 Samuel 26. There is no reason to doubt that it was written during those ten dreadful years, when Saul and his crew beset David". He adds, "The scope of this ode is clearly a prayer for grace to restrain his temper and his tongue in a time of wanton injuries received from those whom he had never wronged".

For the purposes of meditation and study the ten verses of the Psalm may be divided into five equal parts. In verses 1-2 the Psalmist asks for Jehovah's acceptance of his prayer. In verses 3-4 he prays that his tongue and his mind might be restrained, his heart and his thoughts preserved from wrong. In verses 5-6 he asks that if he should need reproof it might come from the righteous, and not from others. In verses 7-8 he describes, poetically, the sad state, but yet the trust, of the persecuted. The concluding verses 9-10 are a renewed prayer for his own preservation and for the punishment of the wicked.

Verses 1-2: The Prayer Introduced

Appropriately, the first word in the Psalm is a divine title, the great name Jehovah. David addresses Jehovah directly, saying twice, "Lord, I cry unto thee…I cry unto thee". The various phrases in v.1 are familiar throughout the Psalter. "I cry unto thee", is found in five Psalms (28.2; 56.9; 61.2; 86.3; 141.1). "Make haste" is found on six occasions (38.22; 40.13; 70.1, 5; 71.12; 141.1). "Give ear" is an appeal which recurs twelve times from its first occurrence in Psalm 5.1 until its final appearance in Psalm 143.1. These are the pleadings of a man in earnest prayer, and David now asks that they may ascend to heaven as incense. The lifting up of the hands in prayer was a familiar gesture, signifying the lifting up of the heart to God. See the comment on this at Psalm 134.2. The evening sacrifice was the offering of a lamb as a burnt offering, from which there ascended a sweet savour (Num 28.4). The Psalmist desires that his intercessions might be as acceptable to God as was that sweet savour which rose from the altar.

Verses 3-4: Guard My Mouth, My Lips, My Heart.

David again appeals to Jehovah. "Set a watch, O Lord, before my mouth;

keep the door of my lips". He is simply asking that his speech might be divinely guarded. In the injustice of the circumstances, threatened by those who were his enemies without cause, it would have been easy to speak hastily and rashly, using words which might afterwards be regretted. His prayer is that he might be spared this. Is there an implication in his request that perhaps he doubted his own ability to keep his lips suitably sealed? As Spurgeon says, "That mouth had been used in prayer, it would be a pity it should ever be defiled with untruth, or pride, or wrath; yet so it will become unless carefully watched...David feels that with all his own watchfulness he may be surprised into sin, and so he begs the Lord Himself to keep him".

How important then is the heart! It is, of course, "deceitful above all things, and desperately wicked" (Jer 17.9). "Keep thy heart with all diligence", wrote David's wise son Solomon, "for out of it are the issues of life" (Prov 4.23). Well the Psalmist knew that he needed divine aid, that his heart might not be inclined to any evil thing. He begs that he may never practise wickedness with wicked men, nor does he ever wish to be tempted by their delicacies. The sinful indulgences of the wicked must never become the pleasures of the child of God, to the ruin of character and testimony for the Lord. Such fleshly pursuits, while tempting and alluring to the natural man, are inconsistent with a life of godliness, and the Psalmist wisely asks to be disinclined from them. Albert Barnes says, "The word here rendered "dainties" properly refers to things which are pleasant, lovely, attractive, which give delight or pleasure. It may embrace all that the world has to offer to give pleasure or enjoyment". It was this that Moses gave up, "choosing rather to suffer affliction with the people of God" (Heb 11.25). What a wise choice! He consequently found greater riches than were in the court of the Pharaoh.

Verses 5-6: Let the Righteous Correct Me!

The Psalmist is willing enough, and humble enough, to admit that at times he may need correction, but he prays that any necessary reproof should come from the righteous. It would be hard to accept reproof from the ungodly, but if the godly man corrected him then that would be a kindness. Reproof and chastisement are never pleasant, but rebuke from a righteous man would come as an excellent anointing oil, it would not break his head and he would not refuse it (JND). Then, if those who had reproved him were ever suffering, and needed prayer, he would pray for them. He would not resent their former rebukes, or hold against them that they had dared to correct him. He would not cease to pray for them in their troubles. "Faithful are the wounds of a friend" (Prov 27.6). Is there here, also, a timely word for those who would administer rebuke to the erring? Correction need not be cruel or harsh. It should come like anointing oil upon the head, gently wooing and guiding the sinning saint back into the right way (Gal 6.1).

The difficulties in v.6 are acknowledged by all commentators and varying suggestions have been made as to the meaning. Who are the "judges" referred to? What is meant by "their" judges? What is meant by their being "overthrown"? Where, or what, are the "stony places"? Who are "they" who will hear the sweet words of the Psalmist? The following explanations are offered, remembering that others have differing views of the matter.

The judges to whom the Psalmist refers must surely be the rulers of the nation, Saul and his cohorts, the officers of the realm. "Their judges", suggests that many of the people accepted and acknowledged this rule, and stood in opposition to David. Keeping in mind the circumstances of 1 Samuel 24 and 26, those were difficult times for David, hunted, pursued, by Saul and several thousands of his men. Yet, David had the assurance that one day they would be overthrown. The "stony places" may be simply poetic, but there may be an allusion to the rocky caves where Saul had been in David's power and could easily have been slain, but David spared him. Nevertheless, David was the rightful heir to the kingdom and Saul would eventually be dethroned. The rest of the verse is prophetic; "They shall hear my words; for they are sweet". It was but a short time after the death of Saul that the people turned to David. The sweet Psalmist of Israel became their king and was a prophet also. They had to admit that his words were "sweet" (5276). They were pleasant, and indeed delightful, for such is the meaning of this word.

Verses 7-8: The Trials and the Trust of the Persecuted

These verses, like the preceding, are difficult to interpret, and different commentators have different views. Some of these require alternative renderings to the AV, changes in the wording and in the punctuation. The following suggestions are agreed by several expositors to be the intended meaning, in support of which see Barnes, Fausset, Plumer, Cohen, Spurgeon, and Kirkpatrick.

In graphic language David describes how he and his faithful followers have been persecuted. "Our bones are scattered at the grave's mouth". This is "sheol" (7585) the grave-land. It need not be a reference to physical death but rather a poetic way of speaking of the sad conditions and feelings of David and his followers. Barnes expresses it well, saying, "We are, indeed, now like bones scattered in the places of graves; we seem to be weak, feeble, disorganised. We are in a condition which of itself seems to be hopeless: as hopeless as it would be for dry bones scattered when they were buried to rise up and attack an enemy. The reference is to the condition of David and his followers as pursued by a mighty foe".

The metaphor then changes. Although "wood" is not in the original text but has been supplied by the translators, the picture does seem to be of splinters and chips of wood lying scattered on the earth. Some however, omit "wood" and think that the Psalmist speaks of the ploughing and harrowing which cleaves and breaks up the earth. Whichever is the true intent, the message is similar; David and his faithful were strewn about, weak, and apparently helpless. There is, however, an important "But"!

"But mine eyes are unto thee, O GOD the Lord". Notice that he again uses the title of Psalm 140.7. Jehovah, the Proprietor, Ruler, and Governor of the Universe, is David's refuge, and in Him he confides. With his eyes fixed on Jehovah he pleads, "Leave not my soul destitute". According to Strong the word "destitute" (6168) signifies "to be left uncovered, bare, exposed". David needed shielding from his many foes, and only Jehovah could provide this. This Psalmist had learned, in the darkest experiences of life, to place his confidence expectantly in Jehovah, and in Him alone.

Verses 9-10: The Final Prayer

In closing, David now asks to be kept from the snares and gins which the workers of iniquity had set for him. These two words "snares" and "gins" have appeared in Psalm 140.5, but while the word "gin" (4170) is the same, meaning "a trap", the word here rendered "snare" is really the Hebrew YAD (3027), meaning "hand". David's concluding prayer is that the hand that had been raised against him, and the snare that had been set for him, might both be defeated in their evil designs, and that those who plotted to ensnare him might fall into their own trap. The closing petition needs no explanation, "Let the wicked fall into their own nets, whilst that I withal escape". He did indeed escape, and lived to bring to his people the sweet words of which he had spoken.

PSALM 142

Introduction

This Psalm is the last of the "Maschil" Psalms. Thirteen Psalms are entitled "Maschil", meaning "wisdom; doctrine; instruction". For a further note on these see the introduction to Psalm 32 which is the first of the Psalms so called. The other Maschil Psalms are 42, 44, 45, 52, 53, 54, 55, 74, 78, 88 and 89. That man is most qualified to instruct others who has himself already trodden the same difficult path and has gathered experimental knowledge of the Lord. David was so fitted. Matthew Henry says, "He calls this prayer *Maschil*, 'a psalm of instruction', because of the good lessons he had himself learned in the cave, learned on his knees, and so learned that he desired to teach others".

The Psalm is assigned to David, and, although the Davidic authorship has been queried by some, there seems to be no good reason to doubt that the son of Jesse is indeed the petitioner. It is also called "A Prayer". Three other Psalms have the word "prayer" in their titles, and on this see notes on the title of Psalm 17. The title states that this was a prayer of David when he was in the cave. No particular cave is indicated or identified here, but it is well known that David had two cave experiences and that these are recorded in 1 Samuel 22 and 24. The first was the cave Adullam when he fled from Achish, King of Gath. The second was the cave at En-gedi where he had taken refuge from Saul. Fausset says that "the Psalm is suited to the people of God when they are in the cave-like darkness of trials and persecutions".

These seven short verses require little in the way of division, but several commentaries observe in verses 1-4 the complaint, and in verses 5-7 the prayer. This suggested arrangement is followed here.

Verses 1-4: The Complaint

Like many Psalms of David, Psalm 142 is really a cry for help. He speaks of "my supplication; my complaint; my trouble; my cry". Twice in the opening verse he speaks of "my voice", and notice the repetition when he says, "Unto the Lord with my voice", and then, "With my voice unto the Lord". The two references to his voice, and the mention of his cry, suggest that he cried aloud. It was not a silent petition, but an audible call to Jehovah from the loneliness of the cave, whether Adullam or En-gedi. Notice that his cry becomes "supplication" (2603). This is a plea for mercy, for grace, for pity, for favour. How downcast he must have felt in the cave, as he later says.

David poured out his complaint (7879) to the Lord. This word denotes the meditations, the musings, of his troubled heart. He made it all known to the Lord, poured it out without reserve. Note the very similar language in the title of Psalm 102, the prayer of an afflicted man who likewise pours out his complaint before the Lord. David told the Lord his trouble (6869). This word is elsewhere rendered "distress; affliction; anguish; tribulation". Poor David! As Plumer remarks, he had been "brought into circumstances of overwhelming grief and solicitude…His monarch and his father-in-law had become his most malignant foe".

It was, however, consolation to the Psalmist in his grief to know that Jehovah knew the way ahead, and He well knew that on that path the adversaries had cunningly laid a hidden snare for his child. These men were ever intent on trapping and stumbling this righteous man. David might be overwhelmed in his spirit, feeble and faint, dejected and forlorn, but this he knew, that the Lord was fully acquainted with the path that lay before him. The omniscient One knows and understands the hearts and ways of all, His people and their enemies alike.

Yet David felt so helpless and alone. As Spurgeon says, "How pleased were his enemies to see the friend of God without a friend! How sad was he to be utterly deserted in his utmost need! Can we not picture David in the cave, complaining that even the cave was not a refuge for him, for Saul had come even there? Hopeless was his looking out, we shall soon see him looking up". There was no champion at his right hand to defend him. There was no advocate by his side to plead for him. No one wanted to know him and no man cared for his soul. No one seemed to care whether he lived or died. He did, of course, have a few faithful followers, but, comparing his small band to the thousands of Israel, he speaks as though there were none. How like the lament of Paul is this; "This thou knowest, that all they which are in Asia be turned away from me" (2 Tim 1.15). Refuge failed for the Psalmist. This word "refuge" (4498) denotes a place of escape, a place to which to flee in danger. "Refuge" in the next verse is a different word.

Verses 5-7: The Prayer

The complaint is finished now. Again he says, as in v.1, "I cried unto thee, O Lord". When human help failed there was help in Jehovah. He must look to Him alone. He exclaims, "Thou art my refuge" (4268). The unfailing Jehovah was his shelter from the storm, his hope and trust in danger. The Lord was not only a shelter, he was David's portion (2506), his inheritance in the world. "The land of the living" is a phrase found fifteen times in the OT from Job to Ezekiel, signifying this world of the living in contrast to the grave-land of the dead. The expression occurs four times in the Psalter: Psalms 27.13; 52.5; 116.9; 142.5. An exile in his own land, banished from what was rightfully his, nevertheless David had a portion – Jehovah Himself!

"Attend unto my cry", he now pleads. "Give ear", he is asking. "Give heed to my cry" (RSV). He had been brought very low. Barnes comments, "I am reduced greatly; I am made very poor. The language would be applicable to one who had been in better circumstances, and who had been brought down to a condition of danger, of poverty, of want. It is language which is commonly applied to poverty". The Psalmist's persecutors (7291), those who so relentlessly pursued him, were stronger than he. "Deliver me", he cries. It is a call for rescue. He prays to be released from his prison. Is this an allusion to the cave? Or is it the dungeon of despair? Or is it both?

Observe the noble motives which prompt the Psalmist's prayer. It is not solely for his own comfort that he desires deliverance. It is, he says, "That I may praise thy name". If he should be delivered, then that would bring honour to Jehovah's name, and he envisages the righteous gathering around him, celebrating the bountiful dealings of God with him. Dr Gill expresses it beautifully, saying, "The righteous shall compass me about. In a circle, like a crown, as the word signifies; when delivered they should flock to him and come about him to see him and look at him as a miracle of mercy, whose deliverance was marvellous; and to congratulate him upon it, and to join with him in praise unto God for it".

PSALM 143

Introduction

This Psalm is the last of those seven which are styled "The Penitential Psalms". The others are Psalms 6, 32, 38, 51, 102 and 130. Perhaps the saddest of these, and the best known, is Psalm 51. This present Psalm is entitled "A Psalm of David", to which the LXX adds, "When he was persecuted by his son". Plumer comments that, as well as the Septuagint, the Arabic, the Ethiopic and the Vulgate versions, with many commentaries, all refer it to the rebellion of Absalom.

The style and tone of the Psalm, and the circumstances of its composition, have created a similarity to the preceding Psalm 142. Since David was a fugitive from both Saul and the rebellious Absalom, this likeness is understandable.

Because there is no specific reference to sin in the Psalm, and no expression of repentance, some have wondered why it should be termed penitential, but there is throughout a sorrowful spirit, a thirsting after God, and prayers for deliverance and guidance, which are all characteristic of the penitent. Perhaps, too, there is an implied prayer for pardon when he speaks of justification, and of the righteousness of God, and when he prays, "Quicken me", which may be a request for recovery or revival.

The only "Selah" in the Psalm, at the close of verse 6, is the last "Selah" in the Psalter. It creates a natural division of the twelve verses into two equal parts. Verses 1-6 are a lament, in which the Psalmist describes the desolation of his heart. Verses 7-12 are a prayer in which he asks, "Hear me; deliver me; teach me; lead me; quicken me". There is a sad earnestness in the Psalm, in which it is easy to feel the deep sorrow of a man who is being persecuted and pursued by his own son.

Verses 1-6: The Lament

The Psalmist's immediate appeal is to Jehovah. "Hear my prayer", he pleads, and then, as in the first verse of the previous Psalm, he speaks of his supplications, asking that the Lord might give ear (238), that He might hearken. The word "supplications" (8469), however, is a different word from that of Psalm 142.1. Here it is simply the thought of entreaty. The Psalmist is pleading with Jehovah for answer to his prayer. David presents no personal merits that he should be heard, but invokes the faithfulness and the righteousness of God. As Plumer says, "*Faithfulness*, in fulfilling His promises. *Righteousness*, in taking sides with David against his unreasonable foes. Having graciously promised, God is now righteously bound to help those who obey His will and rely on Him".

The expression, "Enter not into judgment with thy servant", is a veiled acknowledgement of sin. If Jehovah should enter a case against him, and deal with him in strict justice, this servant would be found as guilty as other men, for in the sight of God no man alive can be pronounced righteous or just in his natural state. The believer today has, of course, the joy of knowing that Another, a sinless One, Jesus, has, by His death, provided a basis whereby God can remain just, and yet be the justifier of him who believes (Rom 3.26). The cross maintains God's righteousness, and yet allows Him to justify the believing sinner.

Having pleaded the faithfulness and the righteousness of God, David now appeals to be heard for another reason. The enemy had persecuted him. He felt as if he had been hurled to the ground, to be trampled into darkness like one already dead. Adam Clarke translates this, "dark places", and suggests that "This may be understood of David's taking refuge in caves and dens of the earth, to escape from his persecuting son; yea, even to take refuge in the tombs, or repositories of the dead". Would Jehovah, for this reason, hear the cry of His suffering servant? Was it any wonder that, as in Psalm 142.3, his spirit was overwhelmed within him? His very heart was desolate (8074), devastated, appalled and astonished at what was happening to him.

In such sad circumstances, David says, "I remember…I meditate…I muse". He has time, in his lonely exile, to recall former days. He thinks upon the dealings of God with him in earlier years. Although they may at times be used interchangeably, yet there are two different Hebrew words for "works" in v.5. The first (6467) has reference to what God has done. The second (4639) refers to the things which He has made. The first is His gracious providence, rendered by JND as, "thy doing". The second is rather His power in creation as the heavens are the work of His fingers in Psalm 8.3. David muses upon all this for comfort in his distress.

This weary saint thirsted for God. He stretched out his hands in earnest appeal to God, striving as if to reach Him who was his only consolation in his sorrow. Like parched land thirsting for water, David longed for refreshment from the Lord. He was indeed a weary man in a weary land, and only God could help. The last "Selah" in the Psalter now calls for a pause, for time to think, time to ponder, and, as has been mentioned, it divides the twelve verses of the Psalm equally, and most appropriately.

Verses 7-12: The Prayer

David's complaint has now been stated. He has made his case known to the One who knew it all already, but whose ear is ever open to listen to the breathings of His afflicted people, the lispings of His children in their need. David's prayer is intense and urgent. "Hear me speedily, O Lord", he begs. His spirit was failing and it was imperative that he should have help soon. He dreads the hiding of Jehovah's face from him. This "hiding of the face" is a common expression in the Psalms, denoting a refusal to hear, or entertain a request. His only hope was in the Lord, and if the Lord did not hear and answer, his fear was that life itself was in danger. There is an implication that his health was failing with his spirit. "Them that go down into the pit", is a description of those who die and are buried. Would this be his portion? If Jehovah did not respond to his prayer and hasten to his aid, then this was indeed a sad possibility, that he might die in exile.

There are two petitions in v.8, both beginning with the same word, and each one followed by an argument or reason for the petition. The first prayer is, "Cause me to hear thy lovingkindness in the morning". This is simply a plea for an early enjoyment of the goodness and kindness of God. "In the morning" may mean "quickly", or "soon", or it may imply, symbolically, a glad morning when the night of suffering is passed. There is a similar thought in Psalm 90.14. This first petition is backed by the argument: "for in thee do I trust". This was the hope of the beleaguered Psalmist, that, for his trust in God during the dark night of persecution, he might be granted to know the lovingkindness of the Lord in a brighter morning.

The second petition is, "Cause me to know the way wherein I should walk". How important was this morally, that he should walk a path pleasing to the Lord. How important also it was literally, when the man was being pursued daily by the supporters of his rebellious son. David needed divine guidance to remain safe until the revolt had been crushed. Adam Clarke takes this literal understanding of the text, reading, "Absalom and his partisans are in possession of all the country. I know not in what direction to go, that I may not fall in with them: point out by Thy special providence the path I should take". The second request is followed by this reason for it: "for I lift up my soul unto thee". David held up his life to the Lord, looking to Him, to be fashioned for His pleasure, according to His will.

His pleadings continue, "Deliver me, O Lord". The Psalmist had many adversaries, too many for him. Jehovah must help and deliver. "I flee unto thee to hide (3680) me", he cries. The word means, "cover me; conceal me; protect me". Ruthless enemies hunted him daily, and David fled. He was no coward, but he was prudent. This was not so much flight from them as flight to Jehovah. There he would find safe refuge until the troubles were past and life in the kingdom was resumed as before. Until then he would continue to trust.

Yet again there are two petitions in one verse as David prays, "Teach me…lead me". These are frequent and familiar requests throughout the Psalms. "Teach me", occurs fourteen times, most of these being in Psalm 119. "Lead me", is found eleven times. The two requests, brought together in this verse, are the last occurrences of these in the Psalter. Note that David's prayer is not, "Teach me to *know* thy will", but, "Teach me to *do* thy will". A man might know what the will of the Lord is, and yet not obey that will. Knowledge must be followed by obedience. Observe his very personal relationship with Jehovah, in that he can call Him, "My God".

The prayers for teaching and leading are joined by the expression, "Thy spirit is good". Some, as JND, RSV, JPS, Plumer, Davies, Cohen, Delitzsch, and others, prefer, "Thy good Spirit". He longs for the gracious ministry of God's Spirit to lead him. "Lead me into the land of uprightness" may be similar to Psalm 23.3, "He leadeth me in the paths of righteousness", but a very practical interpretation is more likely here. "The land of uprightness" is, literally, "an even land; level ground; level country". The phrase occurs as a geographical term in Deuteronomy 4.43, translated, "plain country". How tired David must have been of the rocks and caverns and dens of the mountains through which he was hunted. How he must have longed to feel safe again in open country.

"Quicken me" is another phrase often recurring in the Psalms, especially in Psalm 119 where it is found seven times. It is a prayer for revival or recovery, perhaps a plea of the downcast Psalmist to be lifted out of his depression and despondency. He prays that Jehovah might, for the sake of His name and His righteousness, bring him out of his trouble, his distress. Note that again David pleads no personal merit, and yet again his motives are pure. His deliverance must be for God's glory and the honour of His name.

The final appeal in the Psalm is for the defeat and destruction of those who oppressed him. To this he adds, "For I am thy servant". Surely one who was the servant of God, devoted to the cause of God, would be granted divine protection and the deliverance for which he prayed.

PSALM 144

Introduction

Like Psalm 135, this Psalm has been compared to a mosaic. It is a colourful mingling of prayer and praise, with many quotations from, or allusions to, other Psalms. The title assigns it to David, and there is no valid reason for doubting that it is indeed his. Certain critics however, seem to query almost every Psalm attributed to David, so that many conservative expositors often deem it necessary to refute the criticism and defend David as the rightful owner and author of these compositions. Plumer speaks of general agreement here, citing more than twenty ancient versions and commentaries which all support the Davidic authorship of Psalm 144.

That it appears to be a compilation of so many citations from other Psalms, and that certain words are used which are considered to be marks of later composition, are reasons advanced by some for doubting that David wrote this Psalm. The suggestion is made that some unknown Psalmist of a later date gleaned verses and expressions from earlier Psalms and wove them together into a new Psalm. To this hypothesis Hengstenberg skillfully replies, and he deserves to be quoted in full. He writes, "An objection has been brought against the Davidic authorship from the 'traces of reading' it contains. But one would need to consider more exactly, what sort of reading is here to be thought of. It is only the Psalms of David which form the groundwork of this new Psalm. But that it is one of David's peculiarities to derive from his earlier productions a foundation for new ones, is evident from a variety of facts, which, if any doubt must still be entertained on the subject, would obtain a firm ground to stand upon in this Psalm, which *can* only have been composed by David. The way and manner of the use made of such materials is to be kept in view. This is always of a spirited and feeling nature, and no trace anywhere exists of a dead borrowing". He goes on to dismiss any thought of such borrowing, pointing out that in the second part of the Psalm there is no dependence anyway, upon any earlier Psalms. He concludes by saying of the critics, that they then "betake themselves to the miserable shift of affirming that the Psalmist borrowed this part of the Psalm from a poem now lost". Alexander says, "The Davidic origin of this Psalm is as marked as that of any in the Psalter".

To the title "of David" the LXX adds, "against Goliath", and some think that the sword of v.10 may be a reference to the sword of the giant (1 Sam 17.51).

The fifteen verses may be divided as follows. In verses 1-2 the Psalmist sings the greatness of Jehovah, with an array of glorious titles. Verses 3-4 are an immediate contrast, speaking of the insignificance and frailty of man. In verses 5-8 he appeals for divine intervention and rescue from the enemy. In verses 9-11 he again sings praises and again prays for deliverance. Verses 12-15 describe the happy portion of that people whose God is Jehovah.

Verses 1-2: The Greatness of Jehovah

The Psalm begins with an outburst of praise, "Blessed be the Lord". He can best praise the Lord who knows the Lord in a personal way, as the Psalmist does, and his intimate knowledge and experience of the Lord is evidenced by his use of the personal pronoun "my". He employs this pronoun over and over again, each being a testimony to what Jehovah is to him or has done for him. "My strength" (6697), he says. This word is many times translated "rock", as in Psalm 18.31, 46. The AV rendering here of "strength" is perhaps more in keeping with what follows. Jehovah has been the Psalmist's strength in battle, teaching his hands to war and his fingers to fight. Only divine help could have made the shepherd boy of Bethlehem so victorious in battle and such a champion for Israel. Although the suggestion has been made that "fingers" may be a reference to the use of the bow, this does not seem necessary. Hands and fingers are just a parallelism for David's engagement and skill in battle, enabled by the Lord.

He now calls Jehovah, "My goodness...my fortress; my high tower...my deliverer; my shield". See the similar passage in the early verses of Psalm 18. These glories of the Lord, considered respectively, denote One who, in His goodness, is all goodness and mercy to His people. He is their fortress, their stronghold and castle, for protection from the enemy. As their high tower He is their safe retreat, a refuge in the heights, their security from the foe. He is their deliverer from trouble, and He is their shield, their sure defence from the adversary. All of these blessings David appropriates to himself, and this brings forth due praise from him. Jehovah had subdued the nation under David in the happier days of his reign. Plumer points out that the word "subdued" is not to be taken in a bad sense, and he quotes Calvin, who says, "When a people yields a cordial and willing obedience to the laws, all subordinating themselves to their own place peaceably, this signally proves the divine blessing".

Verses 3-4: Man's Insignificance and Frailty

To those readers who are familiar with the Psalms, a parallel with Psalm 8.4 will be at once apparent here; but why should this reference to man's insignificance be so suddenly introduced at this point? Surely the remembrance of man's weakness and frailty can only magnify the contrasting greatness of God, and, likewise, any consideration of the glory of God can only emphasise the utter weakness of man. All of this, then, extols the wonder of that divine condescension which takes notice of man and comes to his aid.

But what is man anyway? He is like to vanity (1892), like a breath, like a vapour that appears for a little while and then vanishes away (Jas 4.14). He may gather some fame about him. He may accumulate wealth and power and reputation, and he may have ambitious plans, but soon he is gone. There is a most interesting play upon words here. "Man" (120) is ADAM, and "vanity" (1892) is HEBEL, more commonly recognised in the name "Abel". Adam is as Abel! All men are alike, essentially short-lived. Man is like a shadow, now present, now gone, with no abiding substance. No worth in man can occasion God's interest in him. How gracious then of Jehovah to take notice of him.

Verses 5-8: Prayer for Deliverance

David enjoyed so much as King of Israel, but he was in constant trouble from men within and without his kingdom, and he needed the help of God at all times. He prays, "Bow thy heavens, O Lord, and come down". Notice a similar passage in Psalm 18.9. There, however, the verbs indicate what has been accomplished. Here it is a prayer that God would again descend, and intervene for his people. Such was His power that the mountains would smoke at His touch. This had happened literally at Sinai at the giving of the law in Exodus 19.18. This may now be used an expression of Jehovah's might, but if the mountains are here used figuratively, then the appeal is to One who can subdue earthly potentates and powers, crush empires and emperors, with but the touch of His hand or the breath of His mouth. David is asking that God may come as in a storm, sending forth arrows of lightning to scatter and destroy his adversaries.

Whatever was the nature of the Psalmist's then present troubles, he feels as if he is in deep waters, being deluged by adversity. His plea is that Jehovah might stretch forth his hands and deliver him. Note that "hands" is a plural word; he needs the fulness of divine power to rescue him from these deep waters of trouble. He speaks of "strange children". These are aliens, foreigners, strangers to the covenant. This may be a reference to Philistines, or Edomites, or to other surrounding nations at enmity with Israel, but there were also those treacherous men of his own nation, who were, as Calvin suggests, "Strangers, not in respect of generic origin, but character and disposition".

These men spoke vanity (7723). This is not the vanity of v4. Here it is a different word, meaning "falsehood" and "lies". Their speech was emptiness, not worthy to be believed. Their promises were worth nothing, not to be depended upon. Their right hand, the hand usually lifted in solemn affirmation of the word spoken, was a right hand of deceit and fraud. They were deceivers and liars, hypocrites and schemers, and from them David asks to be delivered.

Verses 9-11: Renewed Praise and Prayer

"A new song!" A fresh burst of praise! It was the music of his heart as he contemplated the deliverance of which he felt confident and assured. The AV speaks of "a psaltery and an instrument of ten strings", but notice that the word "and" is in italics, having been supplied by the AV translators. If it is omitted then there is one instrument here, not two, "a psaltery, an instrument of ten strings". The Psalmist refers to the lute, the typical ten-stringed harp of the Hebrews. This is, of course, David's personal and private devotion. The son of Jesse was the sweet Psalmist of Israel (2 Sam 23.1). He was expert on the harp, and with this accompaniment he must often have rendered his praises to the Lord.

The God whom David praised was a sovereign God. He could give salvation to kings, but he also gave victory to the shepherd lad from Bethlehem. In humility the Psalmist speaks of himself as "David his servant". David had been delivered from the hurtful sword. "Hurtful" (7451) is translated "evil" and "wickedness" more than five hundred times in the AV. Some relate this sword, as has been noted, to the sword of Goliath, but it is more likely to be figurative of the cruelty of his enemies and the death which they planned for him.

Verse 11, the closing verse of this section of the Psalm, with its references to "strange children" and "the right hand of falsehood", is an almost exact repetition of these phrases in vv. 7 and 8. Some repetitions are vain, as Jesus taught, but some are expressions of earnestness, emphases of those things which are heavy on the heart and mind of the writer. So it must be with David. Treacherous alien adversaries were ever with him and he cannot refrain from mentioning them again so soon.

Verses 12-15: Happy People!

David now envisages a happy and prosperous kingdom, the foreign foes having been purged from it. Perhaps the picture he paints was realised more fully in the days of his son Solomon, and will be fulfilled completely in the reign of that greater Son of David, the Messiah. Nevertheless, David has ambitions for his realm and he graphically describes the ideal kingdom. He embraces the whole life of the nation in his holy anticipation. He speaks of their sons and their daughters, their granaries, their flocks and their herds.

"That our sons may be as plants grown up in their youth". David is a master of metaphor. This is a prayer that the young men of Israel may develop suitably, strong physically and upright morally, well established and vigorous, healthy and manly. It was indeed an ambitious prayer, a prayer which must be echoed as the heart's desire of every spiritual parent today.

"That our daughters may be as corner stones, polished after the similitude of a palace". Now he is thinking of the beauty and elegance of the sculptured pillars of a palace or temple. Barnes says, "The comparison is a very beautiful one, having the idea of grace, symmetry, fair proportions: that on which the skill of the sculptor is most abundantly lavished".

"That our garners may be full". He longs for good harvests, for plentiful provision which would ensure a contented people. He pictures corn, wheat, and barley in plenty, with the granaries filled and famine unknown. It may be argued that these are ideal conditions, and so they are. See the ultimate realisation of them described in the Messianic Psalm 72.

"That our sheep may bring forth thousands and ten thousands in our streets". He envisages healthy flocks, with ewes and lambs in abundance. "Streets" has caused a problem for some. Sheep lambing in the streets? It simply indicates, as Plumer explains, "Places beyond the domicil, outside of the family enclosure, highways or fields".

"That our oxen may be strong to labour". He turns to the herd now. The oxen were the servants of man. The husbandman was so dependent upon them for ploughing, threshing, and the drawing of loads. They were also the burden bearers. He prays that they might be strong to so labour, and that there might be no breaking in by marauders, no theft, no aggression or hostile intrusions, and no consequent outcry in the streets. It must be said that some commentators understand this "strong to labour" as referring to strength in the bringing forth of their young. JND and RSV actually translate it so, but it is a minority view of the passage.

So the Psalm concludes. "Happy is that people, that is in such a case: yea, happy is that people, whose God is the Lord". No exposition is needed, except to say that this word "happy" means "blessed", and, while the words are different in the Hebrew, nevertheless it can be said that this Psalm begins with a blessed God and ends with a blessed people. Then, as Plumer writes, "The last clause of the Psalm furnishes an instance where it would have been better to transfer the word *Jehovah*; *whose God is Jehovah,* not Baal, not Ashtaroth, not living or dead men, not angels, but the self-existent, independent, eternal, unchangeable Jehovah".

PSALM 145

Introduction

This Psalm is entitled "David's *Psalm* of Praise". Note that "Psalm" is in italics. The translators have supplied it, but "Psalm of Praise" is a translation of one Hebrew word. This is, literally, "David's Praise", or, "David's Praise-Song" and no other Psalm has this word in its title. "Praise" (8416) is T[e]HILLA, the plural of which, T[e]HILLIM, is the title of the whole Book of Psalms. Psalm 145 is all praise. It sings thanksgiving and praise to Jehovah for His glory and His majesty, His greatness and goodness, His grace and mercy, His power and compassion. There are no complaints or imprecations. There are no expressions of sorrow or grief. It is therefore a fitting introduction to the five remaining Psalms in the Psalter, which are sometimes called "The Hallelujah Psalms" because they begin and end with the word, "Hallelujah", the call, "Praise ye the Lord".

De Burgh remarks that in the preceding Psalm "there commenced a strain of praise which continues uninterrupted to the end of the Psalter". Horne comments, "Hitherto, in this divine book, we have been presented with checkered scenes of danger and deliverance, distress and mercy. The voice of complaint hath sometimes been succeeded by that of thanksgiving; and praise, at other times, hath terminated in prayer. But now…the days of mourning are ended". The closing verses of Psalm 144 seemed to anticipate the kingdom, and now the King Himself is extolled.

This is not only the last Psalm to bear the name of David in its title, it is also the last of the alphabetical Psalms. Its acrostic arrangement is almost perfectly regular, each of its twenty-one verses commencing with the appropriate letter of the Hebrew alphabet in sequence. There are, however, twenty-two Hebrew letters, so that one letter is missing here, the Hebrew letter NUN, whose place would have been between the thirteenth and fourteenth verses.

The reason for this omission is not clear. There is nothing to lead to the belief that a strophe has been lost, and so, several explanations for the missing letter have been suggested. First, since there is no lyrical or rhythmic value in the acrostic pattern, that form of composition was probably adapted as an aid to memorisation, and the omission of one letter in the heart of the Psalm may well have been deliberate as an unusual jolting of the memory, lest the repetition of the verses should become mechanical. Second, Hengstenberg, with whom De Burgh seems to agree, suggests that the twenty-one verses resultant from an intended omission of one letter, permits the Psalm to be divided into three equal strophes of seven verses each. Third, commenting on this latter suggestion, and on the claim that the three sevens would put the stamp of perfection upon the Psalm, F.W. Grant takes the very opposite view, saying, "I cannot but conclude that the gap is meant to remind us that the fulness of praise is not complete without other voices which are not found here". He refers, as he goes on to say, to the New Testament church and the heavenly saints. Perhaps the comment of Delitzsch is very wise when he writes, "We are contented to see in the omission of the NUN-strophe an example of the freedom with which the Old Testament poets are wont to handle this kind of form". He then refers to the irregularity of other alphabetical portions of Scripture.

Many commentators point out that the LXX has supplied a strophe beginning with the missing letter NUN. It reads, "Faithful is Jehovah in all His words, and holy in all His works". There is, of course, nothing wrong with these sentiments, but the strophe is rejected by most expositors, as being simply an attempt by the translators to supply a strophe which they mistakenly think has been lost.

The following division of the Psalm, suggested and followed by others, is adapted here as well suited to profitable meditation. As has already been said, the Psalm is all praise to Jehovah. Verses 1-7 are praise for His greatness. Verses 8-10 are praise for His goodness. Verses 11-13 are praise for His glory. Verses 14-16 are praise for His providence, and verses 17-21 are praise for His saving grace.

Verses 1-7: Praise for His Greatness

Perhaps the opening words of the Psalm encapsulate its whole theme; "I will extol thee, my God, O king". To "extol", is to lift high, to exalt, and this is David's intention throughout the whole Psalm, to raise Him high whom he calls, "My God, O king". The Psalm begins with David's personal exercise, but soon he anticipates that others will join with him in his praise of Jehovah. Note the four "I wills" in the opening verses. "I will extol thee...I will bless thy name...I will bless thee...I will praise thy name". As has been observed in other Psalms, the name of the Lord is a synonym for Himself, as he has made Himself known to men. David appreciates every such revelation of God. He has spoken of them often, and in keeping with what he knows he blesses the Lord. The praise begun now continues daily on earth and the echoes of it reverberate through eternity. Twice he says, "For ever and ever...for ever and ever". The praise of the saints will resound eternally, in perpetuity, everlastingly, without end. It is good to remember that David was himself a king, but he is happy to give allegiance to One greater than he, "My God, O king". Spurgeon remarks, "(His) royalty...our loyalty"!

The praise of Jehovah must be in keeping with His greatness. "Great is the Lord"; it follows, therefore, that He is "greatly to be praised". The three words rendered "great", "greatly", and "greatness" in v.3 of the AV are different words in the Hebrew text, but each of them accurately conveys the thought of greatness. For, "greatly", JND has, "exceedingly". Great is Jehovah, and exceedingly to be praised. The greatness of Jehovah is unsearchable (2714), it is past finding out, defying all human investigation. With David the Psalmist, Paul the apostle is, of course, in full agreement, saying, "How unsearchable are his judgments, and his ways past finding out" (Rom 11.33). It is greatness which has been more fully declared in Jesus, of whom Paul said that he preached "the unsearchable riches of Christ" (Eph 3.8).

"One generation shall praise thy works to another". There is now here another word for "praise" (7623). This is an interesting word, rendered "laud" by several versions. It has the thought of triumph in it, and also the idea of glorying. The Psalmist is predicting that one generation shall triumph in the works of the Lord and shall commend them to the succeeding generation so that there may be a continual praising for what He has done. This was a pattern and a principle in Israel, and indeed among the early Christians, that the great things of God should be taught by fathers to children, and to the children's children. Paul exhorts the same thing when writing to Timothy, as he says, "The things that thou hast heard of me...the same commit thou to faithful men, who shall be able to teach others also" (2 Tim 2.2). The mighty acts of Jehovah must be published by all generations of His people. Note that David has begun his praise in the singular, but is now anticipating that generation after generation, myriads upon myriads of God's people, will sing that praise down the ages and into eternity.

What an array of great words and tributes does David now gather together within the confines of one verse. In v.5 he speaks of "the glorious splendour of thy majesty, and of thy wondrous works" (JND). Literally, "The splendour of the glory of thy majesty". Here is a cluster of jewels indeed, "Glory, splendour, majesty, wonder". As another has said, quoted by Spurgeon, "What a cumulus of glowing terms does Holy Writ seek to display the excellence of Deity" (Martin Geier). How the Psalmist has learned God! When he says, "I will speak" (7878), this is no ordinary word for "speak" that he uses. This is not incidental talk. The word denotes a prior musing, meditating, pondering, and now he expresses the thoughts which he has had concerning the King. Although the original Hebrew word is not the same, yet the thought is exactly that of Psalm 45.1 "My heart is inditing a good matter: I speak of the things which I have made touching the king".

Observe how he moves from the personal to the general, and then returns to the personal again. "I will speak...And men shall speak...and I will declare". These mighty acts of Jehovah must be told and retold. There have been, he says, "terrible acts" (3372), fearful wonders that ought to bow the hearts of men in fear, in reverence and awe. Again he speaks of that greatness, which, in v.3, he has said is unsearchable. He must declare it. He will declare it. As best he knows it he will tell out that greatness of his God. He will declare it, and men will declare it, and so the greatness of Jehovah will be published abroad.

Once again, in v.7, he speaks of greatness, and now it is yet another word! By the "great (7727) goodness" of the Lord, is meant, "abounding goodness". The greatness of God manifests itself in many ways. The greatness of His Person is sometimes seen in His terrible acts, but it may also be experienced in His great goodness to men. So, the Psalmist says, men shall "abundantly utter" (5042) the memory of these things, pouring forth their testimony to the goodness of God, as water flows out from a fountain or spring. This is spontaneous praise, men singing aloud, from their hearts, of the righteousness and goodness of God. Gratefully and fervently the redeemed of the Lord will recount their happy recollections of the goodness He has shown them.

Verses 8-10: Praise for His Goodness

David has introduced the thought of God's goodness when speaking of His greatness. The subject of His goodness is now continued and developed. There is grace, compassion, longsuffering, and tender mercies. This is great goodness indeed, as the Psalmist has said in the preceding verse. The RSV rendering of v.8 is especially beautiful, "The Lord is gracious and merciful, slow to anger and abounding in steadfast love". One feature of the greatness of God's goodness is that He is good to all. Not only to all men, but to all His works. His tender mercies are universal. He sends sunshine and rain to all, snow in winter and heat in summer. On every continent He cares for beasts and birds, fruits and flowers, grass and trees, giant mammals and tiny insects. He is good to all without partiality. Thomas Watson says, "Sweet dewdrops on the thistle as well as on the rose"! One day, in millennial bliss, all His works shall join with all His saints to acknowledge with gratitude His goodness to them, and to bless and praise Him.

Verses 11-13: Praise for His Glory

Perhaps already in the Psalm there have been allusions to the splendour of the kingdom. Now it is specific. In these three verses, the Psalmist speaks of the glory and majesty of a kingdom which is everlasting, a dominion which will endure throughout all generations. The glory (3519) of the kingdom is its honour, its dignity, and its wealth. Righteousness and peace kiss each other in the bliss of this kingdom (Ps 85.10). This will be the grand theme of conversation among men. They shall "speak of the glory" and they shall "talk of thy power". The glory of any kingdom is dependent upon the greatness of the King, and so it is the might and power of Jehovah that ensures the endurance of the splendour of His kingdom.

"The sons of men" (120), literally, "the sons of Adam", must be acquainted with the mighty acts of Jehovah. The glory and majesty of His kingdom must be made known to all. The kingdom is a kingdom for all ages. It will never end. In God's purpose, and in His prophetic programme, there will be an earthly phase of the kingdom for one thousand years (Rev 20.2, 3, 4, 5, 6, 7). This is commonly referred to as "the Millennium", but it is important to emphasise that this is but a phase of a kingdom which is everlasting. Even the great Nebuchadnezzar had to acknowledge this, saying, "I blessed the most High, and I praised and honoured him that liveth for ever, whose dominion is an everlasting dominion, and his kingdom is from generation to generation" (Dan 4.34).

Verses 14-16: Praise for His Providence

The Psalmist now points out that both the greatness and goodness of the Creator are shown in His constant care for His creatures. This is especially precious to His own, His people. "The Lord upholdeth all that fall". This is characteristic of Him. Barnes points out that "The word here used is a participle, literally, *The Lord sustaining*, that is, the Lord is a Sustainer or Upholder of all that fall". How poor David knew this, personally and experimentally. Paul knew it too. "Chief of sinners", he called himself, yet Jehovah in majestic grace reached down from the glory to arrest him and save him.

He not only upholds those that are fallen, or falling, He lifts those that are bowed down. He cheers the downcast, and David knew this too. How often he had cried, "Why art thou cast down, O my soul? and why art thou disquieted within me?" (Ps 42.5, 11; 43.5). The Lord will not break the bruised reed, or quench the smoking, smouldering flax (Is 42.3). He will tend, and mend, and heal His failing people.

Every creature is dependent on the Creator. All must look to Him for their sustenance. "The eyes of all wait upon thee". He does not fail or disappoint them but gives them their meat in due season. This is reminiscent of Psalm 104.27, a great Psalm, where, in vv. 10-30 particularly, this universal care and provision of the Lord for His creatures is expounded in lovely detail.

Jehovah opens His hand and with divine beneficence supplies the desire of every living thing. There is nothing stinted or measured with God's provision. As is often said, it does not enrich Him to withhold or impoverish Him to give. So He does not give grudgingly, but provides liberally for the need of all, and, as Spurgeon remarks, "These verses refer to natural providence; but they may equally well apply to the stores of grace, since the same God is king in both spheres". Indeed, "The Lord is good to all".

Verses 17-21: Praise for His Saving Grace

Four times in these five verses the great name of Jehovah appears. The praise of the Psalmist, of the saints, and of the universe must be directed to Him. Here is a twofold reason for that praise, "Jehovah is righteous in all his ways, and holy (2623) in all his works". The word here rendered "holy" does indeed often mean just that, but it may also be translated "kind", and is so rendered by JND, RSV and YLT, and "gracious" by the JPS, ASV and the NKJV. Jehovah then, in Himself, in His ways, and in His works, has this delightful blending of righteousness and kindness. His justice is tempered by grace. Not that He can ever overlook sin, but in His great grace He has provided a basis whereby He can remain just, and yet justify the sinner whom His righteousness might otherwise have condemned. The Just One has died for the unjust (1 Pet 3.18). Righteousness is satisfied, and kindness has wrought salvation for the unjust. Jehovah is just in all His ways, and kind in all His works.

It is yet a further token of His grace that, having pardoned the erring, the Lord now stays near to them. He may indeed be the God of glory, dwelling in the heavens, but He would not be remote from His people. He desires to be near to those who call upon Him. That is, of course, those who call in sincerity, in truth. There may be, on the part of some, an insincere, hypocritical profession of godliness, as there was with the Pharisees in the Saviour's day. This nearness, this presence of the Lord, is promised only to those who call upon Him in truth, and He knows perfectly the true condition of each heart. As Delitzsch says, "He remains at a distance from the hypocrites, just as their heart remains far from Him". The complaint against some in Isaiah's day was, "This people draw near me with their mouth, and with their lips they do honour me, but have removed their heart far from me" (Is 29.13). It is they who have created the distance.

Jehovah hears the cries of His people and fulfils the desire of those who reverence Him. This does not mean that He will grant their every wish. He did not do so for David, or for Paul. What is good and godly in the prayers of those who ask, He will grant. James says, "Ye ask, and receive not, because ye ask amiss" (Jas 4.3). So, those who fear Him always say, "If the Lord will", knowing that what is in His good will for them He will give to them. He delights to hear the cries of His saints and to save them in all the vicissitudes of life.

In v.20 there appears the only reference to the wicked in this Psalm. This is a Psalm of greatness and goodness, of compassion and kindness, of grace and glory, of righteousness and truth. There has been no occupation with the wicked at all, and no occasion even to mention them until now. Here they are introduced into the Psalm to show the contrasting dealings of God with those who love Him and those who choose wickedness. He can preserve and He can destroy. Those who love Him are those who fear Him. These He preserves, keeps, watches over and cares for, but the wicked

He will destroy. It is a sad thought, in such a Psalm of praise, that there are those who reject all Jehovah's goodness and prefer wickedness, and will ultimately perish.

The Psalm ends as it began. David praises personally and calls upon all flesh to join with him in blessing the Lord. Praise to His holy name will go on and on, for ever and ever, echoing and re-echoing throughout the heavens and a renewed earth. The song which begins in time is eternal, it will never end. Hallelujah!

PSALM 146

Introduction

This is the first of those five Psalms commonly called "The Hallelujah Psalms". They are the final Psalms of the Psalter. Each begins, and ends, with a "Hallelujah", and, appropriately, they ring with praise right through until the end of the Book of Psalms. Spurgeon, with characteristic quaintness, and with an allusion to Bunyan's Pilgrim's Progress, says, "We are now among the Hallelujahs. The rest of our journey lies through the Delectable Mountains". Dr Cohen entitles this Psalm, "God the Helper". His introduction to it is very brief as he writes, "Several affinities may be noted between this Psalm and its predecessor. It is general in character and seemingly unconnected with any special circumstances. The theme is that in God alone is an unfailing source of help to be discovered".

No author is identified in the Psalm. Some believe that it was sung at the dedication of the second temple, and because of this it has been attributed to Haggai and to Zechariah. Others, however, while acknowledging that it could indeed have been sung at that time, nevertheless are content to see it as a Psalm of David like the preceding Psalm.

Division of the ten verses is hardly necessary, and somewhat difficult, since the Psalm is a unified whole. It may, though, for the purpose of meditation and study, be divided into two equal parts as follows. Verses 1-5 call for the praise of Him who alone is to be trusted as the true Helper of His people. Verses 6-10 tell of His grace and power, who is the Protector, Provider and Preserver of those who trust Him.

Verses 1-5: Praise Him, and Trust Him

The Psalm may well be a congregational hymn, a call to the people for their collective worship of Jehovah, but it is very personal too. The Psalmist is well entitled to so summon the praise of others, for He himself sings his own praise to the Lord. The first "Praise ye the Lord" is, as has been noted,

"Hallelujah". It is, literally, *Hallelu-Jah,* "Praise ye Jah", this being a shortened, but not diminished, form of Jehovah. The Psalmist, calling on others, now addresses his own soul, saying, "Praise the Lord, O my soul". He responds immediately, answering, "I will praise the Lord as long as I live". This does not simply mean, "during my lifetime", and lest any should so misunderstand what he is saying, he now adds, "I will sing praises unto my God while I have any being". This goes beyond the present life, into the next, and into eternity. He knows that to perpetuity this will be his occupation, to join with all saints in singing praises to the Lord.

Those who find reasons to praise the Lord have also found reasons for trusting Him. Those attributes and virtues which call for the praise of the saints are the grand basis for their dependence and hope in Jehovah. Therefore, the Psalmist exhorts, "Put not your trust in princes, nor in the son of man". Note that the little word "nor" is italicised. Omit it and a paraphrase of the Psalmist's argument is this, "Put not confidence in princes, for even though he may be a noble, yet the prince is but a son of man (120), a son of Adam". There is no assured or permanent help in man. T.W. Davies makes the interesting point that this word "help" (8668) is cognate with the proper names "Joshua" and "Jesus", and that the Hebrew word is usually rendered "salvation". It is folly, therefore, to trust in frail men. Princes may rule, and their nobility may indeed command respect from men, but, as Jonah said, giving thanks in anticipation of divine deliverance, "Salvation is of the Lord" (Jonah 2.9).

Man at his best is but mortal. "He returneth to his earth". One day he will breathe his last breath and his flesh will return to dust (Gen 3.19). Note that the Psalmist speaks of "his" earth. On this, Barnes has the helpful comment, "It is *his* as that from which he was made: he turns back to what he was...The earth – the dust – the grave is "*his*"...it is *his* as the only property which he has in reversion. All that a man – a prince, a nobleman, a monarch, a millionaire – will soon have will be his grave, a few feet of earth. *That* will be his by right of possession; by the fact that for the time being he will occupy it, and not another man. But that, too, may soon become another man's grave, so that even there he is a tenant only for a time. He has no permanent possession even of a grave. How poor is the richest man!" How foolish to place trust there!

"In that very day", the Psalmist says, "his thoughts perish". On the day of his death the plans and purposes of a man cease. On that day his intentions and schemes are brought to an abrupt end. How this was illustrated in the case of the rich farmer whose story Jesus told (Lk 12.16-21). His ground brought forth plentifully. His barns were too small. "This will I do", he planned. He would pull down his barns and build greater. There he would store his fruits. He would say to his soul, "Soul, thou hast much goods laid up for many years; take thine ease, eat, drink, and be merry". But God said, "Thou fool!". In one night his plans were rudely aborted.

Surely the Psalmist has proved his point, that it is vain to trust in any man, since power and wealth and all human ambitions are so very fragile and temporary. Happy is that man who has the God of Jacob for his help (5826). This word "help" is different from the word of v.3. Here it denotes "succour; help meet for the occasion". In the matter of the saints' trust, then "The God of Jacob" is a most appropriate title. It is found thirteen times in the Psalms and this is the last occurrence of it. Jacob, of course, knew all about frailty and need. He built his altar to "God, who answered me in the day of my distress, and was with me in the way which I went" (Gen 35.3). He is blessed who trusts the God of Jacob, "whose hope is in the LORD (3068) his God (430)", in Jehovah Elohim, the Eternal, Ever-Existing, Self-Sufficient Mighty One.

Verses 6-10: Jehovah, Protector, Provider and Preserver of His People

Although He is "The God of Jacob", this does not mean that Jehovah is the God of Israel only. He is the Creator of heaven, earth and sea, and is therefore the God of all creatures that inhabit this threefold dominion of His. He has creatorial rights to be trusted by men. He has moral rights also, for He "keepeth truth for ever". He is eternally true to every promise and every covenant that ever He made with man. Then, too, He has what might be called judicial rights, for He has a renown for executing judgment for the oppressed, justice for those that have been exploited or defrauded. When other officers of law cannot be trusted, Jehovah can. Again, as the great Provider for the needy, Jehovah orders seedtime and harvest, commanding the fruitfulness of the ground for food for the creature. Then, as the Protector of those unjustly bound, "The Lord looseth the prisoners". This is so reminiscent of the opening ministry of Messiah in the Nazareth synagogue, proclaiming liberty to the captives. Compare the prophecy of Isaiah 61.1 with the record of the Saviour's ministry in Luke 4.18.

The Psalmist continues to give reasons why the Lord should be both praised and trusted. Note that the great name Jehovah stands here, in vv. 7-9, at the head of five consecutive lines of the Psalm, both in Hebrew and in English. It occurs three times in v.8, "Jehovah openeth the eyes of the blind: Jehovah raiseth them that are bowed down: Jehovah loveth the righteous". How much of this was evident in the ministry of Jesus. For several reasons, usually attributed to sand, wind, glaring sun and excessive heat, blindness was a common affliction in Israel. Frequently during His ministry Jesus gave sight to the blind. Although physical blindness appears to suit the context, some do understand this blindness in the Psalm as being spiritual blindness. Of course, Jehovah also opens the darkened minds of men, bringing light and new vision into the life.

Those that are "bowed down" are the despondent and the despairing. These, too, knew the gracious ministry of the Saviour when He was here. He, who was the perfect Servant of Jehovah, brought a true revelation of Jehovah's heart to men. He comforted the mourner, cheered the downcast, and encouraged those who were discouraged. His love for the righteous was clearly seen too, approving and commending where appropriate, and condemning without reserve when there was hypocrisy or evil.

Jehovah has always been the great Preserver and Guardian of the stranger (1616). This word means "alien" or "sojourner", but almost certainly implies one who was a foreigner in Israel. There are some seventy references to the stranger in the Pentateuch, the five Books of Moses. Jehovah made a difference between His own people and the stranger, yet He insisted that the stranger in the land should be respected, saying, "Thou shalt neither vex a stranger, nor oppress him: for ye were strangers in the land of Egypt" (Ex 22.21). "Also thou shalt not oppress a stranger: for ye know the heart of a stranger, seeing ye were strangers in the land of Egypt" (Ex 23.9). How true it is, "The Lord preserveth the strangers".

In many a home the father is deceased. Little children become orphans and wives become widows. In divine compassion Jehovah relieves such, surrounding them, supporting them, upholding them. He would be a Father to the fatherless children and a Husband to the widow. But, in sharp contrast, "the way of the wicked he turneth upside down". "The way of the wicked doth he subvert" (JND). He reverses or upsets the way of those who are intent on wickedness. Barnes comments, "The Hebrew word here means to bend, to curve, to make crooked, to distort, then, to overturn, to turn upside down...The idea here is, that their path is not a straight path; that God makes it a crooked way; that they are diverted from their design; that through them He accomplishes purposes which they did not intend".

The Psalm closes on a triumphant note, "The Lord shall reign for ever". His triumph is assured and it is eternal. Then, to make this great fact good to His people, the Psalmist proclaims, "Thy God, O Zion!". It is thy God who will reign eternally, from generation to generation. As Dr Cohen says, "This phrase does not invest the aspiration with a nationalistic character. From His chosen centre, Zion, God will reign over all peoples who will unite in recognition of His Kingship". As in many Psalms, there is here an anticipation of Messiah's millennial reign, the earthly phase of an eternal kingdom.

With such grand assurances and hopes as have been portrayed in the Psalm, what more can now be said except, as in the closing word, "Hallelujah!". "Praise ye the Lord".

PSALM 147

Introduction

Psalm 147 is the second of the five "Hallelujah Psalms" which conclude the Psalter, so called because they begin and end with the word "Hallelujah".

This lovely Psalm is a meditation on the goodness and the power of Jehovah displayed in His creation and revealed in a special way to Israel. Thoughts of such greatness and goodness evoke due praise from the Psalmist, and from God's people.

There is no general agreement as to the date of composition or the identity of the author of this Psalm. Many commentators, principally because of v.2, regard it as being of a late post-exilic date, and, like Psalm 146, ascribe it to Haggai and Zechariah. Others however, like the conservative Dr Gill, are happy to see it as Davidic, and regard v.2 as prophetic, looking even beyond the recovery from the Babylonian captivity to the glory of Jerusalem in the time of the Messiah.

With regard to the numbering of the Psalms, and with reference to an apparent break in this Psalm at the end of v.11, it may be helpful to quote both W.S. Plumer and Adam Clarke. Plumer explains, "The Septuagint and the versions which follow it, unite Psalms 9 and 10 into one, and so, to make the number 150 they divide Psalm 147 into two, making Psalm 146 end at v.11 and Psalm 147 begin at v.12. Of course the numbers of all the Psalms between the ninth and this do not in these versions agree with the Hebrew, as the Douay in a note admits". Adam Clarke writes, "It may be necessary to remark that all the Versions, except the Chaldee, divide this Psalm at the end of the eleventh verse, and begin a new Psalm at the twelfth. By this division the number of the Psalms agrees in the Versions with the Hebrew, the former having been, until now, one behind".

For the purpose of the present exposition, the Psalm is divided as follows. In verses 1-6 Jehovah is praised for His care for Jerusalem, for outcasts, and for those who mourn. Verses 7-11 sing of His provision for His creatures and His pleasure in His people. Verses 12-20 praise the power of His Word, both in nature and in grace.

Verses 1-6: Jehovah's Care for His People

The opening "Hallelujah" is a call to praise, and immediately the Psalmist gives three reasons for the singing of Psalms of praise. It is good; it is pleasant; it is comely. The word "praise" occurs three times in the first verse of the AV, and although these are actually three different Hebrew words, yet the word "praise" in each case seems acceptable as an English translation. JND however, renders the second word "psalms" instead of "praise". Having summoned the people to praise, for the three reasons given, the rest of the Psalm now expands upon other particular matters which should draw forth due praise to Jehovah.

Although v.2 must have been, so very appropriately, the song of the captives returned from the Babylonian exile, yet it must not be restricted or confined to these. It has always been characteristic of Jehovah to build up, establish, the city where He had placed His name. Jerusalem has been, over the many centuries of its history, coveted, besieged, fought over, and destroyed, more than any other city in the world, but Jehovah has a constant care for Jerusalem and repeatedly it has risen from its ruin. "The Lord doth build up Jerusalem". Similarly, it has always been true of Him that "He gathereth together the outcasts of Israel". Again, this was especially the case with the returning exiles, but then, David himself had been an outcast in his day and he knew experimentally that Jehovah cared for exiles and delighted to restore them. Prophetically, this lovely verse still has a delightful future fulfilment, when a remnant nation of Israel shall be gathered from out of the nations to a home in the Land which the Lord has purposed for them and promised to them. Compare Isaiah 11.12 and 56.8.

How precious it is to know that He who cares for nations and cities, cares also for the individual child of God. As Spurgeon remarks, "The Lord is not only a Builder, but a Healer; He restores broken hearts as well as broken walls". So says the Psalmist, "He healeth the broken in heart". He knows the sorrows of His people and He knows what broken-heartedness is. Did not the Saviour Himself say, "Reproach hath broken my heart" (Ps 69.20)? The wounds which He heals are, of course, the wounds of the spirit rather than of the flesh.

Notice the gracious intermingling here of tenderness and power. He who builds the city is the same One who binds the broken heart, and it is He also who "telleth the number of the stars". Saints and stars are alike in His hand and in His care. But "telleth" (4487) does not simply mean that He knows, and can tell, how many stars there are. The word signifies that He assigns their number, He decides and determines how many there are to be. "He calleth (7121) them all by their names" suggests the thought of a roll call. He can, in His might as their Creator, summon these heavenly bodies to appear before Him and they must answer, as an army of soldiers answers when the roll is called. This agrees exactly with Isaiah 40.26.

This calls forth from the Psalmist the exclamation, "Great is our Lord and of great power". The two words translated "great" are different in the Hebrew. While the first (1419) does signify "greatness" in the normally accepted sense of the word, the second (7227) has the thought of "abundance". Jehovah is great, and abounding in power. There follows, in this verse, an interesting play upon words, referring back to v.4. "He telleth the number of the stars...his understanding is infinite". The words "number" and "infinite" are different renderings of the same Hebrew word (4557). The stars are, of course, innumerable (Gen 15.5), but Jehovah who made them knows their number. His understanding, then, is like the stars, beyond measure, infinite, greater than human knowledge. The practical application of this power of Jehovah is that, in His greatness, He can lift up the meek and He can cast down the wicked, and He does. The RSV rendering is very expressive; "The Lord lifts up the downtrodden, he casts the wicked to the ground". He who controls the stars controls mortals also.

Verses 7-11: Jehovah's Provision for His Creatures

Again the Psalmist summons the praise of the saints. He exhorts that with voice and harp they should sing their thanksgiving to the Lord. Jehovah has moved toward His people in great goodness and His people should now move towards Him in gratitude. As Spurgeon says, "Jehovah is ever engaged in giving, let us respond with thanksgiving". In His greatness Jehovah creates the clouds in preparation for necessary rain. Every raindrop is an evidence of His goodness. He waters the earth which accordingly brings forth grass for the cattle, and even the hill country has its share of pastureland for the beasts which roam there. He cares for the mountainsides which are so often beyond the reach of human care and cultivation. He not only provides food for the beasts of the field but He also hears the cry of the young raven, and He feeds these too. The raven! Ceremonially unclean, insignificant and worthless as far as man is concerned, but Jehovah hears their cry and provides for them.

In His essential greatness the Lord takes no pleasure in the pretended greatness of men. Perhaps in v.10 there is a reference to both cavalry and infantry, but neither the strength of the war-horse or the legs of the fleet-footed warrior hold any appeal for Jehovah. His interest is in moral features rather than the physical, and so, "The Lord taketh pleasure in them that fear him". Those who trust Him and hope in His mercy and love are those who bring Him pleasure. It has been demonstrated that He provides for all His creatures, and it pleases Him that men should acknowledge this and trust Him alone for all their need. It gives Him pleasure to be trusted.

Verses 12-20: The Power of His Word

The summons to praise is renewed. Jerusalem is personified and the exhortation is addressed to the city, "Laud Jehovah, O Jerusalem; praise thy God, O Zion" (JND). There now follows a lengthy list of reasons for the praise of Jehovah.

"He hath strengthened the bars of thy gates". Walls and gates were so necessary for the safety and security of the city. Of great importance were the bars, the fastenings, of the gates, assuring the utmost protection against marauders. The inhabitants must be secure, and also the storehouses of grain and other provisions. Jehovah would accordingly protect His city and His people.

"He hath blessed thy children within thee". The citizens of Jerusalem were the apple of His eye. He desired safety and prosperity for them. The inhabitants of Zion were the objects and subjects of divine blessing.

"He maketh peace in thy borders, and filleth thee with the finest of the wheat". Jehovah is the God of Peace and He bequeaths this peace to His saints. One of the most beautiful benedictions of the NT is that of Paul in

2 Thessalonians 3.16, “Now the Lord of peace himself give you peace”. In another place the Psalmist exhorts, “Pray for the peace of Jerusalem: they shall prosper that love thee” (122.6). By “the finest of the wheat” is meant the fatness and fulness of a rich harvest.

“He sendeth forth his commandment upon earth: his word runneth very swiftly”. When Jehovah commands, the elements must obey. How this was manifested in the Saviour’s calming of the waters of the Lake Galilee. “Peace”, He commanded, “be still”. His word ran swiftly indeed, for at once there was a great calm. Storm and waves, winds and water, obeyed His word.

“He giveth snow like wool: He scattereth the hoarfrost like ashes”. He who gives the wheat in harvest also sends the snow in winter. The snowflakes fall gently, softly, covering the earth like white fleecy wool. He spreads the white frost upon the earth as easily as men scatter ashes. Frost and snow may not be so common in Israel as in other parts of the world, but they are certainly not unknown. The Psalmist’s readers would know exactly what he meant.

“He casteth forth his ice like morsels: who can stand before his cold”. By “morsels” is meant “crumbs”. The imagery is of a man scattering crumbs of bread upon the ground, and in like manner Jehovah scatters showers of hail. What man can stand against the severity of extreme cold that Jehovah might choose to send. Such coldness has been known to kill men.

“He sendeth out his word, and melteth them: he causeth his wind to blow, and the waters flow”. The same powerful word which sends out the snow and the hail can also melt them. Jehovah has the right to issue fresh orders and melt the ice which has gripped the earth at His earlier command. At His word the south wind will blow, the temperature will rise, and the ice will turn to flowing waters.

“He sheweth his word unto Jacob, his statutes and his judgments unto Israel”. This word of Jehovah’s power which has commanded earth and the elements, which has ordered rain and hail, sun and snow, in summer and winter, is the word by which He has revealed Himself to His own people. He is the God of Jacob and the God of Israel. He is the God who has in sovereignty chosen Jacob, and from him has created the nation of Israel. No other nation on earth was so privileged as this nation. He had made known His statutes and His judgments to His chosen people and to none other. How special indeed they were to Him.

The Psalmist has rehearsed all these great things for this purpose, that the people should praise the Lord. He has listed reason after reason for this praise and it seems almost to be expected that now, in a joyful conclusion of the Psalm, he should exclaim once again, at the end as at the beginning, “Hallelujah!”. “Praise ye the Lord”.

PSALM 148

Introduction

This lovely Psalm, the central one of the five "Hallelujah" Psalms, is alive with praise throughout its fourteen verses. Praise echoes and re-echoes from heaven to earth, and, as if intelligent creatures were insufficient to render the adoration due to Jehovah, the Psalmist calls on things inanimate to join in the great universal symphony of praise.

No author is identified, nor date of composition. As with the preceding Psalms, many commentators assign it to a late date, after the exile, but again Dr Gill speaks for others when he writes, "This Psalm seems to have been written about the same time, and by the same person, as the preceding; even the Psalmist David, when he was in profound peace, and at rest from all his enemies; and the kingdom of Israel was in a well settled and prosperous condition".

Prophetically, and ultimately, the Psalm must refer to the times of the Messiah, that great millennial day, when, as Psalm 72 says, the whole earth shall be filled with His glory, and men everywhere, with Israel, will unite in praise of the King. It is both interesting and profitable to read the Psalm in conjunction with Revelation 5.

The praise begins in the heavens and then descends to earth, until there is presented a scene similar to that of the morning of the incarnation of the Saviour - "A multitude of the heavenly host, praising God, and saying, Glory to God in the highest, and on earth peace, good will toward men" (Lk 2.13-14).

Little is required in the way of division, or even of exposition or explanation, but the first six verses deal with praise from the heavens and the last eight verses with praise from the earth, all culminating in the closing verse with the praises of Jehovah's peculiar people, the children of Israel. With reference to this, T.W. Davies comments, "There is nothing national in the Psalm except in the last verse. It is a universal song of praise". Kirkpatrick writes, "Let every heavenly being and every heavenly body unite to praise Him Who created them and sustains them (vv. 1-6). Let earth with all its phenomena and all its inhabitants praise Him for the revelation of His majesty (vv. 7-13). Especially has He given His people ground for praising Him by restoring them to honour (v.14)".

Verses 1-6: Praise from the Heavens

The Psalm commences with the "Hallelujah" which is a general call for praise. The Psalmist soon proceeds to invite praise in a detailed, particular manner, from a variety of sources, but this opening *Hallelu-Jah* is a summons to all to join in praise of Jah. This is a contracted, though not a diminished or diluted, form of Jehovah, as has been noticed in preceding Psalms.

"Praise ye the Lord from the heavens, praise him in the heights". The anthem of praise is sounded first of all from the heavens, from the heights. Note it is "heavens", in the plural. The Rabbis, with the Jewish Talmud, spoke of seven heavens. Paul spoke of three (2 Cor 12.2). The "heights" is a poetic synonym for "heavens". This is not vain repetition, but rather emphasis, which may also have had an antiphonal purpose, a form of responsive singing by two choirs.

Another similar repetition now follows, "Praise ye him, all his angels: praise ye him, all his hosts". There are, in the language of Revelation 5.11, "ten thousand times ten thousand, and thousands of thousands" of angelic beings. With seraphim and cherubim these are the hosts of the Lord. These are all summoned to begin the paean of praise which will soon resound throughout the universe.

Heavenly bodies now join with heavenly beings in the praise. Sun, moon, and shining stars, the created light bearers, unite in the song. The "heavens of the heavens" are the loftiest heavens of all, the highest of the high, a superlative similar to "King of kings", or "Holy of Holies". The Psalmist is reaching, in thought, into the uttermost heights to search for voices to praise Jehovah. The "waters that are above the heavens" seems to be a reference to Genesis 1.6-8, perhaps the rain clouds in the heights. All the celestial bodies have reason to praise Jehovah for He is their Creator and Sustainer. By His command they have their being. By that same word they are established and they have decreed bounds which they cannot pass. Albert Barnes expresses it so well when he writes, "The word rendered "decree" here seems to be used in the sense of limit or bound; and the idea is, that He has bound them by a fixed law; He has established laws which they are compelled to observe...by which they are held from flying off. He has marked out orbits in which they move; He has so bound them that they perform their revolutions with unerring accuracy in the very path which He has prescribed. So accurate are their movements that they can be predicted with exact precision; and so uniform that any succession of ages does not vary or affect them". "Praise Him, ye heavens".

Verses 7-13: Praise from the Earth

"Praise ye the Lord from the heavens" the Psalm began. "Praise the Lord from the earth", it continues. Earth's answer to the heavens is like a mirror image. Earth responds to heaven and joins in the praise. Dragons (8577), sea monsters from the deeps, unite with the extremes of fire and hail. Snow clouds and mists, with the stormy winds, all move at His command, fulfilling His Word, and now add their praise of their Creator. Mountains and hills, fruitful trees and giant cedars, alike must render due adoration. Living creatures all, beasts and cattle, animals wild and domestic, with things that creep and birds that fly, all are summoned to join in the praise.

To the higher intelligences of earth the call now extends, beckoning the kings of the earth, with their kingdoms their peoples and nations, with earthly princes and rulers. Young men with their maidens, old men with their children, must all unite to praise the Lord. Maclaren says, "The young man's strong bass, the maiden's clear alto, the old man's quavering notes, the child's fresh treble, should blend in the song". Therefore let them praise the name of the Lord. His name alone must be exalted in its excellence. He must be extolled above the earth and the heaven from which the praise is emanating.

Verse 14: Praise from His People Israel

How tenderly are God's people described here; "His saints; even of the children of Israel, a people near unto him". He has made them what they are. He has lifted up the horn of His people; that is, He has given them their dignity and their power. Surely they have a duty, an obligation, to render praise to Him. Above all others, Israel has reason to praise Jehovah, and the last word of the Psalm is, especially to them, a renewed, final, summons to praise – "Hallelujah!".

PSALM 149

Introduction

As the preceding Psalm was a general call to all the inhabitants of heaven and earth to unite in praise of Jehovah, this call to praise is more particularly for Israel. With such a call the previous Psalm concluded and it has been suggested that the closing verse of Psalm 148 may possibly have been the seed from which this Psalm developed (Kidner). Who should praise Him like His chosen people Israel?

Many commentators use the word "jubilant" to describe this Psalm, for so it is. Spurgeon says, "The tone is exceedingly jubilant and exultant. All through one hears the beat of the feet of dancing maidens, keeping time to the timbrel and harp".

The Psalm sings of triumph and joy, of salvation and glory, and of course the reader is still among the "Hallelujahs". There is, though, in spite of the rejoicing, a certain imprecatory spirit in the Psalm, which calls for vengeance on Israel's foes. Davies comments, "The spirit of the Psalm is vindictive in a high degree, reminding one more of the Book of Esther than of the Sermon on the Mount". This might be said of many Psalms, since the spirit of the new covenant has in so many ways risen above the spirit of the old, bringing characteristic differences between the two, as between the natural and the spiritual. As Delitzsch says, commenting on certain atrocities which have been committed, and justified by this Psalm, "We see that a Christian cannot make such a Psalm directly his own, without disavowing the apostolic warning, 'The weapons of our warfare are not carnal' (2 Cor 10.4). The praying Christian must therefore transpose the letter of this Psalm into the spirit of the New Covenant".

As for a division of the nine verses, between the "Hallelujahs" with which the Psalm begins and ends, verses 1-5 are a summons to the nation to praise Jehovah for His care for, and His pleasure in, His people, and verses 6-9, in triumphalism, anticipate the destruction of Israel's foes.

Verses 1-5: A New Song

The opening "Hallelujah" is now a familiar call to praise. This summons is for Israel in particular, and so the Psalmist says, "Let Israel rejoice". There is a congregation (6951) of saints (2623) who must sing, an assembly of the godly and faithful who should readily respond to the call for praise. It is a "new song" which they sing. This expression is found six times in the Psalter, of which this is the last occurrence. It is also found in Psalms 33.3; 40.3; 96.1; 98.1; 144.9. When Jehovah does some new thing for the nation, or for the individual servant, then there is occasion for a new song. It cannot be known which particular event is celebrated here, but, whatever it was, it called for a new song from Israel.

Israel must rejoice in Him that made them. That Israel should be different to surrounding nations was always the purpose of God. He had made these people what they were. By their own might or skill they could never have risen to the high privileged ground to which He had brought them. No, He had made them! He was their Maker. He had brought them into existence as a nation, brought them out of bondage to their present joy, and He was their King. They were the children of Zion. They belonged to the favoured city where He had placed His name. Truly they must rejoice and sing.

The children of Zion would praise the Lord with singing and dancing, with timbrel and harp. The timbrel (8596) was that which is now commonly called the tambourine. The harp (3658) is, in some other versions, often translated "lyre". With regard to the dance, some commentators, as Adam Clarke, Albert Barnes, Fausset, and Gill, doubt whether this is a true and proper rendering of the word here, and point out that a common marginal reading is "the pipe", a wind instrument such as a flute or fife. However, dancing "before the Lord" (2 Sam 6.14) was, for Old Testament saints, a spontaneous, wholehearted, joyful expression of praise, which may still be witnessed in Israel on the evening before the Sabbath and on festive occasions. Such physical expressions of praise do not belong to the new dispensation, but the wholeheartedness and joy must be admired by those who today unite in worship in spiritual song. See comments on Psalm 150.3-5.

Jehovah takes pleasure in His people. It seems but proper, then, that His people should take pleasure in Him, and praise Him. His care for Israel and His deliverance of them from their many trials, must be proof that He takes pleasure in them. He beautifies the meek with salvation. He adorns His beloved people. They may be humble and poor, afflicted and needy, but they are still His people, and He beautifies them with salvation. This has been true of the nation, and it is also true of the individual. Peter speaks of "the ornament of a meek and quiet spirit" (1 Pet 3.4). How many a rough and vile sinner has been transformed by the gospel, so that the physical appearance, the happy glowing countenance, reveals what God has done in salvation.

Let the saints, the godly, rejoice in this glory and beauty. "Let them sing aloud upon their beds". If the earlier call had been to the congregation, encouraging the praises of the assembly, here the individual saint is exhorted to bring his own personal praise, in the privacy of his own chamber. Let their songs in the night ascend to Him whom they love and serve. Whether corporately, collectively, congregationally, or personally and individually, the saints must rejoice and praise.

Verses 6-9: The Holy War

Israel's enemies were many. Surrounding nations constantly vexed Israel. Now, with the praises of God in their mouth and a two-edged, all-devouring sword in their hand, the saints confidently anticipate the destruction of their foes. It would be righteous retribution, this execution of vengeance upon the heathen (GOYIM - 1471). These heartless adversaries were the Gentile peoples who knew not Jehovah. It was right that they should be punished for their treatment of God's people. Their kings and their nobles would be chained in fetters of iron, signifying inescapable judgment. Such judgment would be in accord with the written Word and the promises of God. Had not their prophet Isaiah, among others, predicted, in writing, the punishment of Israel's enemies (Is 65.6)?

All His saints would share in this honour, the honour of association with the Mighty Jehovah who had vanquished all the adversaries of His people. Here again is a prophetic view of that glorious advent of Messiah, when His enemies shall lick the dust, when all kings shall fall down before Him, and all nations shall serve Him (Ps 72.9, 11). What an honour to be then associated with Him, King of kings and Lord of lords. There can be but one joyful conclusion to such a Psalm as this – "Hallelujah!".

PSALM 150

Introduction

Psalm 150 is a fitting doxology to the whole Book of Psalms. It is an inspired crescendo, a grand finale. What lovely tributes have been paid to this delightful Psalm. Spurgeon writes, "We have now reached the last summit of the mountain chain of Psalms. It rises high into the clear azure, and its brow is bathed in the sunlight of the eternal world of worship". Oesterley calls it, "The grandest symphony of praise to God ever composed on earth". Maclaren says, "This noble close of the Psalter rings out one clear note of praise, as the end of all the many moods and experiences recorded in its wonderful sighs and songs. Tears, groans, wailings for sin, meditations on the dark depths of Providence, fainting faith and foiled aspirations, all lead up to this. The Psalm is more than an artistic close of the Psalter; it is a prophecy of the last result of the devout life, and in its unclouded sunniness as well as in its universality, it proclaims the certain end of the weary years for the individual and the world. 'Everything that hath breath' shall yet praise Jehovah".

This last Psalm of the Psalter may be compared with the first, which also has six short verses. Psalm 1 begins with "Blessed…". Psalm 150 begins and ends with "Hallelujah". The praise of this closing Psalm is the fruit of the blessedness of the opening Psalm. In this way they complement each other.

The word "praise" occurs thirteen times in this Psalm. After the first "Hallelujah" there are twelve more exhortations to praise, sufficient for all the tribes of Israel. If it is noted that there are really three "Hallelujahs" in vv. 1 and 6, then this leaves ten other references to praise. Delitzsch remarks upon this tenfold encouragement to praise, he thinks that it is significant, and says, "for ten is the number of rounding off, completeness, exclusiveness".

The six verses need not be divided. They are a unified call to praise. The praise is local, yet universal, on earth and in heaven. The entire Psalm is praise, and, as the Wycliffe Commentary says, "Not merely the priests and Levites nor merely the congregation, but all the creatures of time and space which have breath are included in this choir of choirs. The Psalter ends, but the melody lingers on as the worshippers continue to chant "Hallelujah, Praise ye the Lord".

Verses 1-6: Hallelujah! Hallelujah! Hallelujah!

The Psalm begins with the now familiar *Hallelu-Jah*, which is immediately followed by an unfamiliar *Hallelu-El*. As Adam Clarke points out, "In many places we have the compound word "Hallelujah", praise ye Jehovah; but this is the first place in which we find "Halleluel", praise God, or the strong God. Praise Him who is Jehovah, the infinite and self-existent Being; and praise Him who is God, El, or Elohim, the great God in covenant with mankind, to bless and save them unto eternal life". Three questions now arise, Where should He be praised? Why should He be praised? How should He be praised?

Where should He be praised? There is a dual answer. "Praise God in his sanctuary: praise him in the firmament of his power". Those who see a parallelism here understand the sanctuary to be the holy place where God dwells, His heavenly habitation. It is more likely, however, and of more direct relevance to the worshippers, that the sanctuary is the earthly temple. Still, whichever is intended, the God of the heavens is the God of the earthly sanctuary too.

If the question, "Where should He be praised?", has a dual answer, so the question, "Why should He be praised?", has a dual answer also. "Praise him for his mighty acts: praise him according to his excellent greatness". He must be praised for what He does, but He must also be praised for what He is. Perhaps this has been the twofold theme of the whole Psalter, the intrinsic worth and eternal personal glory of Jehovah, and the wonder of what He has wrought as Creator of the universe, and as Deliverer, Redeemer, and Preserver of His people. This dual theme of praise will never end. Forever and forever His glorified saints will extol Him for what He is and for what He has done.

Now the third question arises, "How should He be praised?". The six exhortations which follow, have, of course, particular reference to the worshippers of the Psalmist's day. They are more relevant to the people and the days of the old covenant than to the saints of the new spiritual dispensation. These material accompaniments and adjuncts to the worship of those earlier days have now been superseded by the spiritual exercises of those who with psalms, hymns, and spiritual songs, make melody in their hearts, singing with grace in their hearts to the Lord (Eph 5.19; Col 3.16). David Dickson points out that the instruments mentioned here were but shadows of better things to come, and he writes, "The plurality and variety of these instruments were fit to represent divers conditions of the spiritual man, and of the greatness of his joy to be found in God, and to teach what stirring up should be of the affections and powers of our soul, and of one another unto God's worship; what harmony there should be among the worshippers, what melody each should make in himself, singing to God with grace in his heart, and to show the excellency of God's praise, which no means nor instrument, nor any expression of the body joined thereto, could sufficiently set forth in these exhortations to praise God with trumpet, psaltery, etc". Believers today, therefore, should draw on all their faculties and powers to render, in priestly exercises, due praise to God.

"Praise him with the sound of the trumpet". The "trumpet" (7782) was the "shofar", the ram's horn. It was not really an accompaniment to singing, but was employed for calling the people together. It is an interesting fact that the "shofar" was perhaps the earliest instrument to be used by the children of Israel, and is the only Hebrew instrument to be retained by them today for use on solemn occasions (See Lev 25.9). The "shofar", and the silver trumpets of Numbers 10, were the first instruments for which divine directions were given. The trumpet sound was loud and clear, giving an unmistakable call, and for this reason the figure of the trumpet is used by Paul in 1 Corinthians 14.8 and 15.52.

"Praise him with the psaltery and harp". These require little comment, except to say that the psaltery (5035) was really very similar to the harp (3658). Thomas Le Blanc, quoted by Spurgeon, explains, "The psaltery was a ten-stringed instrument. It is constantly mentioned with the harp. The psaltery was struck with a plectrum, the harp more gently with the fingers". Viewed typically, they perhaps represent differing forms or expressions of praise, which may sometimes be loud and exuberant, and at other times more mellow, quiet and subdued.

"Praise him with the timbrel and dance". The "timbrel" (8596) was a woman's instrument, a tambourine or hand-drum (Ex 15.20). The tambourine and the dance have already been mentioned in Psalm 149.3. Refer to the remarks upon these at that verse in this Commentary.

"Praise him with stringed instruments and organs". These are general terms denoting the various kinds of instruments. Some have strings, some have pipes, wind instruments. They produce their melodies in different ways. Spurgeon, with his usual characteristic quaintness, comments, "Many men, many minds, and these as different as strings and pipes; but there is only one God, and that one God all should worship".

"Praise him upon the loud cymbals". The word "cymbal" (6767) comes from a root with the idea of vibrations. It was a hollow circular plate or dish of brass, and, when clanged together, these produced a loud ringing sound which punctuated the music at determined moments during the symphony.

"Praise him upon the high sounding cymbals". That there must have been different types of cymbals is obvious enough, but it is not clear just how they differed. It is probable that different shapes and sizes of cymbals produced different tones and a variety of volume of sound. "High sounding" (8643) seems to indicate cymbals which were, as some think, "those of a larger make, struck above the head, and consequently emitting a louder sound" (Adam Clarke).

In a fitting conclusion to this Psalm, and to all the Psalms, the Psalmist now exclaims, "Let every thing that hath breath praise the Lord". The trumpets and pipes have been blown, the strings of harp and lute have been swept, the tambourines and cymbals have sounded, and now, a final, triumphant, summons for praise that goes beyond the boundaries of Israel and calls upon men everywhere to unite in praise of Jah. Then, a last, loud, lingering, joyful "Hallelujah!". "Praise ye the Lord".

The beloved apostle John saw the fulfilment of it and wrote, "And every creature which is in heaven, and on the earth, and under the earth, and such as are in the sea, and all that are in them, heard I saying, Blessing, and honour, and glory, and power, be unto him that sitteth upon the throne, and unto the Lamb for ever and ever" (Rev 5.13).

This concludes Book 5 of the Psalms

AFTERWORD

The long journey of both reader and writer through the Psalter is now over. There have been hills and valleys throughout the journey. There have been tears and trials, joys and sorrows, triumphs and tragedies, doubts and fears, songs and sighs, sunshine and showers. There have been heights of glory and depths of gloom. There has been elation and depression. We have seen ourselves, but we have seen Christ. We have looked into our own hearts but we have looked also at the majesty of God. From the delectable mountains there have been visions of the Promised Land, and there has been, too, a sad and solemn insight into the doom of the ungodly. This has all produced wonder and worship, gratitude and praise. Perhaps the words of the venerable Adam Clarke are a suitable conclusion to it all. He writes, at the close of his Commentary, "Of such peculiar importance did the Book of Psalms appear to our blessed Lord and His apostles, that they have quoted nearly fifty of them several times in the New Testament. There is scarcely a state in human life that is not distinctly marked in them, together with all the variety of experience which is found, not merely among pious Jews, but among Christians, the most deeply acquainted with the things of Christ".